Critical Studies in Organization and Bureaucracy

Revised and Expanded Edition

*Edited by Frank Fischer
and Carmen Sirianni*

Temple University Press

PHILADELPHIA

Temple University Press, Philadelphia 19122
Copyright © 1984 by Temple University. All rights reserved
Published 1984. Revised and expanded edition 1994
Printed in the United States of America

Library of Congress Cataloging-in-Publication Data
Critical studies in organization and bureaucracy / edited by Frank
Fischer and Carmen Sirianni.—Rev. and expanded ed.
    p.   cm.
Includes bibliographical references.
ISBN 1-56639-121-0. — ISBN 1-56639-122-9 (pbk.: alk. paper).
1. Bureaucracy.   2. Organizational behavior.   I. Fischer, Frank,
1942–   II. Sirianni, Carmen.
HD38.4.C74   1994
302.3'5—dc20   93-7403

Contents

Preface to the
Revised Edition

The second edition of this book, like the first, grows primarily out of our experience teaching about organizations in a variety of undergraduate and graduate settings. Originally we decided to collaborate on a collection of critical studies in organization because most of the mainstream texts did not seem very helpful in analyzing the crises in organizational theory and organizational life, and because even the best of the collections that included critical studies were often too densely theoretical to be of use in most classroom settings. As students we ourselves had often shunned courses in organizations for these very reasons, and as teachers we then found ourselves struggling to make the experience relevant, critical, and empowering, without at the same time losing important theoretical questions in pop sociological analyses of life in the bureaucracy. Judging from our many conversations with other teachers of courses in organizations, the dilemma we faced was not uncommon.

We thus structured our book primarily around a set of accessible case studies of specific organizations, and we have retained this format in the second edition as we have enriched and revised the selection of cases. After an initial section that introduces students to classical writings in organization theory, we present case studies from a great variety of settings in public, private, and nonprofit sectors. Each of these analyses has a critical edge, though they draw upon a range of theoretical perspectives and shun either simple ideological labels or naive organizational alternatives. Our years teaching and studying organizations have convinced us even more than when we began that the world of organizations is both highly, even obdurately, complex and accessible to everyday understanding and collective change. No single theoretical perspective is adequate to these tasks, nor is an approach to organizational alternatives that is not self-critical and willing to confront the problems raised by other perspectives. For reasons of space and coherence, we have not been able to include all the perspectives in organizational theory that we do find useful—that would make for a very different kind of volume. But we have tried to provide a good critical introduction that can motivate and inform further study.

Issues most central to the critical tradition have guided our selections: power and empowerment, forms of control and resistance, class and gender, political economy of bureaucratic systems, technology and domination, social movement and alternative organizational forms. As we argued at much greater length in the introductory essay to our first edition, these themes challenge mainstream approaches along a whole range of dimensions. (We do not think all organization theory neatly falls into critical or mainstream, but these terms are convenient shorthand for our purposes here.) Mainstream approaches often rationalize and obscure the power of managerial and other elites on the basis of presumed administrative and technological imperatives, particularly of narrowly conceived notions of technical efficiency. They usually fail to link organizational dynamics to the relations of class and power in larger political economies, and abstract from history and context in seeking value-neutral and universal laws of organizational development. Conflict and resistance are either glossed over or analyzed as dysfunctions that can be corrected by technical and social-psychological fixes. And the consultants who do the fixing and revise the theory tend to employ positivistic research methodologies that exclude any genuine voice for the research subjects themselves and refuse any alternative rationalities that might be present in their actions. And when mainstream approaches have concerned themselves with alternatives, it has almost always been alternatives developed by those who seek to buttress existing power relations, including the power to frame the problems themselves.

Although key critical questions emerged in the classical writings of Weber, Marx, Michels, and others, organizational thinkers and social actors of recent decades have challenged the assumptions of mainstream organizational thought on virtually every dimension. Indeed, the claims of superior efficiency of bureaucratic and scientific management models have been exploded not only within organizational analyses but in the larger public and even corporate discourse. And this crisis occurs in the midst of more direct challenges to the assumptions of class, power, gender, race, and technique embedded deeply in mainstream approaches, and has opened up space for a richer debate than ever before on the possibilities of postbureaucratic and postindustrial organizational forms than can respond to the crises of efficiency and quality simultaneously with the crises of inclusion and democratization. But although this new terrain of rethinking and reform offers much hope, it also generates its own perils and makes critical approaches to the postbureaucratic innovations of today as necessary as to the bureaucratic ones of yesterday.

In attempting to enrich the selections, we have consulted with many who have taught dynamic courses that included our first edition, and we have drawn upon recent scholarship that has proven successful in our own teaching. The introductions to each section in the text give fuller synopses of each essay; let us note here several changes that stand out.

We have included in this edition more on both gender and race. Joan Acker's "Reproducing Hierarchy: Job Evaluation and Comparable Worth in State Government" (Chapter 13) examines how hierarchical gender classifications can reproduce themselves even in attempts to reverse this through comparable worth and job evaluation by rank-and-file employees. Louise Lamphere and Guillermo Grenier, in "Women, Unions, and Participative Management: Organizing in the Sunbelt" (Chapter 11), examine the underside of some human relations and teamwork strategies, especially as these are used to intimidate and disempower women and minorities in low-paid jobs. Part II on forms of control and divisions of labor is thus richer in its attention to race, gender, and ethnicity, as well as its attention to reforms that may themselves reproduce control and hierarchy. The issue of gender, power, and tokenism, which Rosabeth Moss Kanter takes up in Part III in "Women and Power in Organizations" (Chapter 17), is now complemented by a psychodynamic and cultural analysis that links the specific histories of gender and race in the United States to the problems of mentoring among blacks and whites, in David Thomas's "Mentoring and Irrationality: The Role of Racial Taboos" (Chapter 18). And race and gender receive further attention in Part IV on organizational alternatives and social change. Robert Moses et al., in "The Algebra Project: Organizing in the Spirit of Ella" (Chapter 26), show how the community organizing traditions of the civil rights movement inspired by the empowering methods of black feminist Ella Baker are relevant in today's educational reforms, and they provide a case study of how innovative math-science pedagogies emerged in a multiracial choice school in the Cambridge, Massachusetts, public school system. In "Learning Pluralism: Democracy and Diversity in Feminist Organizations" (Chapter 29), Carmen Sirianni examines how feminist organizations from the 1960s to the 1990s have been engaged in a long process of democratic innovation, and of learning how to manage the problems associated with various methods of empowering members and representing diverse voices. His analysis ranges over a variety of types of feminist organizations and examines these learning processes in the light of the concerns of recent feminist and democratic political theories. Gary Delgado, in "Internal Organization and Social Structure in Community Organizing: The Case of ACORN" (Chapter 30), examines an important model of community organizing and leadership development, and looks at the intersection of the classic problem of oligarchy with race and gender in the multiracial network of low-income community organizations known as ACORN. David Osborne and Ted Gaebler, in "Community-Owned Government: Empowering Rather than Serving" (Chapter 25), examine innovative ways of "reinventing government" by debureaucratizing structures and empowering citizens, and by returning government services to the community, from neighborhood-oriented policing to tenant management and ownership of public housing. Rather than disempowering clients through rationing and control, as Michael Lipsky's classic analysis reveals (in "The Rationing of Services in Street-Level Bureaucracies," Part III, Chapter 15), programs, as Osborne and Gaebler show, can be designed to empower even the inner-city welfare mother who is often their foremost victim.

In addition to these last four selections, Part IV has been expanded still further, to reflect our belief that critical analysis has the burden as well as the opportunity to show how things might be different, as well as to bring critical insight to bear on the alternatives themselves. We have included "The Collectivist Organization: An Alternative to Rational-Bureaucratic Models" (Chapter 24) by Joyce Rothschild, who examines an egalitarian and democratic ideal type in light of recent experiences, and analyzes the limits and constraints as well as the strengths of such forms. Robert Howard and Leslie Schneider, in "Worker Participation in Technological Change" (Chapter 27), compare innovative organizational strategies of employee participation in the design and implementation of new technologies in the United States and Norway. Drawing upon case studies from a variety of industries, including telecommunications, postal, and banking services, they demonstrate the limits of technocentric and organization-centered models and the potential of empowering designs aimed at broad social interests, such as skill development, customer service, gender equity, and industrial democracy. Daniel Mazmanian and Jeanne Nienaber, in "Fishbowl Planning: Environmental Regulation, Economic Development, and Democratic Technique" (Chapter 31), provide a case study of a very innovative program of public participation developed in the Seattle District of the Army Corps of Engineers, which shows the potential of mobilizing expert resources, public interest and environmental groups, and varied economic interests in a community-based discourse and open planning process aimed at achieving consensual resolution of conflicting perspectives on development and conservation. Barry Rabe's "Beyond NIMBY: Participatory Approaches to Hazardous Waste Management in Canada and the United States" (Chapter 32) analyzes successful facility siting and management approaches in the province of Alberta, which instituted early and extensive public participation, as well as other comprehensive strategies that helped the province move beyond familiar gridlock. The possibilities of transplanting this model to the United States, where environmental organizations are stronger and political culture more adversarial, are explored.

Several other essays have been added to further enrich the selections. In Part III, Susan Moore Johnson's "Teaching and Learning in a

Bureaucratic School" (Chapter 16) analyzes the dynamic of street-level bureaucracy in urban school systems and thus frames the organizational challenge of school reform today. Charles Perrow and Mauro Guillén, in "The AIDS Crisis and Organizational Failure" (Chapter 23), examine the serious organizational failures in the early responses to the AIDS crisis of private and public health care systems, and federal and municipal agencies. In Part II, Frank Fischer's "Organizational Expertise and Bureaucratic Control: Behavioral Science as Managerial Ideology" (Chapter 12) has been revised for this edition. And Vicki Smith's "Manufacturing Management Ideology: Corporate Culture and Control in Financial Services" (Chapter 14) examines the broad theme of corporate culture, control, and ideology in the postindustrial setting of financial services undergoing crisis and downsizing, and thus broadens Part II in a new direction.

We have remained committed in this edition to a volume that can be of use to a diverse group of students in a wide range of courses. It can serve students of organizations and bureaucracy in sociology and political science departments, as well as those in administratively oriented professional programs that require study of organizational behavior. As either primary text or supplemental reading, it speaks to the issues raised in professionally oriented public administration programs, labor and management studies, and human and social services.

Michael Ames, editor-in-chief of Temple University Press, has encouraged us to do this revised edition, and we are grateful for his kind support and keen insight over the years. Many of the authors have provided us assistance beyond the gracious sharing of their work, and numerous others have shared their pedagogical insights on how to make the study of organizations engaging and empowering. Much of the content of this volume is designed to provide the basis for critical empowerment and participatory engagement in the face of bureaucratic hierarchies that no longer serve us very well, and we hope that it can enrich and enliven the process of learning itself.

PART I

Classical Problems and Perspectives

This section presents a selection of classic discussions of bureaucracy and organization.

Max Weber's essay is probably the most well-known classic of all, and it set the stage for most subsequent thinking. It is no accident that such a major contribution on bureaucracy came out of Germany; the Prussian bureaucracy was renowned the world over and had provided the context for Hegel and Marx's analyses in the nineteenth century. In this selection, Weber discusses the general features of the bureaucratic type, some of the reasons for its development, its advantages over previous types of organization, and why, once established, it is extremely difficult to destroy. While Weber himself favored legislative controls over bureaucracies, he was quite pessimistic about the long-term prospects for reigning in bureaucratic power.

Karl Marx, though usually not considered a theorist of organization per se, had a number of acute insights into bureaucracy, and his general analysis on social development provided a point of reference for many of the debates that were to follow. In his discussion of the "spirit of bureaucracy" from 1843, Marx develops a stinging critique of the Prussian bureaucracy. Though written in the dense philosophical style of his youth, Marx's basic points are clear enough. Bureaucracy, obsessed with its power and its formalism, views the world as an object to be administered and extends its tentacles as far as it is able to reach. Marx notes bureaucracy's formal characteristics: hierarchy and secrecy. He explains how the levels of the bureaucracy mutually deceive each other; how bureaucrats, concerned above all with their own careers, mask their own interests as general interests of state; and how the bureaucratic meaning of things is often quite different from the real meaning. Marx's own hopes for the complete elimination of bureaucracy are more fully revealed in his discussion of the radically democratic organizational features that he 1 perceived in the Paris Commune, the municipal system that was developed by the mass of Parisian citizens in rebellion against their own centralized and insensitive state in 1871. The Paris Commune subsequently became the symbol of an alternative form of participatory government for many radicals throughout the world.

Robert Michels directly addressed himself to Marx and attempted to show that real democracy in organizations is impossible, although many social struggles would continue to dress themselves in its mantle. Based on his analysis of the Social Democratic party and the trade unions under the kaiser, Michels argues that oligarchy, or rule by a clique of leaders who do all they can to protect their own position in the organization, is inevitable. For profound organizational and pyschological reasons, oligarchy asserts itself as an "iron" sociological law.

Much of the labor turmoil in the early decades of this century, in both Europe and the United States, was a motivating concern behind the next essay. Frederick Taylor, known as the father of scientific management, developed a set of principles for what he considered the best and most efficient way to organize production. While few adopted Taylor's views totally, they did have a profound impact on organization thinking and on the reality of work organization in the lives of many people. Taylor argued not only that management should have complete authority over the organization of work, but also that tasks should be simplified and fragmented as much as possible and that the brain work should be concentrated in the hands of management.

In the 1970s, after it became clear that Taylorist principles, far from dead, had even spread to various forms of white collar work, Harry Braverman undertook a reevaluation of the significance of Taylorism. His study was particularly timely, in light of the rising degree of dissatisfaction among both blue- and white-collar workers not only in the United States, but in many other major industrial countries. Since its publication in 1974, Braverman's analysis has become a classic, and perhaps the most cited piece, in the study of the modern workplace. Braverman attempts to show that the real meaning of Taylorism lies not in some neutral organizational precepts about efficiency, but in the struggle by management to secure control over the workplace and to lower the cost of labor. The fragmentation of work and the separation of conception and execution are not inevitable features of the modern workplace and advanced technology, but reflect management's interest in profit and control.

In a classic essay of the human relations school, Roethlisberger and Dickson develop an analysis of the organization as having both a human and a technical side, an informal as well as a formal one. On the basis of their famous studies at the Hawthorne Plant of Western Electric, the authors argue that the network of personal relations and the "nonrational" sentiments are crucial for understanding what makes an organization function—and what makes workers often resist the demands of management. Although the value of human relations theory has been much debated (Part I, Chapter 6), there can be little doubt that Roethlisberger and Dickson alerted organization theory to the necessity for studying the informal human side of organizations as well as the formal and technical features.

In the final selection, Alvin Gouldner, a major figure in the revival of critical thinking in American sociology, addresses himself to the various types of bureaucracy in industrial settings. The three types (mock, representative, and punishment-centered) reflect different degrees of agreement or conflict between workers and management. The values legitimating them are different, and the consequences of violating them also vary. Gouldner's analysis attempts to expand Weber's theory by uncovering those aspects of bureaucracy that concern human relations, consent, and democratic process in addition to authority, efficiency, and expertise.

1

Bureaucracy

Max Weber

Characteristics of Bureaucracy

Modern officialdom functions in the following specific manner:

I. *There is the principle of fixed and official jurisdictional areas, which are generally ordered by rules, that is, by laws or administrative regulations.*

1. The regular activities required for the purposes of the bureaucratically governed structure are distributed in a fixed way as official duties.
2. The authority to give the commands required for the discharge of these duties is distributed in a stable way and is strictly delimited by rules concerning the coercive means, physical, sacerdotal, or otherwise, which may be placed at the disposal of officials.
3. Methodical provision is made for the regular and continuous fulfillment of these duties and for the execution of the corresponding rights; only persons who have the generally regulated qualifications to serve are employed.

In public and lawful government these three elements constitute "bureaucratic authority." In private economic domination, they constitute bureaucratic "management." Bureaucracy, thus understood, is fully developed in political and ecclesiastical communities only in the modern state, and, in the private economy, only in the most advanced institutions of capitalism. Permanent and public office authority, with fixed jurisdiction, is not the historical rule but rather the exception. This is so even in large political structures such as those of the ancient Orient, the Germanic and Mongolian empires of conquest, or of many feudal structures of state. In all these cases, the ruler executes the most important measures through personal trustees, table-companions, or court-servants. Their commissions and authority are not precisely delimited and are temporarily called into being for each case.

Reprinted from *From Max Weber: Essays in Sociology*, edited and translated by H. H. Gerth and C. Wright Mills. Copyright 1946 by Oxford University Press, Inc.; renewed 1973 by Hans H. Gerth. Reprinted by permission of the publisher.

II. *The principles of office hierarchy and of levels of graded authority mean a firmly ordered system of super- and subordination in which there is a supervision of the lower offices by the higher ones.* Such a system offers the governed the possibility of appealing the decision of a lower office to its higher authority, in a definitely regulated manner. With the full development of the bureaucratic type, the office hierarchy is monocratically organized. The principle of hierachical office authority is found in all bureaucratic structures: in state and ecclesiastical structures as well as in large party organizations and private enterprises. It does not matter for the character of bureaucracy whether its authority is called "private" or "public."

When the principle of jurisdictional "competency" is fully carried through, hierarchical subordination—at least in public office—does not mean that the "higher" authority is simply authorized to take over the business of "lower." Indeed, the opposite is the rule. Once established and having fulfilled its task, an office tends to continue in existence and be held by another incumbent.

III. *The management of the modern office is based on written documents ("the files"), which are preserved in their original or draught form.* There is, therefore, a staff of subaltern officials and scribes of all sorts. The body of officials actively engaged in a "public" office, along with the respective apparatus of material implements and the files, make up a "bureau." In private enterprise, "the bureau" is often called "the office."

In principle, the modern organization of the civil service separates the bureau from the private domicile of the official, and, in general, bureaucracy segregates official activity as something distinct from the sphere of private life. Public monies and equipment are divorced from the private property of the official. This condition is everywhere the product of a long development. Nowadays, it is found in public as well as in private enterprises; in the latter, the principle extends even to the leading entrepreur. In principle, the executive office is separated from the household, business from private correspondence, and business assets from private fortunes. The more consistently the modern type of business management has been carried through the more are these separations the case. The beginnings of this process are to be found as early as the Middle Ages.

It is the peculiarity of the modern entrepreneur that he conducts himself as the "first official" of his enterprise, in the very same way in which the ruler of a specifically modern bureaucratic state spoke of himself as "the first servant" of the state.[1] The idea that the bureau activities of the state are intrinsically different in character from the management of private economic offices is a continental European notion and, by way of contrast, is totally foreign to the American way.

IV. *Office management, at least all specialized office management— and such management is distinctly modern—usually presupposes thorough and expert training.* This increasingly holds for the modern executive and employee of private enterprises, in the same manner as it holds for the state official.

V. *When the office is fully developed, official activity demands the full working capacity of the official, irrespective of the fact that his obligatory time in the bureau may be firmly delimited.* In the normal case, this is only the product of a long development, in the public as well as in the private office. Formerly, in all cases, the normal state of affairs was reversed: Official business was discharged as a secondary activity.

VI. *The management of the office follows general rules, which are more or less stable, more or less exhaustive, and which can be learned.* Knowledge of these rules represents a special technical learning which the officials possess. It involves jurisprudence, or administrative or business management.

The reduction of modern office management to rules is deeply embedded in its very nature. *The theory of modern public administration, for instance, assumes that the authority to order certain matters by decree— which has been legally granted to public authorities—does not entitle the bureau to regulate* the matter by commands given for each case, but only to regulate the matter abstractly. This stands in extreme contrast to the regulation of all relationships through individual privileges and bestowals of favor, which is absolutely dominant in patrimonialism, at least in so far as such relationships are not fixed by sacred tradition.

The Position of the Official

All this results in the following for the internal and external position of the official:

I. *Office holding is a "vocation."* This is shown, first, in the requirement of a firmly prescribed course of training, which demands the entire capacity for work for a long period of time, and in the generally prescribed and special examinations which are prerequisites of employment. Furthermore, the position of the official is in the nature of a duty. This determines the internal structure of his relations in the following manner: Legally and actually, office holding is not considered a source to be exploited for rents or emoluments, as was normally the case during the Middle Ages and frequently up to the threshold of recent times. Nor is office holding considered a usual exchange of services for equivalents, as is the case with free labor contracts. Entrance into an office, including one in the private economy, is considered an acceptance of a specific obligation of faithful management in return for a secure existence. It is decisive for the specific nature of modern loyalty to an office that, in the pure type, it does not establish a relationship to a *person*, like the vassal's or disciple's faith in feudal or in patrimonial relations of authority. Modern loyalty is devoted to impersonal and functional purposes. Behind the functional purposes, of course, "ideas of culture-values" usually stand. These are *ersatz* for the earthly or supra-mundane personal master: ideas such as "state," "church," "community," "party," or "enterprise" are thought of as being realized in a community; they provide an ideological halo for the master.

The political official—at least in the fully developed modern state—is not considered the personal servant of a ruler. Today, the bishop, the priest, and the preacher are in fact no longer, as in early Christian times, holders of purely personal charisma. The supra-mundane and sacred values which they offer are given to everybody who seems to be worthy of them and who asks for them. In former times, such leaders acted upon the personal command of their master; in principle, they were responsible only to him. Nowadays, in spite of the partial survival of the old theory, such religious leaders are officials in the service of a functional purpose, which in the present-day "church" has become routinized and, in turn, ideologically hallowed.

II. *The personal position of the official is patterned in the following way:*

1. Whether he is in a private office or a public bureau, the modern official always strives and usually enjoys a distinct *social esteem* as compared with the governed. His social position is guaranteed by the prescriptive rules of rank order and, for the political official, by special definitions of the criminal code against "insults of officials" and "contempt" of state and church authorities.

The actual social position of the official is normally highest where, as in old civilized countries, the following conditions prevail: a strong demand for administration by trained experts; a strong and stable social differentiation, where the official predominantly derives from socially and economically privileged strata because of the social distribution of power; or where the costliness of the required training and status conventions are binding upon him. The possession of educational certificates—to be discussed elsewhere[2]—are usually linked with qualification for office. Naturally, such certificates or patents enhance the "status element" in the social position of the official. For the rest this status factor in individual cases is explicitly and impassively acknowledged; for example, in the prescription that the acceptance or rejection of an aspirant to an official career depends upon the consent ("election") of the members of the official body. This is the case in the German army with the officer corps. Similar phenomena, which promote this guild-like closure of officialdom, are typically found in patrimonial and, particularly, in prebendal officialdoms of the past. The desire to resurrect such phenomena in changed forms is by no means infrequent among modern bureaucrats. For in-

stance, they have played a role among the demands of the quite proletarian and expert officials (the *tretyj* element) during the Russian revolution.

Usually the social esteem of the officials as such is especially low where
the demand for expert administration and the dominance of status conventions are weak. This is especially the case in the United States; it is
often the case in new settlements by virtue of their wide fields for
profit-making and the great instability of their social stratification.

2. The pure type of bureaucratic official is *appointed* by a superior
authority. An official elected by the governed is not a purely bureaucratic
figure. Of course, the formal existence of an election does not by itself
mean that no appointment hides behind the election—in the state, especially, appointment by party chiefs. Whether or not this is the case does
not depend upon legal statutes but upon the way in which the party
mechanism functions. Once firmly organized, the parties can turn a
formally free election into the mere acclamation of a candidate designated by the party chief. As a rule, however, a formally free election is
turned into a fight, conducted according to definite rules, for votes in
favor of one of two designated candidates.

In all circumstances, the designation of officials by means of an election among the governed modifies the strictness of hierarchical subordination. In principle, an official who is so elected has an autonomous
position opposite the superordinate official. The elected official does not
derive his position "from above" but "from below," or at least not from a
superior authority of the official hierarchy but from powerful party men
("bosses"), who also determine his further career. The career of the
elected official is not, or at least not primarily, dependent upon his chief
in the administration. The official who is not elected but appointed by a
chief normally functions more exactly, from a technical point of view,
because, all other circumstances being equal, it is more likely that purely
functional points of consideration and qualities will determine his selection and career. As laymen, the governed can become acquainted with
the extent to which a candidate is expertly qualified for office only in
terms of experience, and hence only after his service. Moreover, in every
sort of selection of officials by election, parties quite naturally give
decisive weight not to expert considerations but to the services a follower
renders to the party boss. This holds for all kinds of procurement of
officials by elections, for the designation of formally free, elected officials
by party bosses when they determine the slate of candidates, or the free
appointment by a chief who has himself been elected. The contrast,
however, is relative: Substantially similar conditions hold where legitimate monarchs and their subordinates appoint officials, except that the
influence of the followings are then less controllable.

Where the demand for administration by trained experts is considerable, and the party followings have to recognize an intellectually de-

veloped, educated, and freely moving "public opinion," the use of unqualified officials falls back upon the party in power at the next election. Naturally, this is more likely to happen when the officials are appointed by the chief. The demand for a trained administration now exists in the United States, but in the large cities, where immigrant votes are "corralled," there is, of course, no educated public opinion. Therefore, popular elections of the administrative chief and also of his subordinate officials usually endanger the expert qualification of the official as well as the precise functioning of the bureaucratic mechanism. It also weakens the dependence of the officials upon the hierarchy. This holds at least for the large administrative bodies that are difficult to supervise. The superior qualification and integrity of federal judges, appointed by the president, as over against elected judges in the United States is well known, although both types of officials have been selected primarily in terms of party considerations. The great changes in American metropolitan administrations demanded by reformers have proceeded essentially from elected mayors working with an apparatus of officials who were appointed by them. These reforms have thus come about in a "Caesarist" fashion. Viewed technically, as an organized form of authority, the efficiency of "Caesarism," which often grows out of democracy, rests in general upon the position of the "Caesar" as a free trustee of the masses (of the army or of the citizenry), who is unfettered by tradition. The "Caesar" is thus the unrestrained master of a body of highly qualified military officers and officials whom he selects freely and personally without regard to tradition or to any other considerations. This "rule of the personal genius," however, stands in contradiction to the formally "democratic" principle of a universally elected officialdom.

3. Normally, the position of the official is held for life, at least in public bureaucracies; and this is increasingly the case for all similar structures. As a factual rule, *tenure for life* is presupposed, even where the giving of notice or periodic reappointment occurs. In contrast to the worker in a private enterprise, the official normally holds tenure. Legal or actual life-tenure, however, is not recognized as the official's right to the possession of office, as was the case with many structures of authority in the past. Where legal guarantees against arbitrary dismissal or transfer are developed, they merely serve to guarantee a strictly objective discharge of specific office duties free from all personal considerations. In Germany, this is the case for all juridical and, increasingly, for all administrative officials.

Within the bureaucracy, therefore, the measure of "independence," legally guaranteed by tenure, is not always a source of increased status for the official whose position is thus secured. Indeed, often the reverse holds, especially in old cultures and communities that are highly differentiated. In such communities, the stricter the subordination under the arbitrary rule of the master, the more it guarantees the maintenance of the conventional seigneurial style of living for the official. Because of the very absence of these legal guarantees of tenure, the conventional esteem for the official may rise in the same way as, during the Middle Ages, the esteem of the nobility of office[3] rose at the expense of esteem for the freemen, and as the king's judge surpassed that of the people's judge. In Germany, the military officer or the administrative official can be removed from office at any time, or at least far more readily than the "independent judge," who never pays with loss of his office for even the grossest offense against the "code of honor" or against social conventions of the salon. For this very reason, if other things are equal, in the eyes of the master stratum the judge is considered less qualified for social intercourse than are officers and administrative officials, whose greater dependence on the master is a greater guarantee of their conformity with status conventions. Of course, the average official strives for a civil-service law, which would materially secure his old age and provide increased guarantees against his arbitrary removal from office. This striving, however, has its limits. A very strong development of the "right to the office" naturally makes it more difficult to staff them with regard to technical efficiency, for such a development decreases the career-opportunities of ambitious candidates for office. This makes for the fact that officials, on the whole, do not feel their dependency upon those at the top. This lack of a feeling of dependency, however, rests primarily upon the inclination to depend upon one's equals rather than upon the socially inferior and governed strata. The present conservative movement among the Badenia clergy, occasioned by the anxiety of a presumably threatening separation of church and state, has been expressly determined by the desire not to be turned "from a master into a servant of the parish."[4]

4. The official receives the regular *pecuniary* compensation of a normally fixed *salary* and the old age security provided by a pension. The salary is not measured like a wage in terms of work done, but according to "status," that is, according to the kind of function (the "rank") and, in addition, possibly, according to the length of service. The relatively great security of the official's income, as well as the rewards of social esteem, make the office a sought-after position, especially in countries which no longer provide opportunities for colonial profits. In such countries, this situation permits relatively low salaries for officials.

5. The official is set for a *"career"* within the hierarchical order of the public service. He moves from the lower, less important, and lower paid to the higher positions. The average official naturally desires a mechanical fixing of the conditions of promotion: if not of the offices, at least of the salary levels. He wants these conditions fixed in terms of "seniority," or possibly according to grades achieved in a developed system of expert examinations. Here and there, such examinations actually form a character *indelebilis* of the official and have lifelong effects on his career. To this

is joined the desire to qualify the right to office and the increasing tendency toward status group closure and economic security. All of this makes for a tendency to consider the offices as "prebends" of those who are qualified by educational certificates. The necessity of taking general personal and intellectual qualifications into consideration, irrespective of the often subaltern character of the educational certificate, has led to a condition in which the highest political offices, especially the positions of "ministers," are principally filled without reference to such certificates. . . .

Technical Advantages of Bureaucratic Organization

The decisive reason for the advance of bureaucratic organization has always been its purely technical superiority over any other form of organization. The fully developed bureaucratic mechanism compares with other organizations exactly as does the machine with the non-mechanical modes of production.

Precision, speed, unambiguity, knowledge of the files, continuity, discretion, unity, strict subordination, reduction of friction and of material and personal costs—these are raised to the optimum point in the strictly bureaucratic administration, and especially in its monocratic form. As compared with all collegiate, honorific, and avocational forms of administration, trained bureaucracy is superior on all these points. And as far as complicated tasks are concerned, paid bureaucratic work is not only more precise but, in the last analysis, it is often cheaper than even formally unremunerated honorific service.

Honorific arrangements make administrative work an avocation and, for this reason alone, honorific service normally functions more slowly; being less bound to schemata and being more formless. Hence it is less precise and less unified than bureaucratic work because it is less dependent upon superiors and because the establishment and exploitation of the apparatus of subordinate officials and filing services are almost unavoidably less economical. Honorific service is less continuous than bureaucratic and frequently quite expensive. This is especially the case if one thinks not only of the money costs to the public treasury—costs which bureaucratic administration, in comparison with administration by notables, usually substantially increases—but also of the frequent economic losses of the governed caused by delays and lack of precision. The possibility of administration by notables normally and permanently exists only where official management can be satisfactorily discharged as an avocation. With the qualitative increase of tasks the administration has to face, administration by notables reaches its limits—today, even in England. Work organized by collegiate bodies causes friction and delay and requires compromises between colliding interests and views. The administration, therefore, runs less precisely and is more independent of superiors; hence, it is less unified and slower. All advances of the Prussian administrative organization have been and will in the future be advances of the bureaucratic, and especially of the monocratic, principle.

Today, it is primarily the capitalist market economy which demands that the official business of the administration be discharged precisely, unambiguously, continuously, and with as much speed as possible. Normally, the very large, modern capitalist enterprises are themselves unequalled models of strict bureaucratic organization. Business management throughout rests on increasing precision, steadiness, and, above all, the speed of operations. This, in turn, is determined by the peculiar nature of the modern means of communication, including, among other things, the news service of the press. The extraordinary increase in the speed by which public announcements, as well as economic and political facts, are transmitted exerts a steady and sharp pressure in the direction of speeding up the tempo of adminstrative reaction towards various situations. The optimum of such reaction time is normally attained only by a strictly bureaucratic organization.[5]

Bureaucratization offers above all the optimum possibility for carrying through the principle of specializing administrative functions according to purely objective considerations. Individual performances are allocated to functionaries who have specialized training and who by constant practice learn more and more. The "objective" discharge of business primarily means a discharge of business according to *calculable rules* and "without regard for persons."

"Without regard for persons" is also the watchword of the "market" and, in general, of all pursuits of naked economic interests. A consistent execution of bureaucratic domination means the leveling of status "honor." Hence, if the principle of the free-market is not at the same time restricted, it means the universal domination of the "class situation." That this consequence of bureaucratic domination has not set in everywhere, parallel to the extent of bureaucratization, is due to the differences among possible principles by which polities may meet their demands.

The second element mentioned, "calculable rules," also is of paramount importance for modern bureaucracy. The peculiarity of modern culture, and specifically of its technical and economic basis, demands this very "calculability" of results. When fully developed, bureaucracy also stands, in a specific sense, under the principle of *sine ira ac studio*. Its specific nature, which is welcomed by capitalism, develops the more perfectly the more the bureaucracy is "dehumanized," the more completely it succeeds in eliminating from official business love, hatred, and all purely personal, irrational, and emotional elements which escape calculation. This is the specific nature of bureaucracy and it is appraised as its special virtue.

The more complicated and specialized modern culture becomes, the more its external supporting apparatus demands the personally detached and strictly "objective" *expert*, in lieu of the master of older social structures, who was moved by personal sympathy and favor, by grace and gratitude. Bureaucracy offers the attitudes demanded by the external apparatus of modern culture in the most favorable combination. As a rule, only bureaucracy has established the foundation for the administration of a rational law conceptually systematized on the basis of such enactments as the latter Roman imperial period first created with a high degree of technical perfection. During the Middle Ages, this law was received along with the bureaucratization of legal administration, that is to say, with the displacement of the old trial procedure which was bound to tradition or to irrational presuppositions, by the rationally trained and specialized expert. . . .

The Concentration of the Means of Administration

The bureaucratic structure goes hand in hand with the concentration of the material means of management in the hands of the master. This concentration occurs, for instance, in a well-known and typical fashion, in the development of big capitalist enterprises, which find their essential characteristics in this process. A corresponding process occurs in public organizations.

The bureaucratically led army of the Pharaohs, the army during the later period of the Roman republic and the principate, and, above all, the army of the modern military state are characterized by the fact that their equipment and provisions are supplied from the magazines of the war lord. This is in contrast to the folk armies of agricultural tribes, the armed citizenry of ancient cities, the militias of early medieval cities, and all feudal armies; for these, the self-equipment and the self-provisioning of those obliged to fight was normal.

War in our time is a war of machines. And this makes magazines technically necessary, just as the dominance of the machine in industry promotes the concentration of the means of production and management. In the main, however, the bureaucratic armies of the past, equipped and provisioned by the lord, have risen when social and economic development has absolutely or relatively diminished the stratum of citizens who were economically able to equip themselves, so that their number was no longer sufficient for putting the required armies in the field. They were reduced at least relatively, that is, in relation to the range of power claimed for the polity. Only the bureaucratic army structure allowed for the development of the professional standing armies which are necessary for the constant pacification of large states of the plains, as well as for warfare against far-distant enemies, especially enemies overseas. Specifically, military discipline and technical training can be normally and fully developed, at least to its modern high level, only in the bureaucratic army.

Historically, the bureaucratization of the army has everywhere been realized along with the transfer of army service from the propertied to the propertyless. Until this transfer occurs, military service is an honorific privilege of propertied men. Such a transfer was made to the native-born unpropertied, for instance, in the armies of the generals of the late Roman republic and the empire, as well as in modern armies up to the nineteenth century. The burden of service has also been transferred to strangers, as in the mercenary armies of all ages. This process typically goes hand in hand with the general increase in material and intellectual culture. The following reason has also played its part everywhere: The increasing density of population, and therewith the intensity and strain of economic work, makes for an increasing "indispensability" of the acquisitive strata[6] for purposes of war. Leaving aside periods of strong ideological fervor, the propertied strata of sophisticated and especially of urban culture as a rule are little fitted and also little inclined to do the coarse war work of the common soldier. Other circumstances being equal, the propertied strata of the open country are at least usually better qualified and more strongly inclined to become professional officers. This difference between the urban and the rural propertied is balanced only where the increasing possibility of mechanized warfare requires the leaders to qualify as "technicians."

The bureaucratization of organized warfare may be carried through in the form of private capitalist enterprise, just like any other business. Indeed, the procurement of armies and their administration by private capitalists has been the rule in mercenary armies, especially those of the Occident up to the turn of the eighteenth century. During the Thirty Years' War, in Brandenburg the soldier was still the predominant owner of the material implements of his business. He owned his weapons, horses, and dress, although the state, in the role, as it were, of the merchant of the "putting-out system," did supply him to some extent. Later on, in the standing army of Prussia, the chief of the company owned the material means of warfare, and only since the peace of Tilsit has the concentration of the means of warfare in the hands of the state definitely come about. Only with this concentration was the introduction of uniforms generally carried through. Before then, the introduction of uniforms had been left to a great extent to the arbitrary discretion of the regimental officer, with the exception of individual categories of troops to whom the king had "bestowed" certain uniforms, first, in 1620, to the royal bodyguard, then, under Frederick II, repeatedly.

Such terms as "regiment" and "battalion" usually had quite different meanings in the eighteenth century from the meanings they have today. Only the battalion was a tactical unit (today both are); the "regiment" was then a managerial unit of an economic organization established by the colonel's position as an "entrepreneur." "Official" maritime ventures (like the Genoese *maonae*) and army procurement belong to private capitalism's first giant enterprises of far-going bureaucratic character. In this respect, the "nationalization" of these enterprises by the state has its modern parallel in the nationalization of the railroads, which have been controlled by the state from their beginnings.

In the same way as with army organizations, the bureaucratization of administration goes hand in hand with the concentration of the means of organization in other spheres. The old administration by satraps and regents, as well as administration by farmers of office, purchasers of office, and, most of all, administration by feudal vassals, decentralize the material means of administration. The local demand of the province and the cost of the army and of subaltern officials are regularly paid for in advance from local income, and only the surplus reaches the central treasure. The enfeoffed official administers entirely by payment out of his own pocket. The bureaucratic state, however, puts its whole administrative expense on the budget and equips the lower authorities with the current means of expenditure, the use of which the state regulates and controls. This has the same meaning for the "economics" of the administration as for the large centralized capitalist enterprise.

In the field of scientific research and instruction, the bureaucratization of the always existing research institutes of the universities is a function of the increasing demand for material means of management. Liebig's laboratory at Giessen University was the first example of big enterprise in this field. Through the concentration of such means in the hands of the privileged head of the institute, the mass of researchers and docents are separated from their "means of production," in the same way as capitalist enterprise has separated the workers from theirs.

In spite of its indubitable technical superiority, bureaucracy has everywhere been a relatively late development. A number of obstacles have contributed to this, and only under certain social and political conditions have they definitely receded into the background. . . .

The Permanent Character of the Bureaucratic Machine

Once it is fully established, bureaucracy is among those social structures which are the hardest to destroy. Bureaucracy is the means of carrying "community action" over into rationally ordered "societal action." Therefore, as an instrument for "societalizing" relations of power, bureaucracy has been and is a power instrument of the first order—for the one who controls the bureaucratic apparatus.

Under otherwise equal conditions, a "societal action," which is methodically ordered and led, is superior to every resistance of "mass" or even of "communal action." And where the bureaucratization of administration has been completely carried through, a form of power relation is established that is practically unshatterable.

The individual bureaucrat cannot squirm out of the apparatus in which he is harnessed. In contrast to the honorific or avocational "notable," the professional bureaucrat is chained to his activity by his entire material and ideal existence. In the great majority of cases, he is only a single cog in a ever-moving mechanism which prescribes to him an essentially fixed route of march. The official is entrusted with specialized tasks and normally the mechanism cannot be put into motion or arrested by him, but only from the very top. The individual bureaucrat is thus forged to the community of all the functionaries who are integrated into the mechanism. They have a common interest in seeing that the mechanism continues its functions and that the societally exercised authority carries on.

The ruled, for their part, cannot dispense with or replace the bureaucratic apparatus of authority once it exists. For this bureaucracy rests upon expert training, a functional specialization of work, and an attitude set for habitual and virtuoso-like mastery of single yet methodically integrated functions. If the official stops working, or if his work is forcefully interrupted, chaos results, and it is difficult to improvise replacements from among the governed who are fit to master such chaos. This holds for public administration as well as for private economic management. More and more the material fate of the masses depends upon the steady and correct functioning of the increasingly bureaucratic organizations of private capitalism. The idea of eliminating these organizations becomes more and more utopian.

The discipline of officialdom refers to the attitude-set of the official for precise obedience within his *habitual* activity, in public as well as in private organizations. This discipline increasingly becomes the basis of all order, however great the practical importance of administration on the basis of the filed documents may be. The naive idea of Bakuninism of destroying the basis of "acquired rights" and "domination" by destroying public documents overlooks the settled orientation of *man* for keeping to the habitual rules and regulations that continue to exist independently of the documents. Every reorganization of beaten or dissolved troops, as well as the restoration of administrative orders destroyed by revolt, panic, or other catastrophes, is realized by appealing to the trained orientation of obedient compliance to such orders. Such compliance has been conditioned into the officials, on the one hand, and, on the other hand, into the governed. If such an appeal is successful it brings, as it were, the disturbed mechanism into gear again.

The objective indispensability of the once-existing apparatus, with its peculiar, "impersonal" character, means that the mechanism—in contrast to feudal orders based upon personal piety—is easily made to work for anybody who knows how to gain control over it. A rationally ordered system of officials continues to function smoothly after the enemy has occupied the area; he merely needs to change the top officials. This body of officials continues to operate because it is to the vital interest of everyone concerned, including above all the enemy.

During the course of his long years in power, Bismarck brought his ministerial colleagues into unconditional bureaucratic dependence by eliminating all independent statesmen. Upon his retirement, he saw to his surprise that they continued to manage their offices unconcerned and undismayed, as if he had not been the master mind and creator of these creatures, but rather as if some single figure had been exchanged for some other figure in the bureaucratic machine. With all the changes of masters in France since the time of the First Empire, the power machine has remained essentially the same. Such a machine makes "revolution," in the sense of the forceful creation of entirely new formations of authority, technically more and more impossible, especially when the apparatus controls the modern means of communication (telegraph, et cetera) and also by virtue of its internal rationalized structure. In classic fashion, France has demonstrated how this process has substituted *coups d'état* for "revolutions": all successful transformations in France have amounted to *coups d'état*. . . .

The Power Position of Bureaucracy

Everywhere the modern state is undergoing bureaucratization. But whether the *power* of bureaucracy within the polity is universally increasing must here remain an open question.

The fact that bureaucratic organization is technically the most highly developed means of power in the hands of the man who controls it does not determine the weight that bureaucracy as such is capable of having in a particular social structure. The ever-increasing "indispensability" of the officialdom, swollen to millions, is no more decisive for this question than is the view of some representatives of the proletarian movement that the economic indispensability of the proletarians is decisive for the measure of their social and political power position. If "indispensability" were decisive, then where slave labor prevailed and where freemen usually abhor work as a dishonor, the "indispensable" slaves ought to have held the positions of power, for they were at least as indispensable as officials and proletarians are today. Whether the power of bureaucracy as such increases cannot be decided *a priori* from such reasons. The drawing in of economic interest groups or other non-official experts, or the drawing in of nonexpert lay representatives, the establishment of local, inter-local, or central parliamentary or other representative bodies, or of occupational associations—these *seem* to run directly against the bureaucratic tendency. How far this appearance is the truth must be discussed in another chapter rather than in this purely formal and typological discussion. In general, only the following can be said here:

Under normal conditions, the power position of a fully developed bureaucracy is always overtowering. The "political master" finds himself in the position of the "dilettante" who stands opposite the "expert," facing the trained official who stands within the management of administration. This holds whether the "master" whom the bureaucracy serves is a "people," equipped with the weapons of "legislative initiative," the "referendum," and the right to remove officials, or a parliament, elected on a more aristocratic or more "democratic" basis and equipped with the right to vote a lack of confidence, or with the actual authority to vote it. It holds whether the master is an aristocratic, collegiate body, legally or actually based on self-recruitment, or whether he is a popularly elected president, a hereditary and "absolute" or a "constitutional" monarch.

Every bureaucracy seeks to increase the superiority of the professionally informed by keeping their knowledge and intentions secret. Bureaucratic administration always tends to be an administration of "secret sessions": In so far as it can, it hides its knowledge and action from criticism. Prussian church authorities now threaten to use disciplinary measures against pastors who make reprimands or other admonitory measures in any way accessible to third parties. They do this because the pastor, in making such criticism available, is "guilty" of facilitating a possible criticism of the church authorities. The treasury officials of the Persian shah have made a secret doctrine of their budgetary art and even use secret script. The official statistics of Prussia, in general, make public only what cannot do any harm to the intentions of the power-wielding bureaucracy. The tendency toward secrecy in certain administrative fields follows their material nature: Everywhere that the power interests of the domination structure toward *the outside* are at stake, whether it is an economic competitor of a private enterprise, or a foreign, potentially hostile polity, we find secrecy. If it is to be successful, the management of diplomacy can only be publicly controlled to a very limited extent. The military administration must insist on the concealment of its most important measures; with the increasing significance of purely technical aspects, this is all the more the case. Political parties do not proceed differently, in spite of all the ostensible publicity of Catholic congresses and party conventions. With the increasing bureaucratization of party organizations, this secrecy will prevail even more. Commercial policy, in Germany for instance, brings about a concealment of production statistics. Every fighting posture of a social structure toward the outside tends to buttress the position of the group in power.

The pure interest of the bureaucracy in power, however, is efficacious far beyond those areas where purely functional interests make for secrecy. The concept of the "official secret" is the specific invention of bureaucracy, and nothing is so fanatically defended by the bureaucracy as this attitude, which cannot be substantially justified beyond these specifically qualified areas. In facing a parliament, the bureaucracy, out of a sure power instinct, fights every attempt of the parliament to gain knowledge by means of its own experts or from interest groups. The so-called right of parliamentary investigation is one of the means by which parliament seeks such knowledge. Bureaucracy naturally welcomes a poorly informed and hence a powerless parliament—at least in so far as ignorance somehow agrees with the bureaucracy's interests. . . .

Notes

1. Frederick II of Prussia.
2. Cf. *Wirtschaft und Gesellschaft* (Tübingen, 1922), pp. 73 ff. and part II [German editor's note].
3. *Ministerialen.*
4. Written before 1914 [German editor's note].
5. Here we cannot discuss in detail how the bureaucratic apparatus may, and actually does, produce definite obstacles to the discharge of business in a manner suitable for the single case.
6. *Erwerbende Schichten.*

2

The Spirit of Bureaucracy *and* Beyond Bureaucracy: The Paris Commune

Karl Marx

The Spirit of Bureaucracy

The "state formalism" of bureaucracy is the "state as formalism," and Hegel has described it as such formalism. Since this "state formalism" constitutes itself as an actual power and becomes its own *material* content, it is obvious that "bureaucracy" is a web of *practical* illusions or the "illusion of the state." The spirit of bureaucracy is thoroughly Jesuitical and theological. The bureaucrats are the state's Jesuits and theologians. Bureaucracy is the priest's republic.

Since bureaucracy is the "state as formalism" in its *essence*, it is also the state as formalism in its *purpose*. For bureaucracy the actual purpose of the state therefore appears as a purpose *against* the state. The spirit of bureaucracy is the "formal state spirit." Bureaucracy makes the "formal state spirit" or the *actual* spiritlessness the categorical imperative. Bureaucracy considers itself the ultimate finite purpose of the state. Since bureaucracy converts its "formal" purposes into its contents, it everywhere comes in conflict with "real" purposes. It is, therefore, compelled to pass off what is formal for the content and the content for what is formal. The purposes of the state are changed into purposes of bureaus and vice versa. Bureaucracy is a circle no one can leave. Its hierarchy is a *hierarchy of information*. The top entrusts the lower circles with an insight into details, while the lower circles entrust the top with an insight into what is universal, and thus they mutually deceive each other.

Bureaucracy is the imaginary state beside the real state, the spiritualism of the state. Hence everything has a double meaning, a real and a bureaucratic meaning, just as knowledge and also the will are something double, real, and bureaucratic. What is real is dealt with in its

"The Spirit of Bureaucracy" is reprinted from *Writings of the Young Marx on Philosophy and Society,* edited by Loyd Easton and Kurt Guddat (Garden City: Doubleday, 1967), 185–187, with permission from the editors. "Beyond Bureaucracy: The Paris Commune" is reprinted from *Writings on the Paris Commune,* by Karl Marx and Friedrich Engels, edited by Hal Draper (New York: Monthly Review Press, 1971), 69–78. Copyright © 1971 by Hal Draper. Reprinted by permission of Monthly Review Foundation.

bureaucratic nature, in its otherworldly spiritual essence. Bureaucracy possesses the state's essence, the spiritual essence of society, as its *private property*. The universal spirit of bureaucracy is the *secret*, the mystery sustained within bureaucracy itself by hierarchy and maintained on the outside as a closed corporation. The open spirit and sentiment of patriotism, hence, appear to bureaucracy as a *betrayal* of this mystery. So *authority* is the principle of its knowledge, and the deification of authority is its *sentiment*. But within bureaucracy *spiritualism* becomes a *crass materialism*, the materialism of passive obedience, of faith in authority, of the *mechanism* of fixedly formal activity, fixed principles, views, and traditions. For the individual bureaucrat the state's purpose becomes his private purpose of *hunting for higher positions* and *making a career* for himself. In one respect he views actual life as something *material*, for *the spirit of this life has its separate existence* in bureaucracy. Bureaucracy, therefore, must aim to make life as material as possible. In another respect, life insofar as it becomes the object of bureaucratic treatment is material for him, for his spirit is not his own, his purpose lies outside, his particular existence is the existence of the bureau. The state then only exists in various fixed bureau-spirits whose connection is subordination and passive obedience. *Actual* knowledge seems lacking in content, just as actual life seems dead, since this imaginary knowledge and this imaginary life pass for real. So the bureaucrat must treat the actual state Jesuitically, no matter whether this Jesuitism is conscious or unconscious. It is necessary, though, that the Jesuitism, aware of its antithetical position, then achieves self-consciousness and becomes intentional.

While the bureaucracy is in one sense this crass materialism, its crass spiritualism is shown in its trying *to do everything*, that is, in its making *will* the causa prima, because it is merely *active* particular existence, derives its content externally, and thus can demonstrate its existence only through forming and limiting this content. For the bureaucrat the world is a mere object of his concern. . . .

Beyond Bureaucracy: The Paris Commune

On the dawn of the 18th of March, Paris arose to the thunderburst of "Vive la Commune!" What is the Commune, that sphinx so tantalising to the bourgeois mind?

> "The proletarians of Paris," said the Central Committee in its manifesto of the 18th March, "amidst the failures and treasons of the ruling classes, have understood that the hour has struck for them to save the situation by taking into their own hands the direction of public affairs. . . . They have understood that it is their imperious duty and their absolute right to render themselves masters of their own destinies, by seizing upon the governmental power."

But the working class cannot simply lay hold of the ready-made State machinery, and wield it for its own purposes.

The centralised State power, with its ubiquitous organs of standing army, police, bureaucracy, clergy, and judicature—organs wrought after the plan of a systematic and hierarchic division of labour—originates from the days of absolute monarchy, serving nascent middle-class society as a mighty weapon in its struggles against feudalism. Still, its development remained clogged by all manner of mediaeval rubbish, seignorial rights, local privileges, municipal and guild monopolies and provincial constitutions. The gigantic broom of the French Revolution of the eighteenth century swept away all these relics of bygone times, thus clearing simultaneously the social soil of its last hindrances to the superstructure of the modern State edifice raised under the First empire, itself the offspring of the coalition wars of old semi-feudal Europe against modern France. During the subsequent *régimes* the Government, placed under parliamentary control—that is, under the direct control of the propertied classes—became not only a hotbed of huge national debts and crushing taxes; with its irresistible allurements of place, pelf, and patronage, it became not only the bone of contention between the rival factions and adventurers of the ruling classes; but its political character changed simultaneously with the economic changes of society. At the same pace at which the progress of modern industry developed, widened, intensified the class antagonism between capital and labour, the State power assumed more and more the character of the national power of capital over labour, of a public force organised for social enslavement, of an engine of class despotism. After every revolution marking a progressive phase in the class struggle, the purely repressive character of the State power stands out in bolder and bolder relief. The Revolution of 1830, resulting in the transfer of Government from the landlords to the capitalists, transferred it from the more remote to the more direct antagonists of the working men. The bourgeois Republicans, who, in the name of the Revolution of February, took the State power, used it for the June massacres, in order to convince the working class that "social" republic meant the Republic ensuring their social subjection, and in order to convince the royalist bulk of the bourgeois and landlord class that they might safely leave the cares and emoluments of Government to the bourgeois "Republicans." However, after their one heroic exploit of June, the bourgeois Republicans had, from the front, to fall back to the rear of the "Party of Order"—a combination formed by all the rival fractions and factions of the appropriating class in their now openly declared antagonism to the producing classes. The proper form of their joint-stock Government was the *Parliamentary Republic*, with Louis Bonaparte for its President. Theirs was a *régime* of avowed class terrorism and deliberate insult toward the "vile multitude." If the Parliamentary Republic, as M. Thiers said, "divided them (the different fractions of the ruling class) least," it opened an abyss between that class and the whole body of society outside their spare ranks. The restraints by which their own divisions had under former *régimes* still checked the State power, were removed by their union; and in view of the threatening upheaval of the proletariat, they now used that State power mercilessly and ostentatiously as the national war-engine of capital against labour. In their uninterrupted crusade against the producing masses they were, however, bound not only to invest the executive with continually increased powers of repression, but at the same time to divest their own parliamentary stronghold—the National Assembly—one by one, of all its own means of defence against the Executive. The Executive, in the person of Louis Bonaparte, turned them out. The natural offspring of the "Party-of-Order" Republic was the Second Empire.

The empire, with the *coup d'état* for its certificate of birth, universal suffrage for its sanction, and the sword for its sceptre, professed to rest upon the peasantry, the large mass of producers not directly involved in the struggle of capital and labour. It professed to save the working class by breaking down Parliamentarism, and, with it, the undisguised subserviency of Government to the propertied classes. It professed to save the propertied classes by upholding their economic supremacy over the working class; and, finally, it professed to unite all classes by reviving for all the chimera of national glory. In reality, it was the only form of government possible at a time when the bourgeoisie had already lost, and the working class had not yet acquired, the faculty of ruling the nation. It was acclaimed throughout the world as the saviour of society. Under its sway, bourgeois society, freed from political cares, attained a development unexpected even by itself. Its industry and commerce expanded to colossal dimensions; financial swindling celebrated cosmopolitan orgies; the misery of the masses was set off by a shameless display of gorgeous, meretricious and debased luxury. The State power, apparently soaring high above society, was at the same time itself the greatest scandal of that society and the very hotbed of all its corruptions. Its own rottenness, and the rottenness of the society it had saved, were laid bare by the bayonet of Prussia, herself eagerly bent upon transferring the supreme seat of that *régime* from Paris to Berlin. Imperialism, is, at the same time, the most prostitute and the ultimate form of the State power which nascent middle-class society had commenced to elaborate as a means of its own emancipation from feudalism, and which full-grown bourgeois society had finally transformed into a means for the enslavement of labour by capital.

The direct antithesis to the empire was the Commune. The cry of "social republic," with which the Revolution of February was ushered in by the Paris proletariat, did but express a vague aspiration after a Republic that was not only to supersede the monarchical form of class-rule, but class-rule itself. The Commune was the positive form of that Republic.

Paris, the central seat of the old governmental power, and, at the same time, the social stronghold of the French working class, had risen in arms against the attempt of Thiers and the Rurals to restore and perpetuate that old governmental power bequeathed to them by the empire. Paris could resist only because, in consequence of the siege, it had got rid of the army, and replaced it by a National Guard, the bulk of which consisted of working men. This fact was now to be transformed into an institution. The first decree of the Commune, therefore, was the suppression of the standing army, and the substitution for it of the armed people.

The Commune was formed of the municipal councillors, chosen by universal suffrage in the various wards of the town, responsible and revocable at short terms. The majority of its members were naturally working men, or acknowledged representatives of the working class. The Commune was to be a working, not a parliamentary, body, executive and legislative at the same time. Instead of continuing to be the agent of the Central Government, the police was at once stripped of its political attributes, and turned into the responsible and at all times revocable agent of the Commune. So were the officials of all other branches of the Administration. From the members of the Commune downwards, the public service had to be done at *workmen's wages*. The vested interests and the representation allowances of the high dignitaries of State disappeared along with the high dignitaries themselves. Public functions ceased to be the private property of the tools of the Central Government. Not only municipal administration, but the whole initiative hitherto exercised by the State was laid into the hands of the Commune.

Having once got rid of the standing army and the police, the physical force elements of the old Government, the Commune was anxious to break the spiritual force of repression, the "parson-power," by the disestablishment and disendowment of all churches as proprietary bodies. The priests were sent back to the recesses of private life, there to feed upon the alms of the faithful in imitation of their predecessors, the Apostles. The whole of the educational institutions were opened to the people gratuitously, and at the same time cleared of all interference of Church and State. Thus, not only was education made accessible to all, but science itself freed from the fetters which class prejudice and governmental force had imposed upon it.

The judicial functionaries were to be divested of that sham independence which had but served to mask their abject subserviency to all succeeding governments to which, in turn, they had taken, and broken, the oaths of allegiance. Like the rest of public servants, magistrates and judges were to be elective, responsible, and revocable.

The Paris Commune was, of course, to serve as a model to all the great industrial centres of France. The communal *régime* once established in Paris and the secondary centres, the old centralised Government would in the provinces, too, have to give way to the self-government of the producers. In a rough sketch of national organisation which the Commune had no time to develop, it states clearly that the Commune was to be the political form of even the smallest country hamlet, and that in the rural districts the standing army was to be replaced by a national militia, with an extremely short term of service. The rural communes of every district were to administer their common affairs by an assembly of delegates in the central town, and these district assemblies were again to send deputies to the National Delegation in Paris, each delegate to be at any time revocable and bound by the *mandat impératif* (formal instructions) of his constituents. The few but important functions which still would remain for a central government were not to be suppressed, as has been intentionally mis-stated, but were to be discharged by Communal, and therefore strictly responsible agents. The unity of the nation was not be broken, but, on the contrary, to be organised by the Communal Constitution and to become a reality by the destruction of the State power which claimed to be the embodiment of that unity independent of, and superior to, the nation itself, from which it was but a parasitic excrescence. While the merely repressive organs of the old governmental power were to be amputated, its legitimate functions were to be wrested from an authority usurping pre-eminence over society itself, and restored to the responsible agents of society. Instead of deciding once in three or six years which member of the ruling class was to misrepresent the people in Parliament, universal suffrage was to serve the people, constituted in Communes, as individual suffrage serves every other employer in the search for the workmen and managers in his business. And it is well known that companies, like individuals, in matters of real business generally know how to put the right man in the right place, and, if they for once make a mistake, to redress it promptly. On the other hand, nothing could be more foreign to the spirit of the Commune than to supersede universal suffrage by hierarchic investiture.

It is generally the fate of completely new historical creations to be mistaken for the counterpart of older and even defunct forms of social life, to which they may bear a certain likeness. Thus, this new Commune, which breaks the modern State power, has been mistaken for a reproduction of the mediaeval Communes, which first preceded, and afterwards became the substratum of, that very State power. The Communal Constitution has been mistaken for an attempt to break up into a federation of small States, as dreamt of by Montesquieu and the Girondins, that unity of great nations which, if originally brought about by political force, has now become a powerful coefficient of social production. The antagonism of the Commune against the State power has been mistaken for an exaggerated form of the ancient struggle against over-centralisation. Peculiar historical circumstances may have prevented the classical development, as in France, of the bourgeois form of government, and may have allowed, as in England, to complete the great central State organs by corrupt vestries, jobbing councillors, and ferocious poor-law guardians in the towns, and virtually hereditary magistrates in the counties. The Communal Constitution would have restored to the social body all the forces hitherto absorbed by the State parasite feeding upon, and clogging the free movement of, society. By this one act it would have initiated the regeneration of France. The provincial French middle class saw in the Commune an attempt to restore the sway their order had held over the country under Louis Philippe, and which, under Louis Napoleon, was supplanted by the pretended rule of the country over the towns. In reality, the Communal Constitution brought the rural producers under the intellectual lead of the central towns of their districts, and these secured to them, in the working men, the natural trustees of their interests. The very existence of the Commune involved, as a matter of course, local municipal liberty, but no longer as a check upon the, now superseded, State power. It could only enter into the head of a Bismarck, who, when not engaged on his intrigues of blood and iron, always likes to resume his old trade, so befitting his mental calibre, of contributor to *Kladderadatsch* (the Berlin *Punch*), it could only enter into such a head, to ascribe to the Paris Commune aspirations after that caricature of the old French municipal organisation of 1791, the Prussian municipal constitution which degrades the town governments to mere secondary wheels in the police-machinery of the Prussian State. The Commune made that catchword of bourgeois revolutions, cheap government, a reality, by destroying the two greatest sources of expenditure—the standing army and State functionarism. Its very existence presupposed the non-existence of monarchy, which, in Europe at least, is the normal incumbrance and indispensable cloak of class-rule. It supplied the Republic with the basis of really democratic institutions. But neither cheap Government nor the "true Republic" was its ultimate aim; they were its mere concomitants.

The multiplicity of interpretations to which the Commune has been subjected, and the multiplicity of interests which construed it in their favour, show that it was a thoroughly expansive political form, while all previous forms of government had been emphatically repressive. Its true secret was this. It was essentially a working-class government, the produce of the struggle of the producing against the appropriating class, the political form at last discovered under which to work out the economic emancipation of labour. . . .

Except on the last condition, the Communal Constitution would have been an impossibility and a delusion. The political rule of the producer cannot coexist with the perpetuation of his social slavery. The Commune was therefore to serve as a lever for uprooting the economical foundations upon which rests the existence of classes, and therefore of class-rule. With labour emancipated, every man becomes a working man, and productive labour ceases to be a class attribute.

It is a strange fact. In spite of all the tall talk and all the immense literature, for the last sixty years, about emancipation of Labour, no sooner do the working men anywhere take the subject into their own hands with a will, than uprises at once all the apologetic phraseology of the mouthpieces of present society with its two poles of Capital and Wages Slavery (the landlord now is but the sleeping partner of the capitalist), as if capitalist society was still in its purest state of virgin innocence, with its antagonisms still undeveloped, with its delusions still unexploded, with its prostitute realities not yet laid bare. The Commune, they exclaim, intends to abolish property, the basis of all civilisation! Yes, gentlemen, the Commune intended to abolish that class-property which makes the labour of the many the wealth of the few. It aimed at the expropriation of the expropriators. It wanted to make individual property a truth by transforming the means of production, land and capital, now chiefly the means of enslaving and exploiting labour, into mere instruments of free and associated labour.—But this is Communism, "impossible" Communism! Why, those members of the ruling classes who are intelligent enough to perceive the impossibility of continuing the present system—and they are many—have become the obtrusive and full-mouthed apostles of co-operative production. If co-operative production is not to remain a sham and a snare; if it is to supersede the Capitalist system; if united co-operative societies are to regulate national production upon a common plan, thus taking it under their own control, and putting an end to the constant anarchy and periodical convulsions which are the fatality of Capitalist production—what else, gentlemen, would it be but Communism, "possible" Communism?

The working class did not expect miracles from the Commune. They have no ready-made utopias to introduce *par décret du peuple*. They know that in order to work out their own emancipation, and along with it that higher form to which present society is irresistibly tending by its own economical agencies, they will have to pass through long struggles, through a series of historic processes, transforming circumstances and men. They have no ideals to realise, but to set free the elements of the new society with which old collapsing bourgeois society itself is pregnant. In the full consciousness of their historic mission, and with the heroic resolve to act up to it, the working class can afford to smile at the coarse invective of the gentlemen's gentlemen with the pen and inkhorn, and at the didactic patronage of well-wishing bourgeois-doctrinaires, pouring forth their ignorant platitudes and sectarian crotchets in the oracular tone of scientific infallibility.

When the Paris Commune took the management of the revolution in its own hands; when plain working men for the first time dared to infringe upon the Governmental privilege of their "natural superiors," and, under circumstances of unexampled difficulty, performed their work modestly, conscientiously, and efficiently—performed it at salaries the

highest of which barely amounted to one-fifth of what, according to high
scientific authority, is the minimum required for a secretary to a certain
metropolitan school board—the old world writhed in convulsions of rage
at the sight of the Red Flag, the symbol of the Republic of Labour,
floating over the Hôtel de Ville.

3
Oligarchy

Robert Michels

Democracy is inconceivable without organization. A few words will
suffice to demonstrate this proposition.

A class which unfurls in the face of society the banner of certain
definite claims, and which aspires to the realization of a complex of ideal
aims deriving from the economic functions which that class fulfills, needs
an organization. Be the claims economic or be they political, organization
appears the only means for the creation of a collective will. Organization,
based as it is upon the principle of least effort, that is to say, upon the
greatest possible economy of energy, is the weapon of the weak in their
struggle with the strong.

The chances of success in any struggle will depend upon the degree to
which this struggle is carried out upon a basis of solidarity between
individuals whose interests are identical. In objecting, therefore, to the
theories of the individualist anarchists that nothing could please the
employers better than the dispersion and disaggregation of the forces of
the workers, the socialists, the most fanatical of all the partisans of the
idea of organization, enunciate an argument which harmonizes well with
the results of scientific study of the nature of parties.

We live in a time in which the idea of cooperation has become so firmly
established that even millionaires perceive the necessity of common
action. It is easy to understand, then, that organization has become a vital
principle of the working class, for in default of it their success is *a priori*

From *Political Parties* (New York: Free Press, 1964), 61–62, 65–73, 167–168, 170–173,
187, 354, 364–371. Reprinted with the permission of The Free Press, a Division of
Macmillan, Inc. from *Political Parties* by Robert Michels, translated by Eden and Cedar
Paul. Copyright © 1962 by The Crowell-Collier Publishing Company.

b/c of weakness

impossible. The refusal of the worker to participate in the collective life of his class cannot fail to entail disastrous consequences. In respect of culture and of economic, physical, and physiological conditions, the proletarian is the weakest element of our society. In fact, the isolated member of the working classes is defenseless in the hands of those who are economically stronger. It is only by combination to form a structural aggregate that the proletarians can acquire the faculty of political resistance and attain to a social dignity. The importance and the influence of the working class are directly proportional to its numerical strength. But for the representation of that numerical strength organization and coordination are indispensable. The principle of organization is an absolutely essential condition for the political struggle of the masses.

unions?

Yet this politically necessary principle of organization, while it overcomes that disorganization of forces which would be favorable to the adversary, brings other dangers in its train. We escape Scylla only to dash ourselves on Charybdis. Organization is, in fact, the source from which the conservative currents flow over the plain of democracy, occasioning their disastrous floods and rendering the plain unrecognizable. . . .

It is obvious that such a gigantic number of persons belonging to a unitary organization cannot any practical work upon a system of direct discussion. The regular holding of deliberative assemblies of a thousand members encounters the gravest difficulties in respect of room and distance; while from the topographical point of view such an assembly would become altogether impossible if the members numbered ten thousand. Even if we imagined the means of communication to become much better than those which now exist, how would it be possible to assemble such a multitude in a given place, at a stated time, and with the frequency demanded by the exigencies of party life? In addition must be considered the physiological impossibility even for the most powerful orator of making himself heard by a crowd of ten thousand persons.[1] There are, however, other reasons of a technical and administrative character which render impossible the direct self-government of large groups. If Peter wrongs Paul, it is out of the question that all the other citizens should hasten to the spot to undertake a personal examination of the matter in dispute, and to take the part of Paul against Peter.[2] By parity of reasoning, in the modern democratic party, it is impossible for the collectivity to undertake the direct settlement of all the controversies that may arise.

Hence the need for delegation, for the system in which delegates represent the mass and carry out its will. Even in groups sincerely animated with the democratic spirit, current business, the preparation and the carrying out of the most important actions, is necessarily left in the hands of individuals. It is well known that the impossibility for the people to exercise a legislative power directly in popular assemblies led the democratic idealists of Spain to demand, as the least of evils, a system of popular representation and a parliamentary state.[3]

Originally the chief is merely the servant of the mass. The organization is based upon the absolute equality of all its members. Equality is here understood in its most general sense, as an equality of like men. In many countries, as in idealist Italy (and in certain regions in Germany where the socialist movement is still in its infancy), this equality is manifested, among other ways, by the mutual use of the familiar "thou," which is employed by the most poorly paid wage-laborer in addressing the most distinguished intellectual. This generic conception of equality is, however, gradually replaced by the idea of equality among comrades belonging to the same organization, all of whose members enjoy the same rights. The democratic principle aims at guaranteeing to all an equal influence and an equal participation in the regulation of the common interests. All are electors, and all are eligible for office. The fundamental postulate of the *Déclaration des Droits de l'Homme* finds here its theoretical application. All the offices are filled by election. The officials, executive organs of the general will, play a merely subordinate part, are always dependent upon the collectivity, and can be deprived of their office at any moment. The mass of the party is omnipotent.

At the outset, the attempt is made to depart as little as possible from pure democracy by subordinating the delegates altogether to the will of the mass, by tieing them hand and foot. In the early days of the movement of the Italian agricultural workers, the chief of the league required a majority of four-fifths of the votes to secure election. When disputes arose with the employers about wages, the representatives of the organization, before undertaking any negotiations, had to be furnished with a written authority, authorized by the signature of every member of the corporation. All the accounts of the body were open to the examination of the members, at any time. There were two reasons for this. First of all, the desire was to avoid the spread of mistrust through the mass, "this poison which gradually destroys even the strongest organism." In the second place, this usage allowed each one of the members to learn bookkeeping, and to acquire such a general knowledge of the working of the corporation as to enable him at any time to take over its leadership.[4] It is obvious that democracy in this sense is applicable only on a very small scale. In the infancy of the English labor movement, in many of the trade unions, the delegates were either appointed in rotation from among all the members, or were chosen by lot.[5] Gradually, however, the delegates' duties became more complicated; some individual ability becomes essential, a certain oratorical gift, and a considerable amount of objective knowledge. It thus becomes impossible to trust to blind chance, to the fortune of alphabetic succession, or to the order of priority, in the choice of a delegation whose members must possess certain peculiar personal aptitudes if they are to discharge their mission to the general advantage.

Such were the methods which prevailed in the early days of the labor movement to enable the masses to participate in party and trade-union administration. Today they are falling into disuse, and in the development of the modern political aggregate there is a tendency to shorten and stereotype the process which transforms the led into a leader—a process which has hitherto developed by the natural course of events. Here and there voices make themselves heard demanding a sort of official consecration for the leaders, insisting that it is necessary to constitute a class of professional politicians, of approved and registered experts in political life. Ferdinand Tönnies advocates that the party should institute regular examinations for the nomination of socialist parliamentary candidates, and for the appointment of party secretaries.[6] Heinrich Herkner goes even farther. He contends that the great trade unions cannot long maintain their existence if they persist in entrusting the management of their affairs to persons drawn from the rank and file, who have risen to command stage by stage solely in consequence of practical aptitudes acquired in the service of the organization. He refers, in this connection, to the unions that are controlled by the employers, whose officials are for the most part university men. He foresees that in the near future all the labor organizations will be forced to abandon proletarian exclusiveness, and in the choice of their officials to give the preference to persons of an education that is superior alike in economic, legal, technical, and commercial respects.[7]

Even today, the candidates for the secretaryship of a trade union are subject to examination as to their knowledge of legal matters and their capacity as letter-writers. The socialist organizations engaged in political action also directly undertake the training of their own officials. Everywhere there are coming into existence "nurseries" for the rapid supply of officials possessing a certain amount of "scientific culture."

. . . It is undeniable that all these educational institutions for the officials of the party and of the labor organizations tend, above all, towards the artificial creation of an *élite* of the working class, of a caste of cadets composed of persons who aspire to the command of the proletarian rank and file. Without wishing it, there is thus effected a continuous enlargement of the gulf which divides the leaders from the masses.

The technical specialization that inevitably results from all extensive organization renders necessary what is called expert leadership. Consequently the power of determination comes to be considered one of the specific attributes of leadership, and is gradually withdrawn from the masses to be concentrated in the hands of the leaders alone. Thus the leaders, who were at first no more than the executive organs of the collective will, soon emancipate themselves from the mass and become independent of its control.

Organization implies the tendency to oligarchy. In every organization, whether it be a political party, a professional union, or any other association of the kind, the aristocratic tendency manifests itself very clearly. The mechanism of the organization, while conferring a solidity of struc-

ture, induces serious changes in the organized mass, completely inverting the respective position of the leaders and the led. As a result of organization, every party or professional union becomes divided into a minority of directors and a majority of directed.

It has been remarked that in the lower stages of civilization tyranny is dominant. Democracy cannot come into existence until there is attained a subsequent and more highly developed stage of social life. Freedoms and privileges, and among these latter the privilege of taking part in the direction of public affairs, are at first restricted to the few. Recent times have been characterized by the gradual extension of these privileges to a widening circle. This is what we know as the era of democracy. But if we pass from the sphere of the state to the sphere of party, we may observe that as democracy continues to develop, a backwash sets in. With the advance of organization, democracy tends to decline. Democratic evolution has a parabolic course. At the present time, at any rate as far as party life is concerned, democracy is in the descending phase. It may be enunciated as a general rule that the increase in the power of the leaders is directly proportional with the extension of the organization. In the various parties and labor organizations of different countries the influence of the leaders is mainly determined (apart from racial and individual grounds) by the varying development of organization. Where organization is stronger, we find that there is a lesser degree of applied democracy.

Every solidly constructed organization, whether it be a democratic state, a political party, or a league of proletarians for the resistance of economic oppression, presents a soil eminently favorable for the differentiation of organs and of functions. The more extended and the more ramified the official apparatus of the organization, the greater the number of its members, the fuller its treasury, and the more widely circulated its press, the less efficient becomes the direct control exercised by the rank and file, and the more is this control replaced by the increasing power of committees. Into all parties there insinuates itself that indirect electoral system which in public life the democratic parties fight against with all possible vigor. Yet in party life the influence of this system must be more disastrous than in the far more extensive life of the state. Even in the party congresses, which represent the party-life seven times sifted, we find that it becomes more and more general to refer all important questions to committees which debate *in camera*.

As organization develops, not only do the tasks of the administration become more difficult and more complicated, but, further, its duties become enlarged and specialized to such a degree that it is no longer possible to take them all in at a single glance. In a rapidly progressive movement, it is not only the growth in the number of duties, but also the higher quality of these, which imposes a more extensive differentiation of function. Nominally, and according to the letter of the rules, all the acts of the leaders are subject to the ever vigilant criticism of the rank and file.

In theory the leader is merely an employee bound by the instruction he receives. He has to carry out the orders of the mass, of which he is no more than the executive organ. But in actual fact, as the organization increases in size, this control becomes purely fictitious. The members have to give up the idea of themselves conducting or even supervising the whole administration, and are compelled to hand these tasks over to trustworthy persons specially nominated for the purpose, to salaried officials. The rank and file must content themselves with summary reports, and with the appointment of occasional special committees of inquiry. Yet this does not derive from any special change in the rules of the organization. It is by very necessity that a simple employee gradually becomes a "leader," acquiring a freedom of action which he ought not to possess. The chief then becomes accustomed to dispatch important business on his own responsibility, and to decide various questions relating to the life of the party without any attempt to consult the rank and file. It is obvious that democratic control thus undergoes a progressive diminution, and is ultimately reduced to an infinitesimal minimum. In all the socialist parties there is a continual increase in the number of functions withdrawn from the electoral assemblies and transferred to the executive committees. In this way there is constructed a powerful and complicated edifice. The principle of division of labor coming more and more into operation, executive authority undergoes division and subdivision. There is thus constituted a rigorously defined and hierarchical bureaucracy. In the catechism of party duties, the strict observance of hierarchical rules becomes the first article. The hierarchy comes into existence as the outcome of technical conditions, and its constitution is an essential postulate of the regular functioning of the party machine.

It is indisputable that the oligarchical and bureaucratic tendency of party organization is a matter of technical and practical necessity. It is the inevitable product of the very principle of organization. Not even the most radical wing of the various socialist parties raises any objection to this retrogressive evolution, the contention being that democracy is only a form of organization and that where it ceases to be possible to harmonize democracy with organization, it is better to abandon the former than the latter. Organization, since it is the only means of attaining the ends of socialism, is considered to comprise within itself the revolutionary content of the party, and this essential content must never be sacrificed for the sake of form.

In all times, in all phases of development, in all branches of human activity, there have been leaders. It is true that certain socialists, above all the orthodox Marxists of Germany, seek to convince us that socialism knows nothing of "leaders," that the party has "employees" merely, being a democratic party, and the existence of leaders being incompatible with democracy. But a false assertion such as this cannot override a sociological law. Its only result is, in fact, to strengthen the rule of the leaders, for it serves to conceal from the mass a danger which really threatens democracy.

For technical and administrative reasons, no less than for tactical reasons, a strong organization needs an equally strong leadership. As long as an organization is loosely constructed and vague in its outlines, no professional leadership can arise. The anarchists, who have a horror of all fixed organization, have no regular leaders. In the early days of German socialism, the *Vertrauensmann* (homme de confiance) continued to exercise his ordinary occupation. If he received any pay for his work for the party, the remuneration was on an extremely modest scale, and was no more than a temporary grant. His function could never be regarded by him as a regular source of income. The employee of the organization was still a simple workmate, sharing the mode of life and the social condition of his fellows. Today he has been replaced for the most part by the professional politician, *Berzirksleiter* (U.S. ward-boss), etc. The more solid the structure of an organization becomes in the course of the evolution of the modern political party, the more marked becomes the tendency to replace the emergency leader by the professional leader. Every party organization which has attained a considerable degree of complication demands that there should be a certain number of persons who devote all their activities to the work of the party. The mass provides these by delegations, and the delegates, regularly appointed, become permanent representatives of the mass for the direction of its affairs.

For democracy, however, the first appearance of professional leadership marks the beginning of the end, and this, above all, on account of the logical impossibility of the "representative" system, whether in parliamentary life or in party delegation. . . .

Those who defend the arbitrary acts committed by the democracy, point out that the masses have at their disposal means whereby they can react against the violation of their rights. These means consist in the right of controlling and dismissing their leaders. Unquestionably this defense possesses a certain theoretical value, and the authoritarian inclinations of the leaders are in some degree attenuated by these possibilities. In states with a democratic tendency and under a parliamentary regime, to obtain the fall of a detested minister it suffices, in theory, that the people should be weary of him. In the same way, once more in theory, the ill-humor and the opposition of a socialist group or of an election committee is enough to effect the recall of a deputy's mandate, and in the same way the hostility of the majority at the annual congress of trade unions should be enough to secure the dismissal of a secretary. In practice, however, the exercise of this theoretical right is interfered with by the working of the whole series of conservative tendencies to which allusion has previously been made, so that the supremacy of the autonomous and sovereign masses is rendered purely illusory. The dread by which Nietzsche was at one time so greatly disturbed, that every individual might become a functionary of the mass, must be completely dissipated in face of the truth that while all have the right to become functionaries, few only possess the possibility.

With the institution of leadership there simultaneously begins, owing to the long tenure of office, the transformation of the leaders into a closed caste.

Unless, as in France, extreme individualism and fanatical political dogmatism stand in the way, the old leaders present themselves to the masses as a compact phalanx—at any rate whenever the masses are so much aroused as to endanger the position of the leaders.

The election of the delegates to congresses, etc., is sometimes regulated by the leaders by means of special agreements, whereby the masses are in fact excluded from all decisive influence in the management of their affairs. These agreements often assume the aspect of a mutual insurance contract. In the German Socialist Party, a few years ago, there came into existence in not a few localities a regular system in accordance with which the leaders nominated one another in rotation as delegates to the various party congresses. In the meetings at which the delegates were appointed, one of the big guns would always propose to the comrades the choice as delegates of the leader whose "turn" it was. The comrades rarely revolt against such artifices, and often fail even to perceive them. Thus competition among the leaders is prevented, in this domain at least; and at the same time there is rendered impossible anything more than passive participation of the rank and file in the higher functions of the life of the party which they alone sustain with their subscriptions.[8] Notwithstanding the violence of the internecine struggles which divide the leaders, in all the democracies they manifest vis-à-vis the masses a vigorous solidarity. "They perceive quickly enough the necessity for agreeing among themselves so that the party cannot escape them by becoming divided."[9] This is true above all of the German social democracy, in which, in consequence of the exceptional solidity of structure which it possesses as compared with all the other socialist parties of the world, conservative tendencies have attained an extreme development.

When there is a struggle between the leaders and the masses, the former are always victorious if only they remain united. At least it rarely happens that the masses succeed in disembarrassing themselves of one of their leaders. . . .

There is no indication whatever that the power possessed by the oligarchy in party life is likely to be overthrown within an appreciable time. The independence of the leaders increases concurrently with their indispensability. Nay more, the influence which they exercise and the financial security of their position become more and more fascinating to the masses, stimulating the ambition of all the more talented elements to enter the privileged bureaucracy of the labor movement. Thus the rank and file becomes continually more impotent to provide new and intelligent forces capable of leading the opposition which may be latent among the masses.[10] Even today the masses rarely move except at the command of their leaders. When the rank and file does take action in conflict with the wishes of the chiefs, this is almost always the outcome of a misunderstanding. The miners' strike in the Ruhr basin in 1905 broke out against the desire of the trade-union leaders, and was generally regarded as a spontaneous explosion of the popular will. But it was subsequently proved beyond dispute that for many months the leaders had been stimulating the rank and file, mobilizing them against the coal barons with repeated threats of a strike, so that the mass of the workers, when they entered on the struggle, could not possibly fail to believe that they did so with the full approval of their chiefs.

It cannot be denied that the masses revolt from time to time, but their revolts are always suppressed. It is only when the dominant classes, struck by sudden blindness, pursue a policy which strains social relationships to the breaking-point, that the party masses appear actively on the stage of history and overthrow the power of the oligarchies. Every autonomous movement of the masses signifies a profound discordance with the will of the leaders. Apart from such transient interruptions, the natural and normal development of the organization will impress upon the most revolutionary of parties an indelible stamp of conservatism.

The thesis of the unlimited power of the leaders in democratic parties, requires, however, a certain limitation. Theoretically the leader is bound by the will of the mass, which has only to give a sign and the leader is forced to withdraw. He can be discharged and replaced at any moment. But in practice, as we have learned, for various reasons the leaders enjoy a high degree of independence. It is none the less true that if the Democratic Party cannot dispense with autocratic leaders, it is at least able to change these. Consequently the most dangerous defect in a leader is that he should possess too blind a confidence in the masses. The aristocratic leader is more secure than the democratic against surprises at the hands of the rank and file. It is an essential characteristic of democracy that every private carries a marshal's baton in his knapsack. It is true that the mass is always incapable of governing; but it is no less true that each individual in the mass, in so far as he possesses, for good or for ill, the qualities which are requisite to enable him to rise above the crowd, can attain to the grade of leader and become a ruler. Now this ascent of new leaders always involves the danger, for those who are already in possession of power, that they will be forced to surrender their places to the newcomers. The old leader must therefore keep himself in permanent touch with the opinions and feelings of the masses to which he owes his position. Formally, at least, he must act in unison with the crowd, must admit himself to be the instrument of the crowd, must be guided, in appearance at least, by its goodwill and pleasure. Thus it often seems as if the mass really controlled the leaders. But whenever the power of the leaders is seriously threatened, it is in most cases because a new leader or a new group of leaders is on the point of becoming dominant, and is inculcating views opposed to those of the old rulers of the party. It then seems as if the old leaders, unless they are willing to yield to the opinion of the rank and file and to withdraw, must consent to share their power with the new arrivals. If, however, we look more closely into the matter, it is not difficult to see that their submission is in most cases no more than an act of foresight intended to obviate the influence of their younger rivals. The submission of the old leaders is ostensibly an act of homage to the crowd, but in intention it is a means of prophylaxis against the peril by which they are threatened—the formation of a new elite. . . .

As soon as the new leaders have attained their ends, as soon as they have succeeded (in the name of the injured rights of the anonymous masses) in overthrowing the odious tyranny of their predecessors and to attaining to power in their turn, we see them undergo a transformation which renders them in every respect similar to the dethroned tyrants. Such metamorphoses as these are plainly recorded throughout history. In the life of monarchical states, an opposition which is headed by hereditary princes is rarely dangerous to the crown as an institution. In like manner, the opposition of the aspirants to leadership in a political party, directed against the persons or against the system of the old leaders, is seldom dangerous. The revolutionaries of today become the reactionaries of tomorrow. . . .

The principle that one dominant class inevitably succeeds to another, and the law deduced from the principle that oligarchy is, as it were, a preordained form of the common life of great social aggregates, far from conflicting with or replacing the materialist conception of history, completes that conception and reinforces it. There is no essential contradiction between the doctrine that history is the record of a continued series of class struggles and the doctrine that class struggles invariably culminate in the creation of new oligarchies which undergo fusion with the old. The existence of a political class does not conflict with the essential content of Marxism, considered not as an economic dogma but as a philosophy of history; for in each particular instance the dominance of a political class arises as the resultant of the relationships between the different social forces competing for supremacy, these forces being of course considered dynamically and not quantitatively.

Leadership is a necessary phenomenon in every form of social life. Consequently it is not the task of science to inquire whether this phenomenon is good or evil, or predominantly one or the other. But there is great scientific value in the demonstration that every system of leadership is incompatible with the most essential postulates of democracy. We are now aware that the law of the historic necessity of oligarchy is primarily based upon a series of facts of experience. Like all other scientific laws, sociological laws are derived from empirical observation. In order, however, to deprive our axiom of its purely descriptive character, and to confer upon it that status of analytical explanation which can alone transform a formula into a law, it does not suffice to contemplate from a unitary outlook those phenomena which may be empirically established; we must also study the determining causes of these phenomena. Such has been our task.

Now, if we leave out of consideration the tendency of the leaders to organize themselves and to consolidate their interests, and if we leave also out of consideration the gratitude of the led towards the leaders, and the general immobility and passivity of the masses, we are led to conclude that the principal cause of oligarchy in the democratic parties is to be found in the technical indispensability of leadership.

The process which has begun in consequence of the differentiation of functions in the party is completed by a complex of qualities which the leaders acquire through their detachment from the mass. At the outset, leaders arise *spontaneously*; their functions are *accessory* and *gratuitous*. Soon, however, they become *professional* leaders, and in this second stage of development they are *stable* and *irremovable*.

It follows that the explanation of the oligarchical phenomenon which thus results is partly *psychological*; oligarchy derives, that is to say, from the psychical transformations which the leading personalities in the parties undergo in the course of their lives. But also, and still more, oligarchy depends upon what we may term the *psychology of organization itself*, that is to say, upon the tactical and technical necessities which result from the consolidation of every disciplined political aggregate. Reduced to its most concise expression, the fundamental sociological law of the political parties (the term "political" being here used in its most comprehensive significance) may be formulated in the following term: "It is organization which gives birth to the dominion of the elected over the electors, of the mandataries over the mandators, of the delegates over the delegators. Who says organization, says oligarchy."

Every party organization represents an oligarchical power grounded upon a democratic basis. We find everywhere electors and elected. Also we find everywhere that the power of the elected leaders over the electing masses is almost unlimited. The oligarchical structure of the building suffocates the basic democratic principle. That which *is* oppresses *that which ought to be*. For the masses, this essential difference between the reality and the ideal remains a mystery. Socialists often cherish a sincere belief that a new *élite* of politicians will keep faith better than did the old. The notion of the representation of popular interests, a notion to which the great majority of democrats, and especially the working-class masses of the German-speaking lands, cleave with so much tenacity and confidence, is an illusion engendered by a false illumination, is an effect of mirage. In one of the most delightful pages of his analysis of modern Don Quixotism, Alphonse Daudet shows us how the "brav' commandant" Bravida, who has never quitted Tarascon, gradually comes to persuade himself, influenced by the burning southern sun, that he has been to Shanghai and has had all kinds of heroic adventures.[11] Similarly the modern proletariat, enduringly influenced by glib-tongued persons intellectually superior to the mass, ends by believing that by flocking to the poll and entrusting its social and economic cause to a delegate, its direct participation in power will be assured.

The formation of oligarchies within the various forms of democracy is the outcome of organic necessity, and consequently affects every organization, be it socialist or even anarchist. Haller long ago noted that in every form of social life relationships of dominion and of dependence are created by Nature herself.[12] The supremacy of the leaders in the democratic and revolutionary parties has to be taken into account in every historic situation present and to come, even though only a few and exceptional minds will be fully conscious of its existence. The mass will never rule except *in abstracto*. Consequently the question we have to discuss is not whether ideal democracy is realizable, but rather to what point and in what degree democracy is desirable, possible, and realizable at a given moment. In the problem as thus stated we recognize the fundamental problem of politics as a science. Whoever fails to perceive this must, as Sombart says, either be so blind and fanatical as not to see that the democratic current daily makes undeniable advance, or else must be so inexperienced and devoid of critical faculty as to be unable to understand that all order and all civilization must exhibit aristocratic features.[13] The great error of socialists, an error committed in consequence of their lack of adequate psychological knowledge, is to be found in their combination of pessimism regarding the present, with rosy optimism and immeasurable confidence regarding the future. A realistic view of the mental condition of the masses shows beyond question that even if we admit the possibility of moral improvement in mankind, the human materials with whose use politicians and philosophers cannot dispense in their plans of social reconstruction are not of a character to justify excessive optimism. Within the limits of time from which human provision is possible, optimism will remain the exclusive privilege of utopian thinkers.

The socialist parties, like the trade unions, are living forms of social life. As such they react with the utmost energy against any attempt to analyze their structure or their nature, as if it were a method of vivisection. When science attains to results which conflict with their apriorist ideology, they revolt with all their power. Yet their defense is extremely feeble. Those among the representatives of such organizations whose scientific earnestness and personal good faith make it impossible for them to deny outright the existence of oligarchical tendencies in every form of democracy, endeavor to explain these tendencies as the outcome of a kind of atavism in the mentality of the masses, characteristic of the youth of the movement. The masses, they assure us, are still infected by the oligarchic virus simply because they have been oppressed during long centuries of slavery, and have never yet enjoyed an autonomous existence. The socialist regime, however, will soon restore them to health, and will furnish them with all the capacity necessary for self-government. Nothing could be more antiscientific than the supposition that as soon as socialists have gained possession of government power it will suffice for the masses to exercise a little control over their leaders to secure that the interests of these leaders shall coincide perfectly with the interests of the led. This idea may be compared with the view of Jules Guesde, no less antiscientific than anti-Marxist (though Guesde proclaims himself a Marxist), that whereas Christianity has made God into a man, socialism will make man into a god.[14]

The objective immaturity of the mass is not a mere transitory phenomenon which will disappear with the progress of democratization *au lendemain du socialisme*. On the contrary, it derives from the very nature of the mass as mass, for this, even when organized, suffers from an incurable incompetence for the solution of the diverse problems which present themselves for solution—because the mass *per se* is amorphous, and therefore needs division of labor, specialization, and guidance. "The human species wants to be governed; it will be. I am ashamed of my kind," wrote Proudhon from his prison in 1850.[15] Man as individual is by nature predestined to be guided, and to be guided all the more in proportion as the functions of life undergo division and subdivision. To an enormously greater degree is guidance necessary for the social group.

From this chain of reasoning and from these scientific convictions it would be erroneous to conclude that we should renounce all endeavors to ascertain the limits which may be imposed upon the powers exercised over the individual by oligarchies (state, dominant class, party, etc.). It would be an error to abandon the desperate enterprise of endeavoring to discover a social order which will render possible the complete realization of the idea of popular sovereignty. In the present work, as the writer said at the outset, it has not been his aim to indicate new paths. But it seemed necessary to lay considerable stress upon the pessimist aspect of democracy which is forced on us by historical study. We had to inquire whether, and within what limits, democracy must remain purely ideal, possessing no other value than that of a moral criterion which renders it possible to appreciate the varying degrees of that oligarchy which is immanent in every social regime. In other words, we have had to inquire if, and in what degree, democracy is an ideal which we can never hope to realize in practice. A further aim of this work was the demolition of some of the facile and superficial democratic illusions which trouble science and lead the masses astray. Finally, the author desired to throw light upon certain sociological tendencies which oppose the reign of democracy, and to a still greater extent oppose the reign of socialism.

The writer does not wish to deny that every revolutionary working-class movement, and every movement sincerely inspired by the democratic spirit, may have a certain value as contributing to the enfeeblement of oligarchic tendencies. The peasant in the fable, when on his death-bed, tells his sons that a treasure is buried in the field. After the old man's death the sons dig everywhere in order to discover the treasure. They do not find it. But their indefatigable labor improves the soil and secures for them a comparative well-being. The treasure in the fable may well symbolize democracy. Democracy is a treasure which no one will ever discover by deliberate search. But in continuing our search, in laboring indefatigably to discover the undiscoverable, we shall perform a work which will have fertile results in the democratic sense. We have seen, indeed, that within the bosom of the democratic working-class party are born the very tendencies to counteract which that party came into existence. Thanks to the diversity and to the unequal worth of the elements of the party, these tendencies often give rise to manifestations which border on tyranny. We have seen that the replacement of the traditional legitimism of the powers-that-be by the brutal plebiscitary rule of Bonapartist parvenus does not furnish these tendencies with any moral or aesthetic superiority. Historical evolution mocks all the prophylactic measures that have been adopted for the prevention of oligarchy. If laws are passed to control the dominion of the leaders, it is the laws which gradually weaken, and not the leaders. Sometimes, however, the democratic principle carries with it, if not a cure, at least a palliative, for the disease of oligarchy. When Victor Considérant formulated his "democratico-pacificist" socialism, he declared that socialism signified, not the rule of society by the lower classes of the population, but the government and organization of society in the interest of all, through the intermediation of a group of citizens; and he added that the numerical importance of this group must increase *pari passu* with social development.[16] This last observation draws attention to a point of capital importance. It is, in fact, a general characteristic of democracy, and hence also of the labor movement, to stimulate and to strengthen in the individual the intellectual aptitudes of criticism and control. We have seen how the progressive bureaucratization of the democratic organism tends to neutralize the beneficial effects of such criticism and such control. None the less it is true that the labor movement, in virtue of the theoretical postulates it proclaims, is apt to bring into existence (in opposition to the will of the leaders) a certain number of free spirits who, moved by principle, by instinct, or by both, desire to revise the base upon which authority is established. Urged on by conviction or by temperament, they are never weary of asking an eternal "Why?" about every human institution. Now this predisposition towards free inquiry, in which we cannot fail to recognize one of the most precious factors of civilization, will gradually increase in proportion as the economic status of the masses undergoes improvement and becomes more stable, and in proportion as they are admitted more effectively to the advantages of civilization. A wider education involves an increasing capacity for exercising control. Can we not observe every day that among the well-to-do the authority of the leaders over the led, extensive though it be, is never so unrestricted as in the case of the leaders of the poor? Taken in the mass, the poor are powerless and disarmed vis-à-vis their leaders. Their intellectual and cultural inferiority makes it impossible for them to see whither the leader is going, or to estimate in advance the significance of his actions. It is, consequently, the great task of social education to raise the intellectual level of the masses, so that they may be enabled, within the limits of what is possible, to counteract the oligarchical tendencies of the working-class movement.

In view of the perennial incompetence of the masses, we have to recognize the existence of two regulative principles: 1. The *ideological* tendency of democracy towards criticism and control; 2. The *effective* counter-tendency of democracy towards the creation of parties ever more complex and ever more differentiated—parties, that is to say, which are increasingly based upon the competence of the few.

To the idealist, the analysis of the forms of contemporary democracy cannot fail to be a source of bitter deceptions and profound discouragement. Those alone, perhaps, are in a position to pass a fair judgment upon democracy who, without lapsing into dilettantist sentimentalism, recognize that all scientific and human ideals have relative values. If we wish to estimate the value of democracy, we must do so in comparison with its converse, pure aristocracy. The defects inherent in democracy are obvious. It is none the less true that as a form of social life we must choose democracy as the least of evils. The ideal government would doubtless be that of an aristocracy of persons at once morally good and technically efficient. But where shall we discover such an aristocracy? We may find it sometimes, though very rarely, as the outcome of deliberate selection; but we shall never find it where the hereditary principle remains in operation. Thus monarchy in its pristine purity must be considered as imperfection incarnate, as the most incurable of ills; from the moral point of view it is inferior even to the most revolting of demagogic dictatorships, for the corrupt organism of the latter at least contains a healthy principle upon whose working we may continue to base hopes of social resanation. It may be said, therefore, that the more humanity comes to recognize the advantages which democracy, however imperfect, presents over aristocracy, even at its best, the less likely is it that a recognition of the defects of democracy will provoke a return to aristocracy. Apart from certain formal differences and from the qualities which can be acquired only by good education and inheritance (qualities in which aristocracy will always have the advantage over democracy—qualities which democracy either neglects altogether, or, attempting to imitate them, falsifies them to the point of caricature), the defects of democracy will be found to inhere in its inability to get rid of its aristocratic scoriæ. On the other hand, nothing but a serene and frank examination of the oligarchical dangers of democracy will enable us to minimize these dangers, even though they can never be entirely avoided.

The democratic currents of history resemble successive waves. They break ever on the same shoal. They are ever renewed. This enduring spectacle is simultaneously encouraging and depressing. When democracies have gained a certain stage of development, they undergo a gradual transformation, adopting the aristocratic spirit, and in many cases also the aristocratic forms, against which at the outset they struggled so fiercely. Now new accusers arise to denounce the traitors; after an era of glorious combats and of inglorious power, they end by fusing with the old dominant class; whereupon once more they are in their turn attacked by fresh opponents who appeal to the name of democracy. It is probable that this cruel game will continue without end.

Notes

1. Roscher, p. 351.
2. Louis Blanc, "L'état dans une démocratie," *Questions d'aujourd'hui et de demain* (Paris: Dentu, 1880), vol. iii, p. 144.
3. Cf. the letter of Antonio Quiroga to King Ferdinand VII, dated January 7, 1820 (Don Juan van Halen, *Mémoires*, Renouard, Paris, 1827, Part II, p. 382).
4. Egidio Bernaroli, *Manuale per la constituzione e il funzionamento delle leghe dei contadini*, Libreria Soc. Ital., Rome, 1902, pp. 20, 26, 27, 52.
5. Sidney and Beatrice Webb, *Industrial Democracy* (German edition), Stuttgart, 1898, vol. i, p. 6.
6. Ferdinand Tönnies, *Politik und Moral*, Neaer Frankfort Verlag, Frankfort, 1901, p. 46.
7. Heinrich Herkner, *Der Arbeiterfrage*, Guttentag, Berlin, 1908, 5th ed., pp. 116, 117.
8. Similar phenomena have been observed in party life in America (Ostrogorsky, *La Démocratie*, vol. 2, p. 196).
9. Trans. from Antoine Elisée Cherbuliez, *Théorie des Garantis constitutionelles* (Paris: Ab. Cherbuliez, 1838), vol. 2, p. 253.
10. Thus Pareto writes: "If B [the new élite] took the place of A [the old élite] by slow infiltration, and if the social circulation is not interrupted, C [the masses] are deprived of the leaders who could incite them to revolt." (Trans. from Vilfredo Pareto, *Les Systèmes socialistes*, Giard and Brière, Paris, 1892, vol. i, p. 35).
11. Alphonse Daudet, *Tartarin de Tarascon*, Marpon et Flammarion, Paris, 1887, p. 40.
12. Ludwig von Haller, *Restauration der Staatswissenschaften*, Winterthur, 1816, vol. i, pp. 304 et seq.
13. Werner Sombart, *Dennoch!* (Jena: Fischer, 1900), p. 90. Cf. also F. S. Merlino, *Pro e contro il Socialismo*, pp. 262 et seq.
14. Jules Guesde, *La Problème et la Solution*, Libr. du Parti Socialiste, Paris, p. 17.
15. Charles Gide et Charles Rist, *Histoire des Doctrines économiques depuis les Physiocrates jusquà nos jours*, Larose et Tenin, Paris, 1909, p. 709.
16. Victor Considérant, *Principes du Socialisme. Manifeste de la Démocratie au xix Siècle*, Librairie Phalanstérienne, Paris, 1847, p. 53.

4
Scientific Management

Frederick W. Taylor

The writer has found that there are three questions uppermost in the minds of men when they become interested in scientific management.

First. Wherein do the principles of scientific management differ essentially from those of ordinary management?

Second. Why are better results attained under scientific management than under the other types?

Third. Is not the most important problem that of getting the right man at the head of the company? And if you have the right man cannot the choice of the type of management be safely left to him?

One of the principal objects of the following pages will be to give a satisfactory answer to these questions. . . .

Before starting to illustrate the principles of scientific management, or "task management" as it is briefly called, it seems desirable to outline what the writer believes will be recognized as the best type of management which is in common use. This is done so that the great difference between the best of the ordinary management and scientific management may be fully appreciated.

In an industrial establishment which employs say from 500 to 1000 workmen, there will be found in many cases at least twenty to thirty different trades. The workmen in each of these trades have had their knowledge handed down to them by word of mouth, through the many years in which their trade has been developed from the primitive condition, in which our far-distant ancestors each one practised the rudiments of many different trades, to the present state of great and growing subdivision of labor, in which each man specializes upon some comparative small class of work.

The ingenuity of each generation has developed quicker and better methods for doing every element of the work in every trade. Thus the methods which are now in use may in a broad sense be said to be an

Reprinted from "The Principles of Scientific Management," in *Scientific Management,* by Frederick Winslow Taylor (New York: Harper & Row, 1939), 30–48, 57–60. Copyright 1911 by Frederick W. Taylor; renewed in 1939 by Louise M. S. Taylor.

evolution representing the survival of the fittest and best of the ideas which have been developed since the starting of each trade. However, while this is true in a broad sense, only those who are intimately acquainted with each of these trades are fully aware of the fact that in hardly any element of any trade is there uniformity in the methods which are used. Instead of having only one way which is generally accepted as a standard, there are in daily use, say, fifty or a hundred different ways of doing each element of the work. And a little thought will make it clear that this must inevitably be the case, since our methods have been handed down from man to man by word of mouth, or have, in most cases, been almost unconsciously learned through personal observation. Practically in no instances have they been codified or systematically analyzed or described. The ingenuity and experience of each generation—of each decade, even, have without doubt handed over better methods to the next. This mass of rule-of-thumb or traditional knowledge may be said to be the principal asset or possession of every tradesman. Now, in the best of the ordinary types of management, the managers recognize frankly the fact that the 500 or 1000 workmen, included in the twenty to thirty trades, who are under them, possess this mass of traditional knowledge, a large part of which is not in the possession of the management. The management, of course, includes foremen and superintendents, who themselves have been in most cases first-class workers at their trades. And yet these foremen and superintendents know, better than anyone else, that their own knowledge and personal skill falls far short of the combined knowledge and dexterity of all the workmen under them. The most experienced managers therefore frankly place before their workmen the problem of doing the work in the best and most economical way. They recognize the task before them as that of inducing each workman to use his best endeavors, his hardest work, all his traditional knowledge, his skill, his ingenuity, and his goodwill—in a word, his "initiative," so as to yield the largest possible return to his employer. The problem before the management, then, may be briefly said to be that of obtaining the best *initiative* of every workman. And the writer uses the word "initiative" in its broadest sense, to cover all of the good qualities sought for from the men.

On the other hand, no intelligent manager would hope to obtain in any full measure the initiative of his workmen unless he felt that he was giving them something more than they usually receive from their employers. Only those among the readers of this paper who have been managers or who have worked themselves at a trade realize how far the average workman falls short of giving his employer his full initiative. It is well within the mark to state that in nineteen out of twenty industrial establishments the workmen believe it to be directly against their interests to give their employers their best initiative, and that instead of working hard to do the largest possible amount of work and the best quality of work for their employers, they deliberately work as slowly as they dare while they

at the same time try to make those over them believe that they are working fast.[1]

The writer repeats, therefore, that in order to have any hope of obtaining the initiative of his workmen the manager must give some *special incentive* to his men beyond that which is given to the average of the trade. This incentive can be given in several different ways, as, for example, the hope of rapid promotion or advancement; higher wages, either in the form of generous piecework prices or of a premium or bonus of some kind for good and rapid work; shorter hours of labor; better surroundings and working conditions than are ordinarily given, etc., and, above all, this special incentive should be accompanied by the personal consideration for, and friendly contact with, his workmen which comes only from a genuine and kindly interest in the welfare of those under him. It is only by giving a special inducement or "incentive" of this kind that the employer can hope even approximately to get the "initiative" of his workmen. Under the ordinary type of management the necessity for offering the workman a special inducement has come to be so generally recognized that a large proportion of those most interested in the subject look upon the adoption of some one of the modern schemes for paying men (such as piece work, the premium plan, or the bonus plan, for instance) as practically the whole system of management. Under scientific management, however, the particular pay system which is adopted is merely one of the subordinate elements.

Broadly speaking, then, the best type of management in ordinary use may be defined as management in which the workmen give their best *initiative* and in return receive some *special incentive* from their employers. This type of management will be referred to as the management of "*initiative and incentive*" in contradistinction to scientific management, or task management, with which it is to be compared.

The writer hopes that the management of "initiative and incentive" will be recognized as representing the best type in ordinary use, and in fact he believes that it will be hard to persuade the average manager that anything better exists in the whole field than this type. The task which the writer has before him, then, is the difficult one of trying to prove in a thoroughly convincing way that there is another type of management which is not only better but overwhelmingly better than the management of "initiative and incentive."

The universal prejudice in favor of the management of "initiative and incentive" is so strong that no mere theoretical advantages which can be pointed out will be likely to convince the average manager that any other system is better. It will be upon a series of practical illustrations of the actual working of the two systems that the writer will depend in his efforts to prove that scientific management is so greatly superior to other types. Certain elementary principles, a certain philosophy, will however be recognized as the essence of that which is being illustrated in all of the practical examples which will be given. And the broad principles in which the scientific system differs from the ordinary or "rule-of-thumb" system are so simple in their nature that it seems desirable to describe them before starting with the illustrations.

Under the old type of management success depends almost entirely upon getting the "initiative" of the workmen, and it is indeed a rare case in which this initiative is really attained. Under scientific management the "initiative" or the workmen (that is, their hard work, their good-will, and their ingenuity) is obtained with absolute uniformity and to a greater extent than is possible under the old system; and in addition to this improvement on the part of the men, the managers assume new burdens, new duties, and responsibilities never dreamed of in the past. The managers assume, for instance, the burden of gathering together all of the traditional knowledge which in the past has been possessed by the workmen and then of classifying, tabulating, and reducing this knowledge to rules, laws, and formulæ which are immensely helpful to the workmen in doing their daily work. In addition to developing a *science* in this way, the management take on three other types of duties which involve new and heavy burdens for themselves.

These new duties are grouped under four heads:

First. They develop a science for each element of a man's work, which replaces the old rule-of-thumb method.

Second. They scientifically select and then train, teach, and develop the workman, whereas in the past he chose his own work and trained himself as best he could.

Third. They heartily cooperate with the men so as to insure all of the work being done in accordance with the principles of the science which has been developed.

Fourth. There is an almost equal division of the work and the responsibility between the management and the workmen. The management take over all work for which they are better fitted than the workmen, while in the past almost all of the work and the greater part of the responsibility were thrown upon the men.

It is this combination of the initiative of the workmen, coupled with the new types of work done by the management, that makes scientific management so much more efficient than the old plan.

Three of these elements exist in many cases, under the management of "initiative and incentive," in a small and rudimentary way, but they are, under this management, of minor importance, whereas under scientific management they form the very essence of the whole system.

The fourth of these elements, "an almost equal division of the responsibility between the management and the workmen," requires further explanation. The philosophy of the management of "initiative and incentive" makes it necessary for each workman to bear almost the entire responsibility for the general plan as well as for each detail of his work, and in many cases for his implements as well. In addition to this he must do all of the actual physical labor. The development of a science, on the other hand, involves the establishment of many rules, laws, and formulæ which replace the judgment of the individual workmen and which can be effectively used only after having been systematically recorded, indexed, etc. The practical use of scientific data also calls for a room in which to keep the books, records,[2] etc., and a desk for the planner to work at. Thus all of the planning which under the old system was done by the workman, as a result of his personal experience, must of necessity under the new system be done by the management in accordance with the laws of the science; because even if the workman was well suited to the development and use of scientific data, it would be physically impossible for him to work at his machine and at a desk at the same time. It is also clear that in most cases one type of man is needed to plan ahead and an entirely different type to execute the work.

The man in the planning room, whose specialty under scientific management is planning ahead, invariably finds that the work can be done better and more economically by a subdivision of the labor; each act of each mechanic, for example, should be preceded by various preparatory acts done by other men. And all of this involves, as we have said, "an almost equal division of the responsibility and the work between the management and the workman."

To summarize: Under the management of "initiative and incentive" practically the whole problem is "up to the workman," while under scientific management fully one-half of the problem is "up to the management."

Perhaps the most prominent single element in modern scientific management is the task idea. The work of every workman is fully planned out by the management at least one day in advance, and each man receives in most cases complete written instructions, describing in detail the task which he is to accomplish, as well as the means to be used in doing the work. And the work planned in advance in this way constitutes a task which is to be solved, as explained above, not by the workman alone, but in almost all cases by the joint effort of the workman and the management. This task specifies not only what is to be done but how it is to be done and the exact time allowed for doing it. And whenever the workman succeeds in doing his task right, and within the time limit specified, he receives an addition of from 30 per cent to 100 percent to his ordinary wages. These tasks are carefully planned, so that both good and careful work are called for in their performance, but it should be distinctly understood that in no case is the workman called upon to work at a pace which would be injurious to his health. The task is always so regulated that the man who is well suited to his job will thrive while working at this rate during a long term of years and grow happier and more prosperous, instead of being overworked. Scientific management consists very largely in preparing for and carrying out these tasks.

The writer is fully aware that to perhaps most of the readers of this paper the four elements which differentiate the new management from the old will at first appear to be merely high-sounding phrases; and he would again repeat that he has no idea of convincing the reader of their value merely through announcing their existence. His hope of carrying conviction rests upon demonstrating the tremendous force and effect of these four elements through a series of practical illustrations. It will be shown, first, that they can be applied absolutely to all classes of work, from the most elementary to the most intricate; and second, that when they are applied, the results must of necessity be overwhelmingly greater than those which it is possible to attain under the management of initiative and incentive.

The first illustration is that of handling pig iron, and this work is chosen because it is typical of perhaps the crudest and most elementary form of labor which is performed by man. This work is done by men with no other implements than their hands. The pig-iron handler stoops down, picks up a pig weighing about 92 pounds, walks for a few feet or yards and then drops it onto the ground or upon a pile. This work is so crude and elementary in its nature that the writer firmly believes that it would be possible to train an intelligent gorilla so as to become a more efficient pig-iron handler than any man can be. Yet it will be shown that the science of handling pig iron is so great and amounts to so much that it is impossible for the man who is best suited to this type of work to understand the principles of this science, or even to work in accordance with these principles without the aid of a man better educated than he is. And the further illustrations to be given will make it clear that in almost all of the mechanic arts, the science which underlies each workman's act is so great and amounts to so much that the workman who is best suited actually to do the work is incapable (either through lack of education or through insufficient mental capacity) of understanding this science. This is announced as a general principle the truth of which will become apparent as one illustration after another is given. After showing these four elements in the handling of pig iron, several illustrations will be given of their application to different kinds of work in the field of the mechanic arts, at intervals in a rising scale, beginning with the simplest and ending with the more intricate forms of labor.

One of the first pieces of work undertaken by us, when the writer started to introduce scientific management into the Bethlehem Steel Company, was to handle pig iron on task work. The opening of the Spanish War found some 80,000 tons of pig iron placed in small piles in an open field adjoining the works. Prices for pig iron had been so low that it could not be sold at a profit, and it therefore had been stored. With the opening of the Spanish War the price of pig iron rose, and this large accumulation of iron was sold. This gave us a good opportunity to show the workmen, as well as the owners and managers of the works, on a fairly large scale the advantages of task work over the old-fashioned day work and piece work, in doing a very elementary class of work.

The Bethlehem Steel Company had five blast furnaces, the product of which had been handled by a pig-iron gang for many years. This gang, at this time, consisted of about seventy-five men. They were good, average pig-iron handlers, were under an excellent foreman who himself had been a pig-iron handler, and the work was done, on the whole, about as fast and as cheaply as it was anywhere else at the time.

A railroad switch was run out into the field, right along the edge of the piles of pig iron. An inclined plank was placed against the side of a car, and each man picked up from his pile a pig of iron weighing about 92 pounds, walked up the inclined plank and dropped it on the end of the car.

We found that this gang were loading on the average about 12½ long tons per man per day. We were surprised to find, after studying the matter, that a first-class pig-iron handler ought to handle between 47 and 48 long tons per day, instead of 12½ tons. This task seemed to us so very large that we were obliged to go over our work several times before we were absolutely sure that we were right. Once we were sure, however, that 47 tons was a proper day's work for a first-class pig-iron handler, the task which faced us as managers under the modern scientific plan was clearly before us. It was our duty to see that the 80,000 tons of pig iron was loaded onto the cars at the rate of 47 tons per man per day, in place of 12½ tons, at which rate the work was then being done. And it was further our duty to see that this work was done without bringing on a strike among the men, without any quarrel with the men, and to see that the men were happier and better contented when loading at the new rate of 47 tons than they were when loading at the old rate of 12½ tons.

Our first step was the scientific selection of the workman. In dealing with workmen under this type of management, it is an inflexible rule to talk to and deal with only one man at a time, since each workman has his own special abilities and limitations, and since we are not dealing with men in masses, but are trying to develop each individual man to his highest state of efficiency and prosperity. Our first step was to find the proper workman to begin with. We therefore carefully watched and studied these seventy-five men for three or four days, at the end of which time we had picked out four men who appeared to be physically able to handle pig iron at the rate of 47 tons per day. A careful study was then made of each of these men. We looked up their history as far back as practicable and thorough inquiries were made as to the character, habits, and the ambition of each of them. Finally we selected one from among the four as the most likely man to start with. He was a little Pennsylvania Dutchman who had been observed to trot back home for a mile or so after his work in the evening about as fresh as he was when he came trotting down to work in the morning. We found that upon wages of $1.15 a day he had succeeded in buying a small plot of ground, and that he was engaged in putting up the walls of a little house for himself in the morning before starting to work and at night after leaving. He also had the reputation of being exceedingly "close," that is, of placing a very high value on a dollar. As one man whom we talked to about him said, "A penny looks about the size of a cart-wheel to him." This man we will call Schmidt.

The task before us, then, narrowed itself down to getting Schmidt to handle 47 tons of pig iron per day and making him glad to do it. This was done as follows. Schmidt was called out from among the gang of pig-iron handlers and talked to somewhat in this way:

"Schmidt, are you a high-priced man?"

"Vell, I don't know vat you mean."

"Oh yes, you do. What I want to know is whether you are a high-priced man or not."

"Vell, I don't know vat you mean."

"Oh, come now, you answer my questions. What I want to find out is whether you are a high-priced man or one of these cheap fellows here. What I want to find out is whether you want to earn $1.85 a day or whether you are satisfied with $1.15, just the same as all those cheap fellows are getting."

"Did I vant $1.85 a day? Vas dot a high-priced man? Vell, yes, I was a high-priced man."

"Oh, you're aggravating me. Of course you want $1.85 a day—everyone wants it! You know perfectly well that that has very little to do with your being a high-priced man. For goodness' sake answer my questions, and don't waste any more of my time. Now come over here. You see that pile of pig iron?"

"Yes."

"You see that car?"

"Yes."

"Well, if you are a high-priced man, you will load the pig iron on that car tomorrow for $1.85. Now do wake up and answer my question. Tell me whether you are a high-priced man or not."

"Vell—did I got $1.85 for loading dot pig iron on dot car tomorrow?"

"Yes, of course you do, and you get $1.85 for loading a pile like that every day right through the year. That is what a high-priced man does, and you know it just as well as I do."

"Vell, dot's all right. I could load dot pig iron on the car tomorrow for $1.85, and I get it every day, don't I?"

"Certainly you do—certainly you do."

"Vell, den, I was a high-priced man."

"Now, hold on, hold on. You know just as well as I do that a high-priced man has to do exactly as he's told from morning till night. You have seen this man here before, haven't you?"

"No, I never saw him."

"Well, if you are a high-priced man, you will do exactly as this man tells you tomorrow, from morning till night. When he tells you to pick up a pig and walk, you pick it up and you walk, and when he tells you to sit down and rest, you sit down. You do that right straight through the day. And what's more, no back talk. Now a high-priced man does just what he's told to do, and no back talk. Do you understand that? When this man tells you to walk, you walk; when he tells you to sit down, you sit down, and you don't talk back at him. Now you come on to work here tomorrow morning and I'll know before night whether you are really a high-priced man or not."

This seems to be rather rough talk. And indeed it would be if applied to an educated mechanic, or even an intelligent laborer. With a man of the mentally sluggish type of Schmidt it is appropriate and not unkind, since it is effective in fixing his attention on the high wages which he wants and away from what, if it were called to his attention, he probably would consider impossibly hard work.

What would Schmidt's answer be if he were talked to in a manner which is usual under the management of "initiative and incentive"? say, as follows:

"Now, Schmidt, you are a first-class pig-iron handler and know your business well. You have been handling at the rate of 12½ tons per day. I have given considerable study to handling pig iron, and feel sure that you could do a much larger day's work than you have been doing. Now don't you think that if you really tried you could handle 47 tons of pig iron per day, instead of 12½ tons?"

What do you think Schmidt's answer would be to this?

Schmidt started to work, and all day long, and at regular intervals, was told by the man who stood over him with a watch, "Now pick up a pig and walk. Now sit down and rest. Now walk—now rest," etc. He worked when he was told to work, and rested when he was told to rest, and at half-past five in the afternoon had his 47½ tons loaded on the car. And he practically never failed to work at this pace and do the task that was set him during the three years that the writer was at Bethlehem. And throughout this time he averaged a little more than $1.85 per day, whereas before he had never received over $1.15 per day, which was the ruling rate of wages at the time in Bethlehem. That is, he received 60 per cent higher wages than were paid to other men who were not working on task work. One man after another was picked out and trained to handle pig iron at the rate of 47½ tons per day until all of the pig iron was handled at this rate, and the men were receiving 60 percent more wages than other workmen around them.

The writer has given above a brief description of three of the four elements which constitute the essence of scientific management: first, the careful selection of the workman, and, second and third, the method of first inducing and then training and helping the workman to work according to the scientific method. Nothing has as yet been said about the science of handling pig iron. The writer trusts, however, that before leaving this illustration the reader will be thoroughly convinced that there is a science of handling pig iron, and further that this science amounts to so much that the man who is suited to handle pig iron cannot possibly understand it, nor even work in accordance with the laws of this science, without the help of those who are over him.

The law is confined to that class of work in which the limit of a man's capacity is reached because he is tired out. It is the law of heavy laboring, corresponding to the work of the cart horse, rather than that of the trotter. Practically all such work consists of a heavy pull or a push on the man's arms, that is, the man's strength is exerted by either lifting or pushing something which he grasps in his hands. And the law is that for each given pull or push on the man's arms it is possible for the workman to be under load for only a definite percentage of the day. For example, when pig iron is being handled (each pig weighing 92 pounds), a first-class workman can only be under load 43 percent of the day. He must be entirely free from load during 57 percent of the day. And as the load becomes lighter, the percentage of the day under which the man can remain under load increases. So that, if the workman is handling a half pig weighing 46 pounds, he can then be under load 58 per cent of the day,and only has to rest during 42 per cent. As the weight grows lighter the man can remain under load during a larger and larger percentage of the day, until finally a load is reached which he can carry in his hands all day long without being tired out. When that point has been arrived at this law ceases to be useful as a guide to a laborer's endurance, and some other law must be found which indicates the man's capacity for work.

When a laborer is carrying a piece of pig iron weighing 92 pounds in his hands, it tires him about as much to stand still under the load as it does to walk with it, since his arm muscles are under the same severe tension whether he is moving or not. A man, however, who stands still under a load is exerting no horse-power whatever, and this accounts for the fact that no constant relation could be traced in various kinds of heavy laboring work between the foot-pounds of energy exerted and the tiring effect of the work on the man. It will also be clear that in all work of this kind it is necessary for the arms of the workman to be completely free from load (that is, for the workman to rest) at frequent intervals. Throughout the time that the man is under a heavy load the tissues of his arm muscles are in process of degeneration, and frequent periods of rest are required in order that the blood may have a chance to restore these tissues to their normal condition.

To return now to our pig-iron handlers at the Bethlehem Steel Company. If Schmidt had been allowed to attack the pile of 47 tons of pig iron without the guidance or direction of a man who understood the art, or science, of handling pig iron, in his desire to earn his high wages he would probably have tired himself out by eleven or twelve o'clock in the day. He would have kept so steadily at work that his muscles would not have had the proper periods of rest absolutely needed for recuperation, and he would have been completely exhausted early in the day. By having a man, however, who understood this law, stand over him and direct his work, day after day, until he acquired the habit of resting at proper intervals, he was able to work at an even gait all day long without unduly tiring himself.

Now one of the very first requirements for a man who is fit to handle pig iron as a regular occupation is that he shall be so stupid and so phlegmatic that he more nearly resembles in his mental make-up the ox than any other type. The man who is mentally alert and intelligent is for this very reason entirely unsuited to what would, for him, be the grinding monotony of work of this character. Therefore the workman who is best suited to handling pig iron is unable to understand the real science of doing this class of work. He is so stupid that the word "percentage" has no meaning to him, and he must consequently be trained by a man more intelligent than himself into the habit of working in accordance with the laws of this science before he can be successful.

The writer trusts that it is now clear that even in the case of the most elementary form of labor that is known, there is a science, and that when the man best suited to this class of work has been carefully selected, when the science of doing the work has been developed, and when the carefully selected man has been trained to work in accordance with this science, the results obtained must of necessity be overwhelmingly greater than those which are possible under the plan of "initiative and incentive."

Notes

1. The writer has tried to make the reason for this unfortunate state of things clear in a paper entitled "Shop Management," read before the American Society of Mechanical Engineers.

2. For example, the records containing the data used under scientific management in an ordinary machine shop fill thousands of pages.

5
The Real Meaning of Taylorism

Harry Braverman

First Principle

"The managers assume . . . the burden of gathering together all of the traditional knowledge which in the past has been possessed by the workmen and then of classifying, tabulating, and reducing this knowledge to rules, laws, and formulae. . . ."[1] We have seen the illustrations of this in the cases of the lathe machinist and the pig-iron handler. The great disparity between these activities, and the different orders of knowledge that may be collected about them, illustrate that for Taylor—as for managers today—no task is either so simple or so complex that it may not be studied with the object of collecting in the hands of management at least as much information as is known by the worker who performs it regularly, and very likely more. This brings to an end the situation in which "Employers derive their knowledge of how much of a given class of work can be done in a day from either their own experience, which has frequently grown hazy with age, from casual and unsystematic observation of their men, or at best from records which are kept, showing the quickest time in which each job has been done."[2] It enables management to discover and enforce those speedier methods and shortcuts which workers themselves, in the practice of their trades or tasks, learn or improvise, and use at their own discretion only. Such an experimental approach also brings into being new methods such as can be devised only through the means of systematic study.

This first principle we may call the *dissociation of the labor process from the skills of the workers*. The labor process is to be rendered independent of craft, tradition, and the workers' knowledge. Henceforth it is to depend not at all upon the abilities of workers, but entirely upon the practices of management.

Reprinted from *Labor and Monopoly Capital*, by Harry Braverman (New York: Monthly Review Books, 1974), 112–121.

Second Principle

"All possible brain work should be removed from the shop and centered in the planning or laying-out department. . . ."[3] Since this is the key to scientific management, as Taylor well understood, he was especially emphatic on this point and it is important to examine the principle thoroughly.

In the human, as we have seen, the essential feature that makes for a labor capacity superior to that of the animal is the combination of execution with a conception of the thing to be done. But as human labor becomes a social rather than an individual phenomenon, it is possible—unlike in the instance of animals where the motive force, instinct, is inseparable from action—to divorce conception from execution. This dehumanization of the labor process, in which workers are reduced almost to the level of labor in its animal form, while purposeless and unthinkable in the case of the self-organized and self-motivated social labor of a community of producers, becomes crucial for the management of purchased labor. For if the workers' execution is guided by their own conception, it is not possible, as we have seen, to enforce upon them either the methodological efficiency or the working pace desired by capital. The capitalist therefore learns from the start to take advantage of this aspect of human labor power, and to break the unity of the labor process.

This should be called the principle of the *separation of conception from execution*, rather than by its more common name of the separation of mental and manual labor (even though it is similar to the latter, and in practice often identical). This is because mental labor, labor done primarily in the brain, is also subjected to the same principle of separation of conception from execution; mental labor is first separated from manual labor and, as we shall see, is then itself subdivided rigorously according to the same rule.

The first implication of this principle is that Taylor's "science of work" is never to be developed by the worker, always by management. This notion, apparently so "natural" and undebatable today, was in fact vigorously discussed in Taylor's day, a fact which shows how far we have traveled along the road of transforming all ideas about the labor process in less than a century, and how completely Taylor's hotly contested assumptions have entered into the conventional outlook within a short space of time. Taylor confronted this question—why must work be studied by the management and not by the worker himself; why not *scientific workmanship* rather than *scientific management?*—repeatedly, and employed all his ingenuity in devising answers to it, though not always with his customary frankness. In *The Principles of Scientific Management*, he pointed out that the "older system" of management makes it necessary for each workman to bear almost the entire responsibility for the general plan as well as for each detail of his work, and in many cases for his implements as well. In addition to this he must do all of the actual physical labor. The development of a science, on the other hand, involves the establishment of many rules, laws, and formulae which replace the judgment of the individual workman and which can be effectively used only after having been systematically recorded, indexed, etc. The practical use of scientific data also calls for a room in which to keep the books, records, etc., and a desk for the planner to work at. Thus all of the planning which under the old system was done by the workman, as a result of his personal experience, must of necessity under the new system be done by the management in accordance with the laws of the science; because even if the workman was well suited to the development and use of scientific data, it would be physically impossible for him to work at his machine and at a desk at the same time. It is also clear that in most cases one type of man is needed to plan ahead and an entirely different type to execute the work.[4]

The objections having to do with physical arrangements in the workplace are clearly of little importance, and represent the deliberate exaggeration of obstacles which, while they may exist as inconveniences, are hardly insuperable. To refer to the "different type" of worker needed for each job is worse than disingenuous, since these "different types" hardly existed until the division of labor created them. As Taylor well understood, the possession of craft knowledge made the worker the best starting point for the development of the science of work; systematization often means, at least at the outset, the gathering of knowledge which *workers already possess*. But Taylor, secure in his obsession with the immense reasonableness of his proposed arrangement, did not stop at this point. In his testimony before the Special Committee of the House of Representatives, pressed and on the defensive, he brought forth still other arguments:

> I want to make it clear, Mr. Chairman, that work of this kind undertaken by the management leads to the development of a science, while it is next to impossible for the workman to develop a science. There are many workmen who are intellectually just as capable of developing a science, who have plenty of brains, and are just as capable of developing a science as those on the managing side. But the science of doing work of any kind cannot be developed by the workman. Why? Because he has neither the time nor the money to do it. The development of the science of doing any kind of work always required the work of two men, one man who actually does the work which is to be studied and another man who observes closely the first man while he works and studies the time problems and the motion problems connected with this work. No workman has either the time or the money to burn in making experiments of this sort. If he is working for himself no one will pay him while he studies the motions of some one else. The management must and ought to pay for all such work. So that for the workman, the development of a science becomes impossible, not because the workman is

not intellectually capable of developing it, but he has neither the time nor the money to do it and he realizes that this is a question for the management to handle.[5]

Taylor here argues that the systematic study of work and the fruits of this study belong to management for the very same reason that machines, factory buildings, etc., belong to them; that is, because it costs labor time to conduct such a study, and only the possessors of capital can afford labor time. The possessors of labor time cannot themselves afford to do anything with it but sell it for their means of subsistence. It is true that this is the rule in capitalist relations of production, and Taylor's use of the argument in this case shows with great clarity where the sway of capital leads: Not only is capital the property of the capitalist, but *labor itself has become part of capital.* Not only do the workers lose control over their instruments of production, but they must now lose control over their own labor and the manner of its performance. This control now falls to those who can "afford" to study it in order to know it better than the workers themselves know their own life activity.

But Taylor has not yet completed his argument: "Furthermore," he told the Committee, "if any workman were to find a new and quicker way of doing work, or if he were to develop a new method, you can see at once it becomes to his interest to keep that development to himself, not to teach the other workmen the quicker method. It is to his interest to do what workmen have done in all times, to keep their trade secrets for themselves and their friends. That is the old idea of trade secrets. The workman kept his knowledge to himself instead of developing a science and teaching it to others and making it public property."[6] Behind this hearkening back to old ideas of "guild secrets" is Taylor's persistent and fundamental notion that the improvement of work methods by workers brings few benefits to management. Elsewhere in his testimony, in discussing the work of his associate, Frank Gilbreth, who spent many years studying bricklaying methods, he candidly admits that not only *could* the "science of bricklaying" be developed by workers, but that it undoubtedly *had been:* "Now, I have not the slightest doubt that during the last 4,000 years all the methods that Mr. Gilbreth developed have many, many times suggested themselves to the minds of bricklayers." But because knowledge possessed by workers is not useful to capital, Taylor begins his list of the desiderata of scientific management: "First. The development—by the management, not the workmen—of the science of bricklaying."[7] Workers, he explains, are not going to put into execution any system or any method which harms them and their workmates: "Would they be likely," he says, referring to the pig-iron job, "to get rid of seven men out of eight from their own gang and retain only the eighth man? No!"[8]

Finally, Taylor understood the Babbage principle better than anyone of his time, and it was always uppermost in his calculations. The purpose of work study was never, in his mind, to enhance the ability of the worker, to concentrate in the worker a greater share of scientific knowledge, to ensure that as technique rose, the worker would rise with it. Rather, the purpose was to cheapen the worker by decreasing his training and enlarging his output. In his early book, *Shop Management*, he said frankly that the "full possibilities" of his system "will not have been realized until almost all of the machines in the shop are run by men who are of smaller calibre and attainments, and who are therefore cheaper than those required under the old system."[9]

Therefore, both in order to ensure management control and to cheapen the worker, conception and execution must be rendered separate spheres of work, and for this purpose the study of work processes must be reserved to management and kept from the workers, to whom its results are communicated only in the form of simplified job tasks governed by simplified instructions which it is thenceforth their duty to follow unthinkingly and without comprehension of the underlying technical reasoning or data.

Third Principle

The essential idea of "the ordinary types of management," Taylor said, "is that each workman has become more skilled in his own trade than it is possible for any one in the management to be, and that, therefore, the details of how the work shall best be done must be left to him." But, by contrast: "Perhaps the most prominent single element in modern scientific management is the task idea. The work of every workman is fully planned out by the management at least one day in advance, and each man receives in most cases complete written instructions, describing in detail the task which he is to accomplish, as well as the means to be used in doing the work. . . . This task specifies not only what is to be done, but how it is to be done and the exact time allowed for doing it. . . . Scientific management consists very largely in preparing for and carrying out these tasks."[10]

In this principle it is not the written instruction card that is important.* Taylor had no need for such a card with Schmidt, nor did he use one in

---

*This despite the fact that for a time written instruction cards were a fetish among managers. The vogue for such cards passed as work tasks became so simplified and repetitious as to render the cards in most cases unnecessary. But the concept behind them remains: it is the concept of the direct action of management to determine the process, with the worker functioning as the mediating and closely governed instrument. This is the significance of Lillian Gilbreth's definition of the instruction card as "a self-producer of a predetermined product."[11] The worker as producer is ignored; management becomes the producer, and its plans and instructions bring the product into existence. This same instruction care inspired in' Alfred Marshall, however, the curious opinion that from it,

many other instances. Rather, the essential element is the systematic pre-planning and pre-calculation of all elements of the labor process, which now no longer exists as a process in the imagination of the worker but only as a process in the imagination of a special management staff. Thus, if the first principle is the gathering and development of knowledge of labor processes, and the second is the concentration of this knowledge as the exclusive province of management—together with its essential converse, the absence of such knowledge among the workers—then the third is the *use of this monopoly over knowledge to control each step of the labor process and its mode of execution.*

As capitalist industrial, office, and market practices developed in accordance with this principle, it eventually became part of accepted routine and custom, all the more so as the increasingly scientific character of most processes, which grew in complexity while the worker was not allowed to partake of this growth, made it ever more difficult for the workers to understand the processes in which they functioned. But in the beginning, as Taylor well understood, an abrupt psychological wrench was required.* We have seen in the simple Schmidt case the means employed, both in the selection of a single worker as a starting point and in the way in which he was reoriented to the new conditions of work. In the more complex conditions of the machine shop, Taylor gave this part of the responsibility to the foremen. It is essential, he said of the gang bosses, to "nerve and brace them up to the point of insisting that the workmen shall carry out the orders exactly as specified on the instruction cards. This is a difficult task at first, as the workmen have been accustomed for years to do the details of the work to suit themselves, and many of them are intimate friends of the bosses and believe they know quite as much about their business as the latter."[13]

Modern management came into being on the basis of these principles. It arose as theoretical construct and as systematic practice, moreover, in the

workers could learn how production is carried on: such a card, "whenever it comes into the hands of a thoughtful man, may suggest to him something of the purposes and methods of those who have constructed it."[12] The worker, in Marshall's notion, having given up technical knowledge of the craft, is now to pick up the far more complex technical knowledge of modern industry from his task card, as a paleontologist reconstructs the entire animal from a fragment of a bone!

*One must not suppose from this that such a psychological shift in relations between worker and manager is entirely a thing of the past. On the contrary, it is constantly being recapitulated in the evolution of new occupations as they are brought into being by the development of industry and trade, and are then routinized and subjugated to management control. As this tendency has attacked office, technical, and "educated" occupations, sociologists have spoken of it as "bureaucratization," an evasive and unfortunate use of Weberian terminology, a terminology which often reflects its users' view that this form of govenment over work is endemic to "large-scale" or "complex" enterprises, whereas it is better understood as the specific product of the capitalist organization of work, and reflects not primarily scale but social antagonisms.

very period during which the transformation of labor from processes based on skill to processes based upon science was attaining its most rapid tempo. Its role was to render conscious and systematic, the formerly unconscious tendency of capitalist production. It was to ensure that as craft declined, the worker would sink to the level of general and undifferentiated labor power, adaptable to a large range of simple tasks, while as science grew, it would be concentrated in the hands of management.

Notes

1. Frederick Taylor, *The Principles of Scientific Management* (New York: 1967), 36.
2. Ibid., 22.
3. Frederick Taylor, "Shop Management," *Scientific Management* (New York and London: 1947), 98–99.
4. Taylor, *Principles of Scientific Management*, 37–38.
5. "Taylor's Testimony before the Special House Committee," Taylor, *Scientific Management*, 235–236.
6. Taylor, Ibid.
7. Taylor, Ibid., 75, 77.
8. Taylor, *Principles of Scientific Management*, 62.
9. Taylor, "Shop Management," *Scientific Management*, 105.
10. Taylor, *Principles of Scientific Management*, 39, 63.
11. Lillian Gilbreth, "The Psychology of Management (1914)," *The Writings of the Gilbreths*, William R. Spriegel and Clark E. Myers, eds. (Homewood, Ill.: 1953), 404.
12. Alfred Marshall, *Industry and Trade* (London: 1919, 1932), 391–393.
13. Taylor, "Shop Management," *Scientific Management*, 108.

6

Human Relations and the Informal Organization

Fritz J. Roethlisberger and William J. Dickson

The Two Major Functions of an Industrial Organization

An industrial organization may be regarded as performing two major functions, that of producing a product and that of creating and distributing satisfactions among the individual members of the organization. The first function is ordinarily called economic. From this standpoint the functioning of the concern is assessed in such terms as cost, profit, and technical efficiency. The second function, while it is readily understood, is not ordinarily designated by any generally accepted word. It is variously described as maintaining employee relations, employee good will, cooperation, etc. From this standpoint the functioning of the concern is frequently assessed in such terms as labor turnover, tenure of employment, sickness and accident rate, wages, employee attitudes, etc. The industrial concern is continually confronted, therefore, with two sets of major problems: (1) problems of external balance, and (2) problems of internal equilibrium. The problems of external balance are generally assumed to be economic; that is, problems of competition, adjusting the organization to meet changing price levels, etc. The problems of internal equilibrium are chiefly concerned with the maintenance of a kind of social organization in which individuals and groups through working together can satisfy their own desires.

Ordinarily an industrial concern is thought of primarily in terms of its success in meeting problems of external balance, or if the problems of internal equilibrium are explicitly recognized they are frequently assumed to be separate from and unrelated to the economic purpose of the enterprise. Producing an article at a profit and maintaining good employee relations are frequently regarded as antithetical propositions. The results of the studies which have been reported indicated, however, that these two sets of problems are interrelated and interdependent. The

Reprinted from *Management and the Worker*, by Fritz J. Roethlisberger and William J. Dickson (Cambridge: Harvard University Press, 1939), 552–562, by permission of the publisher. Copyright © 1938, 1967 by the President and Fellows of Harvard College.

kind of social organization which obtains within a concern is intimately related to the effectiveness of the total organization. Likewise, the success with which the concern maintains external balance is directly related to its internal organization.

A great deal of attention has been given to the economic function of industrial organization. Scientific controls have been introduced to further the economic purposes of the concern and of the individuals within it. Much of this advance has gone on in the name of efficiency or rationalization. Nothing comparable to this advance has gone on in the development of skills and techniques for securing cooperation, that is, for getting individuals and groups of individuals working together effectively and with satisfaction to themselves. The slight advances which have been made in this area have been overshadowed by the new and powerful technological developments of modern industry.

The Technical Organization of the Plant

In looking at an industrial organization as a social system it will first be necessary to examine the physical environment, for this is an inseparable part of any organization. The physical environment includes not only climate and weather, but also that part of the environment which is owned and used by the organization itself, namely, the physical plant, tools, machines, raw products, and so on. This latter part of the factory's physical environment is ordered and organized in a certain specified way to accomplish the task of technical production. For our purposes, therefore, it will be convenient to distinguish from the human organization this aspect of the physical environment of an industrial plant and to label it the "technical organization of the plant." This term will refer only to the logical and technical organization of material, tools, machines, and finished product, including all those physical items related to the task of technical production.

The two aspects into which an industrial plant can be roughly divided—the technical organization and the human organization—are interrelated and interdependent. The human organization is constantly molding and recreating the technical organization either to achieve more effectively the common economic purpose or to secure more satisfaction for its members. Likewise, changes in the technical organization require an adaptation on the part of the human organization.

The Human Organization of the Plant

In the human organization we find a number of individuals working together toward a common end: the collective purpose of the total organization. Each of these individuals, however, is bringing to the work situation a different background of personal and social experiences. No two individuals are making exactly the same demands of their job. The demands a particular employee makes depend not only upon his physical needs but upon his social needs as well. These social needs and the sentiments associated with them vary with his early personal history and social conditioning as well as with the needs and sentiments of people closely associated with him both inside and outside of work.

The Individual

It may be well to look more closely at the sentiments the individual is bringing to his work situation. Starting with a certain native organic endowment the child is precipitated into group life by the act of birth. The group into which the child is born is not the group in general. The child is born into a specific family. Moreover, this specific family is not a family in isolation. It is related in certain ways to other families in the community. It has a certain cultural background—a way of life, codes and routines of behavior, associated with certain beliefs and expectations. In the beginning the child brings only his organic needs to this social milieu into which he is born. Very rapidly he begins to accumulate experience. This process of accumulating experience is the process of assigning meanings to the socio-reality about him; it is the process of becoming socialized. Much of the early learning period is devoted to preparing the child to become capable of social life in its particular group. In preparing the child for social participation the immediate family group plays an important role. By the particular type of family into which the child is born he is "conditioned" to certain routines of behavior and ways of living. The early meanings he assigns to his experience are largely in terms of these codes of behavior and associated beliefs. As the child grows up and participates in groups other than the immediate family his leanings lose, although never quite entirely, their specific family form. This process of social interaction and social conditioning is never-ending and continues from birth to death. The adult's evaluation of his surroundings is determined in a good part by the system of human interrelations in which he has participated.

The Social Organization of the Plant

However, the human organization of an industrial plant is more than a plurality of individuals, each motivated by sentiments arising from his own personal and private history and background. It is also a social organization, for the members of an industrial plant—executives, technical specialists, supervisors, factory workers, and office workers—are interacting daily with one another and from their associations certain patterns of relations are formed among them. These patterns of relations, together with the objects which symbolize them, constitute the social organization of the industrial enterprise. Most of the individuals who live among these patterns come to accept them as obvious and necessary truths and to react as they dictate. Both the kind of behavior that is expected of a person and the kind of behavior he can expect from others are prescribed by these patterns.

If one looks at a factory situation, for example, one finds individuals and groups of individuals who are associated at work acting in certain accepted and prescribed ways toward one another. There is no complete homogeneity of behavior between individuals or between one group of individuals and another, but rather there are differences of behavior expressing differences in social relationship. Some relationships fall into routine patterns, such as the relationship between superior and subordinate or between office worker and shop worker. Individuals conscious of their membership in certain groups are reacting in certain accepted ways to other individuals representing other groups. Behavior varies according to the stereotyped conceptions of relationship. The worker, for example, behaves toward his foreman in one way, toward his first-line supervisor in another way, and toward his fellow worker in still another. People holding the rank of inspector expect a certain kind of behavior from the operators—the operators from the inspectors. Now these relationships, as is well known from everyday experiences, are finely shaded and sometimes become complicated. When a person is in the presence of his supervisor alone he usually acts differently from the way he acts when his supervisor's supervisor is also present. Likewise, his supervisor acts toward him alone quite differently from the way he behaves when his own supervisor is also there. The subtle nuances of relationship are so much a part of everyday life that they are commonplace. They are taken for granted. The vast amount of social conditioning that has taken place by means of which a person maneuvers himself gracefully through the intricacies of these finely shaded social distinctions is seldom explicitly realized. Attention is paid only when a new social situation arises where the past social training of the person prevents him from making the necessary delicate interpretations of a given social signal and hence brings forth the "socially wrong" response.

In the factory, as in any social milieu, a process of social evaluation is constantly at work. From this process distinctions of "good" and "bad," "inferior" and "superior," arise. This process of evaluation is carried on with simple and ready generalizations by means of which values become attached to individuals and to groups performing certain tasks and operations. It assigns to a group of individuals performing such and such a task a particular rank in the established prestige scale. Each work group becomes a carrier of social values. In industry with its extreme diversity of occupations there are a number of such groupings. Any noticeable similarity or difference, not only in occupation but also in age, sex, and nationality, can serve as a basis of social classification, as, for example, "married women," the "old-timer," the "white-collared" or clerical worker, the "foreign element." Each of these groups, too, has its own value system.

All the patterns of interaction that arise between individuals or between different groups can be graded according to the degree of intimacy involved in the relationship. Grades of intimacy or understanding can be arranged on a scale and expressed in terms of "social distance." Social distance measures differences of sentiment and interest which separate individuals or groups from one another. Between the president of a company and the elevator operator there is considerable social distance, more for example than between the foreman and the benchworker. Social distance is to social organization what physical distance is to physical space. However, physical and social distance do not necessarily coincide. Two people may be physically near but socially distant.

Just as each employee has a particular physical location, so he has a particular social place in the total social organization. But this place is not so rigidly fixed as in a caste system. In any factory there is considerable mobility or movement. Movement can occur in two ways: the individual may pass from one occupation to another occupation higher up in the prestige scale; or the prestige scale itself may change.

It is obvious that these scales of value are never completely accepted by all the groups in the social environment. The shop worker does not quite see why the office worker, for example, should have shorter hours of work than he has. Or the newcomer, whose efficiency on a particular job is about the same, but whose hourly rate is less than that of some old-timer, wonders why service should count so much. The management group, in turn, from the security of its social elevation, does not often understand what "all the fuss is about."

As was indicated by many of the studies, any person who has achieved a certain rank in the prestige scale regards anything real or imaginary which tends to alter his status adversely as something unfair or unjust. It is apparent that any move on the part of the management may alter the existing social equilibrium to which the employee has grown accustomed and by means of which his status is defined. Immediately this disruption will be expressed in sentiments of resistance of the real or imagined alterations in the social equilibrium.

From this point of view it can be seen how every item and event in the industrial environment becomes an object of a system of sentiments. According to this way of looking at things, material goods, physical events, wages, hours of work, etc., cannot be treated as things in themselves. Instead they have to be interpreted as carriers of social value. The meanings which any person in an industrial organization assigns to the events and objects in his environment are often determined by the social situation in which the events and objects occur. The significance to an employee of a double-pedestal desk, of a particular kind of pencil, or of a handset telephone is determined by the social setting in which these objects appear. If people with double-pedestal desks supervise people with single-pedestal desks, then double-pedestal desks become symbols of status or prestige in the organization. As patterns of behavior become crystallized, every object in the environment tends to take on a particular social significance. It becomes easy to tell a person's social place in the organization by the objects which he wears and carries and which surround him. In these terms it can be seen how the introduction of a technical change may also involve for an individual or a group of individuals the loss of certain prestige symbols and, as a result, have a demoralizing effect.

From this point of view the behavior of no one person in an industrial organization, from the very top to the very bottom, can be regarded as motivated by strictly economic or logical considerations. Routine patterns of interaction involve strong sentiments. Each group in the organization manifests its own powerful sentiments. It is likely that sometimes the behavior of many staff specialists which goes under the name of "efficiency" is as much a manifestation of a very strong sentiment—the sentiment or desire to originate new combinations—as it is of anything strictly logical.

This point of view is far from the one which is frequently expressed, namely, that man is essentially an economic being carrying around with him a few noneconomic appendages. Rather, the point of view which has been expressed here is that noneconomic motives, interests, and processes, as well as economic, are fundamental in behavior in business, from the board of directors to the very last man in the organization. Man is not merely—in fact is very seldom—motivated by factors pertaining strictly to facts or logic. Sentiments are not merely things which man carries around with him as appendages. He cannot cast them off like a suit of clothes. He carries them with him wherever he goes. In business or elsewhere, he can hardly behave without expressing them. Moreover, sentiments do not exist in a social vacuum. They are the product of social behavior, of social interaction, of the fact that man lives his life as a member of different groups. Not only does man bring sentiments to the business situation because of his past experiences and conditioning outside of business, but also as a member of a specific local business organization with a particular social place in it he has certain sentiments expressing his particular relations to it.

According to this point of view, every social act in adulthood is an integrated response to both inner and outer stimuli. To each new concrete situation the adult brings his past "social conditioning." To the extent that this past social conditioning has prepared him to assimilate the new experience in the culturally accepted manner, he is said to be "adjusted." To the extent that his private or personal view of the situation is at variance with the cultural situation, the person is called "maladjusted."

The Formal Organization of the Plant

The social organization of the industrial plant is in part formally organized. It is composed of a number of strata or levels which differentiate the benchworker from the skilled mechanic, the group chief from the department chief, and so on. These levels are well defined and all the formal orders, instructions, and compensations are addressed to them. All such factors taken together make up the formal organization of the plant. It includes the systems, policies, rules, and regulations of the plant which express what the relations of one person to another are supposed to be in order to achieve effectively the task of technical production. It prescribes the relations that are supposed to obtain within the human organization and between the human organization and the technical organization. In short, the patterns of human interrelation as defined by the systems, rules, policies, and regulations of the company, constitute the formal organization.

The formal organization of an industrial plant has two purposes: it addresses itself to the economic purposes of the total enterprise; it concerns itself also with the securing of cooperative effort. The formal organization includes all the explicitly stated systems of control introduced by the company in order to achieve the economic purposes of the total enterprise and the effective contribution of the members of the organization to those economic ends.

The Informal Organization of the Plant

All the experimental studies pointed to the fact that there is something more to the social organization than what has been formally recognized. Many of the actually existing patterns of human interaction have no representation in the formal organization at all, and others are inadequately represented by the formal organization. This fact is frequently forgotten when talking or thinking about industrial situations in general. Too often it is assumed that the organization of a company corresponds to a blueprint plan or organization chart. Actually, it never does. In the formal organization of most companies little explicit recognition is given to many social distinctions residing in the social organization. The blueprint plans of a company show the functional relations between working units, but they do not express the distinctions of social distance, movement, or equilibrium previously described. The hierarchy of prestige values which tends to make the work of men more important than the work of women, the work of clerks more important than the work at the bench, has little representation in the formal organization; nor does a blueprint plan ordinarily show the primary groups, that is, those groups enjoying daily face-to-face relations. Logical lines of horizontal and vertical co-ordination of functions replace the actually existing patterns of interaction between people in different social places. The formal organization cannot take account of the sentiments and values residing in the social organization by means of which individuals or groups of individuals are informally differentiated, ordered, and integrated. Individuals in their associations with one another in a factory build up personal relationships. They form into informal groups, in terms of which each person achieves a certain position or status. The nature of these informal groups is very important, as has been shown in the Relay Assembly Test Room and in the Bank Wiring Observation Room.

It is well to recognize that informal organizations are not "bad," as they are sometimes assumed to be. Informal social organization exists in every plant, and can be said to be a necessary prerequisite for effective collaboration. Much collaboration exists at an informal level, and it sometimes facilitates the functioning of the formal organization. On the other hand, sometimes the informal organization develops in opposition to the formal organization. The important consideration is, therefore, the relation that exists between formal and informal organizations.

To illustrate, let us consider the Relay Assembly Test Room and the Bank Wiring Observation Room. These two studies offered an interesting contrast between two informal working groups; one situation could be characterized in almost completely opposite terms from the other. In the Relay Assembly Test Room, on the one hand, the five operators changed continuously in their rate of output up and down over the duration of the test, and yet in a curious fashion their variations in output were insensitive to many significant changes introduced during the experiment. On the other hand, in the Bank Wiring Observation Room output was being held relatively constant and there existed a hypersensitivity to change on the part of the worker—in fact, what could almost be described as an organized opposition to it.

It is interesting to note that management could draw from these studies two opposite conclusions. From the Relay Assembly Test Room experiment they could argue that the company can do almost anything it wants in the nature of technical changes without any perceptible effect on the output of the workers. From the Bank Wiring Observation Room they could argue equally convincingly that the company can introduce hardly any changes without meeting a pronounced opposition to them from the workers. To make this dilemma even more striking, it is only necessary to recall that the sensitivity to change in the one case occurred in the room where no experimental changes had been introduced whereas the insensitivity to change in the other case occurred in the room where the operators had been submitted to considerable experimentation. To settle this question by saying that in one case the situation was typical and in the other case atypical of ordinary shop conditions would be to beg the question, for the essential difference between the two situations would again be missed. It would ignore the social setting in which the changes occurred and the meaning which the workers themselves assigned to the changes.

Although in both cases there were certain informal arrangements not identical with the formal setup, the informal organization in one room was quite different from that in the other room, especially in its relation to the formal organization. In the case of the Relay Assembly Test Room there was a group, or informal organization, which could be characterized as a network of personal relations which had been developed in and through a particular way of working together; it was an organization which not only satisfied the wishes of its members but also worked in harmony with the aims of management. In the case of the Bank Wiring Observation Room there was an informal organization which could be characterized better as a set of practices and beliefs which its members had in common—practices and beliefs which at many points worked against the economic purposes of the company. In one case the relation between the formal and informal organization was one of compatibility; in the other case it was one of opposition. Or to put it another way, collaboration in the Relay Assembly Test Room was at a much higher level than in the Bank Wiring Observation Room.

The difference between these two groups can be understood only by comparing the functions which their informal organizations performed for their members. The chief function of the informal group in the Bank Wiring Observation Room was to resist changes in their established routines of work or personal interrelations. This resistance to change, however, was not the chief function of the informal group in the Relay Assembly Test Room. It is true that at first the introduction of the planned changes in the test room, whether or not these changes were logically in the direction of improvement, was met with apprehension and feelings of uneasiness on the part of the operators. The girls in the beginning were never quite sure that they might not be victims of the changes.

In setting up the Relay Assembly Test Room with the object of studying the factors determining the efficiency of the worker, many of the methods and rules by means of which management tends to promote and maintain efficiency—the "bogey," not talking too much at work, etc.—were, in effect, abrogated. With the removal of this source of constraint and in a setting of heightened social significance (because many of the changes had differentiated the test room girls from the regular department and as a result had elevated the social status within the plant of each of the five girls) a new type of spontaneous social organization developed. Social conditions had been established which allowed the operators to develop their own values and objectives. The experimental conditions allowed the operators to develop openly social codes at work and these codes, unhampered by interference, gave a sustained meaning to their work. It was as if the experimenters had acted as a buffer for the operators and held their work situation steady while they developed a new type of social organization. With this change in the type of social organization there also developed a new attitude toward changes in their working environment. Toward many changes which constitute an unspecified threat in the regular work situation the operators become immune. What the Relay Assembly Test Room experiment showed was that when innovations are introduced carefully and with regard to the actual sentiments of the workers, the workers are likely to develop a spontaneous type of informal organization which will not only express more adequately their own values and significances but also is more likely to be in harmony with the aims of management.

Although all the studies of informal organization at the Hawthorne Plant were made at the employee level, it would be incorrect to assume that this phenomenon occurs only at that level. Informal organization appears at all levels, from the very bottom to the very top of the organization.[1] Informal organization at the executive level, just as at the work level, may either facilitate or impede purposive cooperation and communication. In either case, at all levels of the organization informal organizations exist as a necessary condition for collaboration. Without them formal organization could not survive for long. Formal and informal organizations are interdependent aspects of social interaction.

Note

1. C. I. Barnard, *The Functions of the Executive* (Cambridge: Harvard University Press, 1938), 223–24.

7
Three Patterns of Bureaucracy

Alvin W. Gouldner

1. Mock Bureaucracy: The "No-Smoking" Rule

Analysis of the plant rules can begin by turning to the "no-smoking" regulations. As comments of people in the plant emphasized, one of the most distinctive things about this rule was that it was a "dead letter." Except under unusual circumstances, it was ignored by most personnel.

Thus, while offering a cigarette to a worker, one of the interviewers asked:

> *What about the "No-Smoking" signs? They seem to be all over the place, yet everyone seems to smoke.*
>
> (Laughing) Yes, these are *not really Company rules*. The fire insurance writers put them in. The office seems to think that *smoking doesn't hurt anything*, so they don't bother us about it. That is, of course, until the fire inspector (from the insurance company) comes around. Then as soon as he gets into the front office, they call down here and *the word is spread round for no smoking*.

The workers particularly seemed to enjoy the warning sent by the front office, for they invariably repeated this part of the story. For example, another worker remarked:

> We can smoke as much as we want. When the fire inspector comes around, *everybody is warned earlier.* . . . The Company doesn't mind.

Since under ordinary circumstances no one attempted to enforce this rule, it entailed little or no tension between workers and management. On the contrary, the situation was one which strengthened solidarity between the two groups. Their joint violation of the no-smoking rule, and their cooperative effort to outwit the "outsider," the insurance company, allied them as fellow "conspirators."

It seems evident from the above quotations that *one* of the things leading to rejection of the no-smoking rule, by workers and management alike, was that this regulation was initiated by an *outside* group. The workers usually distinguished between rules voluntarily initiated by the Company or plant management and those which, for one or another reason, management was compelled to endorse. Nonetheless, there were certain rules with which workers complied, even though local management was not viewed as responsible for their introduction.

One of these regulations governed the mining of gypsum ore. It specified that different "checks" (which were little numbered placards) had to be placed on each load of gypsum that was sent up from the mine. As a miner explained:

> You get a 'Number 1' check for General Gypsum and a 'Number 5' for royalty. They (the Company) have to pay ten cents a ton to everyone whose land they use. You can see *they're not doing this 'cause they want to; it's got to be done this way.*

Though [it presented] something of a nuisance, miners were ready to conform to this rule, and did so, despite the fact that it sprang from "outside" pressure. They conformed because the system enabled them to "check up" on their tonnage output and, since their earnings were geared to this, on their income.

Enforcement of the no-smoking rule would, of course, subject workers to an annoyance which, for some of them, was more than trifling. To demand that a man give up smoking would be much like asking him to stop chewing his fingernails. As a surface painter said:

> You can't stop a man from smoking. He has to. *It keeps him from getting nervous.* You just can't stop a man from smoking if he wants to.

Had conformance to this rule been demanded, a powerful and clear-cut legitimation would have been needed. As the above painter added:

> Safety is another story. The men won't resist that. *It's for their own good. They don't want accidents, if they can help it.* It's not like smoking.

Similarly, the labor relations director at the main office remarked:

> In plants where there is a *real danger of fire*, the men can be gotten to give up smoking.

In this plant, though, since there was little flammable material around, workers could see "no good reason" why they should stop smoking. In other words, workers do not believe that management has the right to institute *any* kind of a rule, *merely because they have the legal authority to do so.* A rule must also be legitimate in terms of the group's *values*, and will be more readily accepted if it is seen as furthering their own ends. Workers rejected the no-smoking rule, in part, because it could not be justified by rational considerations; it did not effectively attain something *they* valued and wanted.

This, however, was only a part of the picture. What would have happened, or what did people in the situation believe would happen, if the no-smoking rule would be enforced? Enforcement of the rule was generally expected to *sharpen* status distinctions within the plant. This was suggested, for example, by the comments of a foreman, who was explaining why the no-smoking rule was ignored:

> You see, they got a permit to smoke in the office. *The men feel if they can smoke up there, they can smoke down here* (in the factory).

In brief, enforcement of the no-smoking rule would heighten the visibility of existent status differences, allowing to one group obvious privileges denied to another. This relates to the "screening function" of the rules, and their role in blurring unacceptable status distinctions. Apparently, where enforcement of rules *unveils* status distinctions, as in this case, rather than masking them, the rule is neglected.

There is a difference between this situation and the "check" system in the mine. When miners conformed to the check regulation, their status was not impaired. Quite the contrary; for an important attribute of their status, namely their income, was made all the more secure by conforming to the checking rules. Conformance to the no-smoking regulations, however, would threaten, not fortify, the status of most production workers and even their supervisors.

Only on one occasion did management seek compliance with the no-smoking rule. This occurred when the insurance inspector made his tour through the plant. The worker who violated the rule *at this time* was bombarded with sharp criticism by his peers. As one board worker complained:

> There are a few guys who didn't even stop smoking when the inspector comes around. They are troublemakers, and *we let them know where they get off.*

During these routine inspections, as in the routine conduct of the "checking" system in the mine, workers viewed management's enforcement of the rule as compelled; that is, "they're not doing this 'cause they want to." The inspection was *not* seen as an occasion joyfully seized upon by management to increase its control over the workers. On the other hand, workers who "*violated*" the no-smoking rule under ordinary conditions were not viewed by supervisors as "troublemakers" giving vent to their hostilities. Instead, workers who smoked were viewed as being in the grip of an uncontrollable "human" need, for smoking was presumably required to quell their "nervousness."

Briefly, then, the no-smoking rule is a pattern possessing the following fairly obvious characteristics:

1. Usually, the rule was neither enforced by plant management nor obeyed by workers.

2. As a rule, it engendered little tension and conflict between the two groups and in fact seemed to enhance their solidarity.
3. Both the customary violation of the rule, as well as the occasional enforcement of it, were buttressed by the informal sentiments and behavior of the participants.

As point "two" above suggests, this pattern was partly anchored in the "leeway function" of the rules. That is, informally friendly and cooperative attitudes toward management were evoked insofar as management *withheld* enforcement of the rules. While the above discussion has already suggested some clues as to *how* this pattern was brought about, it will be helpful to wait and consider other rules before a summary analysis, which sifts out the underlying variables, is attempted.

This pattern has been called "mock bureaucracy," for many of the bureaucratic cues were present—rules, posters calling for their enforcement, and inspections—but in the ordinary day-to-day conduct of work, this bureaucratic paraphernalia was ignored and inoperative. In terms of the plant's recognized work divisions or departments, it is evident that the mine, rather than the surface factories, more closely approximated mock bureacracy. Finally, it may be noted that "mock bureaucracy" was the organizational counterpart of the "indulgency pattern." The indulgency pattern refers to the criteria in terms of which the plant was judged by workers as "lenient" or "good." Together, these criteria comprised an implicit description of mock bureaucracy. To put it the other way around, mock bureaucracy refers to the kind of social relations that emerge if the norms of the indulgency pattern are administratively implemented.

2. Representative Bureaucracy: The Safety Rules

The safety operations comprised a sphere which was more bureaucratically organized than any other in the plant. This was not, of course, the only respect in which safety regulations differed from other rules; nevertheless, it is a key factor that deserves consideration.

As a preliminary indication of the high degree of bureaucracy in this sphere, attention may be given first to the sheer quantity of rules included under the heading of safety. These were more numerous and complex than rules governing any other distinctive activity. There were, for example, sizeable lists of safety regulations which applied to the plant as a whole, while there were others which applied only to specific divisions of the factory. Thus, in the mine, there were specific rules concerning the use and handling of dynamite caps. In the mill, there were rules specifying the manner in which the large dehydrating vats were to be cleaned out. Still other rules, indicating proper procedure to be followed if a tool fell into the mixture, applied only to the board building.

Not only was the system of safety rules complex, but considerable stress was placed upon conformity to them. Unlike the no-smoking rules, the safety regulations were not a "dead letter." Specific agencies existed which strove energetically to bring about their observance. These agencies placed continual pressure upon both workers and management, and sought to orient the two groups to the safety rules during their daily activities. For example, the Company's main office officially defined accident and safety work as one of the regular responsibilities of foreman and supervisors. As the Company's safety manual asserted:

> The foreman must accept the responsibility for the accidents that occur in his department . . . (and) he should be provided with the *knowledge* (sic) he needs to carry it out. (Our emphasis—A. W. G.)

A complex system of "paper work" and "reports," so symptomatic of developed bureaucracy, was centered on the safety program. Thus, in the event that a compensable accident occurred, foremen were directed to prepare a complete report. The safety manual specified the detailed information which this report had to contain: (1) the specific unsafe condition involved in the accident; (2) the specific unsafe working practice committed by the injured worker or some other employee; (3) what the foreman had done, or recommended should be done, to prevent a similar accident.

In addition to these reports, records were also kept of *all* first aid cases. Both accident reports and first aid records were given regular and careful review by a "safety engineer" who worked out of the Company's main office.

Another instrument designed for generating conformance to the safety program was the closely planned and regularly conducted "safety meeting." Usually, this was presided over by the "safety and personnel manager" employed by the local plant. Such meetings were supposed to limit themselves to a thorough examination of the accidents which had occurred, the analysis of the outstanding accident-producing practices and conditions in the plant, and the suggestion of ways and means of correcting them. Actually, as will be noted later, the meetings sometimes discussed other subjects having little connection with safety work.

A final indication of the extent to which safety work was bureaucratized is that it was organized by, and was the responsibility of, a specific, continually existent office, 'the safety and personnel manager" in the plant. On the basis of his *superior and specialized knowledge*, he was expected to detect unsafe acts or conditions in the plant, and to call them to the attention of the appropriate foreman.

No other ongoing program in the plant was as highly bureaucratized. The "no-absenteeism" rule, for example, was not backed up with anything like the careful system of statistics and reports which were prepared for accidents. In fact, there were no absenteeism statistics kept in the plant. No other program in the plant had the galaxy of rules, special meetings, posters, inspections, or special supervisors in the main office and local plant. Indeed, until Peele's arrival, the only thing that the men in the plant thought of as "rules" were the safety regulations. As one foreman said: "It is the one thing they really work on."

3. Punishment-Centered Bureaucracy:
The No-Absenteeism Rule

"Punishment-centered bureaucracy" is distinguished from "mock" and "representative" bureaucracy in that responses to deviations take the form of *punishments*. This particular type is composed of two sub-patterns, depending on *who* exercises the punishment and who receives it. In one case, management utilizes punishments, directing them against workers. In the other case, workers subject management to punishments when the latter deviates. The first case can be called the "disciplinary" pattern. The second subtype can be termed the "grievance" pattern, for the union-grievance machinery is one of the most commonly used instruments by means of which workers inflict punishments on management.

[We focus here on the "disciplinary" pattern, the best example of which was the "no-absenteeism" rule, whose violations were specifically punished.]

Management on all levels of authority was hostile to absenteeism. While workers had varying feelings about the no-absenteeism rule, few of them welcomed it. Since we are not paid for time off, some workers asked rhetorically, why should management complain? As was already emphasized, absenteeism was traditionally valued by the miners, and they solidly closed their ranks to squash a challenge to this ancient prerogative. Many values important to workers were satisfied by absenteeism: for example, they could spend more time with their families, repair their homes, do spring plowing, hunt and fish, visit around, get drunk, or just rest. It was also a personalized and individual way of giving vent to dissatisfactions that arose in the course of working. At any rate, absenteeism was one way workers realized values that at any given moment might be more important to *them* than management's need for regular, predictable production.

The social status of worker and management alike was involved in the tug-of-war centering around the no-absenteeism rule. The foreman who was short-handed, due to absenteeism or any other reason, faced the danger of being unable to fill his production quota. No one in the plant was exempt from meeting this obligation, for "production comes first." Supervisors enforced the no-absenteeism rule, partly, therefore, because it enabled them to satisfy their chief status-obligation, keeping production going.

The no-absenteeism regulation also meant that the worker had to *account* for what he did *outside* of the plant. Under this rule the worker had, in effect, to receive his supervisor's permission to go to a wedding, attend a funeral, or stay home with a sick relative, whom he must now prove was really sick. The no-absenteeism rule challenged the workers' control over a wide range of out-of-plant behavior, bringing it within the purview of the foreman. As such, the rule was experienced as an extension of managerial power into an illegitimate area.

When the worker returned from an absence, the supervisor had to decide whether the worker's behavior was punishable. He was not formally interested in the causes of absenteeism, as he was of accidents, with the object of removing them. The investigation of an absence simply determined whether or not a worker would be punished.

The supervisor operated on the assumption that some absences were not "excusable." He believed that they evidenced the worker's "irresponsibility," marking him as a person who knowingly and deliberately evaded his obligations. The supervisor did not assume, as he did with respect to safety violations, that the absent worker was unwittingly careless, or ignorant of the requirements. As one foreman said emphatically:

> They know God-damned well they're not supposed to be out without a good excuse. What can we do with them but get tough?

Workers responded in much the same way when they felt that the requirements of the "bidding system" had been evaded by supervisors. Since the bidding rules had been incorporated into the contract and since, time and again, the union committee had called these provisions to management's attention, their neglect tended to be viewed as malicious and deliberate. As one mill worker said in such a situation, *"They're just asking for trouble."* Like management, workers responded by getting "tough." The rules, therefore, served to legitimate the punishment of those deemed to be *willfully* deviant and deliberately aggressive.

In fine, then, the punishment-centered bureaucratic pattern was characterized by the following features:

1. The rules about which the pattern was organized were *enforced*, but primarily by *one group*, either workers or management, rather than by both.
2. Adjustment to the rules was not attained by ignoring them, nor by "educating" the deviant or involving him in the rule's administration, but by *punishing* him.
3. The pattern was associated with considerable conflict and tension.

It may now be clear that this pattern was given its name because it is organized around the punishment-legitimating functions of bureaucratic rules, and is intimately associated with "close supervision."

Summary of Factors Associated with the Three Patterns of Bureaucracy

	Mock	Representative	Punishment-Centered
1. Who Usually Initiates the Rules?	The rule or rules are imposed on the group by some "outside" agency. *Neither* workers nor management, neither superiors nor subordinates, identify themselves with or participate in the establishment of the rules or view them as their own. e. g.—The "no-smoking" rule was initiated by the insurance company.	*Both* groups initiate the rules and view them as their own. e. g.—Pressure was exerted by union *and* management to initiate and develop the safety program. Workers and supervisors could make modifications of the program at periodic meetings.	The rule arises in response to the pressure of *either* workers or management, but is *not jointly* initiated by them. The group which does not initiate the rule views it as imposed upon it by the other. e. g.—Through their union the workers initiated the bidding system. Supervisors viewed it as something to which the Company was forced to adhere.
2. Whose Values Legitimate the Rules?	*Neither* superiors nor subordinates can, ordinarily, legitimate the rule in terms of their own values.	Usually, *both* workers and management can legitimate the rules in terms of their own key values. e. g.—Management legitimated the safety program by tying it to *production*. Workers legitimized it via their values on personal and bodily welfare, maintenance of income, and cleanliness.	*Either* superiors or subordinates alone consider the rule legitimate; the other may concede on grounds of expediency, but does not define the rule as legitimate. e. g.—Workers considered the bidding system "fair," since they viewed it as minimizing personal favoritism in the distribution of jobs. Supervisors conformed to it largely because they feared the consequences of deviation.

Summary of Factors Associated with the Three Patterns of Bureaucracy—*Continued*

Mock	Representative	Punishment-Centered

3. Whose Values Are Violated by Enforcement of the Rules?

Mock

Enforcement of the rule violates the values of *both groups.*

e. g.—If the no-smoking rule were put into effect, it would violate the value on "personal equality" held by workers and supervisors, since office workers would still be privileged to smoke.

Representative

Under most conditions, enforcement of the rules entails violations of *neither* group's values.

e. g.—It is only under comparatively *exceptional* circumstances that enforcement of the safety rules interfered with a value held by management, say, a value on production.

Punishment-Centered

Enforcement of the rules violates the values of only one group, *either* superiors or subordinates.

e. g.—The bidding rules threatened management's value on the use of skill and ability as criteria for occupational recruitment.

4. What Are the Standard Explanations of Deviations from the Rules?

Mock

The deviant pattern is viewed as an expression of "uncontrollable" needs or of human nature."

e. g.—People were held to smoke because of "nervousness."

Representative

Deviance is attributed to ignorance or *well-intentioned carelessness*—i. e., it is an unanticipated byproduct of behavior oriented to some other end, and thus an "accident." This we call a "utilitarian" conception of deviance.

e. g.—Violation of the safety rule might be seen as motivated by concern for production, rather than by a deliberate intention to have accidents. If, for example, a worker got a hernia, this might be attributed to his ignorance of proper lifting technique.

Punishment-Centered

In the main, deviance is attributed to *deliberate* intent. Deviance is thought to be the deviant's *end*. This we call a "voluntaristic" conception of deviance.

e. g.—When a worker was absent without an excuse, this was *not* viewed as an expression of an uncontrollable impulse, or as an unanticipated consequence of other interests. It was believed to be *willful.*

5. What Effects Do the Rules Have upon the Status of the Participants?

Ordinarily, deviation from the rule is status-enhancing for workers and management *both*. Conformance to the rule would be status-impairing for both.

e. g.—Violation of the no-smoking rule tended to minimize the visibility of status differentials, by preventing the emergence of a privileged stratum of smokers.

Usually, deviation from the rules impairs the status of superiors *and* subordinates, while conformance ordinarily permits both a measure of status improvement.

e. g.—The safety program increased the prestige of workers' jobs by improving the cleanliness of the plant (the "good house-keeping" component), as well as enabling workers to initiate action for their superiors through the safety meetings. It also facilitated management's ability to realize its production obligations, and provided it with legitimations for extended control over the worker.

Conformance to or deviation from the rules leads to status gains *either* for workers or supervisors, but not for both, and to status losses for the other.

e. g.—Workers' conformance to the bidding system allowed them to escape from tense relations with certain supervisors, or to secure jobs and promotions without dependence upon supervisory favors. It deprived supers of the customary prerogative of recommending workers for promotion or for hiring.

6. Summary of Defining Characteristics or Symptoms

(a) Rules are neither enforced by management nor obeyed by workers.
(b) Usually entails little conflict between the two groups.
(c) Joint violation and evasion of rules is buttressed by the informal sentiments of the participants.

(a) Rules are both enforced by management and obeyed by workers.
(b) Generates a few tensions, but little overt conflict.
(c) Joint support for rules buttressed by informal sentiments, mutual participation, initiation, and education of workers and management.

(a) Rules enforced by either workers or management, and evaded by the other.
(b) Entails relatively great tension and conflict.
(c) Enforced by punishment and supported by the informal sentiments of *either* worker or management.

PART II

Forms of Control and Divisions of Labor

The essays in this section concern themselves with managerial strategies to control the labor process, contested divisions of labor, and forms of ideology and consent. From Taylorism and the human-relations school to modern technocratic and corporate culture, and even many participative-management and comparable-worth approaches, these essays reveal the conservative managerial and gendered biases that shape historical and contemporary transformations of work.

Richard Edwards's essay analyzes the labor process as the site of historic confrontations between labor and capital. Responding to theoretical issues raised by Braverman's analysis of Taylorism, managerial control, and the degradation of workers' skills, Edwards seeks to preserve and reformulate the role of class conflict and workers' own active strategies in the analysis of the labor process. He examines the historical development and succession of several major forms of control (simple, technical, and bureaucratic), as workers and managers confront each other in dynamic conflict at the point of production, and the way new forms emerge amidst the crises of the old. Crises in current technical and bureaucratic forms of control set the context for recent innovative responses by managers and workers.

Peter Rachleff's essay examines a specific case of management strategy in the public sector to use new technologies for mail sorting to undercut the gains postal workers had made in the early 1970s. Offering a vivid glimpse of workplace struggles in the public sector, the essay examines congressional and managerial strategic responses to the postal workers' nationwide strike during the Nixon administration. Illustrating how machine technologies helped postal administrators disrupt informal workplace groups, increase control through large-scale reorganization, and undermine postal unions, Rachleff stresses both the economic dysfunctions and human alienation resulting from wholesale automation, as well as worker resistance to managerially defined reorganization and mechanization.

Michael Burawoy's study of a machine shop in Chicago—the very one **83** that appeared in Donald Roy's classic studies of the 1950s—shows how workers actively participate in transforming their managerially imposed quotas into a game. The game of "making out," though it serves managerial goals of profit and control, is arranged with a good deal of flexibility by the various groups involved. Burawoy demonstrates how the logic of making out permeates workers' shop-floor culture and restructures the patterns of conflict between labor and management. In contrast to some other critics of the labor process, Burawoy argues that work is structured in such a way that workers actively consent to their own domination.

Louise Lamphere and Guillermo Grenier examine the innovation of participative-management teams that promises to empower and upgrade workers and yet is used as part of managerial control strategies among economically vulnerable men and women (primarily Hispanic) workers engaged in a campaign of unionization. HealthTech (a pseudonym for a major health products corporation in the Southwest) has many of the trappings of progressive corporate culture, including flexitime, open-door policies, and teams led by "facilitators." Yet many of the women workers, especially those to whom union organization and legally protected "rights-to-know" about chemical exposure at work have appeal as basic empowerment strategies, experience the team meetings as personally invasive and manipulative, and as psychologizing problems and mobilizing workers against each other. The interviews reveal—in the voices of the women themselves—how these innovations are experienced, both by the women who find them oppressive and disempowering, and those who find them humanizing and empowering. Because the authors locate their study in the context of a union drive, they are also able to explore some misconceptions about why it is so difficult to organize women workers.

Frank Fischer's essay portrays the managerial bias that has shaped the development of social science's contribution to organizational analysis, both its theory and its methodology. Focusing on the contribution of organizational psychology and the human-relations school to the development of modern organization theory, he demonstrates the ideological support that the theory has provided for management throughout its history of struggle with labor over industrial workplace control. Fischer concludes by pointing to the contemporary uses of psychological techniques to combat unionization in both private and public organizations.

Joan Acker's essay examines an ambitious attempt in the state of Oregon to rethink gendered job classifications and pay structures to bring them into line with the challenge of the comparable-worth movement to male-female inequities. But despite the fact that feminists had a considerable presence on the task force that supervised the reclassification projects, and that representative groups of female and male rank-and-file workers constituted the teams that reexamined each job classification in terms of different kinds of skills, gendered hierarchies were nonetheless reproduced. Acker shows how powerful the value of hierarchy itself proved to be in the attempt to develop a consistent and believable classification. Not only were some of the deepest assumptions about gender and hierarchy reproduced by the consultants' guide charts and conceptions about what supervisors in contrast to those they supervise actually do at work, but face-to-face interaction of men and women in the teams and the decision rules they adopted to facilitate their work helped to accomplish much the same result. Acker's account is a sobering and useful one for feminists and trade unionists who have tried to undo some of the gendered inequities of the workplace through a strategy of comparable worth, and it points to the need for more refined strategies.

Vicki Smith's essay provides a case study of a major West Coast bank whose strategic management response to downsizing and restructuring is a program of corporate-culture and management seminars for the middle managers upon whom much of the burden of reorganization fell. Smith vividly portrays the training programs designed to reform the way that middle management thinks about supervision of employees, and in particular how such programs try to get them to abandon bureaucratic supervision and evaluation techniques in the name of ideals of flexibility, personal judgment, and individualization inspired by corporate-culture approaches. But the new ideals turn out to be perceived as more arbitrary, manipulative, and problematic than the old ones that secured managerial legitimacy, and middle managers are themselves resistant. The management seminars, however, provide little room for even the voice of the middle managers and deflect any criticism of strategic management's decisions and mistakes that may have led to failures in the marketplace. In addition to extending critical analysis of the labor process and authority to the financial-services sector, Smith provides a complex view of the conflicts within management itself over the structure of authority and control, as well as a welcome demystification of much of what passes for progressive corporate-culture programs.

8

Forms of Control
in the Labor Process:
An Historical Analysis

Richard C. Edwards

For the last several years, discussions of the labor process have tended to take as their starting point Harry Braverman's *Labor and Monopoly Capital*. Most writers have accepted Braverman's thesis of the degradation of work; a few have criticized it. Yet despite the book's brilliant insights, the weaknesses in its analysis are becoming increasingly visible. Most important are the following:

1. The book fails to take account of labor responses to the new forms of "degraded" work that employers have developed. In Braverman's story, new, fragmented, de-skilled methods of work are developed and implemented by capitalists, with drastic effects on workers but with little apparent resistance. No impact results from what resistance does occur. Unions play no role, and there is no class struggle.

2. The book accepts or seems to accept writings on management theory as evidence for actual developments on the shop or office floor. The most important example is Braverman's reading of Frederick Taylor's writings as though they described real processes rather than simply Taylor's thinking and theories. The book has therefore taken what are clearly ideological sources of information and treated them as though the processes they describe were real.

3. The book's basic premise of "de-skilling" remains problematical. It seems clear that de-skilling has occurred in the traditional craft trades, including the machinists' tradition out of which Braverman himself came. It also seems correct to emphasize the tendency for capitalists to replace high-skill (or more precisely, high-wage) labor with low-skill (low-wage) labor whenever possible. Nonetheless, the development of both the forces and relations of production continually throw up new products, new technologies, and a demand for re-skilled, especially educated labor as well as de-skilled

Originally appeared as "The Social Relations of Production at the Point of Production." Reprinted from *Work and Labor*, a special issue of *The Insurgent Sociologist* 8, nos. 2–3 (Fall 1978): 109–125, by permission of the publisher.

labor. Thus accumulation must be seen as simultaneously de-skilling and re-skilling the labor force. Rather than the simple, one-way process that Braverman describes, we must recognize this more complicated, two-way movement.

Admitting this point immediately changes our analysis of the trends in the composition of the American working class. The historical tendency can no longer be the simple one of the creation of an ever-increasing mass of unskilled or low-skilled workers. Rather, craft work declines, educated labor emerges, and the overall impact on the working class—whether it is becoming more homogeneous or more differentiated—is at least ambiguous.

4. The book fails to be clear as to whether modern techniques of production (carrying with them their inherent de-skilling, degradation of work, etc.) are inevitable consequences of technical economies of scale. The most consistent reading of the book, I would argue, would necessarily interpret the new methods of production as more efficient. In part, of course, the new methods simply permit (in Braverman's theory) the use of low-skill workers, but this begs the central question of whether such techniques do not also result in higher productivity. If this reading is accurate, then the demise of craft and other production in which workers have a knowledge of the entire production process is sad but "progressive." Capitalism is only the messenger, the vehicle for these necessary advances in society's productive capacity. Yet this reading seems quite at odds with the vitriol that Braverman displays when he records management's quest for control, and his suggestion, in several places, that degradation results from the specifically capitalist organization of production.
5. The book fails to make any distinctions between monopoly capital and non-monopoly capital. Indeed, the "monopoly capital" of the title turns out to be monopoly capital*ism*, i.e., capitalism in the present period. Yet how the book's analysis relates to monopoly capitalism rather than simply to capitalism remains entirely unclear. There is no evidence or reasoning introduced to suggest that monopoly capital in particular impinges upon the labor process in any way different from contemporary non-monopoly capital—or, for that matter, different from an earlier competitive capital. Of course the more recent managers are more sophisticated than (e.g.) their 19th-century counterparts, but the transition to monopoly capitalism does not seem to have altered the *logic* of the labor process.
6. While the book appears to provide an historical argument, starting with the development of management ideas in the 19th century and

pursuing their realization in the present, in fact there exists no real historical content to the analysis. For example, between Taylorism and the present came, among other historical processes, the organization of workers in the mass production industries into industrial unions. This historic achievement, the goal of the labor and left-wing movements for the preceding several decades, does not in any way impinge on Braverman's "historical" argument.

These six omissions (and others) are serious flaws indeed in any analysis of the labor process. Just as Paul Baran and Paul Sweezy in *Monopoly Capital* excise the sphere of production from their analysis of modern capitalism, so it seems Harry Braverman has left class conflict out of his analysis of the labor process. The relations of production simply unfold as ever more systematic (and horrifying) applications of the Babbage principle. This rather mechanical logic is all the more surprising since it was Braverman himself who insisted that Marx's distinction between labor and labor power (between work done and the capacity to do work) was the essential starting point for any analysis of the labor process. But surely the relevance of this distinction is precisely the workers' ability—individually, in small groups, and collectively—to resist and in consequence to re-shape employers' schemes to transform labor power into labor. Workers do not have unlimited power, but then neither do capitalists, and Braverman's story needs to be amended to take account of the real constraints on capitalists.

In this paper I cannot deal with all these issues, but I will try to suggest an alternative formulation of the dynamics of the labor process which begins to get at some of the problems in Braverman's analysis.[1] The central departure from Braverman's analysis can be quite simply stated. Whereas Braverman concerned himself primarily with the *technical* aspects of the development of the labor process—"technical" in the sense of workers' relations to the physical process of production—my analysis will focus on the developing *social* relations of production at the point of production. This analysis, rather than contradicting Braverman's work, instead incorporates and builds upon it. The 20th century has witnessed the emergence of two divergent tendencies: (1) the development of production technology has tended to abolish old craft skills and obliterated distinctions among work tasks, . . . thereby also reducing skills distinctions among workers; but (2) the development of the social relations of the workplace has tended to create new divisions (and institutionalize pre-existing ones) based on the social organization of the workplace. As a result, the working class has become both more homogeneous as a mass of machine operatives and re-divided by the social organization of production. What Braverman leaves out is the capitalist firm as a social system, one embodying technical and social relations of production. This is what must be studied if we are to understand the dynamics of the labor process and the formation of the modern American working class. The rest of this paper is devoted to providing a sketchy and schematic framework for such an investigation.

1. The Labor Process

Capitalists are in business to make profits, and to do that they organize society's production. They begin by converting their funds for investment (money capital) into the raw materials, labor, machinery, etc., needed for production; they organize the labor process itself, whereby the constituents of production are transformed into useful products or services; and then, by selling the products of labor, they re-convert their property back to money form. If the money capital obtained at the end of this cycle exceeds that invested initially, the capitalists have earned a profit.

Each step in this sequence is fraught with uncertainties, and none more so than production itself. In organizing the labor process, employers seek to carry out two very different tasks. The first is what might be termed the coordination of social production. Any production process that involves many persons must be consciously directed so that each person's labor meshes with or contributes to the labor of the other producers. Such coordination is required in all societies.

The second task derives more particularly from the class nature of the capitalist labor process. Employers not only coordinate, they must also compel. They must compel because, while workers produce the firm's output, it is capitalists who own or appropriate the output. Capitalists must therefore convince workers, through means subtle or brutal, to produce goods that they (the capitalists) will profit from. That is, capitalists must seek to convert the labor power they have purchased in the marketplace into useful labor under conditions in which the possessor of the labor power has little to gain from providing useful labor. Indeed, competition among capitalists makes such compulsion not merely a matter of individual choice or greed but rather an economic necessity. Capitalists are forced to extract as much useful labor from their workers as possible; those employers who fail to do so or do it badly will usually be driven out of business.

What employers strive to achieve is minimum *per unit* costs of production. After all, it is the total unit cost that is deducted from the selling price to yield the "residual," the capitalist's profit. Profit maximizing, particularly if it is intensified and enforced by market competition, thus sets in motion a continuing search for new methods of production, new sources of labor, new ways of organizing the labor process that will reduce unit costs. In this search, the capitalist has few biases: whatever reduces unit costs and increases profits is seized upon.

It must be noted, however, that de-skilling and the increasing use of low-skill, low-wage labor is only *one* avenue for reducing unit costs. Consider in particular that portion of total unit costs that derives from the labor input, i.e., the unit labor cost. This portion of the firm's costs clearly depends upon two quantities: the price (wage) or labor power, and the productivity of labor power. Minimizing one of these elements (e.g., the wage) does not minimize their ratio. Specifically, it may pay the firm to pay a wage higher than the least possible wage if the result is a more than proportionate increase in productivity. Of course, if wages can be reduced with effect on, or with an increase in, productivity, then cutting wages will be profit-maximizing; but if lower wages bring forth lower productivity, then the profit-maximizing strategy depends on the magnitudes involved.

This distinction between minimizing wages and minimizing per unit labor costs is not simply a point in theory; as should become clear below, the history of the labor process in the 20th century cannot be understood without it. This distinction assumes such importance because labor, unlike all the other ingredients of production, does not come available to capitalists as a purchasable commodity. Labor power can be bought, but between the purchase of labor power and the real appropriation of useful labor comes a wedge; the will, motivation, and consciousness of the worker drastically affect the work force's productivity. Hence the employer's second task in organizing production: the extraction of labor from labor power.

This second task must be understood as one which applies primarily to the firm's workforce at large, or at least to substantial portions of it. For any individual or any small group of workers, wider market mechanisms come into play. Any worker who produces significantly less than the "norm," or indeed who produces less than the most eager substitute among the unemployed, will simply be replaced; here, the market and the "reserve army" enforce production levels. But as I argue below, the use of the reserve-army sanction as a "first-resort" mechanism for extracting labor has produced resistance to the limitations on capitalists as well as obedience from workers. In all cases the employer's prerogative to hire and fire remains the ultimate sanction, but, especially among big employers, different methods serve to organize work on a day-to-day basis.

In some cases, the second task may be trivial. It is trivial, for example, if employers can directly contract for labor rather than labor power. If it is possible to specify in advance all of the duties to be performed, then the employer can simply purchase the product or service of labor. Likewise, employers may pay only for work actually done if each worker's output is independent; here, piece-rate pay may compel adequate production. Other workplace schemes may be directed towards the same end.

In general, however, capitalists have found it neither practical nor profitable to rely on such devices. Only rarely can every worker's duties be exhaustively specified when the worker is hired. Piece-rate pay has limited application and frequently engenders conflict over the rates themselves. In both cases, evaluation of whether the contracted work was properly done raises further problems. Moreover, such workers are likely to be using company-provided tools or machinery, so even if a "slow" worker receives a low wage, the capitalist cannot be indifferent to the under-utilization of the capital. Other schemes (profit sharing, distributing company stock to workers, more elaborate incentive schemes) also fail. Most importantly, all these devices founder because their targets, the workers, retain their ability to resist. Typically, then, the second task—extracting work from employees who have no direct stake in profits—remains to be carried out in the workplace itself.

The social division into workers and capitalists thereby lays the foundation for continuing conflict in the labor process, as employers attempt to extract the maximum effort from workers [who] necessarily resist their bosses' impositions. Conflict ensues over how work shall be organized, what work pace shall be established, what conditions producers must labor under, what "rights" workers shall enjoy, how the various employees of the enterprise shall relate to each other. The workplace becomes a perpetual battleground.

The struggle in the workplace has a closely-intertwined parallel in the bargaining that goes on in the marketplace. Here conflict concerns wages, as labor and capital contend over the reward for the laborer's time. Sometimes this bargaining occurs collectively (e.g., between unions and industry representatives); at other times it takes an individual form (between job applicant and employer). At times wage bargaining creates a crisis; at other times it assumes an entirely pacific form. But here too the clash of interests persists.

Thus, in the old slogan, "a fair day's work for a fair day's pay," both elements become matters of conflict. "A fair day's work" is as much an issue for bargaining, resistance, and struggle as is the "fair day's pay." The old Wobbly demand said it more cogently if less completely: "Good Pay or Bum Work!"

The "war" on the shop and office floor may take many forms. At times it is open warfare, mutually joined; more commonly, it is a cold war, or some variant of guerrilla operations and peaceful co-existence. Frequently it is not consciously recognized as battle at all. The combatants sometimes perceive the clash in class terms, but more often they view it within an individual or small-group framework. But whether acute or dormant, the conflict remains.

Conflict in the labor process occurs under definite historical circumstances—or, what is the same, within a specific economic and social context. Most importantly, production is part of the larger process of capital accumulation, i.e., the cycle of investment of prior profits, organization of production, sale of produced commodities, realization of profits (or loss), and reinvestment of profits. This process constitutes the fundamental dynamic of a capitalist economy. But capital accumulation, while it remains the basic theme, gets played out with substantial variations. A whole set of factors—the degree of competition among capitalists, the size of corporations, the extent of trade union organization, the level of class consciousness among workers, the impact of governmental policies, the speed of technological change, and so on—influence the nature and shape and pace of accumulation. Taken together, these various forces provide both possibilities and constraints for what can occur within the workplace. What was possible or successful in one era may be impossible or disastrous in another. Conflict at work, then, must be understood as a product both of the strategies or wills of the combatants and of definite conditions not wholly within the grasp of either workers or capitalists. As Marx put it, "People make their own history, but they do not make it just as they please; they do not make it under circumstances chosen by themselves, but under circumstances directly found, given, and transmitted from the past."[2]

Conflict occurs within definite limits imposed by a social and historical context, yet this context rarely yields a precise determination of work organization. After technological constraints, the discipline of the market, and other forces have been taken into account, there remains a certain indeterminacy to the labor process. This "space" for the working out of workplace conflict is particularly evident within the large corporation, where "external" constraints have been reduced to a minimum. Here especially, the essential question remains: how shall work be organized?

Outside the firm, relations between capitalists and workers take the form of demanders and suppliers of the commodity "labor power;" that is, the "equality" of market relations prevails. Inside the firm, relations between capitalists and workers take the form of boss and bossed; that is, a *system of control* prevails. Any system of control must embody three elements: (1) the direction of work tasks, (2) the evaluation of the work done, and (3) the rewarding and disciplining of workers.

I distinguish below between three historically important and essentially quite different ways of organizing these three elements. The first is what I term "simple control": capitalists exercise power openly, arbitrarily, and personally (or through hired bosses who act in much the same way). Simple control formed the organizational basis of 19th century firms and continues today in the small enterprises of the more competitive industries. The second is "technical control": the control mechanism is embedded in the physical technology of the firm, designed into the very machines and other physical apparatus of the workplace. The third is "bureaucratic control": control becomes embedded in the social organization of the enterprise, in the contrived social relations of production at the point of production. These last two systems of control constitute "structural" forms of control, in the sense that the exercise of power becomes institutionalized in the very structure of the firm and is thus made impersonal. Structural control, as explained below, provides the rationale for the organization of workplace[s] in big corporations today.

This typology of control embodies both the pattern of historical evolution and the array of contemporary methods for organizing work. On the one hand, each form of control corresponds to a definite stage in the development of the "representative" or most important firms, and so the systems of control correspond to or characterize stages of capitalism. On the other hand, capitalist production has developed unevenly, with some sectors pushing far in advance of other sectors, and so each type of control exists alongside the others in the economy today.

Since the transformation of the workplace in the 20th century is largely a story of the organization of work in large corporations in the advanced countries, I restrict the discussion below to that topic. Workers in small firms, as well as most large corporations' employees in Third World countries, continue to face older, more direct, less institutionalized forms of control.

The labor process becomes an arena of class conflict. Faced with chronic resistance to their efforts to compel production, employers over the years have attempted to resolve the matter by reorganizing, indeed revolutionizing, the labor process itself. Their goal remains profits; their strategies aim at establishing structures of control at work. That is, capitalists have attempted to organize production in such a way as to minimize workers' opportunities for resistance and even to alter workers' perceptions of the desirability of opposition. Work has been organized, then, to contain conflict. In this endeavor employers have sometimes been successful.

2. Towards New Systems of Control

The conditions of work in capitalist enterprises have changed as capitalism itself has changed. In both cases, evolution has not overturned the fundamental relations that exist between capitalist and worker. But just as capitalism has proceeded from a competitive to a monopoly phase, so also have the organization of workers in production and the circumstances of their employment passed from one developmental stage to another. And it is important to note that the latter process has occurred largely as a result of the class nature of capitalist production, rather than as the result of anything "inevitable" or "natural" in either technology or the operation of large organizations.

During the 19th century much production was still carried on by skilled craftsmen, who established their own working conditions, protected the quality of their products, and limited access to their industry through craft rules, customs, apprenticeships, and the like. They were subject to market forces, of course, yet within the unit of production they themselves or their craft traditions served to organize the labor process. But as a population dependent on wages emerged, capitalists could increasingly out-compete petty producers by taking control of the labor process directly. Production itself, as well as the sale of commodities, became organized by capitalists.

Most 19th-century businesses were small and subject to relatively tight discipline from competition in their product markets. The typical firm had few resources and little energy to invest in creating more sophisticated management structures. A single entrepreneur, usually flanked by a small coterie of foremen and managers, ruled the firm. They exercised power personally, intervening often in the labor process to exhort workers, bully and threaten them, reward good performance, hire and fire on the spot, favor loyal workers, and generally act as despots, benevolent or otherwise. They had a direct stake in promoting production, and they combined both incentives and sanctions in an idiosyncratic and unsystematic mix. There was little structure to how power was exercised, and workers tended to be treated arbitrarily. Since workforces were small and the boss was both close and powerful, workers had little chance collectively to oppose his rule. Generally, workers could do little more than attempt to protect dying craft traditions or engage in informal efforts to restrict output.

In terms of the three elements of a control system listed above, analysis shows that each element tended to reveal simply another feature of the personal relation between capitalist (or other bosses) and workers. In specifying what tasks were to be done, the boss directly delineated the jobs and assigned workers to them. Where production involved unstandardized or batch-type processes, this direction typically involved continuous supervision, as in gang-labor. Where production was routinized, personal direction still involved assignment and reassignment of workers to different work stations. Evaluations also occurred continuously and could scarcely be distinguished from direction; certainly few separate evaluation procedures existed. Rewarding and disciplining tended to be somewhat more structured (firms often established wages schedules, for example), yet even here the arbitrary and unconstrained power of the capitalist to punish workers meant that workers were constantly subject to personal rule. Control was, in effect, a system of direct and immediate tyranny, from which little relief was possible. Indeed, those outside the factory gates—the reserve army—stood as ready replacements for any workers who rebelled against such tyrannical power.

This system of *simple control* survives today in the small-business sector of the American economy. It has necessarily been amended by the passage of time and by borrowings of management practices from the more advanced corporate sector, but it retains its essential principles and mode of operation. We readily see it in the mom-and-pop grocery store, but it is also apparent in small manufacturing concerns. For example, a small guitar factory in Kansas employs some 50–60 workers, all of whom know the owner well. Indeed, the owner acts as "head workman" in some cases, occasionally building the specialized one-of-a-kind guitars ordered by show-business celebrities. The workers build the more standardized instruments, each doing a small operation on the 10 or so guitars produced every day. In directing their labor, in evaluating their performance, in rewarding and disciplining them, the owner (and the few other bosses present) rely on the personal relations of the factory to control work. The impact of simple control can also be seen in a Boston-area electronics plant, a plant employing some 500 workers. As described by Ann Bookman, the owner and the top-level foreman rule the roost in direct personal ways, exhorting or threatening workers to produce more, watching closely how hard workers work, assigning workers to easy or tough work stations depending on the foreman's fancy, and handing out or withholding pay raises, permission to take time off, overtime, etc., as rewards and disciplines.[3] Once again, personal despotism rules the workplace.

The system of simple control is not the principal organizing device in today's corporate sector. Toward the end of the 19th century, tendencies toward concentration of capital undermined the practice; some firms grew too large for effective simple control. As firms began to employ thousands of workers, the distance between capitalists and workers expanded and the intervening space was filled by growing numbers of foremen, general foremen, supervisors, superintendents, and other petty managers. The unplanned, willy-nilly expansion of intermediate bosses produced an exaggerated harshness on the shop floor—what one observer has aptly termed "the foreman's empire."[4] Here, foreman and hired bosses ruled nearly without restraint, assuming most of the powers formerly exercised by the entrepreneur. They hired and fired, assigned work, set pay rates, disciplined recalcitrants, and drove the work pace. They acted as petty tyrants, dispensing and withholding the various sanctions at their command.

But whereas immediate tyranny had been more or less successful when conducted by entrepreneurs (or foremen close to them), the system did not work well when staffed by hired bosses. The new bosses were caught in the middle of intensifying workplace conflict. On one side, foremen came into conflict with the employers. The new bosses exercised many of the workplace powers of entrepreneurs, but they nonetheless remained hired hands, not capitalists. The interests of capitalists and petty bosses diverged, and foremen began to use their power for their own ends. Owners experienced increasing difficulty in controlling production through these unreliable intermediaries. Sometimes termed "organizational uncoupling," substitution of the foreman's interests for those of the capitalist understandably destroyed the foreman's allegiance to the system.

On the other side, and undoubtedly more serious, the foremen also came into increasingly serious conflict with the workers. Intensified competition—"cutthroat" competition, as it was known—among manufacturers led them to press ever harder in their efforts to extract greater production from their workers. But the firm's workforce had grown much bigger, and with expansion and speed-up came increased consciousness. Then, too, the entrepreneur had profited directly from increased productivity, and a small capitalist's success often derived as much from eliciting cooperation and loyalty from his employees as from exercising the whip. But for foremen, no comparable incentive existed, and the historical evidence demonstrates that simple control via hired bosses produced brutal, severe punishment, abusive supervision, and few positive compensations. The industrial regime had become harsher, and the mix of incentives and sanctions had swung to nearly total reliance on the negative.

These developments inside the firm both reflected and interacted with a broader reorganization occurring throughout the American economy: the transition from the small-business, competitive capitalism of the 19th century to the corporate monopoly capitalism of the 20th. The driving force of capital accumulation pushed successful firms first to merge and then to attempt to make their new positions profitable. This tendency toward centralization increasingly produced a dichotomy in the economy's industrial structure. Big firms with great market power dominated most major industries, while small firms with little market power survived in their interstices and along their periphery. The dual economy was born.

The transition also unleashed powerful oppositional forces. The maturing labor movement and an emergent Socialist Party organized the first serious challenge to capitalist rule. From the Homestead and Pullman strikes at the beginning of the period to the great 1919–1920 steel strike that closed it, workers fought with their bosses over control of the actual process of production. Intensifying conflict in society at large and the specific contradictions of hierarchical control in the workplace combined to produce an acute "crisis of control" on the shop floor.

The large corporations fashioned the most far-reaching response to this crisis. During the conflict, big employers joined small ones in supporting direct repression of their adversaries. But the large corporations also began to move in systematic ways to reorganize work. They confronted the most serious problems of control, but they also commanded the greatest resources with which to attack the problems. Their size and substantial market power released them from the tight grip of short-run market discipline and made possible for the first time planning in the service of long-term profits. Their initial steps—welfare capitalism, scientific management, company unions, industrial psychology, etc. constituted experiments, trials with serious errors inherent in them, but useful learning experiences nonetheless. In retrospect, these efforts appear as beginnings in the corporations' larger project of establishing more secure control over the labor process.

The new methods of organization that big employers developed were more formalized, more consciously contrived, more structured; they were, in fact, *structural* forms of control. Two possibilities existed: the more formal, consciously contrived controls could be embedded either in (1) the physical structure (technology) of the labor process, or in (2) its social structure. In time, employers used both. They found the advantages of structural control (whether in its technical or social variant) to be two-fold. On the one hand, it made the control system less visible to workers, more hidden and institutional; control became a product not of capitalist employment relations, but rather of "technology" or the scale of "modern industry." On the other hand, structural control provided a means for controlling the "intermediate layers," those extended lines of supervision and power.

Technical control tended to emerge out of the employer's attempts to control conflict in the "bluecollar" or production operations of the firm, whereas bureaucratic control grew out of similar conflicts in the burgeoning "white-collar" or administrative functions. Yet, as I argue below, no such simple identification is possible today. The incompleteness of technical control and the increasingly factory character of administrative work has largely obliterated such distinctions.

3. Technical Control

How something is produced is in large part dictated, of course, by the nature of the product and by the known and available technologies for producing it. Thus lumbering tends to be dispersed in the forests while auto assembly is concentrated indoors, building jet-liners tends to involve a stationary work-object while radio-assembly uses a moving line. In this sense, considerations of the physical efficiency of a technique—for example, the number of times steel has to be reheated as it is processed—distinguish superior from inferior methods. Yet these types of technical considerations by themselves are insufficient for determining what technologies will actually be used.

It is well known that most industries face a variety of possible techniques, and that the relative costs or required inputs will influence which technology is chosen. For example, steel-making can be performed in huge automated factories with much machinery and little labor, as can be seen now in the advanced countries where labor is expensive; or it can be produced in primitive hearths, with greater labor inputs and less machinery, as, for example, in some underdeveloped countries today or in the advanced countries 75 years ago, where machinery is or was expensive. Thus, *within* the known and available technologies, considerable choice is possible.

What is less well known is that there is an important social element in the development and choice of technique as well[, j]ust as it is true that firms confront a range of techniques which tend to provide greater or lesser possibilities for control over their workforces. That is, capitalists may prefer one technique over another because it gives them a strengthened hand in transforming labor power into useful labor. The preferred technique need not be more efficient, but it must be more *profitable*. What is profitable depends on the extent to which purchased commodities (including labor power) result in salable output. Consider, for example, two production techniques, A and B. Technique A is highly efficient, permitting three workers to produce 10 units per day, but it also gives workers substantial power to set their own pace. Technique B is less efficient, permitting three workers to produce at most 8 units per day, but the technology establishes this pace as an invariant daily rate. The two techniques are identical with respect to the per unit use of other inputs. If we take as the "labor input" the labor actually done, the first technique is more efficient. However, if technique A's workers use their control over the labor process to limit how much useful labor they tender in each working day, they do not affect the efficiency of the technique but they do affect the level at which it can be run. For example, they may actually produce only 7 units a day. Technique A remains the more efficient one, but technique B becomes more profitable, since for the same *purchased* inputs, the capitalist winds up with more output in technique B.

Thus, while it remains true that capitalists undoubtedly seek those technologies which are most profitable, we now must admit that there are several considerations which enter into the calculations of profitability. One is physical efficiency, the ratio of the physical output to the material inputs; another is the cost of the various inputs and the value of outputs; yet a third is the extent to which any technology provides managers leverage in transforming labor power into labor done. The way in which the third consideration—control—came to be considered is revealing of the whole process which has revolutionized work in the capitalist era.

Technical control involves designing machinery and planning the flow of work to minimize the labor/labor-power problem. This process occurs simultaneously with the attempt to maximize the purely physically based possibilities for achieving efficiencies. Thus a social dimension—the inherent class nature of capitalist production—is added to the evolution of technology.

Technical control is "structural" in the sense that it is embedded in the technological structure or organization of production. Technical control can be distinguished from simple mechanization, which merely increases the productivity of labor without altering the elements of control. Thus, for example, use of an electric rather than manual typewriter increases the speed with which a secretary works, but it does not alter how the secretary is directed to the new task, how his or her work is evaluated, or what the rewards or disciplining will be. Mechanization often brings with it technical control, as the worker loses control of the pace or sequence of tasks, but this consequence must nearly always be understood to be the result of the *particular* (capitalist) design of the technology and not as an inherent characteristic of machinery *in general*.

Technical control may also be distinguished from simple machine pacing, although the latter may be considered simply as technical control applied to the individual worker. Machine pacing occurs whenever a worker must respond to, rather than set, the pace at which the machinery is being operated. Building a production pace into machinery has long been a tactic used by employers to try to gain control of the labor process. Yet so long as the machinery affects just one worker or one work team, the conflict over pace and rhythm continues to revolve around and focus on these workers and their boss. For example, such machinery typically can in fact be operated at various speeds, and in this sense it requires bonus schemes, piece-rates, incentive pay, etc., to set the pace. Even where machinery has only one speed, boss and workers can nonetheless agree to turn it off for rest periods, if the machinery in question utilizes only workers in this workplace. The social organization surrounding such machine pacing continues to be that of simple control.

Technical control only emerges when the entire production process of the plant, or large segments of the plant, are based on a technology which paces and directs the labor process. In this case, the pacing and direction of work transcend the particular workplace and are thus beyond the power of even the immediate boss; control here is truly "structural."

Toward the end of the 19th century, the crisis created by the contradiction of simple control set off a search for more powerful and sophisticated mechanisms. This experimentation, often identified with "scientific management" or "Taylorism," both went far beyond the theories and stopped far short of the often silly applications put forward by Frederick Taylor and his followers. In essence, although the scientific management movement self-consciously adopted the rhetoric of mechanical engineering, the actual contribution of Taylor and his followers to the design of machinery was quite small. Yet in the plants and offices of the large corporations, the notion of technical control was by no means ignored. The advantages of continuous flow production beckoned.

While all the corporations at the turn of the century groped toward new structures to control their workers, each firm and each industry faced somewhat different circumstances. In some, the product—whether blast furnace heat, a harvester, or a railroad sleeping car—seemingly involved single-unit or small-batch production; here employers saw little chance to exploit technical possibilities for control, although they did engage in a titanic struggle to break the power of the skilled crafts workers. In these industries simple control was solidified, and the corporations turned to the bribes of bonus schemes, incentive pay, and welfare capitalism to create a more sophisticated control structure. But in other industries, notably meat-packing, electrical products, and autos, the flow of production was more direct. There technology was first recognized as a basis for wider, *structural* control.

Textile manufacturers in the 19th century had developed the basis for technical structuring of the first of the three elements of any control system, the technical direction of the work tasks. The other elements of the control system were less well worked out. In these mills, workers found themselves yoked to machinery which determined their work pace. There was little room for resistance in the workplace, and, lacking a strong union, the workers accepted the work or left.

Meat-packing was another early industry to adopt continuous-flow production—this time as a disassembly line. When Swift, Armour, and other Chicago packers began using refrigeration to revolutionize slaughtering and meat-packing, the old shop-based, small-batch techniques of the abattoir gave way to continuous flow. Investigating the packing houses for a British medical journal, one observer put it as follows:

> Outside the big factory buildings there are long, inclined, boarded passages up which the animals are driven. Thus the pigs are brought up to the height of the second floor. As they enter the main building each pig is caught by one of the hind legs. With rope and loop-knot and hook it is slung up, the head downwards and the neck exposed, at a convenient height for the slaughterer to strike. With great rapidity the suspended pigs are pushed on to a sort of passage about four feet broad where their throats are slashed open as they pass along. . . . Within less than a minute the dying pig reaches a long tank full of scalding water and in this the palpitating body is thrown. . . . Standing in the damp and steam, men armed with long prongs push the swine along. By the time when the hogs have floated down to the other end of the boiling-water tank they are sufficiently scalded for the bristles to be easily extracted. They are now put on a moveable counter or platform and as the hogs pass along other workers scrape the bristles off their backs. . . . At a subsequent stage the body is opened and the intestines are removed.[5]

From the perspective of control, the benefits of such production were immediate and obvious. By establishing the pace at which hogs were driven up the passages and onto the slaughter platform, managers could set the pace of work for the entire workforce. There were, of course, limits, both physical and worker-imposed ones, but each supervisor no longer has primary responsibility for directing the workers. Instead, the line now determined the pace, and the foreman had merely to get workers to follow that pace. Our observer makes this point quite explicit:

> When [the animal is] strung up, the machinery carries [it] forward and men have to run after it to cut its throat, while others follow with great pails to catch the blood; and all this without interrupting the dying animal's journey to . . . the next process of manufacture. . . . On they go from stage to stage of manufacture and the men have to keep pace with them.[6]

Thus by 1905 the essentials of continuous flow production, including the possibilities for controlling workers, were established in meat-packing.

With each worker fixed to a physical location in the production process, contact between and among workers nearly ceased. Whereas before workers had made the workday pass more quickly by talking, reading to each other, etc., now each worker simply tended his or her machine. Of particular interest to their employers was the fact that workers had little opportunity to discuss common grievances, compare foremen, exchange views on pay rates or job conditions, etc. Thus, despite their physical proximity, workers had little chance to communicate.

But if continuous flow production appeared first in textiles, meat-packing, lamp-production, and elsewhere, it was the Ford assembly line which brought the technical direction of work to its fullest potential. The automobile industry had its origin in the bicycle plants, where each team (a skilled mechanic and his helpers) performed all the operations necessary to assemble bicycles from separate parts. Carried over into auto plants, this organization slowly gave way as the assembly process began to be broken into parts; each team now added only a limited range of parts to the product, which was then passed on to another team. But it was not until the Highland Park plant opened in 1913 that the endless conveyor finally abolished the craft pretensions of the Ford workers.

The Ford line resolved technologically the essential first task of any control system: it provided unambiguous direction as to what operation each worker was to perform next, and it established the pace at which the worker was forced to work. Henry Ford himself emphasized this aspect of the line by stating as one of his three principles of "progressive manufacture": "The delivery of work instead of leaving it to the workmen's initiative to find it."[7]

Ford might well have added that the line's "delivery of work" also relieved his foremen of having to push work onto the workers, as was the case in simple control. H. L. Arnold studied the plant in great detail in

1914, and his report provides an excellent source for understanding how the new methods worked out in practice. Ford introduced the first chain-driven "endless conveyor" to assemble magnetos, and Arnold (and co-author L. F. Faurote) wrote, "The chair drive [i.e., continuous assembly] proved to be a very great improvement, hurrying the slower men, holding the fast men back from pushing work on to those in advance, and acting as an all-around adjustor and equalizer."[8]

The Ford line created a "technological necessity" in the sequence of tasks which were to be performed. Despite the fact that many assembly sequences were physically possible, no choice attached to the order in which workers did their jobs: the chassis or magneto or engine under construction came past a worker's station, lacking the part inventoried at that station; it would soon move on to other stations where it would gain every other part. The obvious necessity of adding the part in question at this station was thus established. Arnold and Faurote expressed this point as follows:

> Minute division of operations is effective in labor-cost reducing in two ways: first, by making the workmen extremely skillful, so that he does his part with no needless motions, and secondly, by training him to perform his unvaried operation with the least possible expenditure of will-power, and hence with the least brain fatigue.[9]

Thus the line hemmed in the worker, establishing a situation in which only one task sequence was possible.

Similarly, the line established a "technological presumption" in favor of the line's work pace. Struggle between workers and bosses over the transformation of labor power into labor done was no longer a simple and direct *personal* confrontation; now the conflict was mediated by the production technology itself. Workers had to oppose the pace of the line, not the (direct) tyranny of their bosses. The line thus established a technically-based and technologically-repressive mechanism to be used to keep workers at their tasks.

The substitution of technical for human direction and pacing of work simultaneously revolutionized the relation between foreman and work-ers. Arnold and Faurote explained that

> [The Highland Park plant] has applied team work [i.e., division of labor] to the fullest extent, and by this feature in conjunction with the arrangement of successive operations in the closest proximity, so as to minimize trans-portation and to *maximize the pressure of flow of work, it succeeds in maintaining speed without obtrusive foremanship.*[10]

The line eliminated "obtrusive foremanship," that is, close supervision in which the foreman simultaneously directed production, inspected and approved work, and disciplined workers. In its place, the line created a situation in which the foreman was relieved of responsibility for the first element of the control system. This change marked an important first step away from the simple control model which granted the foreman all the prerequisites of an "entrepreneur" within his own shop. Instead, the line brought with it the first appearance of structural control.

The importance of this change is indicated by the small number of "straw-bosses" and foremen needed to supervise the Ford workplace. In 1914 about 15,000 workers were employed at all the Ford plants. Leaving aside the top management, this large force was overseen by just 255 men ranking higher than "workman," including: 11 department foremen, 62 job foremen, 84 assistant foremen, and 98 sub-foremen (straw-bosses). Thus there was one foreman (all ranks) for each 58 workers, an impossible ratio except in a situation in which the foremen no longer directed the sequence of pacing of work.[11]

The foreman in technical control is thus transformed into an *enforcer* of the requirements and dictates of the technical structure. On the assembly line he or she monitors workers to keep them at their tasks—the foreman no longer is busy initiating tasks. The foreman penalizes exceptions to the normal flow of work, rather than personally directing that flow. Moreover, this enforcement is seen as being required by the larger structure. Exceptional circumstances aside, the foreman cannot personally be held responsible for the oppressiveness of the production process. If the legitimacy of the line is accepted, then the necessity for the foreman's job follows. The actual power to control work is thus vested in the line itself rather than in the person of the foreman, and the power relations are made more invisible. Instead of control appearing to flow from boss to workers, control emerges from the much more impersonal "technology."

Technical control has since come to be based upon a much more sophisticated technology, of course, than that which was available when the Ford line was introduced. The most dramatic changes in technology have occurred as a result of the invention of new devices to control or "program" machinery, including the increasingly pervasive linking of mini- or micro-computers to machines. Yet rather than producing qualitative differences, this new technology is best understood as simply expanding the potential contained in the concept of technical control.

But technical control by itself was not a sufficient advance over simple control to resolve the crisis of control within the firm, and it is not difficult to see why. Technical control provided the possibility of embedding in the technical structure the first element of all control systems (progressively directing the worker to further tasks), but it did little to change the second and third elements (evaluating work performance and enforcing compliance). In early forms of technical control, for example, supervisors had the power to discharge workmen immediately and at will. The second and third elements of control changed little.

Thus technical control by itself was not destined to be the ultimate wrinkle in corporate control. For one thing, it still left open the issue of how to motivate workers. If anything, the Ford plants represented a step *backwards* on this score, since the massive layoffs needed to "discipline" those workers who failed to produce according to the line's speed provoked increasingly intense hostility and resistance. The carrot was largely absent, the stick ever-present. The chief weapon, often even a first-resort disciplining device, was the "reserve army of the unemployed." Less drastic penalties (docking pay, suspension, etc.) also existed, but their usefulness varied directly with the potency of the supervisor's major sanction, dismissal. The only real motivator in this system was the worker's fear of being sacked.

But if dismissal was to be feared, either as a threat or as a fact, it was necessary that there be many substitute workers able and available to fill the jobs. The lack of plausible replacements was precisely what had given the old skilled workers their power, and had led, by way of reaction, to their demise. Similarly, in times of tight labor markets (such as during war), workers were relatively confident both that replacements could not easily be found and that, if fired, workers could find other jobs.

Thus, in technical control no less than in simple control, employers had a powerful incentive to make their workers as interchangeable and substitutable as possible. The continuing mechanization eroded the need for skills anyway, making the workforce more uniformly composed of unskilled and semi-skilled machine operatives. But the strictly *control* aspects of work reorganization contributed a further impetus to the homogenizing process.

The tendency to create a common (and degraded) status for all workers was evident in the labor policies of the early Ford plants. The famous Five Dollar Day which Ford announced in 1914 seemed to be a real advance, since $5 was substantially above other wages being paid to factory labor. Yet the higher wage was not essential for filling the company's vacancies; although it did create an enormous labor surplus. The day after the announcement there were 10,000 people outside the gates clamoring for jobs; for months afterward, as Francesca Maltese reports, the job-seekers "continued to clog the entrances to Ford's employment offices."[12] The lesson was not lost on the people employed inside the gates: the Company would have no trouble finding replacements for recalcitrant workers.

Similarly, other Ford labor policies attempted to generate a "ready reserve" of surplus labor. Thus it is no coincidence that the first large-scale entry of blacks into northern industrial employment was in the Ford plants. By 1926 Ford employed 10,000 black workers, over 90 percent of Detroit's black industrial labor force. The Company cast its net even further, drawing into potential employment the physically handicapped (generously labelled "substandard men"), young boys, and others. It was energetic in establishing a recruiting bureau to attract workers from other cities. Thus technical control both continued the need for surplus labor as a ready disciplinarian, and strengthened its derivative, the increasing substitutability and homogenizing of the labor force.

The attempt to generate highly visible pools of surplus labor was a response to the crisis of control on the shop floor, and it affected primarily the blue-collar workers. But technical control's influence extended also to the lower-level clerical staff, and here technical control introduced a new stimulus towards homogenization.

The corporation in part addressed the problem of controlling the white-collar staff by reorganizing their work along the lines of technical control. The routinization of clerical work has been extensively investigated elsewhere, and it need not be repeated here.[13] The essential point is that many clerical workers—those performing key-punching, typing of forms, and other standardized operations—were transformed into operatives of simple machines. Given the nearly universal nature of high school education by 1930, they could easily be replaced, and they became subject to the discipline of the reserve army. They had been reduced to the level of homogeneous labor.

But even as the new system solved some of the corporation's labor problems, it created other and more serious ones. Technical control yoked the entire firm's labor force (or each of the major segments thereof) to a common pace and pattern of work set by the productive technology. In so doing, technical control resolved for the individual workplace and the individual foreman the problem of translating labor power into labor. But it did so at the cost of raising this conflict to the plant-wide level. Thus the basic conflict was *displaced*, not eliminated.

At first this displacement was not realized. Throughout the 1910's and even more so during the relatively conflict-free 1920's, technical control appeared to have decisively turned the power balance in favor of the capitalists. Individual sabotage, disputes between workers and their foremen, and grumbling over wages continued, of course, but these could be managed and the power of technology drove the work pace.

The flaw in this naïveté was exposed dramatically and at heavy costs to the capitalists. Irving Bernstein describes what happened in the auto plants.

> On December 28 [1936] a sudden sit-down over piece-rate reductions in one department in Cleveland swept through the plant and 7000 people stopped work; Chevrolet body production came to a complete halt. On December 30 the workers in Flint sat down in the huge Fisher One and the smaller Fisher Two plants. Combined with the stoppage in Cleveland, this forced the closing of Chevrolet and Buick assembly operations in Flint. On December 31 the UAW sat down at Guide Lamp in Anderson, Indiana. . . . By the end of the first week of the new year, the great General Motors automotive system had been brought to its knees.[14]

The cost of lifting the shop-floor conflict out of the individual workplace and raising it to the plant-wide level was not apparent. Technical control linked together the plant's workforce, and when the line stopped, every worker necessarily joined the strike. Moreover, in a large, integrated manufacturing operation, such as auto production, a relatively small group of disciplined unionists could cripple an entire system by shutting down a part of the line.

Technical control thus took relatively homogeneous labor—unskilled and low-skilled workers—and technologically linked them together in production. This combination proved to be exceptionally favorable for building unions. The Flint strike was not the first sit-down, nor were such strikes confined to plants with moving lines. But the sit-downs were most effective in the mass-production industries of autos, electrical products, rubber, and textiles. More broadly, "quickie" sit-downs (strikes of a few minutes or an hour or two), sabotage, wildcats, and other labor actions were much more effective in plants organized according to technical control.

The CIO success of the 1930's clearly resulted in part from wider factors not considered here: the depression, the increasing concentration of industry, the conscious activity of militant union organizers. Yet the rise of industrial unionism was also significantly a response to technical control, and it marked the beginning of an effective limitation on that system.

These limits were nowhere more clearly revealed than at GM's Lordstown (Ohio) Vega plant several decades later.[15] GM had come to Lordstown with the intention of achieving a dramatic speedup in output. Its strategy was two-pronged. First, GM re-designed the plant and machinery to accommodate production at roughly 100 cars per hour (one every 36 seconds); this rate represented a 40 percent increase over the one-a-minute average that prevailed in most of its plants. Second, the company recruited a new labor force, one without long traditions of struggle to restrict industrial output. The plan didn't work.

The 1972 revolt at Lordstown gained much publicity and even notoriety, and justifiably so, but mostly the event attracted attention for the wrong reasons. On one side, Lordstown was declared atypical (and hence not really worrisome) because of the youthfulness of the workers (average age 24), because of the plant's counter-culture ambience, and because of the workforce's lack of industrial experience and discipline. On the other side, Lordstown was heralded as the new wave of working-class revolt for precisely the same reasons. Yet what really should have been noted was that Lordstown may have represented technical control's final gasp as an ascendant control system. The most advanced industrial engineering went into the design of the plant, but only resistance and the breakdown of control came out. Undoubtedly youth, counter-culture, and lack of industrial conditioning contributed to GM's problems, but it is precisely for such populations that technical control is designed.

Machine-pacing and de-skilling through use of "smart" machines continue, and it is even expanding in the lower-level clerical occupations. Moreover, in the "new" areas of investment—the U.S. South and the Third World, for example—technical control remains a first principle for factory organization. Equally, in the economy's small-firm periphery such organization remains important. But technical control can never again by *itself* constitute an adequate control system for the core firm's main industrial labor force.

Indeed, in its principal areas of application, technical control has evolved into a more mixed system, with unions playing a decisive (even if limited) role. The second and third elements of control become *jointly* administered by management and unions (with unions as junior partners). Evaluation and reward/discipline become matters for mutual determination in accordance with collectively bargained rules, procedures, and protections. Arbitrary dismissal and other punishments are limited by arbitration and grievance machinery; job "rights" become contractual obligations rather than "privileges" dispensed by bosses; wages and benefits are established within an overall contract structure. Technical control thus becomes supplemented, in the unionized sector of industry, by the elaborate administrative mechanisms achieved by unions to protect workers from the ravages of the earlier, more pure system of technical control.

The resistance engendered by technical control set off a new search for methods of controlling the workplace. In firms like IBM, Polaroid, Xerox, Gillette, and others, management devised a different system of structural control, this time based on the social or organizational structure of the firm. The result is what is here termed *bureaucratic control.*

4. Bureaucratic Control

The defining feature of bureaucratic control is the institutionalization of hierarchical power. "Rule of law"—the firm's law—replaces "rule by supervisor command" in the direction of work tasks, in the principles for evaluation of those tasks, and in the exercise of the firm's power to enforce compliance. Work activities become defined and directed by a set of work criteria: the rules, procedures, and expectations governing particular jobs. Thus for the individual worker, his or her job tends to be defined more by formalized job descriptions or "work criteria" attached to the job (or, more precisely, by the interpretation given to those criteria by his or her supervisor and higher levels of supervision) than by specific orders, directions, and whims of the supervisor. Moreover, it is against those criteria that the worker's performance is measured. Finally, company rules and procedures carefully spell out the penalties for poor performance and, more importantly, the rewards for adequate performance.

The criteria contain both written and unwritten requirements, and the essential characteristic is just that the worker is able to ascertain them and that they are highly stable. The firm no longer alters the worker's tasks and responsibilities by having the supervisor tell the worker to do something different; rather, it "creates a new job" or "redefines the job." From these criteria derive the "customary law" notions of "equity" or "just cause" in firing, promotion, and job assignment.

Top-echelon management retain their control over the enterprise through their ability to determine the rules, set the criteria, establish the structure, and enforce compliance. For the latter concern (enforcing compliance), bureaucratic organization again marked a departure from simple control. In simple control, power is vested in individuals and exercised arbitrarily according to their discretion, but with bureaucratic control power becomes institutionalized by vesting it in official positions or roles and permitting its exercise only according to prescribed rules, procedures, and expectations. Rules governing the exercise of power become elements of the work criteria defining supervisor's jobs. Superiors as well as subordinates become accountable to top-down control; the system thus broadens its reach to the "intervening layers" of petty officials.

Work activities can never be completely specified by job criteria in advance, and "rule of law" can never completely replace "rule of command" in an hierarchical enterprise. Some situations or problems always arise which need to be handled in an ad hoc, particularistic way, and so supervisors can never be content merely to evaluate and never to instigate. The shift to bureaucratic control must therefore be seen as a shift toward relatively greater dependence on institutionalized power, and bureaucratic control comes to exist alongside and be reinforced by elements of simple control. Bureaucratic control becomes, then, the predominant system of control, giving shape and logic to the firm's organization, although not completely eliminating elements of simple control.

The imposition of bureaucratic control in the monopoly firm had four specific consequences for the social relations of the firm.

1. The power relations of hierarchical authority were made invisible, submerged and embedded in the structure and organization of the firm, rather than visible and openly manifest in personal, arbitrary power.

2. Bureaucratic control, because of its emphasis on formal structure and status distinctions, made it possible to differentiate jobs more finely. Organizational as well as technical (i.e., production) aspects of jobs defined their status. Each job appeared more unique and

individualized by its particular position in the finely graded hierarchical order, by the job criteria which specified work activities, and by its distinct status, power, responsibilities, and so on. Elements of the social organization of the firm which differentiated between jobs were emphasized, while those which created commonality diminished.

These two changes tended to erode the bases for common worker opposition. Increasingly the individual worker came to face an impersonal and massive organization more or less alone. In general, the work environment became less conducive to unions and strike or other opposition activities. In those bureaucratized industries where unions remained (or were subsequently organized), more and more the unions accepted the organization of work and directed their energies toward non-control issues (wages, fringe benefits, and procedures for promotion, hiring, and firing). Even where unions turned their attention to the work activities themselves, their efforts were mainly defensive, directed toward making the job criteria more explicit and openly articulated; while this tended to undermine the authority of arbitrary foremen, it strengthened the legitimacy of the overall structure. As the common bases of work experience declined, so did the possibility for united worker action concerning control over work.

3. The role of the supervisor was transformed from that of active instigator, director, and overseer of work activities to that of monitor and evaluator of the worker's performance. The superior now judged the subordinate's work according to the work criteria. Moreover, the supervisor's own work—his or her use of sanctions, for example—became subject to much greater evaluation and control from above.

4. Bureaucratic control has made possible, and indeed fostered, career ladders and institutional rewards for tenure and seniority within the firm—that is, what labor market economists have called "internal labor markets." These mechanisms by which job vacancies are filled—for example, job bidding systems, regularized promotion procedures requiring periodic supervisors' evaluations, customs restricting job access to apprentices or assistants, and "management development" programs—all tend to tie the worker to continued employment in the firm. Good jobs up the job ladder become available only for workers who stay with the firm. In all these ways, the firm structures relations so that identification with the company pays off, while resistance is penalized.

This new system of control appears in modified or partial form in many corporations, but it is seen most clearly in the "modern management" firms that have consciously planned it. Polaroid is a good illustration.[16]

Each job within the Polaroid plants has been analyzed and summarized in an "approved description" (or, in the case of salaried employees, an "exempt compensation survey"). Such descriptions, in addition to stating pay, location, and entry-requirement characteristics for each job, set forth in considerable detail the tasks which the worker must perform. That is, the company writes down in these descriptions the rules, procedures, and expectations that I have referred to more broadly as "work criteria."

One such description is that for the job of a machine operator who assembles SX-70 film. All the regular duties of such operatives are set forth in considerable detail, including the operation of the "automatic assembly machine," responsibility for "clearing jams" and making adjustments, monitoring the machine's output, maintaining the machine, etc. In addition, precise direction is given for responsibilities in the event of the crew chief's absence (the operative is responsible). Finally, even the "irregular" duties are spelled out: training new operators, conducting special tests for management to improve productivity or quality, and so on.

It might be thought that the company would find it profitable to make such a careful listing of duties and responsibilities only for management or skilled positions. But the job description indicates that "SX-70 Film Assembly Operator" is rated only at the level of PCV-13; from the company's wage schedule one can see that roughly half of the hourly workers—not to mention the salaried employees—have higher-level jobs.

The content of each job, what the worker is supposed to do while at work, is thus formalized and made explicit and routine in these "approved descriptions." In contrast to simple control, where bosses assign work tasks by command, or to technical control, where sequencing is engineered into the machinery, bureaucratic control at Polaroid directs production through work criteria. In large part these are *written* rules and directives. They may also include unwritten procedures that the company inculcates during training programs. But what is central is that whatever their form, they emanate from the contrived formal organizational structure of the firm.

Of course bureaucratic control never fully replaces direct and personal command, and Polaroid's compensation manual is careful to point out that any approved description "does not attempt to define all elements of a position. It defines Main Function, Regular Duties, and Irregular Duties." Implicitly, Irregular Duties or even the occasional Exceptional Circumstances may require efforts outside the job description, and as we shall see, the evaluation procedure permits plenty of scope for supervisors to reinforce cooperation in such matters.

Yet the fact that bureaucratic specification of tasks is less than complete should not obscure the tremendous importance of what it does do.

The fine division and stratification of Polaroid's workers, in combination with the carefully articulated job descriptions (work criteria), establish each job as a distinct slot with clearly defined tasks and responsibilities. A presumption of work and its specific content—that is, a presumption of what constitutes a "fair day's work"—has been established.

Directing the worker is only the first control-system element. At Polaroid, great attention is given to the second element as well. Polaroid appraises every worker's performance on a regular schedule. Undoubtedly supervisors on the job consistently monitor, assess, and reprimand or praise workers as production occurs. Yet more formally, at least once per year, supervisors must evaluate each worker's performance.

Polaroid's bureaucratic control immediately provides the structure for evaluation. Workers are evaluated on the tasks and duties laid out in the job description. Although (e.g.) the significance of any particular task or the severity of the assessment undoubtedly varies with the supervisor, the job description provides a limited, explicit, and set basis for rating each worker's performance.

The criteria, and what the worker is supposed to do on the job, are known by both worker and boss; so also is the evaluation. Evaluation is an open process, with the final supervisor's rating available for the worker's inspection.

Formalizing and making explicit the basis for evaluation also in turn permit Polaroid's first-line and intermediate supervisors to be evaluated themselves. Their appraisals of subordinates can be subjected to higher-up scrutiny.

For example, a "production manager" at Polaroid normally supervises 10 to 25 production workers. In addition to directing and monitoring production, he or she must "interpret and administer personnel policies. Select, train, and evaluate individual and team performance. Initiate actions on merit increases, promotions, transfers, disciplinary measures." Yet in all these activities the production manager reports to a "general supervisor—production" whose job it is to "select and train first-line supervisors. Evaluate performance of supervisors and determine actions on salary and promotion. Review and approve supervisor determinations on merit increases, promotions, disciplinary measures." Hence the first-line supervisor's room for maneuver is restricted by the imposition of inspection by higher command.

The content as well as the form of Polaroid's evaluation provides insight into its control system. Each worker is rated in each of four equally important categories on a seven-point scale, with the seven levels defined as performances appropriate to the seven pay steps built into each job classification. Of the four categories, only the fourth ("skill and job knowledge") deals with whether the employee is capable of doing the assigned job. One category treats the quantity of work done. The remaining two categories—"quality" (meaning the worker's dependability and thoroughness) and "work habits and personal characteristics"—are concerned with work behavior rather than actual production achieved. These categories rate the degree to which the employee is responding appropriately to the work criteria and to the bureaucratic organization of the workplace.

A separate category in the evaluation checks up on "attendance and punctuality." Here mere judgments are not enough, and the form demands more precise information: a space is left for percentages and frequencies. Once again Polaroid is not measuring output but instead compliance with rules.

The formal system of evaluation does not perfectly mirror the actual system, of course, and personality clashes, favoritism, and personal jealousies often occur. Yet formalizing evaluation—making it periodic and written, basing it on established criteria, opening it to the employee's inspection, subjecting it to higher scrutiny—tends to limit and constrain the arbitrariness of the system.

Within the bureaucratic control system, as in any control system, it is insufficient simply to set out the tasks and later check to see whether they have been done; capitalists require rewards and sanctions to elicit or compel behavior in accord with their needs. Polaroid's policies demonstrate the considerable advance in sophistication and subtlety which bureaucratic control allows over prior systems.

The company's power to hire and fire underlies its ability to get purchased labor power transformed into labor done. This power comes into play in a couple of ways. Insubordination and other explicit "violations of company rules and of accepted codes of proper behavior" (to use the company's language) can trigger immediate dismissal. Dismissal also threatens workers who get bad evaluations. The company states that the evaluations are designed to weed out "mediocrity," and, of course, "mediocre" job performance is determined by how faithfully the worker fulfills the work criteria. In addition to periodic reviews—new employees after three months, older workers at least once a year—both old and new workers are on almost continuous probation. So the penalty for failing to comply with stated performance standards is readily evident.

Yet even though bureaucratic control at Polaroid continues the historic capitalist right to deprive workers of their livelihood, this power has been re-shaped by the bureaucratic form. Exceptional violations aside, workers can be dismissed only if, after receipt of written warnings specifying the improper behavior, they continue to "misbehave." Moreover, higher supervisory approval is required and any grievance can be appealed. Thus even the process of dismissal has become subjected to the rule of (company) law.

If bureaucratic control has re-shaped the power to fire (and other negative sanctions), it has brought even greater change by introducing elaborate positive rewards to elicit cooperation from the workers. At

Polaroid, the structure of rewards begins with the seven possible pay steps within each job. Each of these steps represents a five-percent increment over the previous pay. After having been hired into a particular job, the worker is expected in a period of months to pass through the first two ("learning") steps. What is actually to be learned is not so much job skills as "work habits, attendance, attitude, and other personal characteristics" which Polaroid sees as necessary for dependable performance. Moreover, the learning may occur more on the side of the company (learning whether the new worker has acquired the proper work habits through prior schooling or jobs) than on the part of the employee.

As he or she demonstrates "mastery" of the "normal work routine," the worker moves up into the middle three ("experienced") pay steps. At these levels, work "quality can be relied on," the worker is "reliable," and "good attendance [has been] established;" or more simply, "personal characteristics are appropriate to the job." Progress is by no means automatic, but the worker who tries reasonably hard, who makes little trouble, and is an "average performer" moves, in time, through these steps.

Finally, there remain the final two ("exceptional") pay steps for workers who set "examples . . . to others in methods and use of time" and who suggest ways of "improving job methods" and "increasing effectiveness of the group." These workers need to show "cooperation, enthusiasm, [and exceptional] attitude." Supervisors are reminded that there must be "special justification for 'outstanding' ratings such as these."

The pay steps within each job classification thus establish a clear reward (up to 30 percent higher pay) for workers who obey the rules, follow the work criteria, cooperate, and in general do their jobs without creating difficulty. Yet the pay scales within job classifications are merely a prelude to rewards available to those who move up the corporate hierarchy—that is, who transfer to new job categories.

"It is [Polaroid's] general policy to fill job openings by promotion from within the Company. . . ." The mechanism for filling jobs is a posting system. The company lists each job, along with skill requirements and other job characteristics, on bulletin boards. Employees wishing to move to the new job can "bid" for the job, setting in motion a process of application, interview, and selection. Unlike many union plants, Polaroid's selection is not based solely on seniority, although "seniority should always be considered." Instead, jobs are filled by "the persons considered to be among the most qualified;" qualifications include, among other things, work habits and attendance.

Thus, through the posting system, Polaroid's 15 hourly and 10 salaried grades of jobs come to represent a second scale of rewards for the enterprising employee. Although no employee can realistically expect to start at the bottom and rise to the top—such stories better support myth than represent reality—the salary differential nonetheless suggests the range of rewards available to the employee who accepts the system: the top pay, at $160,644 annually (in 1975), is over 28 times the lowest pay of $5678 per year. More to the point, the top hourly pay ($9.26) more than triples the bottom ($3.01), and the pay of the 30-35 percent of the firm's workforce which is salaried rises from the top hourly pay.

Yet even the within-job and between-job differentials do not complete the positive incentives which Polaroid dangles before its workers. Every employee who stays at the job for five years earns an additional five-percent bonus. Seniority is also a factor in being able to obtain job transfers and promotions. Finally, the company's lay-off policy is based on an elaborate "bumping" system in which seniority is the key criterion. For example, during the 1975 recession nearly 1600 employees were laid off; employees in departments where there was no work bumped less senior workers in other departments or even in other plants.

Polaroid's structure thus provides tremendous rewards—higher pay, more rights, greater job security—to workers who accept the system and seek, by individual effort, to improve their lot within it. Moreover, the considerable rewards to workers who stay long periods at Polaroid insure that this identification will be a long-term affair. Organizing efforts to build a union at Polaroid have failed due in large measure to this structure.

To be understood fully, Polaroid's organization of its workers must be seen as a system—a structure in which power is institutionalized and the various elements of control fit together. Most importantly, it is the sytem which directs work, monitors performance, and rewards cooperation or punishes recalcitrance. Insofar as it works, people only carry out roles that the system assigns them, with circumscribed responsibilities and "proper" modes of behavior. By contrivance, Polaroid's exercise of power has been embedded in the firm's social relations.

One of the clearest manifestations of the systematic character of control is the elimination of arbitrary and capricious rule by bosses. Most importantly, supervisors' treatment of their underlings, including their evaluation of workers' performance, is subjected to scrutiny and is regulated by higher-ups. That treatment is also constrained from below, as workers have rights: they can file a grievance when they feel the rules are not being followed, they can inspect their supervisors' evaluations of them, they can demand explanations when they have been passed over for a job they bid on. Except for the highest echelons (where people can change the system itself), superiors as well as subordinates are enmeshed in the system.

A second feature of Polaroid's system is worth emphasizing. As its major way of motivating workers, the company has explicitly moved away from reliance on negative sanctions, on penalizing failure, and moved toward positive incentives, toward rewarding cooperation. All elements of control—not only rewards but the very structure of jobs and the process of evaluation as well—have been bent to make these incentives efficacious. This feature is especially striking relative to prior systems of control. Of course for troublemakers or chronic slackers the sack is still always available; but the attractions of the sophisticated range of promotions, step pay raises, seniority bonuses, and other positive rewards work for most employees.

The positive incentives, the relief from capricious supervision, the right to appeal grievances and bid for jobs, the additional job security from seniority—all these make the day-by-day worklife of Polaroid's workers more pleasant. They function as an elaborate system of bribes, and like all successful bribes, they are attractive. But they are also corrupting. They push workers to pursue their self-interests in a narrow way as individuals, and they stifle the impulse to struggle collectively for those same self-interests.

All this elaboration of job titles and rules and procedures and rights and responsibilities is, of course, neither accidental nor benevolent on Polaroid's part. It is simply a better way to do business. As workers are isolated from each other and as the system is made distinct from bosses who supervise it, the basic capitalist-worker relation tends to shrink from sight. The capitalist's power has been effectively embedded in the firm's organization.

For a time, bureaucratic control appeared to have resolved the problem of control—it was the first system without contradictions. Indeed, at present the corporations that have carried it furthest have been quite successful in forestalling unionism and in containing worker resistance. Yet this success is deceptive. While the opposition to bureaucratic control remains more a potential than a pressing reality, it is growing and already we can begin to see the main lines of attack. This opposition appears as the demand for workplace democracy.[17]

Workers' response to bureaucratic control, in the U.S. at least, has resulted primarily in individual and small-group discontent rather than collective action. This individualistic opposition emerges in part from the failure of the labor movement to challenge new forms of control. In the absence of a well-articulated critique, the systemic roots of experiences producing individual resentment remain obscure. The lack of a collective response can also be partially traced, however, to the inherent properties of bureaucratic control; its stratification and re-division of workers makes collective action more difficult. Workers' failure to respond collectively is, then, a measure of bureaucratic control's success in dividing workers. Together with the lack of a self-conscious movement challenging it, bureaucratic control has resulted in individual, not collective, opposition.

Thus bureaucratic control has created among American workers vast discontent, dissatisfaction, resentment, frustration, and boredom with their work. We do not need to recount here the many studies measuring alienation: the famous HEW-commissioned report, *Work in America*, among other summaries, has already done that. It argued, for example, that the best index of job satisfaction or dissatisfaction is a worker's response to the question: "What type of work would you try to get into if you could start all over again?" A majority of both white-collar workers and blue-collar workers—and an increasing proportion of them over time—indicated that they would choose some different type of work. This overall result is consistent with a very large literature on the topic.[18] Rising dissatisfaction and alienation among workers, made exigent by their greater job security and expectation of continuing employment with one enterprise, directly create problems for employers (most prominently, reduced productivity).

Individual or small-group opposition cannot by itself, however, seriously challenge employer control. Such opposition has existed throughout the history of capitalism without posing a real problem. Only the *collective* power of workers can effectively threaten the organized power of capitalists. Moreover, productivity loss by itself is not so serious either, since capitalists depend on average, not peak, productivity. What makes the rising individual frustration with capitalist control a source of potentially revolutionary change is the fact that an *alternative, higher-productivity* method of organizing work beckons. That truth emerges from the many experiments with worker self-management. An astonishingly high proportion of such experiments result in (a) relaxing of management's prerogative to make the rules, and (b) higher productivity.[19] The former is the peril that capitalists face in introducing workers' management; the latter is the lure, and it has proved to be a powerful attraction.

Capitalists themselves are led, even forced, to introduce the very schemes that threaten their grip. They have been the most important force behind actual experiments in workplaces. They have sponsored innumerable efforts in job enrichment, job enlargement, Scanlon Plans, worker self-management, worker-employer co-management, etc. Thus the logic of accumulation increasingly drives capitalists to try to unlock the potential productivity which lies inside economically secure producers who both identify with their enterprise and govern their work activities themselves. They try to obtain this higher output "on the cheap," by granting limited amounts of each of the needed components: some security within the overall capitalist context of insecurity, partial identification with work within the relations of private ownership, and limited self-government within authoritarian enterprise.

The trouble is that a little is never enough. Just as some job security leads to demands for guaranteed lifetime wages, so some control over workplace decisions raises the demand for industrial democracy. Thomas Fitzgerald, Director of Employee Research and Training at GM's Chevrolet Division and a former GM first-line supervisor, stated this point directly; Fitzgerald explained to the readers of the *Harvard Business Review* that, once workers begin participating,

> the subjects of participation . . . are not necessarily restricted to those few matters that management considers to be of direct, personal interest to employees. . . . [A plan cannot] be maintained for long without (a) being recognized by employees as manipulative or (b) leading to expectations for wider and more significant involvement—"Why do they only ask us about plans for painting the office and not about replacing this old equipment and rearranging the layout?" Once competence is shown (or believed to have been shown) in say, rearranging the work area, and after participation has become a conscious, officially sponsored activity, *participators may very well want to go to topics of job assignment, the allocation of rewards, or even the selection of leadership. In other words, management's present monopoly [of control] can in itself easily become a source of contention.*[20]

That this concern is no idle threat is evident from an incident in the 1960's at Polaroid. The company set up a special worker-participation project involving some 120 film-pack machine operators. The production requirements did not seem especially promising for the experiment; making the new film packs called for high-quality operation of complex machinery in the face of a pressing deadline. Workers on the project spent one hour each day in special training, two hours doing coordinating work, and five hours operating the machinery. According to Polaroid's "organization development" consultant, the film was brought into production on time, and "most people think we would never have gotten it out otherwise." Nonetheless, the experiment was liquidated, not for efficiency reasons but rather because democracy got out of hand. Ray Ferris, the company's training director, explained: "[The experiment] was *too* successful. What were we going to do with the supervisors—the managers? We didn't need them anymore. Management decided it just didn't want operators that qualified."[21]

5. The Present Situation

The social relations of the workplace can only be understood as a product of an on-going dialectic. The unfolding logic of the accumulation process creates new circumstances for both capitalists and workers, circumstances embodying both new constraints and new possibilities. On the one hand, capitalists are pushed by competition to seek new ways to reduce unit labor costs at the same time that the concentration of capital gives them new resources with which to conduct this search. On the other hand, workers are subject to new forms of control while they continually press for their needs based on what they experience, what they perceive, what they think possible. Together, capitalists and workers clash in the sphere of production over the general issue of the transformation of labor power into labor. More concretely, capitalists and workers struggle over the pace of work, workplace "rights," issues of safety, relief from the immediacy of the reserve army sanction, and myriad other specific aspects of capitalist production.

This history of accumulation and class conflict provides and "transmits from the past" definite circumstances which impinge upon the present. Contemporary labor processes are subject to three quite distinct sets of the social relations of production at the point of production: simple control, technical control, and bureaucratic control. Each system contains within it important variations on the general theme of the exploitation of wage-labor.

The existence of distinct systems of control in the labor process has far-reaching implications for the formation of the modern American working class. For one thing, the nature of workers' resistance to workplace tyranny differs markedly depending upon the organization of the workplace. In simple control, workers tend to struggle against the effects of boss's personal despotism. In technical control with joint management/ union administration, workers resist the technically-imposed production pace as well as struggle for expansion and enforcement of the collectively-bargained "rights." In bureaucratic control, workers are beginning to press for the introduction of workplace democracy. Thus, in these workplace-specific struggles, the needs and demands of workers turn out to be quite different because the manner of the workers' exploitation also differs.

The effects of these divisions in the labor process extend far beyond the workplace. They provide an immediate basis for the oft-noted segmentation of labor markets and the more widely observed division (or "fractionalizing") of the American working class. They even, I argue elsewhere, impart a new (i.e., post-1945) dynamic to American politics.[22]

This, then, is the element of the labor-process dialectic that Braverman misses. Technical aspects of production—de-skilling, degradation of work, creation of a mass of machine-operatives, etc.—can only be understood within this simultaneous development of the social relations of production. For, fundamentally, capitalism is not driven by technology but rather by the imperatives of appropriating surplus labor.

Notes

1. See my *Contested Terrain: The Transformation of the Workplace In the 20th Century* (New York: Basic Books, 1979) for a more extended treatment.

2. Karl Marx, *The Eighteenth Brumaire of Louis Bonaparte*, in Robert C. Tucker, ed., *The Marx-Engels Reader* (New York: Norton, 1972), 457.

3. Ann Bookman, *The Process of Political Socialization Among Women and Immigrant Workers* (unpublished Ph.D. thesis, Harvard University, 1977).

4. Daniel Nelson, *Managers and Workers* (Madison, Wisc.: University of Wisconsin Press, 1975), Ch. III.

5. *The Lancet*, no. 4246 (January 14, 1905), 120.

6. *Ibid.*, 122.

7. Henry Ford, "Progressive Manufacture," *Encyclopedia Britannica* (Cambridge: Cambridge University Press, 1927).

8. H. L. Arnold and L. F. Faurote, *Ford Methods and the Ford Shops* (New York: The Engineering Magazine Co., 1915).

9. *Ibid.*, 245.

10. *Ibid.*, 6, 8 (emphasis added).

11. *Ibid.*, 2, 46.

12. Francesca Maltese, "Notes Towards a Study of the Automobile Industry," in R. Edwards, M. Reich, and D. Gordon, eds., *Labor Market Segmentation* (Lexington, Mass.: D. C. Heath, 1975).

13. See Harry Braverman, *Labor and Monopoly Capital* (New York: Monthly Review Press, 1974).

14. Irving Bernstein, *Turbulent Years: A History of the American Worker, 1933–1941* (Boston: Houghton Mifflin, 1970), 524–525.

15. Stanley Aronowitz, *False Promises* (New York: McGraw-Hill, 1972), Ch. 1.

16. All quotations, data, etc., concerning Polaroid are taken from internal documents that the company made available to me.

17. I consider here only the workplace-oriented opposition. In *Contested Terrain* I consider the broader and potentially more revolutionary opposition, rooted in bureaucratic control, that appears in the political sphere.

18. See, for example, Special Task Force to the Secretary of Health, Education, and Welfare, *Work in America* (Washington, D.C.: U.S. Government Printing Office, 1972), and Harold Sheppard and Neal Herrick, *Where Have All the Robots Gone?* (New York: Free Press, 1972).

19. See David Jenkins, *Job Power* (New York: Doubleday, 1973), and Juan Espinosa and Andrew Zimbalist, *Economic Democracy* (New York: Academic Press, 1978).

20. Thomas Fitzgerald, "Why Motivation Theory Doesn't Work," *Harvard Business Review*, July–August 1971, 42 (emphasis added).

21. In Jenkins, op. cit., 313–315.

22. See my *Contested Terrain*.

9
Machine Technology and Workplace Control: The U.S. Post Office

Peter Rachleff

The availability, development, and introduction of new technologies has long provided management with a powerful weapon in its quest to control workplaces. The implementation of various machine technologies has helped management disrupt workers' informal workplace organization, reorganize production, routinize work, increase the office's control over the shop, and undermine trade unionism. In the past decade, labor and social historians, radical economists, and sociologists have helped shed light on this process. Among the more important studies have been those of Harry Braverman,[1] Dan Clawson,[2] Andrew Zimbalist,[3] Joan Greenbaum,[4] David Montgomery,[5] Richard Edwards,[6] Stephen Marglin,[7] Bryan Palmer,[8] and Jeremy Brecher.[9]

Most of these studies are grounded in research in the private sector—the steel industry, the auto industry, data processing, machine shops, the manufacture of electrical products, longshoring, and others. An examination of the United States Postal Service since its reorganization in the early 1970s demonstrates that similar forces have been at work in the public sector as well. Postal management turned to wholesale reorganization in the face of growing demands and militancy on the part of postal workers in the late 1960s and early 1970s. The replacement of human labor by machines and the regimentation of remaining labor processes through machines became the order of the day. Postal facilities were relocated from urban centers to concrete parking lots in suburbia. Management designed and introduced new technologies that disrupted work groups and social networks of support within postal facilities, reorganized production, and centralized management's control. The quality of work and of the nation's mail service plummeted; however, the introduction of these new technologies served management by significantly shifting the

This is a revision of an article that first appeared in *Radical America* 16, nos. 1–2 (Jan.–April 1982): 79–90, and is reprinted by permission of the editors.

balance of power in its direction. This is the story that emerges from transcripts of congressional oversight hearings (held annually to review the United States Postal Service's budget) and from interviews with management officials, research and development staffers, union officials, and rank-and-file postal workers from all over the country.

For nearly two hundred years, the United States Post Office had functioned as a federal agency and as such had been largely immune from the pressures for higher profits and capital accumulation facing business enterprises. The delivery of the nation's mail relied almost exclusively on manual labor, with management in the hands of political appointees. Congress determined policies governing the Post Office Department, established appropriations for running it, and evaluated its performance. In July 1971, with the passage of the Postal Service Reorganization Act, all of this changed. Once seemingly immune to goals of business and distant from the havoc created by new technology, in the decade of the 1970s the postal service now moved into the economic mainstream.

As the volume of all mail more than doubled between 1940 and 1970, and first-class mail tripled in volume, the postal service compensated by adding to its workforce, becoming the second largest employer in the entire country. Postal facilities became increasingly crowded with both mail and workers, and the quality both of service and of working conditions went steadily downhill. In 1969 a postal-union official told a House of Representatives committee:

> The average mail handler working in one of these poorly lit, dirty, cluttered, depressing and inefficient operations, usually bears the brunt of the Post Office's backwardness. He finds himself lugging around an 85- to 100-pound sack that could be transported far more efficiently and easily by machines operated by mail handlers. Many of our major post offices are so inadequate for today's needs that mail handlers and other postal employees are literally falling all over one another trying to get their job done.

In 1970, this deterioration of the postal service came to a head for both management and workers. Drawing strength and confidence from the movement of public-employee unionism in the 1960s, rank-and-file postal workers, from mail handlers to letter carriers, defied their national union leaders and launched a nationwide wildcat strike. For one week, the nation's mail was disrupted as postal workers held firm and, in some cities, threatened to expand their strike to other dissatisfied public employees. Administrators, meanwhile, had become convinced—some before, some during the strike—that full-scale "reorganization," wedded to massive capital improvements, mechanization, and "modernization," was the solution to their problems.

Postal workers were united in their quest for significant wage increases. At the time, their average annual income fell well below the Department of Labor's minimum standards for a family of four. There were even stories of full-time workers receiving public assistance. Postal workers had no intention of going back to work, whatever their union leaders told them, until they got their due. It did not take long for management to make conciliatory noises, as even Wall Street tottered on the brink of shutdown. President Nixon told the public that postal workers had been underpaid for the past twenty-three years. Within the halls of Congress, rumors of substantial wage increases were leaked out. Even then, even after all this talk, it took the deployment of 25,000 federal troops into the New York City postal facilities—the very center of the strike—to finally push postal workers back to the job.

Postal management, for its part, was thinking beyond the immediate termination of the strike to full-scale reorganization. An elaborate plan took shape, whose implementation would change the postal service from top to bottom. Part of this plan was, first, the convincing of union officials that their members' demands for decent wages and working conditions could only be met through reorganization and mechanization, and then, secondly, to use the union leaders to convince their members of the same. Over the 1970s, the first would prove easier to accomplish than the second.

In 1971, a new semi-independent United States Postal Service was born, with a new "nonpolitical" management structure and new corporate goals. The new USPS was given "broad borrowing authority," the right to float bonds to finance capital improvements. "Efficiency," cost-cutting, attrition, mechanization, productivity, and "self-sufficiency" became the watchwords of the new management. Here, then, was the ultimate answer to the threat which had been posed in the 1970 national wildcat.

One of the first steps taken by USPS was to seek binding collective bargaining agreements with a limited number of nationwide trade unions, along industrial rather than craft lines. With rapid job transformation and work reorganization in the offing, postal management knew that an industrial-union structure would prove more amenable to the job loss and transfers that would result. The agreements also specifically denied postal workers the right to strike. A highly formalized grievance procedure with arbitration as the final step was negotiated for solving questions that arose under the contracts. Each agreement contained a "management rights" clause patterned after those in private industry. It read, in part:

> The Employer shall have the exclusive right, subject to the provisions of this Agreement and consistent with applicable laws and regulations:
>
> A. To direct employees of the Employer in the performance of official duties;
>
> B. To hire, promote, transfer, assign, and retain employees in positions within the Postal Service and to suspend, demote, discharge, or take other disciplinary actions against such employees;
>
> C. To maintain the efficiency of the operations entrusted to it;

D. To determine the methods, means, and personnel by which such operations are to be conducted.

In short, the USPS was given a free hand to "reorganize" postal work as it saw fit.

Mechanization was seen as the way to reduce the total labor costs of the USPS, which management feared would outstrip its ability to pay—especially in light of the wage concessions that had been necessary to end the 1970 wildcat. Many hoped that mechanization would eventually bring immunity to the disruption of strikes. Frederick R. Kappel, then chair of the USPS Board of Governors, was asked by a congressional committee in early 1973:

Q: What would we do if we had an occurrence of the strike of a couple of years ago? Do we have any machinery now that would work any better than we had before?

Mr. Kappel responded:

A: No, we do not. I do not know what you could do about it. I think we have some mechanization, but it only feeds into a place where there isn't any, and I think we are still in a very serious condition should a strike occur.

Zip codes, originally intended primarily for use by large-volume mailers, were now promoted for adoption by all users of the postal service. Postal management also began a long—and ongoing—campaign for relative uniformity in envelope and postcard dimensions. The focus of management's attention rested on dreams of a mechanized post office. Peter Dorsey, then the regional postmaster for New York and later the USPS's primary strategist in its mechanization campaign, told a congressional committee in 1973: "I suppose the ideal thing would be to have a long conglomeration of equipment hooked up sequentially where you could dump raw mail in one end and have it come out sorted to the carrier at the other end."

The early 1970s saw the piecemeal introduction of such notions, with chaotic and catastrophic results. New machines were installed in antiquated and overcrowded postal facilities in major cities. Moe Biller, then president of the New York Metro local postal workers union, told a congressional committee in 1973:

The mechanization program, which runs into billions, will yet prove the biggest bust of all. You can't quarrel with the idea of mechanization in 1973, just as we're all for motherhood and against sin. Let's look at the New York experience in this regard. The introduction of letter-sorting machines into the general post office, a building built in 1910. That is a crying shame. The noise is unbearable. The machines are not cleaned enough; frequently there are paper lice. . . . The workers on these machines have mostly nightwork and most of them work weekends even though, initially, management advertised these jobs as mostly weekends off. Management's comment? The people must be where the mail is.

At the same time, during the early seventies, the new postal management also adopted the strategy of reducing total labor costs through attrition, actively encouraging early retirement and even imposing a hiring freeze in 1972. They sought quick results, and they got them: 55,000 postal employees opted for early retirement. In New York for example, total postal personnel fell by 13 percent between 1970 and 1973. Needless to say, such across-the-board reductions failed to mesh with the mechanization program and created even more chaos in the postal service. Letter carriers certainly didn't have their loads lightened. With their ranks reduced, they found their routes lengthened, their traditional work patterns disrupted by such directives as crossing lawns rather than walking on sidewalks, and their actual work observed by timekeepers and monitored by devices in their vehicles. Local union officials across the country reported an increase in heart attacks among letter carriers. Inside postal facilities, the reduced work forces were called upon to put in long overtime hours, actually increasing labor costs of many facilities. New York regional postmaster Peter Dorsey admitted to Congress in 1973: "We may have gone too far, we were hell bent on saving money as opposed to service." James H. Rademacher, then president of the National Association of Letter Carriers, summed it all up in his testimony before the same committee: "We can state without fear of contradiction by the general public that the level of mail service is at the worst stage in history and the quality of the nation's mail service is the poorest it has ever been." Indeed, no one contradicted him.

By 1973, the business-oriented management of the new USPS had introduced new machines in existing postal facilities with high mail volumes and had reduced their total workforce through an attrition campaign. All observers, inside and outside the postal service, were agreed: the immediate results had been disastrous. The USPS was no closer to "self-sufficiency" than it had been in 1970 at its establishment. The quality of mail service had become a national scandal. And working conditions inside postal facilities had deteriorated even further. Despite the no-strike clause in the contract, management feared another major disruption of the nation's mails upon the contract's expiration in 1973. Apparently, the business-oriented management's new strategies had backfired all around.

In this context, postal management moved to drastically reorganize the postal system, seeking to *create* large accumulations of mail in specific locations. A single, centralized facility would process all the originating mail for a given geographical region. And the entire range of new mail-handling and processing machines would be installed in these new buildings, constructed according to new, "modular" specifications. Similar plans were laid for the construction of twenty-one new bulk-mail facilities, which would transform the handling of parcels and other non-first-class items. Peter Dorsey, now promoted to senior assistant postmaster general for operations despite his problem in New York, reported in 1974:

> Inside a Bulk Mail Center or Auxiliary Service Facility we will replace today's manual single sorting operations with high-speed machine processing designed to maintain a continuous flow of mail through the facility. Our aim is to reverse the present 80 percent manual, 20 percent mechanical ratio in processing bulk mail. . . .
>
> Put very simply, the basic idea behind the national Bulk Mail Service is to centralize mail processing so that it is more efficient to utilize mechanization.

Thus relocation and mechanization became inseparable strategies as postal management moved to put the service on a more businesslike basis. Without relocation to concentrate the mails, mechanization would not be profitable—and without mechanization, relocation would make no sense at all.

Having reorganized the workplace and the whole mail-handling system, management established standards for the output expected from each type of job within the post office. It also prescribed the most "efficient" methods for performing individual tasks. Now it resorts to discipline or discharge for those who fail to meet the standards or refuse to follow established methods.

In the short span of one decade the U.S. Post Office Department, a federal agency which provided an essential service, was reorganized, and in the process of that reorganization it acquired new goals.

The Postal Service Moves to the Suburbs

It was part of postal management's overall strategy to locate many of the new facilities for accumulating mail outside of central cities. Publicly, postal officials offered a range of weak excuses for this major decision. Traffic was too congested in central cities, they argued, and it would slow the transportation of mail to and from the new facilities. But it turned out that many of the new locations were on major commuter arteries, and no less prone to traffic tie-up than urban streets. Land was too expensive in the cities, they also argued. But then they went out and paid exorbitant sums for suburban acreage. Of course, under the new United States Postal Service structure, they did not really have to convince anyone of the justice of their argument. What was behind their strategic relocation of major postal facilities?

The center of the 1970 wildcat had been in the major postal facilities in large cities. In Detroit, Pittsburgh, Philadelphia, and New York, some 50 to 75 percent of the workers—and strikers—had been black. Moving to the suburbs was designed to alter the composition of the workforces at the major postal facilities. Forest Park, Illinois, for example, was selected as the site for a new facility to replace the major Chicago center. In the old post office, a majority of the employees were black. In Forest Park, a lengthy commute from South Chicago, there were no black families—not one. It was unlikely that many black postal workers would make the transfer. Similar concerns were voiced in city after city.

The suburban location of the new facilities would alter the composition of the workforce in other ways as well. Many workers would choose not to transfer, either seeking jobs elsewhere in the postal system or retiring altogether. Administrators would thus have considerable latitude in hiring new workers or reassigning veteran workers, and, with their strengthened hand, could shape the workforce more in accordance with their own preference and needs. An added weapon, of course, was that workers transferring in had to be able to master the operation of new machinery. The location of new facilities at some distance from the currently operating centers therefore gave management a tremendous opportunity to reorganize the workforces inside the centers of the postal system.

But the implications of this relocation extended even further, for it simultaneously undermined two major sources of postal workers' strength. With the reorganization of work and the workforce which accompanied relocation, informal work groups which had developed over many years were suddenly torn apart. Men and women who had come to trust and understand each other would never work together again. Moving to a new facility was an individual decision, and many chose not to go. Even accepting reassignment offered little promise of keeping work groups together, for the new machines in the new facilities demanded a reorganization of the work itself. Management in the new, mechanized facilities could thus operate, at least initially, with little concern for the workplace powers developed by experienced work groups.

The impact of relocation was even more wide-ranging. Traditionally, the bars, taverns, and restaurants surrounding a large workplace have served as centers of socializing and discussion by the workers employed there. These establishments, and the neighborhood within which they are located, have been a critical element to whatever strengths their patrons and residents exercised at work. The old, central-city postal facilities were situated within such a framework, one which helped consolidate and extend the postal workers' immediate work-group relationships. But the new facilities were constructed "in the middle of nowhere," surrounded by miles of concrete in every direction.

The new postal facilities were not located in the heart of any neighborhoods, surrounded by various social institutions. Nor have such institutions developed. Most postal workers live too far away from the new facilities to be willing to add to their time away from home by hanging around after work. The prospect of an hour's drive in heavy traffic is enough to sour any man or woman on relaxed socializing.

One postal worker gave the following account of a postal relocation in Pennsylvania:

> The GMF is on the outskirts of town. While the facility is only 2.5 miles from the old building, the setting is totally different. The old building is three blocks from the center of Lancaster. A convenience store and sandwich shops are literally across the street or around the corner. Banks and stores in the downtown area can be walked to during lunch break or after work. Numerous bars and taverns are within walking distance.
>
> In contrast, the GMF is surrounded by acres of grass and farmland. There is no store or sandwich shop within walking distance. Employees are thus subtly encouraged to stay in the building. Except for the administrative offices, there are no windows in the building. The building consists of a one story, 156,000 square foot concrete slab. The warehouse atmosphere is cold and sterile.

Postal management officials have designed these bleak facilities in such a way as to maximize their control over workers. The results are strikingly similar to a prison yard. (Postal workers noted that even the newly remodeled facilities in central cities look very much like fortresses and prisons.)

On the basis of efficiency and financial return on the dollars invested, however, the relocation strategy did not make a particularly good showing. The bulk mail centers soon became the subject of much public criticism. In February 1979 the nationally syndicated columnist Jack Anderson sent one of his staff into a bulk mail center as a postal employee and then published the following impressions, under the headline "BULK MAIL CENTER: AUTOMATED NIGHTMARE."

> The bulk mail center is a machine-powered world modeled after Charlie Chaplin's movie, "Modern Times." Automated carts filled with mail run along trolley tracks, heedless of parcels that fall off and people who get in the way. Overhead trays carry mail through the building, tipping their contents into chutes on command from the control room.
>
> Operators in the control room can tell how the mail is moving by watching the flow on video screens. Unfortunately the screens don't show the plight of a worker frantically trying to load a truck as fast as the conveyor belt spews the mail out. It also doesn't show the assemblyline workers who can't keep pace with the relentless machines and can't shut off or slow down the conveyor belt. The parcels often spill off the belt onto the floor, where they may remain for days.
>
> Employees at the Washington center have their own wry slogan: "You mail 'em, we maul 'em." It's not the humans who are doing the mauling, though; it's the machines. Like the sack shake-out rig that empties parcels—including those marked "Fragile—Glass"—from mail sacks and lets them fall four feet onto a belt.

Packages that get jammed in the automatic conveyors are ripped apart. Attempts are made to patch them up, but the many Humpty Dumpty irreparables end up in a parcel graveyard—a room designated "loose in the mail" and off-limits to all but a few employees. Our reporter got inside for a look around, and found thousands of items from books to homemade Christmas presents. There were so many books that they had been arranged by topic on metal shelves. . . .

The billion-dollar bulk mail system was supposed to save the Postal Service $300 million a year. Recent estimates have now reduced the potential savings to $40 million—a return of 4 percent on the money invested.

Nor is there any evidence that the bulk mail system saves time. A package en route from El Paso to Midland, Tex., for example, is sent 1,483 miles out of the way to be processed by a bulk mail center.

When Machines Replace People

Traditionally, mail had been sorted manually by experienced clerks, working in "teams" around a shared table. Each person had to memorize complex sorting "schemes," and all were able to gain virtually 100-percent accuracy. A great deal of pride and experience went into learning "schemes," and tight-knit informal work groups developed within the post office. All this was wiped out by the introduction of letter-sorting machines (LSMs).

Now clerks sit before keyboards and screens. Letters—already faced, cancelled, and placed in position—appear on the screen at the rate of one per second. Reading the zip code, the clerk then types the appropriate code on the keyboard. Each clerk sits, fixated before the automatically placed screen, in a separate cubbyhole. Communication with workmates is virtually impossible. The LSMs are very noisy—so noisy that many operators contend they exceed OSHA noise levels. At any rate, the level of noise presents a major obstacle to normal conversation. But that doesn't concern postal management, since normal conversation among LSM operators is prohibited in most facilities.

The new LSMs rely on electronic memory banks, which allow operators to sort mail into an immediate 277 separations, far superior to the 77 which had been standard under the manual-sort system. The new machines reduce the number of sorts necessary overall, and, intermeshed with the accumulation of mail volumes in a limited number of locations, their use made possible a significant reduction in the sorting workforce employed in mail processing. The LSM alone, according to postal management, was at least 57 percent more productive than the manual sorting system.

Nowhere in management's productivity claims did it count the human toll. LSM operators have complained of hearing loss, eyesight impairment, and various stress-related disorders. Some even developed serious personal problems as a result of the job.

> I hated the job and everything about it so much, that I took it out (unwittingly) on those around me. When I finally bid off that dehumanizing LSM, my wife told me how completely different I was and how thankful she was I had gotten off—and then she told me she didn't know how much more she could have taken had I stayed on the machine: only then did I learn how close I had come to ruining my marriage.

The letter-sorting machine was not introduced alone. Rather it was interfaced with a host of other innovations, which brought mail processing close to a continuous flow operation. Mechanical cullers, face-cancellers, and edgers fed mail into the LSMs. Operators processed letters at the rate of one every second, and trays were automatically swept, the letters bagged for transportation to their post office of destination. The labor needed for first-class mail handling dropped sharply.

Postal management was—and still is—very interested in yet another innovation which could be interfaced with the LSM, further boosting productivity and displacing labor. This technological wonder—the optical character reader, or OCR—has long held a particular fascination for postal management. The San Francisco sectional center manager pulled no punches when he told a congressional committee in 1973: "The only piece of machinery that we have no problem with is the OCR. But as long as you put a human being at one of those LSMs, we do have a problem because it is getting this human being adjusted to the machinery."

While there are technical problems to be overcome before the OCR can be introduced on a system-wide basis, when it does come the OCR will eliminate the LSM operator's job.

This, then, is the modern facility where most first-class mail is processed. Clearly, it has cost postal workers a great deal. Interestingly, it has not seemed to solve the USPS's problems. More mail than ever is sent through private carriers. Overnight delivery remains a pipe dream for most first-class mail. Postal rates have continued to climb, while the goal of "self-sufficiency" remains as elusive as ever. Missent mail floats throughout the system. But there is no denying that this reorganization has strengthened postal management's hand vis-a-vis its employees. In this sense, and in no other, the reorganization of first-class mail processing can be termed a "success."

The second main area of postal reorganization and mechanization has been bulk mail. Changes in this area have proven even more disastrous for postal workers.

In the early 1970s, the new management of the USPS earmarked more than $1 billion for the construction of a complete, integrated, mechanized bulk mail system. Twenty-one BMCs and eleven Auxiliary Service Facilities were to be constructed by the mid-1970s. Here, as with the relocation of major postal facilities, management's public justification was questionable. The stated goal was to win back the parcel-post business which had been lost to UPS and other private carriers. However, a study commissioned by the Postal Service itself in 1973 had concluded that, even if it worked perfectly, the new bulk-mail system, with its complicated rerouting of packages over thousands of miles between facilities, would never be competitive with UPS within a 600-mile range of delivery—precisely the area in which UPS has captured the largest share of USPS business. Even before the new bulk-mail system became operational, then, it was clear to postal management that it could not magically recapture the lost business.

But this did not deter postal management. The new system—with its centralized control, relocation of centers to suburban areas, recomposition of the workforce, and reorganization of work—remained attractive to them. Despite a series of construction delays and equipment failure, the new system was put into operation in the later 1970s. George R. Cavell, the first program director of the Bulk Mail Processing Department, explained to Congress what was supposed to happen in each facility:

> The equipment in question consists of high-speed sorting machines into which parcels are introduced from a series of automatic induction units. When the machinery is running, unsorted parcels are brought on conveyors to employees who, by operating simple keyboards, feed the zip code of each package into a computer. Once a package has been through this key code operation, it is automatically transferred to one of a number of shallow trays mounted on chair-driven carriages. These trays move by at a rate of 160 per minute, and, following an oval path, carry the packages past a series of slides each of which leads to a different collection point. The computer "remembers" which individual collection point each package is destined for, and as the tray comes up to the particular slide into which its package should be deposited, the computer activates a tripping device that tilts the tray and lets the parcels slide out.

It sounds pretty smooth. But in 1976, Representative Charles Wilson opened his subcommittee's hearings on the Bulk Mail System by calling it, "a dream gone sour, or, more appropriately, a management blunder of the first magnitude, which will cost the American public millions of dollars."

Witnesses told Wilson's subcommittee of packages caught between conveyor rollers, parcels being run over by containers, small parcels being damaged in induction unit slides by heavier parcels, and packages being smashed upon dropping from sack shake-out machines. William Anderson, deputy director of the General Government Division of the GAO, which had just released its study of the bulk mail system, testified: "We believe much of the damage is caused by the equipment in the centers. Unlike the other problems the Postal Service may have, the personnel have very little to do with this one. It's just a case of the machinery."

Missent and misdirected parcels remained a much larger percentage of total volume than was expected as well. Instead of the targeted maximum of 5 percent, for example, the Washington, D.C., regional facility was rarely below 10 percent in 1975 and 1976, and occasionally above 20 percent.

The BMC's were also quite unsafe. Accident rates were high from the day the centers opened, and they have remained high to the present day. In 1978, for example, USPS figures ranged between twelve and fourteen injuries per million work hours, triple the nationwide average. The brand new buildings with brand new machinery were proving as unsafe as the old, antiquated facilities which were being closed. GAO investigator William Anderson testified in 1976:

> The walkways are really tough to stick to and then these towveyors are moving downward. There are a lot of instances, and I know we had to dodge them all over the place walking through the plant here. The work floor is just so crowded, and these things are coming sporadically and if you don't keep your—if you're not intent all the time on trying to spot a coming towveyor, I can understand how people can be getting hurt.

It is unfortunate indeed that frequently the public placed the responsibility for postal services inefficiencies on the postal employees rather than on poor management and ineffective machinery. Employees who have traditionally prided themselves on both speed and accuracy in handling the nation's mails have thereby been hit hard from both sides. The new technology has eliminated jobs and degraded those that remain. And when the new technology fails, the workers get blamed.

Summoning up the USPS's success in making the mails more efficient, one union leader made the following critique in 1976:

> What has $3 billion in plant and mechanization accomplished? The Bulk Mail System cost $1 billion and high speed letter sorting machines, and other mechanization cost nearly $2 billion. Let's look at the Postal Service when it was labor intensive. During that time, missent, misdirected and damaged mail amounted historically to about ½ of 1 percent of the volume during the decade preceding the Postal Reorganization Act of 1970. Today the Bulk Mail System damage rate is 1 percent and the missent is approximately 5 percent. This error rate is machine error, not human error. In the letter sorting machine operation the error rate (machine) is 4 percent.

Who now thinks of "self-sufficiency" as a feasible goal for the USPS? Postal rates increase, subsidies increase, and postal service remains a public laughing stock. It is now important to ask ourselves why these have been the results of the new strategies of postal management.

One is tempted to answer the question glibly by dismissing the USPS's condition as merely another typical example of government bureaucracy in action. To be sure, instances of mismanagement, ignorance, stupidity, and perfidy can be cited ad infinitum. But, was there not a method to this madness? Are there not some long-run advantages to management which will outweigh the costs and confusion which we have noted? It seems so.

The one critical, shared feature of the measures taken by the new business-oriented management was that they all attacked postal workers' sources of power. Not only was the workforce reduced and the postal unions tightly restricted, but the attack also targeted the informal work groups, the neighborhoods around the postal facilities, and the once-crucial importance of the workers' skill and knowledge to the daily operations of the postal service. Work was simplified, mechanized, routinized, and subjected to the automatic pace of machines and the centralized control of management. Parking lots look like prison yards, surrounded by high gates. Management's concern with gaining control dictated the strategies which have resulted in the continuing deterioration of the quality of postal service, but these same strategies now place management in the driver's seat for determining, without challenge or interruption, the future of the postal service.

Use of machine technology has put postal management in the driver's seat for the moment; however, it also has generated new levels of opposition and awareness among postal workers and their unions. At the national level, officials of the American Postal Workers Union (APWU) and the National Association of Letter Carriers (NALC) have begun discussing a merger of their organizations. Local union officials from both organizations have launched a variety of collaborative ventures, from classes on "labor and technology" for shop stewards to public demonstrations. Rank-and-file groups have published local level shop newspapers and have laid the foundation for national networks. Some have promoted the dissemination of information and critical analyses on management strategies, from machine technologies to quality circles and participation schemes. And some of these rank-and-file groups have affiliated themselves with similar groups from other industries, within both the public and private sectors. These concerns have given birth to new visions of the role of machine technologies in the organization of work, the purpose of this industry, and the nature of its management. An editorial in a rank-and-file paper from Maryland, for instance, concluded:

> We would run the PO democratically. The first step would be the elimination of all craft distinctions, and the equalization of salaries for all postal workers. All supervisory and managerial positions would be filled by democratic vote, all would be subject to recall, and would receive salaries no higher than the rest of the workers. . . . All rules and regulations concerning work, salary, etc. would be decided democratically. . . . The postal service would remain as the property of the people of the US, run and operated by the workers as a non-profit service to the public.[10]

Notes

1. Harry Braverman, *Labor and Monopoly Capital: The Degradation of Work in the Twentieth Century* (New York: Monthly Review Press, 1974).

2. Dan Clawson, *Bureaucracy and the Labor Process: The Transformation of U.S. Industry, 1860–1920* (New York: Monthly Review Press, 1980).

3. Andrew Zimbalist, *Case Studies on the Labor Process* (New York: Monthly Review Press, 1979).

4. Joan Greenbaum, *In the Name of Efficiency: Management Theory and Shopfloor Practice in Data-Processing Work* (Philadelphia: Temple University Press, 1979).

5. David Montgomery, *Workers Control in America* (Cambridge: Cambridge University Press, 1979).

6. Richard Edwards, *Contested Terrain: The Transformation of the Workplace in the Twentieth Century* (New York: Basic Books, 1979).

7. Stephen A. Marglin, "What Do Bosses Do?" *Review of Radical Political Economics* 6, no. 2 (Summer 1974): 33–60.

8. Bryan Palmer, "Class, Conception and Conflict: The Thrust for Efficiency, Managerial Views of Labor, and the Working Class Rebellion, 1903–1922," *Review of Radical Political Economics* 7, no. 2 (Summer 1975): 31–49.

9. Jeremy Brecher, "Uncovering the Hidden History of the American Workplace," *Review of Radical Political Economics* 10, no. 4 (Winter 1978): 1–23.

10. Editorial by Dan Betman, *Union Dispatch*, Prince Georges, Md., local of APWU. The editorial continued in these words: "[Our] proposal is really very simple. Get rid of the current make-up of the Postal Service, the PMG, the Board of Governors, the whole mess. In its place, turn over the operation and running of the Postal Service to the only people who know how to run it correctly—the people who do the work day in and day out. This could be done by working through the Union structure. Let the Congress stake us to just three years Postal Subsidy to cover the period of reorganization, and we would be breaking even at the end of those 3 years.

"The problem with the PO isn't the hopeless situation of trying to provide a cheap, efficient service to the people and it is not with the workers themselves. The real problem is with top management who sit down in L'Enfant Plaza in air conditioned and carpeted offices and play around with computers, adding machines, pushing a lot of paper and juggling a lot of figures. The problem is that they don't know the first thing of what it is like on the workroom floor, of what it is like actually trying to move the mail. The average worker on the floor knows more about his/her job than any so-called "expert" and there is nothing that cannot be learned by the workers about the rest of the operations. . . .

"The problem with the PO is not the workers. The problem is the system under which the PO is run. Even the politicians who are hell-bent upon destroying the Postal Service say this. Their solution is give it away to business and the public and workers be damned. We see the same problem but offer a different solution, one that can provide a cheap, reliable service to the public and safeguard our welfare, our safety and our livelihood. So, Mr. PMG, give away the postal service, not to those who only want to use it for their own profit, but to those who are the only ones capable enough and caring enough to do the job."

10

Organizing Consent on the Shop Floor: The Game of Making Out

Michael Burawoy

Making Out—A Game Workers Play

In this section I propose to treat the activities on the shop floor as a series of games in which operators attempt to achieve levels of production that earn incentive pay, in other words, anything over 100 percent. The precise target that each operator aims at is established on an individual basis, varying with job, machine, experience, and so on. Some are satisfied with 125 percent, while others are in a foul mood unless they achieve 140 percent—the ceiling imposed and recognized by all participants. This game of making out provides a framework for evaluating the productive activities and the social relations that arise out of the organization of work. We can look upon making out, therefore, as comprising a sequence of stages—of encounters between machine operators and the social or nonsocial objects that regulate the conditions of work. The rules of the game are experienced as a set of externally imposed relationships. The art of making out is to manipulate those relationships with the purpose of advancing as quickly as possible from one stage to the next. . . .

After the first piece has been OK'd, the operator engages in a battle with the clock and the machine. Unless the task is a familiar one—in which case the answer is known, within limits—the question is: Can I make out? It may be necessary to figure some angles, some short cuts, to speed up the machine, make a special tool, etc. In these undertakings there is always an element of risk—for example, the possibility of turning out scrap or of breaking tools. If it becomes apparent that making out is impossible or quite unlikely, operators slacken off and take it easy. Since they are guaranteed their base earnings, there is little point in wearing themselves out unless they can make more than the base earnings—that is, more than 100 percent. That is what Roy refers to as goldbricking. The other form of "output restriction" to which he refers—quota restric-

---

Reprinted from Michael Burawoy, *Manufacturing Consent* (Chicago: University of Chicago Press, 1979), 51, 57–61, 63–67, 71–73, with permission of the publisher. © 1979 by the University of Chicago.

tion—entails putting a ceiling on how much an operator may turn in— that is, on how much he may record on the production card. In 1945 the ceiling was $10.00 a day or $1.25 an hour, though this did vary somewhat between machines. In 1975 the ceiling was defined as 140 percent for all operations on all machines. It was presumed that turning in more than 140 percent led to "price cuts" (rate increases), and . . . this was indeed the case.

In 1975 quota restriction was not necessarily a form of restriction of *output*, because operators *regularly* turned *out* more than 140 percent, but turned *in* only 140 percent, keeping the remainder as a "kitty" for those operations on which they could not make out. Indeed, operators would "bust their ass" for entire shifts, when they had a gravy job, so as to build up a kitty for the following day(s). Experienced operators on the more sophisticated machines could easily build up a kitty of a week's work. There was always some discrepancy, therefore, between what was registered in the books as completed and what was actually completed on the shop floor. Shop management was more concerned with the latter and let the books take care of themselves. Both the 140 percent ceiling and the practice of banking (keeping a kitty) were recognized and accepted by everyone on the shop floor, even if they didn't meet with the approval of higher management.

Management outside the shop also regarded the practice of "chiseling" as illicit, while management within the shop either assisted or connived in it. Chiseling (Roy's expression, which did not have currency on the shop floor in 1975) involves redistributing time from one operation to another so that operators can maximize the period turned in as over 100 percent. Either the time clerk cooperates by punching the cards in and out at the appropriate time or the operators are allowed to punch their own cards. In part, because of the diversity of jobs, I managed [as a participant-observer] to avoid punching my cards. At the end of the shift I would sit down with an account of the pieces completed in each job and fiddle around with the eight hours available, so as to maximize my earnings. I would pencil in the calculated times of starting and finishing each operation. No one ever complained, but it is unlikely that such consistent juggling would have been allowed on first shift.[1]

How does the present situation compare with Geer? As Roy describes it, the transfer of time from one operation or job to another was possible only if they were consecutive or else were part of the same job though separated in time. Thus Roy could finish one job and begin another without punching out on the first. When he did punch out on the first and in on the second, he would already have made a start toward making out. Second, if Roy saved up some pieces from one shift, he could turn those pieces in during his next shift only if the job had not been finished by his day man. Accordingly, it was important, when Roy had accumulated some kitty on a particular job, that he inform Joe Mucha. If Mucha could, he would try to avoid finishing the job before Roy came to work. Shifting time between consecutive jobs on a single shift was frequently fixed up by the foreman, who would pencil in the appropriate changes. Nonetheless, stealing time from a gravy job was in fact formally illicit in 1945.

> Gus told me that Eddie, the young time study man, was just as bad, if not worse, than the old fellow who gave him the price of one cent the other day. He said that Eddie caught the day man holding back on punching off a time study job while he got ahead on a piecework job. He turned the day man in, and the day man and the time cage man were bawled out.
> "That's none of his damn business. He shouldn't have turned in the day man," exclaimed Gus angrily.
> Gus went on to say that a girl hand-mill operator had been fired a year ago when a time study man caught her running one job while being "punched in" on another. The time study man came over to the girl's machine to time a job, to find the job completed and the girl running another.
> Stella has no use for time study men. She told me of the time Eddie caught Maggie running one job while being punched in on another. Maggie was fired.[2]

These examples suggest that, while chiseling went on, it was regarded as illegitimate at some levels of management.

What can we say about overall changes in rates over the past thirty years? Old-timers were forever telling me how "easy we've got it now," though that in itself would hardly constitute evidence of change. To be sure, machines, tooling, etc., have improved, and this makes production less subject to arbitrary holdups, but the rates could nonetheless be tighter. However, an interesting change in the shop vernacular does suggest easier rates. Roy describes two types of jobs, "gravy" and "stinkers," the former having particularly loose and the latter particularly tight rates. While I worked in the small-parts department, I frequently heard the word "gravy" but never the word "stinker." Its dropping out of fashion probably reflects the declining number of jobs with very tight rates and the availability of kitties to compensate for low levels of output. How do Roy's own data on output compare with 1975 data? Recomputing Roy's output on piecework in terms of rates rather than dollars and cents, I find that during the initial period, from November to February, his average was 85 percent and that during the second period, from March to August, it was 120 percent.[3] During the first six months of 1975, the average for the entire plant was around 133.5 percent. For the different departments this average varied from 142 percent among the automatic screw machines and automatic lathes to 121 percent in the small-parts department, where I worked. The small-parts department functions as a labor reservoir for the rest of the plant because turnover there is high, rates are notoriously tight, and it is the place where newcomers normally begin. Nonetheless, of all the departments, this one probably most closely resembles Roy's Jack Shop in terms of machines and type of work. Thus, overall rates are indeed easier to make now, but my experiences in my own department, where most of my observations were made, bore a close resemblance to Roy's experiences.[4]

What is the foreman's role in all these operations? He is seen by everyone but senior plant management as expediting and refereeing the game of making out. As long as operators are making out and auxiliary workers are not obstructing their progress, neither group is likely to invite authoritarian interventions from the foreman. For their part, foremen defend themselves from their own bosses' complaints that certain tasks have not been completed by pointing out that the operators concerned have been working hard and have successfully made out. We therefore find foremen actively assisting operators to make out by showing them tricks they had learned when they were operators, pointing out more efficient setups, helping them make special tools, persuading the inspector to OK a piece that did not exactly meet the requirements of the blueprint, and so on. Foremen, like everyone else on the shop floor, recognize the two forms of output restriction as integral parts of making out. When operators have made out for the night and decide to take it easy for the last two or three hours, a foreman may urge more work by saying, "Don't you want to build up a kitty?" However, foremen do not act in collusion with the methods department and use the information they have about the various jobs and their rates against the operators, because rate increases would excite animosity, encourage goldbricking, increase turnover, and generally make the foreman's job more difficult. . . .

The Organization of a Shop-Floor Culture

So far we have considered the stages through which any operation must go for its completion and the roles of different employees in advancing the operation from stage to stage. In practice the stages themselves are subject to considerable manipulation, and there were occasions when I would complete an operation without ever having been given it by the scheduling man, without having a blueprint, or without having it checked by the inspector. It is not necessary to discuss these manipulations further, since by now it must be apparent that relations emanating directly from the organization of work are understood and attain meaning primarily in terms of making out. Even social interaction not occasioned by the structure of work is dominated by and couched in the idiom of making out. When someone comes over to talk, his first question is, "Are you making out?" followed by "What's the rate?" If you are not making out, your conversation is likely to consist of explanations of why you are not: "The rate's impossible," "I had to wait an hour for the inspector to check the first piece," "These mother-fucking drills keep on burning up." When you are sweating it out on the machine, "knocking the pieces out," a passerby may call out "Gravy!"—suggesting that the job is not as difficult as you are making it appear. Or, when you are "goofing off"—visiting other workers or gossiping at the coffee machine—as likely as not someone will yell out, "You've got it made, man!" When faced with an operation that is obviously impossible, some comedian may bawl out, "Best job in the house!" Calling out to a passerby, "You got nothing to do?" will frequently elicit a protest of the nature, "I'm making out. What more do you want?" At lunchtime, operators of similar machines tend to sit together, and each undertakes a postmortem of the first half of the shift. Why they failed to make out, who "screwed them up," what they expect to accomplish in the second half of the shift, can they make up lost time, advice for others who are having some difficulty, and so on—such topics tend to dominate lunchtime conversations. As regards the domination of shop-floor interaction by the culture of making out, I can detect no changes over the thirty years. Some of the details of making out may have changed, but the idiom, status, tempo, etc., of interaction at work continue to be governed by and to rise out of the relations in production that constitute the rules of making out.

In summary, we have seen how the shop-floor culture revolves around making out. Each worker sooner or later is sucked into this distinctive set of activities and language, which then proceed to take on a meaning of their own. Like Roy, when I first entered the shop I was somewhat contemptuous of this game of making out, which appeared to advance Allied's profit margins more than the operators' interests. But I experienced the same shift of opinion that Roy reported:

> Attitudes changed from mere indifference to the piecework incentive to a determination not to be forced to respond, when failure to get a price increase on one of the lowest paying operations of his job repertoire convinced him that the company was unfair. Light scorn for the incentive scheme turned to bitterness. Several months later, however, after fellow operator McCann had instructed him in the "angles on making out," the writer was finding values in the piecework system other than economic ones. He struggled to attain quota "for the hell of it," because it was a "little game" and "keeps me from being bored."[5]

Such a pattern of insertion and seduction is common. In my own case, it took me some time to understand the shop language, let alone the intricacies of making out. It was a matter of three or four months before I began to make out by using a number of angles and by transferring time from one operation to another. Once I knew I had a chance to make out, the rewards of participating in a game in which the outcomes were uncertain absorbed my attention, and I found myself spontaneously cooperating with management in the production of greater surplus value.

Moreover, it was only in this way that I could establish relationships with others on the shop floor. Until I was able to strut around the floor like an experienced operator, as if I had all the time in the world and could still make out, few but the greenest would condescend to engage me in conversation. Thus, it was in terms of the culture of making out that individuals evaluated one another and themselves. It provided the basis of status hierarchies on the shop floor, and it was reinforced by the fact that the more sophisticated machines requiring greater skill also had the easier rates. Auxiliary personnel developed characters in accordance with their willingness to cooperate in making out: Morris was a lousy guy because he'd always delay in bringing stock; Harry was basically a decent crib attendant (after he took my ham), tried to help the guys, but was overworked; Charley was an OK scheduling man because he'd try to give me the gravy jobs; Bill, my day man, was "all right" because he'd show me the angles on making out, give me some kitty if I needed it, and sometimes cover up for me when I made a mess of things. . . .

The Dispersion of Conflict

I have shown how the organization of a piecework machine shop gives rise to making out and how this in turn becomes the basis of shop-floor culture. Making out also shapes distinctive patterns of conflict. Workers are inserted into the labor process as individuals who directly dictate the speed, feed, depth, etc., of their machines. The piece wage, as Marx observed, "tends to develop on the one hand that individuality, and with it the sense of liberty, independence, and self-control of the labourers, on the other, their competition one with another."[6] At the same time, the labor process of a machine shop embodies an opposed principle, the operator's dependence on auxiliary workers—themselves operating with a certain individual autonomy. This tension between control over machinery and subordination to others, between productive activities and production relations, leads to particular forms of conflict on the shop floor.

I have already suggested that pressures to make out frequently result in conflict between production and auxiliary workers when the latter are unable to provide some service promptly. The reason for this is only rarely found in the deliberate obstructionism of the crib attendant, inspector, trucker, and so one. More often it is the consequence of a managerial allocation of resources. Thus, during the period I worked on the shop floor, the number of operators on second shift expanded to almost the number on first shift, yet there was only one truck driver instead of two; there were, for most of the time, only two inspectors instead of four; there were only two foremen instead of four; and there was only one crib attendant instead of two or three. This merely accentuated a lateral conflict that was endemic to the organization of work. The only way such lateral conflict could be reduced was to allow second-shift operators to provide their own services by jumping into an idle truck, by entering the crib to get their own fixtures, by filling out their own cards, by looking through the books for rates or to see whether an order had been finished, and so one. However, these activities were all regarded as illegitimate by management outside the shop.[7] When middle management clamped down on operators by enforcing rules, there was chaos.

In the eyes of senior management, auxiliary workers are regarded as overhead, and so there are continual attempts to reduce their numbers. Thus, as already recounted, the objective of the quality-control manager was to reduce the number of inspectors. Changes in the philosophy of quality control, he argued, place increasing responsibility on the worker, and problems of quality are more effectively combatted by "systems control," design, and careful check on suppliers, particularly suppliers of castings. But, so long as every operation had to have its first piece checked, the decline in the number of inspectors merely led to greater frustration on the shop floor.

A single example will illustrate the type of conflict that is common. Tom, an inspector, was suspended for three days for absenteeism. This meant that there was only one inspector for the entire department, and work was piling up outside the window of Larry (another inspector). I had to wait two hours before my piece was inspected and I could get on with the task. It was sufficiently annoying to find only one inspector around, but my fury was compounded by the ostentatious manner in which Larry himself was slowing down. When I mentioned this to him, jokingly, he burst forth with "Why should I work my ass off? Tom's got his three days off, and the company thinks they are punishing him, but it's me who's got to break my back." In this instance, conflict between Tom and the company was transmuted into a resentment between Tom and Larry, which in turn provoked a hostile exchange between Larry and me. "Going slow," aimed at the company, redounds to the disadvantage of fellow workers. The redistribution of conflict in such ways was a constant feature of social relations on the shop floor. It was particularly pronounced on second shift because of the shortage of auxiliary workers and the fact that the more inexperienced operators, and therefore the ones most needing assistance, were also on that shift.

Common sense might lead one to believe that conflict between workers and managers would lead to cohesiveness among workers, but such an inference misses the fact that all conflict is mediated on an ideological terrain, in this case the terrain of making out. Thus, management-worker conflict is turned into competitiveness and intragroup struggles as a result of the organization of work. The translation of hierarchical domination into lateral antagonisms is in fact a common phenomenon throughout industry, as was shown in a study conducted on a sample of 3,604 blue-collar workers from 172 production departments in six plants scattered across the United States:

> Work pressure in general is negatively correlated to social-supportive behavior, which we have called cohesive behavior, and positively related to competitive and intra-group conflict behavior. Cohesive behavior is generally untenable under high pressure conditions because the reward structure imposed by management directs employees to work as fast as they can individually.[8]

The dominant pattern of conflict dispersion in a piecework machine shop is undoubtedly the reconstitution of hierarchical conflict as lateral conflict and competition. However, it is by no means the only redistribution of conflict. A reverse tendency is often found when new machinery is introduced that is badly coordinated with existing technology. Here lateral conflict may be transformed into an antagonism between workers and management or between different levels of management. . . .

Conclusion

Between Geer Company of 1945 and Allied Corporation thirty years later, the labor process underwent two sets of changes. The first is seen in the greater individualism promoted by the organization of work. Operators in 1975 had more autonomy as a result of the following: relaxed enforcement of certain managerial controls, such as inspection of pieces and rate-fixing; increased shop-floor bargaining between workers and foremen; and changes in the system of piece rates—changes that laid greater stress on individual performance, effort, and mobility, and allowed more manipulations. The second type of change, related to the first, concerns the diminution of hierarchical conflict and its redistribution in a number of different directions. As regards the relaxation of conflict between worker and management, one notes the decline in the authority of the foreman and the reduction of tensions between those concerned with enforcement of quality in production and those primarily interested in quantity. The greater permissiveness toward chiseling, the improvement of tooling and machines, as well as easier rates, have all facilitated making out and in this way have reduced antagonism between worker and shop management.[9] The employment of fewer auxiliary workers, on the other hand, has exacerbated lateral conflict among different groups of workers.[10]

These changes do not seem to support theories of intensification of the labor process or increase of managerial control through separation of conception and execution. What we have observed is the expansion of the area of the "self-organization" of workers as they pursue their daily activities. We have seen how operators, in order to make out at all, subvert rules promulgated from on high, create informal alliances with auxiliary workers, make their own tools, and so on. In order to produce surplus value, workers have had to organize their relations and activities in opposition to management, particularly middle and senior management. . . . Workers actively struggle *against* management to defend the conditions for producing profit. For Cornelius Castoriadis, this represents the fundamental contradiction of capitalism:

> In short, it [the deep contradiction] lies in the fact that capitalism . . . is obliged to try and achieve the simultaneous exclusion and participation of people in relation to their activities, in the fact that people are forced to ensure the functioning of the system half of the time *against* the system's own rules and therefore in struggle against it. This fundamental contradiction appears constantly wherever the process of management meets the process of execution, which is precisely (and par excellence) the social moment of production.[11]

But if the self-organization of workers is necessary for the survival of capitalism, it also questions the foundations of capitalism.

> When the shop-floor collective establishes norms that informally sanction both "slackers" and "speeders," when it constantly constitutes and reconstitutes itself in "informal" groups that respond to both the requirements of the work process and to personal affinities, it can only be viewed as actively opposing to capitalist principles new principles of productive and social organization and a new view of work.[12]

But is making out as radical as Castoriadis claims? Or is it, as Herbert Marcuse would argue, a mode of adaptation that reproduces "the voluntary servitude" of workers to capital? Are these freedoms and needs, generated and partially satisfied in the context of work and harnessed to the production of surplus value, a challenge to "capitalist principles"? Does making out present an anticipation of something new, the potential for human self-organization, or is it wholly contained within the reproduction of capitalist relations?[13] We can begin to answer such questions only by examining more closely the relationship between making out and the essence of the capitalist labor process—the simultaneous obscuring and securing of surplus value.

Notes

1. My day man, Bill, never penciled in the time but always got his cards punched in on the clock at the time office. This restricted his room for manipulation; but since he was very experienced on the miscellaneous job, this did not reduce his earnings by very much. When I filled in for him on first shift, I did in fact pencil in the times, and no one complained. This may have been a reflection of my power, since, with Bill away, hardly anyone knew how to do the various jobs or where the fixtures were. By penciling in the times, I reckoned I could earn the same amount of money as Bill but with less effort.

2. Donald Roy, "Restriction of Output in a Piecework Machine Shop," Ph.D. diss., Univ. of Chicago, 1952, p. 240.

3. Ibid., table 4, p. 94.

4. During the week 17 November to 23 November 1975, there were sixteen radial-drill operators in the small-parts department. Their average "measured performances" for the entire year (or for the period of the year since they had begun to operate a radial drill) were as follows (all figures are percentages): 92, 108, 109, 110, 111, 112, 115, 116, 119, 125, 133, 137, 139, 141, 142. The average was 120 percent, which turns out to be precisely Roy's average in his second period. Moreover, the average period spent on a radial drill in the *first eleven months of 1975* among these sixteen operators was of the order of six months, though a number of these operators had probably been operating radial drills for years. The data do not suggest significant differences between the rates on radial drills in Geer's Jack Shop and on radial drills in Allied's small-parts department.

5. Donald Roy, "Work Satisfaction and Social Reward in Quota Achievement," *American Journal of Sociology* 57 (1953), 509–10.

6. Karl Marx, *Capital* Vol. I (New York: International Publishers, 1967), p. 555.

7. I vividly recall being bawled out by a manager who came into the time office long after he should have gone home. He found me going through the books to see how many pieces had been handed in on a particular operation. Second-shift shop-floor management allowed and even encouraged operators to look these sorts of things up for themselves rather than bother the time clerks, but senior management regarded this as a criminal act.

8. Stuart Klein, *Workers under Stress: The Impact of Work Pressure on Group Cohesion* (Lexington: University of Kentucky Press, 1971), p. 100.

9. A similar argument [is] made by Tom Lupton, *On the Shop Floor* (Oxford: Pergamon Press, 1963), pp. 182–83. Though Lupton fails to see the organization of work as the consequence and object of struggles between workers and managers, among workers and among managers, his characterization of the *functions* of the "fiddle" are illuminating.

10. In interpreting these changes we will repeatedly come up against a difficult problem, namely, the degree to which Roy's observations reflect the exigencies of wartime conditions. For example, during the war, government contracts encouraged the overmanning of industry, since profits were fixed as a percentage of costs. Boosting costs did not change the rate of profit. As a consequence, we should not be surprised to discover cutbacks in personnel after the war. Thus, Roy informs us that after V-J Day, just before he left Geer, there was a reorganization in which foremen were demoted and the setup function was eliminated (Roy, "Restriction of Output," pp. 60, 219). Hostility of workers to the company must have been, at least in part, engendered by wartime restraints on union militancy and by the choking-off of the grievance machinery.

11. Paul Cardan (alias Cornelius Castoriadis), *Redefining Revolution* (London: Solidarity Pamphlet 44, n.d.), p. 11.

12. Cornelius Castoriadis, "On the History of the Workers' Movement," *Telos* no. 30 (Winter 1976–77): 35.

13. See, for example, Herbert Marcuse, *One-Dimensional Man* (Boston: Beacon Press, 1964), chap. 1; *An Essay on Liberation* (Boston: Beacon Press, 1969); *Eros and Civilization* (Boston: Beacon Press, 1955), chap. 10.

11

Women, Unions, and Participative Management: Organizing in the Sunbelt

Louise Lamphere and Guillermo Grenier

As more and more working mothers enter the labor force, the structure of industries that employ women is changing. Not only are apparel and electronics firms establishing "runaway shops" in Mexico, the Caribbean, and Southeast Asia, but corporations with branch plants remaining in the United States are "modernizing" their management policies. With the increasing popularity of "quality circles" (adapted from Japanese models), firms have enthusiastically embraced various forms of "participative management" policies that purport to give workers a measure of control over their work environment. Yet beneath the ethic of participation is often a clear anti-union stance. Women who work in these firms are facing a new workplace where modern plant equipment is often combined with management policies that limit women's ability to organize.

In this article we examine the use of participative-management policies during a union drive at a new plant in the Southwest. Since the plant workforce was dominantly female and included a large proportion of Hispanic women workers, many of whom were mothers, the case helps us to understand the complex interrelationship among labor activism, gender, and ethnicity. We argue that no one factor accounts for the union's loss by a two-to-one vote. Participative management techniques, the firm's use of legal and illegal anti-union tactics, and the economic vulnerability of young women workers all played a role. In addition, the union's failure to campaign for community support may have been a factor. More important, our interpretation emphasizes the process of the union drive itself and the factors at work in building workers' consciousness of the need for a union, as well as the timing of later management countertactics. A promising start was turned around by a stepped-up, highly orchestrated anti-union campaign.

Reprinted from *Women and the Politics of Empowerment,* edited by Ann Bookman and Sandra Morgen (Philadelphia: Temple University Press, 1988), 227–56.

On the one hand, it could be argued that Hispanic or Chicana women are difficult to unionize because of their lack of commitment to the labor force, language and customs different from mainstream workers, and deference to authority. On the other hand, recent research on Mexican-American women workers in California and Texas has indicated that they have been active participants in early apparel, food processing, and cannery strikes; in farm worker struggles; and in the Farah strike in the early 1970s.[1] Those who have studied Chicano families have recently attacked the "traditionalism argument," suggesting that women's lack of commitment to the workplace is more an outcome of the lack of opportunity in particular local economies than of adherence to values that keep women at home.[2] Finally, there is evidence that women are no less likely to vote for unions than are men, other conditions being equal.[3]

Certainly, Hispanic women in Sunbelt City[4] do not fit the stereotype of peripheral women workers. Census data indicate that Hispanic women in Sunbelt City entered the labor force in greater numbers between 1960 and 1970, and by 1980, 49.8 percent of Hispanic women were working outside the home.[5] In this urban area, few Hispanics are recent immigrants. Many families trace their roots in the state back to early Spanish settlement, most identify themselves as "Spanish" and not as Mexican or Mexican-American, and the majority of those under thirty years of age use English at home and at work. The women we interviewed at HealthTech and other industrial plants are examples of what might be termed the Southwest's "new women workers"—that is, young Hispanic women who are not taking time out to rear their children before returning to the labor force, but who are committed to retaining jobs that are necessary to support their families, even though they have preschool children.

In the case we will discuss, many Hispanic women (along with a number of Anglo and black women) were able to "see through" the "high-involvement" structure and perceive the need for a union to represent them in gaining higher wages and a real voice in policies. However, union supporters were not able to gain a majority of the needed votes for a union in the face of management's strategies. The reasons lie, we argue, partly in a powerful combination of participative-management policies and legal and illegal tactics, and partly in the economic vulnerability of these new women workers.

R. B. Freeman and J. L. Medoff have argued that managers of U.S. firms in recent years have increased their opposition to unions through the use of three strategies: (1) positive labor relations such as wage increases and improvements in fringe benefits; (2) tough legal campaigns to convince workers that they should vote against a union; and (3) illegal actions, such as the firing of union activists.[6] Their review of the literature suggests that the use of legal tactics, particularly leaflets and other communications with workers, the delay of a union election, and the use of consultants to fight unionization all tend to influence the results of an election in the direction of defeating the union.[7] More important, Freeman and Medoff argue that illegal tactics, such as firing workers, have an even more chilling impact on union campaigns. They estimate that unfair labor practices account for from one-fourth to one-half of the decline in the number of National Labor Relations Board (NLRB) elections won by unions over the past thirty years.[8]

Freeman and Medoff give little attention in their book to "positive labor relations" and their impact on union drives, partly because these are harder to measure than the use of anti-union communication and consultants (as examples of legal campaign practices used by management) and the number and type of NLRB charges filed by a union (as a measure of "illegal" practices). We believe that the new stress on participative management, particularly if it organizes informal social relations in the plant and puts them more under the control of management, has the potential of making loyal company supporters out of employees. Participative-management policies are thus a new form of "positive labor relations," one that is possibly as important as fringe-benefit packages, profit-sharing plans, or wage increases in warding off pro-union sentiment.

The Role of the Researcher

This article has emerged from material collected during two different research projects. In 1982–83 Louise Lamphere was coprincipal investigator on a National Sciences Foundation (NSF)–funded project to study the impact of female employment on families where the mother worked full time in a production-level job in the apparel and electronics industries. Dual-worker couples and single mothers—all with children under school age—were interviewed about their jobs, their work histories, and how they arranged household and child-care tasks in order to cope with the woman's full-time employment.[9] Women workers at HealthTech were included in the study since it was a new plant whose work process was very similar to that of apparel plants.

Permission to interview workers was given after an interview with the plant manager by Peter Evans, a coprincipal investigator. The manager then referred project members to the plant's social psychologist. In initial discussions with the psychologist, Lamphere was told that there was a union drive but was asked specifically not to discuss unions with workers. In initial interviews, therefore, Lamphere and her coworkers maintained the role of "detached researchers." Since we had pledged confidentiality to both the plant manager and the employees, we felt we could not turn over names, phone numbers, or interview material to the union organizers, although, as the drive progressed through the last few months of 1982, we became more and more sympathetic with the union cause. Lamphere was not in Sunbelt City during the last months of the campaign but was able to interview several additional workers whose names she got through the union organizer. These later interviews give a better sense of the role of the campaign in the lives of two of the ten women interviewed by those working on the NSF project.

Guillermo J. Grenier's role began as a researcher and was transformed into that of a pro-union spokesperson at a crucial juncture in the campaign, although his research interests remained throughout. During the fall of 1982 Grenier began conducting research on participative management structures—particularly the "teams" being used at HealthTech—for his doctoral degree in sociology. With the help of the plant social psychologist he was able to observe team meetings and talk with supervisors during the course of the union campaign. In the early months he acted as an unpaid research assistant to the social psychologist, taking up his suggestion to investigate the role that the teams played in the firm's anti-union campaign. When the firm's lawyer became concerned that Grenier's notes might be subpoenaed for an NLRB hearing, Grenier submitted a proposal to the company requesting permission to research "small group dynamics in an industrial setting." He informally agreed with the psychologist that he would keep the firm's anti-union strategy as a secondary focus of his research.

As Grenier gathered more information, particularly about the manipulative techniques used in team meetings and the company's firing strategy, he became convinced that there was nothing inherently "proworker" about the new design environment. After a great deal of soul searching, he spoke out against the activities of the company at a public forum organized by the union in April 1983. His comments resulted in the firing of the social psychologist and were important in eventually gaining a positive judgment from the NLRB concerning a number of worker grievances.

After his public statement Grenier was barred from the plant, but he was able to conduct interviews with a number of union activists, both male and female. Thus, his data include rich details on management tactics during the campaign as well as postelection analysis by a number of those who sided with the union. Our two roles emerged out of very different circumstances. Lamphere and her coworkers were interviewing workers in their homes, and the structure of their project, plus Lamphere's promise to avoid the topic of unionism, pushed her to collect data only on work and family. Grenier's association with the plant psychologist led him in just the opposite direction and gave him access to information that in turn could be useful for the union. In this article we see these two sets of data as complementary. By focusing on women's work and family lives on the one hand and the team structure and union drive on the other, we are able to analyze the interaction between management and women workers as it was shaped during the course of the union campaign.

The Setting

The union drive we analyze took place in 1982 and 1983 in a new branch plant of HealthTech located in Sunbelt City. The city's economy is based primarily on military and government jobs and the city's position as a commercial center. Within the past ten years the city has begun to attract branch plants of large corporations, primarily in apparel and electronics. Recently, several plants have been built with modern equipment, richly carpeted offices, and the latest in computer technology. In addition, a number of plants have introduced aspects of participative management, making Sunbelt City somewhat a "laboratory" for the management of the future.

Thus when HealthTech opened its doors in 1981, it was one of the most innovative plants in the city, operating on what management terms a "high-involvement" philosophy and also hiring a workforce that was 90 percent female and 65 percent Hispanic.

The "high-involvement" philosophy at HealthTech had several ingredients. As in two or three other plants in the area, benefits for production and nonproduction employees were equal, there were no time clocks, and the plant had something like "flex-time" in that workers could be late and make up the time at the end of the day. Also, the plant manager maintained an "open-door" policy by which any worker could talk with him about issues of concern. However, HealthTech had gone beyond these forms of participation to completely restructure the labor process around small groups called "teams," which in principle were involved in hiring, training, evaluating, and firing fellow workers.

Workers at the HealthTech plant were involved in making surgical sutures. Trainees learned to attach surgical thread on curved steel needles (a process called "swaging") through the use of "learning curves." Each week the trainee was given a production goal of completing so many dozen swaged needles each day; the number increased until the employee reached " 100 percent efficiency." The learning curves used at HealthTech are very similar to production curves used in apparel plants across the country. Although not paid on a piece rate as garment workers are, HealthTech workers were, in effect, pushing against a clock and trying to "make their numbers," increasing their production on a daily basis.

Each department was divided into "production teams" of twelve to fourteen workers. The plant operated on two shifts. Six or seven members of each team worked from 7 A.M. to 3 P.M.; the rest worked evenings from 3 to 11 P.M. The team decided on a rotation schedule, which normally meant that individuals worked two weeks on days and two weeks on nights. Teammates often took breaks or lunch together, and the team met weekly to discuss issues of concern. Building production around small groups meant that management rather than workers created the "informal work" group long ago discovered by the human relations school of management psychology.[10]

In addition, implementation of the "team concept" meant a massive restructuring of the cultural categories through which work and management–worker relations were interpreted. Each team had a "facilitator," not a "supervisor." The "facilitator" was thus not a "boss" but someone who helped improve the interpersonal relationships on the team and aided individuals with their productivity. The team itself was supposed to have an important role in decision making. Two team members interviewed prospective employees (after they had been interviewed by a personnel administrator and the facilitator), and if the evaluation they brought back to the team meeting was negative, the person was not hired.

Weekly team meetings between the facilitators and workers were held at the time of the shift change (between 2:30 and 3:30 P.M.). A good deal of time was spent in these meetings discussing the production quotas of individual team members and the team as a whole. Whereas in a more traditional plant the supervisor or trainer would be responsible for exhorting the worker to do better, discussion of "numbers" in the team meetings involved the use of negative comments by coworkers, and thus public embarrassment, as methods of motivating a worker to perform better. In addition, as part of the "team support evaluation," team members rated one another on whether they "work hard to reach production."

After a two-month probationary period, and for each six-month period thereafter, team members participated in the evaluation of a new teammate. Evaluations were based on "quality," "quantity," "attendance," and "team support." Each team member filled out a form on the worker being evaluated and checked, among other things, whether that worker showed "a positive attitude toward the job," took an "active part in team evaluations," and understood "the team concept/open communication philosophy." In other words, team members were asked to evaluate their peers on social behavior and attitudes unrelated to the production process itself. These evaluations were discussed in the team meeting, and a poor evaluation sometimes resulted in a raise refusal or a termination (especially at the point of the first evaluation after sixty days of employment).

This redefinition of the work environment—turning bosses into facilitators and workers into "team members" who are peers and who control their work lives—mystifies the hierarchical relations that in fact remain. As our data show, during a union drive workers were carefully screened by management before team members talked to them, firings were initiated by managers and were often carried out without the consent of workers, and the interaction in team meetings was orchestrated by the "facilitator."

Women Workers at Healthtech

During the course of the NSF Sunbelt industrialization study, we interviewed ten female HealthTech workers. Four were single parents and six were married. Like the other forty-seven women interviewed as part of the project, all had children under school age and all worked full time in a production job. Economically, the HealthTech workers did not differ significantly from women who worked at apparel and electronics plants in Sunbelt City. All had a history of labor-force participation before obtaining the HealthTech job. Most had worked at low-paying service-sector jobs, and the HealthTech position was the highest-paying and most stable job they had had. Like our other production workers, these women had typically been employed since high school in fast-food restaurants, in children's clothing and shoe stores, in day-care centers, or in jobs such as dental assistant or motel maid. Several had some industrial experience as well as a history of jobs in the service sector. They had been employed as sewing machine operator, material sorter, or packer at one of the apparel plants in Sunbelt City. One single mother had been employed for several years at a HealthTech plant in another state and had requested transfer to the new Sunbelt City plant.

The ten HealthTech workers we interviewed were all earning between $5.00 and $5.80 per hour, depending on seniority and shift. The four single parents' salaries (of $10,000–$11,600 a year) were the major support for themselves and their children; all had only one child. However, their pay was not high enough for them to live on their own. One woman lived with her sister and the sister's boyfriend, another with a cousin, a third with her mother, and a fourth with both parents. In the case of the six married workers, the woman's salary contributed almost half or, in two cases, more than half of the couple's income. In three couples the husband had faced several months of unemployment during 1982, so that in these three families the wife's employment at HealthTech was a particularly critical stabilizing factor. Family incomes ranged from $12,500 to $23,600 per year; three of the couples were classified in our larger study as being in a "precariously stable" economic position and three as being in a "stable" position. Median income for the thirty-eight couples (twenty-three Hispanic and fifteen Anglo) in our larger study was $22,300. In other words, the Health-Tech women tended to be in families with incomes in the lower half of our sample and in situations where the husbands' jobs were less stable and the wives' hourly pay not as high as the pay in some of the electronics and electrical equipment plants. For both single parents and couples, female employment was an absolutely crucial aspect of the family's economic situation.

Of the ten women interviewed, five supported the union and five did not. Since the final union vote was 141 against the union and 71 for the union, our sample is biased in the direction of union supporters. However, since we were not focusing on the union issue, we did not realize until writing this article that our sample included proportionately more union supporters than found in the workforce. The ten women, however, represent the range of participation in the drive—including a very vocal antiunionist, two members of the union organizing committee, and several women who were quiescent during the campaign.

Among the ten women we spoke with, our interviews show that there were few significant differences in their attitudes toward being a working mother. Instead, feelings about their jobs had been deeply influenced by their own work experiences and by the union campaign. In other words, the interview data suggest that women bring to work quite similar views about how work and family fit or do not fit together, but that attitudes toward the job are shaped in the workplace. These women were committed to both their roles as workers and their roles as mothers, which created some ambivalence when the two roles came into conflict. For example, all ten agreed or strongly agreed that "women need to work to help their families keep up with the high cost of living." Most agreed (but not strongly) that "working is an important part of my life that would be hard for me to give up." In addition, most felt (though not strongly) that "even if I didn't need the money, I would continue to work." All agreed or strongly agreed that "I feel that anybody who works in my line of work ought to feel good about herself." All these items indicated the importance of working outside the home.

Other items, however, showed that being a mother often conflicted with being a worker. For example, all felt that "working mothers miss the best years of their children's lives." They also felt the pressures of the "double day." All but one interviewee agreed (or strongly agreed) that "I have sometimes felt it was unfair that I have to work and also spend so much time taking care of my home and my children." They also agreed that "I sometimes think I cannot do enough for my family when I work." On the other hand, all but two felt that "family responsibilities have *not* interfered with my getting ahead at work." In other words, both union and nonunion supporters in our sample were committed to jobs outside the home but felt the pressures of combining two roles, feeling the double burden of housework and child care and regretting not being able to spend more time with their children.

Union and nonunion supporters differed more in how they felt about their HealthTech jobs. The views of union supporters had in several cases been influenced by the campaign itself and some of the issues that had been raised about wages and conditions during its course. For one supporter of the union, her treatment by management during the campaign led her to quit her job after the union lost the election.

Union supporters and nonunion supporters valued the same aspects of work. For example, nine of the ten listed job security among the top three important aspects of any job. Good pay and ease of getting to and from work were the next most important attributes, whereas good supervisors, opportunities for promotion, challenging work, and no conflicts with family responsibilities were each mentioned only twice.

In contrast, union supporters had a much more negative view of their HealthTech jobs, feeling that their jobs were less secure (perhaps because of their union support) and that they were not well paid. Nonunion supporters were overwhelmingly positive about their jobs, all five feeling that their positions had job security ("very true") and high pay ("very true" or "true"). They also felt that they had good supervisors and opportunities for promotion. They were slightly more positive about their jobs in terms of how little they conflicted with family responsibilities and how challenging the work was. Three union supporters felt strongly that schedules that demanded working on alternating shifts conflicted with their family responsibilities, and one felt that she was unable to work at her own pace because of the pressure to meet production goals ("pressure in meeting numbers"). Three union supporters felt it was "not true" or "not true at all" that they had a good supervisor.

Activism for and against the Union:
Lucille, Bonnie, and Annette

The similarity in our interviewees' economic situation and attitudes toward combining work and motherhood, and their differences in on-the-job experience suggest that attention should be focused on the workplace and management's strategies during the campaign. The interaction between the work process, the team structure, and the facilitators' tactics to curb union support reveal a great deal about the forces that shaped the range of support and nonsupport for a union that was evidenced in our small sample. This range of opinion and activism can best be illustrated by contrasting Lucille, an anti-union interviewee, with Bonnie and Annette, both strong union supporters.

Both Lucille and Bonnie were among the first workers hired when the HealthTech firm moved to Sunbelt City during 1981. Lucille, an Hispanic, and Bonnie, an Anglo, were both mothers of three children. Neither husband had a good-paying job and both women's HealthTech incomes were a major source of support for the family. Both Lucille and Bonnie were chosen from more than nine hundred initial applicants and were on the first teams formed. Lucille was assigned to drill swaging (Team A) and Bonnie to channel swaging (Team A).[11]

Lucille learned the drill-swaging technique quickly and was asked to train new employees in the drill department in March. She continued training until December 1981 and then began a period of thirteen weeks' "demonstration" (that is, swaging and winding the newly attached needles and thread at 100 percent efficiency for a period of thirteen weeks). Lucille was the first person in the plant to "demonstrate," and she found the pressure severe. She felt that people on her team were not supportive and that she was not given credit or praise for finishing her demonstration (and getting a raise). This did not dampen her overall enthusiasm for her job, however; she gave her work top ratings on all aspects from pay to supervisor to job security.

Lucille described what she liked about the job:

> What do I like about it? . . . Feeling important as far as what we are making and how it associates with other people. . . . I like everything about that job. The management people, they are so nice, they are just so down-to-earth people. They are not really your bosses as much as your friends. They have never taken that superior attitude over us. Never. They don't have any more benefits than we do. Their benefits are equal to ours. . . . They have an open-door policy. Any time we want to, we can go up and talk to them.

Not only did Lucille do well on her job and feel positive about the management, but she also had a positive assessment of the team structure. She had no difficulty rotating shifts (working both days and evenings, usually two weeks at each); she enjoyed the team meetings and felt positive about her role in hiring decisions: "I really enjoy them . . . because you get to communicate real good with the people on your own team, plus with your facilitator, and you get input with everything that goes on. There is really nothing that you can't talk about in your team meeting."

Lucille also responded positively to her role in interviewing prospective workers: "I interviewed most of the first people that got hired. . . . It was fun. I'd never done it before and it was really interesting and I really enjoyed it. I highly recommend it."

With these opinions about the company, the participative-management policies, and the team system, it is not surprising that Lucille took an active role against the union when it became an issue. She described how the union issue emerged in her team:

> Well, there was quite a bit of conflict, because there was a couple on our team that wanted the union. And the rest didn't want the union, and there was some that didn't care one way or the other or didn't know enough about it to care. . . . We changed the minds of the ones that wanted the union . . . about six or seven weeks ago. . . . The union stopped being

> pushy. They are being really quiet. I don't know what they are planning, but they are being really quiet. What we did was, several of us from different departments got together and started an antiunion committee. And we had our own meetings and passed our own flyers.

Bonnie's experiences were quite different. At first she was quite nervous about doing well in her job.

> I was really scared at first. Because it's very tedious, you know. Right down into the machine. It really took me a month or so to get into it. I really thought I was going to lose it. . . . All that producing. You only had so many days to produce that much. And if you don't make it . . . well, "goodbye." So I was really kind of panicked, but I picked up on it. . . . There was so much to learn that it was really quite scary.

However, Bonnie did well enough to become a trainer of new employees. She was only one of two of the original twelve team members who was still employed by the spring of 1983. Since the channel swaging job was harder than drill swaging, taking eighteen months to master, and since Bonnie spent a good deal of time training others, she had not gone through her demonstration period by the time her third child was born in April 1983 (two years after she was hired).

Bonnie initially responded favorably to team philosophy. As Bonnie said, "I thought it was kind of nice. It might be kind of fun. It was all new to me: to have somebody . . . if you had a problem in your team you could have somebody to help you out." However, Bonnie became disillusioned by the team process. The facilitator for the Channel Department Teams A and B (who was later fired) often tried to provoke conflict among workers. In addition, Bonnie felt it was embarrassing for the workers to have to justify their low production numbers or explain their troubles with the machines during a public meeting. Bonnie described the meetings of Team A.

> And he was always on us about numbers. It was always his job if our numbers didn't come up. And why did we do so poorly that week. And we'd have to go around the table. And I really hated that. If your numbers were 80 percent for the week and the week before, and that week you did only 67 percent, you know, "Why did you do 67 percent? You are supposed to be at 80." At the time our machines seemed to be breaking down constantly. Down time [would count against us]. But yes, well, that got to be kind of an "old excuse."

Participating in a firing was also a difficult process for Bonnie. She described her feelings about firing one male team member who had been unable to meet his production quotas.

> Well, it's terrible. That person is sitting right there. . . . It was for his numbers. He really was a good worker and a good person . . . to get along with and everything. But his numbers weren't there. He'd had some trouble with his machine, and I guess it had just gotten down to the wire

and they had to fire him. I guess we all agreed that if this was what we are supposed to do, we've got to do it. If you don't make your numbers, you've got to go. Either [the facilitator's] going to fire him or the team was going to fire him, and that was one of our things, . . . knowing that we would have to hire and fire . . . hoping that we would never have to fire. . . . It was awful.

On the whole, Bonnie liked her job, but she often felt that there were some unfair aspects of the production system, such as having difficulties with the machine and "lost time" count against her in meeting her production quotas.

I enjoyed the job. Because it was kind of a challenge. I always . . . like I say, I always watch the clock. If I could do something in 25 minutes or less, I felt real good about it. . . . I did not like when my machine broke down. Or if I had to do re-work. I did not like that counted against me. I didn't think that it was my fault that the machine broke down and I had to work on it . . . but I enjoyed the people there.

By the summer of 1982 several members of Channel A and B were having doubts similar to Bonnie's about the participatory nature of the team structure. Their expectations that the team concept would create a positive kind of work environment were not fulfilled. They found that workers' advice concerning improvements was not heeded, and many came to feel that the team philosophy was a "charade," especially when they were given lines to rehearse in preparation for a plant tour by visiting executives.

Late in June 1982 six workers from Teams A and B formed an organizing committee with the goal of unionization. By 27 July a group of fifteen workers had written to the plant manager that they favored a union and asked for a debate to take place on the issue of unionization. These workers included Bonnie and three of her female teammates from Channel Team A, three workers from Channel Team B, four from the Devices Department, and one from the Vault Department. Three members of the Drill Department, including two of Lucille's teammates, signed the letter. Since most were from the earliest group of employees hired and almost half were from the Channel Department (the most difficult job with the most demanding production numbers and the most production problems), these workers had begun to develop a critique of how production was administered in the plant. In addition, a number had begun to "see through" the team structure. Possibly because of the way in which the facilitator of Channel Teams A and B administered his teams, workers felt that their participation was only on the surface and actually under the control of management.

Through the next few months, support for the union grew. A union organizer from the national office began to contact workers, emphasizing the high wages at other unionized company plants even though there were few differences in the cost of living. The organizing committee began to pass out leaflets, and by October 25, when a signed leaflet was handed out, the committee's membership had expanded to include twenty-one workers. Sixteen were women, including ten Hispanic women, four Anglos, one black, and one Asian woman. All five men were Hispanic. Again, about half of the committee members (eleven) were from Channels A and B; several more had been added from Drill (two on Team C and one on Team F), but support in the Devices Department had dropped, and the committee had lost the male worker in the Vault Department. The teams in Channel were becoming strongholds, and there was now additional scattered support in other departments.

Annette was one of the new members of Team B who signed the October 25 leaflet, the day after it was handed out. She was an Hispanic single parent who was living with her sister and her sister's boyfriend, and whose $5.62-an-hour job was supporting her and her four-year-old son. She and one other team member worked permanently on the evening shift, which allowed her team members more weeks on days in the overall rotation schedule. At the time of our interview, she had been having machine problems and her numbers were low. "When gut first came in to Channel Swaging, I was the first one to work with it. I had to learn. The facilitator had me trying different dyes to find out which dyes the needles worked best with and stuff like that. So my numbers dropped then, too." Along with several other union supporters, Annette had a well-developed critique of the production quota system and the learning curves. She would have preferred a straight incentive system and bonus pay, but she also felt that the numbers were too high. "They are always comparing us to the other plant. . . . But their swagers have been there an average of fifteen to twenty years, and we've only been swaging a year or a year and a half."

She had been hired in September 1981, six months after Bonnie had started on Team A. Her feelings about the team meetings were similar to Bonnie's: "It would be just like one big 'tattle-tale session.' That's the way our other facilitator . . . the one before José. He had the meetings being conducted like that. It got to where everybody was fighting with each other and everything." Annette's complaints, like Bonnie's, were based both on her perception that difficulties with production were unfairly treated and her sense that the team concept was really not "participation."

At the time of our interview Annette had just been warned that if her numbers did not improve, she would be suspended for three days. She felt that this reprimand was related to her union support, "Because they are getting kind of nervous because the union wants to get in. So they are doing anything to get rid of the people that are for. . . . Like, I'm on the union committee . . . so . . . I'm not going to give a reason to get rid of me." Annette's suspicion was correct. As union activity increased, the company's anti-union strategies went into high gear.

Management's Anti-Union Strategies

Management presented its high-involvement structure and philosophy as incompatible with a union. One company document stated, "We give everyone a chance to represent themselves without a 'third party' such as a union." Through formal and informal communications, management emphasized that a union would interfere with the effort to get everyone to participate, and the company would therefore "lose flexibility" in implementing the high-involvement design. In management's decision to come to Sunbelt City, the lack of a "strong union environment" had been a factor. Although other branch plants in both the East and the Southwest are unionized, the company would not have located the new plant in an area with a union environment. In addition, the larger corporation of which HealthTech is a part had located plants in Singapore and Taiwan in order both to avoid unions and to pay cheaper wages.

Most important, the company calculated that if it could keep the union out for three years, it would save $5 million in wages, benefits, and administration. And when it reached its employee limit of five hundred, it would save over $10 million every three years.

Freeman and Medoff's framework for analyzing anti-union strategies, as described earlier, provides a useful starting point for our analysis. They focus on three types of strategies: positive employee relations, a tough legal campaign, and illegal tactics. However, the notion of "positive labor relations" needs to be expanded to include ways the company used the team structure to push a pro-company and anti-union position. This was called by the plant psychologist the "proactive" approach—an approach in which the facilitator orchestrates and initiates the discussion of the union at team meetings and in that way gets across certain ideas about the union to employees.

In addition, however, this "proactive" or positive labor relations approach was supplemented with informal "negative" relations as well, activities that were not illegal and were not focused on disseminating anti-union information. Called the "individual conflict approach" by the plant psychologist, this was an approach in which management attempted to isolate individuals already known to be pro-union at the team and individual levels. Pro-union workers were to be isolated from other team members and confronted individually concerning their own attitudes.

In Freeman and Medoff's scheme the tough legal campaign involves giving workers information not necessarily solicited by them but nevertheless important in informing them about the anti-union stance of the company. At HealthTech this included a barrage of leaflets, bulletins read in team meetings, team discussions to bring out anti-union views, an anti-union contest, and movies that stressed strikes as well as conflict that was purportedly created by union activity.

There were two sets of illegal tactics that had a profound impact on the election's outcome, as we shall see. First, the firing of pro-union employees created a climate of fear among workers. Second, the questioning of new applicants in order to screen out those with pro-union attitudes virtually assured the pro-company stance of the substantial number of workers hired during the final months of the union's campaign.

The team system became the organizational foundation for developing and implementing these three strategies. The informal relations between facilitator and team members and the more formal team meetings became the context in which management implemented both its proactive and its legal information-disseminating activities. The use of the team as part of management's anti-union strategies can best be illustrated by what happened to Drill Teams A, B, and C, where one supervisor, Dennis, used his team meetings to persuade workers to adopt the company point of view.

In Drill Team A, as we have already reported, Lucille was active in the forming of the pro-company organization. She also played an important role as an anti-union spokesperson during team meetings. For example, Andres, one of the two pro-union members of the team, reported that at a team meeting in September 1982, Lucille had asked, "How far would the union go to get into the plant?" In response, Dennis pulled out a piece of paper and said something like, "Oh, by the way, I've got something to read you about the union." Dennis read that a union in New York had gotten its members a twenty-five-cent raise. "Is this the kind of union you want representing you?" he asked. Andres retorted, "Why don't you stick to the facts of what the union has done at other HealthTech plants and what it can do here, and not some other union at another place?"

Elena, another anti-unionist, responded, "If you're not happy with the company, why don't you resign?" She continued her attack, almost yelling at Andres. Dennis did not speak up. "He allowed the wolf pack to attack me," Andres commented. Such acrimonious conflict meant that workers became reluctant to speak out, afraid of being ridiculed or even fired.

In Drill Team B pro-union support seemed stronger and was quietly developing among the group that worked consistently on the day shift (all women, including two Hispanic mothers we interviewed). At a team meeting on 17 September 1982, Dennis, the facilitator, took action to bring out any anti-union views which might be expressed publicly by team members. He mentioned a television show of the previous evening:

"Speaking of TV, did anyone see the piece on Coors on '60 Minutes' last night?" A couple of workers responded that they had, as did a female personnel administrator who had been invited to come to the meeting. She was encouraged to give her views.

> It showed how the union keeps trying to get in at the Coors plant in Colorado, even when the workers don't want anything to do with it. It was real funny because they showed how they got all the employees in a great big room asking them what they thought of the company, and every single one of them said how much they liked working for the company, how much the company was trying to help them and all that stuff. . . . They showed all the stuff the company was doing for the workers—the gym they had set up, the benefits and all that. . . . And it was a really good show."

The administrator's speech was sufficient to bring out anti-union sentiments from three other workers.

After the union leaflet of 25 October and the union's letter to the company naming the organizing committee, the company moved more quickly to use the team meetings as a context for fighting pro-union settlement and to isolate pro-union people. As the social psychologist said on 27 October, "But today . . . we have lifted the 'hold' we have had on facilitators. Instead of having to depend on employees to bring things up about the union, to try to keep the union out, we are letting facilitators go. They can do what they want on the union issue."

Dennis, for example, stepped up his "proactive strategy," which was also combined with the "individual conflict approach" to isolate pro-union workers. The first target was Rosa, a member of Drill Team C who was one of two pro-union employees on the Compensation Committee, which dealt with the wage and evaluation system. During a team meeting Dennis "tore the leaflet apart" and then asked for comments. As Rosa reported:

> Tracy spoke up. She said, "I don't feel Rosa should be on the Compensation Committee because I don't feel she is trustworthy enough now to express what we feel or want." She said my name had been on the union leaflet with other people she thought were not trustworthy enough because we were not for the HealthTech philosophy, compensation plan or team concept. . . . When she got through I said that I'd voluntarily step down from the committee. I didn't want to be on it if people felt that way about it. Plus, I suspected that I was being set up. Tracy had always been my friend. People said we were like sisters, that we even looked like sisters.

Dennis refused to let Rosa step down and said that the other teams should have a chance to decide this issue. The next day at a meeting of about seventy-five members of the whole Drill Department (Teams A–F) Dennis raised the issue of Rosa's resignation and asked for comments. Tracy again stood up and accused Rosa, "almost yelling." Several other anti-union employees hollered agreement, and then Rosa was asked to stand up and be identified. Finally, Anne, a teammate, defended Rosa's performance on the committee, and Rosa was asked her opinion. "I feel I'm being harassed for my political opinion," she said, "and that is discrimination." Tracy later said, "You know they forced me to do that, don't you," and asked Rosa, "Do you forgive me?" Rosa replied that she would never forgive her.

Anne, in fact, felt that Dennis had subtly used the team as a way of "getting at" the union supporters.

> I think he tried to create conflict. There really were some hard-core [anti-union] people in our team. This is only a guess. But I think he got those people aside and said, "This is what I want you to do—bring up such and such an issue. When I'm talking about something, cut in." . . . These people *had* to be put up. I think that Tracy was put up to do what she did to Rosa. She was supposed to be her best friend. And for her to turn around and do that. Somebody had to put her up to that.

With these tactics, Dennis was able to keep union support in his three teams limited to two workers in Drill Team A (Lucille's team), a small group of three or four in Team B, and a small group in Team C (including Rosa, Anne, and three others). In contrast, the Channel A and B teams, during the fall of 1982, continued to give their new facilitator, José, a difficult time. Pro-union women either brought up criticisms of the company directly or, if this tactic did not result in any change or dialogue, refused to participate. Team B was perhaps the most successful in this tactic. One team member, Dee, said, "He said that Team B was too loud or something. Every time we tried to say something, he would shut us up. Then if we weren't going to say something, he'd tell us, 'Why don't you talk?' So, he said, 'You guys just don't function as a team.' "

Annette, the single parent mentioned earlier, explained how the team had developed its own informal support network. "We've gotten closer and we look out for each other, like we are supposed to be doing . . . like what they are saying. You know, disciplining each other and stuff like that. But [José's] getting upset, because he doesn't really know what's going on."

Thus Team B was very successful in becoming united around the issue of the union and in confronting their facilitator. Channel A and B had been the center of union sentiment from the beginning, and José, the new facilitator, had come from a union plant, so perhaps was not as committed as others to fighting the union in team meetings.

A measure of the union's support in early December 1982 was the fact that ninety-three workers (both women and men) signed a petition asking the company to investigate a bad smell that was pervading the production area of the plant. Workers were fearful that ETO, the dangerous chemical that was used to sterilize the sutures, might have seeped into the air filter system in the "clean room" in which the workers worked. The petition stated:

> We, the undersigned, want to know the names of the chemicals causing the bad smell in the plant. We are upset over the complaints of headaches, teary eyes, and nausea resulting from the odor, and we are very concerned about the effects of these chemicals on pregnant women and their unborn children. We have a right to know what chemicals we are being exposed to.

Phrased as a women's issue and backed by union supporters, this petition was signed by fifty-four Hispanic women and twenty-two Anglo and black women.[12] Not all of the Hispanic and Anglo women who eventually voted for the union signed the petition. Thirty-seven Hispanic women and seven non-Hispanic women did sign it but later did not vote for the union. The company responded to the petition by arguing that ETO is not a compound with a smell and that, although they were looking into the cause of the odor, it was not hazardous to workers' health. A statement to this effect was read in all the team meetings. With this strong response on the part of the company, the issue eventually faded into the background. However, the petition represents a high point in terms of support for an issue that the union brought to the fore. By this time about 49 percent of the workers had signed union cards. The union decided to wait for card signing to increase beyond the 50-percent mark, a point that never came. Both the petition and the card signing may have represented more antimanagement feeling than actual willingness to support the union. In any case, from this period on, the company began to be more successful in eroding the growing union sentiment.

Despite the strong support on the ETO issue and the signing of union cards, most facilitators remained in control of their teams. The tactics that Dennis used with Drill Teams A, B, and C were beginning to have an effect and to keep workers who had been in the plant for a year or more from defecting to the union. Facilitators were using the rhetoric surrounding the "high-involvement" philosophy to isolate union supporters. Pro-union workers had "bad attitudes," were not really "team members" or did not believe in the "team concept" and thus were not trustworthy. To be pro-union was to be against the company and against the high-involvement philosophy. The attempt to redefine union supporters as being against the team concept and thus "losers" was another way of strengthening the informal basis of support for the company. More important, however, was the company's major illegal strategy: firing pro-union workers.

The evidence presented by Freeman and Medoff suggests that illegal tactics such as firing pro-union workers have the most devastating impact on union campaigns. Other tactics that would have a negative impact would be surveillance of union supporters during work hours and discrimination against pro-union applicants for jobs. Firings in themselves might result in a negative reaction to the company, a galvanizing of sympathy for the union, and stronger support. We must ask, therefore, why firings would result in fear and compliance rather than resistance on the part of women workers. The effect of firings and other illegal tactics, we argue, is more damaging to a union drive when the company had already laid the basis for support for its anti-union position in the interpersonal relationships between workers and management. Channel Teams A and B may have been strongholds of union support, but the tactics of Dennis and other facilitators had laid the groundwork for anti-union sentiment in other teams, something that could be built on if strong union supporters could be fired. The team system at HealthTech and its use by management to support anti-union workers and isolate union supporters set the context in which firings would have a particularly negative impact on the union drive.

As early as 5 November 1982, the plant psychologist talked to Guillermo J. Grenier about the possibility of firing some of the pro-union workers. He said that because the company was restricted legally in how much it could do to stop the union, it would have to act surreptitiously. He referred to one employee whom the company was getting ready to fire as a "fat slob" in the Drill Department. They were toying with ideas about firing her and hoped to put the union in a "no win" situation by doing it. In fact, the company succeeded in firing this woman because the doctor's excuse that she used to account for an absence did not cover the correct time period. A male union supporter was also fired but was later reinstated because of inconsistencies in the policies for making up absences that had been used to justify his termination.

Sometime in November management met with corporate lawyers who recommended using firing as an anti-union strategy. The first two firings had been "trial balloons" to see what the union would do when its supporters were fired for objective reasons. Additional firings were planned, probably to take place after Christmas, since the company "did not want to come across like Scrooge," firing people right before the holidays.

However, on 16 December two women on the Channel B team who were union supporters were fired for "falsifying company records." A worker named Maria had phoned to tell her friend Linda to log her in on the computer, that she would be five minutes late; however, she arrived at work at 8:00 rather than 7:05 A.M. At the end of the day Maria's facilitator called her into the back room and confronted her with the situation.

> I went back there and I talked to him, and he said somebody had seen me clocked in. And I said I'd go look on my time sheet. "But Linda clocked you in early," he said. "Ya, I told her to clock me in, because I'm going to be five minutes late at the most." And he goes, "You're not supposed to

do that." There wasn't no rules. Everybody clocks each other in. They knew about it too.

The next day Maria was dismissed, despite the fact that her time sheet (as opposed to the computer) recorded her 8:00 A.M. entry into the plant. Maria suspected that her firing was the result of her name's being on the 25 October leaflet. And according to the social psychologist, the plant manager had decided to fire these women because it would be a good symbolic gesture, a good way to scare other pro-union employees.

Thus by Christmastime four of the twenty-one employees who had signed the 25 October leaflet had been fired and another had been forced to resign from the Compensation Committee following a large meeting in which she had been publicly embarrassed and had been left visibly shaken.

Worker Resistance

Women workers who were pro-union, and their male peers, did not knuckle under to the company's anti-union strategies. A number of "unfair labor practice" charges were filed with the NLRB on 27 October alleging that workers were being interrogated, threatened with loss of benefits if a union was formed, and threatened with firing. Additional charges were filed after the 6 November firings and after the firings of Maria and Linda on 19 December.

Nevertheless, the union was working in a climate of fear. It was clear that supporting the union could mean being threatened with a suspension if one's numbers were down (as in Annette's case) or being fired through the strict application of company policy that had been more leniently applied to nonunion supporters (as in the case of Maria and Linda). The first months of the union campaign (between July and October) had resulted in a concentration of supporters in the Channel A and B teams, with some support among some of the Drill teams and in Devices. Between October and December the company stepped up its tactics, adding illegal activities to the full range of other strategies, including the manipulation of attitudes in team meetings and the more straightforward dissemination of information through leaflets and the bulletin board. The union was thus faced with the need to persuade more workers to join the union in a threatening atmosphere. In addition, the company was continuing to expand its workforce and was carefully screening new employees to make sure they would be anti-union when they entered the plant. The union committee continued to meet in January and February, and at the end of February an open meeting was held at a local hotel.

In the meantime, a mechanic who had not previously been associated with the union drive was fired for talking back to his supervisor. This mechanic and a coworker had written to the plant manager in mid-February expressing support for the union. The firing enlisted a great deal of sympathy from workers. The union's filing of an "unfair labor practice" charge on the mechanic's behalf gained his support and that of several other workers in early March. In addition, the union had advertised in the local newspapers seeking information on applicants who had been interrogated about their union views during interviews or training. Clearly, the union was continuing to take an aggressive legal stand in trying to protect workers who had been discriminated against for their views or support of the union drive.

The union also conducted a trip for five production workers (two anti-union, two undecided, and one scared to take a side) to the company's unionized plant in the eastern United States. Although they were not able to see the inside of the plant, the workers met with one hundred union employees and made a videotape of the meeting that was later shown to the Sunbelt City workers at a union-sponsored meeting. All five workers who made the trip were persuaded to take the union's side.

As Rosa's friend Anne said,

> What really opened my eyes was going to [the East] and seeing what they had over there. It's not an individual team over there. It's one big team over there. It opened my eyes, and that was towards the end of the campaign. . . . We need somebody to represent us—to back us up—that's what we need. . . . You go up and talk to them. And after you have that talk, he still has the final say. You have nobody—no other recourse to talk to. You have no other alternative. Who's going to fight for you . . . against the company. And that's basically why I got involved with the union.

Lorraine, a single parent who worked in Devices, had worked at another HealthTech plant for five years and had been a union member. She was the only worker who had transferred from a union plant in another city to the new Sunbelt City plant. In order to do so she had had to drop out of the union, and she had found it necessary to mention her difficulty in resigning from the union in order to become hired. She was advised not to talk about the union, but by February 1983 she was becoming involved with the union campaign. She explained the reasons for the trip and its impact on the drive.

> 'Cause the company had bad-mouthed the union really bad, so bad that everybody was afraid of the union. So they sent five of us and we went to [another company plant]. And when we came back, we told them. And a lot of people turned for us and for the union. [But] there was a lot of people that wouldn't . . . that's where the tension developed.

In March, sensing that it was not gaining much additional support, the union filed with the NLRB for an election. Between that date and the date of the election, 18 May, the company continued to pursue its tactics of isolating pro-union employees but also moved in several ways to step up its public anti-union campaign.

Conclusion of the Union Drive

Since late fall of 1982 the plant psychologist had been making a concerted effort to identify union supporters and then to isolate them. In December he reported to Guillermo J. Grenier that facilitators were watching pro-union workers, and when they saw them talking to anti-union or neutral people, they would go up and interrupt the conversation. The point, he explained, was to control the influence and interactions of the pro-union people.

During this period the company began to rate all the employees on their stance on the union. "Plus one" and "plus two" were the pro-company employees and "minus one" and "minus two" were the pro-union employees. Undecided employees or those the company could not figure out were listed as zeros. The company was continuing to increase the pressure on pro-union employees and, in the words of the plant psychologist, was "withdrawing status from them using a strong psychological approach." The company was trying to separate the "winners," or anti-union people, from the "losers," the pro-union people.

Women workers reacted in different ways to this strategy of isolating the union supporters. Anne said,

> Some people react different to scare tactics. Me—stand up and fight. That's the way I am. If someone threatens me, I . . . especially if I am boxed in a corner . . . I come out and fight. Some people don't. They give into the threat. And I think that's what a majority of the people did do. They were afraid. Afraid of losing their jobs. Afraid of the . . . humiliation you were put through . . . and you were humiliated. All these things added up and they just didn't want to go through with it. So they went to the side they thought would win.

Others took rejection by management more personally. Lorraine, the single parent in Devices, was in a large department where the facilitator had come from another plant, bringing many employees with him. Their loyalty to him partially accounted for the low proportion of union supporters (eight out of twenty-six). Lorraine herself felt that she was particularly ostracized by management when they realized that she had become pro-union.

> They ignored me. Before the campaign started, they were always inviting me to go here and there. Then afterwards . . . not even a "Hi." . . . They'd come onto the production floor and they'd stand like [in groups of] two or

three and make faces and stand like they were talking about me. And that would bother me. Because they had never done it before.

As the election approached, the company engaged in a more open expression of anti-union sentiment. Some of the activities had all the earmarks of the "tough legal campaign." In April the company initiated a union strike contest, asking employees to guess how many strikes the union had engaged in between 1975 and 1983. Memos from the plant manager were frequently circulated to employees, and plantwide meetings were held. At one meeting in May a film on union violence was shown. The motto of the campaign became "Be a Winner! Vote No."

Lorraine felt strongly about how the company handled this part of the campaign and the image of the union that it presented.

> I wouldn't have portrayed the image that these people would. This is a free country. Everybody could do what they want. Sure there's rules . . . but they don't have to go around treating us like that. . . . You couldn't say certain things. You couldn't bring in certain papers. I would have let people bring in their papers; you know equal—both sides. But it wasn't equal. Only one side. And that wasn't right. That wasn't a fair way.

The union's one important strategy during this period was to hold a public meeting on 12 April organized by a group of lawyers and community leaders concerned over the course of the union campaign. As mentioned earlier, Guillermo J. Grenier read a statement at this meeting arguing that the teams were being used as part of the company's "union-busting" strategy. Shortly afterward the plant social psychologist and the personnel director were dismissed, and Grenier's statement was used by the union in pressing its NLRB charges.

Despite the public exposure of the company's strategies, on election day, 18 May 1982, the union lost, getting only 71 votes; 141 employees voted against the union, and 11 votes were contested.

Why Did the Union Lose?

In order to understand why the union, in the end, was not able to gain the support of the majority of the company's production workers, it is important to assess the company's heavy-handed strategies in relation to the composition of the labor force. Of the 220 employees in the bargaining unit, 65 percent were Hispanics and 35 percent non-Hispanics (including Anglos, blacks, native Americans, and Asians). Seventy-nine percent of the workforce (174 out of 220) were female, including 119 Hispanic women and 55 non-Hispanic women (68.4 percent and 31.6 percent of the female production workforce). Of the 174 female workers, 46 percent of the women had children (N = 80), 27 percent had no children (N = 47), and we had no data on whether the remaining 27 percent had children or were childless (N = 47). In other words, this was a workforce dominantly composed of working mothers, mostly of Hispanic descent.

In the end proportionately more non-Hispanic women (Anglos, blacks, and native Americans) and more men (Hispanic and Anglo) voted for the union than did Hispanic women. The proportion of Hispanic women who voted for the union was lower than that in the overall bargaining unit. Thus, while the female labor force was 68.4 percent Hispanic (^{119}/174), only 28 Hispanic women or 23.5 percent voted for the union (^{28}/119) (see Table 11–1 and Table 11–2).

If we look at the mothers (both married and single) in the bargaining unit, the picture is more striking. Of the 80 women who we knew were mothers, only 30 (or 37.5 percent) voted for the union. And of the 60 Hispanic mothers, only 17 (or 28.3 percent) voted for the union (see Table 11–3).

If we take the ETO petition mentioned earlier as an indication of the support the union had gained by early December, before the firings became a successful management strategy, we can see that the union lost 37 Hispanic women (including 18 mothers) and 7 non-Hispanic women (including 5 mothers) who had been willing to sign the petition but did not vote for the union five months later. Clearly the union had been able to raise an important woman's issue and galvanize women's support. However, the company in response was able to defuse the issue during a period in which it fired 2 Hispanic women. The message conveyed during the period between December and February was that support for the union could mean losing a job. Hispanic women, including a significant number of mothers, dropped from the potentially pro-union ranks. Had these 37 Hispanic and 7 Anglo, black, and Asian women voted for the union, the union would have garnered 115 votes, enough to win the election.

Table 11–1
Voting Patterns among Female Workers

Vote	Hispanic		Non-Hispanic		Total	
	N	*Percentage*	*N*	*Percentage*	*N*	*Percentage*
Pro-Union	28	23.5	22	40	50	28.7
Anti-Union	91	76.5	33	60	124	71.3
Total	**119**	**100.0**	**55**	**100**	**174**	**100.0**

Note: These figures are estimates. We had a list of 221 eligible to vote and were able to identify 65 of 71 probable voters from petitions signed by workers who favored union policies and from the information given us by the union organizer.

Table 11–2
Voting Patterns among Male Workers

	Hispanic		Non-Hispanic		Total	
Vote	*N*	*Percentage*	*N*	*Percentage*	*N*	*Percentage*
Pro-Union	12	52.2	10	45.5	22	48.8
Anti-union	11	47.8	12	54.5	23	51.2
Total	**23**	**100.0**	**22**	**100.0**	**45**	**100.0**

Note: These figures are estimates. We had a list of 221 eligible to vote and were able to identify 65 of 71 probable voters from petitions signed by workers who favored union policies and from the information given us by the union organizer.

Table 11–3
Voting Patterns among Mothers (N = 80)

	Hispanic		Non-Hispanic		Total	
Vote	*N*	*Percentage*	*N*	*Percentage*	*N*	*Percentage*
Pro-Union	17	28.3	13	65	30	37.5
Anti-union	43	71.7	7	35	50	62.5
Total	**60**	**100.0**	**20**	**100**	**80**	**100.0**

Note: These figures include both single parents and married mothers, so we cannot assume that these mothers were the sole support of their children, but on the basis of the NSF interviews we can assume that their incomes were vital in supporting their families.

The union was able to attract the support of some Hispanic women, but others were either interested only initially or failed to support the union at all. Although the NSF interviews were not designed to explicate the issue of union support, they do offer some clues to these varying reactions. For some, workplace difficulties provided a context for galvanizing support especially within teams formed early in Health Tech's history. For example, we interviewed Valerie and Delores in Drill Team B. On this team, anti-union sentiment was strongest among the six members who worked on the evening shift. Unlike in other teams whose members rotated on a one- or two-week basis, enough Drill Team B members were willing to work evenings that the six who preferred to work days could do so without rotating. Both Valerie and Delores felt that shift rotation was the biggest disadvantage of the job, and both became union supporters because they felt the union would be able to abolish the rotation system. As Valerie said:

> When we do have to go nights, it's a real big problem. One of the biggest problems I have there. . . . It's hard, because baby-sitter wise, no baby sitter's going to want . . . okay, these two weeks you can take her and then for two hours the next two weeks. I've got to find somebody that can take her at nights. And that's hard on my husband, it's hard on my little girl.

Delores was equally adamant that the rotating shift system interfered with her time with her family and kept her away from her five-year-old daughter. Though neither reported difficulties with her job, Valerie rated pay, supervisors, and opportunities for promotion low (3 on a scale of 4), and Delores felt that the plant was not a safe place to work at night because of the dark, unprotected parking lot. In addition, she felt that her job conflicted with her family responsibilities when she had to work nights, and she felt a great deal of pressure in meeting her "numbers." Valerie also felt that the team meetings were "not working," that workers were not getting anything out of them. Despite these relatively negative comments about the job, the crucial issue for both women in supporting the union was shift rotation and its impact on them as mothers. For both these women, the union was able to capitalize on their frustrations and keep their allegiance, despite the climate of fear induced by the firings and other unfair labor practices.

Other Hispanic workers were part of teams more under the control of supervisors, worked in operations not so difficult as Channel or Drill Swaging, or may have been screened for anti-union sentiments when they were hired. Perhaps typical of the kinds of women workers the union did not win over were Regina, Grace, Karen, and Jenny—the four non-union supporters, in addition to Lucille, who were interviewed for the NSF project. Regina and Grace were Hispanic single parents, while Karen was an Anglo married to an Hispanic and Jenny was part native American married to an Anglo. Economically they were in situations similar to those of the union supporters we interviewed. Regina and Grace were single parents like Annette and Lorraine. Jenny's husband had periods of unemployment not dissimilar to Bonnie's and Valerie's spouses. Karen herself had had a series of service-sector jobs, and although her husband had a stable position at a mental health center, his pay was low.

However, all had been at HealthTech for a shorter time than the union supporters (with the exception of Lorraine, who had been a union member elsewhere). And all were in departments where there was a low level of union support (Foil/Overwrap, Drill D, and Devices). Several of these women had complaints about their jobs. Grace did not like working on rotating shifts, and Regina also mentioned that working on two shifts was a major disadvantage of the job. Karen was nervous about her evaluations and did not like the way the teams were being used. Despite these disadvantages, each rated her job higher than union supporters rated theirs. The negative aspects of the job were outweighed by financial need and job security. These were the kinds of women whom the union needed to win over in order to win the election. But it was difficult to do so in the face of the atmosphere successfully created by the company, partially since these women were in team contexts where there were few pro-union voices. In the end, we cannot say for sure why these four women did not vote for the union, but we can assess the impact of the firm's strategies on the female work force as a whole.

In Freeman and Medoff's framework the firings and the delay of the election would account for the union's loss. But in the HealthTech context workers were also part of a team structure in which facilitators were hard at work using a number of tactics to keep workers from turning pro-union. The December firings had created a climate of fear. Although there was a show of support when the mechanic was fired in February, only thirty-seven workers signed the petition, all of them strong union supporters. The fact that the NLRB put off hearings on the firings and other unfair labor practices so that none of these workers was reinstated by the time of the election allowed the company to keep the upper hand. Certainly screening of new applicants had an important impact. The union drew only a smattering of support from teams formed late in the campaign—that is, from Drill Teams D, E, F, and G (2 votes) and from Channel C and D (3 votes). The anti-union votes in these six teams amounted to 52, more than one-third of the anti-union support.

Given the economic vulnerability of Hispanic women, particularly mothers, we can see how the team structure and management tactics created a climate in which it was risky for those not already committed to the union to vote for it.

Seeking Community Support

The union did not attempt to counter the company's strategies by seeking support from church and community institutions early in the campaign. The head organizer believed that shop-floor issues were the major ones in the drive and that the media might be more sympathetic to the company's position were the campaign taken outside the workplace. However, a few weeks before the election, the union, perhaps because it knew it needed more votes, attempted to mobilize community support through a public meeting and letters from religious and political figures. For example, the archbishop's office issue a letter that said:

> An important union election is taking place at HealthTech this week. By getting a Union at this plant, wage earners would gain increased bargaining power, would improve their wages and job rights and would be better able to provide for their families. Support for those who are seeking union representation would advance the cause of workers' rights and human dignity here at home and would be consistent with the Church's teachings about the dignity of labor.

In addition, the former lieutenant governor sent letters to workers and held poorly attended meetings hoping to educate workers on the benefits of unions. His last letter was sent to all employees and said in part:

> I strongly believe that a Union at HealthTech would have a positive impact which would benefit not only HealthTech members but also the entire

community. First, union membership would mean higher wages. Higher wages would mean more money into the economy. In addition, a union would help the state establish itself as a state interested in the kind of industry which provides fair wages and good working conditions.

The letter came at a time when workers were being bombarded with material from the company, including handouts about the impact of a strike on wages, a handout charging that the union had a history of filing unfair labor practices, and a paycheck insert stating what union dues would mean in terms of lost pay.

Support from the church and community leaders came too late to change anyone's mind. In an atmosphere in which NLRB charges were not being heard, fired workers had not been reinstated, and the risks of a union were being clearly emphasized by the company, workers who had not been won over to the union side undoubtedly saw union support as too risky. These workers included many Hispanic women, mothers as well as single individuals.

Conclusions

There is a long-standing literature on human relations and small-group behavior in industrial settings, beginning with the famous Hawthorne experiments at Western Electric in the 1930s. Various forms of the human relations perspective, which include a personnel department to fit workers to jobs and various forms of psychological testing and counseling, are part of the structure of most firms. More recently, social scientists have focused on various forms of control exercised by management over workers.[13] The issue of workplace participation has received recent attention, but little has been done to analyze how new participative-management structures can reorganize the labor process as well as the social relations of the workforce to create new forms of management control.

In the HealthTech case, rather than relying on an hierarchical authority structure with large departments under a supervisor who reported to area supervisors and a plant manager, management structured production around small teams of twelve to fourteen members under the guidance of a "facilitator" who was to "facilitate" the human relations within the group, urging workers to help each other increase output as well as to participate in the hiring, evaluation, and firing of their peers.

The team structure was an attractive control mechanism because of its apparently humanizing effect on a bureaucratized and hierarchical work environment. The team structure helped to "debureaucratize" work; and rules and regulations were less formal and appeared to be the responsibility of workers. Peer pressure was institutionalized as the major control mechanism. Workers felt they had more responsibility for the performance of others. Yet the facilitator remained in charge, wielding power in an informal but real way. Managing the discussion of union issues and isolating those with pro-union views were just two examples of the ways in which facilitators attempted to control worker attitudes.

Furthermore, the team structure fragmented the labor force. This had both positive and negative aspects. As the union drive developed, the close interaction among team members in addition to difficulties workers faced in meeting production quotas helped to build pro-union sentiment in some teams. As one manager said, the team under some circumstances can be just like a juvenile gang. On the other hand, since teams were relatively isolated from each other, the team structure could hinder the spread of pro-union sentiment. In some teams facilitators were able to neutralize pro-union activists and keep them from convening other workers. The few activists became isolated and silenced in teams dominated by pro-company workers. The company continued to hire new workers, carefully screening them for any union support. As one facilitator said, "We hire anti-union people by screening for them, and it's my job to see to it that they stay that way."

Thus it is important to emphasize the process of the campaign as it interacted with workers' experience of the labor process, the team structure, and the economic vulnerability of a female, predominantly Hispanic workforce. In the early months of the campaign the company probably made some mistakes. Facilitators were new at their jobs; some had had experience in traditional plants or lacked strong anti-union views. Difficulties with the production process plus some obvious evidence that workers were not so powerful as they had been led to believe allowed a number of the first workers hired to "see through" the team philosophy. As the drive progressed to a second stage, management turned to more traditional tactics to keep the union out: (1) legal tactics, particularly bulletins and discussions to persuade workers that their company did not need a union; and (2) illegal actions, including the screening of new workers for pro-union views and the firing of union activists. These were implemented within the team structure that had the potential of isolating the pro-union teams from teams more directly under the control of supervisors and filled with new, carefully screened recruits.

With the beginning of this second stage (starting with the pre-Christmas firings), it became apparent that supporting the union would mean, at the least, being branded as having a bad attitude or being against the "team concept" and, at the most, losing one's job. The plant psychologist and facilitators attempted to control the interactions of pro-union activists by interrupting their conversations with other workers. They rated workers on a scale of "pro-company" to "anti-company" to keep track of their own support. The careful screening of new employees and the use of team meetings by facilitators made it possible to win over many employees to the company's view. Here, taking key words and phrases from the notions surrounding "team support" and the "team concept" and using them to judge pro-union workers as "anticompany" and as "losers" was probably effective. However, the economic threat of job loss was more critical to showing neutral employees what was at stake.

During the last two months, under a barrage of leaflets, meetings, and movies (the more traditional techniques of the tough union campaign), the dangers of losing one's job became more salient. From the company's point of view, spending $1 million on the campaign was well worth it. For most women in the plant, this job was the best job they had ever had. They could put up with team meetings, keep their "numbers" up, and deal with the more strictly enforced absentee policy if it meant remaining in what was basically a high-paying job in a clean, new plant with good benefits and job security.

The defeat of the union cannot be blamed on the passivity of women workers, traditional Hispanic values, or the lack of women's commitment to their jobs. Instead, many women (including Hispanic women) forged strategies of resistance in attempting to fight for union representation. That an initially promising campaign turned to defeat is the result of a number of factors: the team structure in combination with the heavyhanded legal and illegal tactics of management in the context of an economically vulnerable workforce. That the union did not succeed is a measure both of the company's power and of the importance that women placed on retaining their jobs in an atmosphere of considerable conflict and threat.

Notes

1. C. Duron, "Mexican Women and Labor Conflict in Los Angeles: The ILGWU Dressmakers' Strike of 1933," *Aztlan* 15, no. 1 (1984): 145–61; Vicki L. Ruiz, *"Obreras y Madres:* Labor Activism among Mexican Women and Its Impact on the Family," in Ignacio García and Raquel Rubio Goldsmith, eds., *La Mexicana/Chicana,* Renato Rosaldo Lecture Series Monograph, vol. 1 (Tucson: University of Arizona 1985); Vicki L. Ruiz, "Working for Wages: Mexican Women in the Southwest, 1930–80," Working Paper no. 19 (Tucson: Southwest Institute for Research on Women, University of Arizona, 1986); L. Coyle, G. Hershatter, E. Honig, "Women at Farah: An Unfinished Story," in Magdalena Mora and Adelaida R. Del Castillo, eds., *Mexican Women in the United States: Struggles Past and Present,* Occasional Paper no. 2 (Los Angeles: Chicano Studies Research Center Publications, University of California, 1980), 117–43.

2. P. Zavella, "The Impact of 'Sun Belt Industrialization' on Chicanas," *Frontiers* 8, no. 1 (1984): 21–28, esp. 21 and 22.

3. R. B. Freeman and J. L. Medoff, *What Do Unions Do?* (New York: Basic Books, 1984), 227.

4. We have used a pseudonym for both the city and the plant; we have also changed the names of individuals whom we interviewed in order to protect their privacy.

5. In the 1950s and 1960s the labor force participation rate of Hispanic women was lower than that of Anglo women, but by 1970 the rate was 40 percent, only 3 percentage points behind the Anglo rate. In 1980, 42.6 percent of married Hispanic women with children under the age of six were employed, and 54.7 percent of those with children between six and eighteen held jobs.

6. Freeman and Medoff, *What Do Unions Do?*, 231.

7. Ibid., 233–36.

8. Ibid., 238.

9. The project was titled "Women's Work and Family Strategies in the Context of 'Sunbelt' Industrialization," NSF Grant no. BNS 8112726. In addition to Louise Lamphere, Patricia Zavella, Jennifer Martinez, and Peter Evans conducted some of the interviews used in this article.

10. Elton Mayo, *The Human Problems of an Industrial Civilization* (New York: Macmillan, 1933); F. J. Roethlisberger and W. Dickson, *Management and the Worker* (Cambridge: Harvard University Press, 1939).

11. Drill and channel swaging are two different methods of attaching a surgical needle to a gut or silk cord. The channel technique took eighteen months to master; the drill technique took twelve.

12. Nine men, including five Hispanic men, also signed the petition. Four of the ninety-three signatures were illegible.

13. Harry Braverman, *Labor and Monopoly Capital* (New York: Monthly Review Press, 1974); Richard Edwards, *Contested Terrain: The Transformation of the Workplace in the Twentieth Century* (New York: Basic Books, 1979).

12

Organizational Expertise and Bureaucratic Control: Behavioral Science as Managerial Ideology

Frank Fischer

During the past two decades an increasing number of writers have turned their attention to the ideological role of the social sciences.[1] In general, this work has evolved from an epistemological critique of the social sciences' dominant methodological orientation, empiricism. Such critiques range from an assault on the traditional "value-neutral" conception of an empirical science, which rules out social and political evaluation, to an attempt to locate an interest in sociotechnical control within social science methodology itself.[2] Various writers have ascribed ideological consequences to such a methodology, ranging from a bias toward social stability and the status quo to political domination and repression.

One of the areas of social science that has come under relatively sharp criticism is the field of organizational theory. The purpose of this discussion is to illustrate the ideological character of one major component of organization theory, organizational psychology and the human relations school.

Ideology and Authority

To put the issue bluntly, organizational psychology emerged to facilitate the bureaucratic processes of twentieth-century corporate capitalism. As unabashed students of industrial efficiency and stable work relations, its first theorists laid the groundwork for a discipline designed to supplement and support the bureaucratic mode of authority and control. Since then the study of organizational behavior has never swung far from the narrowly defined objectives of corporate organization. Always closely affiliated with a school of business or an institute of labor relations, the discipline has emerged as one of the most well-financed but carefully insulated areas of social research.

The outcome, as Paul Goldman explains, is an organization theory that has "by its assumptions and procedures systematically narrowed its field of inquiry and, consequently, presented an incomplete and distorted picture of organizational reality."[3] Similarly, Alasdair MacIntyre maintains that the methodology of organization theory itself has become the ideology of bureaucratic authority. In his words, organizational science represents little more than an "ideological expression of that same organizational life which the theorists are attempting to describe."[4] For both Goldman and MacIntyre, the result of this narrowed field of interest is an elite-oriented ahistorical theory that is insulated from the critical concepts of social and political theory, particularly the concepts of power, authority, and class.

By distorting the picture of workplace realities, organization theory has taken on the standard functions of an ideology, in both the descriptive and the pejorative meanings of the term. As a workplace ideology, organization theory has conventionally represented a managerial "worldview." In this sense, it has programmatically embodied the interests, values, and objectives of the professional-managerial classes.

For example, Daniel Bell defines ideology in programmatic terms as "a way of translating ideas into action" and explains a *total* ideology" as "an all inclusive system of comprehensive reality," which includes "a set of beliefs, infused with passion, that seeks to transform the way of life."[5]

A total ideology, as such, is a program or plan of action based on an explicitly systematic model or theory of how society works, which is held with more confidence (passion) than the evidence for the theory or model warrants.

It is when we raise this issue of warrantability that an ideology loses its descriptive or nonjudgmental function and takes on a pejorative connotation. In the pejorative sense, the term is used when agents in the society are deluded about themselves, their position in society, or their interests. Jürgen Habermas, for instance, speaks of an ideology as a "world picture" that stabilizes or legitimizes authority and domination.[6] It is by virtue of the fact that it supports or justifies reprehensible social institutions, unjust social practices, relations of repressive authority, exploitation, or domination that a form of consciousness is an ideology.

Ideologies in organizations, in this regard, must be understood as efforts to justify the struggle for power and authority. Generated by conditions of conflict and contradiction, Organizational ideologies as defined by Reinhard Bendix function as "attempts by leaders of enterprises to justify the privilege of voluntary action and association for themselves, while imposing upon all subordinates the duty of obedience and of service to the best of their ability."[7]

The objective here is to offer an interpretation of the ideological functions of organizational psychology and the human relations movement. Bringing the perspective of the political and social theorist to bear on an "applied" behavioral science, I intend to show how the human relations movement, cloaked in the garb of scientific warrantability, has served to ideologically translate images of repressive authority into a widely accepted form of workplace consciousness.

Authority in Organization Theory

For Max Weber, the founder of modern organizational sociology, the problems of power and authority lay at the very heart of bureaucratic organization. Weber's principal objective was essentially to both describe and legitimate the replacement of "old world" forms of state authority based on traditional and charismatic leadership with a "rational-legalistic" mode of authority that facilitated industrial development.[8]

Based on emotion and mystique, rather than calculation and orderly change, the traditional and charismatic forms of monarchial and clerical authority thwarted the development of profit maximizing in the wider society. To replace these earlier forms, Weber sought to both describe and promote an alternative mode of authority based on fixed rules and routines, which he called "legal-rational" authority. As the foundation of managerial power in both state and industrial organizations, rational authority is linked to clearly defined, procedurally determined rules and regulations for coordinating relationships among administrative units.

For analytical purposes, Weber posited an ideal model of bureaucracy as the quintessential form of legal-rationalistic authority. This legal-rationalistic model represented the purest form of administrative control. As an analytical construct, it emerged as the basic conceptual foundation of organizational analysis. Contemporary theory, however, has underplayed Weber's emphasis on authority as a form of *power,* stressing instead the *efficient* aspects of legal-rationalistic authority. In a turn from Weber's social and political perspective on bureaucracy, the modern literature has adopted a narrower orientation: Bureaucratic administration is represented more as a model of technical efficiency than as a form of power and domination.

At this point, Weber's conception of bureaucracy as a model of efficiency converges with the emerging "value-neutral" science of management, designed to uncover the efficient rules governing the rational pursuit of goals. In the process, Weber's modern-day followers have underplayed his original concept of authority. Shunning his broad political perspective on entrepreneurial legitimation, they have restricted the concept of authority to an emphasis on its functional contribution to efficient organization practices, such as the uses of hierarchy, technical competence, and leadership.

Organizational Authority and Class Conflict

Bendix is one of the few theorists in the mainstream literature who has maintained Weber's early emphasis on power and authority. On the basis of a comparative examination of managements' justifications for workplace authority in major industrial countries, Bendix defines the function of a management ideology this way:

> Such ideologies interpret the facts of authority and obedience so as to neutralize or eliminate the conflict between the few and the many in the interest of a more effective exercise of authority. To do this, the exercise of authority is either denied altogether on the ground that the few merely order what the many want; or it is justified with the assertion that the few have qualities of excellence which enable them to realize the interest of the many.[9]

In the United States the problem of legitimating management assumed special import. Managers in the United States faced a particular dilemma or contradiction. On the one hand, democratic ideologies stress liberty and equality for all. On the other, large masses of workers had to submit to the arbitrary authority of the enterprise's managers, backed up by local and national police forces and legal power, for ten to twelve house a day, six days a week. Moreover, in face of this fact, the workers' right to form unions of their own was severely limited or simply prohibited.

The problem, as Bendix put it, was this: How could a managerial elite legitimate its own privileges while imposing a harsh subservience upon its subordinates? The solution was sought at the level of symbols. Designed "as weapon[s] . . . in the struggle for industrialization," managerial ideologies emerged to confer advantage upon the privileged capitalist class.

Before industrialization, managers took little interest in the attitudes of their workers. Only when workers became antagonistic did early industrialists intervene in the works process. And then, to stem the tide of rebellion, they principally relied upon the prerogatives of ownership, backed by the physical force of the state. After the turn of the century, however, there was a dramatic turn to the promulgation of managerial ideologies to foster the compliance of labor. In this place of the struggle, as DiTomaso points out, the loyalty of the workers, or at least the pretension of loyalty, becomes as important as doing a good job.[10] Rather than only specifying rules and regulations to govern various work situations, managerial ideologies function to promote an atmosphere or attitude of loyalty. As Bendix explains, they are aimed at the spirit rather than the letter of the rules.

The purpose of the remaining discussion is to illustrate the role of one managerial ideology—human relations theory—in class conflict at the level of the workplace.

Scientific Authority and Class Conflict

In the textbook conception of the human relations movement, its task has been to compensate for the empirical deficiencies of scientific management through the introduction of the methods and techniques of behavioral science.[11] Accepting the basic postulates of classical organization theory, the neoclassical human relations school sought to empirically build the *human* element into Frederick Taylor's "machine model" of management. In this regard, human relations psychologists attempted to scientifically modify Taylorism by introducing the role of individual behavior and the concept of the "informal group."

In addition to the general introduction of behavioral science methodology, the lasting theoretical contribution of neoclassical human relations theory clearly has been its conceptualization of informal group processes. In contrast to the focus upon formal hierarchical structures within scientific management, neoclassical theory emphasized informal work groups, defined as the natural social groups that emerge in the workplace. Unaccounted for by the formal table of organization, such groupings appear, according to human relations theory, as a response to the worker's social need to associate with others. Generating an internal culture of norms for group conduct, the informal group can serve as an agency for worker identification, socialization, and control.

From the viewpoint of management, the informal group operates as a system of status and communication capable of thwarting managerial policy and control. In this respect, human relations theorists have often sought ways to coordinate the activities of the formal and informal organizations. William Scott puts it this way:

> Management should recognize that the informal organization exists, nothing can destroy it, and so the executive might just as well work with it. Working with the informal organization involves not threatening its existence unnecessarily, listening to opinions expressed for the group by the leaders, allowing group participation in decision-making situations, and controlling the grapevine by prompt release of accurate information.[12]

What none of this says is that in practice human relations psychology actually took hold as a response to the earlier successes of labor unions by the 1920s. Mainstream theorists are correct to see human relations as a response to the limitations of scientific management, but not for the reasons of science alone. Rather than a theoretical problem in experimental design, we must first look at human relations in the context of scientific management's experience with worker unrest.

By 1915 there was growing opposition to Taylorism and scientific management. One result was a major strike against scientific-management practices at the government's Watertown Arsenal. The strike prompted extensive congressional hearings that elevated Taylorism to the level of national concern.

At the root of the problem was the issue of workplace control. As Harry Braverman and Dan Clawson have illustrated, to understand scientific management properly, one must penetrate its scientific rhetoric and recognize it as a response to labor's authority over actual work process.[13] Above all else, scientific management emerged as a managerial strategy to gain greater control of the workplace during the labor struggles that accompanied rapid industrialization, especially from 1880 to 1920.

Fundamentally, Taylor recognized that capitalists could never win the struggle with labor under the divided authority that characterized nineteenth-century workplace organization. As long as capitalists continued to take for granted that the workers' craft organizations would retain control of the details of the labor process, they were forced to depend on the voluntary cooperation and active initiatives of these workers. Taylor recognized that capitalists had to conceive and implement an alternative organization of production. That clearly became the task of scientific management. The functions of scientific management experts were twofold. First, they were to enter the workplace to learn (through time and motion studies) what the *workers* already knew: how to plan and direct the details of the work process. Second, through managerial planning and analysis, Taylorites were to employ this newly gained knowledge to "efficiently" redesign the production process under *management* control.

Although Taylorism in the standard textbook is presented only as a stage in the scientific evolution of organization theory, its *real* contribution was less the development of scientific techniques for measuring work processes than the construction of a new mode of organizational control. In fact, according to Clawson, Taylor never conducted anything that approximated a scientific experiment. Thus, while Taylorism was able to show productivity increases, there is little basis for telling whether such increases resulted from *improved* work procedures or were obtained merely by speeding up the existing practices.

Scientific management's primary contribution to the work process was thus to wrest authority from the craft organization of the nineteenth century and to place it in the hands of a newly emerging profession of management. As a set of *practical* procedures for the shop floor, however, it was less than a success. Labor found fault with it for political reasons, while management troubled over its technical failures. From management's point of view, Taylorites had properly identified the issue of workplace authority, but, as Richard Edwards put it, they "had not found quite the right mechanism."[14] The human relations movement can be understood as the culmination of a series of interrelated attempts to find the "right mechanism." Early interest in human relations by industrialists can, in fact, be interpreted as a response to the upsurge of organized labor, significantly facilitated by hostilities toward Taylorism itself.

Hugo Munsterberg's industrial psychology was the earliest forerunner of the human relations movement. As father of the newly emerging discipline, Munsterberg couched his 1913 book, *Psychology and Industrial Efficiency,* in language borrowed from Taylor's *Principles of Scientific Management.* Writing at the height of national interest in scientific management, Munsterberg intended to elevate the study of human behavior to the same level of concern. The central focus of his book was to develop psychological techniques to identify the "best possible man" for the job.[15] Despite major opposition by many industrialists to psychological techniques, others began to recognize the need for the development of a "scientific personnel management" as a logical extension of Taylorism.

With the increasing pace of labor instability in the second decade of the century, particularly reflected in the problems of work stoppages, absenteeism, and turnover, this concern was expressed in the emergence of specialists to aid line managers in the selection and testing of workers as well as to perform other functions such as the administration of wages. The development of such specialists was one of the first steps in the widespread growth of the personnel department as a primary organizational function. Munsterberg's industrial psychology set the agenda, touching off study in vocational counseling and placement testing in both business and public administration.

Industrial psychology and the "personnel movement" received big pushes during both World War I and its aftermath. Facilitated by discussion between Munsterberg and government officials—including President Woodrow Wilson, as well as the secretaries of both commerce and labor—psychological techniques were widely put to use during the government's war efforts. Not only were soldiers tested and selected by psychological techniques, such methods were also extended to job analysis and problems of morale. After the war, facing the enormous task of making a transition to a peacetime economy, military and government psychologists were turned loose to work on the problem of industrial personnel. Psychological consulting developed into a thriving business.

During the same period another approach gave credibility to the importance of the human dimension of organization, or what came to be known as the "labor problem." Dubbed "welfare capitalism," it involved bribing workers with selected nonjob benefits to undercut the militance created by the oppressive, alienating conditions of factory work, especially those associated with the newly emerging system of assembly-line production.[16]

Henry Ford, the founder of "welfare capitalism," startled the industrial world in 1914 with the announcement of a bold and unprecedented program.[17] To both win the loyalty of his workers and spur productivity, Ford agreed to more than double hourly production wages. Ford's "welfare" scheme was, however, largely designed to undercut a growing labor crisis wrought by assembly-line techniques, which were introduced to the industrial world by Ford himself. While the assembly line dramatically increased the rate of production, it had the simultaneous effect of increasing the ranks of the unions, particularly the ranks of the militant Industrial Workers of the World (IWW) at the Ford plant.

Ford's pay increase solved his basic labor problem. Because the new wage scale was so much higher than prevailing wages, it enlarged the pool or labor from which the company could choose. Moreover, because workers were now anxious to hang on to their jobs, it was easier for the plant to increase the pace of production. But this was only the beginning. To further ensure labor tranquility, Ford required participating workers to submit to the ministrations of his "Sociological Department." Basically, this meant that workers agreed to permit one or more of the department's 100 investigators—or "advisors"—to inspect their homes for cleanliness, to monitor their drinking habits, to investigate their sex lives, and generally to ensure that their leisure time was used "properly."

Heralded as a success by the business community, Ford's experiment proved a point. If management would devote time, effort, and a little money to the consideration of the human element of business, production and profits would rise. It was at least equivalent to the introduction of better machinery.

The lesson was not wasted on the larger community. Organizations of prominent industrialists (such as the National Civic Federation) incorporated "welfare capitalism" into their strategies for "harmonizing" the interests of labor and capital. Designed to combat a combination of tight labor markets and socialist union militance (both of which threatened military production in the coming world war), the capitalist welfare program "represented a sophisticated, well-financed, and widely implemented plan for controlling labor."[18] It continued well into the mid-1920s.

Closely related to the idea of welfare capitalism was the concept of the "company union." The chief stimuli for company unions were the labor settlements negotiated during the war. While army psychologists were busy developing techniques for selection and control, the government mandated companies to introduce "work councils" or "plans of representation" in the hope of stemming the dramatic rise of labor militance threatening to cripple military production. After the United States entered the war, President Wilson established the War Labor Board and a new labor policy mandating worker council participation in labor-management arbitration. In exchange for peace, specifically a moratorium on strikes, labor was guaranteed the right to organize and bargain collectively through the representation plan.[19]

However, the policy had a loophole. Because the law was vague on the type of labor organization permitted by the War Labor Board, big companies turned eagerly to a new experiment, the "company union." To meet the War Labor Board's requirement for a "work council" or "plan of representation," many large corporations quickly set up their own company-controlled unions before real unions could be established.

The idea of a company union was simple: establish a formal grievance procedure within the context of rigorously defined limits. Given a channel for expression of legitimate grievances, "loyal" workers would not be driven to join a labor union. As such, these channels represented a substantial roadblock to independent unions as well as extensive possibilities for company propaganda. The administration of the company plan became an important function of newly emerging personnel departments.

During the war the government's War Industry Board set up special procedures to facilitate and promote the training of "employment managers," often essential for the administration of the company union. In all plants manufacturing munitions, war supplies, and ships, the government mandated the existence of a personnel department. Although "labor administration" had begun to slowly emerge before the war, the managerial requirements generated by the war were the primary catalyst behind the full-scale appearance of personnel departments. This functions included recruiting, testing, selection, training, discipline, grievance procedures, research, company unions, and welfare provisions. One writer estimates that over 200 departments were added during this period.[20]

Although the company council and the personnel department were too transparent to stifle the intense workplace conflicts of the depression era, they were highly effective in delaying unionism during the postwar decade. Furthermore, they offered valuable lessons that advanced the human relations movement, the most important of which was the legacy of the grievance procedure. Corporate capitalists came to realize that formal grievance appeals procedures were actually quite useful. Rather than a threat to management prerogatives, they could be used to protect management's authority. Not only did they permit the company to redress individual grievances at little cost, such procedures also focused attention on individual cases rather than on company policy itself. Often this prevented grievances from festering into union militance.

From these activities—psychological testing, personnel administration, welfare capitalism, and company unions—emerged a growing recognition of the value of the human element, particularly in regard to the use of grievance procedures and the supervision of workers' needs. Yet these practical techniques were not provided with theoretical underpinnings until the final development that cinched the success of the human-relations movement: the Hawthorne experiments and the writings of Elton Mayo.

The Hawthorne studies, usually posited as the starting point for the human-relations tradition in conventional theory, were initiated and publicly financed by the congressionally chartered National Research Council of the National Academy of Sciences.[21] At the outset, the project began as an experiment in scientific management at the Western Electric Company near Chicago, a plant well known for its opposition to organized labor. The purpose of the Hawthorne experiments was to determine the effects of lighting on work performance.

To summarize a lengthy and complex set of investigations, the light experiments were conducted on two groups of women. One group was placed in a test room where the intensity of illumination was varied, and the other group worked in a control room with a supposedly constant environment. The investigation was to determine the specific conditions governing work efficiency.

The results were baffling to the researchers: Productivity increased in both rooms. The predicted correlations between lighting and output in the test room were thus undermined. In fact, to the astonishment of the investigators, the production of the women in the test room continually increased whether the lighting level was raised, was retained at the original level, or even was reduced so low that the workers could barely see. Obviously, some variables in the research were not being held constant under experimental controls. Something aside from the level of illumination was causing the change in productivity.

That something turned out to be the "human" variable. After additional experiments, Elton Mayo theorized that the variations were a function of the changing "mental attitude" of the group. The women in the test room of the experiment, as it turned out, had formed an "informal" social groups that enjoyed the attention of the supervisors and developed a sense of participation in the project. Believing that they had been specially chosen to participate in an important experiment, the women in the test group informally banded together to provide the researchers with their best performance, even in the face of worsening physical conditions.

From all the theories about the Hawthorne studies, the most important finding for management has been recognition of the *supervisory* climate. Mayo hypothesized that the experiments, having taken an interest in the workers, had assumed the role of de facto supervisors. This led to a second series of studies designed to examine the effects of supervision. Largely under the direction of a Harvard research team headed by Fritz Roethlisberger and William Dickson, these experiments initiated an "interviewing program" to further explore the connection between morale and supervision.

With the aim to improve supervisory techniques, the researchers sought to reeducate shop-floor supervisors by teaching them to play the role accidentally assumed by the experimenters in the original light studies. During this second phase, counselors were appointed to the various departments under investigation. No educational or professional experience was required, though the company gave them in-plant training. The principal requirement for counselors was that they be well likely by the people in the department. The counselor's function was to deal with the workers' *attitudes* toward their problems, but not the problems themselves. As Loren Baritz explained, "Regardless of all the technical gobbledygook that has been written about the function of the counselor, it all simmers down to a plain injunction that he was to listen to any problem of any employee, good worker or not; that he was not to give advice or argue; and that he should make no promises about remedial action."[22]

In short, the counselor, who was not to be guided by a problem- or efficiency-oriented approach, was just to listen to the employee. According to a Western Electric publication, the counselor "was to watch constantly for signs of unrest and to try to assuage the tension of the worker by discussion before the unrest became active." Counselors were to try to dilute or redirect dissatisfaction by helping the employees to think along "constructive lines." Through this process of adjusting people to situations, rather than situations to people, management hoped that absenteeism, low production, high turnover, grievances, and militant unionism could be reduced, if not avoided.

In addition, the company hoped to achieve a secondary benefit from the counseling program. One of the major themes throughout its interest in the role of counseling, as Baritz stated, "was that a well-trained counselor would be a likely candidate for promotion to a supervisory position, and it was thus hoped that counseling would . . . provide a recruitment pool for managerial positions."[23] In short, the counseling program could serve as a managerial screening device.

The Hawthorne studies probably remain the most widely analyzed and discussed experiments in the history of the social sciences. Many have criticized the findings for methodological errors; writers such as Alex Carey have argued that no valid generalizations emerged from the experiments, while others such as Paul Blumberg maintain that the Harvard researchers failed to see the real implications of their experiments.[24] As Donald Wren points out, however, most of the complaints have generally missed the overarching implications of the study: Regardless of their validity, the experiments opened up "new vistas" for supervision. Management could train supervisors to establish a harmonious work climate, free of idiosyncratic, personal authority.[25] This link between supervision, morale, and productivity became the foundation of academic human relations theory.

For Mayo, the Hawthorne studies offered nothing less than a foundation for a new *political* vision of industrial civilization. Basic to his philosophy was the view that twentieth-century industrial institutions were organized for conflict rather than cooperation. Class politics under capitalism, as he saw it, was nothing more than a "confused struggle of pressure groups [and] power blocs." In his own conception of the ideal community, small cooperative social groupings would replace the need for community.

Mayo maintained that the cooperation of individuals and groups is the supreme principle of the ideal community. Cooperation, he wrote, is a "balanced relation between various parts of the organization, so that the avowed purpose for which the whole exists [defined as the 'common interest'] may be conveniently and continuously fulfilled." Where there are different groups interests, even certain inevitable conflicts, their elimination is merely a matter of "intelligent organization that takes careful account of all the group interests involved."[26]

Much of Mayo's political and social theorizing was based on a "psychopathological" analysis of industrial life. Essentially, he argued that workers tend to be motivated by emotions and generalized feelings, while management acts on the basis of logic and rationality. Unable to find satisfactory outlets for the expression of personal dissatisfactions in their work lives, workers became preoccupied with latent "pessimistic reveries," which are manifestly expressed as an apprehension of authority, restriction of output, and a variety of other forms of behavior that reduce morale and output. According to Mayo, industrial society, as presently organized, leads to the social maladjustment of workers and eventually to obsessively irrational behavior, including the formation of adversarial unions.

For Mayo, social class conflict is thus a "deviation" from the normal state of human actions and attitudes. For instance, he argued that "Marx detested 'the bourgeoisie' on grounds that will someday probably be shown to have been personal." Similarly, he described labor leaders as psychological deviates: "These men had no friends. . . . They had no capacity for conversation. . . . They regarded the world as a hostile place. . . . In every instance the personal history was one of social privation—a childhood devoid of normal and happy association in work and play with other children."[27]

Class conflict was, therefore, little more than a primitive expression of human imperfections. In Mayo's ideal community there would be no need for political confrontations between labor and capital: "Where cooperation is maintained between the individual and his group, the group and the union, the union and management, the personal sense of security and absence of discontent in the individual run high."[28]

The remedy for class conflict is the proper application of psychological techniques. The objective is to eliminate class tensions through the development of "social skills" education. With the proper introduction of human relations oriented supervisors and psychological counselors, workers' desires for recognition, security, and the expression of grievances would be adequately fulfilled, obviating the need for union representation altogether.

For Mayo, as well as later Mayoists, the obligation for cooperation always remains in the hands of the management.[29] As the embodiment of logic and rationality, management always knows best. Its interests are thus presented as synonymous with the interests of the organization and society as a whole. For this reason, according to Baritz, Mayo bothered to discuss the role of unions only twice in all his writings.

Given the implications of his theory, Mayo was eager to justify human relations research to corporate management. From his academic post at the Harvard Graduate School of Business, he sought to convince top management that he knew their problems, understood their needs, and sympathized with their goals. Human relations techniques were presented as a means for discovering the true causes of management's problems, which could be revealed by nondirective psychological skills training. As Baritz stated, "Management was encouraged and instructed to enter not only the intellectual, social, and financial lives of the workers, but through counseling, to expose their most personal thoughts and aspirations."[30] In short, management's problems were caused more by management's failure to convert the worker to its point of view than by labor's failure to understand the principles of cooperation.

Given the managerial basis of his theory, it did not take long for Mayo to find staunch supporters. By the 1940s his work was widely viewed as the theoretical successor to scientific management. In industry generally, as Peter Drucker and others have pointed out, the human relations philosophy was widely adopted as the creed of the modern personnel department.[31] By the 1950s groups such as the American Management Association asserted that human relations skills and supervisory training were the most important ingredients of good workplace management. Moreover, a quick look at the curriculum of any contemporary management program, not to mention industrial psychology departments, will attest to the enduring value of the conviction.

As the theoretical capstone of the human relations movement, Mayo's work succinctly expressed the culmination of a thirty-year search for the "right mechanism," from the rise of industrial psychology and personnel administration to the development of company unions and welfare capitalism. From the foregoing discussion, it is clear that Mayo's contribution was much more than an empirical step in the evolution of modern organization theory. Regardless of the experimental orientation of the Hawthorne studies, Mayo's most profound contribution was to lift the findings to the level of a managerial *ideology*.

Not only does human relations philosophy offer a justification for the dominance of management over labor, it also provides psychological techniques for blurring the realities of workplace control. As a managerial worldview, it posits the logical, "rational" authority of management over the "irrational," psychologically immature behavior of workers and their unions. Management is the agent of cooperation, while unions are the embodiment of social and political conflict.

In programmatic terms, human relations ideology masks a strategy to stabilize or legitimate managerial authority and domination. Through the manipulation of the organization's psychological climate, the purpose is to promote an atmosphere of attitude of loyalty to management. Although never stated formally, the specific objective is to blur the worker's consciousness of the general issues of power, authority, and class; particular unjust practices; and repression.[32] The union is depicted as an external interloper between the worker and management, and workers are socialized to accept a paternalistic conception of "management-knows-best." In psychological terms, management is portrayed as the all-knowing, benevolent father who offers guidance and protection to his children, the workers.

Finally, human relations theory, like ideologies in general, came to be accepted with more confidence than the evidence would warrant. This is attested to by the number of studies that have shown the Hawthorne experiments to be either unscientific or inconclusive at best. As Carey put it after his detailed study of the purported evidence, one wonders "how it is possible for studies so nearly devoid of scientific merit, and conclusions so little supported by the evidence, to gain so influential and respected a place within the scientific disciplines and to hold this place so long."[33]

The answer is found in the theory's ideological appeal, especially to those who have generally funded organizational research. No one has more succinctly expressed this appeal than Michael Rose. Describing Mayoism as the "twentieth century's most seductive managerial ideology," Rose has captured its appeal in these words: "What, after all, could be more appealing than to be told that one's subordinates are nonlogical; that their uncooperativeness is a frustrated urge to collaborate; that their demands for cash mark a need for your approval; and that you have a historic destiny as a broker of social harmony?"[34]

In 1949 the United Auto Workers' (UAW) monthly education magazine expressed the union's hostility to human relations: "The prophet is Elton Mayo, a Harvard University professor who has been prying into the psychiatric bowels of factory workers since around about 1925 and who is the Old Man of the movement." Further satirizing management's devotion to Mayoism, they continued:

> The Bible is the book, the Human Problems of an Industrial Civilization. The Holy Place is the Hawthorne Plant of the Western Electric Company (the wholly owned subsidiary of one of the nation's largest monopolies, the AT and T). At Hawthorne, Ma Bell, when she wasn't organizing company unions, allowed Professor Mayo to carry on experiments with a group of women workers for nine years.[35]

Criticizing Mayo's assertion that the women produced more because of the expressed interest the supervisors and psychologists took in their personal problems, they sarcastically concluded that his finding "is the greatest discovery since J. P. Morgan learned that you can increase profits by organizing a monopoly, suppressing competition, raising prices and reducing production." While the union's view offers little to refine our understanding of the human relations approach, it does help to convey the labor-management tensions that it was designed to address.

Beyond the UAW, however, the human relations school was greeted by labor with relative silence. Given the fact that human relations techniques were motivated by a desire to undercut the growth of unionism, it is surprising that they never elicited the full outcry that was accorded to Taylorism. In part, this was probably because psychological techniques are more subtle than the industrial engineer's stopwatch. The human relations approach, therefore, appears as a less explicit threat and in many quarters may have passed over the heads of union leaders. Another reason may be the fact that by the 1940s the leaders of organized labor had substantially moved toward a more conciliatory relationship with management. Unions, as a result of Gompers's legacy, concentrated on wage gains and left workplace authority to management.

Workplace Psychology Today

Before closing, it is interesting to offer a brief update on the use of human-relations techniques in the contemporary workplace. As might be anticipated, the movement is still very much alive today, although it is now dressed in a more sophisticated theoretical language.

By 1960 human relations theory was said to be on the wane. As modern organizational theory began to shift its emphasis to top-level managerial concerns, such as strategic planning and systems analysis, the human relations tradition was seemingly relegated to a story in the history of organization theory. To the degree that its contribution lived on, it was subsumed under specialized areas of industrial and personnel psychology.

During the 1970s, however, when recessionary conditions began to put new pressures on corporate profit margins, management unleashed the most explicit offensive against trade unions since the 1930s. In the process, the concerns of human relations practitioners began to resurface on the managerial agenda. Sometimes called the "new industrial relations," the offensive has essentially taken two principal forms, one quite sophisticated and the other rather crude. Respectively, they have involved the development of Quality of Work Life (QWL) programs and a new type of management consulting aimed explicitly at union busting. Both are easily recognized as carrying forward the basic objectives that motivated the earlier human relations movement. Here, in the closing section of this chapter, we point to a few of the basic aspects of these two developments.

First, we turn to QWL programs, which have grown dramatically in the U.S. workplace in recent years. Most major corporate employers in the United States now have established some form of program that falls under the QWL rubric. They have also grown quite rapidly in the public sector. In 1983, for example, the secretary of the International Association of Quality Circles estimated that over 135,000 QWL circles operated at 8,000 locations in the United States, involving approximately 1 million workers.

There are a number of good things that can be said about QWL programs. Compared with earlier human relations approaches, they are based on a much broader understanding of the workers' relationship to organizations and jobs. QWL programs, in this respect, are built upon a number of important advances in organizational psychology, particularly those identified with "human-resources psychology." The human-resources approach, grounded in the theories of Douglas McGregor and

Frederick Herzberg, among others, has focused primarily on the task of "job enrichment." Perhaps the most important aspect of this work has been the recognition that at times it may be the organization—not the individual—that needs to be changed.

Moreover, in recent years QWL programs have incorporated innovative techniques from other social and cultural contexts. Especially significant has been the appropriation of "quality circle" concepts and techniques from the Japanese. Quality-circle programs, often credited with boosting Japan's rate of industrial productivity, are basically a set of methods designed to turn workers into organizational problem solvers. In many places in the United States QWL programs have, in fact, become synonymous with quality circles.

In it essential, however, to see QWL programs in the political-economic context that gave rise to their wide-scale adoption. While much of the popular discussion of these programs emphasizes the role of modern psychological theories, the reason for the dramatic growth of QWL programs can be traced to the economic crisis of the late 1970s. Here, of course, it is impossible to discuss these economic difficulties in any detail. Suffice it to say that aggressive competition from foreign producers began to make clear the fact that the unilateral rule of the world economy by U.S. corporations was coming to an end. Indeed, the situation began to raise questions about the general health of the American economy. Much of the discussion has centered on industry's declining rate of productivity, especially when compared with that of Japan. In particular, this posed serious questions about U.S. labor-management practices. Many of the corporation's critics argued that productivity had fallen because of rigid managerial structures, often responsible for worker apathy and alienation. Corporate leaders also focused on worker apathy but largely blamed the presence of unions in the workplace. Both groups, however, sought a solution through the "new industrial relations." For many concerned with worker apathy, it offered a new set of techniques for reviving worker motivation. For those who pointed to the unions, it was seen as a new opportunity for reasserting management's social control of the workplace.[36]

The result has been the dramatic growth of QWL programs, and many of the experiences with these schemes have been remarkably similar to those associated with the earlier human relations programs. Corporations rapidly hired human-resources specialists to hurriedly put these new programs in place at the same time that they launched a major attack on the unions. Typically, this took the form of demanding major contract concessions in the name of declining growth and productivity. In place of the cutbacks, corporate managers offered Quality of Work Life programs.

Many QWL programs were put into place so quickly that they caught many people—including union leaders—off guard. Structures, guidelines, and training were seldom worked out in advance. Lip service was initially paid to the idea that QWL programs were for job satisfaction, but, as Parker points out, this was largely to mollify workers and unions who objected.[37] Later, after programs were well established, many companies openly declared increasing productivity and economic competitiveness to be the goal of QWL programs. By the 1980s little was heard about job enrichment per se. Today it is significant only insofar as it leads to well-defined productivity gains.

Union leaders, despite the fact that they are primary targets of QWL programs, have seldom been openly hostile to these programs. High levels of unemployment and dwindling union membership put union leaders and their staffs on the defensive. Under these conditions, unions have had very little influence over the shape of the programs. This, of course, was clearly an important component of the corporate strategy.

There is an unmistakable déjà vu associated with these QWL programs. For many corporate leaders, it is clearly a second opportunity to shape the human side of work for their own political advantages. The strategy is more sophisticated but the basic objective differs very little from that of human-relations theory. Essentially, the tactic is to get workers involved in the production process. As one consultant put it: The goal is to get workers to think and act like managers without, at the same time, sharing managerial power. Basic to the approach is an attempt to blur the conflicts between labor and management. The hidden message, as another consultant puts it, is that "we're all in it together." Unions may have been necessary in an earlier period, but the times have changed. In short, leave the union and join the "corporate family."

Finally, we turn to the new breed of management consultants explicitly engaged in a much more obvious form of union busting. Like human-resource psychologists, these new consultants purport to specialize in the application of updated human relations techniques. But unlike human-resource psychologists, who generally stand behind the guise of disinterested science, these "human relations consultants" are much more politically explicit in their efforts to assist management in tightening administrative control. In significant part, they have done this by wedding specific techniques of behavioral psychology to the classical political problems of industrial relations. The result has been the growth of a small industry devoted to the techniques of employee manipulation and union busting. It is estimated by labor sources that they are presently assisting management to oppose about two-thirds of all union organizing drives, including efforts in both the private and the public sectors.

As in the Mayoist tradition, their approach is grounded in a basic ideological opposition to the labor movement. Emphasizing a new vision of "humanistic" workplace relations, introduced by an "enlightened" and "benevolent" management, the new approach focuses on eliminating conflict between workers and management by good communications and improved supervision. Through a variety of techniques designed to socialize and "indoctrinate" workers to management's point of view, particularly during union-organizing drives, these specialists (like their predecessors) often establish the informal group as the central focus of their assault.

According to these consultants, up to 90 percent of all organizing drives are initiated by informal employee groups rather than by union organizers. Recognizing that unionization is the product of troubles that first find expression in the organization's informal groups, such modern-day consultants are quick to advise management on the merits of an internal grievance process to undercut such channels of communication. As with the earlier human relations movement, the purpose is to isolate and stifle dissatisfaction before it festers to the widespread dissent that fosters unionization.[38]

Only in recent years have unions begun to take steps to counter the union-busting firms. For instance, union charges that such consultants are abusing the nation's labor laws has prompted the House Education and Labor Committee's subcommittee on labor-management relations to conduct hearings that linked such consultants to unfair labor practices and union busting.[39]

Concluding Perspectives

Max Horkheimer wrote that "the surface appearance or even the thesis of a doctrine rarely offers a clue to the role it plays in society."[40] The developments presented here clearly show that organization theory can be offered as evidence to substantiate his premise. In sharp contrast to an objective science of organizational behavior, what emerges from the history of organizational psychology is a picture of ideological corruption. Both wittingly and unwittingly, organizational psychology has evolved into a tool of manipulation and control in the ongoing struggle for command of the workplace.

The example of human relations theory thus demonstrates the need for a *political* theory of organizational science. Though the articulation of such a theory is beyond the scope of the present chapter, from the foregoing analysis it is nonetheless possible to specify a number of factors that must be included in such a theory. Consider, for example, the relationship between organizational expertise and class politics.

An adequate theory of the role of organizational expertise must begin with the premise that knowledge has become a critical resource in the politics of class struggle, both inside and outside the workplace. In an age of bureaucratic organizations, characterized by hierarchy and functional compartmentalization, the very premises that determine political consciousness and class conflict are significantly shaped by the control of knowledge and information. Therefore, political scientists and sociologists must examine organizational psychology not only for its contribution to work processes but also for its critical force in shaping the political attitudes and actions of the working classes.

Second, in the elaboration of such a theory, one must recognize the complexity of the role of organizational expertise in the larger class struggle between capital and labor.[41] Men like Mayo were more than "tools" of capitalist power. While human relations psychology, like scientific management, has helped to mitigate the capitalists' conflicts with labor, it must be perceived as the commodity of a *new* class vying for position in the evolving world of bureaucratic capitalism.

Here we can benefit from Stark's analysis of scientific management.[42] Like scientific management, human relations theory must be understood as an emergent ideology of organizational psychologists bent upon earning a niche for themselves in the structures of modern industrial society. Positioned between capital and labor, they have sought the basis for a new professional recognition and autonomy by mediating class conflict. In this regard, Baritz, too, has shown that industrial and human-relations psychologists required little prodding by the leaders of industry and government. Like the industrial engineers before them, they sought to legitimate themselves as members of a new professional-managerial strata. The justification for the role was to be provided by the experimental knowledge of human relations research developed by the industrial and organizational psychology community. Appeals to the "objective" laws of human behavior provided the basic ideological underpinnings for the psychologist's autonomy; psychological measurement offered the necessary data for display of their expertise; and the newly developed departments of personnel administration established an organizational base of operations.

Finally, a few comments should be made about the role of government. From the foregoing discussion, it is clear that the federal government has consistently sponsored the development of managerially biased organizational techniques. Thus the focus of labor-relations policy should be extended beyond its primary emphasis on collective bargaining to include government's role in shaping specific workplace practices. Like the scientific-management approach introduced at the government's Watertown Arsenal, the major strides in the development of industrial psychology, personnel management, and company unions were facilitated by the government's war efforts and later through public financing, as exemplified by the Hawthorne studies. Today, the research offices of the federal government, particularly those of the army and navy, remain among the most significant financial contributors to organizational research.

Consideration of these various elements leads to the following conclusion: If organization theory is to contribute to the construction of a socially just society, it must more directly confront the political motivations that shape its uses. In the realm of practice, social scientists must begin with the understanding that theory does not directly dictate practice. Unable to control the implications of their own words, they must recognize that even the most humanistic techniques can be employed to further unjust ends. Only with such caveats clearly in mind can organizational theorists realistically hope to address the need for legitimate practical reforms.

Notes

1. The distinction between the social and the behavioral sciences is largely a matter of professional convention. In large part, the term *behavioral science* was introduced to refer to those disciplines that strive for a rigorous, objectively detached, empirical orientation, in contrast to the "softer," more value-laden, and less scientific disciplines. For instance, political science is typically designated as a social science while psychology is considered to be a behavioral science. It has been argued that the distinction was contrived in part to dissociate specific disciplines and approaches from the more contentious and controversial concerns typically surrounding the social sciences, thus increasing their social respectability. On the ideological role of these sciences, see, for example, Robin Blackburn, ed., *Ideology in Social Science* (London: Fontana, 1972).

2. On the critique of "value-neutrality," see Frank Fischer, *Politics, Values, and Public Policy: The Problem of Methodology* (Boulder, Colo.: Westview, 1980). For an attempt to locate an interest in sociotechnical control in social-science methodology, see Herbert Marcuse, *One-Dimensional Man* (Boston: Beacon, 1964).

3. Paul Goldman, "Sociologists and the Study of Bureaucracy: A Critique of Ideology and Practice," *The Insurgent Sociologist* 3 (Winter 1978): 21.

4. Alasdair MacIntyre, "Social Science Methodology as the Ideology of Bureaucratic Authority," in *Through the Looking-Glass,* ed. Maria J. Falco (Washington, D.C.: University Press of America, 1979), 42.

5. Daniel Bell, "The End of Ideology in the West," in *The End of Ideology Debate,* ed. Chaim I. Waxman (New York: Funk and Wagnalls, 1968), 88, 96.

6. Jürgen Habermas, *Toward a Rational Society* (Boston: Beacon, 1970).

7. Reinhard Bendix, *Work and Authority in Industry* (New York: John Wiley, 1956), xxiii; Michael E. Urban, "Bureaucracy, Contradiction, and Ideology in Two Societies," *Administration and Society* 10, no. 1 (May 1978): 49–85.

8. Max Weber, *The Theory of Economic and Social Organization* (New York: Oxford University Press, 1947).

9. Bendix, *Work and Authority in Industry,* 13.

10. Nancy DiTomaso, "The Organization of Authority in the Capitalist State," *Journal of Political and Military Sociology* 6 (Fall 1978): 189–204.

11. William G. Scott, "Organization Theory: An Overview and Appraisal," *Organizations,* ed. Joseph A. Litterer (New York: John Wiley, 1969), 15–29.

12. Ibid., 20.

13. Harry Braverman, *Labor and Monopoly Capital* (New York: Monthly Review Press, 1974); Dan Clawson, *Bureaucracy and the Labor Process* (New York: Monthly Review Press, 1980), 47.

14. Richard Edwards, *Contested Terrain* (New York: Basic Books, 1979), 104.

15. Donald A. Wren, *The Evolution of Management Thought* (New York: Ronald Press, 1972), 195–208.

16. Stuart Brandeis, *American Welfare Capitalism, 1880–1940* (Chicago: University of Chicago Press, 1976).

17. Loren Baritz, *The Servants of Power: A History of the Use of Social Science in American Industry* (Middletown, Conn.: Wesleyan University Press, 1960), 32–35; Braverman, *Labor and Monopoly Capital,* 149.

18. Edwards, *Contested Terrain,* 95.

19. Ibid., 105–10.

20. Henry Eilburt, "The Development of Personnel Management in the United States," *Business History Review* 33 (Autumn 1959): 345–64.

21. Baritz, *Servants of Power,* 76–116; Wren, *Evolution of Management Thought,* 275–99.

22. Baritz, *Servants of Power,* 105.

23. Ibid.

24. Alex Carey, "The Hawthorne Studies: A Radical Criticism," *American Sociological Review* 32 (June 1974): 403–16; Paul Blumberg, *Industrial Democracy* (New York: Schocken, 1976), 14–46; A. J. M. Sykes, "Economic Interest and the Hawthorne Researchers," *Human Relations* 18 (August 1965): 253–63.

25. Wren, *Evolution of Management Thought,* chaps. 13 and 14.

26. Elton Mayo, *The Social Problems of an Industrial Civilization* (London: Routledge, 1949), 128; Mayo, *The Political Problems of Industrial Civilization* (Cambridge, Mass.: Harvard University Printing Office, 1947).

27. Mayo, *The Social Problems of an Industrial Civilization,* 24; Baritz, *Servants of Power.*

28. Mayo, *The Social Problems of an Industrial Civilization,* 111.

29. For a good illustration of the anti-trade-union interpretation of the Hawthorne findings, see T. North Whitehead, *Leadership in a Free Society* (Cambridge, Mass.: Harvard University Press, 1936), 155.

30. Baritz, *Servants of Power,* 115.

31. Peter Drucker, *The Practice of Management* (New York: Harper & Row, 1954), 273–88.

32. For a discussion of how the vocabulary of human relations experts blurs the facts of organizational power, see C. Wright Mills, "The Contributions of Sociology to Studies of Industrial Relations," *Proceedings of the First Annual Meeting of the Industrial Relations Association* (1948), 212–13.

33. Carey, "Hawthorne Studies," 403.

34. Michael Rose, *Industrial Behaviour; Theoretical Development since Taylor* (London: Allen Lane, 1975), 124.

35. Quoted by Baritz, *Servants of Power,* 11–15.

36. Guillermo J. Grenier, *Inhuman Relations: Quality Circles and Anti-Unionism in American Industry* (Philadelphia: Temple University Press, 1988).

37. Mike Parker, *Inside the Circle* (Boston: South End Press, 1985).

38. See, for example, Steve Lagerfeld, "The Pop Psychologist as Union Buster," *American Federationist,* November 1981, pp. 6–12; Damon Stetson, "New Kind of Law Firm Keeping Labor at Bay," *New York Times,* 25 October 1981, p. 53.

39. Committee on Education and Labor, House of Representatives Oversight Hearings Before the Subcommittee on Labor-Management Relations, 96th Congress, 1st session, *Pressures in Today's Workplace,* 4 vols. (Washington, D.C.: Government Printing Office, 1979).

40. Max Horkheimer, *The Eclipse of Reason* (New York: Oxford University Press, 1947), 85.

41. For an illustration of a Marxist attempt to explain organizational psychology in terms of the larger class struggle between capital and labor, see Walter R. Nord, "The Failure of Current Applied Behavioral Science—A Marxian Perspective," *Journal of Applied Behavioral Science* 10, no. 4 (October, November, December 1974): 557–78.

42. David Stark, "Class Struggle and the Transformation of the Labor Process: A Relational Approach," *Theory and Society* 9 (January 1980): 102.

13
Reproducing Hierarchy: Job Evaluation and Comparable Worth in State Government

Joan Acker

With the hiring of Hay Associates the state of Oregon purchased a complete job-evaluation system based on "traditional organizational designs." According to one member of the Hay team, "The Guide Charts were developed over time by working with a number of different managers in different organizations. The Guide Charts represent a composite of the value systems of managers from various organizations. They are reflective of traditional organizational designs" (Task Force Minutes, 25 April 1984:8). Traditional organizational designs emerged with the development of the large corporation and the search for better ways, more scientific ways, to manage production, as any history of management or of organizational theory attests (see, for example, Clegg and Dunkerley, 1980; Mouzelis, 1967). These designs are intended to provide control over work and workers; they can be seen as instruments used by capital in the continuing conflict between classes (Edwards, 1979).[1] Thus, in the job-evaluation stage, the project moved to an arena already defined in management terms.

The focus was on technical work during this phase of the project, and much of it went on with little public conflict. The crux of doing good comparable worth, many of us thought, was in producing unbiased, sex-neutral job evaluations. To that end, project participants were committed to doing the best technical work possible, and this required cooperation. Backstage, in the continuing discussions of other issues such as control of the project, collective bargaining, and how a new classification system would be structured, class and gender tensions were alive. These could be detected in meetings of the steering committee, in meetings between management and union representatives, and in rum-

---

From Joan Acker, *Doing Comparable Worth: Gender, Class, and Pay Equity* (Philadelphia: Temple University Press, 1989), ch. 3.

blings from state agencies and male employees questioning the aims and the justification for all this work.

Some technical issues did, however, become major open political arguments, focused on the questionnaire, the relative weighting of factors, the definition of factors, and the evaluation process itself. As could be expected, management and consultants tended to side together against Task Force feminists. These conflicts revealed how deeply embedded are both gender and class inequalities in organizational hierarchies. Observations of the job-evaluation process also revealed how job evaluation reproduces hierarchy, a feature of organizational structure that was, with a minor and unsuccessful exception, unchallenged by any project participant. I argue, as do Hay consultants, that the central accomplishment of job evaluation is the recreation of an acceptable hierarchy, a believable system of inequality.[2] The meaning of *acceptable* and *believable* is discussed below. Such a legitimate system of inequality can tolerate the raising of some wages, but the demands of hierarchy also limit the degree to which this method can reduce the wage gap between women and men.

In this chapter I discuss in some detail the process of job evaluation and how it structured a somewhat revised system of inequality. Although the material is detailed, even technical, it is important to an understanding of comparable worth and of the intertwining of class and gender. The Hay system and similar ones, such as the Willis system, have been used in a number of successful comparable-worth efforts: Hay in Minnesota and San Jose, Willis in the state of Washington. Although they tend to reproduce a traditional hierarchy and can be accused of gender bias, these job-evaluation methods still usually show that female-dominated jobs are paid less than male-dominated jobs with similar scores. Detailed knowledge about how these systems work can provide a basis for developing evaluation schemes that better reflect the content of women's jobs. Moreover, knowledge about the internal structure of job-evaluation instruments and the process of their use can reveal ideology and image that help to produce hierarchy and wage inequality in work organizations.

The work at this stage was complex, including developing a job-content questionnaire, reviewing and modifying the Hay Guide Charts, pretesting the questionnaire and the Guide Charts, training state employees to fill out the questionnaire, distributing and collecting the questionnaires, analyzing the questionnaires and writing job descriptions, selecting and training job-evaluation teams, carrying out the job evaluations, and assessing their quality. All of this was accomplished in nine months, and by the end of August 1984, 32,000 state employees, filling every position included in the study, had completed questionnaires, and evaluations of 350 benchmark job groups had been carried out. Other parts of the project were overlapping, and the grouping of jobs was part of the later classification work as well as a preparation for job evaluation.

The Hay Guide Chart–Profile Method of Job Evaluation

The development of elaborate bureaucratic systems, including personnel departments, job descriptions, and job evaluation, began before World War II. It accelerated during and after the war as a consequence of government regulations that required certain kinds of accounting about employees, and of the rapid development of a profession of personnel experts that actively promoted its products, as well as of an interest in control of labor (Baron, Dobbin, and Jennings, 1986). The Hay Guide Chart–Profile Method of Job Evaluation was a particularly successful part of this development. According to Oregon consultants and published descriptions (McAdams, 1974; Treiman, 1979; Bellak, 1982; Farnquist, Armstrong, and Strausbaugh, 1983), the Hay method developed over many years beginning in the 1940s, in an inductive process aimed at helping employers to establish equity within their firms.[3] Working with Hay consultants, employers identified the factors most important to them in jobs within their organizations. These were the knowledge required by the job, the thinking required to solve the problems the job faces, and the responsibility assigned to the job. Jobs could be ranked on these factors. Later, a system for determining the distance between ranks was worked out, and the whole complex of decisions on the factors was put into Guide Chart form (Barker, 1986; Bellak, 1982).

This system "is used by more than 4,000 profit and nonprofit organizations in some thirty countries with Western or westernized cultures" (Bellak, 1982:1; Bureau of National Affairs, 1984). For example, a 1976 survey of British employers found that 79 percent used job evaluation. The Hay Guide Chart–Profile method was the most frequently used specific scheme (Thakur and Gill, 1976:18). The International Labour Office (1986:107) reported that the Hay method was used to evaluate technical, professional, and managerial jobs in two-fifths of U.S. enterprises. Without doubt, this is an important tool for rationalizing managerial judgments about work positions. As Hay consultants emphasize, this method focuses on characteristics of the job, not on characteristics of the job holder, such as education, skill, or pay. Thus it is a system for constructing a structure of empty place and, in that sense, could be seen as defining the locations in the internal stratification of a class structure.

It is not surprising that the Hay method, as a management technology originally devised to produce a consistent ranking of jobs, builds hierarchy into the charts. As Treiman notes (1979), this hierarchy is also the managerial hierarchy. The managerial slant of the Guide Charts (Barker, 1986) worried Task Force feminists because, given that few women are in upper managerial positions, a weighting toward managerial tasks would underemphasize other—and more female—functions.

An examination of the structure of the factors shows in detail how this occurs.

The Guide Charts are matrices that measure components of each major factor. There is a separate chart for each factor, Know-How, Problem Solving, Accountability, and Working Conditions. Each major factor has subfactors, so that a total of eleven decisions must be made about each job (Table 13–1). Each level of each component is defined in generic language and in language specific to a particular employer. The evaluation process starts with qualitative decisions about, for example, the amount of technical knowledge, managerial knowledge, and human-relations skills involved in a job. These qualitative decisions come together to indicate the particular, quantitative location of the job within the Know-How matrix. Similar judgments are made for the other factors, and the scores on the three factors are summed. Working conditions are scored and added, particularly when blue-collar jobs are among those being evaluated.

Know-How is composed of (1) practical procedures, specialized techniques, and knowledge necessary to perform the job, (2) managerial knowledge needed to integrate and harmonize diversified functions, and (3) human-relations skills, "active, practicing person-to-person skills" (Bellak, 1982:1). Eight levels of knowledge are arrayed along the left

Table 13–1
Job-Evaluation Factors, Hay Guide Chart–Profile Method

1. Know-How—Knowledge and skills, however gained
    Technical
    Managerial
    Human Relations*
2. Problem Solving—Complexity and autonomy of problems
    Thinking Environment (autonomy)
    Thinking Challenge (complexity)
3. Accountability—Levels of responsibility for outcomes
    Freedom to Act
    Impact—how directly the job affects organizational goals
    Magnitude in budgetary or program impact terms
4. Working Conditions†
    Hazardous working conditions
    Physical effort
    Physical environment

*Oregon modifications to Human Relations Skills and Knowledge: four levels instead of three.

†Oregon modifications to Working Conditions:
  Sensory effort, such as having to pay close attention to electronic monitoring devices, added to physical effort.
  Work Demands subcategory added:
    Time Demands—extreme time pressures in job
    Role Loading—conflicting and contradictory expectations
    Emotion Loading—heavy involvement with people who are violent, disoriented, psychotic, or responsibility for action in extreme, life-threatening situations.

side of the chart, while four levels of managerial skills are along the top. Human-relations skills are arrayed as subscales to Managerial Know-How, with—in most Hay Charts—three levels of Human Relations within each Managerial level.

Technical knowledge and skill potentially contributes the most points to the Know-How score. This includes knowledge about things, people, and management. Managerial Know-How is the application of the managerial knowledge already scaled under Technical Know-How; it is measured primarily by the diversity of functions to be integrated. For example, the hospital manager responsible for personnel, billing, and supply would have to integrate more functions than the manager in charge of only one of those departments. Managerial Know-How often parallels hierarchical position. Human Relations skills add the smallest number of points to the total Know-How score. The three levels of Human Relations skills start with a basic level where common courtesy is needed for normal contacts and providing information. At the next level such skills are important for understanding, influencing, or serving people and causing action or understanding. At the third level such skills are critical for successful job performance. Taken as a whole, the Know-How chart emphasizes managerial skills and knowledge and thus favors male-dominated jobs.

The numbering system is complex. Numbers in the charts rise by 15-percent increments as complexity increases. Each cell in the matrix contains three numbers. In using the charts to evaluate a job, one first determines the appropriate cell then identifies the appropriate number within the cell. Both Technical and Managerial Know-How judgments are more significant than Human Relations judgments for arriving at the Know-How factor score. A change in judgment on Technical or Managerial Know-How from one cell to another changes a score by 32 percent, whereas movement from one cell to another on a Human Relations judgment alters the score by only 15 percent. Thus, a dimension that may have particular importance in female-dominated jobs has the least possibility of adding points in the basic structure of the charts. Other problems with Human Relations are discussed below.

The second factor, Problem Solving, is scored as a percentage of Know-How because it is defined as an application of Know How: "You think with what you know" (Bellak, 1982:1). Problem Solving has two dimensions, Thinking Environment and Thinking Challenge. Thinking Environment is defined as "freedom to think," the degree to which the job allows or requires independent problem solving. The scale goes from little freedom, jobs that are constrained by strict rules and procedures, to a great deal of freedom, jobs that are not even constrained by the most general organizational policies and goals. The levels seem to rise in parallel with usual organizational hierarchies.

Thinking Challenge refers to the degree of complexity in the problems to be solved. Complexity rises from simple jobs with a few delineated tasks to highly complex jobs. Again, the procedure is to choose a cell in the matrix and a number, in this case, a percentage, within the chosen cell. Two percentages are presented in each cell, giving evaluators a chance to carefully modulate their estimate of the problem-solving complexity demanded by the job.

Accountability is the third factor. It measures the "effect of the job on end results of the organization" (Bellak, 1982:3). Accountability is a more complex concept than responsibility. It has three subfactors. First, Freedom to Act refers to the extent of control the job has over its main goal. Second, Impact measures the "extent to which the job can directly affect actions necessary to produce results" (Bellak, 1982:3). Magnitude, the third subfactor, has to do with the proportion of the total organization affected by the primary emphasis of the job. Accountability is also presented in matrix form, and, as with Know-How, three separate judgments are necessary to locate a job within a cell of the matrix. A final judgment picks one of the three numbers in the cell. As with Know-How, both Problem Solving and Accountability replicate in their construction the hierarchy of most organizations.

Working Conditions is the final factor, added to the others where jobs to be evaluated have physical demands or environmental hazards.

Factor weighting in the Guide Charts is not immediately evident because of the complex structure of the charts.[4] That is, weights are embedded in the internal structure of the charts. Know-How appears to have the heaviest weight. However, in different jobs factors may be weighted differently. Most obviously, Problem Solving is a proportion of Know-How, but it is a varying proportion; consequently, the relative weights of the two factors vary. Some jobs are heavier on Accountability and some are heavier on Problem Solving. According to consultants, Know-How tends to have a heavier weight for lower-level jobs, with Problem Solving and Accountability contributing proportionately more to scores for higher-level jobs. When Working Conditions is used, it has a heavier weight and contributes more to the total score of lower-level than of higher-level jobs. Analyzing total Hay scores for 355 benchmark jobs in the Oregon study, Barker (1986:261) found that the average contribution of each factor to the total score was Know-How, 60.9 percent; Problem Solving, 17.3 percent; Accountability, 20.4 percent; and Working Conditions, 1.4 percent.

In sum, the structure of the Hay charts and the definition of factors is heavily weighted toward Technical and Managerial Know-How. These dimensions of the Know-How factor, both reflective of images of the male worker, whether a skilled craftsman, an engineer, or a manager, contribute the most to the Know How score. Know-How is counted again in the Problem Solving factor, which is calculated as a percentage of Know-How. Some elements in Accountability are closely related to knowledge and may actually be tapping the same dimension again. Each chart is arranged in a hierarchical manner, evoking images of bureaucratic structure. Images of class are also embedded in the Managerial dimension and in the Accountability factor. This was the system Task Force feminists wanted to alter.

Modifying the Guide Charts

Gender issues were uppermost in the minds of feminists involved as the Task Force and the Advisory Group discussed with Hay consultants modifications of their Guide Charts to better reflect the values "bias-free, sex-neutral." Task Force feminists had a heavy investment in achieving these modifications. One of the unique features of the Oregon project was that it was the first one in which consciously feminist values would be applied in the job-evaluation phase. As one Task Force member put it, "The critical aspect of the study, whether it is a success or a failure, will depend on whether bias can be eliminated" (Task Force meeting, 7 Dec. 1983).

Task Force feminists and their feminist constituency were aware of the contradictions embedded in the use of a management tool to attempt to counteract inequities caused by years of management—and union—business as usual. A method to consistently apply managerial values would be employed to upset some of those values. Criticisms of *a priori* systems, such as Hay Associates' Guide Chart–Profile Job Evaluation System, had pointed to some of the problems, and Task Force members had read these analyses (see Treiman, 1979; Schwab, 1980; Remick, 1979, 1981, 1984; Treiman and Hartmann, 1981).

According to Remick (1984:110), "Job evaluation systems are designed to reflect prevailing wages in their choice of factors, weighting of factors and salary setting practices." To the extent that prevailing wages reflect historically produced discrimination against women, point-factor scores may also reflect this discrimination. As Treiman and Hartmann (1981:81) suggest, "It is possible that the process of describing and evaluating jobs reflects pervasive cultural stereotypes regarding the relative worth of work traditionally done by men and work traditionally done by women."

In spite of the high probability that *a priori* job-evaluation methods contain an inbuilt cultural devaluation of women's work, these systems have consistently demonstrated, as discussed above, that female-dominated jobs are underpaid when compared with male-dominated jobs with similar point scores. This consistent result reveals one type of devaluation: job elements that are rewarded in male-defined jobs are not equally rewarded when these same elements are found in female-defined jobs. For example, a certain level of knowledge and skill in a nursing job may earn fewer dollars than the same level of knowledge and skill in an engineering job. Consistent application of a measurement of knowledge and skill to both the nursing job and the engineering job, and a comparison of the scores and salaries of the two jobs, should reveal the magnitude of this type of discrepancy.

Another type of devaluation discussed in the literature is probably not tapped so well by *a priori* systems (Remick, 1984). This devaluation occurs when aspects of women's jobs that are valuable for organizational functioning are not evaluated, either because no factor captures these job components, or because operational definitions of factors refer only to components of male jobs. For example, Remick (1984:107; see also Barker, 1986; Steinberg and Haignere, 1987) points to a number of dimensions along which male-typed and female-typed jobs differ. Some elements characteristic of female jobs, such as responsibility for persons rather than for property, may not only be absent from job-evaluation systems but may actually be negatively rewarded in salary setting (see, for example, Pierson, Koziara, and Johannesson, 1984).

Task Force feminists wanted to make sure that our job-evaluation system would give points for these hidden and undervalued dimensions of women's jobs. This was one way of meeting the legislative require-ment to produce a bias-free, sex-neutral evaluation. Hay had agreed to some modifications of their instrument along these lines, as noted above. All other parts of the project would also be scrutinized for bias. One of the best protections against bias, we thought, was to do all of the technical work as carefully and systematically as possible, with ongoing review of the quality of the work.

The structure of the Hay charts presented formidable difficulties to Task Force feminists who were committed to modifying them to remove gender bias. Feminists pushed the consultants on the question of sex bias and identified places in the charts that could be altered: the Human Relations subscale, Working Conditions, and the definitions of criteria for the Technical Knowledge and Accountability scales. However, changes to this complex system would have to be minor, we understood. As one consultant put it, they would be glad to build us a completely new system starting from the values of the state of Oregon, but that would cost far more than the $104,000 that Hay had bid, and take far longer than the scheduled thirteen or fourteen months.

In a large public work session devoted to modifying the charts, the consultant defined the goal of the meeting as "fine tuning, to address and resolve problems," to customize the charts for Oregon. Some feminists disagreed with this notion of the meeting's goals. They saw the task as the rooting out of sex discrimination. As one Advisory Group member said, "Over the past 40 years in our culture there has been discrimination against women in setting salaries. If so, one could argue that the Hay system, if it is a good system, if it has accurately captured the values of the culture, it is likely to be a sex discriminating system, because the culture has sex discrimination in it" (Advisory Group meeting, 14 March 1984).

Although the consultants had agreed to cooperate in the task of slightly modifying the charts, they reiterated with conviction that their system contains no bias and that it is only discriminatory pricing of jobs that introduces unjustified wage differences between the sexes. "It is our experience that the point spread [within the clerical series and within the blue collar series] is identical . . . but the employers for a variety of reasons have chosen to put a lower dollar value on a 150-point clerical job than they put on a 150-point blue collar job. So the issue is not the point evaluation, but that the employer is paying very differently for the same content in different occupational areas" (Advisory Group, 14 March 1984).

The feminist majority on the Task Force and feminists on the Advisory Group were not covinced, and they pursued the matter of the Human Relations scale, pushing for alterations that would increase its weight, or its contribution to the total score. There were two issues, the number of levels in the scale and the definitions of the levels. As one Advisory Group member pointed out, Human Relations had only three levels in the Guide Chart as compared with Freedom to Act, which had twenty-six levels.[5] The possible variation, and thus the possible impact on the total score, was much higher for Freedom to Act than for Human Relations.[6]

Feminists proposed that the number of levels in the Human Relations scale should be increased from three to five. This would give some additional weight to the Human Relations subfactor. Feminists also proposed modifying the definition of Human Relations. They wanted to include skills needed in mediating relationships with coworkers, supervisors, and the public, as well as maintaining cooperative processes with irate clients and disturbed patients. They were particularly concerned about the definition given by a consultant to the first level of human relations: "overt friendliness or common courtesy." With a three-level scale, most workers, including most clerical and human service aide jobs, would fall in this lowest slot. But this would undervalue the skills needed to maintain common courtesy in the face of anger, fear, and hostility, and it would make it impossible to distinguish between jobs with such demands and those without them.

Hay definitions of Human Relations seemed linked to levels of bureaucratic function, focusing on supervisory and managerial tasks of motivating and training. Some consultants pointed out that asking whether a job has the power to reward and punish may help to place the job on Human Relations. According to the consultants, the first level requires personal interaction dealing essentially with facts. The second and third levels require different intensity of use of skills to cause behavioral changes in individuals or groups. Task Force feminists, while not denying that managers and psychotherapists need Human Relations skills, held out for definitions that would give more recognition to those skills involved in lower-level jobs.

This was not an idle exercise. Two full days of meetings were devoted to this and the issue of Working Conditions, in addition to significant parts of other lengthy meetings. Hay consultants argued against increasing the number of levels for a number of reasons: (1) Human Relations were never undervalued in the Hay system, (2) evaluators cannot make distinctions between more than three levels of skill, (3) increasing Human Relations to five levels would result in overcounting relative to managerial skills, and (4) it would reduce the point difference between managerial and nonmanagerial jobs, leading to problems in management recruiting.

The consultants went to great lengths to convince the Task Force. For example, they devised an exercise for the Task Force and the Advisory Group. In this exercise, all were invited to take part in the evaluation of two jobs, those of a social worker and an engineer. The only difference between the locations of the two jobs on the charts was that the social work job was given a "3" on Human Relations, while the engineering job got a "1." This high location on Human Relations, argued the consultants, would result in a ripple effect through other factors, producing for the social worker a score 35.5 percent higher than the score for the engineer. The Hay system, they said, compares one job with another and asks, "Does this difference make sense?" Most organizations, they continued, were unwilling to pay a 35 percent difference for human-relations skills. Some feminists were angry with this exercise because it contained the unexplored assumption that assigning a "3" on Human Relations must lead to increasing scores on Technical Know-How and Problem Solving. Thus, they argued, the consultants had been deliberately misleading. Tensions were very high during this controversy, marking its significance in the conflict between management interests and women's interests.

A related issue had to do with the internal numbering of the charts. Expansion of Human Relations from three to five levels would require reordering the numbers within the cells. Because Human Relations is a subscale of Management Know-How, this reordering could reduce the point differences between management and nonmanagement jobs. The consultants believed that this was the most damaging probable outcome of enlarging Human Relations. In spite of the consultants' warnings, the Task Force majority voted to compare a five-level and a three-level scale in the pretest of the evaluation process. The pretest showed that use of a five-point scale altered the rank ordering of some jobs, as the consultants had predicted.

The battle over three or five levels of Human Relations continued in the Task Force and Advisory Group meetings. Management representatives sided with the consultants. Union people and feminists were on the other side. This was an emotional struggle. Clearly, important interests were embedded in a minor technical issue: Should there be three or five levels in a subscale? Finally, in a close Task Force vote, a compromise of four levels was passed. The consultants reworded the descriptions, but not as much as Task Force feminists had intended. There were some modifications in wording for the two highest levels in the scale, but no recognition of skills such as mediating, conciliating, and supporting necessary in many clerical and service jobs. Comparison of the Human Relations definitions offered by Hay at the beginning of the project and those finally used show little difference (see Table 13–2).

Controversy also arose over Working Conditions. Hay definitions of Working Conditions, as in most systems, were developed to evaluate blue-collar jobs (Remick, 1979). In the Working Conditions chart, physical effort was defined by such things as lifting heavy weights, and the work environment was defined as unpleasant or hazardous only when heat, cold, rain, or exposure to such dangers as toxic chemicals or speeding cars were necessary job components. The ordinary office environment was defined as normal, essentially benign. Such definitions were not peculiar to the Hay system; they were and are simply part of the taken-for-granted understanding of work. Feminists on the project were unwilling to accept this common understanding. They wanted to include frequent lifting of smaller weights, continuous hand motions, and concentrated staring at a computer screen as physical effort. Sitting continuously in one place and being confined in a poorly ventilated and noisy office were other Working Conditions feminists tried to include in the definitions.

Table 13–2
Hay Associates Human-Relations Definitions, Comparison of Scales

3-Level Scale Suggested at Beginning	4-Level Scale Used in Oregon Project
1. *Basic:* ordinary courtesy and effectiveness in dealing with others through normal contacts, and request for, or providing information.	1. *Incidental:* Communication skills are incidental to the nature of the job duties performed.
2. *Important:* Understanding, influencing, and/or serving people are important considerations in performing the job; causing action or understanding in others.	2. *Basic:* Skills in communicating factual information are necessary in the job.
3. *Critical:* Alternative or combined skills in understanding, developing, and motivating people are critical to successful job performance.	3. *Important:* Skills in understanding and influencing, motivating, counseling, or training people are important job components.
	4. *Critical:* Skills in motivating, developing, understanding, persuading, and/or counseling people are critical for effective job performance.

Task Force feminists also argued that many state jobs involve a great deal of stress, that stress is frequently a component of lower-level women's jobs, and that it should be compensated, or counted in job evaluation. Hay consultants answered that job stress is picked up in factors such as Know-How. Part of the knowledge base of the psychologist position, for example, is how to deal with people who are emotionally disturbed. They emphasized the importance of avoiding double counting particular aspects of jobs in the evaluation process. In addition, the consultants countered, we must distinguish between characteristics of jobs and characteristics of the people who fill the jobs. Job evaluation has to do with jobs, not with their occupants. One person might find a job stressful, while another would simply love the challenge of the same set of tasks. State management voiced other concerns. Stress can be a basis for workers' compensation claims. Management worried that if we were to admit, by including it in the job-evaluation process, that stress exists in certain jobs, this might put the state in greater jeopardy.

The Task Force finally decided to measure stress by including something called "Work Demands" in the Working Conditions factor. This terminology, suggested by the consultants, seemed neutral enough to avoid the implication that the state was putting its workers in danger of psychological damage. The content of Work Demands also seemed to capture some of the elements in female-dominated jobs that feminists had identified as hidden and undervalued. For example, secretaries frequently have to follow the orders of several bosses or answer telephones and meet typing deadlines at the same time; psychiatric aides do much of the face-to-face work with severely disturbed patients. Work Demands were defined as "mental alertness and mental energy required by the intensity, continuity and complexity of work being performed." They were further specified as "Time Demands: the build up of work that must be accomplished under generally inflexible timelines. Frequent interruptions, if characteristic of the job, may contribute to work demands. Role Loading: having to perform in multiple, critical roles, or two or more incompatible roles, and Emotion Loading: the provision of direct services to individuals experiencing physical or emotional distress" (Task Force Minutes, 27 June 1984).

Management members of the Task Force and Personnel were solidly opposed to Work Demands; however, this factor was included in the charts by a majority vote. Again, the clear taking of sides on this issue and the time and energy devoted to it hint at a significance for maintaining existing hierarchical relations.

In the arguments over Human Relations and Working Conditions factors, the consultants concerns focused on legitimacy: what makes sense, what is believable. The consultants seemed particularly sensitive to the reactions of managers and professionals, opposing changes that might decrease the point differences in the hierarchy as well as changes that might alter the rank order assumed to make sense. For example, changes that could place people-caring jobs higher than some technical jobs were impossible on the grounds that such changes were not rational, not in accord with what any person could see was sensible.

Task Force feminists, on the other hand, were facing competing legitimacy claims of a sophisticated local and national feminist community. This community shared a literature critical of systems such as Hay and a goal of eliminating deeply embedded sex bias. The importance of these competing claims is underscored by the amount of time and effort the Task Force, the Advisory Group, and Hay consultants spent on working out relatively minor variations in the Guide Charts. Given the complex internal stratification of organizations such as the state of Oregon, the consultants' concerns were well founded, for as the project unfolded perhaps the greatest threat to its legitimacy turned out to be changes that upset the existing internal stratification structure. Thus, legitimacy was on the side of the status quo, creating a contradiction for feminists working for change. To be successful, the project had to be accepted by diverse groups, but the means to acceptance undermined the possibility for change.

The final modifications to the Hay Guide Charts were modest: four rather than three levels of Human Relations skills, a Work Demands subfactor in Working Conditions to measure some aspects of job stress, the inclusion of continuous and rapid movements in the definition of muscular effort, and the addition of sensory effort to Working Conditions (see Table 13–1). In addition, the Working Conditions chart was restructured by the consultants to include the new subfactor. This was not the end of it; as we shall see, the consultants achieved their aims to minimize changes in their system by giving operational definitions to the changes that made them almost impossible to use in the actual evaluation process.

Reproducing Hierarchy: Job-Evaluation Training and Practice

Job evaluation itself is the core of the process of reproducing the (on paper) hierarchy. What is actually evaluated is a job description, and preparing the job description is called job documentation. This step in the process is discussed in the literature as a possible source of bias. The completed Oregon questionnaires were, on the whole, of high quality—workers seemed to describe their jobs fully and without bias. Although it was a tremendous undertaking, it was the least conflict-ridden part of the project. I discuss it briefly here as a necessary prelude to job evaluation.

Job Documentation

Job classes had to be described before they could be evaluated. A job class is an aggregate of similar positions. Some job classes, such as secretary, contain several thousand positions. Others, such as ship's cook, contain only one. So that the job classes could be described, information on each position had to be obtained and composite descriptions based on the position information had to be written. To get this basic information, we developed and pretested a questionnaire, using a prototype provided by Hay as a beginning point.

The questionnaire was designed to elicit the information necessary to use the Hay method. Items included a listing of all job duties, types of contacts with clients, public, and coworkers, position in the organizational structure, problems and difficulties on the job, and characteristics of working conditions.

The going was smooth until we got to the question of supervisory review of workers' questionnaires. Here the management point of view differed from the trade-union and feminist perspective. Feminists and trade unionists were concerned about confidentiality and the possibility that workers might feel constrained to answer the questions the way they thought the supervisor would approve. Thus, we thought, the validity of the data was in jeopardy with supervisory review. Unions were also afraid that the questionnaires might be used in a punitive way if available to supervisors.

Personnel advocates, although they agreed that supervisors should not be allowed to alter workers' answers, argued strenuously that supervisory review was essential if management support of the project was to be preserved. Supervisors have the responsibility to assign tasks; therefore, they have the right to review the adequacy of workers' descriptions of their tasks, was the argument. Another worry motivated Personnel's insistence on supervisory review. "The supervisor assigns the work and yet what often happens is either the supervisor doesn't know what the employee is doing or the employee has taken on responsibilities which are not immediately obvious to the supervisor. Sometimes you will find a situation where the employee is running the office and the supervisor is not" (Personnel Director, Task Force meeting, 1 Feb. 1984). Such a situation, according to Personnel, might have to be resolved by higher management in order to get a description of duties appropriate to the position. This suggests that Personnel may have expected to use the study to identify and rectify deviations from an orderly, rational model. The aim seemed not to be to identify and reward workers who were doing more skilled and responsible work than their positions required, but rather to police and clean up the system. This was an indication that the goals of pay equity and upgrading the status of women's work were subject to displacement by other agendas, such as the control goals of management.

Hay consultants sided with Personnel. As far as they were concerned, supervisory review was a quality check; supervisors were most likely to add tasks that workers had forgotten, rather than to challenge or criticize the workers' job descriptions. Moreover, they argued that confidence in the study would be damaged if supervisory authority was undermined. With the weight of these legitimacy arguments, Task Force feminists and union representatives went along with supervisory review, with the important proviso that supervisors were not to change any answers on workers' questionnaires.

In fact, workers had few problems in completing the questionnaires. Supervisors, on the whole, agreed with workers' views of their tasks. No supervisors were found to have abandoned their responsibility to underlings. Hay consultants were right. The success of this stage of the project was largely due to a tremendous educational effort by the Personnel Division, whose staff held 459 information and training sessions throughout the state. Every state employee was given time off to attend such a session, which included an explanation of comparable worth and detailed information about how to fill out the questionnaire. Some unions held separate meetings with their members to further instruct them in accurately describing their jobs. In addition, every state employee was given two hours of work time to fill out the questionnaire. In sum, state management had committed considerable resources to the study.

The Job-Evaluation Process

Job evaluation is the process of applying the values expressed in the evaluation instrument, in this case the charts, to actual jobs. It is the transformation process that links the charts' complex imagery of work to the living hierarchy of workers. Thus, knowledge about how it is done provides some additional understanding about how hierarchies of power and reward are reproduced in contemporary large organizations. I briefly describe the Hay job-evaluation method, as it was used in Oregon, to set the context for the discussion of the ways in which training for job evaluation and the process itself reinforced the managerial hierarchy already evident in the structure of the charts.[7]

To do job evaluation using this method, several people sit down around a table. Each has in front of her a job description and a set of Guide Charts. To the side is a blackboard. There is a team leader or facilitator and a recorder who takes detailed notes on all decisions. Each person reads the job description and then makes a preliminary decision about where to place the job in the Technical Knowledge scale of the Know-How chart. The team leader begins the discussion on the placement of the job in the chart and discussion continues until there is agreement or, failing that, a vote. One person stands at the blackboard and writes the decision there. Each scale in each chart is, in turn, similarly considered until all are done and a total score determined. Once the total has been achieved, the relationships among the factor scores are scrutinized to see that they make sense, that the factors have the proper relationship to each other, as I discuss below. The charts are daunting, but it is possible to learn to use them efficiently; one evaluation may take from fifteen to forty-five minutes.

Evaluations are done through a consensus-creating method. Learning the method and developing the ability to apply job-content information to the charts takes four or five days of intensive work with a trainer. There is a continuous monitoring of the process by team leaders who are in touch with consultants. Consultants returned for several additional sessions with the evaluators. In a sense, training is a constant process. Hay consultants emphasized that there were no right or wrong assessments, of course always within the implicit limits of what makes sense. The training was to assure that evaluators were consistently making judgments based on the values of the organization.

Legitimacy concerns structured the composition of the teams and the choice of the evaluators. Although I emphasize the political legitimacy issues, technical quality was also important and linked to legitimacy, for believable evaluations could not be attained with work of poor quality. Three teams of six evaluators, a team leader, and a recorder met four days per week for five weeks in the summer of 1984 to do the benchmark evaluations for the state of Oregon. Team members were experienced workers from a variety of agencies and a variety of levels within the agencies. Nominated by management and unions and appointed by the Task Force, they represented the best: people who had broad knowledge, intelligence, and energy, they were respected by supervisors and coworkers alike. Their evaluations of a representative benchmark group of state jobs would provide the framework within which Personnel Division staff would evaluate and rank all other jobs. Their reputations in state employment would lend credibility to the scores. This approach was recommended by Hay consultants as their usual method of doing the initial, or benchmark, evaluations.

The consultants also recommended the distribution of types of jobs and evaluators among the three teams. Each team had equal or nearly equal numbers of women and men. Team 1 members were clerical and blue-collar workers, and they evaluated clerical, blue-collar, and lower-level service jobs. Team 2 was made up of middle-level professionals and supervisors whose assignment was to evaluate supervisory jobs. On Team 3 were professionals and paraprofessionals with a strong representation from health and care agencies. They evaluated jobs from these areas and some other professional jobs. This division made sense: The evaluators were examining types of work with which they were familiar.

On the other hand, this division had consequences in regard to class and gender cleavages. Women and men confronted each other over the differences between working-class jobs, clerical, and blue collar. Sharp differences emerged, but also some mutual support across gender lines. Clerical workers, however, did not have the opportunity to compare clerical jobs with management jobs higher than the first-line supervisor.

Therefore, no confrontation with structural anomalies at this level was possible. That is, instances in which there might be a blurring of responsibility across the clerical-management divide could not become visible and problematic. As I discuss below, this division of labor did not avert a rather disturbing compression of professional, supervisory, and management scores, an outcome that the consultants steadily warned would be potentially disastrous.

Doing job evaluation is an intense experience because it requires making clear distinctions between jobs on levels of complexity within each factor and subfactor. Evaluators make multiple judgments using qualitative criteria. It is exacting and demanding work, analogous to coding qualitative data in research. Moreover, in the Hay process, as in many others, the decisions are group decisions. Hay consultants structure the groups to facilitate the achievement of consensus. Each group facilitator keeps the work going along, sums up, and sometimes mediates disputes. Group recorders make systematic notes on the bases for all decisions, creating a detailed record of the process that can be used as a basis for a quality check, or for reconsidering an evaluation if that is necessary. Other elements in the group process contribute to reaching agreements.

Most evaluators, according to my experience and observation on the Oregon project, come to feel an internal pressure to assess jobs fairly and consistently. At the same time, there is a push toward conformity that may be in conflict with the internalized commitment to fairness. When team members disagree strongly about where to place a particular job on a particular factor, tensions within and between evaluators may rise. Reluctance to seem contentious, as well as a desire to meet the quota for expected numbers of evaluations for the day, may push toward capitulation, while the pressure to be fair may push toward holding out. Differences of opinion may be resolved by getting more information on a job, looking at its organizational chart location, or consulting the description of the knowledge and experience required to enter the job. Sometimes the evaluators implicitly negotiated with each other on points for a factor or subfactor. Sometimes consensus could not be reached and the team had to vote.

Agreement is facilitated by the emergence of decision rules within the group. For example, when the group has decided that all true supervisors get a "4" on Human Relations, that decision is made quickly and routinely. The more decision rules, the faster the evaluation. Evaluators comment on their skill in using the rules, saying "we're on target" or "I was out of line." However, decision rules cannot be made for many job dimensions, and team members may disagree on what the rule should be, even if, in principle, a rule could be made.

Sore thumbing, an important part of the Hay system, serves to correct errors in the evaluations. When evaluations are completed and total scores are ranked, some jobs may stick out like a sore thumb. Thus, sore thumbing involves comparing scores for different jobs to see if their relative placement makes sense. Inconsistency in application of evaluation criteria will turn up in total or subscores that appear to be either too high or too low in relation to what evaluators and consultants know about how the job compares with others. In sore thumbing, the shape of jobs is also examined. Shape refers to the relative scoring on the three main factors. So, for example, if a research job had an Accountability score higher than its Problem Solving score, this shape would alert evaluators to an error. Research jobs should be higher on Problem Solving than on Accountability because their main function is to supply information to the organization, not to make operational decisions. Hay uses a final, independent check of the quality and consistency of evaluations called *correlation*. This involves a detailed comparison of scores from a particular customer, such as the state of Oregon, with scores arrived at in other applications of the Hay method, and an examination of the decision-making process that resulted in any scores that seem inconsistent or at great variance with other scores for similar jobs.

Consensus and sore thumbing can be seen as methods of attaining validity and reliability. These processes help to assure that female-dominated jobs are evaluated consistently on the same criteria as male-dominated jobs, but, at the same time, they help to assure that rankings do not unduly upset organizational hierarchies. One of the tests of validity is whether or not the scores reflect the established hierarchy within job or occupational families. Validity in another sense is established as team members discuss the placement of jobs on the charts, putting jobs with similar degrees of complexity in the same chart locations. At the same time, consistency of judgment or reliability is also established. The process has results similar to those of the process of establishing inter-rater reliability. Differing judgments are reviewed, discussed, and resolved, producing a consistent interpretation and application of criteria.

This part of the process accounts for some of the success in using job evaluation to locate and remedy undervaluation of women's work. My observation indicates that, within the confines of the values it represents and replicates, job evaluation is what it purports to be: a systematic, consistent, and open process of applying a set of values in the assessment of the content of jobs. Making qualitative decisions about values is a difficult process, but it can be done. The important question is, What are the values (Remick, 1984)? It is to this that I now return.

Methods of Reproducing Hierarchy

Managers' values, encoded in the Guide Charts, appear to be so carefully ranked that hierarchy itself emerges as a predominant value. The job-evaluation training and process further assured the replication of a managerially oriented hierarchy in several ways, through operational definitions given to factors, through instructions about avoiding over-counting, through the use of organizational charts, and through insistence on consistent relationships between factors.

Operational Definitions

Training began with the instruction that evaluators would measure the value to the organization of one job class as compared with another along a range from the most complex and most valuable to the least complex and least valuable. Operational definitions of levels of complexity were partially established through illustrating the types of jobs found at a particular level. For example, Level B on Technical Know-How might fit a chauffeur or a production typist. Another example comes from training to use the "Impact" subscale of the Accountability factor. Impact was a difficult concept, referring to the importance of the job to the end result intended, or the overall reason for the existence of the job. The illustration of the levels of impact replicated an established hierarchy of jobs:

Level of Impact	Job
Remote	Data entry operator
Remote/contributory	Computer operator
Contributory	Programmer
Contributory/shared	Systems analyst
Primary	Head of electronic data processing

Depending upon the specific set of choices made on the Accountability Guide Chart, and one was the Impact choice, there could be a 150- to a 200-point distance between the data entry operator and the head of electronic data processing on this one factor. Thus, the structure of the charts and the decision rules learned in training both helped to ensure that a believable hierarchy would emerge in the process. All these examples meant that some jobs were pegged at particular levels even before evaluation began.

Impact was also interesting because it contained one level that could have reflected a democratic organization of work. This was the "Shared" level, defined as "participating with others (except own subordinates and superiors), within or outside the organizational unit in taking action." "Shared" could have been used to describe—and give points for—jobs that functioned within a team approach in a work unit. However, by definition sharing of decision making could be conceived as happening only between equals in the organizational structure, and these were held to be rare occurrences.

Managerial Know-How was defined in terms of the specific managerial location of particular jobs. To manage is to carry out an integrative function, such as coordinating the work of the Welfare Division and the Corrections Division, but jobs that were not managerial in the organizational chart could not be evaluated above the lowest level of Managerial Know-How. Thus, the coordination of services that a ward clerk might carry out or the program coordination assigned to many professional jobs could not be recognized with extra points for an integrative function. Such jobs are often held by women.

Operational definitions preserved hierarchy in another way, in making distinctions between supervisors and nonsupervisors and between custodial and treatment personnel. An implicit assumption in evaluation was that a supervisor should have a higher point score than her subordinates. Even though the supervisor's technical Know-How might be at the same level as that of the supervisee, greater knowledge about management might push the supervisor's technical Know-How score higher. In addition, Problem Solving and Accountability would probably add points to the supervisor's score. Also, supervisors motivate other workers, and this aspect of the job would place them higher on the Human Relations scale than other workers. Therefore, deciding who was or who was not a supervisor was important for the emergent ranking.

The problem for the job evaluators was that not all supervisory functions are located in jobs titled "supervisor." There are lead workers who organize work and motivate coworkers. There are secretaries who supervise clerical assistants. There are professional workers who supervise one or two other workers. In addition, in the universities there are many clerical workers at various levels who hire, fire, and supervise work-study students.[8]

The evaluation teams, with the help of the consultants, developed rules to deal with this complexity: a lead worker gets a "3" on Human Relations. A "true supervisor" supervises five or more workers, and 75 percent to 80 percent of the job's activities have to do with supervision. A true supervisor also hires, fires, and disciplines. Such a supervisor gets a 4 on Human Relations. However, if fewer than five workers are supervised, the Human Relations score may be lower. The secretary who supervises part-time student workers, even if she oversees 15 to 20 workers, is seen simply as a lead worker and does not get extra evaluated points above the "3" on Human Relations that went automatically to lead workers. Nevertheless, there was some accommodation in the evaluation process to the organizational reality that the supervisory function is partially distributed into nonsupervisory jobs. Many of these jobs are female-dominated, and adding some extra points for supervision may be one of the sources of scores that show that these jobs have been undervalued.

The distinction between custodial and treatment jobs also arose in the process of operational definition. This distinction was confounded or cross-cut by the distinction between supervisors and nonsupervisors. Again, the distinction has implications for point scores given to primarily women's jobs. It also has implications for the maintenance of class differences in the organizational hierarchy.

Custodial jobs are those low-level positions in state institutions, homes for the mentally retarded, mental hospitals, prisons, that have the responsibility for minute-by-minute care of inmates. These positions are nonsupervisory and seen as unskilled and routine. A decision about whether or not a position was "just custodial" was critical for deciding the level of complexity on the Technical Knowledge dimension of Know-How and thus was critical for determining the total number of points assigned to a job.

The assumptions embedded in the distinction between custodial and treatment reflect the undervaluation of people-caring functions in some female-dominated jobs noted by Remick (1984). The distinction is also rooted in a particular medical model. One assumption of this model is that treatment is separate from routine care and something that is applied in particular times and places by people other than the routine caregivers. Occupational status, reinforced by advanced training, becomes linked to the distinction between treatment and custodial care, with the knowledge and skill needed for custodial work being further devalued in comparison with the professional knowledge of treatment personnel.

This notion was widely challenged in the 1950s and 1960s by the movement to create therapeutic communities and by the recognition that unrelieved custodial care, as in some mental hospitals, could exacerbate and make chronic conditions that might otherwise have subsided after an acute phase (for instance, Jones, 1976). In the therapeutic community all who had any contact with a patient were part of the treatment team, and every moment of the patient's stay became part of the process of treatment. The aides who spent their days with patients were to be part of the treatment team, participating in team planning of therapeutic approaches and developing skills on the job. This new ideology of care had an impact in Oregon, as elsewhere. The survival of the notion of custodial care in job-evaluation definitions may simply reflect the failure of attempts to create therapeutic communities. Perhaps routine care is still the insensitive and unresponsive management of human bodies. On the other hand, the Oregon job-evaluation process suggests that the term *custodial* may inaccurately convey what some employees actually do, and may be required to do, in these sorts of jobs.

For example, kitchen aides and laundry workers often have to work with mentally retarded inmates who are assigned to the kitchen or laundry to learn some basic skills. These low-level, "unskilled" workers have considerable "responsibility in practice" for encouraging and monitoring the performance of the inmates. Yet, skills needed to carry out these tasks are not reflected in the knowledge and experience requirements of the jobs, in the organizational level of the job, or in its rewards. In the actual job-evaluation process such jobs were given some points for the Human Relations skills needed in supervising inmates, or students, as they are called, but there was little recognition in Technical Know-How points for the knowledge that this required.

The most significant example of the use of operational definitions in the reproduction of hierarchy is the undermining of the major Task Force effort to eliminate sex bias in the Guide Charts through changing Human Relations and Working Conditions. In spite of the many hours of discussion in Task Force and Advisory Group meeting, and in spite of the majority decisions in both groups that a broadening of the Human Relations scale should be the policy of the state of Oregon, in the benchmark evaluations the consultant's definition of three levels of Human Relations skills prevailed.[9] The consultants achieved this outcome through the training for the use of the four-level scale. They defined Level One to include only those jobs in which practically no human contact occurs. This level was called "Incidental" and referred to the person who sits in a room all alone and gets direction from pieces of paper shoved under the door. Of course, there are practically no jobs that are so isolated, so that the Incidental level was rarely used by the evaluators. This left a three-level scale that did not allow a distinction between, for example, a clerical worker who must interact with several bosses in the office and a highway maintenance worker who must get along with others on the work crew.

The three-level scale was frustrating to the job evaluators who tried to recognize the caring and mediating tasks in many female-dominated jobs. I discuss this in some detail below. Several Task Force feminists observed the consultants' training sessions and were aware of this maneuver to save the consultants' three-level scale. The Task Force members did not interfere, primarily from considerations of legitimacy. Hay had been hired partly to give respectability and authority to the project. Initial training took place in a large public room with a number of observers. An open challenge in that setting would, we felt, undermine and slow down the process. Consequently, no challenge was made.

The consultants also shaped in the training process the use of the revised Working Conditions factor. Work Demands were interpreted as a way to add points for only the most severe conditions. For Time Demands, the criterion, in general, was, "Is this a drop-dead situation?" For example, a hostage negotiator in a prison riot would experience Time Demands. Role Loading was defined in private sector, managerial terms as, for example, a job in which the incumbent was required to do long-term planning for a company and at the same time be responsible on a daily basis for production. The suggestion that many workers in human-service jobs experience role loading or conflict when they have to act as enforcers of laws for the state and supportive helpers for the client was not adopted in the definition of role loading. Emotion Loading was defined as applying only to jobs in crisis medical care or treatment of extremely difficult psychiatric problems. Thus, the potential for altering the hierarchy of jobs through evaluating often hidden aspects of women's work was subverted by the actions of the consultants.

Double Counting

The predetermined hierarchy was also maintained through avoidance of overcounting or double counting. Trainers frequently emphasized the dangers of overcounting. For example, Emotion Loading, a component of the Work Demands subfactor of Working Conditions, could be used to double or triple count some aspects of jobs. Emotional stress might be implicitly accounted for under Human Relations, in Problem Solving, or even in the Technical Know-How subfactor where knowledge about psychological problems would be credited. Evaluators were warned that giving points for the same content under different factors could distort the rankings. As I have discussed above, double or triple counting on managerial tasks appears to be clearly built into the Guide Charts, but this was not seen as problematic. The stricture against double counting on the new subfactors or the redefined subfactors, therefore, acted to preserve the hierarchy, with its managerial slant, already built into the charts.

Use of Organizational Charts

When evaluators were in doubt about the complexity of a job, there were precedents set in the training to refer to the organizational chart. The charts were especially helpful when there were numerous bureaucratic levels and little apparent difference in job content between levels. For example, an agency might have district supervisors deployed geographically and a supervisor of these supervisors; the two job descriptions might look quite similar. Location in the organizational hierarchy could then help to peg the appropriate number of points for the factors, keeping in mind that supervisors ought to have more points than those beneath them, and fewer points than those above them in the hierarchy. Place in the hierarchy could also indicate formal responsibility and thus contribute to assessment of the accountability factor. Other criteria, such as licensing and other laws, were used to locate accountability. Registered nurses (RNs), for example, are legally responsible for patient well-being, in contrast to licensed practical nurses (LPNs). Although LPNs might do substantially the same things as RNs, almost everyone agreed, they could not have as high ratings on any of the factors because of the differences in legal responsibility. Thus, we can differentiate between formal or bureaucratic responsibility and responsibility in practice. Responsibility in practice was never recognized in awarded points at a level equal to bureaucratic responsibility, although the evaluation teams discussed these differences extensively. Here is another way, then, that the replication of the organizational hierarchy was guaranteed in the practical process of job evaluation.

Relationships between Factors

Just as there are usual rankings of jobs produced by the Hay system, there are also usual relationships between the factors for any particular job. Technical Know-How, as the trainers insisted, cannot be lower than Problem Solving (Thinking Challenge and Freedom to Think) or than the Freedom to Act dimension of the Accountability chart. These relationships were justified on logical grounds: Problem Solving and action cannot occur in the absence of knowledge about the problem and possible courses of action. Similarly, if the freedom to think is very constrained in a job, it is not reasonable to believe that the job has a high level of freedom to act. Action implies some prior thought in this context. However, as discussed above, factor interrelationships are not uniform. Certain types of jobs have common internal patterns. Some emphasize accountability or results, others problem solving or generating information; still others have a balance between requirements to produce results and to produce information. Thus, each job has a characteristic profile. Examination of this profile and comparison with other knowledge about a job provides a validity check on the evaluation.

Training included instructions in achieving the proper internal consistency. Sometimes Technical Know-How had to be adjusted to make it consistent with Problem-Solving, or Problem-Solving had to be adjusted to make it consistent with elements in Accountability. Sometimes these relationships did not make sense to the evaluators. For example, some clerical worker evaluators insisted that certain clerical jobs had problem-solving demands far too high to be consistent with the Technical Know-How they saw in the job. The Hay trainers would not accept this job "shape," arguing that this represented irrational and defective job design. By force of argument they convinced the recalcitrant clerical workers that this aberration in their jobs should not be reflected in the evaluations. Thus, at least at this point, an organizational logic was imposed over the evaluators' perceptions of job content, possibly obscuring an important characteristic of some female-dominated jobs, that they have to deal with problems that in the formal structure are in the provinces of their supervisors and that they are not rewarded for this work. This push toward consistent relationships across factors and subfactors also, of course, was another strand in the tightly woven fabric of hierarchy. In sum, through careful and forceful instruction in defining and assessing job content in terms of evaluation factors, the consultants gave concrete meaning to the abstract words in the Guide Charts. The production of a conventional gender and class hierarchy was reinforced by the ideas about gender that evaluators revealed.

Gender Images in Job Evaluation

Images of masculinity and femininity are associated with sex-segregated jobs, as popular knowledge and a large body of recent research attest (for example, Cockburn, 1983, 1985; Game and Pringle, 1984). Writers on comparable worth identify such images as one source of bias in job evaluation (for example, Remick, 1984; Steinberg and Haignere, 1987). Gender images are part of the ideology that supports male dominance; at the same time, images of masculinity and femininity are part of the ideology justifying existing class relations, for they provide part of the rationale that makes life worth living.[10]

Efforts to combat this ideology in job evaluation take the issue to the table around which sit women and men contending over the worth of their work. When people argue about the content and difficulty of the work process, the terms they use suggest their assessments of the work and how they differentiate it from other work. In my observations of job evaluation I could see clearly some of the ways in which typical female work is undervalued. Disagreements in the team that evaluated clerical and blue-collar jobs provide most of the data. On this team several experienced clerical workers, two of whom were feminists, confronted some highly articulate blue-collar workers. Their clashes of opinion resulted in long discussions of job content.

These interactions between the women and men on the clerical and blue-collar team revealed something about how jobs become gendered. Women and men often disagreed about the content of female-defined jobs, but usually, although not always, agreed about male-dominated jobs. An asymmetry in the process emerged early. Women were willing, on the whole, to accept the men as authorities on male-defined jobs. Women deferred to the men, asked them to explain and evaluate the content of male jobs. Consequently, men talked more than women and directed the evaluation of male jobs. Often they argued for higher scores on Know-How for male-dominated jobs. However, the men did not defer to the superior knowledge of the women about female-dominated clerical and service jobs. There was much more dialogue across gender lines about women's jobs. The men were skeptical and contentious. The women often responded by refusing to budge. Sometimes tensions escalated and everyone became uncomfortable. The women reported distress at having to be so combative and adamant with the men, but they usually stuck to their positions, both out of the belief in the correctness of their ideas, and out of dedication to representing the interests of all clerical workers.

Technical Know-How and Human Relations skills were contested areas in which cultural images were revealed. Contrasting pictures of male and female work were implicit in different language used to describe the jobs, both in the written job composites and in the group discussions. Low-level women's jobs were called entry-level positions, while such male jobs were apprentice positions. Women's jobs were more often described as simple, routine, repetitive, and detailed; men's jobs were more often tricky, intricate, broad, and strenuous. Women were described as making judgments, interpreting, resolving, and verifying. Men were troubleshooting, negotiating, installing, and repairing. Above all, male blue-collar workers were journeymen. The designation *journeyman* implied a certain basic level of Know-How. "This is a journeyman-level job" carried meanings of autonomy, respect, skill, and long apprenticeship or training. Also, journeymen are troubleshooters. In contrast, even the highest-level clerical jobs, Administrative Assistant or Management Assistant, had no such implications. Assistants, after all, are only assistants. Moreover, these jobs have no apprenticeship and little formal training. Even the job descriptions used in evaluation tended to devalue by prescribing for almost all but entry-level clerical jobs a minimum experience requirement of only two years, while four years' apprenticeship and several years of experience were often required for male journeyman-level jobs.

Men on the evaluation team saw clerical work in a much different light than did the women. According to the male image, much clerical work is typing and checking for accuracy. This is only a repetitive production job, in their estimation. Anyone with a high school education can type and write letters, they thought. Women evaluators, in contrast, saw these jobs as much more complex. Workers who primarily did typing had to edit and proofread, rather than just check for errors. They needed to know how to choose the format and to construct new formats. Often typing was combined with receptionist work, and the pressure of completing reports and manuscripts combined with answering the telephone and responding to people at the front desk required a cool head and the competence to do several things simultaneously. These were the arguments of the women evaluators.

The organizational knowledge that women could see in some clerical jobs was completely invisible to the men. A case in point is the institution unit clerk, the person who does the clerical work on a hospital ward (see Sacks, 1984). The women argued that the person in this job has "to be pretty well versed in the operations of the whole place to do the job." The ward clerk coordinates appointments for patients, often has to explain what is going on to a distressed family and to the patient, and is the only clerical person in the unit. In addition, this work cannot be learned in a year or two, according to the women evaluators. The men countered that the work may seem complex, but it is not. Doctors and nurses do the explaining, and scheduling is not difficult. You just answer the phone and note down the times. The women won their point on Know-How; the men conceded finally that perhaps the ward clerk needs to know about the structure of the hospital. However, the women lost on their attempt to raise the scoring on Problem Solving and Accountability for this job. One woman evaluator, depressed as she left the day's evaluation session, said that she felt as though she had betrayed the people to whom she was committed.

The blue-collar workers also had difficulty in seeing the complexity of bureaucratic tasks. For example, the state has a number of jobs that process records, verifying information, applying eligibility rules, routing forms, answering questions about rules, explaining regulations. "I don't see them making decisions; if they make a mistake it just comes back to them," said a blue-collar man. The women contended that rules have exceptions—to apply rules one must have knowledge about the exceptions. Moreover, a broader knowledge about how programs work is necessary in order to apply rules intelligently. The men countered that situations dictate procedures and that records specialists just had to fit things into categories. Women do production, they do not troubleshoot. They do not have to solve problems and make decisions.

The most extreme example of this view emerged in the evaluation of the stenographic court reporter who makes a verbatim record of court proceedings. Evaluators agreed that the stenographic system involves a fairly high degree of knowledge. However, the application of that knowledge was interpreted as routine. The sounds in the courtroom are processed through the reporter's brain, coming out as symbols on a tape. Indeed, "this person is a sophisticated machine." Therefore, points on problem solving are minimized: "You don't have to understand it to write it down." Women evaluators objected to this interpretation of the court reporter's job, but the male view prevailed. Evaluators faced similar problems with the word processing job. Working at a word processor is not very complex, they decided, although more complex than doing ordinary production typing. Some argued that production typing is really more complex because with word processing the knowledge about formating, document style, and even spelling may be in the machine. This was a topic of some ambiguity, and it seems that in this Oregon group, the question of whether the new technology deskills or requires new skills had not been resolved.

The ambiguity of the technology, the difficulty in deciding about deskilling, reflect the social components in the definition of skill. The links between skill and masculinity have been demonstrated in a number of studies (Phillips and Taylor, 1986; Game and Pringle, 1984; Cockburn, 1983). Male workers act to preserve the perception of their own work as skilled work, even when the tasks have been simplified through technological change. The definition of male work as skilled is maintained by contrasting it with female work, which is, often by definition, not skilled. The process of saving male superiority, in this job-evaluation case, was two sided—arguing both for the complexity and difficulty of male jobs and for the simplicity of female jobs.

Comparing clerical jobs at any level with skilled blue-collar jobs, these male workers usually placed the female jobs lower in an implicit scale of complexity of knowledge and problem solving. They were also highly skeptical about claims that many office jobs need high human-relations skills to keep the flow of work going smoothly. The invisibility to the men of many aspects of women's jobs came out in heated exchanges over Human Relations skills in the course of lengthy discussions of higher-level office jobs. The women on the team maintained that such jobs require Human Relations skills above the level of "common courtesy" or basic effectiveness in relating to others. Office conflicts must be managed, often several bosses must be placated, information must be extracted from and given to the public, liaison with other departments must be established and maintained, and arrangements and decisions must be facilitated. The blue-collar men argued first that these functions were not the basic purposes of the jobs, so should not be credited, and, second, that in any case, the level of Human Relations skill required was not greater than that required of a member of a bridge maintenance crew. After all, it is essential that bridge workers be able to communicate with each other; to talk with the public requires no greater skill. To the men, the women were only arguing that secretaries or administrative assistants had to be nice and polite for longer periods of time than the bridge worker, not that there was anything qualitatively different about the work. The men, in addition, could not see the levels of skill that the women could see and thus could not differentiate between different levels and types of office work. As one said in this debate, "the skills are no more than you would expect on the street."

The disputes over Human Relations skills were related to the way that the consultants restricted the choices on the scales, which I have discussed above. With the first level effectively eliminated by defining it as involving no human contact, the second level became "common courtesy." Level three was used for lead workers and for jobs such as the ordinary registered nurse or the supervisor of small groups, and level four, "critical," was reserved for jobs in which most of the work was done through human relations, such as psychiatric therapy. Thus, the women on the team who were aware of the invisible work in many female-dominated jobs had no latitude in the scale. The clerical worker evaluators attempted to use the numbering patterns in the Know-How chart to recreate a four-level scheme in order to differentiate between types of clerical jobs and between clerical and blue-collar jobs. They did this by giving the maximum points possible, within the Guide Chart limitations, to jobs deemed to have heavy human-relations obligations. This solution was not satisfactory, and most of the acrimonious debates centered on this strategy. The women were dedicated to the comparable-worth goal and argued their points fiercely. The men were equally adamant and, indeed, never gave in. Their concern was that, in comparison with female jobs, the male jobs would be undervalued.

The women identified several components of Human Relations, qualities of behavior such as responsiveness and tactfulness, task components, such as facilitating and explaining, and actors in interaction, coworkers, the public, bosses. To the men, it was all the same. A file clerk's job was no different than a secretary's. The stance of the men in this part of the evaluation was constructed with reference to their own public, other blue-collar workers, and with reference to the symbolic value of the image of journeyman. As one said, "the men at work will never believe that an administrative assistant is at a journey level."

Working Conditions were another matter, for here the discussions and outcomes reflect class-based rather than gender-based disagreements. Male evaluators sided with female on the question of Working Conditions in the office, against the management-oriented advice of consultants. The consultants had defined the office environment as normal, and a normal environment gets no points, by definition. Even though many clerical workers had stated in their questionnaires that windowless rooms, windows that do not open, poor artificial ventilation, dust and fumes made their work environments at least unpleasant, the definitions on the physical environment dimension made it impossible to give points for this. Ironically, while evaluations were in progress, a state office building was closed for several days because workers had become ill from some unidentified fumes in the ventilating system.

The concept of the office as normal contrasts with the idea of an outdoor workplace as not normal, or at least as unpleasant. Thus, blue-collar work is likely to be given job-evaluation points when it is located outside. Sensory-muscular effort descriptions are, similarly, more applicable to male jobs than to female jobs. Typist jobs that required virtually full-time keyboard work qualified for points on muscular effort. Sitting in front of a video monitor for seven or eight hours a day was considered to involve sensory effort. However, very few jobs had these characteristics. The operational definitions from the consultants meant that working with arms and hands extended brought no points unless this position was almost constantly maintained. But, "you ache after awhile when using a keyboard," according to one clerical worker. She and others thought that Working Conditions points should be given for jobs that were primarily typing jobs even if the workers had other responsibilities that took them away from the keyboard for periods of time. But the consultants disagreed. Since the consultants were in a position of authority and they were guiding the job-evaluation process, their position usually prevailed, as it did in this case.

Evaluators tried to give points for jobs that were extremely sedentary or extremely boring. This effort was led by a man on the team who, early in his working life, had been briefly a file clerk. He argued that extremely routine jobs require a high degree of focus and attention and that workers must find some way to play mental games that help to keep them at the tasks.[11] "Does the state of Oregon want to pay for boredom?" said one consultant. "No one is comfortable justifying to taxpayers paying for boredom." Of course, the routine jobs, such as file clerk, that stimulated this discussion were all female-dominated jobs. Again, evaluators were unsuccessful in their attempts to modify the Hay system.

The new dimension of Working Conditions devised for the Oregon project, Work Demands, faced the greatest difficulties in evaluation. The consultants' definitions had made Work Demands into a factor that would only rarely be found in any job and one that would primarily occur in only high-level jobs, such as top managers or executives of the World Bank, as one consultant suggested. Points for Work Demands were given to only 20 of the 346 benchmark jobs. These were primarily jobs dealing with people under severe physical or emotional strain. The stress inherent in many clerical jobs (Stellman and Henifin, 1983) did not appear as a compensable factor.

Evaluators, especially those looking at blue-collar and clerical jobs, spent a lot of time discussing working conditions. These deliberations had little effect on the final scores, since the points actually awarded in the evaluations of Working Conditions varied only from 1 to 16, as compared with the variation of points awarded for Know-How, which ranged from 56 to 400 points. These differences in awarded points are one reason for Barker's (1986) finding that Working Conditions accounted for only 1.4 percent of the average total Hay score. Thus, the relative weights of the factors in the Hay system vary as a consequence of the points awarded in the actual use of the scales, as well as in the range of possible points built into the scales. This is one of the additional ways that particular values are built into the process. To "overvalue" working conditions would be to reduce the distance between managerial and nonmanagerial jobs.

Results

At the end of the benchmark evaluation process, when Hay consultants examined the ranking of scores and compared it with other applications of their method, they found that Oregon scores were, on the whole, quite similar to those of other employers. The scores of some clerical jobs were too low when compared with blue-collar jobs, according to the consultants, suggesting that the gender images of the blue-collar men had prevailed in the evaluation process. Some of these scores were raised in the sore-thumbing process. Scores on Human Relations followed a conventional pattern: Level One was used for only 11 out of 355 job classes evaluated. Clerical jobs were all evaluated at Level Two, with the exception of the Executive Administrative Secretary, who was Level Three. Level Three on Human Relations was given to lead workers and many human service jobs. All higher-level managerial jobs and human-service professional jobs dealing with sensitive emotional problems rated a Level Four.

Preliminary analysis of job-evaluation scores and wages showed pay differences between female- and male-dominated jobs with similar scores, despite our failure to make even slight modifications in the Hay method to better reflect the content of women's jobs. For example, Laundry Worker 2, 78 percent female and with a point score of 95, earned an average salary of $973 per month. Laborer 3, 11 percent female and with a point score of 98, had an average salary of $1,214 per month (Table 13–3). Other selected illustrations of benchmark scores for

Table 13-3
Female- and Male-Dominated Jobs by Point Scores and Average Monthly Pay, 1984, Oregon (selected examples)

New Classification	Point Score	% Female	Monthly Pay
Laundry Worker 2	95	78.60	$ 973
Laborer 3	98	11.10	1,214
Administrative Specialist 4	125	90.14	1,030
Hospital Worker 3	127	81.25	1,069
Printer 1	124	28.57	1,299
Equipment Technician 1	125	0.00	1,507
Administrative Specialist 5	143	81.96	1,170
Dental Assistant 1	143	100.00	979
Bindery Worker 2	142	21.43	1,526
Secretary 1	165	100.00	1,218
Administrative Specialist 7	165	97.55	1,128
Locksmith	166	0.00	1,616
Equipment Technician 2	165	7.10	1,581
Administrative Specialist 9	203	60.87	1,475
Dental Assistant 2	203	100.00	1,127
Electrician	208	0.00	1,952
Carpenter	208	1.39	1,809
Registered Nurse 3	275	92.10	1,882
Engineer 3	275	3.70	1,886

Note: These job classifications are from the proposed classification plan. The Administrative Specialist series contained jobs that, in current classification terms, were Clerical Assistant, Clerical Specialist, and assorted other clerical classifications.

proposed new job classifications are given in Table 13–3. On the whole, the results were quite consistent with those in other studies. We have no way of estimating how much higher scores for female-predominant jobs might have been had we successfully modified the Hay process.

Discussion: The Technical Reproduction of Hierarchy and Gender-Class Politics

Job evaluation reproduced Oregon's job hierarchy but also revealed gender-based divisions within class processes. Many lower-level women's jobs had less pay than men's jobs with similar point scores. However, the resulting estimates of underevaluation were probably low because efforts to reduce sex bias in the Hay system failed. Political questions about what should be valued in women's jobs were confronted, in this stage of the project, in terms of the technical structure of the Guide Charts, the definitions of factors, and the process of evaluation. Evaluation requires detailed interpretations of the abstract definitions of job factors as these are applied to concrete definitions of actual jobs. Consultants teach and supervise the use of conventional definitions that reproduce hierarchy. Skills in verbal interpretation, complex experience-based knowledge, and the ability to convince are parts of a consultant's competence. Feminists, unfamiliar with job evaluations, attempting to intervene from the outside, were no match for the consultants on their own technical ground. The consultants knew their system and understood how certain technical changes could reverberate through the whole process, altering widely accepted hierarchical relationships. Altering these relationships too much would threaten the legitimacy of the job-evaluation system, which is built upon and expresses managerial values. The consultants could not let that happen and used their technical knowledge and expertise to circumvent the threat.

It was the legitimacy of their system, its public appearance of reasonableness, that the consultants were protecting as they made virtually impossible the implementation of any of the modifications sought by Task Force feminists. The hierarchy was somewhat rearranged, but only as a consequence of consistent application of the evaluation method to both female-dominated and male-dominated jobs, not as a consequence of altering the method to reduce sex bias. The consultants were able to further ensure, through their training of evaluators and their extensive quality-control methods, that there was no basic disturbance of the conventional ordering. This was their responsibility to the project, not only a matter of the self-interest of consultants, as part of their task was to confer legitimacy on the Oregon comparable-worth effort. The need for legitimacy placed Task Force feminists in a contradictory situation. They too needed legitimacy for the project, but legitimacy achieved at the cost of reducing sex bias in job evaluation conflicted with their feminist goals.

Feminists would have avoided this contradiction if there had been a commitment within the state administration to decrease overall inequality (Acker, 1987). No such commitment existed, as was obvious as management representatives sided with the consultants against increasing points for human-relations skills and job stress in low-paid jobs. Moreover, in the process there was much discussion by consultants and managers about the need for more, not less, inequality. That is, managers in the public sector are paid much less than those in the private sector, and public sector professionals are also underpaid in relation to the private market. No support existed among such employees for even further increasing their disadvantage in comparison with other managers and professionals through a reduction of hierarchy internal to the state.

These are expressions of class interests, not simply interests in preserving status hierarchy. Thus, class processes are intrinsic to hierarchical processes, and the reproduction of gender inequality is also accomplished within these same processes. In the political contest over the technical reproduction of hierarchy, the class interests of the consultants and of state management prevailed over the gender interests of feminists and the gender and class interests of those working women they intended to represent.

The language used by consultants in explaining and defending their system reveals managerial assumptions about hierarchies and jobs. Hierarchy is natural, and the test of whether a particular ranking is correct is common sense. Common sense is what any reasonable person can see is right. In all probability, it is close to the hierarchical ordering that exists. Jobs are abstract categories with no occupants, and job evaluation assesses jobs, not workers. Characteristics of workers, which vary, should not be confused with characteristics of jobs. For example, stress may be the reaction of certain workers, not an element in a job. Thus, such stress could not be evaluated. Such concepts of jobs and hierarchies contributed to difficulties in changing the valuation of women's jobs.

Examination of the job-evaluation process suggests some of the ways that specifically female- and male-class positions are reproduced, and thus, some of the concrete processes through which class structures are constituted as gendered structures. Cockburn (1983) has described the historical process through which the gendering of work was constructed in one industry, printing, as a defense against processes of deskilling that were threatening to devalue men's work and to deprive male workers of their gendered identities. In this comparable-worth project, we have a brief glance at a related phenomenon, the verbal strategies male workers used to try to avoid a devaluation of their skills. Such a devaluation would come from decreasing the differentials between male skills and female skills. Although scores would eventually affect relative earnings, I do not believe that these job evaluators had money in mind when they fought against attributing knowledge and some degree of complexity to clerical work. They were concerned with respect, getting their due. Admitting that certain female jobs might be worthy of a similar respect seemed to be demeaning to them. Their refusal to believe the women evaluators probably also reveals something about their regard for female knowledge and about the invisibility of dimensions of women's jobs, which are seen as auxiliary, assisting, supporting, without any agency of their own.

Job content that is supervisory, coordinating, mediating, or therapeutic is often obscured, not only in male minds, but in the abstract ordering of positions and in the documentation that supports and legitimizes that ordering. The formal hierarchy specifies that managerial and supervisory functions are located at certain levels. Job descriptions used for job evaluations in Oregon indicate, however, that supervisory responsibilities are part of many nonsupervisory jobs. This observation is confirmed for Great Britain in a recent study that found that "those who are not classified as supervisors nevertheless perform a wide variety of supervisory tasks" (Rose, Marshall, Newby, and Vogler, 1987:17). Among the nonsupervisors, nonmanual employees had the highest proportion of supervisory duties. Although this British study does not give information on the exact jobs with these supervisory duties, it is probable that many of them are female-dominated.

The Oregon data also suggest that clerical work is much more various than is implied by the term, as indicated by the initial division of six job categories into more than eighty. Knowledge and skill specifications for such jobs often do not fully reflect the variations in complexity in many lower-level female-dominated jobs. This observation is contrary to the idea, widely accepted by sociologists (for example, Glenn and Feldberg, 1979; Crompton and Jones, 1984), that clerical work has been deskilled. Some clerical work is certainly unskilled and deskilled; other clerical work is not. The hierarchical location of all clerical work obscures variation and the dispersion of supervisory tasks to lower levels. The theoretical question of what constitutes class boundaries and where they might be located becomes more complicated when the work of women is entered into the analysis, for if supervisory responsibilities are widely dispersed downward in organizations, the supervisor-nonsupervisor divide may not constitute a good indicator of class boundaries (Rose, Marshall, Newby, and Vogler, 1987).

The assignment of job-evaluation points to all job classifications and all individual positions in state employment, a profoundly political process in bureaucratic clothes, was the first step on the road to true comparable worth. Issues of sex bias in job evaluation were joined early, and the feminists and trade unionists lost. The hiring of Hay Associates, though it was the best choice given the limitations of time, money, and political legitimacy, abdicated the ground to a conservative management approach. Since even this approach revealed more undervaluation of women's work than the state administration was willing or able to deal with, the question of male and managerial bias in the evaluation system paled in significance in comparison with the difficult issues of building and implementing a new classification and compensation system. These steps were even more obviously political.

Notes

1. There are, of course, other interpretations of the emergence and nature of hierarchical organizational design, particularly those that see it as an emergent feature of all attempts to organize complex activities on a large scale (for instance, Abrahamsson, 1985) or as necessary for efficiency under those conditions. I obviously am more convinced by the analyses that emphasize the control aims of these organizational forms.

2. A survey of British employers in 1976 (Thakur and Gill) confirmed that this is one of the purposes employers have in mind when they institute job evaluation. Asked why they had introduced job evaluation, almost all employers replied, "to get a fair pay structure." Fifty-five percent used job evaluation "to establish a system of job hierarchy" (1976:14).

3. See Barker (1986) for a thorough discussion of the history of the Hay system.

4. See Lichtenstein (1984) and Barker (1986) for an analysis of the implicit weights in the Hay Guide Charts.

5. See Lichtenstein (1984) for further analysis of the effects of levels and numbering patterns in the Hay Guide Charts.

6. The impact of a factor on the total score is determined by the number of levels that are actually used in evaluations (Aaron and Lougy, 1986). If only two levels in Freedom to Act were actually all that were ever used, it would contribute less to the total variance of scores than Human Relations if all three levels were used.

7. I observed 81 of the 355 benchmark evaluations and, in addition, listened to sore-thumbing sessions and group discussions on evaluations. In the pretest evaluations I was a member of an evaluation team that discussed or evaluated thirty-two jobs. Most of my observations were of the blue-collar clerical team.

8. A recent British study confirms this finding (Rose, Marshall, Newby, and Vogler, 1987). Using a sample survey of the economically active population, they report that 14 percent of employees without managerial or supervisory status report supervisory or managerial responsibilities.

9. This discussion is based on material from Acker (1987).

10. The argument that beliefs about gender form part of the ideology of capitalism is widespread. See, for example, Harding (1986) and Acker (1988).

11. For an interesting description of this process see Barbara Garson, *All the Livelong Day* (1975).

References

Aaron, Henry J., and Cameran M. Lougy. 1986. *The Comparable Worth Controversy.* Washington, D.C.: The Brookings Institution.
Abrahamsson, Bengt. 1985. "Form and Function in Organization Theory." *Organization Studies* 6, no. 1: 39–53.

Acker, Joan. 1987. "Sex Bias in Job Evaluation: A Comparable Worth Issue." In Christine Bose and Glenna Spitze, eds., *Ingredients for Women's Employment Policy*. Albany: State University of New York Press.

———. 1988. "Class, Gender, and the Relations of Distribution." *Signs* 13, no. 3: 473–497.

Barker, Melissa. 1986. "An Organizational Perspective on Job Evaluation Methods: Implications for Comparable Worth Approaches to Pay Equity." Ph.D. diss., Department of Sociology, University of Oregon.

Baron, James N., Frank R. Dobbin, and P. Deveraux Jennings. 1986. "War and Peace: The Evolution of Modern Personnel Administration in U.S. Industry." *American Journal of Sociology* 92, no. 2: 350–383.

Bellak, Alvin O. 1982. *The Hay Guide Chart–Profile Method of Job Evaluation*. Chicago: The Hay Group.

Bureau of National Affairs. 1984. *Pay Equity and Comparable Worth: A BNA Special Report*. Washington, D.C.: Bureau of National Affairs.

Clegg, Stewart, and David Dunkerley. 1980. *Organization, Class and Control*. London: Routledge & Kegan Paul.

Cockburn, Cynthia. 1983. *Brothers: Male Dominance and Technological Change*. London: Pluto Press.

———. 1985. *Machinery of Dominance*. London: Pluto Press.

Crompton, Rosemary, and Gareth Jones. 1984. *White-Collar Proletariat: Deskilling and Gender in Clerical Work*. Philadelphia: Temple University Press.

Edwards, Richard. 1979. *Contested Terrain*. New York: Basic Books.

Farnquist, Robert L., David R. Armstrong, and Russel P. Strausbaugh. 1983. "Pandora's Worth: The San Jose Experience." *Public Personnel Management* 12: 358–68.

Game, Ann, and Rosemary Pringle. 1984. *Gender at Work*. London: Pluto Press.

Garson, Barbara. 1975. *All the Livelong Day*. New York: Doubleday.

Glenn, Evelyn Nakano, and Roslyn L. Feldberg. 1979. "Degraded and Deskilled: The Proletarianization of Office Work." In A. Zimbalist, ed., *Studies in the Labor Process*. New York: Monthly Review Press.

Harding, Sandra. 1986. *The Science Question in Feminism*. Ithaca, N.Y.: Cornell University Press.

ILO. 1986. *Job Evaluation*. Geneva: International Labour Office.

Jones, Maxwell. 1976. *Maturation of the Therapeutic Community: An Organic Approach to Health and Mental Health*. New York: Human Science Press.

Lichtenstein, Sara. 1984. "Comparable Worth as Multiattribute Utility." Talk given at Judgment and Decision Making Society Meeting, San Antonio, Texas.

McAdams, Kenneth G. 1974. "Job Evaluation and Classification." *Journal of American Water Works Association* 66, no. 7: 405–9.

Mouzelis, Nicos. 1967. *Organization and Bureaucracy*. London: Routledge & Kegan Paul.

Philips, Ann, and Barbara Taylor. 1986. "Sex and Skill." In *Feminist Review*, ed., *Waged Work*. London: Virago.

Pierson, David, Karen Shallcross Koziara, and Russell Johannesson. 1984. "A Policy-Capturing Application in a Union Setting." In Helen Remick, ed., *Comparable Worth and Wage Discrimination*. Philadelphia: Temple University Press.

Remick, Helen. 1979. "Strategies for Creating Sound, Bias-free Job Evaluation Plans." In *Job Evaluation and EEO: The Emerging Issues*. New York: Industrial Relations Counselors.

———. 1981. "The Comparable Worth Controversy." *Public Personnel Management Journal* 10: 371–83.

———. 1984. "Major Issues in *a priori* Applications." In Helen Remick, ed., *Comparable Worth and Wage Discrimination*. Philadelphia: Temple University Press.

Rose, David, Gordon Marshall, Howard Newby, Carolyn Vogler. 1987. "Goodbye to Supervisors?" *Work, Occupations and Society* 1: 7–24.

Sacks, Karen Brodkin. 1984. "Computers, Ward Secretaries, and a Walkout in a Southern

Hospital." In Karen Brodkin Sacks and Dorothy Remy, eds., *My Troubles Are Going to Have Trouble with Me*. New Brunswick, N.J.: Rutgers University Press.

Schwab, Donald G. 1980. "Job Evaluation and Pay Setting: Concepts and Practices." In E. R. Livernash, ed., *Comparable Worth: Issues and Implications*. Washington, D.C.: National Equal Employment Advisory Council.

Steinberg, Ronnie, and Lois Haignere. 1987. "The Undervaluation of Work by Gender and Race: The New York State Comparable Pay Study." In Christine Bose and Glenna Spitze, eds., *Ingredients for Women's Employment Policy*. Albany: State University of New York Press.

Stellman, Jeanne, and Mary Sue Henifin. 1983. *Office Work May Be Dangerous to Your Health*. New York: Pantheon.

Task Force Minutes, State of Oregon. 1985. *Task Force on State Compensation and Classification Equity Minutes*. Salem: State of Oregon Archives.

Thakur, Manab, and Deirdre Gill. 1976. *Job Evaluation in Practice*. London: Institute on Personnel Management.

Treiman, Donald J. 1979. *Job Evaluation: An Analytic Review*. Interim Report of the Equal Employment Opportunity Commission. Washington, D.C.: National Academy of Sciences.

Treiman, Donald J., and Heidi Hartmann, eds. 1981. *Women, Work, and Wages: Equal Pay for Jobs of Equal Value*. Washington, D.C.: National Academy Press.

14

Manufacturing Management Ideology: Corporate Culture and Control in Financial Services

Vicki Smith

Trainers to seminar participants: Any time change is
introduced you experience insecurity. You have to
beware of the comfort zone: you're falling into a
network of despair; you need to pull yourself up and
accept change.

Seminar participant to trainers: I'd rather quit than
extract "stretch" from my employees through your
criteria.

Formula presented by trainers: "SARAH": the stages
managers allegedly pass through when criticized for
their management style:
  S = shock
  A = anger
  R = rejection
  A = acceptance
  H = hope

*—from Management seminars
at American Security Bank*

In corporation after large American corporation, business leaders are
restructuring their operations to maintain competitiveness. They have
placed new objectives such as reducing labor costs—by extracting
concessions from professional and manual workers and increasing
worker productivity across the board (what some call "skimming the fat"
from inflated firms)—at the forefront of top management rhetoric and
policy.
  Corporate leaders now argue for flexibility and change. To set the

performance of U.S. corporations back on track, they warn, firms must change their compensation systems for professional and managerial employees (from bureaucratic systems to meritocracies), transform themselves from rigid bureaucracies to flexible, less hierarchical structures, and shift from centralized to decentralized management practices.[1] These new policies radically challenge the terms and conditions of growth-engendered, bureaucratic, and generous employment contracts: the regularized, stable framework of rules governing wages, promotions, and discipline (Edwards 1979).

Transforming corporate cultures also will lead to more competitive corporate performances, according to this new outlook. The idea that corporate cultures can determine the success or failure of large firms has captured the imagination of business observers, academics, and lay persons alike. Peters and Waterman's *In Search of Excellence* (1984) popularized the successful entrepreneurial cultures of such companies as Hewlett-Packard and Procter and Gamble, while studies of the flexible "art of Japanese management" (Athos and Pascale, 1981; Ouchi, 1981) alerted the public to all that was wrong with rigid American bureaucrats.[2]

The business press has taken up the thread, exploring the virtues and disadvantages of evaluating firms from the cultural vantage point. Pascale (1984) extolled the virtues of this perspective, arguing in *Fortune* magazine that management must pay attention to the culture of the firm because a strong culture "supplements formal rules," whereas a weak culture "can make organizational life capricious." In a more skeptical vein, Uttal (1983), also writing in *Fortune,* cast a wary eye on the "corporate culture vultures": consultants who capitalize on their alleged expertise in repairing and redirecting company cultures.

Belief in the significance of culture has become powerful enough that many of its advocates claim that poor or undermanaged cultures literally can block successful corporate change (*Businessweek,* 14 May 1984; Halloran, 1985). Many companies now try to *transform* bureaucratic orientations, to push managers to become more entrepreneurial and to take more risks, in order to overcome the harmful effects of poor cultures.[3] Top managers try to administer new meaning throughout the firm by manipulating company symbols, myths, and history and to overturn complacency by appealing to the pride and loyalty of all company employees.

American Security's strategic management exploited these claims, using the management training seminars to reshape the bank's culture. The issues debated in these seminars are at the heart of the transformation and possible degradation of managerial, professional, and white-collar employment: a necessary transformation, according to the contemporary management theorists, if U.S. industry is to regain its international competitiveness.

The managers who were the subject of this study did not have a direct formal role in formulating American Security's restructuring processes, although they were targeted as the principal agents for achieving them. Through the training seminars, strategic management inculcated an ideology of nonbureaucratic, coercive management that would secure the legitimacy for, while obscuring, their restructuring agenda. The seminar trainers gave middle managers the tools to ease out growth-based employment policies and mobility opportunities and to usher in an employment framework shaped by constraint, decline, and an ongoing struggle to achieve profitability. Middle managers were charged with the mission of garnering the consent of employees to the daily, not-so-regularized business of the firm.

If the corporate culture program and the new management methods represent the theory of individual judgment or autonomous management, then the seminars and the act of teaching the new program represent the practice, and the trainers the practitioners of individualizing management. In this uniquely collective setting within an otherwise tremendously fragmented social system, middle managers were exposed to the conditions facing other managers and were systematically subjected by the trainers to strategic management's agenda. In addition, the seminar trainers attempted to contain and channel possible resistance to the new managerial agenda by getting managers to discuss their fears of and objections to change and to admit collectively the need for a recreated management. The seminar interactions therefore provide an opportunity to examine the *process* whereby middle managers were targeted as agents and objects of corporate restructuring.

Management Training and Managerial Consent

Management training programs serve, in part, as an arena in which control over, and consent from, management will be gained. Utilizing an elaborate apparatus of in-firm personnel relations, human resources, and management development departments as well as outside consultants, top management in many firms has devoted substantial resources to train managers away from the "point of production" in order to produce and reproduce managerial commitments and ideology.[4]

As early as the 1930s personnel experts in American industry recognized the importance of special training programs for foremen, above and beyond any "managerial expertise" that could be acquired from experiences on the shop floor (Jacoby, 1985). Personnel managers used these programs to reshape foremen's role in a highly volatile political context: top management and personnel specialists believed that foremen's behavior could block, or conversely lead to, unionization of workplaces. "The revival of foremen's training," Jacoby (1985) argues in his study of the emergence of bureaucratic personnel practices, "was industry's plan to use foremen as its first line of defense against unionism" (230).

Training programs attempted to educate foremen about the limitations on their power, encourage them to sell workers on company propaganda, train them in the human-relations approach to make them better managers, and bolster their loyalty to the company (Jacoby, 1985: 230–31). Thus such programs functioned to regulate the arbitrary exercise of power by foremen and to promote a greater identification between the objectives of foremen and the company. Patten (1968) similarly emphasizes the fact that firms, the War Manpower Commission established during World War II, and YMCA foremen's clubs trained foremen in the area of human-relations theory (110–17).

Management training programs emerged concurrently with a new appreciation for "the mind of management" in the early decades of this century. Corporations, unable to assume a managerialist orientation, used these training sessions to professionalize and create an "elite" management (Bendix, 1956:320). The methods used to reshape the managerial orientation—teaching the human-relations approach to managing employees; administering performance ratings of managers through tests and interviews; scheduling weekend, evening, and other regular staff meetings—added up to an agenda of "intensive communication," one aim of which was that managers should manage in a more enlightened and effective fashion.

Some have prescribed training and education programs as a means to gaining managerial-level employees' participation in new corporate goals. One way of smoothing the route to corporate reorganization may be to involve managers in diagnosing current organizational problems. Such organizationwide participation in training programs may increase an overall and coordinated rather than a departmental or competitive, point of view (Argyris, 1955). Furthermore, participation in collective organizational settings is often used to exert top managerial control, contain conflict, and co-opt resistance (Dickson, 1981). By organizing group sessions, "top management can establish a framework for participation which allows them to retain effective control" (Dickson, 1981: 162–63).

The level of financial commitment made by U.S. firms to management training underscores an ongoing preoccupation with securing managerial commitment to and participation in corporate life. According to a 1986 survey, more firms offer formal training programs to middle managers than to any other occupational group, with the exception of executives (69.5 percent of the firms that responded provide training for executives; 68.9 percent provide training for middle managers; and 61.2 percent of the firms offer training to first-line supervisors; the next highest occupational category to which firms provided training was office/clerical at 50.8 percent). Furthermore, in the firms surveyed, middle managers receive on the average more hours of training (44.2 annually) than any other occupational group (see Gordon, 1986b: table 1, p. 49). Another survey concludes that by the year 2000 the average manager will spend eighty-two hours per year in training programs, suggesting that there will be little abatement of this emphasis on training and retraining managers (Fulmer, 1986:70).[5]

Indicated by purely economic measures, American Security Bank's seminars represented an extremely significant deployment of resources. The training seminars were organized by an elaborate management development division, set up in 1983 for the sole purpose of administering the managerial turnaround. The management division was staffed by American Security's management-level employees rather than outside management consultants, although outsiders were initially employed to assist in designing the program. At any given time approximately twenty-five managers were teaching the classes; in addition, several managers and supporting staff ran the operation.

The management development division paid a high price to provide a comfortable, even generous setting for the seminars. For the first two years the seminars were nearly always conducted in resort hotels around the state, where all participants stayed for the entire five days.[6] With all expenses paid at vacation-like locations and paid time off from jobs, the seminar week was seen as a privileged break from work.

In structure and timing, the seminars departed radically from the way in which managers had been socialized in the past, changes that indicated a significant organizational measurement of the training. Before the management training program was introduced in 1983, managers received no regular, systematic training as managers in American Security Bank.[7] Although a manager might have attended one of a number of *thematic* classes at some point in his or her career (such as classes in communications, career planning, and leadership or functionally specialized classes such as credit training or use of on-line computer systems), few had attended *occupational* classes that would prepare them for their new role. Furthermore, participation even in thematic programs was inconsistent across the bank. Employees of the bank were frequently promoted into management positions without first undergoing managerial job training. This historical lack of rigorous socialization of managers throws the new agenda for middle managers into even sharper contrast; the new regime represented a major reallocation of organizational resources to recreating management.

Finally, the use of bank employees to teach the seminars provides testimony to the ideological dimension of the training. Each seminar was run by three trainers, drawn from diverse sectors of the bank. Managers who worked as trainers did so for two years, after which time they returned to the working ranks of management. Coming from diverse organizational locations throughout the bank, the trainers were individuals who had chosen the training position either as a respite from their normal work or because they had been redeployed as a result of restructuring.[8]

Their personal histories with the bank allowed these in-house trainers to claim that they identified with both the plight of managers and the need for new corporate goals; theoretically they possessed the legitimacy to galvanize others to the mission of the training seminar. The trainers and the seminar attendees were, after all, part of the same big American Security "family."

Many of the seminar trainers evinced what amounted to a religious devotion to strategic management's goals, taking extremely seriously their assignment to incorporate middle managers into the fold of corporate change. As one particularly articulate women impressed on me, her purpose in working as a management trainer was to spread [CEO] Wedgewood's message and "give everyone an opportunity to change." Another felt that he had "always been in the role of a change agent, but it was never explicit"; in the role of seminar trainer, he felt that he had found his calling. Even one male trainer who appeared to be somewhat cynical about his "cheerleader" role continually and persuasively turned his acerbic style to the objectives of the seminar, using sarcasm and irreverence to get middle managers to laugh at and criticize themselves.

Despite the sincerity and enthusiasm with which the trainers undertook their mission, their dual structural position imposed a notable tension within the seminar proceedings. On the one hand, the trainers were integrated into the personnel management apparatus of the bank; in this sense they were the agents of strategic management's agenda. On the other hand, their insider status occasionally made them more vulnerable to manager's hostility. Their common position as managers in the bank increased their empathy with middle managers, often leading them to accept passively the full brunt of managers' criticisms about the organizational changes taking place.

Their struggle to reconcile these two facets of their position, to make sense of the hostility showered on them by seminar participants, without, for the most part, condemning those participants, was often painfully apparent. At several very awkward moments in the seminars, the trainers truly lacked answers for the concerns participants were raising. However, this did not stop the trainers from otherwise maintaining a very consistent approach in steering and controlling group discussions.[9]

Inside the Management Seminars: Organization and Politics

My position at a table with the trainers in the back of the seminar room gave me a comprehensive view of the entire seminar proceedings. In contrast, only a handful of participants could see us. Those attending the seminar sat at a U-shaped arrangement of tables: facing each other around the U, the fifteen to twenty-five participants were fully visible to one another. The very formal, even lavish, environment (all the tables had floor-length skirted tablecloths; each place setting had an elegant name card facing outward for all to see; large pitchers of ice water were placed every few feet along the table; and every position had a pile of literature—fat binders full of seminar information—along with pens and pencils imprinted with the company logo) contributed to a sense of important purpose. Indeed, we were all about to embark on the very serious and collective endeavor of reconstructing management.

American Security's management seminars shared many characteristics of human-potential courses; the "take responsibility for your own actions" ethos, so dominant in the human-potential movement, enhanced the objective of individualizing management.[10] Managers participated extensively, as the trainers encouraged them to examine and discuss their feelings about the many changes confronting them. Although there was a high tolerance for "sharing" one's feelings, however, the range of topics and the tone in which they were discussed were closely managed by the seminar trainers.

The trainers walked the participants through a number of curriculum modules and attempted to delimit carefully the directions in which discussions could move. The objectives of the seminar included describing the theory behind the newly instituted Performance Planning, Coaching, and Evaluation system (PPCE), and discussing situational leadership and the new corporate culture, otherwise known as "Vision, Values, and Strategy."

Techniques to regularize management pervaded all aspects of the seminar and its preparation. The standardization of course materials and curriculum created a coherent and professional image of the project at hand. Visual devices such as charts, graphs, and poster-size illustrations were hung around the conference room. Each class member received reams of written material mass-produced for the seminars by the bank's management development division. Consisting of books explaining the use of the PPCE, salary administration, and how to be a career counselor to one's employees, the material also included a number of articles on corporate culture, change, and resistance to change from such business publications as the *Harvard Business Review*.

Before attending the seminar each manager engaged in a self-monitoring exercise by filling out a "leadership practices inventory" (LPI) and administering this same inventory to his or her employees. The inventory assessed how good a leader each manager was from the perspective of both the manager and the people he or she managed. (Inventory items asked whether they managed conflict or change well and whether or not they were good decision makers.) The manager submitted all the inventories to the management development staff, who tallied up the results. The trainers distributed computerized tabulations of each manager's leadership skills, results that were later used to analyze and suggest improvements for the manager's performance.[11]

The trainers began by having participants state their names and what they wanted to gain from the seminar. Managers' statements simultaneously reflected their uneasiness about the very meaning of the managerial role in the context of the bank's crisis and expressed their interest in viable management guidelines. Comments ranged from "I want to learn how to be a good people manager," "I need to learn hands-off managing," and "I want to learn how to get good people to work harder when they don't want to" to "I'm trying to decide whether or not I even want to be a manager," and "I need to learn to cope with the PPCE."[12]

The trainers then proceeded with a presentation that showed how the bank's changes were related to the crisis in the banking industry. Always careful to emphasize the factors external to the firm that were creating a need for a new managerial orientation, the trainers showed the "big picture"—the turbulent environmental and financial conditions facing the bank—and its effects on working conditions in the office and on the shop floor. The discussion of the bank's financial and organizational difficulties, marked factors in particular, parallels the "exposure strategy" cited by Whalley (1986) in his study of engineers. Firms encouraged a "managerialist" orientation by exposing their engineering employees to financial and organizational information about the company's competitive situation (227). Presumably exposure compels employees—professional or managerial—to identify with and work to achieve profitability objectives.

Starting with the principles of the new corporate culture captured in the program of Vision, Values, and Strategy, the trainers demonstrated how the larger direction and profitability of the bank directly affected and were affected by what went on in the bank's many divisions, offices, and branches. They further argued that they could offer concrete tools to enable managers to make a positive contribution to the bank's larger direction.

The trainers introduced the Performance Planning, Coaching, and Evaluation (PPCE) procedure as the mechanism linking corporate strategic plans to daily work processes at all levels of the bank. The procedure would allow middle managers to translate top management's plans for a leaner, more entrepreneurial, nonbureaucratic organization into concrete personnel and employment policies. As one trainer noted, discussing a chart that showed the relationship between corporate business plans and the "action plans" of individual managers, the PPCE "holds this whole scheme together."

Throughout the seminar exercises, managers demonstrated a good understanding of the big picture and agreed with the general need for greater productivity to improve the financial health of the corporation. The consensus emerged that to rectify the current crisis, action was necessary at all levels of the corporation. This consensus is the axis of intramanagement unity, representing the convergence of middle and strategic management interests.

But another consensus emerged, one that united *middle* managers but separated them from strategic management. While lower-level managers agreed with strategic management's agenda for achieving larger profitability objectives, they diverged from that agenda over the methods by which those objectives could be achieved. Although corporate restructuring created very different pressures for different groups of managers, these managers nevertheless agreed that the new managerial orientation would undermine rather than promote long-term consent to the restructuring process; they felt that their ability to elicit productive work behavior was threatened by what they perceived as a skewed definition of entrepreneurialism and an arbitrary set of management methodologies.

Middle managers anticipated heightened politicization resulting from the new emphasis on using individual managerial judgment to push through a new productivity program. In the context of contraction and the decline of organization-wide mechanisms of control, the arbitrary management schemes and the new definition of management on which they were based would weaken bases for managerial authority. The trainers countered these concerns by reinterpreting the organizational politics of corporate restructuring as neutral organizational problems *caused* by individual psychological maladjustment, and to be *solved* by individual managerial judgment.

Extracting Greater Effort: Minimum Job Requirements

Recent theories of corporate structure have blamed lack of productivity and innovation in large corporations on too great a dependence on centralized, bureaucratic rules. Thus some have argued for replacing strictly bureaucratic organization with less hierarchical, more fluid structures that would facilitate decentralized, innovative management action (cf. Kanter's [1983] discussion of the "integrative" corporation). American Security Bank imported elements of this critique of bureaucratic behavior into the new management platform. One attempt to redress the ills of bureaucracy consisted of weaning managers and employees from the allegedly binding and stultifying job descriptions on which position had historically been based.

Emphasis on merely satisfactory job performance, according to the seminar trainers, was a legacy of a profitable, complacent banking environment. Managers who did not look for ways to wring more out of the jobs and the people they managed were encouraging mediocrity. Thus managers should look for ways to "raise the bar": to upgrade *jobs* by raising the "minimum job requirements" (MJRs) for positions. In so doing managers could become innovators in their own units. The trainers argued that middle managers should reorient their thinking away from bureaucratically constricting, standardized job descriptions based on position and focus instead on increasing results in order to contribute to improved corporate performance. This they would do by setting "stretch objectives": upgrading *people* by pushing them to achieve even higher levels of output.[13] In lieu of specific recommendations for upgrading jobs and jobholders, the seminar trainers continually advocated leaving managers alone to upgrade through vigorous and flexible use of management judgment.

The trainers informed me, before "class" began, that the discussions of MJRs were always the most difficult modules of the seminars, because managers held so much "irrational resistance" toward this fundamental change in their orientation to managing. This precaution heightened my anticipation of the module devoted to the MJR. What was it about this topic that could unnerve the trainers so much that they would warn me about it beforehand? Why were middle managers so protective of "across the board" or organizationally consistent MJRs?

The discussions of minimum requirements for a job demonstrate why American Security's managers held a quite rational resistance to the demise of a bureaucratic framework for managing. From middle managers' perspective, company-wide standardized job expectations were important for regularizing their evaluations of employees' performance. The loss of such standards connoted a level of chaos that would undermine the new responsibilities with which these managers were saddled. Yet in the seminars the trainers insisted that the bank, in its current process of change, could no longer come up with positional levels appropriate for the entire corporation. Managers must use their own judgment instead and take responsibility for determining new and higher job expectations.

After introducing the idea that managers should deemphasize minimum job requirements and emphasize increased results, one of the trainers attempted to neutralize the politics of upgrading jobs and individuals. Rather than discuss MJRs as an important benchmark by which managers could consistently evaluate employees, this trainer attempted to get managers to think of MJRs as something merely psychological. Calling MJRs "only a tool, only a consideration in the thought process," she anticipated manager's reluctance to abandon a more centralized framework for managing, acknowledging in a sympathetic voice that "many of you will find it hard to come up with positional MJRs." She went on to place the onus on managers, however, saying, "You as manager need to go through the thought process, figure out what you need. There are very few positions in the corporation for which we can come up with across-the-board MJRs."

She admonished the seminar participants not to expect centralized guidelines in measuring employee performance. Insisting that standardized job requirements were inappropriate for a firm as diverse and changing as rapidly as American Security, this trainer suggested that they were, in fact, the true impediments to productive management; reworking productivity standards through the appropriate thought process was the sign of the truly entrepreneurial manager.

Another trainer hinted at the real purpose behind "deemphasizing" MJRs; he repeated the charge that standardized expectations of employees block innovation and productivity. His approach is telling, for it recasts the productivity problem as a problem of individuals and their psychological propensities. "Let's think about human nature," he argued. "If we just had MJRs, why would people work any harder than just the minimum?"

One trainer, named Kathryn, reiterated that managers should be "raising the bar" (or minimums) of as many jobs as they could. Dave, a seminar participant, argued against managers' role in utilizing personal judgment to shift the boundaries of productivity in this way: "If we don't have a standard, we can't do this." Kathryn insisted that in fact Dave did have a standard—his managerial judgment. Management judgment simply did not carry weight with Dave, however. Thinking ahead to his work situation, Dave touched on the contradiction between the agenda of the seminar (to get managers to increase productivity and to slim down the corporation in a context of contraction and declining rewards) and the tools being offered to managers to achieve that agenda. He insisted that strategic management should execute the new corporate agenda more directly by selling assets and closing unprofitable units, arguing that middle managers did not have the means to manage effectively by individual judgment. To Kathryn's claim that he possessed a valid standard, Dave replied, "No, I don't, but the corporation does. And this is leading to change and downgrading. We cannot manage these processes without a corporate standard."

Middle managers quickly caught on to what it meant in practice to deemphasize standardized job descriptions in the service of higher productivity levels. Helen argued that if everyone in her unit were told that they had different and fluctuating MJRs, she could say goodbye to any possibilities for increasing productivity. Her employees would constantly be at Employee Relations (an employee/management mediating unit within the bank) to force greater consistency in evaluation procedures. Other participants jumped into this discussion, with Mavis asserting that "if there are different MJRs for fourteen different people in similar jobs, there is going to be trouble." A trainer intervened to redirect what had become a very contentious drift, arguing that raising job minimums to different levels for different individuals was a very natural task, simply part of a thought process in which managers logically connected individual job performance with the larger profitability objectives of the firm.[14] "We may be getting off on a tangent. The key is that managers must go through the thought process of knowing what you need for business goals and articulate these minimums to employees. It's a tool."

The trainers' behavior during discussions of MJRs and objectives visibly expressed their discomfort at being the objects of managers' antagonism. They walked nervously around the room, they more frequently interrupted discussions among participants, and they called for unscheduled break intervals at the peaks of heated discussions.

Trainers also used dismissive statements, such as "We may be getting off on a tangent" or "That's an excellent point and I'd like to save that for a future discussion" to defuse "hot points" during the seminars. But this marginalizing tactic did not deter Helen from insisting that concepts such as "thought process" and "individual judgment" were vague and of little help. The trainers might extol the virtues of management theory, claiming it provided an orderly and rational means of gaining greater worker effort, but the difficulty of managing the politics of a speedup were clear to Helen. Her concern, she argued, was not with abstractions and theory, but with "fairness and consistency. The practicality [of managing up employees' performance] is, you'd better know what you're doing."

The seminar trainers used the language of thought process to promote a framework of individual, innovative managerial action, at the same time playing down the negative implications of the new framework. The language allowed the trainers to dilute the significance of both the pressure on middle managers to increase productivity and the lack of centralized guidelines for doing so. In the framework of individualized responsibility, MJRs were no longer a set of guidelines for evaluating job performance: they were no more than an element of the thought process through which managers had to go to increase productivity.

Managers were not agents of a speedup of their employees' work: their role in increasing results was merely part of a thought process in which working to increase productivity steadily was a normal task, to be rationally incorporated into a manager's everyday job. The trainers minimized the import of "raising the bar" by expressing surprise and scoffing at the disturbed responses of the seminar participants. Recasting the political problems of consent and cooperation as simple individual problems, the trainers insinuated that any rational manager should be able to resolve the "minor" conflicts of organizational change.

At the same time, the insistent focus on managerial judgment to increase productivity formalized strategic management's agenda to individualize the responsibility of corporate change. As managers repeatedly voiced their dissent to having to manage each individual employee with less centralized guidance, they met ever greater insistence that they were to use situational leadership to obtain higher performance levels from all employees.

In response to managers apprehensions about the new emphasis on increasing results, one of the trainers cavalierly suggested that managers should simply write in (on employee performance evaluations) as much stretch as possible. After a manager carefully considers all aspects of a position and an employee's capabilities, that manager should "take risks" to "encourage workers to increase output": the trainer asked, "Shouldn't we raise the bar? Don't we ask more of them?" Sandy, a branch manager concerned about the disruptive aspects of both the random application of high stretch levels and the sudden transition from rewards for efforts and seniority to rewards for results, was very agitated as she asked, "How do you arbitrarily raise the bar for someone who has worked with the bank for fifteen years?" The trainer gave a response that reflected the individualizing thrust of situational leadership: "You know management isn't easy. You've got to use J [judgment, often referred to as "the Big J"]. You need to get involved in the process. *We* can't give you a cookbook."

The managers attending the seminars did not disagree with the need to find more effective ways of managing, but they did protest the impact that these particular methods would have on managerial effectiveness and legitimacy. Chris's response further illuminates middle managers' dilemma over the demise of more standardized guidelines in this organizational context. Chris was responsible for over eight indirect reports in an area management group in the retail division. She was an extremely accomplished employee and had received the bank's prestigious "golden pin of merit" (an award given out by the corporate personnel department for outstanding performance); at the end of the week-long seminar her fellow participants voted her "best manager" of their class. Presumably an ideal manager from the perspective of top management, Chris expressed her agreement throughout the seminar for many of top management's goals. But she was also quite articulate about her differences with certain aspects of those goals.

After a particularly long and antagonistic discussion of the process of raising the bar and deemphasizing minimum job requirements in which she urged that managers not penalize employees for managerial misjudgment, Chris attempted to sum up the basis of the group's opposition to the methodologies presented by the trainers: "I think we felt threatened when you said to *take away* the minimum job requirements. You're taking away one of our important measuring tools." Her comment seemed to embolden Ralph, who earlier had expressed anger when the trainers denied the importance of bureaucratic standards. He interjected, "You got my back up over the terminology change. Different areas have different needs and standards. When you admit the importance of MJRs I don't get bent out of shape. I'm going to go back and do things exactly the same way I have been." Judging by the rather defiant murmur that followed his words, this opinion was shared by others as well.

Managing Structural Change

Managers' fears were exacerbated similarly when they were confronted with the demand to increase productivity and set new objectives in the context of "nonnegotiable" changes: loss of personnel and funding and possible workplace closure. These structural transformations complicated managers' role in pressuring employees for greater work effort. And the language and management method of individualization failed to obscure the exploitative nature of the changes taking place, on which individual managerial legitimacy had little bearing.

Barry, for example, had comanaged a branch for several years in the position of branch administrative officer. He insisted that a key problem from his perspective lay in getting his employees to stretch (to become more productive) when the branches were undergoing staff reductions. Barbara, another branch manager, articulately summed up the contradiction inherent in demanding stretch in a context of diminishing resources:

> As managers we're told to cut staff; we're told to turn our tellers and ourselves into quality salespeople; and as managers we are supposed to increase our supervision and general productivity. Branch managers are really figureheads in terms of authority, yet we're under all this pressure: there is not really very much we can do.

These pressures similarly affected Rose, who managed fourteen loan-collection officers in the southern California area. As the loan function was being centralized, her loan officers could not "really give quality customer service. We don't have the expertise or tools any more to give informal answers to customer questions." Further under the gun because her unit was responsible for loan collection at precisely the time that the bank was facing unprecedented loan defaults, Rose expressed great frustration over the fact that at her previous branch, loan officers had been pushed to "sell paper": to lend out money as rapidly as possible.

Rose's lack of control over the way functional changes affected the jobs of her loan officers undermined her ability to understand existing productivity objectives, quite apart from formulating new and higher ones. The transformation of this function held other implications for Rose's job, because an increase in customer complaints (due to confusion over the new organization of the loan process) appeared on her PPCE as one negative measurement of her ability to "manage change." When Rose expressed a great deal of anger about the bank's continuing to make loans when its loan losses were beginning to look severe, Kathryn suggested that Rose should seek innovative ways of facing the managerial challenge and recommended that Rose ask herself, "What can *I* do to help this situation?" This individualistic recommendation triggered a long and heated discussion about managers' actual lack of control over their work situations.

Managers were supposed to manage employees in a context of extreme organizational uncertainty as the structure, labor process, and function of divisions changed unevenly throughout the bank. When managers raised concerns about managing uncertainty, they were given individualizing mechanisms for coping.[15] Middle managers frequently lamented the fact that they were kept in the dark about pending corporate changes. Kathryn, one of the trainers, responded that managers should not reveal their ignorance about the corporate restructuring process to their employees. Good managers, she argued, were opaque and would maintain individual legitimacy by concealing the inadequacy of their knowledge about the decline of the organization.

> Managers should not be transparent. If a manager has to make a decision and it is difficult—for example, if you're involved in a major centralization of functions, or redeployment—when you're communicating these changes to the employee, you should not be transparent. You don't want to be saying "I don't really understand why the company wants us to do this, but . . . ."

Helen, who managed a group of data-entry workers, expressed her frustration with this cryptic approach to managing change. One of the objectives on her PPCE on which *she* would be evaluated was to increase the productivity of her workers. But rumors were sweeping through her unit that some of these positions were going to be eliminated. Her work group had subsequently been severely demotivated (*sic*) and she had been unable to justify stretching on other than purely coercive terms ("no stretching, no jobs"). Thus what was transparent in her position was her lack of control over and knowledge about the fate of the unit and her inability to conceal the exploitative aspects of demands for a greater contribution to the firm.

Her workers plied her with questions about their future. She told her seminar colleagues, "If I don't know why something is happening, I will say I just don't understand." She felt that this bluntness, although it was a kind of manipulation, would lead her far more credibility in the managing process. Kathryn retorted, "What is your gut feeling? Use the Big J; be proactive; think ahead and be more managing and instrumental." Helen responded, "I will try to find out what's happening, but I am often unable to do so."

Kathryn refused to admit any larger organizational responsibility for managers' dilemmas, continuing instead to pin responsibility for managing conflict and change squarely to the shoulders of middle managers.

She expressed an extreme version of the individualist argument. "You're responsible for your own fate," she claimed.

> The corporation may own your job but you own your career. You have to try to manage the situation. If employees think they can see through you, you won't get a commitment from them. The onus is on managers. Managers have to write the PPCEs; you have to be taken seriously. Managers have to support top management. You have to be genuine. We don't want "just compliance" from managers.

Sandy contended that this managerial approach to change was simply irrelevant to her case: her employees discovered their branch was closing only when some workers came by to place a bid on the reconstruction of their building. As one single manager, Sandy rejected the idea that her legitimacy would justify, much less obscure, this type of corporate change.

In the course of the seminar no definitive solutions were given for achieving significantly higher productivity levels when employees and managers were unsure of their occupational outcomes and when managers, with fewer personnel and budgetary resources, lacked legitimate grounds for making employees work harder. When seminar participants persisted in pushing harder to know how they were to extract more from employees with fewer resources and guidelines, the trainers continually redirected responsibility for the solution back onto the managers. As one trainer stated, "We used to use the SPM [Standardized Procedures Manual] as a source for all dos and don'ts. But times have changed. We can't only follow rules; we have to ask ourselves: Does this make sense?"

Nor were managers satisfied that genuinely autonomous exercise of their judgment was unambiguously sanctioned by top management. Managing out looked like a murky process to middle managers, because the consequences of pushing workers to unreasonable limits to increase productivity were clear. If a manager had not clarified and documented every aspect of a work situation to the employee but had nevertheless fired or downgraded him or her, the employee might feel that he or she had been misled and later sue the bank—a turn of events for which the manager would ultimately be held responsible.

Several discussions centered on the procedures and implications of managing out. The trainers used "case studies" to teach managers how to identify and deal with poor performers. Many managers, however, were concerned about the ambiguities of this process. Andy had managed eight people in a branch in the Los Angeles area for seven years. He had been told that if a manager used language such as "might terminate" in an employee's PPCE and a labor board brought a case against the bank for wrongful termination, "the judge might highlight the 'might' and inquire what the alternatives were. It would shore up the employee's case against the manager."

The sensitive nature of managers' position in managing up or out was further driven home by Ken, who had managed four lawyers in the bank's litigation department for three years. As an older man, Ken had a perspective on the firm's legal position gained from many years of private practice outside the bank and from his location in the administrative inner sanctum of the bank. Ken was adamant; once a promise to an employee had been violated, he warned, a manager should anticipate legal action taken by that employee. "You're in a litigation context," he argued, "once a major screwup has happened in personnel policy."

In one module of the seminar, trainers and participants discussed a case study of a female employee who brought a discrimination suit against American Bank. The intention of the discussion was to ascertain who and what had been responsible for bringing on the suit. Tom, one of the trainers, argued that the fault lay with the manager: "Lack of communication is the root cause of the problem. She can file a discrimination suit—but what happens to American Bank when a suit is filed? It gives the corporation a bad image. *Managers should be talking to employees who feel discriminated against.*" Managers would be directly evaluated, on their PPCEs, on how well they used their judgment in avoiding these negative scenarios.

Almost without fail, managers responded with confusion and frustration to trainers' claims that managers must exercise discretion and judgment in dealing with employees. As one participant wryly noted, "We're given discretion about disciplinary action, but if I follow exactly what I want, the bank may be sued. I constantly must look for advice. My *employees* know the SPM—they would be great managers." At which point one of the trainers redirected the discussion: "Let's keep this question in mind. I hope we can answer this during the week. We have to remember the Big J. Your judgment: Can I do this or can't I?" Every so often the contradictions inherent in the Big J would bubble to the surface. When Diane questioned how a manager was to suspend a so-called poor performer, the trainers went to such lengths to caution her that she burst out, "What happened to my judgment as a manager? Suddenly I can't do anything unless I ask seventeen people before I send someone home."

Behind the concerns that managers had about increasing output was the very serious problem of defining output and productivity rates in production contexts that defied easy codification and quantification; this problem characterized many of the work sites within this bank, and of course, many work sites within firms and industries in a "postindustrial" or service-based economy. The fact that managers were being asked to increase productivity when minimal standardized guidelines existed for many jobs in the first place led to a good deal of confusion and frustration, expressed both in the training seminars and in interviews.

Ken, the corporate attorney mentioned above, was furious about the individualizing bias and the vague standards for productivity, in which all responsibility for productivity was deemed to be the middle manager's. When his seminar group was shown a diagram illustrating how each manager was supposed to increase the output of his or her department by getting every employee to stretch, he exclaimed, "How does this get affected if the input is inadequate? When I don't have enough people I cannot increase output."

Trainers insisted that output was the responsibility of the manager. Bill equated output with a manager's efforts, asserting that employees will strive to accomplish what they think the boss wants: "It's the manager who doesn't see the environment properly, who doesn't expect enough stretch, who doesn't give challenging enough assignments." The trainers referred to managers who would not get their employees to stretch as deadwood, old-timers who resisted change. Despite this condemnation, Diane blurted out in frustration that she would rather quit than extract stretch from her employees through the criteria proposed by the trainers.

The individualizing thrust was similarly expressed whenever seminar participants attempted to direct discussion of the current profitability crisis toward strategic management. When trainers admonished them for middle-managerial shortsightedness and for being more self-centered than firm-centered, seminar participants in turn challenged the firm's historical stress on what they called "corporate" as distinct from "moral" values and questioned whether top management was "being honest" about the root causes of the current dilemma.

The trainers trivialized dissenting individuals' efforts by forcing participants to "own" their contesting statements as mere personal opinions, again neutralizing the political issues of organizational restructuring by characterizing the dissenters as organizational miscreants. Anytime participants questioned the incompatibility between the human needs of people who worked in the corporation and the needs of profit making, trainers dismissed the seriousness of the conflicts and reduced them to "breakdown" in managers' communication of the goals of the corporation to individuals.

Managers anticipated many contradictory consequences from having to increase productivity and reduce personnel just as standardized measures to implement this ambitious agenda were disappearing. Thus intramanagement conflict crystallized in a struggle over the very meaning and function of bureaucracy. As strategic management pushed the ideological critique of managerial bureaucrats, middle managers asserted their case for centralized, bureaucratic criteria in order to implement the new agenda. The seminars became a site of struggle over the terms of management: managers challenged the new definition of entrepreneurial management in an environment of contraction and challenged the ways in which they were supposed to extract greater effort from those they managed.

Conclusion

Do the American Security Bank seminar proceedings mirror a battle taking place across the ranks of American corporate management, a struggle over the theory of management and over corporate management practices? Other examples support the claim that corporations use cultural programs to position managers as objects and agents of corporate change in this current era of industrial restructuring. These examples also point to high levels of conflict within management over the new norms contained in cultural platforms.

The very terminology of reporting in business publications suggests a cultural onslaught against middle levels of management, a trend not confined to information, financial, or service industries. One of the most well-publicized efforts deliberately to transform a corporate culture has been that of General Motors Corporation. Changing its culture was a tactical move in a long-term effort to "reinvigorate" the company's business standing (*Businessweek,* 7 April 1986). In its "corporate civil war" (presumably the equivalent of American Security's "cultural revolution"), the auto firm cracked down on a perceived "culture of complacency" and the ethos that permeated what chief executive officer Roger Smith called the "frozen middle" of management. Thawing out that frozen middle by eliminating bureaucratic layers of managers—eliminating one-quarter of its managerial workforce by 1990, to be precise—was one of the central aims of GM's corporate culture program (*Fortune,* 10 November 1986).

A similar effort was undertaken by the Ford Motor Company. The firm administered tests of managerial style and culture in workshops for managers; 76 percent of those tested were classified as "noncreative types," too willing to accept authority (*Wall Street Journal,* 3 December 1985). One observer declared the 1980s the "decade of the cultural revolution" after American Telephone and Telegraph adopted a program for changing its company culture during its breakup (Turnstall, 1986). Prechel's (1986) study of a corporate cultural change in a large steel company yields conclusions much like those drawn in this chapter: the emphasis on changing cultures can be a transitional strategy of almost last resort for top managements in declining and restructuring industries. As Ray (1986) suggests, the arena of culture may constitute the last frontier of control for corporate top management.[16]

The growing attention paid to management ideology and culture reflects a greater preoccupation with reshaping the values of American management to make managers willing ushers of corporate change. But in important ways these new management philosophies obscure organizational changes that undermine rather than promote managers' ability to act as agent of change.[17]

The conflicts taking place in the seminars are significant insofar as they reflect a lack of unity about the means and ends of the new corporate restructuring agenda. But the seminar proceedings also fueled and heightened antistrategic politics. Managers regularly expressed their skepticism about the aims of strategic management as they were transmitted in the seminar. If anything, the seminar heightened their awareness of the contradictions in the new orientation. Frank Cosgrove stated that top management was charging middle managers with reducing the bank's personnel but was hiding this mission behind depoliticized and optimistic language and "opaque" management. In his opinion, strategic management was asking middle management to manage by Theory X under the pretense that it was using Theory Y. In other words, managers were supposed to appear enlightened (the Theory Y manager) yet act in a more coercive fashion (the Theory X manager).[18] One branch manager could find no better term for the management philosophies, presented in the seminar and in the array of management literature distributed through the bank, than "brainwashing."

The theorists of new management philosophies have presented an ideal picture of nonhierarchical participatory corporate structures. They focus almost exclusively on the drawbacks of bureaucracy and criticize managers for preserving bureaucratic rigidity. They minimize or ignore, however, the degree to which bureaucratic norms provide an important source of consent to objectives corporate America is under so much pressure to achieve: such norms ensure rewards and regularize relations within the workplace. Under conditions of organizational contraction, centralization, and the elimination of monetary or mobility incentives, managers may view bureaucratic norms as one of the few sources of their ability to manage. Managers' demand that certain rules be left intact does not necessarily indicate organizational conservatism (although certainly in some cases it may): rather, as American Security Bank's middle managers recognized, their ability to secure consent and gain greater productivity levels depends to some degree on regularized reward and feedback procedures.

The current focus on controlling managers through corporate culture and ideological reform parallels attempts through the scientific-management movement to control lower-level production and clerical workers. Whereas scientific-management programs break down and colonize the physical movements of lower-level workers, corporate culture agendas attempt to specify the precise content and meaning of middle managers' social relations.

Striving to control employees through cultural mechanisms, however, may be limited in the same way that scientific management was limited in its applications to lower levels of workers (Edwards, 1979:97–104). The theory of cultural control frequently ignores such variables as the historical and organizational context of the workplace, the complex and unequal relations between different strata of management, and the relations between managers and those they manage. This theory also ignores the fact that cultures emerge from the actual structures of organizations and work processes; deliberate attempts to transform culture from the top down and at a purely symbolic level may thus face serious obstacles (Ouchi and Wilkins, 1985: 476). The vibrant entrepreneurial cultures that the new management theorists wish to create may be most typical in expanding, growth-based firms and may not be replicable in firms facing serious profitability pressures.

Middle managers' responses to change at American Security can best be explained by the particular organizational context in which they were to exercise the new managerial agenda. Calling for enterpreneurialism, flexibility, and heightened use of discretion, the new agenda simultaneously delimited what an entrepreneur was, how his or her tasks should be executed, and the repercussions of failing to exercise discretion in a way that served the corporations' purposes. In short, the platform of the new corporate culture substituted coercive, individualized responsibility for the autonomy and flexibility of the entrepreneur.

Furthermore, in the view of middle managers, strategic management's definition of arbitrarily inflated productivity standards, opaque management, and flexibility were inviable and potentially costly to the firm. Located at the intersection between the global changes of the firm and the effects of these changes in the bank's various work sites, managers predicted that the new methods would fail. The success of the program depended on exploiting managers' individual legitimacy, but the program itself undermined the legitimacy they needed to achieve corporate objectives.

Ralph, a manager, commented on the difficulties of acting like entrepreneurs and innovators in a context that continually undermined legitimacy, authority, and autonomous action. "We're encouraged to develop entrepreneurship; we're given visions, values, and strategy. But they're unfocused in relation to what managers have to do. When it conflicts with reality it's a problem." And insofar as the seminars were the site of strategic management's attempts to produce new managerial standards that contradicted the realities managers faced every day, the seminars became the site of struggle over the very definition of entrepreneurial behavior and over the terms by which managers were to extract greater effort from employees.

Notes

1. The proponents of a new corporate ideology include, for example, "progressive" management theorists who analyze both organizational structures and management practices (Naisbett, 1982; Kanter, 1983; Brandt, 1986; Kanter, 1987).

2. There has been a significant surge of sociological and organizational research on culture in organizations. Scholarly publications such as the *Administrative Science Quar-*

terly ("Organizational Culture," 1983), *Organizational Dynamics* ("Organizational Culture," 1983), and the *Journal of Management Studies* ("Organizational Culture and Control," 1986) have devoted entire issues to epistemological and methodological discussions of studying organizational and corporate cultures. Few of these studies have traced the ways in which the recent fascination with culture has shaped organizational practices. They have, rather, examined how existing cultural symbols and values impede or facilitate organizational objectives, an important, albeit limited, project. See Wilkins's (1989) critical assessment of corporations' misappropriation of the scholarly studies of corporate culture when top managers desperately try to remedy their organizational problems.

3. See Kimberly and Quinn (1984); Berman (1986); *Restructuring Turnaround* (1987); Martin (1988).

4. This supplements the common view that managers' allegiance to corporate life is predicated on appropriate socialization (class background, business school training), salary, promotion, and occupational conditions that bind professional or managerial employees to the firms in which they work (Perrow, 1986:128).

5. In addition, more firms reported "management skills training," regardless of occupation, as the principal area in which they provide training; the next highest areas of skills training were very closely related to, if not inseparable from, management skills, such as supervision and communications (Gordon, 1986b: p. 54, table 2). This survey was based on a sample of 2,550 firms with a range of 50 to 10,000 or more employees (43.4 percent of the firms had over 2,500 employees; 20.9 percent had over 10,000) (Gordon, 1986a: p. 27, table 2).

6. So, in addition to the several million dollars poured into the management development division, expenditures for the management turnaround included hotel rental and salaries for all employees while they were away at the seminar.

7. One could argue that extensive decentralization had really isolated strategic management from the bank's operations. Only as a result of the new, bankwide emphasis on change did strategic management learn fully about the lower ranks of American Security's managers. When they first announced, with great fanfare, that all managers would attend the new program, they anticipated training 9,000 employees; by 1985 CEO Wedgewood proclaimed that 14,000 managers would attend the program by year's end.

8. The trainers I observed, for example, were from the branch system, systems management, and lending. The trainers were largely a self-selected group. For complex personal and organizational reasons, they had a prior interest in and commitment to working as salespeople for the new corporate culture. Because trainers were ensconced in the seminars for a considerable time, their enthusiasm for the new corporate agenda was not significantly diminished by the "reality factor" other managers faced on their return to the field. Much like the commitments of missionaries in various religious orders, for a two-year period the trainers' work lives were devoted entirely to the seminars. Their enthusiasm was, however, occasionally strained by the participants' antagonism.

9. This type of "processual containment" on the part of the trainers is consistent with the seminar processes described by Jacoby (1985:229) and Hochschild (1983: chap. 6).

10. Recently there has been furor over the introduction of human-potential approaches into the workplace. The *New York Times* reported an increase of lawsuits by employees who feel they have been unduly pressured to participate in activities, such as self-exploration techniques and group therapy, that conflict with their personal or religious values. These activities have been organized toward the goal of increasing workplace productivity. One man who worked for an auto dealership contended, for example, that the teaching of "New Age Thinking to Increase Dealership Profitability" was "inimical to his religious views" (*New York Times,* 17 April 1987). American Security's human-potential side was comparatively toned down.

11. Since the N size of the inventory respondents was generally quite small (most of the inventories ranged from three to six responses), the inventory probably had a function other than to provide a meaningful measurement of a manager's managing skills. Zuboff's work may inadvertently be helpful for understanding the more implicit and coercive

function of such tests. Zuboff (1985) touts the leveling effects of coordinating knowledge of production processes between managerial and nonmanagerial workers. She argues that engaging both workers and supervisors in data generation and evaluation (rather than mystifying the process by leaving it in the hands of managers) makes them "brethren in the data" rather than perpetuates unnecessary relations of power and hierarchy (134). As workers and managers become "brethren" in the act of evaluating managers, one basis of managerial authority—ability to assert the managerial prerogative about knowing what it takes to manage effectively—diminishes greatly. This could be one form of what Blau and Schoenherr (1971) call "insidious control."

12. One indication that strategic management had successfully and informally disseminated the fact that managers were to be critically evaluated for the way they used the PPCE came from the management development division. In an interview one trainer informed me that the division had been "bombarded with phone calls" requesting information about proper use of the PPCE, as managers throughout the bank realized they would be held accountable for and through the PPCE system.

13. In essence, managers were being asked to raise both bottom-line productivity levels for merely satisfactory job performance and the productivity levels that would qualify employees for merit raises. This was part of the "managing up" program.

14. This individualizing tendency was startlingly evident in an unrelated discussion about ranking individual employees. Admonishing managers for their reluctance to give raises and promotions by frankly comparing each and every employee, Kathryn stated, "You simply can't make a commitment [to employees about achieving merit increases in pay]. You articulate this as stretch; *you'll say something very different to every employee* based on their maturity [emphasis added]."

15. Indeed, when one woman manager questioned why managers were not told about pending change, a trainer reversed the challenge, his patronizing tone conveying the distinct impression that her wish to know reflected a deep personality flaw: "The really important thing is, Why is this an important issue to you?"

16. When Pacific Bell (California) decided to change its company culture, it invested $30 million in "leadership development training" sessions (called Krone training after the management consultant who designed it), which all 67,000 of its employees would attend. Many employees filed complaints about the training, claiming that they were coerced into attending. Local media discovered that a major purpose of the training was to forge new, nonconflictual relations with the Communications Workers of America (representing approximately two-thirds of the PacBell workforce) (*San Francisco Chronicle*, 23 March 1987; 27 March 1987).

17. Ray (1989) similarly emphasizes this function of the recent preoccupation with corporate cultures. For Ray, transforming the corporate culture represents an attempt to "socially reskill" managers so that they will work harder interpersonally to get employees to swing their efforts to the larger good of the corporation. That was certainly one goal of American Security Bank's corporate culture agenda. However, the *particular* content of these new ideologies for middle managers must be stressed: the cultural themes revolve around the entrepreneurial manager, who in his or her everyday management practices will take an active role in downsizing the ranks of corporate employees (managerial and nonmanagerial) and will forge ahead to a new, leaner corporate America.

18. Cosgrove was referring to McGregor's (1960) model of the two most prevalent managerial styles.

References

Argyris, Chris. 1955. "Organizational Leadership and Participative Management." *Journal of Business* 28 (1): 1–7.

Athos, Anthony, and Richard Pascale. 1981. *The Art of Japanese Management: Applications for American Executives.* New York: Simon & Schuster.

Bendix, Reinhard. 1956. *Work and Authority in Industry: Ideologies of Management in the Course of Industrialization.* Berkeley and Los Angeles: University of California Press.

Berman, Melissa, ed. 1986. *Corporate Culture and Change.* Report from the Conference Board. Report No. 888. New York: The Conference Board.

Blau, Peter, and Richard Schoenherr. 1971. *The Structure of Organizations.* New York: Basic Books.

Brandt, Steven. 1986. *Entrepreneurs in Established Companies: Managing Toward the Year 2000.* New York: New American Library.

Businessweek. 14 May 1984. "Changing a Corporate Culture." Pp. 130–138.

———. 7 April 1986. "Roger Smith's Campaign to Change the GM Culture." Pp. 84–85.

Dickson, John. 1981. "Participation as a Means of Organizational Control." *Journal of Management Studies* 18 (2): 159–176.

Edwards, Richard. 1979. *Contested Terrain: The Transformation of the Workplace in the Twentieth Century.* New York: Basic Books.

Fortune. 10 November 1986. "GM is Tougher Than You Think." Pp. 56–64.

Fulmer, Robert. 1986. "Educating Managers for the Future." *Personnel* 63 (2): 70–73.

Gordon, Jack. 1986a. "*Training* Magazine's Industry Report 1986." *Training: Magazine of Human Resources Development* 23 (10): 26–28.

———. 1986b. "Where the Training Goes." *Training: Magazine of Human Resources Development* 23 (10): 49–68.

Halloran, Keith D. 1985. "The Impact of Merger and Acquisition Programs on Corporate Identity." *Mergers and Acquisitions* 20 (1): 60–66.

Hochschild, Arlie. 1983. *The Managed Heart.* Berkeley and Los Angeles: University of California Press.

Jacoby, Sanford. 1985. *Employing Bureaucracy: Managers, Unions, and the Transformation of Work in American Industry, 1900–1945.* New York: Columbia University Press.

Kanter, Rosabeth Moss. 1983. *The Changemasters.* New York: Simon & Schuster.

———. 1987. "The Attack on Pay." *Harvard Business Review* 65 (2): 60–67.

Kimberly, John, and Robert Quinn. 1984. *Managing Organizational Transitions.* Homewood, Ill.: Richard D. Irwin.

McGregor, Douglas. 1960. *The Human Side of the Enterprise.* New York: McGraw-Hill.

Martin, Thomas. 1988. "Building a Quality Culture at Westinghouse." Pp. 451–69 in Ralph Kilman and Teresa Covin, eds. *Corporate Transformation: Revitalizing Organization for a Competitive World,* San Francisco: Jossey-Bass.

Naisbett, John. 1982. *Megatrends.* New York: Warner Books.

New York Times. 17 April 1987. "Gurus Hired to Motivate Workers Are Raising Fears of 'Mind Control.' " Sec. 1, p. 10.

"Organizational Culture." 1983. *Administrative Science Quarterly* 28 (3). Special issue.

"Organizational Culture." 1983. *Organizational Dynamics* 12 (2). Special issue.

"Organizational Culture and Control." 1986. *Journal of Management Studies* 23 (3). Special issue.

Ouchi, William. 1981. *Theory Z: How American Business Can Meet the American Challenge.* Reading, Mass.: Addison-Wesley.

Ouchi, William, and Alan Wilkins. 1985. "Organizational Cultures." *Annual Review of Sociology* 11: 457–83.

Pascale, Richard. 1984. "Fitting New Employees into the Company Culture." *Fortune,* 28 May, pp. 28–42.

Patten, Thomas. 1968. *The Foreman: Forgotten Man of Industry.* New York: American Management Association.

Perrow, Charles. 1986. *Complex Organizations: A Critical Essay.* 3d ed. New York: Random House.

Peters, Tom, and Robert Waterman. 1984. *In Search of Excellence: Lessons from America's Best-Run Companies.* New York: Warner Books.

Prechel, Harland. 1986. "Capital Accumulation and Corporate Rationality: Organizational Change in an American Steel Corporation." Ph.D. dissertation, University of Kansas.

Ray, Carol Axtell. 1986. "Corporate Culture: The Last Frontier of Control." *Journal of Management Studies* 23 (3): 287–97.

———. 1989. "Skill Reconsidered: The Deskilling and Reskilling of Managers." *Work and Occupations* 16 (1): 65–79.

Restructuring Turnaround: Experiences in Corporate Renewal. 1987. Business International Research Report. Geneva, Switzerland: Business International.

San Francisco Chronicle. 23 March 1987. "PacBell's New Way to Think." Pp. 1, 6.

———. 27 March 1987. "PacBell 'Kroning'—Figures Soar." P. 1.

Turnstall, W. Brooke. 1986. "The Break-up of the Bell System: A Case Study in Cultural Transformation." *California Management Review* 28 (2): 110–24.

Uttal, Bro. 1983. "The Corporate Culture Vultures." *Fortune,* 17 October, pp. 66–72.

Wall Street Journal. 3 December 1985. "Ford's Leaders Push Radical Shift in Culture as Competition Grows." Pp. 1, 26.

Whalley, Peter. 1986. "Markets, Managers, and Technical Autonomy." *Theory and Society* 15 (1–2): 223–47.

Wilkins, Alan. 1989. *Developing Corporate Character: How to Successfully Change an Organization Without Destroying It.* San Francisco: Jossey-Bass.

Zuboff, Shoshanna. 1985. "Technologies That Informate: Implications for Human Resource Management in the Computerized Industrial Workplace." Pp. 103–39 in Richard Walton and Paul Lawrence, eds. *Human Resources Management: Trends and Challenges.* Boston: Harvard Business School Press.

PART III

Structures, Power, and Practices

The essays in this section examine a broader range of dynamics within organizations and locate these within larger contexts of political structure, political culture, and political economy. Multiple rationalities emerge within organizational structures as these elicit active adaptation and resistance from everyday actors situated differently with respect to power, authority, cultural identities, and numerical proportions. And these everyday interactions—be they of teachers in a bureaucratic urban school system, operators in a nuclear power plant, managers in multicultural organizations, or government administrators in regulatory agencies—can be fully understood only within the larger organizational and political contexts within which they operate.

Michael Lipsky's essay on public service bureaucracies analyzes how street-level bureaucrats, in response to the scarcity of resources and client demand, develop a variety of routines for rationing service. He demonstrates how, under existing structural constraints, it is often dysfunctional for street-level bureaucrats to be more responsive in meeting client needs. Service is rationed by increasing the costs to the clients—in money, time, information, or psychological burdens and degradations. Agencies are quite aware that such routines result in the denial of service to many eligible people; indeed, regulations are often consciously designed with this in mind. Lipsky also reveals the political power relationships involved in waiting and queuing, and the various forms of inequality and bias that result from, or find fertile soil in, the often unconscious patterns of practice of street-level bureaucrats. Those who propose to empower citizens and improve service to clients, as later essays in this volume discuss, must come to grips with ways to reverse the powerful dynamics of everyday practice in street-level bureaucracy that Lipsky examines.

Susan Moore Johnson's essay examines the organizational structures and teacher practices in the typical bureaucratic school system and further enriches Lipsky's analysis by viewing these through the eyes of those who have been designated by their peers as excellent teachers who **259** themselves resist the logic entailed in current arrangements. She examines the range of practices—scheduling, class size, batch processing, departmentalization, specialization, tracking, testing, nonteaching duties, curricular mandates, teacher testing and supervision—that continue to enact the metaphor of "school as factory" that shaped school reform in the early part of the century, even though current rhetoric would disguise and deny this. Giving voice to those who live their critique of such bureaucratic practices every day they walk into the classroom, Johnson's analysis sketches what the real challenges of school reform and teacher empowerment entail.

Rosabeth Moss Kanter's essay on men and women in a large corporation develops a dynamic structural analysis of gendered power relations, and the variety of behavioral responses to them. As with opportunity, power tends to accumulate in an ascending spiral. Power begets more power. And the powerless tend to get caught in a descending spiral. Kanter's purpose is to develop organizational strategies for breaking these cycles, especially as they affect women, by understanding their structural bases rather than imputing them to social psychological or cultural differences. Thus she focuses on organizational features, such as alliances with sponsors, peers, and subordinates, in an effort to show the powerful tendencies at work in marginalizing women and denying them power.

David Thomas's essay takes some of these themes further in his analysis of mentoring relationships, gender, and race. Drawing upon rich interviews among black and white, male and female managers, and his own broad consulting experience in organizations grappling with the challenges and dilemmas of multiculturalism and empowerment, Thomas argues that the dynamics of power are not race- and gender-neutral, or simply determined by structural positions, but embedded in a long history of racial taboos that are still resonant at deeper psychological levels in mentoring relations among black and white men and women. What we might think of as archaic cultural stereotypes and irrational fears about white men's unlimited sexual access to black women, black men's forbidden approaches to white women, or white men's benevolent freeing of black men, prove themselves to be operative in many of the everyday dynamics of mentoring. Thomas shows how an approach that is informed by cultural analysis and historical specificity, as well as psychodynamic depth, can complement structural approaches such as Kanter's. And though he sees value in equal-opportunity legislation and color-blind organizational rules, he also recognizes that these can serve as "social defenses" reinforcing the very taboos that help reproduce racialized and gendered power relations.

Charles Perrow's study of the accident at Three Mile Island nuclear power plant in 1979 raises serious questions about the organizational possibilities of ensuring safety in nuclear systems and proposes a basic reconceptualization of the very notion of an accident. Accidents in such highly complex, interactive, and tightly coupled systems are "normal," in the sense that they are not fully preventable over the course of time. Failures in warning systems, design, and equipment, as well as operator error, are inevitable, take unanticipated forms, and have highly interactive negative effects (negative synergy). Operator mistakes must be viewed as normal and inevitable behavioral responses to systems of such high complexity. Perrow makes a strong case for the argument that the dangers of such technologies are an inherent part of the very organizational systems and rationalities designed to control them, and that they resist elimination by simple improvement of operator training, safety procedures, or equipment design. The problem is in the organizational and technological rationalities themselves, although operators are often conveniently scapegoated to deny this. Perrow's analysis of this particular case not only sheds light on the larger nuclear power industry, including its regulatory bodies whose own failures were clearly revealed in the accident, but has much relevance for nuclear weapons technologies, whose organizational systems are also highly interactive, tightly coupled, and prone to some of the same kind of failures.

Gordon Adams's essay on the "iron triangle" in the military-industrial establishment presents a political analysis of the interorganizational decision-making system at work in national security policy since World War II, and reinforced in many ways during the Reagan administration. Specifically, Adams shows the ways in which Pentagon procurement policies serve both the immediate and long-term interests of the large corporate defense contracting industries and their political allies. Since the nuclear arms race during the Cold War, national security goals, and U.S. foreign policy are incomplete explanations for the enormous growth of military spending up until recent years, Adams argues that the expanding power of the military-industrial complex is promoted and sustained by an iron triangle of mutually beneficial relationships among the Defense Department, corporate contractors, and key members of Congress who have defense plants in their districts or serve on committees that determine defense spending. This interorganizational decision-making process facilitates the flow of money, personnel, information, and influence among the three corners of the triangle. It operates to reinforce the political power of each, and to reinforce their mutual relations, while it shields decision making from effective scrutiny and control in the broader political arena. And although the end of the Cold War has changed some of the rules of the game and created great pressure for defense cuts, the dynamic of the iron triangle remains very powerful and continues to constrain the possibilities for reduction and reconversion.

Steven Kelman's essay provides a comparative perspective on the role of government regulation in the industrial workplace in the United States and Sweden. He focuses here on the differences between U.S. and Swedish compliance patterns and their respective outcomes. Whereas American government inspectors rely on an enforcement or punishment-oriented approach to compliance in an adversarial environment, their Swedish counterparts principally resort to normative inducements and the use of representative labor-management groups at both national and shop-floor levels. Kelman shows that the policy makers' choices between these two alternative control systems are functions of the larger context of cultural and political values in the respective systems. Moreover, the Swedish system works in a less bureaucratic manner because Swedish workers, through collective bargaining and national legislation, have won more rights to participate directly in health and safety committees in their workplaces. The primary outcomes of the two systems differ significantly in their levels of hostility and resentment toward regulation. The American system has generated suspicion and resentment between inspectors and employers, whereas the Swedish system has fostered a more cooperative atmosphere of mutual understanding and assistance. A greater trade union role, in short, has led to a less cumbersome, more cooperative, and comparatively effective system of health and safety regulation at work.

Nancy DiTomaso's essay provides a case study of the United States Department of Labor in two critical periods of its history: 1869–1913 and 1957–1973. Illustrating the value of an historical perspective for organizational analysis, she shows that almost all of the decisions concerning the structure of the Department of Labor are linked to major social and political conflicts in the society at large. Initial decisions about the formation and organization of the Labor Department involved political decisions about who should have access to state power; and subsequent battles to reorganize generally reflected a shifting balance in the political alignments of the system as a whole, and different actors' preferences for centralization and decentralization. As the Labor Department assumes a new prominence with the election of a Democratic administration in 1992, and as a dynamic new secretary focuses on the challenges of labor in a postindustrial and global economy, the kinds of questions raised by Kelman and DiTomaso become ever more important for strategies aimed at democratic empowerment in the workplace around issues of health and safety, skill upgrading, workplace and worklife flexibility, and the transformation of American unionism.

Charles Perrow and Mauro Guillén's essay analyzes the tragic failures of organizations to respond effectively to the AIDS crisis in the early years when the spread of the epidemic might have been substantially slowed. Focusing on both public and private organizations nationally and in New York City (including Congress, the executive branch and local politicians, the Centers for Disease Control, hospitals and the blood supply industry, gay and religious groups), the authors examine several varieties of organizational explanation: (1) the bureaucratic explanation that finds normal organizational failures, especially of an already over-taxed U.S. health care system; (2) an explanation of the specific timing of the Reagan administration's cost cutting that further impacted on normal failures; (3) an ideological explanation that attributes certain constraints on effective response to the Moral Majority's conservative pressure; and (4) an explanation that takes into account some of the unique features of AIDS (intentional behavior, degrees of cultural tolerance linked to class and racial or ethnic minority status, possibilities of unwitting transmission, and link to sexual and other stigmas, which themselves are linked to race, poverty, and intravenous drug use). Perrow and Guillén highlight the peculiar convergence of peril, stigma, and cost, as well as the interactive effects within organizational systems that exacerbated the crisis, such as hospital bed shortages leading to decisions to dismiss AIDS patients, who amidst the crisis of homelessness spread the epidemic even more rapidly in homeless shelters.

15

The Rationing of Services in Street-Level Bureaucracies

Michael Lipsky

Theoretically there is no limit to the demand for free public goods. Agencies that provide public goods must and will devise ways to ration them. To ration goods or services is to establish the level or proportions of their distribution. This may be done by fixing the amount or level of goods and services in relation to other goods and services. Or it may be done by allocating a fixed level or amount of goods and services among different classes of recipients. In other words, services may be rationed by varying the total amount available, or by varying the distribution of a fixed amount. . . .

The rationing of the level of services starts when clients present themselves to the worker or agency or an encounter is commanded. Like factory workers confronted with production quotas, street-level bureaucrats attempt to organize their work to facilitate work tasks or liberate as much time as possible for their own purposes. This is evident even in those services areas in which workers have little control over work flow. For example, police often cannot control work flow because most police assignments are in response to citizen initiated calls.[1] Dispatchers, however, make every effort to permit officers to finish one call before beginning another. Officers often take advantage of this practice by postponing reporting the completion of a call until after they have finished accumulated paperwork. In this way police officers regularize the work flow despite substantial irregularity in requests for assistance.

The way in which work comes to the agency significantly affects the efficiency and pleasantness with which it is accommodated. Official efforts to influence the flow of work vary greatly. They range from the mild advisory of the post office providing patrons with information concerning the times when delays are likely to be longest, to the extreme measures taken by a New York City welfare office that closed its doors at noon rather than admit a greater number of Medicaid applicants than could be processed by available personnel in an eight-hour day.[2]

Reprinted from Michael Lipsky, *Street-Level Bureaucracy* (New York: Russell Sage Foundation, 1980), 87–104, by permission of Russell Sage Foundation and the author.

Clearly there are costs to clients in seeking services. In both of the above examples agencies seek to inform clients of the costs and the problems they will encounter—in the first instance, if they seek assistance during days when post office patronage is heavy; in the second, if in ignorance of the situation they attempt to apply for Medicaid and cannot be accommodated because of the high intake demand relative to intake workers. In many instances even the failure to inform clients of likely costs in seeking service constitutes a consumer complaint.

The highest costs are borne by potential clients who are discouraged from or forbidden access to bureaucratic involvement. While exclusion from client status is usually accomplished on the basis of legal grounds, the population of the excluded or discouraged includes many whose exclusion is a matter of discretionary judgment. The ineligibility of tenants evicted from public housing, students expelled from school, or welfare claimants deemed uncooperative depends not on fixed criteria alone, but also on interactions with street-level bureaucrats.

The Costs of Service

To analyze individual influence it has sometimes proved useful to recognize the relationship between citizens' influence and their command of personal resources such as money, status, information, expertise, and capacity for work.[3] People who have these resources tend to be more powerful than those who do not. When people have them they enhance personal influence. When workers for public agencies have them they may be used to direct or subordinate clients or discourage clients from further interactions with the agency.

Monetary
Street-level bureaucracies can rarely assign monetary costs for services, since by definition public services are free. However, monetary costs *are* imposed in several instructive instances. In income-providing programs citizens' contributions to the income package may be manipulated as policy. Medicare patients may be asked to pay a higher deductible before insurance provisions become operable. Food-stamp recipients may be asked to pay more for their stamps. The effective taxation of earned income in welfare reduces the number of people in contact with this street-level bureaucracy. Clearly differences in monetary costs serve to ration street-level bureaucrats' services.

Programs sometimes force clients to incur monetary costs that discourage them from seeking service. Acquiring records from other agencies to establish eligibility or securing transcripts for appeals can be costly, particularly if travel is involved. Agencies that keep bankers' hours impose monetary costs on working people who cannot appear without losing wages. Appointments sometimes require parents to seek babysitters. Street-level bureaucracies that seek to minimize these penalties introduce evening office hours, or they provide child-care services.

Time

Just as available time is a resource for people in politics, it is also a unit of value that may be extracted from clients as a cost of service. Clients are typically required to wait for services; it is a sign of their dependence and relative powerlessness that the costs of matching servers with the served are borne almost entirely by clients. It is to maximize the efficiency of workers' time that queues are generally established. A primary reason that clinic-based practice is more efficient than home-based practice is simply that it is patients and not physicians who spend time traveling and waiting. Policemen also allocate time costs by stopping to question young people who, while not guilty of any crime, are judged to require reprimanding.[4]

Some teachers in some school systems make home visits to meet with parents, while others schedule parent-teacher conferences after school on specific days set aside for such purposes. (If there are two parents and one or both work, both are unlikely to be able to meet with the teacher.) These alternative perspectives on parent-teacher conferences measure significant differences in the value placed on time of parents and teachers.

Time costs are often assessed by street-level bureaucrats as delay; they are often experienced by clients as waiting. Bureaucracies can reward clients by expediting service, punish them by delaying service. Court postponements can function in this way, as can an increase in the time between intake interviews and placement on the welfare rolls. Importantly, bureaucracies often have little interest in reducing delay, since more expeditious processing would simply strain available resources.

Assessed time costs may also be experienced as inconvenience, although they are levied as procedure. For example, when an agency refuses to receive complaints over the telephone and requires that they be written, it may cut off complaints lodged frivolously or on impulse, but also discourages complainants who would protest if it were easier.[5] Requirements to complete multiple forms and produce extensive documentation function similarly. It is possible to make an argument that since the real costs of delay and elaborate procedures are the activities foregone while waiting, that is, opportunity costs, it is justifiable that poor people wait longer than the more affluent, since the opportunities foregone are less valued by the society.[6] However, at the very least this elitist view is based on a calculus to the terms of which clients have not consented.

Information

Giving or withholding information is another way in which services may be rationed. Clients experience the giving or withholding of information in two ways. They experience the favoritism of street-level bureaucrats who provide some clients with privileged information, permitting them to manipulate the system better than others. And they experience it as confusing jargon, elaborate procedures, and arcane practices that act as barriers to understanding how to operate effectively within the system. The emblematic carrier of this characteristic is the court clerk who runs his words together in an undecipherable litany to the dominance of court procedures over citizens' rights.[7] At the bureaucratic level the giving and withholding of information is most obvious in examining how agencies manipulate their case loads by distributing or failing to distribute information about services.

Conventionally, analysts assess the demand for services by studying client rolls and visits. (Demands are statements directed toward public officials that some kind of action ought to be undertaken.)[8] If it is recognized that manifestations of client involvement may not fully reflect client interests, analysts contrive ways to assess underlying needs, for example, through attitudinal and census surveys. From this assessment administrators and politicians make claims about appropriate levels of services.

However, if it is recognized that organizations normally ration services by manipulating the nature and quantity of the information made available about services, then it is easily seen that demand levels are themselves a function of public policy. Client rolls will be seen as a function of *clients' perception* of service availability and the costs of seeking services. Client demand will be expressed only to the extent that clients themselves are aware that they have a social condition that can, should, and will be ministered to by public agencies.

When New York City reduced acceptance rates for new welfare cases at seven centers by 17 percent it accomplished this feat by tightening the application process. This meant not only more careful scrutiny of applicants' claims, but also more documentation and inquisition was required, which contributed a separate measure of rationing.[9]

This perspective is illustrated by indices of need for legal assistance for domestic problems. When a sample of Detroit residents were asked if they required a lawyer for assistance with some domestic-relations matters, scarcely more than 1 percent answered affirmatively. It would have been difficult to predict from this survey that approximately 40 percent of the clients of legal aid and neighborhood law offices originally sought help with domestic problems.[10]

Needs become manifest when the institutions that might provide assistance send out signals that they stand ready to assist. The 40 percent of the clients who originally sought help with domestic matters might have been only a small portion of the population that could have benefitted from such assistance. Some who could have used such services may have been deterred from seeking them. Since legal services are vastly underfunded, even more dramatic demonstrations of need might have materialized if more lawyers had been available.

Information about service is an aspect of service. Withholding information depresses service demands. For example, the campaign to reform welfare by dramatically increasing the welfare rolls was based on the view that a political movement could help overcome the stigma attached by potential recipients to welfare status. It could provide the information necessary to realize a substantial increase in the number of recipients.[11] The failure of public welfare agencies to make sure potential recipients receive the benefits to which they are entitled contrasts dramatically with the success of social security and Veterans' Administration benefits. The difference is that the clients of these two income support programs—the elderly, and veterans—are not socially stigmatized.[12]

Client statistics may not indicate much about the objective needs of the client population but they reflect a great deal about the organizations that formally cater to those needs.[13] Thus growing demand for adult continuing education partly exists in the felt needs of the adult population, but the demand also is responsive to the publicity generated by colleges and universities and their desire to attract students and their tuition. The demand for emergency police services exists to an unknown degree, but the introduction of a 911 central telephone number and dispatch system makes it more likely that citizens believe the police will respond quickly. After the system is introduced, the increase in 911 calls will be responsive to organizational factors such as publicity about the service and response time as well as more objective factors such as population growth and changes in the age distribution of the population.

Although the dominant tendency is for street-level bureaucracies to attempt to limit demand by imposing (mostly nonmonetary) costs for services, there are some times when they have a stake in increasing their clientele. They will do this through an analogous rationing process, now directed toward increasing utilization.

Agencies are likely to try to increase their clientele when they are newly established and have to prove their ability to put services into operation. Thus the tripling of service complaints when Boston introduced its Little City Halls program was particularly welcome by its sponsors.[14] Efforts to increase clienteles were generally noticeable when central funding sources launched many subordinate service agencies, which saw themselves competing for funds in the next fiscal cycle. Such agencies would "beat the bushes" for clients in order to demonstrate that they were worthy of future support. Community action agencies and neighborhood mental health centers have been cases in point.[15]

Established street-level bureaucracies may also attempt to increase their clientele if they perceive themselves under attack and calculate that demonstrations of significant service provision, or increases in clientele, might aid their cause. Relatedly, street-level bureaucracies may attempt to increase the number of clients when they are competing against other programs with similar objectives. Such agencies perceive that they are competing for the same client pool, and that only the more successful will survive in the next budget cycle.

This competition also is conducive to quasi-legitimate fraud directed toward making the agencies look better. For example, when drug treatment centers were few they could afford to impose rigorous residential requirements, particularly since clients' commitment to their own rehabilitation was considered critical to therapy. When the number of institutions increased in the early 1970s in response to available funding, and the population of drug users started to decline, to increase their clientele the centers began to relax their enrollment requirements (for example, by accepting clients who previously would have been judged too difficult to help). They also relaxed attendance requirements, so that a treatment bed might be occupied by someone who was not in fact a full-time resident of the center. Besides drug treatment centers, other organizations that have competed for larger shares of a fixed client pool include mental health centers funded in the same city, and academic departments competing for students within a university.

In theory this bureaucratic competition might provide precisely what bureaucracies importantly lack—a substitute for market place accountability. This, of course, is the idea behind educational vouchers. However, the healing effects of competition are too often mitigated by the residual bureaucratic aspects of the competing organizations. Faculty members in academic departments with declining enrollments are still protected by the tenure system, rewards for research (and bringing in research grants), and other factors that protect them from being assessed solely on criteria of service to students. Similarly, educational voucher experiments have foundered on teachers' tenure, union opposition, and parental inability to express preferences within the system for lack of information on the implications of the available choices.

Psychological

Bureaucratic rationing is also achieved by imposing psychological costs on clients. Some of these are implicit in the rationing mechanisms already mentioned. Waiting to receive services, particularly when clients conclude that the wait is inordinate and reflects lack of respect, contributes to diminishing client demands.[16] The administration of public welfare has been notorious for the psychological burdens clients have to bear. These include the degradation implicit in inquiries into sexual behavior, childbearing preferences, childrearing practices, friendship patterns, and persistent assumptions of fraud and dishonesty.[17] Nor have these practices been confined to the "unenlightened" 1950s, although some of the more barbaric features of welfare practice, such as the early dawn raids to catch the elusive "man-in-the-house," are no longer practiced.

To take a modest example, women appyling for Aid to Families with Dependent Children at times are required to submit to an interview with lawyers, in which they must agree to assist the welfare department in prosecuting the father of their children. Apparently many women are unwilling to agree to this, since it would jeopardize the tenuous but at least partially satisfactory relationship that they may have with the childrens' father. They fear that the support they currently do receive and the positive benefits of good relations with them would be cut off by alienating the fathers, who may not be making substantial incomes anyway. Applicants are thus forced to lie or risk the loss of an important relationship. The interviews are conducted in a legalistic way with little sympathy for the position of the applicant. Many eligible potential clients do not complete the application process, because they prefer not to suffer these pressures and indignities.[18] Like so many monitoring procedures in welfare, it is unclear if monies recovered through these procedures equal the costs of engaging in them.

Psychological sanctions serve to reduce the demands from clients within the system as well as help to limit those who come into it. The defendant in a lower criminal court who asserts that he or she does not understand the charges will be silenced by the hostile response of the judge or clerk who unenthusiastically attempts to redress the complaint. Teachers, by varying their tone of voice, encourage or discourage pupils from asking questions. A lawyer in responding to clients can communicate the opinion that the inquiry is stupid and the client unworthy of a thoughtful response.

The importance of psychological interactions for rationing service is manifest in the extent to which clients will sometimes seek or approve of service simply because they like the way they are treated. Although they later find against them, sympathetic judges sometimes give thoughtful attention to defendents or complainants with weak cases simply in order to make them feel that they had their day in court. The reported gratitude of citizens who are treated in this way indicate how little people have come to expect from government. It would seem that clients sometimes judge services positively if they are treated with respect regardless of the quality of services. In this connection a study of clients' evaluation of walk-in mental health clinics revealed that "clinic applicants are satisfied with almost any response [from the staff] at first so long as the emotional atmosphere of the contact is comfortable."[19] While seekers of mental health services may be particularly sensitive to the quality of initial client-staff interactions there is every reason to think that these interactions form a substantial part of clients' initial evaluations of schools, courts, police, and other street-level services where there are no clearly defined service products to be obtained.

Queuing

The most modest arrangements for client servicing impose costs on clients. This is evident in the way clients are arranged, or required to present themselves, for bureaucratic processing. Even the most ordinary queuing arrangements—those designed to provide service on a first-come, first-served basis in accordance with universalistic principles of client treatment—impose costs.[20]

Queues that depend upon first-come, first-served as their organizing principle elicit client cooperation because of their apparent fairness, but they may ration service by forcing clients to wait. When clients are forced to wait they are implicitly asked to accept the assumptions of rationing: that the costs they are bearing are necessary because the resources of the agency are fixed. They are also controlled by the social pressures exerted by others who wait. This is one of the functions of the line, waiting room, and other social structures that make it evident that others share the burden of waiting for service.

While resource limitations may be unalterable in the very short run, they are not necessarily immutable. They derive from allocation decisions that consider it acceptable to impose costs on waiting clients. Costs will not be imposed upon clients equally. Long lines processed on a first-come, first-served basis relatively benefit people who can afford to wait, people whose time is not particularly valuable to them, or people who do not have other obligations.

Poor people often suffer in such a system. Not only may clients who appear more affluent get served first because it is thought that the costs of waiting are higher for them,[21] but agencies often paternalistically develop policy as if the costs to the poor were nonexistent. A visit to the waiting room of a welfare office in any inner-city neighborhood is likely to convey the impression that the Welfare Department assumes recipients have nothing else to do with their time. Recipients learn the lesson of people who must seek service from a single source. Like the telephone company, the welfare department is able to pass on to the customer the costs of linking people with service. This system also benefits the average client to the disadvantage of people with extraordinary needs, since initially it has no mechanism for differentiating among clients. However, where the injury to people with extraordinary needs is likely to be severe, as in police work or medical emergencies, the ordering of services is often deliberately structured to search for and respond to this information.

An alternative to the first-come, first-served waiting room or line is the first-come, first-served queue by appointment. This system is also normatively acceptable and theoretically has the advantage of eliminating many of the costs of waiting time. In this queue the costs may appear to be reduced for the average client, but they may still be significant if appointments are crowded together to insure client overlap, as is typically done in health clinics and other medical settings. Crowding appointments may be done for the convenience of bureaucrats whose time is considered more valuable than that of clients, and who thus are guaranteed a flow of clients even if one misses an appointment. The costs of such a queue will also be borne by clients who seek service but cannot afford to wait for it, who are not disciplined enough to make and keep appointments, or who are not sure enough of the likely benefits of service to invest in seeking it. What appears to the street-level bureaucrat as a fair way to allocate time may be seen by the client in the light of past experiences of bureaucratic neglect and taken as a sign that the agency is unlikely to be responsive, or that the problem is unlikely to yield to assistance.

For some clients the costs of waiting may be quite high. In one legal services program approximately 40 percent of eligible clients who received an appointment with a lawyer for the following week did not keep the appointment.[22] This may have been because the problem dissoved during the intervening time, or because merely talking to the intake worker provided a degree of comfort. However, it is equally likely that clients who did not keep their appointments could not keep them but were afraid to say so, were not organized enough to show up at the appointed time, or faced their legal problems without professional advice. Or it may have been that the applicants for assistance interpreted the demand to wait for appointments as a sign that legal services was not likely to be responsive and assumed that, like other public agencies, it would not in the end prove helpful.

In any event, the day a client appears to seek assistance may be the day when he or she is most open to help or the street-level bureaucrat is most likely to be able to intervene successfully. Catherine Kohler Reissman has written about mental health services in an analogous situation. "It is obvious that the disequilibrium created by a crisis is a powerful therapeutic tool that is lost if the situation is allowed to degenerate, through postponement, into a chronic, long-term problem."[23]

Similar to the queue by appointment is the waiting list; clients are asked to wait for what is usually an undetermined amount of time until they can be accommodated. Although it appears to be straightforward on the surface, the waiting-list system has several important latent functions. First, as we have seen in the case of Boston public housing, a waiting list tends to increase the discretion of street-level bureaucrats by providing opportunities to call clients from the waiting list out of turn, or to provide special information that will permit them to take advantage of ways to be treated with higher priority.[24] Waiting lists also permit agencies to give the appearance of service (after all, clients *are* on a waiting list) and to make a case for increased resources because of the backlog of demand.[25] The waiting list appears to record the names of potential clients who are seeking service but cannot be accommodated, although it is obvious to all that many names continue on the list only because the agency has not attempted to discover who is actively waiting and who has long since ceased to be interested.

Some social agencies act as if the waiting list usefully filters potential clients who are truly in need of service and strains out those whose needs are not substantial and who thus drop off. This system of rationing may also provide for a period of time in which spontaneous recuperation may occur, again reserving client spaces only for those who are needy.[26] However, it is uncertain whether continuation on the list is a sign of substantial need or precisely the opposite, a sign that the potential client is successful enough in managing the problem that he or she can wait patiently for services.

A queuing arrangement that maximizes the costs to citizens at the expense of a relatively small number of street-level bureaucrats is employed by lower courts, which typically require defendants to appear on a given day, but notify them only as to the hour they should appear. In a typical situation fifty to one hundred defendants, possibly with a friend or member of their family, must be ready for a hearing or arraignment, with substantial penalties if they do not appear precisely at the beginning of the session (when their names are first called). Here they must wait until the judge arrives, and then wait again while the judge gives priority to defendants in the lockup who may require attorneys, defendants whose attorneys plead that they have to be elsewhere, and defendants whose cases require the testimony of waiting police officers, who themselves are subject to other priorities. Only when [such] priorities are accommodated will the docket be called in alphabetical or some other order.

Defendants may be innocent but by virtue of being arrested are judged guilty enough to pay in time and uncertainty the price that the court exacts for scheduling cases for the primary convenience of the judge. Although practices vary from court to court it is typical that defendants will not be told even approximately when their cases will be called, so that they must wait in the courtroom, possibly for most of the day, until they receive a hearing.[27]. The defendant who has waited through such a day has been instructed in the costs of continued interaction with the court system and must consider whether exercising rights or even pleading innocent in a minor matter, although legally valid, is worth the time and irritation. Some court systems have recently recognized that similar problems, including frequent postponements, inhibit witnesses from appearing and testifying in trials. But the same analysis rarely focuses on defendants and their experiences in court.

This queue by roundup is also typical of jury impaneling, where citizens are called for a week of service and must sit in a jury room awaiting assignment, often for several days, perhaps never to be called. The system officially is justified by the fluctuating and relatively unpredictable demand for jurors, and again is premised on the high value placed on the court's time relative to citizens' time. To insure that there are always people ready to serve, more jurors are called than will be required. If the court could tolerate a postponement now and then for lack of available jurors, and if jurors were called to report serially during the week rather than all at once, less time would be wasted for prospective jurors. But such practices could only be adopted if the time of prospective jurors were accorded more value relative to judges' and lawyers' time than is currently the case.

Clients frequently may be quite willing to pay the costs of waiting. Clients undoubtedly understand that there are times when they will have to wait, unless bureaucracies hire enough staff to meet peak demand. And since demand in most street-level bureaucracies is to some degree unpredictable—even schools often have to hire new teachers or shuffle teacher assignments after school has started—it would be too costly to provide services so that waiting would never occur. Waiting becomes injurious and inappropriately costly only under certain conditions.

Waiting is inappropriate when it exceeds the time generally expected for a service. A person may not resent a two-hour wait in an emergency room to receive a tetanus shot if it is clear that patients with more serious claims are being served first. But the same amount of time spent waiting in line simply to hand in forms to renew a driver's license may be exceedingly irritating. Waiting may also be resented as inappropriate when clients have made an appointment, except when the appointment is considered only an approximation of the time of service (as in the case of office visits to doctors).

Still another situation in which clients resent the costs of waiting arises when they wait unfairly. Thus if a favored client gains access to service more easily than others it will be resented by those who are not favored. Sometimes unfairness in waiting time may be so slight as to go unnoticed by clients. A study of black patients in Chicago hospital emergency rooms revealed that compared to whites waiting time was a little more than three minutes, incurred primarily by claimants with nonemergency conditions who sought help when the emergency room was relatively busy. But this cost is not actually trivial. It is worth noting that a modest three minutes or so, *for the 1,105 blacks in the sample alone*, would add up to a full working day for 2,619 people on a yearly basis,[28] a measure of one of the costs of institutional racism for the blacks of Cook County, Illinois.

Routines and Rationing

The existential problem for street-level bureaucrats is that with any single client they probably could interact flexibly and responsively. But if they did this with too many clients their capacity to respond flexibly would disappear. One might think of each client as, in a sense, seeking to be the one or among the few for whom an exception is made, a favor done, an indiscretion overlooked, a regulation ignored.

This dilemma of street-level bureaucrats is illustrated well by the legal services program. Individually, each attorney is obliged by professional norms to pursue fully the legal recourses available to clients. For impoverished clients this presumably means that attorneys should act on clients' behalf irrespective of cost. Only if this assumption is correct could the provision of legal services begin to redress the balance of power in the legal system, which every observer concedes favors those who command legal resources. But if all clients' legal needs were fully pursued there would be no time for additional clients: The dilemma is exquisite. To limit lawyers' advocacy is to deny poor people equal access to the law. To permit unbounded advocacy is to limit the number of poor people who can have such access. Only a reconstitution of the legal system could overcome the dilemma within the current patterns of inequality: either a radical departure in the amount of subsidies for legal assistance for the poor or a radical simplification of legal procedures.

When confronted with the dilemma of serving more clients or maintaining high quality service, most public managers will experience great pressures to choose in favor of greater numbers at the expense of quality. Their inability to measure and demonstrate the value of a service, when combined with high demand and budgetary concerns, will tend to impose a logic of increasing the quantity of services at the expense of the degree of attention workers can give to individual clients. Street-level bureaucrats, however, may devise ways to sabotage management efforts to reduce interactions with clients. The costs of achieving compliance in the face of workers' resistance may sometimes be more than managers want to pay. An example of such worker resistance is related by Robert Perlman in his study of the Roxbury Multi-Service Center. "Confronted with the complexity and number of demands being made on them, staff members resorted to shielding themselves from the mounting pressures. They extended interviews to postpone or avoid taking the next client. They scheduled home visits in order to avoid intake duty."[29]

Whether street-level bureaucrats oppose efforts to limit their interaction with clients, or whether they accept and encourage such efforts as a way of salvaging an unattractive or deteriorating work situation, is perhaps the critical question on which the quality of public service ultimately depends. Although street-level bureaucrats may sometimes struggle to maintain their ability to treat clients individually, the pressures more often operate in the opposite direction. Street-level practice often reduces the demand for services through rationing. The familiar complaints of encountering "red tape," "being given the run-around," and "talking to a brick wall" are reminders that clients recognize the extent to which bureaucratic unresponsiveness penalizes them.

Routinization rations services in at least two ways. First, set procedures designed to insure regularity, accountability, and fairness also protect workers from client demands for responsiveness. They insulate workers from having to deal with the human dimensions of presenting situations. They do this partly by creating procedures to which workers defer, happily or unhappily. Lawyers and judges, for example, generally accept court procedures that insulate them from erratic client demands. Police officials resist instituting (or more properly, reinstituting) a beat system because they are apprehensive that officers would become too involved with neighborhood residents, and thus perhaps engage in biased behavior. For similar reasons they often oppose assigning officers to the areas in which they reside, and they advocate reasonably frequent changes in assignment.

Social workers may be unhappy with the requirement to process endless paperwork rather than spend time providing client services. But whether happy or unhappy with job routines the fact remains that they serve to limit client demands on the system. The righteous objections of critics that routine procedures detract from primary obligations to serve clients are of little account, since in an important sense it is not useful for the bureaucracies to be more responsive and to secure more clients.

Second, routines provide a legitimate excuse for not dealing flexibly, since fairness in a limited sense demands equal treatment. Unresponsiveness and inflexibility reinforce common beliefs already present that bureaucracy is part of the problem rather than the solution, and they further reduce clients' claims for service or assertions of needs.

When routines lead to predictability they may promote a degree of client confidence. As a public defender lecturing his peers on increasing client trust advised: "It's better to tell a client you will see him in two weeks and then show up, than to reassure him by saying, "I'll stop by tomorrow,' and never show."[30]

But agency practices do not always lead to predictability. When they lead to delay, confusion, and uncertainty they assign considerable costs to clients. At times routines established to protect clients are distorted to minimize contact or services. For example, to insure responsiveness housing inspectors may be required to make more than one effort to contact complainants. However, inspectors may become adept at telephoning complainants when they are unlikely to be home or fail to keep appointments punctually. In Boston this practice "enhanced the prospects of no one being home when the inspector arrived—a practice which when repeated thrice, enabled cases to be dropped."[31]

The significance of practices that subvert predictability, antagonize or neglect clients, or sow confusion and uncertainty is that they are generally *functional* for the agency. They limit client demands and the number of clients in a context where the agency has no dearth of responsibilities and would not in any way be harmed as an agency if clients became disaffected, passive, or refused to articulate demands. Any reduction in client demand is only absorbed by other clients who come forward, or by a marginal and insignificant increase in the capacity of street-level bureaucrats to be responsive to the clients who continue to press.

It is for this reason that we conclude that stated intentions of street-level bureaucracies to become more client-oriented, to receive more citizen input, and to encourage clients to speak out are often questionable, no matter how sincere the administrators who articulate these fine goals. It is dysfunctional to most street-level bureaucracies to become more responsive. Increases in client demands at one point will only lead to mechanisms to ration services further at another point, assuming sources remain unchanged.

The logical but absurd extension of the relationship between demand and services is exemplified by the apocryphal library that reduced costs by closing down. Yet it is a real problem that increased patronage of libraries, museums, zoos, and other agencies providing free goods increases their uncompensated costs when they succeed in becoming more attractive.

Undoubtedly there are dimensions of bureaucratic practice in which increased responsiveness does not add to workers' tasks. Addressing clients politely rather than rudely or indifferently is an area in which greater responsiveness is not necessarily burdensome to the work load. Furthermore, reorganization may result in increasing the responsive capacity of workers. However, most increases in responsiveness—doing more for clients, or even listening to them more—place additional burdens on street-level bureaucrats, who will subvert such developments in the likely absence of any strong rewards or sanctions for going along with them.

There are times when bureaucratic rationing is not simply implicit; limiting clientele or reducing services is the agency's stated policy. In response to reduced budgets or other developments that make client-worker ratios conspicuously high, agencies will reduce the scope of service in several characteristic ways. In reducing services explicitly they will continue to honor the formal norm of universalistic service patterns.

Street-level bureaucracies may reduce services geographically. They may formally narrow the catchment area from which clients are drawn or reduce the number of neighborhoods served by a program. Alternatively, because reductions in service are unpopular, street-level bureaucracies may prefer to reduce the number of centers, effectively cutting services to some areas without formally changing anyone's eligibility. When the borough of Manhattan, for example, consolidated its municipal court system, eliminating district courts in Harlem, it did not formally change access to the court, but informally it substantially increased the costs of using the court system to Upper Manhattan residents.

Services can be limited in terms of clients' personal characteristics. Formally, agencies can change income eligibility levels. Informally, they may limit service by failing to print posters in Spanish or by placing notices in old-age and nursing homes rather than in public housing in order to attract primarily an elderly population.

Street-level bureaucracies also can formally or informally ration services by refusing to take certain kinds of cases. The decriminalization of drunkenness, for example, formally exonerates policemen from dealing with alcoholics (although public disapproval still places pressure on the police to do something about drunks). Informally, departments can limit the clientele if officers choose to ignore public drunkenness, or they can reduce its place in departmental priorities.

Even when limiting services is not explicitly the function of rationing practices, service limitation often is not an unintended consequence of bureaucratic organization. Street-level bureaucrats and agency managers are often quite aware of the rationing implications of decisions about shorter office hours, consolidation of services, more or fewer intake workers, or the availability of information. Consider, for example, the efforts of the Budget Bureau of New York City in 1969 to decrease welfare expenditures. In a document remarkable for our purposes the Bureau suggested several ways to save close to $100 million.[32] In addition to reducing allowance levels, which would supply the bulk of the savings, the bureau recommended four administrative changes. Each would explicitly ration services in some way. A new intake procedure was proposed that would require applicants to be actively seeking jobs prior to the intake interview. This would force people to accept low-wage work, and, it was hoped, "more aggressive utilization of existing leverage over the employables would . . . have a deterrent effect on applications for welfare."[33] The authors recognized that for this innovation to be effective a substantially greater capacity of public employment agencies would be required, but there was no discussion of the costs of achieving this increase.

More frequent recertifications would be conducted to induce recipients who were on the rolls but no longer eligible because of changed circumstances to initiate case closings. (More than half of all case closings were then initiated by clients.) This reform would reduce the time between changes in clients' circumstances and the next reporting period.

Closing seven outreach centers would save some of the costs of running the centers, but more importantly, "larger savings are anticipated from secondary effects. . . . The most important of these is the opportunity *to build up and maintain the maximum legal backlog* between intake and eligibility increasing average backlog from two weeks to a full month."[34] Among other secondary benefits of center closings, the authors of the recommendations expected that "the relative inconvenience to the client of self-maintenance on emergency grants (for which application is normally made at the center more than once a week) may have some deterrent effect on [those] marginally eligible for welfare."[35]

Finally, stronger management audits would introduce greater uniformity in the system and provide better checks on welfare employees, who are portrayed in the document as more interested in enrolling clients than in controlling welfare costs.

Of equal interest are the strategies considered but not recommended. These included reducing intake hours, drastically closing intake centers, and requiring clients to provide increased documentation of birth, wages, rent payments, and other details of eligibility. While these provisions were rejected because they might result in unmanageable backlogs and infringe on clients' legal right to a response to their application within a month, the memo clearly recognizes that these measures would deter application rates by increasing the costs of applying to clients.

Provisions of this memo have been described at some length not because they are themselves remarkable but because they illustrate awareness at the agency planning level of the implications of rationing to limit client demand. It is naive to accept the rhetoric of public officials that their actions have the incidental effect of limiting or discouraging client demands. Rather, the opposite assumption is more useful analytically and more accurate empirically; namely, that public employees and higher officials are aware of the implications of actions taken that effectively increase or decrease client demand. They may deny such intentions publicly, of course, since their jobs require obeisance to norms of public service. They may not favor such policies personally, and they may regret that funding limitations preclude being able to serve more clients. Nonetheless, it is appropriate to assume that public agencies are responsible for the rationing implications of their actions.

In 1976 New York City introduced administrative controls that were credited with reducing the acceptance rate for new welfare applicants by half and terminating 18,000 cases a month. But this was accomplished because eligibles were being turned away "by very negative administration of work and parent-support rules," and because half of those terminated failed to show up for recertification, to respond to mailed questionnaires, or to verify school attendance. Their ineligibility was strictly a matter of difficulty or reluctance to pay the costs of remaining on the rolls until forced to do so. Meanwhile, according to an administrator, welfare centers are "overcrowded," "noisy," and "dirty." Some clients wait four to five hours for service and too often are required to make more than one visit to the center to complete their business. In addition, they don't know the names of people who are serving them."[36] In these and other ways *eligible* clients are asked to pay the costs of seeking relief.

Notes

1. The reactive nature of police work, and police dependence upon citizens in this respect, is stressed in Albert Reiss, *The Police and the Public* (New Haven: Yale University Press, 1971).

2. The latter case is cited by Barry Schwartz, *Queuing and Waiting* (Chicago: University of Chicago Press, 1975), p. 24. This excellent volume provides many insights into issues of priorities in client treatment and the costs of seeking service.

3. See Robert Dahl, "The Analysis of Influence in Local Communities," in Charles Adrian, ed., *Social Science and Community Action* (East Lansing, Mich.: Michigan State University Press, 1960), p. 32.

4. See generally Jonathan Rubinstein, "Suspicions," in *City Police* (New York: Farrar, Straus, 1973).

5. For example, one prosecutor's office that switched from telephone to mail complaint handling in processing white collar crimes experienced a 25 percent reduction in complaints received. Michael Brintnall, "The Allocation of Services in the Local Prosecution of Economic Crime" (Ph.D. diss., Massachusetts Institute of Technology, 1977), chap. 6.

6. See Schwartz, *Queuing and Waiting*, chap. 6.

7. When court clerks use confusing legal language we may call it "bureaucratic language as incantation." M. Edelman, *Political Language: Words that Succeed and Policies that Fail* (New York: Academic Press, 1977), p. 98. But what shall we call the court clerk's chant that strings words together indistinguishably? Perhaps it should be called "incantation as symbolic language." For attempts to deal positively with the rationing effects of legal language, consider the New York state law requiring consumer contracts to be written in clear, understandable language. See *New York Times*, Aug. 11, 1977, p. B1.

8. This is a paraphrase of the definition of demands in David Easton, *A Framework for Political Analysis* (Englewood Cliffs, N.J.: Prentice-Hall, 1965), p. 120.

9. *New York Times*, Sept. 25, 1977.

10. Leon Mayhew, "Institutions of Representation: Civil Justice and the Public," *Law and Society Review* 9, no. 3 (Spring, 1975), p. 403. The discrepancy is so great that it would be difficult to attribute it to differences in the nature of the sample.

11. Richard Cloward and Frances Fox Piven, "A Strategy to End Poverty," *The Politics of Turmoil* (New York: Vintage, 1975), pp. 89–106.

12. Gilbert Steiner, *The State of Welfare* (Washington, D.C.: Brookings, 1971).

13. Kitsuse and Cicourel have written that statistics reflect a great deal about the organizations collecting the statistics. John Kitsuse and Aaron Cicourel, "A Note on the Uses of Official Statistics," *Social Problems* 11 (1963), pp. 131–139. Sometimes the statistics collectors are not the same as those formally charged with providing information about services.

14. Eric Nordlinger, *Decentralizing the City* (Cambridge, Mass.,: Massachusetts Institute of Technology Press, 1972), p. 286.

15. The dynamics of this process are discussed in Michael Lipsky and Morris Lounds, "Citizen Participation and Health Care: Problems of Government Induced Participation," *Journal of Health Politics, Policy and Law* 1, no. 1 (Spring, 1976), pp. 85–111.

16. See the discussion of the psychological implications of waiting in Schwartz, *Queuing and Waiting*, chaps. 1, 8.

17. Virtually every commentary on welfare practices draws attention to the degradation of clients. See Alan Keith-Lucas, *Decisions about People in Need* (Chapel Hill, N.C.: University of North Carolina, 1957); Steiner, *The State of Welfare*; Frances Fox Piven and Richard Cloward, *Regulating the Poor* (New York: Pantheon, 1971), chaps. 4–5.

18. Jeffrey Prottas, *People-Processing: The Street-Level Bureaucrat in Public Service Bureaucracies* (Lexington, Mass.: Lexington Books, 1979). On the continuing relationships between ghetto fathers who have deserted and their families, see Elliot Liebow, *Tally's Corner* (Boston: Little, Brown, 1967).

19. June Grant Wolf, "The Initial Evaluation at a Walk-In Clinic: Applicant's and Evaluator's Perspectives" (Ph.D. diss., Boston University, 1974), p. 76.

20. First-come, first-served "constitutes the normative basis for most forms of queueing." Schwartz, *Queuing and Waiting*, p. 93.

21. Ibid., chap. 6.

22. Carl Hosticka, "Legal Services Lawyers Encounter Clients: A Study in Street-Level Bureaucracy" (Ph.D. diss., Massachusetts Institute of Technology, 1976).

23. Catherine Kohler Reissman, "The Supply-Demand Dilemma in Community Mental Health Centers," *American Journal of Orthopsychiatry* 40, no. 5 (October, 1970), p. 860.

24. See Lipsky, *Street-Level Bureaucracy*, chap. 2.

25. See Jeffrey Galper, *The Politics of Social Services* (Englewood Cliffs, N.J.: Prentice-Hall, 1975), pp. 70–71.

26. Reissman, "The Supply-Demand Dilemma," p. 860.

27. See Schwartz, *Queuing and Waiting*, pp. 26–29.

28. Ibid., chap. 5 and fn. 5, p. 201.

29. Robert Perlman, *Consumers and Social Services* (New York: John Wiley, 1975), p. 77.

30. Speaker, Annual Convention of the National Legal Aid and Defenders Association, Seattle, Washington, November, 1975.

31. Nivola, "Municipal Agency: A Study of Housing Inspectional Service in Boston," chap. 3.

32. "Budget Bureau Recommendations for Savings in the Welfare Budget," March 24, 1969. Unpublished document in author's files.

33. Ibid.

34. Ibid.

35. Ibid.

36. *New York Times*, December 21, 1977.

16
Teaching and Learning in a Bureaucratic School

Susan Moore Johnson

During the early 1900s educational efficiency experts touted what has come to be known as the industrial model of schooling. Schools were likened to factories, students were treated as raw materials, and teachers dealt with like laborers. Although most school reforms fade fairly quickly, this one endured. Throughout the United States administrators applied to public schools practices of accountability drawn from business and industry. They focused on economies of scale and calculated returns on investments. They instituted departmentalized teaching in the form of "platoon schools," devising blocked schedules that rotated teachers from class to class. They constructed tests and rating scales for measuring school efficiency and instituted quantitative measures of teachers' productivity. Raymond E. Callahan concludes that school officials did not succeed in making schools more productive: they achieved economy but only the appearance of efficiency.[1] Although the effort to rationalize schooling failed to better educate children, it was not abandoned, for it reduced costs and enabled school administrators to look responsible in the eyes of the business community.

The image of the school as a factory is no longer fashionable, and today education is rarely characterized as a production process. Schools are known to be complex social organizations, and children to vary in abilities and interests. Educators voice respect for diversity and speak of being responsive to the individual student and recognizing the need for flexible school structures. Features of industrial organization persist nonetheless, and today's schools continue to operate as bureaucracies even though the work that goes on inside them cannot be productively standardized. Blocked schedules, Carnegie units, age-graded classrooms, competency testing, and ability-group tracking remain the norm; open schools and classrooms, the integrated day, interdisciplinary courses, ungraded classes, and modular scheduling are the exception.

The rhetoric of educational mass production is no longer heard, but its structures endure.

Bureaucratic forms in education are resilient because they keep costs down and permit schools to cope with large numbers of students in a seemingly orderly way. They do not, however, meet the needs of teachers and students who are engaged in the business of teaching and learning rather than management and accounting. If schools were structured from the inside out rather than the outside in, if they derived their form from the needs of teachers and students rather than the priorities of administrators and business, they would be smaller, more flexible, and varied organizations.

In this chapter we explore what happens when rationalizing structures are applied to work that is not wholly rational; when schools are organized as if pedagogy could be prescribed, instruction delivered in uniform doses to clients in large groups, and the products of learning measured and summarized for public scrutiny. The public-school teachers interviewed for this study strained to make their schools work on behalf of good teaching, despite school structures that often hampered them from doing so. They committed much energy to coping with institutional constraints, energy that might have been better used in teaching their students. They learned that much of what school departments do in the name of efficiency, productivity, or fiscal responsibility is neither efficient, productive, nor fiscally responsible. They found themselves obliged to prop up ineffective practices and apologize for unrealistic expectations even while they saw their students ill served. Ironically, the factory model of schooling prevails most strongly in those urban schools that enroll the neediest and most diverse populations—the very students who require the individualized approaches to instruction that bureaucratic schools can least deliver.

Although teachers in independent schools of the private sector also encountered some bureaucratic elements in their workplaces, the constraints were far less restrictive than in the public sector. Classes were smaller; instructional loads were lighter; teaching time was disrupted less often; clerical duties were fewer; and instructional autonomy was greater. As a result, teachers expressed more confidence in achieving success with all their students and reported more often that they could teach as they thought they should. But before examining these valued teachers' responses to the bureaucratic features of their workplaces, we should consider in more detail why schools are such poor candidates for mechanistic control.

Why Schooling is Hard to Rationalize

Organizational analysts have observed that work can be successfully rationalized only under certain conditions. First, the work cannot be subject to uncertainty; only in a predictable and unvarying environment can work be routinized reliably.[2] Where there is little uncertainty, as in the paper industry, organizations can safely standardize practice. Where uncertainty increases, as in computer software development, organizations must be able to adapt their responses to sudden and unexpected change. Second, organizations with clear goals can more readily standardize practice than those with unclear or conflicting goals. The organizational purposes of a fire department are far less ambiguous than those of a human rights commission and, consequently, the work of fire fighters can be prescribed more precisely than that of human rights advocates. Third, the technology, or way of doing the work, must be such that it can be planned in advance and clearly specified. An organization that is to provide standardized services or products must be able to ensure conformity of process and consistency of product. McDonald's has developed such a technology for preparing fast food and has devised methods for training its predominantly unskilled, teenage workforce to carry out those procedures. By contrast, the technology of writing poetry is difficult to specify, and creativity cannot be programmed. Fourth, organizations that adapt well to rational structures typically use raw materials of constant quality. Assembly-line production of microchips requires consistently high-quality silicon; given suitable supplies, work can proceed in a routinized manner. By contrast, a chef's raw materials are less constant and predictable, and those who cook must adapt their techniques to the unexpected delivery of unripe avocados or sinewy beef.

When environmental uncertainty is low, goals explicit and achievable, technology narrowly specified, and raw materials consistent, an organization can specialize workers' roles and standardize their activities, whether they are manufacturing frisbees or administering inoculations. However, when uncertainty is great, goals ambiguous or contradictory, technology weak, and raw materials uneven, organizational structures must be more flexible and permit workers to experiment and adapt in doing their work. The structures must allow time for workers to coordinate their efforts and exchange information about progress and problems; they must tolerate inefficiency; and they must be responsive to the demands of an individual client rather than controlled by programmed routines of the service-delivery system.

Schools are clearly organizations of the second sort. They operate in uncertain and sometimes volatile environments. They encounter unexpected budget cuts, sudden arrivals of large immigrant groups, new mandates from state and federal governments, and constant political demands from all segments of the community. Their goals are notoriously ambiguous and conflicting; schools are expected to provide everything for everyone, to teach children both conformity and creativity, to inculcate respect for authority as well as critical thinking. Teachers are simultaneously told to attend to the needs of the individual and the group. They are expected to teach broad concepts, but their students are often tested for proficiency in discrete skills. Nor is there much consensus about the technology of teaching. For some subjects, such as typing, there are tried-and-true approaches. For others, such as creative writing, methods vary widely. Finally, students—the raw materials of school-ing—vary physically, intellectually, socially, and psychologically. As schools reach out to serve increasingly diverse student populations, they necessarily must cope with the even greater variation in ability, interest, and behavior that these students present.

A review of these features of school organizations—the environment, goals, technology, and raw materials—suggests that, if schools are to be effective, they must have adaptive structures, experiment with varied approaches, and prepare for different kinds of outcomes. Theory would lead us to predict that standardized structures and preplanned practices would enable educators to serve only some students and achieve only some goals, that rationalizing instruction overall would be ill advised and ineffective. In some public schools education is not arranged in bureau-cratic fashion or doled out in uniform doses to large groups of students. Joan Lipsitz describes several such middle schools.[3] Theodore Sizer's Coalition of Essential Schools is nurturing similar efforts across the country.[4] Most persons familiar with public education can cite other examples. But these are exceptions, created and maintained at consider-able personal cost to teachers and principals who must contend with strong organizational forces in public education that suppress variation in favor of standardized treatment of students in large schools and classes with uniform, though not necessarily distinguished, outcomes.

Batch Teaching

Although teaching is inherently an interpersonal activity, teachers in our society rarely work with their students one at a time. Rather, they encounter diverse groups of 15 to 40 students. Although elementary-school teachers may work with the same 20 students throughout the day, secondary-school teachers are routinely assigned 125 students in five rotating classes. The teachers in this study regularly noted the constraints of large, diverse classes and demanding course loads and expressed concern about their ability to meet the needs of all their students. In general, classes were both larger and more varied in public than independent schools; teachers in Catholic schools sometimes taught more students at once than did their public-school counterparts, but their classes tended to be more homogeneous in student composition.

Class Size
Research to date on the effects of class size has yielded inconclusive and contradictory results.[5] Lacking clear demonstration that students learn

more in small classes, critics of public education often argue that class size is simply a matter of teachers' self-interest—smaller classes make work easier and protect more jobs. Given the considerable expense of reducing class size, school districts usually avoid the cost unless they encounter strong pressure in the community or at the negotiating table.

Teachers in this study expressed strong opinions about class size, opinions formed by their own experience rather than research findings. They told of large classes forcing them to lecture rather than lead discussions and reducing the time available for them to interact with individual students. They were convinced that class size made a difference in how and what students learned, and they held remarkably consistent notions about what levels of enrollment were intolerable (over 30), acceptable (25–30), preferable (15–25), and ideal (10–15).

Public-school elementary classes generally ranged from 20 to 25 students; the largest regular class represented in this study totaled 30 students.[6] Classes in reading, bilingual education, and special education were smaller, those in physical education or music sometimes larger. At the middle-school and junior-high-school level, class size varied as a result of ability grouping.[7] A mathematics teacher's smallest class included 13 students while her largest had 33. High-school classes also varied in size—7 to 35 students—as a result of both tracking practices and elective offerings in specialized or advanced subjects such as restaurant management or Latin. Class sizes in Catholic schools were similar, although a few elementary-level classes exceeded 30 students. Since some of these schools offered only one class per grade level, a particularly large class was often said to be a temporary demographic quirk. Teachers from Jewish and Quaker schools in the sample reported consistently smaller classes, reflecting their institutions' commitment to personalized instruction. Independent-school classes were often half the size of those in the public sector. With one exception, all teachers interviewed from these schools taught fewer than 20 students in a class, and most had no more than 15. Allen Rondo said that in his school the average class size was about 15: "It varies from four or five in the smaller, upper electives up to, very occasionally, a math class might have twenty." One secondary-school teacher, who said that she had never taught a class with more than 12 students, characterized class size in her school as "very manageable." The sizes of any single teacher's classes also varied in secondary independent schools, but the average size was much smaller than in public and parochial schools. One independent-school teacher's classes ranged from 5 to 14 students, another's from 7 to 18. The smallest classes of most secondary independent schools were half the size of those in public schools, while their largest were approximately two-thirds the size of comparable classes in the public sector.[8]

Public-school teachers generally considered classes with more than 25 students difficult to teach. One elementary-school teacher with 30 students called her class "enormous" and described the practical problem of arranging thirty desks for a class discussion. Another middle-school teacher of 32 students complained that her class was "huge." A middle-school teacher with classes of "about twenty-six to twenty-seven kids" called this "way too many," causing difficulties in "really getting to know them." Teachers generally doubted that policy makers understood the importance of class size. A suburban high-school English teacher said that her assistant superintendent had decided to increase certain college preparatory classes from 25 to 27 students, thus eliminating three sections and "saving the town a lot of money." The change was made in the name of efficiency, but this teacher argued:

> What she has done is create classes that people are uncomfortable teaching, and what they've lost is far greater than anything they've gained by eliminating that half of a position. . . . Numbers make a big difference in any classroom. You know, I can do fine with a class up to twenty-five, really I can. But when it gets over the line of twenty-five, just in terms of physical layout, trying to get those extra seats in, it's a problem. I like to get to every kid at least once a period. The periods are forty-eight minutes long, and you have thirty kids. If I get to everybody, I'm not going to hear much from any one person.

A middle-school mathematics teacher in an economically poor community agreed:

> As you get up into the twenty-twos and twenty-fives and twenty-eights, effective instruction is compromised because we're dealing with kids who, ideally . . . should have individualized instruction in math. . . . They have poor math backgrounds, and they don't have a grasp of mathematical concepts or figures.

He, too, believed there was simply not enough time to go around: "In a class of thirty it's impossible. No matter what anyone tells you, in a forty-five-minute class, it's virtually impossible." Public-school teachers who taught fewer than 20 students at once said that good teaching was possible in that situation. An elementary-school teacher said that classes in her school are typically 18 to 20, which she finds "ideal." A high-school mathematics teacher whose classes averaged fewer than 20 students echoed: "It's really ideal."

Although most public-school teachers thought that classes with fewer than 20 students were ideal, independent-school teachers preferred, and generally expected, classes of no more than 15. Prior experience in private schools had led them to believe that they could and should succeed with all their students,[9] and they often argued that personalized attention was possible only when they were teaching 15 or fewer students. A history teacher in a prestigious day school, who contended that small class size is "the most crucial thing for good teaching," said that there is a "critical number" that permits, even obliges, all students to participate in class discussions. But "when classes get beyond fifteen or sixteen for me, I know that students can slip by. . . . At fourteen, they can't."

Class size, therefore, affected teachers' choice of teaching methods and expectations of success. Classes approaching 30 students were termed manageable, but only with teacher-centered instruction in which teachers took the role of experts delivering information and students became passive recipients, seldom raising questions, offering interpretations, or entering into real discussion with their teachers or peers. Teachers believed that such classes met the needs of only some students some of the time. Those who taught classes of 20 to 25 students said that they had more opportunity to address individuals' interests and needs, and they suggested that reducing class size by even 2 or 3 students made a big difference in their work. Teachers whose classes were smaller than 20 in the public sector and 15 in the private sector were decidedly more optimistic that they could truly reach and teach each of their students.

Class Composition

Numbers were only part of what concerned teachers when they talked about responding to students' needs in large groups, for class size interacts with class composition. A teacher of severely handicapped children may not be able to teach more than 3 students in one class, while in advanced placement mathematics a teacher might feel confident of success with a class of 25.

Student bodies in independent and church-related schools were more homogeneous than those in the public sector by virtue of parents' choices and school admission standards. Many such schools refused to accept students with special learning needs and there were few low-income students, given the high costs of tuition and limited scholarship funds. Therefore, although any group of children is inevitably diverse, the range of abilities, experience, and attitudes toward formal education was reported to be far narrower in the private than the public sector.

City schools were more diverse racially, ethnically, and economically than suburban schools, and even those urban classes that were homogeneous in race or economic background often included students with an array of social, health, and learning problems that required considerable individualized attention. Urban school teachers felt the greatest demands to adapt their teaching to the individual needs of students but were the least able to do so because of large classes.

Handicapped students, present in virtually all public-school teachers' classes, presented particular demands for individualized instruction. A fourth-grade teacher in an urban school argued that her class of 20 was too big, given the large numbers of such students: "On paper, it's a regular mainstreamed classroom, but there are children here who have special needs. . . . That is the greatest source of stress in my work: time, and having children who need more help than the help I can give them." Similarly, a science teacher in an urban middle school, who argued that class size is the single factor that most compromises his effectiveness, explained that the difficulty of teaching many students is augmented when a number of those students present unusual needs:

> I think that it makes any teacher less effective. In my case, I feel that I have a large number of special-ed children. I make tremendous adjustments for them in the classroom. In other classes, the class size might be drastically reduced because of the children going out to special ed, but it's a policy in the school that all children will have science, and I am the science teacher.

The interview data provided testimony of great variation among students, the raw materials of the educators' trade, and teachers were well aware that they could not apply the same set of expectations and teaching practices to all students and expect common outcomes. In fact, they found the notion laughable. Yet schools are organized as if they could and should.

Teaching Load

For secondary-school teachers, the teaching loads—the total number of students and sections they taught—further influenced their ability to teach well. Secondary-school teachers from public and Catholic schools had comparable teaching loads, with 75–130 students in middle and junior high schools and 80–130 students in high schools. By contrast, teachers in secondary independent schools taught a maximum of 70–80 students.[10]

Theodore Sizer has persuasively argued the case for smaller teaching loads in public schools, contending that Horace Smith, his fictitious though typical teacher, "should not have to compromise; he should be responsible for only 80 students at a time, not 120 or 150 or 175, as is common today in many public and parochial schools."[11] A teacher's student load determines the amount of sustained attention available for any individual student. A teacher who considers the learning needs of 75 students simply thinks differently than one concerned with twice that number.

Public- and independent-school teachers also differed significantly in the number of course sections assigned to them, and thus the number of class preparations and hours of stand-up instruction. Most academic teachers in public and Catholic secondary schools taught five classes five times a week. With few exceptions, independent-school teachers taught four courses four or five times each week. Anna Capello compared her schedule as a home-economics teacher with that of her academic colleagues:

> I think I would have a hard time if I were an academic teacher, teaching the same subject every day for five periods. But my schedule is different every

day. I have six classes. I see them two days a week for a total of four periods. I see them longer. They're double periods, which is sometimes difficult, but it also works well when you're preparing food. It gives me flexibility within my curriculum.

She was glad to have longer blocks of time, even though it meant that she was assigned more students.

The combined effects of five large and diverse classes meeting one after another each day exhausted many respondents. The urban high-school teacher who is responsible for 130 students in five sections each day simply cannot provide the attention to class preparation or individualized instruction that is possible for the independent-school teacher with 75 students meeting in four sections, four times each week.

Grouping and Tracking

With small classes, teachers can adapt their instructional approaches to respond to individuals' abilities, learning styles, and levels of motivation. With large classes, they must either accept that they will reach only some students or devise ways to reduce the diversity. The most common response is to group, or track, students by ability. Ironically, this response often leads to a schoolwide system that is both impersonal and inflexible and reinforces the very bureaucratic practices that teachers initially sought to moderate.

Throughout this study, teachers reported grouping students by ability for instructional efficiency. Elementary teachers often regrouped students from one or more classes for reading or mathematics. For example, one urban teacher said that she exchanges students "with another second-grade teacher in our school just so we can have a top math group and a bottom math group and different reading groups, so you can get to a different group of kids."

Middle- and junior-high-school teachers also frequently organized classes into more homogeneous groups. A suburban teacher of social studies and English described the complicated arrangement in her school:

> Social studies is heterogeneous in both seventh and eighth. Science is heterogeneous in seventh, and in eighth it is semi-heterogeneous. There are a couple of top-level science classes. But in math and English, they are definitely tracked into three levels, A, B, C.

Although a few school districts prohibited tracking in the elementary or middle schools, others encouraged it. Most classes at these levels differentiated broadly among groups (advanced, regular, remedial). At an extreme, one urban English teacher, whose largest class had 32 students, reported that there were sixteen different levels in the seventh grade. The school had coped with enormous class size and its accompanying complexity by creating many discrete, homogeneous groups of students. With few exceptions, high-school teachers' academic classes were stratified either by an explicit tracking system that designated courses by level (honors, standard, or basic: Curriculum I, II) or by an elective system that differentiated courses by difficulty (Medieval History, Modern Living).

Most teachers agreed that teaching was more manageable in a homogeneous than a heterogeneous class, because one could prepare materials and approaches that were geared to a greater proportion of the students. Those who taught advanced classes might find the task demanding, but they were not confused about whose needs to meet. The goal of the class was clear and the students able and focused on their work. Many teachers of low-performing students also reported that teaching homogeneous classes was easier than trying to address such students' needs within heterogeneous groups, provided the classes were not too large. But the teachers were well aware that sometimes only the best students profit from such arrangements; that large concentrations of weak students reinforce poor study habits and low expectations among peers; and that average students often get lost in a huge, gray middle. Moreover, the teachers knew that tracking is often socially and academically stigmatizing. Several mentioned that research findings discredit tracking,[12] and some, particularly in elementary and middle schools, said they preferred to work with heterogeneous groups. However, few teachers believed that sufficient individualization was possible given the size and diversity of most public-school classes, and they believed that students' needs could best be met by reducing diversity through grouping students with others of similar interests and abilities. Tracking was the accommodation they made to a school organization that requires batch processing of learners.

Specialization of Teachers

Workers on an industrial assembly line have highly specialized assignments. In manufacturing a product, whether it be a bicycle or a coat, they become experts at particular subtasks such as welding spokes, assembling brakes, cutting sleeves, or making buttonholes. No single person performs the total task; no bicycle or coat bears the stamp of a craftsperson responsible for its construction. At best, an inspector tucks a slip of paper into the carton or pocket to verify that the product meets company standards. An assembly line can produce goods of uniform quality quickly and at far lower cost than items custom made by a single mechanic or tailor for particular customers.

In a school organization modeled on manufacturing, teachers would be experts in computer technology, right-brain learning, phonics, or scientific inquiry, and over the course of thirteen years, students would move from one expert worker to the next to be informed, treated, and tested until they emerged as certifiably educated graduates. Teachers would repeat routine, predetermined tasks rather than adapt their approaches to changing students. In the extreme, all students would pass through the same set of procedures, and those who failed periodic inspections would be rejected. By contrast, schools organized in response to clients would orient their approaches to individuals or small groups of students and fashion instruction to meet their particular needs. Working alone or in teams, teachers would attend to the whole child, considering physical development and social skills as well as capacity to reason abstractly or compute accurately. Predetermined teaching patterns would be replaced with individually fashioned education plans. These organizations would make it possible to diagnose and respond to the students' complex and varied needs, but only at a cost in dollars and inefficiency.

Elementary Schools

Most respondents from elementary schools, both public and private, taught self-contained classes and, thus, could be considered generalists rather than specialists. Teachers who preferred this instructional format valued the opportunity to teach the whole range of subjects to a small group of students. A fifth-grade teacher said that he had been "resisting team teaching. I guess maybe I don't want to let go. I like having the kids in all the different areas." Self-contained classes provide consistent, if unspecialized, attention to student learning. With one teacher responsible for all of a student's major subjects, that student's total instructional experience is more likely to be coordinated and coherent than if several teachers were assigned parts of the total task.

Even in self-contained classes, however, selected students were taken out of class for work with specialized tutors under the auspices of programs in special education, Chapter I, or English as a second language. Four elementary-school teachers of self-contained classes reported that such disruptions were the greatest source of stress in their work. One explained:

> The major problem that teachers have is fragmentation in our day. We have kids going everywhere. They go out to the reading lab, and they go out to Chapter I, and they go out to the resource room. We have kids going in and out all the time, and then you don't know how to make up what they're missing.

One teacher did not question the value of such specialists' work but reflected on the costs of a fragmented schedule: "I have twenty-three interruptions in the course of a week in this room, and I never have my full class together, ever at one time. And parents say to me, 'Well, will my child miss anything?' Well, of course they will. Of course they will."

Classroom teachers saw some irony in the fact that schools increasingly seek to serve the needs of the whole child by interrupting their core instructional time for work with outside specialists. In a few schools, specialists' services were scheduled with a regard for the integrity of core instructional time, and teachers praised those arrangements. One respondent explained that grade-level teachers in his school designate two periods each day for reading and mathematics, which could not be interrupted. Several respondents recommended that special-education programs be modified to bring specialists into the classroom to support instruction there, making students' learning more consistent and classroom teaching more coherent.

Middle and Junior High Schools
The tension between teachers' roles as specialists and generalists increased in grades five through eight of the public schools, which are typically thought to provide a transition between client-centered instruction in the primary grades and subject-centered instruction in the high schools. Few teachers at this level taught self-contained classes; most were assigned to either subject-specific departments or interdisciplinary teams or clusters. The structure of teaching units reflected the extent to which schools and teachers oriented their programs to either the student or the subject.

In some schools teachers were organized by interdisciplinary teaching teams and assigned to work exclusively with a single group of students. Typically, such teams included teachers in English, mathematics, social studies, and science, who together took responsibility for 80–100 students. In the most successful examples these teachers met together regularly, planning and coordinating their curricula and constructing schedules that were consistent with their students' instructional needs. Teachers could monitor students' progress closely, and if one began to fall behind in a particular subject, that teacher might ask his or her colleagues whether they saw evidence of similar problems. Study skills, personal development, and in-class behavior were of concern to all staff, and meetings with parents usually included all teachers rather than just one. Richard Sand, who collaborated with four colleagues in teaching 100 students, described his team's interaction:

> We meet every single day. Basically, we discuss the kids; that's why we're here. We bring up problems. We let each other know what we're doing so we don't all schedule a major test the day before Christmas, things like that. We deal with parents' problems and parents' requests. We have parents come in and talk about the kids. Sometimes we request; sometimes they request.

Teachers who favored this teaching structure valued the coordinated, holistic attention to students that it permitted, as well as the curricular insights that interdisciplinary work offered. Often classes were heterogeneous rather than homogeneous. One teacher called it "very, very healthy for students." Another said that it permitted her to respond quickly with other staff and parents when she saw a problem developing: "There's no lag time."

A departmentalized structure characterizes the organization of most junior high schools. Teachers worked far more closely with colleagues who shared their subject specialty than with teachers from other departments who shared their students. As the day proceeded, students assembled and reassembled for their different classes with different collections of their peers. In departmentalized schools, a fixed schedule subdivided instructional time by subject, and all teachers had to work within the constraints of its uniform blocks. Many teachers liked working with colleagues who had similar academic interests, but several respondents from departmentalized schools expressed concern about the effects of specialization. One said:

> I like [departmentalization], but then there comes a point where, if teachers were working together, we could get more out of students. It seems like we're always fighting the battle alone. It's one teacher, one class, and it's either sink or swim with that class.

This teacher contended that students' experiences were too fragmented under the current departmentalized arrangement:

> They come from elementary schools where they are with the same teacher every day, all day, and then the first day of the seventh grade, they see seven different teachers, and that's the way it is for the rest of the year. I think a lot of kids don't adjust too well. . . . It's tough.

Teachers who had worked in both interdisciplinary and departmental structures generally favored the cluster structure. Richard Sand had taught in both situations and emphatically preferred the team approach, because teachers could quickly identify and deal with problems as they developed:

> It's quick. There's no lag time. Before, if a kid was having a problem, if I remembered, I would speak to another teacher at lunch time or after school or before school. It might be a week. It might be ten days. I might forget completely. We just didn't pick up on some of the problems kids were having. This is, by far, much better.

A teacher whose school had returned to a departmentalized organization regretted the change:

> We had a certain flexibility that we don't have now, the ability to double up, to have two periods without hassling all the other teachers in the school. There were lots of advantages like that. And being able to get together with the members of the team and talk about the kids, being able to send kids back and forth. There were a lot of advantages.

Her school had returned to a departmentalized structure in order to promote schoolwide curriculum development, but most other teachers whose schools had moved from clusters to departments said that the change had been made for financial rather than instructional reasons. As one teacher explained, "They didn't want to pay. We weren't teaching five full periods, which the other schools were." In order to work as they are intended, cluster structures require extra staff time for meeting and coordination, and teachers' preparation periods must be aligned. By contrast, scheduling by departments can be done without assigning joint planning time and, therefore, is less costly both in dollars and administrative effort.

High Schools
Specialization was extensive in the curriculum and schedule of both public and private high schools, where virtually all respondents' work was organized by subject specialties. A high-school English teacher was far more likely to meet and talk regularly with another member of the same department who taught an entirely different group of students than with a mathematics teacher who taught the same students. The curriculum of the large comprehensive public high school was extensive and varied, featuring elective courses in subjects as diverse as Chaucer, Chinese studies, auto repair, and advanced placement physics. Public high schools responded to diverse student needs by offering many courses and alternative paths to graduation. As a result, students' scholastic experiences in most public high schools were highly differentiated, some would say fragmented.[13]

Three teachers in this study taught in schools-within-schools that resembled the cluster structure of some middle and junior high schools. One alternative program for 100 students restricted their course options but enabled them to participate in setting policies and practices for their schooling. One teacher believed the smaller class size, personal commitment, and democratic structure contributed to a community that supported student learning.

A second respondent, in cooperation with a science and mathematics teacher, taught English and social studies to a group of 68 students in a vocational high school. Students attended academic classes one week and vocational classes the next. This teacher thought that the small, tight structure was "good for the kids." He and his colleague were able to monitor students' progress and adapt the schedule to fit their teaching needs: "I like the control that the two of us have. If we want to extend a period or shorten a period, we can do it. We can do anything we want academically. The week we have them, we're in complete control."

A third respondent instituted a cluster program in his school when officials in his suburban district moved the ninth grade to the high school and he became "very concerned" that ninth graders would get "totally lost and fail academically." Under the new arrangement each cluster consisted of English, social studies, and science teachers working with a group of students, "monitoring them socially and academically." Teachers eventually hoped to "get together to do interdisciplinary teaching." The program was working well, though students taking accelerated courses in science and mathematics could not be accommodated in the schedule.

Except in alternative programs such as these schools-within-schools just described, public high schools provide virtually no systematic means for staff to monitor individual students' progress or to intervene when difficulties arise. Counselors with very heavy case loads—typically 250–300 students—were expected to oversee students' course selection, personal and social development, academic achievement, college applications, and career plans. No one really expected them to effectively integrate the complex and highly differentiated structure of the school on students' behalf, and yet no one else was in a position to do so.

As in public high schools, the primary reference group for most independent-school teachers was the department, where collegial interactions centered on curriculum rather than individual students. But because of the small size of these schools, teachers were often assigned to more than one department, thus promoting more exchange across disciplines within the faculty. Allen Rondo estimated that two-thirds of the teachers in his school belong to more than one department. In most independent high schools the entire faculty met regularly to review students' progress one by one. They drew on their varied perspectives as instructors, administrators, advisors, coaches, and dormitory supervisors to identify problems and to devise strategies for intervention. An average of 378 students, compared with 1,262 in public high schools, made such oversight possible and ensured that no student fell between the cracks of the departmental structure. Few public high schools are small enough to make such continuing attention possible. Moreover, faculty who may know less than 10 percent of the student body in large schools can hardly be expected to hold this schoolwide concern for individual students' progress.

Pressures to Departmentalize

For a number of reasons, no high school encountered in this study was organized predominantly by clusters or interdisciplinary teams. Many teachers liked working in departments, with opportunities to teach highly specialized courses that they found both challenging and rewarding. Graduation requirements and standards for college entrance reinforce a departmentalized structure; interdisciplinary courses are misfits in traditional academic accounting systems. Standard departmental structures also survive because alternatives are costly. Faced with budgetary constraints, teachers preferred smaller traditional classes to interdisciplinary innovations. In some cases students resisted interdisciplinary structures. Able and motivated students benefited from specialized academic and vocational coursework, appreciating the opportunity to choose from 150 or more specialized courses; the less able or poorly motivated students who had more to gain from cluster structures were typically less vocal and influential.

Teachers in this study from all levels saw advantages in both specialized and unspecialized school structures. The specialists can hone subject-specific skills that generalists cannot, and the content of instruction may be richer as a result. The sixth-grade teacher who works exclusively as a writing specialist may contribute more to students' learning than he or she could if expected to teach all subjects. The advanced placement physics teacher arguably can offer better training to aspiring engineers than someone teaching general physics to all students.

However, highly differentiated, rationalized schools hindered teachers from integrating students' experiences from different courses or monitoring their progress effectively. Although able, self-motivated students might provide that integration for themselves, many others could not, and the price of specialization may too often be academic fragmentation and social disintegration. Ultimately, teachers' desire to see students progress may be more frustrated than facilitated by specialized structures. With lighter teaching loads and smaller schools, teachers might gain the opportunity to be both specialists and generalists, pursuing their interests and abilities in environmental science and Tolstoy while attending to their students' total schooling experience.

Constraints of Nonteaching Duties

Although some teachers' instructional roles were highly specialized, very few teachers in this study were permitted to specialize exclusively in teaching. If teachers' scarce and precious time were not claimed for extraneous clerical or supervisory duties, they might move more easily between the demands of subject matter and students. Any teacher's time, no matter how devoted she or he may be to students or school, is ultimately limited. Time that is spent monitoring cafeterias, supervising detention, or counting lunch money cannot be effectively spent correcting homework, meeting with parents, or tutoring students. One might expect that school officials who were concerned with efficiency and productivity would see that teachers' time is used for teaching, but often they do not, and teachers routinely function as monitors, security guards, and clerks.

Elementary-school teachers generally believed that their students needed close supervision and sustained care, and they accepted supervisory tasks such as lunch duty, bus duty, and recess duty. Secondary-school teachers perceived less need to monitor students' behavior outside of class, in part because they considered their students to be sufficiently independent to fend for themselves. Many secondary-school teachers said that the greatest source of stress in their work was the shortage of time, and yet virtually all had to reserve forty-five minutes each day for noninstructional tasks. A bilingual teacher who spent third period each day in the main corridor of a large urban high school "guarding the door against intruders" considered herself lucky that it was generally quiet enough there to allow her to grade papers. However, for most teachers, supervisory time was lost time. A foreign-language teacher observed, "My main concern should be my classes and my students, not my study hall. I know I resent having to do that duty." Five of the more experienced public-high-school teachers in the sample had devised ways to substitute instructional or administrative responsibilities for supervisory duties. One who taught twenty-eight periods rather than the standard twenty-five explained, "I'll trade two or three more teaching periods for babysitting detail any day."

The problems of custodial care in public secondary schools are very real. Faculty and administrators cannot depend on positive student norms to ensure socially responsible student behavior as they might in smaller, more homogeneous schools; they cannot leave students to their own devices during free time. School facilities must be protected from disruptive or dangerous intruders. But teachers do not believe that the answer lies in seizing their already scarce professional time.

Extracurricular activities were optional for most public-school teachers, although many respondents participated. By contrast, independent-school teachers at the secondary level were usually required to coach two out of three seasons, a responsibility that some enjoyed as an integral part of their work with students and others disliked because it detracted from their "real work" of teaching. In either case, coaching claimed a great deal of after-school and weekend time. One respondent said that when she finishes teaching each day, she spends "two and one half hours out on the playing field. I spend all Wednesday afternoon at games and all day Saturday at games. It's exhausting. Perhaps if that time weren't consumed by coaching, I could spend more time thinking up new ideas." Another teacher agreed that coaching claims time that otherwise might be spent on classroom teaching: "A good soccer practice takes as long to prepare as a good chemistry class."

Throughout these interviews, teachers distinguished between nonteaching duties that required their expertise and those that did not. Richard Sand observed humorously:

> Student contact stuff we have to do. Standing in bathrooms—I don't think we have to do that. . . . They could bring a gorilla in and chain it to the wall and give it just enough rope to reach the little buggers. The student contact tasks I really don't mind for the most part.

All agreed that collecting money—whether for pictures, insurance, lunches, field trips, or candy sales—should be delegated to aides or secretaries, as should tallying daily racial counts, completing the state-required attendance register, authorizing welfare forms, and filling out truancy cards. Schools varied widely in the extent to which they subjected teachers to such tasks. Some teachers handled no money, while others had to tend several accounts. Two teachers complained about being "insurance agents" without commissions. One second-grade teacher collected lunch money daily and submitted a detailed order for hot and cold lunches, noting preferences for white or chocolate milk and ice cream or chips. She estimated that it took "a good twenty minutes" each morning to get it all right. Some schools simplified attendance procedures with computerized systems, while others required hand-tallied accounts from each classroom teacher. One elementary-school teacher said that she had few such clerical responsibilities: "We've had good leadership along the way that has seen to it that our time is put into working with children. That's probably why I'm still here." By contrast, Gary Stein said that attending to such administrative business in his second-grade classroom consumed half an hour each morning. He regretted the waste: "Time for me is very precious because the rest of the day we're going full steam."

Teachers in some schools were required to file reports listing the number of minutes they intended to devote to each subject, detailed accounts of their compliance with special-education plans, and their own lesson plans for subsequent weeks. Often they suspected that no one read these documents.

Teachers spent additional time on clerical tasks such as typing hand-outs and tests, ordering supplies and books, and photocopying or duplicating materials for class. A few teachers objected to these chores, but most were grateful if they had access to typewriters with ribbons, photocopiers that worked, and purchase orders that would be honored. Gary Stein said that he had managed to

> barter with the principal to get a second field trip on the condition that I take on all additional responsibilities of collecting money, keeping records of money, and getting a final check that is ready to go to the bus company. The only impact on the office is that they call to arrange for the bus and they mail the check that I've given them.

Although much of teachers' routine clerical work could have been performed by others, virtually no public school in this sample had designated aides or secretaries for the purpose.

Curriculum and Pedagogy

If schools were to operate like factories, producing educated students in large batches, teachers would be equipped with standardized curricula and trained in proven pedagogies. In fact, there has been growing optimism in some quarters that such an instructional technology is possible. Proponents of so-called effective teaching practices have sought to describe and prescribe failproof approaches to instruction. However, since 1985, researchers have raised increasing doubts about finding formulas for successful teaching.[14] More recently, those seeking to define a "knowledge base" for professional teachers have found such a definition to be "elusive" despite "a 'dramatic explosion' in research about teaching and learning over the past 20 years."[15] Despite such uncertainty, state officials and school districts throughout the country have become increasingly prescriptive about exactly what and how teachers must teach.

The teachers in this study expressed skepticism about the wisdom of any search for one best pedagogy; they believed the strength of their teaching rested in their ability to diagnose the needs of individual students and classes and to adapt their instructional approaches in response. One junior-high-school teacher said that she did not know how people could survive who rely on a single technology and do "the same thing year after year." She likened them to industrial workers who "work in an automobile plant and put the taillight bulb in every Nova that goes through." She argued that teachers must be responsive to differences among children: "The kids are different every year. They might be the same number, and there might be some of the same problems, but they're all different. Each class that goes through has its own personality. You have to adjust; you have to adapt." Respondents also spoke of the importance of encouraging teachers to feature the strengths of their individual teaching styles. An elementary-school teacher argued: "I don't think there is one way; I really don't. I think that for every person, it's a different way, and I think you need that." Richard Sand contended that "the worst kind of teacher is the teacher who opens the textbook and starts on page one, and at the end of the year wants to get to that last page." An urban middle-school teacher said that he and his principal agree that a good teacher "is one who does as many varied things as are necessary to meet the needs of various kids within the subject areas." A suburban English teacher was disparaging of peers who took pride in a prepackaged approach to technology:

> Their curriculum is more like a machine than anything else. They've got eighty lessons and they've got eighty days, and they click through it. It may be a pretty fancy and elaborate and detailed machine, but I think they're taking pride in something that doesn't warrant any particular pride. I'm not impressed with their curricula. I would like to see them be more motivated, more energetic, rather than trot the kids through this French Revolution for the twelfth year in a row.

Because this research was conducted in Massachusetts, where state officials do not try to regulate teaching directly, few teachers participating in this study said that they were obliged to follow a regimented, preprogrammed curriculum, and most from both the public and private sectors reported exercising a good deal of freedom in their teaching. Private-school teachers were rarely guided by more than rough outlines of course content. One elementary-school teacher, who said that he had a "tremendous amount of freedom," explained that he is constrained only by a "set of ideals and philosophy." A sixth-grade independent-school teacher explained that faculty at her school are

> given the general area, and then they decide what they want to do. I was told to teach classical Greece, and I sat down and looked at what classical Greece meant to me, what it had meant to the previous teacher, and pretty much sorted out what I wanted to do.

An English teacher from an independent high school said that she could choose her books and move at her own pace: "I can digress as I please or do other sorts of special projects as I please." A chemistry teacher in an independent school reported having much the same discretion: "In chemistry classes, I'm pretty much free to take those classes anywhere. . . . I can go fast or slow, and I can spend three months on nuclear power or acids and bases, and nobody would ever question that." Allen Rondo elaborated: "How many tests you give, how you want to do them, even your grading scale. . . . Do you assign homework or do you not? Do you collect it for a grade? That's up to you." Although public-school teachers spoke less confidently about their freedom to teach what and how they wanted, many in this sample did exercise as much discretion as private-school teachers. They were grateful that, unlike their counterparts in states such as Texas, they worked in a place that did not regulate their teaching practice or textbook selection.[16]

The curricula these teachers used were often local products prepared by teachers themselves. Anna Capello mentioned a home-economics "curriculum guide for the city. In fact, I wrote it." A middle-school teacher observed, "We have tremendous control over what we teach. We've designed our curriculum and change it frequently as a department." Another explained, "The prescribed curriculum is there, but it was developed by us in summer workshops a number of years ago. We set it up the way we wanted it. So it still came from us."

Teachers spoke eloquently, even passionately, about their need for autonomy in teaching. An elementary-level teacher in an independent school said, "I love making curricula for kids, for individual kids, for groups of kids, specific to learning styles." A number of respondents said that they would not continue to teach if they lost autonomy in their classrooms. An elementary-school art teacher said that if her supervisor had told her "what to teach and how to teach," she "probably wouldn't be here." A physics teacher who said, "I love the autonomy," argued similarly: "If somebody came in here and told me to teach this way or that way, it wouldn't work—not for good teachers. . . . If you want to set a mine field . . . for failure, that's how you do it." A middle-school teacher whose district had no centralized curriculum said that autonomy "keeps you motivated." She found that prescription "really takes away all desire to [teach]. It's irritating. I invent my own projects in the class and my own goals. It's a lot easier to work that way." A high-school English teacher argued that when "competent people who are enthusiastic about what they're doing" have "creative input so that they actually have an individual stamp, then I think that really you're going to support good teaching. It's self-motivating."

This celebration of autonomy should not be read as a demand for license. Teachers recognized the importance of a coherent program and acknowledged their responsibility to colleagues who would teach their students in subsequent years. A middle-school science teacher who said, "I don't like to be restricted and I'm not" also argued for an articulated curriculum and said that he felt an obligation to children as they moved on to another teacher or grade:

> There are certain basic assumptions that are being made about the material that has been covered, and certain concepts that should be understood in order to deal more effectively with the following grades. So I do follow the curriculum, though I may not teach exactly like many other teachers.

A middle-school mathematics teacher said that he was free to devise units and lessons "within the guidelines of what our curriculum describes. I mean, I can't just go and teach whatever I feel like teaching." A junior-high-school teacher, who said that she had "felt very hemmed in" by a curriculum some years ago, still did not advocate abandoning all guidelines: "I don't think I should be free to wander outside the curriculum even if I don't like it. It's the only way certain expectations can be met." Several teachers mentioned the importance of consistency among schools to permit relatively smooth student transfer from building to building. Others explained the need for agreement within a school about the sequence of skills to be taught. In fact, several respondents criticized the absence of any orderly approach to curriculum in their districts. One said that he had been granted autonomy by default: "I teach the basic things, but if I didn't want to . . . I could teach anything I wanted." He would have preferred some general guidelines. Although the teachers in general prized their autonomy, they also expected to exercise that autonomy within a framework that coordinated their efforts with those of other teachers.

A few public-school districts and a number of Catholic schools had assigned curricula that defined not only the scope but also the sequence of topics to be covered and skills taught. Janice Gagne described the structure in her Catholic school:

> The textbooks follow one on the other. They do want us to go by the textbook. Whatever I find most important within the textbook, I can devote more time or attention to that. . . . You have the manuals. . . . How you [cover the course material] is up to you. But they want it covered. . . .

> So it does put some pressure on you, I think. There are some things that I would rather give more quality time to, rather than worrying about having to get on. There is some pressure there.

Many teachers resented such prescription, and some refused to comply. A public-elementary-school teacher said that he had "played it right by the book" one year and found that he "wasn't satisfied. I had thought maybe they had a magical formula here. I did everything that they said to do. Then I said, 'No way. . . . I can do this much better,' and I have." He reorganized the sequence of stories, introduced novels, and prepared exercises to promote higher-level thinking skills. He reclaimed his autonomy with little difficulty, but others encountered more constraints. Several teachers from one urban district chafed under mandated curricula that specified both content and outcome by grade level and subject. The amount of material to be covered was another serious concern, and some of the teachers eventually rejected the requirements. An English teacher said that her centrally prescribed curriculum was far too comprehensive, but that she had decided not to cover it all: "To me, if I can cover half of it, and they understand half of it fully, I would rather do that than go through one hundred percent and have them understand nothing." Asked whether such adjustments required approval from above, she said, "I don't ask. I just do it." By contrast, a social studies teacher felt very confined by the requirements of the district's prepackaged curriculum. She compared teaching her American history class, where the program was prescribed, to teaching in her "best" class, Afro-American history, "where you don't have all those curriculum and objectives to follow" and she could do "exciting things." In the required course,

> you're a robot and it's an assembly-line kind of thing, where you're not doing anything well. You're just on some kind of a schedule. . . . Trying to cover a whole textbook before the end of the year doesn't leave you any room to do creative kinds of things.

She argued that the prescribed program discouraged creativity among teachers: "You tend to take the safe route out. 'We're on chapter twelve today.' Boom. Boom. Boom. Boom."

Policy makers who advocate prescribed curricula for public schools do so in part beeause they believe that all children should be taught the same things. These teachers would undoubtedly agree that all children should learn to read and compute, that those studying Latin must master the ablative case, and that those studying chemistry must attain an understanding of valences. But there are topics and courses that are less dependent on content, where teachers aim to instill concepts more than content and develop intellectual habits rather than discrete skills.[17] A science teacher who said that he and his collegues were "given a lot of freedom as to what we teach" explained that they had taught meteorology, in part "for our own stimulation." He explained that in earth science the content can vary because "it's the thinking process that we're trying to develop." He, like many other teachers in this study, believed that curricular objectives could be accomplished in various ways and that a good teacher attended both to the learning needs of students and to his or her own ever-evolving interests.

Supervision and Testing

In a mechanized production process, quality control can be obtained either by closely supervising the workers or by inspecting their products.[18] In an effort to exercise closer control over the process and product of public education, some policy makers and school officials have instituted programs to evaluate teaching practices directly by observation or indirectly with student test scores. In Massachusetts, where the data for this study were collected, state officials called for teacher evaluations every other year as well as testing of students' basic skills, relatively modest requirements compared with those of other states. Local school districts administered a variety of other tests. Private schools, which were not subject to the state requirements, administered tests of their own. Most of the teachers said that neither classroom observation nor testing resulted in significant regulation of their work, although some found the programs intrusive and counterproductive. For the most part, the programs provided the semblance, rather than the reality, of control.

Classroom Observation

Formal evaluation procedures that included periodic classroom observation by administrators served as spot checks on teachers' basic competence but did not provide school officials with continuous data about the teachers' compliance with the curriculum or prescribed teaching methods. For the teachers interviewed, observation of their work by administrators was largely symbolic. Most teachers reported that school officials monitored neither what nor how they taught, that they were left alone in their teaching. One urban elementary-school teacher said, "There's no one standing over my shoulder watching me." Gary Stein, who called evaluation "a rote process," said that his principal "really doesn't know what's going on in my classroom." Anna Capello agreed:

> I feel that I'm basically left alone. I think it would have been harder for me to stay if someone was, for lack of a better expression, breathing down my neck all the time. I really feel very independent in that no one is watching me all the time.

An urban English teacher concurred:

No one looks over your shoulder. I could do anything I want and no one says anything. And I mean no one says anything. It's just one of those things. They just take for granted that you're in your classroom, doing what you're supposed to do.

Teachers offered several explanations for this absence of oversight. Some said that their principals and department heads trusted them as professionals. One elementary-school teacher said that her principal had announced to his staff that he had selected them to teach in his school because they were "strong." She agreed: "We are all strong; we all do our job, and we don't need anyone to be looking over our shoulder. So we feel a certain amount of freedom in our school because we all are real professionals and do what we're supposed to do." Similarly, another elementary-school teacher said, "I have a principal who basically respects me and what I do and says, 'I hired you to do this. Do it.' He doesn't get involved." Other teachers attributed the absence of oversight to neglect or lack of interest on the part of school administrators. One suburban elementary-school teacher said, "The fact is, there isn't anybody out there who knows what is happening. I'm not sure they care, either." An art teacher echoed, "I don't know if they care that much, to tell you the truth." These teachers, being respected as they were by administrators, may have experienced less oversight in their work than their peers, but their responses suggest no special treatment. Classroom observations were conducted to meet contractual obligations, but rarely to monitor practice.

Some administrators sought to oversee teaching indirectly by examining documents such as plan books or grade books. Anna Capello said that she had to submit weekly lesson plans but, "the person whom I submit the lesson plans to knows nothing about foods. He's the department head, a former business teacher." One middle-school English teacher said that she had to send a set of compositions to the curriculum supervisor monthly. Gary Stein was required to submit chapter tests in mathematics for review by administrators. None of these teachers complained that such techniques significantly restricted what or how they taught, but complying with administrators' requests for documentation and maintaining the pretense of accounting consumed valuable time.

Student Testing
Standardized tests, a second oversight mechanism, were reported by the teachers to be increasingly prominent in their work. There was considerable evidence that test results influenced some teachers' work, but the respondents themselves seldom viewed the systemwide tests as professional tools enabling them to teach better. Because students vary and develop at different rates, it is difficult to isolate any single teacher's contribution to a student's test scores. However, some teachers believed that tests could be used by administrators to reveal individual teachers'

shortcomings. One said, "If there is a teacher who really isn't making it, the following year when the kids are tested, it really shows, and I think they can pretty well be identified. Maybe not for one year, but if it's a pattern over a period of years, it shows up." Most respondents objected to administrators' using tests to single out individuals. One who acknowledged that it was "beneficial" to identify gaps in students' proficiency said that she did not think it appropriate to "blame the third-grade teacher" for students' being "low in some area." She argued that others must share the responsibility: "She's not the only one who's been teaching math to those children in the last three years. We have first-grade teachers, second-grade teachers, and we have third-grade teachers. They test the children in the third grade."

In the case of academic programs taught exclusively by individuals, several teachers accepted standardized tests of students as appropriate measures of teaching performance. A teacher of advanced physics said that he felt "constrained" by the advanced placement exam, but that this was "fine. I teach to that test. That's supposed to be very bad, but it's an excellent test. I don't mind that at all." Districts seldom administered achievement tests in secondary subject areas and, therefore, teachers' practice was virtually unaffected by testing.

In the middle schools, tests often had greater influence in English and mathematics than in other subject areas. A junior-high-school social studies teacher explained that he was "dealing not so much with skills as with values and concepts, much harder things to test," and, as a result, he was safe from scrutiny: "The pressure is on in math and English. That's what parents think is important. So they don't value us [in social studies] as much, but they don't put as much pressure on us either."

At the elementary level, where reading and mathematics are the core of the curriculum, teachers were much more attentive to standardized tests, a fact that some teachers thought perverted rather than improved classroom teaching. One said,

> The object is that children should learn, that they should start where they are and progress as far as they can during the year. The teachers should put their best effort into that process. You should try to motivate the children to make their best effort. That's what it is all about. But if it hinges on a score at the end of the year—no.

Notably, some of the same respondents who claimed that they are autonomous in their teaching also said that tests affect what and how they teach. A first-grade teacher said that she is "more aware now of getting [her] children prepared for second grade, because I know that the big push is on for competency-based testing." Although she did not believe that she should be "teaching for tests," there was a belief in her district "that if the kids fail, then it's the teacher's fault." She said that she disciplines herself not to be driven by the tests—"I teach my curriculum, what I think is sound and what they need"—but she acknowledges that the prospect of tests influences her work: "In the back of my head, I know that's coming, and I want them to be able to go in and do it." Two elementary-school teachers reported that they had rearranged the sequence of units in their curriculum to ensure that students studied key topics before the tests were administered in the spring. Another teacher, who thought that tests could be used constructively to identify students deficient in basic skills, nevertheless criticized colleagues for overresponding to each year's results:

> The tests come back. They're low in some area. The third-grade teachers get blamed for that. What didn't you do? So they work on the math area, maybe. Then the next year the tests come out, and the math has gone up but the English is down.

Some teachers thought that their districts used tests appropriately to identify strengths and deficiencies in the program. A few who were dismayed by the lack of curricular order in their schools and districts advocated increased testing in order to pinpoint weaknesses in the curriculum. An urban elementary-school teacher said that he and his colleagues had "been unhappy, all of us, very unhappy, about the lack of testing in the city to begin with," and he called it "absurd" that students were "not tested on a regular basis so we can see where they're at when they come into a particular classroom, and where they're at when they leave. We can't follow kids' progress."

Teachers' responses to standardized testing often depended upon whether the results were used by outsiders or by teachers themselves to improve their practice. Many criticized the public's current preoccupation with test scores and the way in which some school officials inappropriately cite test scores as evidence of a faculty's success or failure. One suburban teacher said that her district publicizes high scores with pride—"Aren't we wonderful?"—although the scores can be best explained by the students' privileged backgrounds. By contrast, a teacher from a large urban district criticized administrators who were "very, very concerned" about test scores and encouraged competitive school-by-school comparisons, holding teachers solely responsible for the results. Richard Sand was angered by recent comparisons of schools' scores in local newspapers:

> We just had all the state testing at grades three, seven, and eleven. A year ago, when all this was introduced, it was: "This is to help you better understand what you're doing for the kids. It is not designed for comparisons." Yet in the last three weeks . . . all they did was compare. It is extremely depressing to pick up newspapers and read about schools being weighted by their CAT scores, their SAT scores, when at the same time, we're being told by so-called experts . . . that we have to do more hands-on work with the kids, get out of the schools more. It's the same people saying

these things. "Scores have to go up. Get them out in the world." Yet, if I don't have them here and can't sit down and work with them, I can't help them with their skill problems.

A number of those interviewed recognized the need for some indicators of progress but objected to test scores' being used as the only one that counted. A junior-high-school teacher who said, "Frankly, I resent them" also acknowledged that school officials needed some way to demonstrate progress: "They need somehow to put a candle to it . . . to measure it and quantify it and qualify it. That's very difficult in education."

The context for these teachers' responses must be remembered: at the time of the interviews, state officials had only recently instituted minimum-competency tests permitting district-by-district and school-by-school comparisons, and the scores had, as yet, little influence on important decisions about funding, staffing, or promotion. These were, therefore, low-stakes tests. By contrast, teachers in other states encounter tests that are used to make important decisions. Research by H. Dickson Corbett and Bruce Wilson in Maryland and Pennsylvania indicates that such high-stakes tests move districts to become "more focused on testing than learning."[19] Administrators in these states that were devising strategies to improve test scores expressed concern that they were "compromising a standard of good professional practice."[20] Teachers were spending time preparing students for test taking even while doubting the long-term value of their efforts. The tests tended to become ends in themselves rather than means to better teaching. Richard Sand said of teachers in other states, "They ignore the individual and teach to the tests. That's what is happening. We're very fortunate. We haven't been pushed that way."

The teachers in this study said that tests provided them with general evidence about program success across grades and schools. Some diagnostic, criterion-referenced tests provided more detailed, individualized information about students' performance, which teachers could use in addressing particular students' learning problems, but most standardized tests told teachers little, if anything, more than they already knew. Confronted with a list of summarized scores, teachers were left to guess whether these were complete and valid measures of their efforts, to wonder how changes in their practice might affect test outcomes, and to question whether adjusting their teaching to achieve higher scores was the right and responsible thing to do.

Beyond Bureaucracy

Public schools have been far more bureaucratized than private schools. Indeed, one of the most striking features of independent schools is their very independence. They set their own policies and practices and are not obliged to coordinate their programs or procedures with those of other schools. They do not have to contend with "the people downtown," and they are not beholden to the state for money. Because they are embedded in no larger system prescribing or limiting what they must or can do, teachers in these schools were far less subject to the "large-batch" expectations of specialization, standardization, and oversight. Schools and classes were smaller, teachers were more often responsible for the whole child, curriculum was more flexible, and oversight was modest and indirect. As a result, teachers found that they could adapt their work to the needs of individual students and infuse their teaching with their own academic and personal strengths.

Church-related schools varied in degree of bureaucracy. Some Catholic diocesan school systems rivaled public school-district bureaucracies in formality and complexity. Individual schools and teachers were required to respond first to the larger organization's demands for conformity, efficiency, and accountability; students' needs came second. Other Catholic schools, however, were virtually autonomous and decidedly nonbureaucratic in character, featuring smaller classrooms, unregimented practices, and a focus on individuals rather than large groups.

Teachers in all schools clearly believed that highly bureaucratic schools, whether in the public or private sector, made poor use of them as professionals. Their special interests and expertise were neutralized; they were expected to comply rather than invent. They doubted their students' needs as learners were well met. Why do schools carry on with these attempts to mass-produce learning when they are seen to be futile by those most closely involved? First, only rarely do teachers, those who are most aware of the complexity of instruction, design schools. Formal authority in public education has traditionally rested with those (mostly male) administrators who manage the enterprise rather than with those (mostly female) teachers who provide the service. From the early part of this century, administrators following the industrial model of organization have advocated efficient and productive schools with the greatest possible yield for each educational dollar. Schools are, moreover, embedded in state and local political systems that demand accountability for both what is taught and what (presumably) is learned. School funding formulas, which depend on student enrollments, lead to large classes and large schools. Graduation and certification requirements drive the organization of instruction both directly and indirectly toward standardization. Although large, centralized districts occasionally experiment with alternative schools, those who staff such schools are seldom free to organize teaching and learning solely on behalf of the teachers and learners, for they must coordinate their school practices with others in the district. The cost of alternative, adaptive organizations is another factor. Many administrators who would like to encourage more flexible, client-oriented practices find that they cannot pay the price of smaller classes and instructional loads, teacher aides, schools within schools, or variable schedules. Tight budgets force schools to moderate their expectations and to discount individual differences.[21] Those who seek smaller, less mechanized schools often must look outside the public sector. Finally, nonbureaucratic schools—those lacking schedules, bells, formal curricula, credits, levels, large classes, and teacher-centered instruction—do not look like "real" schools. John Meyer and Brian Rowan have insightfully described the ways in which the rationalized attributes of schools convey legitimacy on an enterprise that is otherwise filled with uncertainty, even failure.[22] Schools may have muddled goals and serve students poorly, but they remain tenable institutions if they *look* like schools, and so those both inside and outside the schools rely on predictable structures, such as bell schedules, tracks, and course credits, to define education, despite much evidence that those structures interfere with the work to be done.

State officials persist in efforts to reform schools by prescribing curriculum and pedagogy; by requiring close observation and rating of teachers; and by imposing high-stakes tests that promote comparisons among classrooms, grades, schools, and districts. These policies are likely to increase the impersonal character of schooling, improve students' capacity to take tests rather than think critically, and continue to drive outstanding teachers out of teaching.

Other reforms offer more promise. Public and private high schools participating in Theodore Sizer's Coalition of Essential Schools are reducing the scope of their curricula to a "limited number of essential skills and areas of knowledge," decreasing teachers' workload to 80 students in order to personalize teaching and learning, and reorganizing the schools so that teachers are generalists first and disciplinary specialists second.[23] Other school districts are attempting to subdivide large urban high schools and create several smaller schools within the same building, where students and teachers can have more continuing contact. Although small school size may limit the breadth of the academic program, advocates contend that students benefit more from the close attention and interdisciplinary teaching that these schools permit. There are also increasing efforts to decentralize school governance throughout the United States. Dade County, Rochester, Chicago, and Boston have transferred substantial powers for setting policy to school-site councils composed of teachers, parents, and administrators, giving public schools the kind of autonomy that typifies independent schools. District offices are being reduced in size, and administrators are being directed to assist rather than control those working at the school site.[24]

These reforms promise to reduce the bureaucratic control of districts and return to the school site the design and control of teaching practice. However, many of the changes needed to personalize schooling also will require new understandings and attitudes on the part of school officials and the public. Important differences exist among both children and teachers, differences that must be valued rather than eradicated. Teaching and learning are complex processes that require large areas of discretionary action. The outcomes are inherently varied; standardization cannot be achieved except at the most superficial level. Variation is not evidence of irresponsibility, nor is standardization a virtue in itself. Much that must be changed in public education must begin with a change of mind.

Nor will the bureaucratic elements of schools be eliminated without money. Large classes and teaching loads, standardized curricula, and tight schedules persist, in part, because they are economical. If teachers are to establish more continuous and intimate relations with students, if they are to participate in both departments and interdisciplinary teams, if they are to replace multiple-choice tests with more meaningful assessments of student achievement, more personnel and more time must be found, and both cost money, which must either be newly allocated or reallocated within education. Those districts with the largest central bureaucracies have also the largest opportunity, for they can redistribute funds that currently support large administrative staffs and purchase more people and time in the schools.[25] In many districts, if less money were spent on efforts to formalize and standardize education and more were spent to permit and promote flexibility and adaptation, schools might, ironically, become more productive.

Notes

1. Raymond E. Callahan, *Education and the Cult of Efficiency* (Chicago: University of Chicago Press, 1962), 178.

2. In their research, Burns and Stalker found "mechanistic" organizational structures in industries that were stable and established, "organic" structures in industries that were more dynamic. Tom Burns and G. M. Stalker, *The Management of Innovation* (London: Tavistock, 1961). Subsequently, Lawrence and Lorsch found that organizational structures were more flexible in the plastics industry than in the packaged-foods or box-container industries; they concluded that these differences in structure reflected differences in environmental uncertainty. Paul R. Lawrence and Jay W. Lorsch, *Organization and Environment: Managing Differentiation and Integration* (Boston: Graduate School of Business Administration, Harvard University, 1967).

3. Joan Lipsitz, *Successful Schools for Young Adolescents* (New Brunswick, N.J.: Transaction Books, 1984).

4. Holly M. Houston, "Restructuring Secondary Schools," in *Building a Professional Culture in Schools,* ed. Ann Lieberman (New York: Teachers College Press, 1988), 109–28.

5. U.S. Department of Education, *Class Size and Public Policy: Politics and Panaceas* (Washington, D.C.: U.S. Government Printing Office, 1986).

6. Nationally, the median class size at the elementary level is 24. Class size in Massachusetts is well below that of other states, such as California. Ibid., 28.

7. Nationally, the median class size at the secondary level is 22. Ibid., 14.

8. For comparisons of class size in the public and private schools of New Jersey, see Pearl R. Kane, *The Teachers College New Jersey Survey: A Comparative Study of Public*

and Independent School Teachers (New York: Teachers College, Columbia University, 1986).

9. See also Arthur G. Powell, "The Conditions of Teachers' Work in Independent Schools: Some Preliminary Observations," in *The Secondary School Workplace,* ed. Milbrey Wallin McLaughlin and Joan Talbert (New York: Teachers College Press, 1990).

10. In her survey of teachers' workloads in public and private schools in New Jersey, Pearl Kane found that the average load for public-school teachers in academic disciplines was 103. The average load in independent day schools was 69, whereas in boarding schools it was 50. Kane, *The Teachers College New Jersey Survey.*

11. Theodore R. Sizer, *Horace's Compromise: The Dilemma of the American High School* (Boston: Houghton Mifflin, 1984), 197.

12. Helen Featherstone, "Organizing Classes by Ability," *Harvard Education Letter* 3, no. 4 (July 1987):1–2. Also see Jeannie Oakes, *Keeping Track: How Schools Structure Inequality* (New Haven: Yale University Press, 1985).

13. See Arthur G. Powell, Eleanor Farrar, and David K. Cohen, *The Shopping Mall High School: Winners and Losers in the Educational Marketplace* (Boston: Houghton Mifflin, 1985).

14. Barbara Neufeld, "Evaluating the Effective Teaching Research," *Harvard Education Letter* 1, no. 5 (November 1985):5.

15. Lynn Olson, "Teaching's 'Knowledge Base' Seen Still Elusive," *Education Week* 7, no. 23 (2 March 1988):7.

16. For a description of such prescriptive curricula, see Linda McNeil, "Exit, Voice, and Community: Magnet Teachers' Responses to Standardization," *Educational Policy* 1, no. 1 (Winter 1987):93–113.

17. Grant Wiggins makes this useful distinction in "10 'Radical' Suggestions for School Reform," *Education Week* 7, no. 24 (9 March 1988):28.

18. Charles Kerchner and Douglas Mitchell have argued that work which we call "labor" can be rationalized and monitored directly, whereas "professional" work is adaptive and can be assessed only indirectly. Douglas E. Mitchell and Charles T. Kerchner, "Labor Relations and Teacher Policy," in *Handbook of Teaching and Policy,* ed. Lee S. Shulman and Gary Sykes (New York: Longman, 1983), 214–38.

19. H. Dickson Corbett and Bruce L. Wilson, "Raising the Stakes on Statewide Mandatory Testing Programs," in *The Politics of Reforming School Administration,* ed. Jane Hannaway and Robert Crowson (New York: The Falmer Press, 1989), 30.

20. Ibid., 33.

21. Theodore Sizer's Coalition of Essential Schools is working to provide alternative structures with no more than modest increases in costs, "an ultimate per pupil cost not to exceed those at traditional schools by more than 10 percent." Houston, "Restructuring Secondary Schools," 127.

22. John W. Meyer and Brian Rowan, "The Structure of Educational Organizations," in *Environments and Organizations: Theoretical and Empirical Perspectives,* ed. M. Meyer and Associates (San Francisco: Jossey-Bass, 1978); the concept of the "real" American high school is developed by Mary Haywood Metz, *"The American High School": A Universal Drama Amid Disparate Experience* (Madison, Wisc.: National Center on Effective Secondary Schools, 1988).

23. Houston, "Restructuring Secondary Schools," 126–27.

24. Lynn Olson, "In San Diego, Managers Forging 'Service' Role," *Education Week* 8, no. 24 (8 March 1989):1.

25. Under a new school reform act, Chicago schools are projected to save $40 million by reducing the size of the central office, savings that will be passed on to the schools. Designs for Change, *The Chicago School Reform Act: Highlights of Senate Bill 1840* (Chicago: Designs for Change, 1989).

17

Women and Power
in Organizations

Rosabeth Moss Kanter

What does make a difference is *power*—power outward and upward in the system: the ability to get for the group, for subordinates or followers, a favorable share of the resources, opportunities, and rewards possible through the organization. This has less to do with how leaders relate to followers than with how they relate to other parts of the organization. It has less to do with the quality of the manager-subordinate relationship than with the structure of power in the wider system. Early theory in organizational behavior assumed a direct relation between leader behavior and group satisfaction and morale, as if each organizational subgroup existed in a vacuum. However, Donald Pelz, in a study at Detroit Edison in the early 1950s, discovered that perceived influence *outside* the work group and upward in the organization was a significant intervening variable. He compared high- and low- morale work groups to test the hypothesis that the supervisor in high-morale groups would be better at communicating, more supportive, and more likely to recommend promotion. Yet when he analyzed the data, the association seemed to be nonexistent or even reversed. In some cases, supervisors who frequently recommended people for promotion and offered sincere praise for a job well done had *lower* morale scores. The differentiating variable that Pelz finally hit upon was whether or not the leaders had power outside and upward: influence on their own superiors and influence over how decisions were made in the department as a whole. The combination of good human relations *and* power produced high morale. Human relations skills coupled with low power sometimes had negative effects on morale.[1] What good is praise or a promise if the leader can't deliver? As other research discovered, both women and men attach more importance to having a competent, rather than a nice, boss—someone who gets things done. A classic study of first-line supervisors showed that more secure (and hence effective) foremen were those who had closer relationships

Reprinted from *Men and Women of the Corporation*, by Rosabeth Moss Kanter (New York: Basic Books, 1977), 168–171, 181–205, by permission of the publisher.

upward in the hierarchy; they had the most frequent exchanges with superiors.[2]

Power begets power. People who are thought to have power already and to be well placed in hierarchies of prestige and status may also be more influential and more effective in getting the people around them to do things and feel satisfied about it. In a laboratory experiment, subordinates were more likely to cooperate with and to inhibit aggression and negativity toward leaders of higher rather than lower status. In a field study of professionals, people who came into a group with higher external status tended to be better liked, talked more often, and received more communications. The less powerful, who usually talked less, were often accused of talking *too much*. There was a real consensus in such groups about who was powerful, and people were more likely to accept direct attempts to influence them from people they defined as among the powerful. Average group members, whether men or women, tended to engage in deferential, approval-seeking behavior toward those seen as higher in power.[3] Thus, people who look like they can command more of the organization's resources, who look like they can bring something that is valued from outside into the group, who seem to have access to the inner circles that make the decisions affecting the fate of individuals in organizations, may also be more effective as leaders of those around them—and be better liked in the process.

Twenty Indsco executives in a sample of managers reached the same conclusion when asked to define the characteristics of effective managers. The question of the relative importance of "people sensitivity," as they put it, provoked considerable debate. Finally, they agreed that "credibility" was more important than anything else. "Credibility" was their term for competence plus power—the known ability to get results. People with credibility were listened to, their phone calls were answered first, because they were assumed to have something important to say. People with credibility had room to make more mistakes and could take greater risks because it was believed that they would produce. They were known to be going somewhere in the organization and to have the ability to place their people in good jobs. They could back up their words with actions. Thus, the ultimate in credibility in the corporate bureaucracy was "the guy who doesn't have to make recommendations; he comes out with a *decision* and all supporting material. Everyone else just says yes or no. . . ."

Credibility upward rather than downward—that is, wider-system power—rendered managers effective, they thought. To have it downward, with subordinates, they must first have it upward, with their own superiors and the people with whom their tasks were interwoven in the matrix. Credibility downward was based on subordinates' belief in their managers' importance, which in turn was based on their political position. People-sensitivity could be an added bonus, but it was considered much less important than power. "Some managers are very successful and very tough," an executive commented. "John Fredericks is as tough as they come but also sensitive to people. His people have gone far, but is that because he's sensitive or because he has clout? It's impossible to untangle." "You can get people to do nearly anything for you if they think you have their interest at heart and will fight for them. They must see that you can produce for them, that the fighting will pay off." And lack of system power could undermine the best of human relations: "Fred Burke came in as an outsider to manage his department, so he didn't know the business and he didn't have the right connections in the company. When he tried to get things from headquarters, he had no clout. Headquarters wanted to talk to the people *under* him because they knew the answers. But sensitive, yes! Christ, I don't know anyone more sensitive than Fred Burke. You've never seen a more sensitive guy; but his people turned against him anyway. They had no respect for him." "What we're saying, I guess," someone tried to summarize the discussion, "is that you need a combination of both—people-skills and credibility." "No," others disagreed. "It's the need to take action that distinguishes effective managers. Having some results at the end of all that people-sensitivity. What good is it if you can't get anything done in Indsco?"

The preference for association with the powerful and the degree to which this preference motivates members of organizations is a function of the degree of dependency built into the organization itself. Where people can do their work rather independently, where they can easily get the things they need to carry out their tasks, where they have a great deal of latitude in decision-making, and where rewards are not so contingent on career mobility, then there need not be the same concern with appropriate political alliances. However, the large, complex hierarchical corporation fosters dependency. . . . In the context of such organizationally fostered dependency, people seem willing to work very hard to reduce it. One way to do this is by allying themselves with the powerful, with people who can make them more independent by creating more certainty in their lives.

Power in an organization rests, in part, on the ability to solve dependency problems and to control relevant sources of uncertainty.[4] This can be true with respect to the system as a whole as well as around individuals. For the system, the most power goes to those people in those functions that provide greater control over what the organization finds currently problematic: sales and marketing people when markets are competitive; production experts when materials are scarce and demand is high; personnel or labor relations specialists when labor is scarce; lawyers, lobbyists, and external relations specialists when government regulations impinge; finance and accounting types when business is bad and money tight.[5] There is a turning to those elements of the system that seem to have the power to create more certainty in the face of dependency, to generate a more advantageous position for the organization. . . .

Alliances: Power through Others

The informal social network that pervades organizations can be very important, as many theorists have pointed out. In a large, complex system, it is almost a necessity for power to come from social connections, especially those outside of the immediate work group. Such connections need to be long-term and stable and include "sponsors" (mentors and advocates upward in the organization), peers, and subordinates.

Sponsors

Sponsors have been found to be important in the careers of managers and professionals in many settings. In the corporation, "sponsored mobility" (controlled selection by elites) seems to determine who gets the most desirable jobs, rather than "contest mobility" (an open game), to use Ralph Turner's concepts.[6] At Indsco, high-level sponsors were known as "rabbis" or "godfathers," two colorful labels for these unofficial bestowers of power.

Sponsors are often thought of as teachers or coaches whose functions are primarily to make introductions or to train a young person to move effectively through the system. However, there are three other important functions besides advice that generate power for the people sponsored. First, sponsors are often in a position to *fight* for the person in question, to stand up for him or her in meetings if controversy is raised, to promote that person for promising opportunities. When there are large numbers of personnel distributed across wide territories, as in Industrial Supply Corporation, there was much advantage to being the favorite of a powerful person who could help distinguish a person from the crowd and argue his or her virtues against those of other people. ("They say the rabbi system is dead," commented a young manager, "but I can't believe we make promotion decisions without it.") Despite a rating system that tried to make the system more open and equitable at lower levels, sponsors could still make a difference. Indeed, one of the problems with not having a powerful manager, Indsco workers thought, was that the manager would not be strong enough to stand up and fight for subordinates in places where they could not fight for themselves.

Second, sponsors often provided the occasion for lower-level organization members to *bypass the hierarchy*: to get inside information, to short-circuit cumbersome procedures, or to cut red tape. People develop a social relationship with a powerful person which allows them to go directly to that person, even though there is no formal interface, and once there, a social interchange can often produce formal results. This could be very important to formal job success in Indsco, to the ability to get things done, in a system where people could easily get bogged down if they had to honor official protocol. One saleman with a problem he wanted to solve for a customer described Indsco as "like the Army, Air Force, and Navy—we have a formal chain of command." The person who could make the decision on his problem was four steps removed from him, not in hierarchical rank but according to operating procedure. Ordinarily, he would not be able to go directly to him, but they had developed a relationship over a series of sales meetings, during which the more powerful person had said, "Please drop by anytime you're at headquarters." So the salesman found an occasion to "drop by," and in the course of the casual conversation mentioned his situation. It was solved immediately. A woman manager used her powerful sponsors in a similar way. Whenever her boss was away, she had lunch with her friends among the corporate officers. This provided an important source of information, such as "secret" salary information from a vice-president. In fact, the manager revealed, "much of what I get done across groups is based on informal personal relations through the years, when there is no formal way to do it."

Third, sponsors also provide an important signal to other people, a form of *reflected power*. Sponsorship indicates to others that the person in question has the backing of an influential person, that the sponsor's resources are somewhere behind the individual. Much of the power of relatively junior people comes not from their own resources but from the "credit" extended to them because there appears to be a more powerful set of resources in the distance. This was an important source of the power of "comers" at Indsco, the "water walkers" and "high fliers" who were on fast tracks because they were high performers with powerful backing. A manager in that position described it this way: "A variety of people become impressed with you. You see the support at several levels; someone seems comfortable with you although he's a vice-president, and he looks you in the eye. You get offered special jobs by powerful people. You're pulled aside and don't have to go through channels. If you can sustain that impression for three to four years, your sphere of influence will increase to the point where you have a clear path for a few miles. You can have anything you want up to a certain level, where the power of the kingpins changes. Here's how it happens. A manager who is given a water walker, knowing that the person is seen as such from above and from below, is put in a no-win situation. If the person does well, everyone knew it anyway. If the person doesn't do well, it is considered the manager's fault. So the manager can only try to get the star promoted, move him or her out as fast as possible; and the manager wants to help accelerate the growth of walkers because someday the manager might be working for them. All of this promotes the star's image." Another rising executive commented, "Everyone attempts to get on the heels of a flier. Everyone who does well has a sponsor, someone to take you on their heels. In my case, I had three managers. All of them have moved but continue to help me. A vice-president likes me. I can count on getting any job up a level as long as he remains in favor."

Those seen as moving accumulated real power because of their connections with sponsors, but they also had to be careful about the way they used the reflected power of the sponsor: "It's an embryonic, gossamer-type thing because four levels up is *far* away, and the connection is very tenuous. It's only a promise of things to come. You can't use it with your own manager, or you get in trouble. The rabbis are not making commitments right now. One guy tried to use his connections with his manager, to cash in his chips too early. The axe fell. He had to go back to zero." Handling relationships with sponsors could be tricky, too. "It's scary because you have to live up to others' expectations. There is great danger if you go up against a godfather. It becomes a father/son issue as well as business. God help you if you are not grateful for the favors given." And, of course, fast trackers can also fall when their sponsors fall if they have not developed their own power base in the interim.

If sponsors are important for the success of men in organizations, they seem absolutely essential for women. If men function more effectively as leaders when they appear to have influence upward and outward in the organization, women need even more the signs of such influence and the access to real power provided by sponsors. Margaret Cussler's and Margaret Hennig's studies of those few women in top management positions in U.S. corporations showed dramatically the importance of sponsorship. A British study concluded that "office uncles" were important in the careers of women in organizations because they offered behavioral advice and fought for the women to be promoted.[7] Ella Grasso, the first woman elected to a state governorship on her own, had a sponsor in John Bailey, who was chairman of the Democratic National Committee from 1961 to 1968. He first spotted her as a political "comer" in the 1950s. Since then he [had] provided advice, campaign help, and introductions to certain circles.[8] At Indsco the same pattern emerged. One woman was brought into her management position at Indsco by a sponsor, a vice-president for whom she had worked as an executive secretary. Her relation to him and the connections she had already made through him made her reception into management quite different from that of other former secretaries. Another secretary who was promoted without sponsorship felt ignored, isolated, and resented after her move, but the first woman's experience was different. Male peers immediately made her one of the gang. During her first week in the new position, she remembered, she was deluged with phone calls from men letting her know they were there if she had any questions, making sure she had a lunch date, and inviting her to meetings.

If sponsors are important for women, they can also be harder to come by. Sponsorship is sometimes generated by good performance, but it can also come, as one of Indsco's fast trackers put it, "because you have the right social background or know some of the officers from outside the corporation or look good in a suit." Some people thought that higher-ups decided to sponsor particular individuals because of identification and that this process almost automatically eliminated women. (There is, indeed, much research evidence that leaders choose to promote the careers of socially similar subordinates.)[9] Men could not identify with women, and very few women currently held top positions. Identification was the issue in these remarks: "Boy wonders rise under certain power structures. They're recognized by a powerful person because they are very much like him. He sees himself, a younger version, in that person. . . . Who can look at a woman and see themselves?" This was a good question. When women acquired sponsors, the reasons were often different from the male sponsor-protégé situation. In one case, officers were looking for a high-performing woman they could make into a showpiece to demonstrate the organization's openness to good women. In another instance, an executive was thought to have "hung his hat on a woman" (decided to sponsor her) to demonstrate that he could handle a "tricky" management situation and solve a problem for the corporation.

Peers

More often neglected in the study of the accumulation of organizational power is the importance of strong peer alliances, although Barry Stein has written about the ways groups can capitalize on the success of a "comer."[10] At Indsco high "peer acceptance," as managers put it, was necessary to any power base or career success. "Individual performers" found their immediate accomplishments rewarded, but their careers stuck . . . because they had not built, nor were seen as capable of building, the kinds of connections necessary for success in ever more interdependent higher-level jobs. "The group needs each other," a sales manager remarked. "To become powerful, people must first be successful and receive recognition, but they must wear the respect with a lack of arrogance. They must not be me-oriented. Instead of protecting their secrets in order to stand taller than the crowd, they are willing to share successes. They help their peers. . . . This is 'leader quality.' "

Strong alliances among peers could advance the group as a whole, as Stein noted in commenting on the fact that certain cohorts sometimes seem to produce all of the leaders in an organization.[11] However, a highly competitive situation could also imbue peer relations with politics and pitfalls. A star performer just promoted to his first management position told me quite proudly how he had just handled his first political battle with a counterpart in his position. One reason he was telling me at such length, he explained, was because he had no one he could tell within the organization. He had decided to take care of the issue by going directly to the other man and working it out with him, then promising him it would go no further. My informant had been the one who was wronged, and he could have gone to his boss or the other person's boss, but he decided that in the long run he was wiser to try to honor peer solidarity and try to build an ally out of the person who had hurt him. "I didn't want to create enemies," he commented. "Some peers look to you for help, to work with you for mutual gain, but others wait for you to stumble so they can bad-mouth you: 'Yeah, he's a sharp guy, but he drinks a lot.' If I had gone against the other guy now, even if I had won, he would have had a knife out for me sometime. Better to do him a favor by keeping quiet, and then he'll be grateful later."

Peer alliances often worked through direct exchange of favors. On lower levels information was traded; on higher levels bargaining and trade often took place around good performers and job openings. In a senior executive's view, it worked like this: "A good job becomes available. A list of candidates is generated. That's refined down to three or four. That is circulated to a select group that has an opportunity to look it over. Then they can make bargains among themselves." A manager commented, "There's lots of 'I owe you one.' If you can accumulate enough chits, that helps you get what you need; but then, of course, people have to be in a position to cash them in."

Subordinates

The accumulation of power through alliances was not always upward-oriented. For one thing, differential rates of hierarchical progress could mean that juniors or peers one day could become a person's boss the next. So it could be to a person's advantage to make alliances downward in the hierarchy with people who looked like they might be on the way up. There was a preference for "powerful" subordinates as well as powerful bosses. Just in the way Bernard Levenson proposed, a manager on the move would try to develop subordinates who could take over, keeping a member of "his team" in place. Professionals and executives needed more junior people loyal to them as much as they needed the backing of higher-level people. Especially higher up, the successful implementation of plans and policies depended heavily upon the activities of those people lower down in the hierarchy who were responsible for the carrying out of day-to-day operations or the translation into specifics of general guidelines. So alliances with subordinates often developed early in careers, anticipating the time when managers would need the support of "their team." There was often a scrambling by managers to upgrade the jobs reporting to them so that they could attract more powerful subordinates. Also, as I have indicated, managers could benefit from speeding up the career of a person already on a fast track.

However, if power was something that not everyone could accumulate, what happened to the powerless?

Accountability without Power: Sources of Bureaucratic Powerlessness

People who have authority without system power are powerless. People held accountable for the results produced by others, whose formal role gives them the right to command but who lack informal political influence, access to resources, outside status, sponsorship, or mobility prospects, are rendered powerless in the organization. They lack control over their own fate and are dependent on others above them—others whom they cannot easily influence—while they are expected by virtue of position to be influential over those parallel or below. Their sense of lack of control above is heightened by its contrast with the demands of an accountable authority position: that they mobilize others in the interests of a task they may have had little part in shaping, to produce results they may have had little part in defining.

First-line supervisors in highly routinized functions often are functionally powerless. Their situation—caught between the demands of a management hierarchy they are unlikely to enter because of low opportunity and the resistance of workers who resent their own circumstances—led classic writers on organizations to describe them as "men in the middle."[12] (However, they are also often "women in the middle.") They have little chance to gain power through activities, since their functions do not lend themselves to the demonstration of the extraordinary, nor do they generate high visibility or solutions to organizational problems. They have few rewards to distribute, since rewards are automatically given by the organization; and their need for reliable performance from workers in order to keep their own job secure limits the exercise of other forms of power. "I'm afraid to confront the employees because they have the power to slack, to slouch, to take too much time," a supervisor of clerical workers said, "and I need them for results. I'm measured on *results*—quantitative output, certain attendance levels, number of reports filed. They have to do it for me." Another one said, "When I ask for help, I get punished because my manager will say, 'But it's your job. If you can't do it, you shouldn't be in that job.' So what's *their* job? Sending me notes telling me it's unacceptable? They're like teachers sending me a report card." First-line supervisors also felt powerless because their jobs were vulnerable during times of recession, while people farther up in the hierarchy seemed secure. They resented the fact that their peers were let go, while higher managers were not. "Why us? Aren't they running the show? Shouldn't they be the ones to suffer if business isn't going well?" And supervisors of secretaries . . . were also rendered powerless by the secretary's allegiance to a boss with more status and clout in the organization.

Occupants of certain staff jobs were similarly organizationally powerless.[13] They had no line authority and were dependent on managers to implement their decisions and carry out their recommendations. Staff programs that managers saw as irrelevant to their primary responsibilities would be ignored. Affirmative action and equal employment opportunity officers often found themselves in this position. Their demands were seen by line people as an intrusion, a distraction from more important business, and the extra paperwork that EEO entailed was annoying. Personnel staff who tried to introduce more rational, universalistic, and equitable systems for job placement for nonexempts also had difficulty selling their programs. . . . These staff activities were seen as destroying a managerial prerogative and interfering with something managers preferred to do for themselves. The aims of personnel people in sending out certain candidates for jobs could conflict with the desires of the manager who would be using the candidate, and when battles resulted, it was often the more prestigious line manager who prevailed.

Regardless of function, people could also be rendered powerless if their own management did not extend opportunities for power downward—if their situations did not permit them to take risks, if their authority was undercut, or if their sphere of autonomous decision-making was limited. There seemed to be a consensus at Indsco that superiors who solved problems themselves or tried to do the job themselves disempowered the managers or professionals under them. Considered ideal, by contrast, was the manager who "never gave anyone an answer; but when you walked out of his office, you had it because he asked you the questions that made you think of it." Many women thus objected to the "protectiveness" that they perceived in their managers, protection that "encased" them "in a plastic bubble," as one put it, and rendered them ineffectual. Anyone who is protected loses power, for successes are then attributed to the helpful actions of others, rather than the person's own actions. Women complained about the "people who want to move walls for me instead of saying, 'Hey, here's a wall. Let's strategize working through it.' " Another said, "You need a lot of exposure to get ahead, a broad base of experience. I don't want to be protected, given the easy management situations, the easy customers, the sure-fire position." And being in a position where decisions were reviewed and authority could be undercut also created powerlessness. A customer service representative faced a situation where she had to tell a customer that she couldn't ship to him because the materials were not available; this was an order that had come down to her. The customer said he would call the immediate manager. The manager backed up the representative, indicating that he would call headquarters but that the rep was right and had the information. So the customer went one step higher in the hierarchy, calling headquarters himself. This time he managed to get a change. Everyone lost credibility, but especially the woman. Nothing diminishes leaders' power more than subordinates' knowledge that they can always go over their heads, or that what they promise has no real clout. A management recruiter advised companies that wanted to ensure the success of new women managers not to inadvertently encourage resistance to the new manager: even seemingly innocuous requests, such as a higher manager asking to be kept informed, could encourage subordinates to bypass the woman and do their reporting higher up.[14]

Powerlessness, finally, was the general condition of those people who could not make the kinds of powerful alliances that helped to manage the bureaucracy. People without sponsors, without peer connections, or without promising subordinates remained in the situation of bureaucratic dependency on formal procedures, routine allocations of rewards, communication that flowed through a multi-layered chain of command, and decisions that must penetrate, as Robert Presthus put it, "innumerable veto barriers."[15] People who reached dead ends in their careers also rapidly lost power, since they could no longer promise gains to those who followed them and no longer had the security of future movement. Powerlessness was also the psychological state of people who, for whatever reason, felt insecure in their functioning as leaders and anticipated resistance rather than cooperation from those whom they were to lead. Indeed, the structural characteristics of modern organizational life tend to produce the symptoms of powerlessness in more and more lower-to-middle managers, supervisors, bureaucrats, and professionals. The chance to engage in the non-routine, to show discretion, to take risks, or to become known, are all less available in the large bureaucracy.

Behavioral Responses to Powerlessness

Controlling Behavior and Close Supervision

Psychoanalyst Karen Horney, in *The Neurotic Personality of Our Time*, described people's neurotic attempt to dominate when they feel anxious or helpless, inferior or insignificant. As a protection and a defense, the psychologically powerless turn to control over others. They want to be right all the time and are irritated at being proven wrong. They cannot tolerate disagreement.[16] In short, they become critical, bossy, and controlling. Some degree of power, in the sense of mastery and control over one's fate, is necessary for feelings of self-esteem and well-being, as Rollo May has indicated.[17] When a person's exercise of power is thwarted or blocked, when people are rendered powerless in the larger arena, they may tend to concentrate their power needs on those over whom they have even a modicum of authority. There is a displacement of control downward paralleling displacement of aggression. In other words, people respond to the restrictivness of their own situation by behaving restrictively toward others. People will "boss" those they can, as in the image of the nagging housewife or old-maid schoolteacher or authoritarian boss, if they cannot flex their power muscles more constructively and if, moreover, they are afraid they really are powerless.

One example of this syndrome comes from research on the leadership style of low-power male Air Force officers. Officers of lower status and advancement potential favored more directive, rigid, and authoritarian techniques of leadership, seeking control over subordinates. Subordinates were their primary frame of reference for their own status assessment and enhancement, and so they found it important to "lord it over" group members. They also did not help talented members of the group get ahead (perhaps finding them too threatening) and selected immediate assistants of mediocre rather than outstanding talent.[18] Similarly, in a French bureaucracy technical engineers in an isolated position with low mobility and low power with respect to directors were, in turn, extremely authoritarian and paternalistic with *their* subordinates.[19]

When people expect to be successful in their influence attempts, in contrast, they can afford to use milder forms of power, such as personal persuasion. Even a little bit of influence is likely to work, and it is so much more pleasant to avoid conflict and struggle. But when people anticipate resistance, they tend to use the strongest kind of weapon they can muster. As Frantz Fanon proposed in *The Wretched of the Earth*, the powerless may come to rely on force, first and foremost.[20] In a series of laboratory studies simulating supervision of three production workers, male subjects who lacked confidence in their own abilities to control the world or who thought they encountered resistance from the mock subordinates used more coercive than persuasive power, especially when resistance stemmed from "poor attitude" (a direct threat to their power) rather than ineptness.[21] We know from other laboratory studies that people are more automatically obedient toward the organizationally powerful than the powerless, regardless of formal position. Subordinates inhibit aggression in the face of power, but they direct more intense aggression to the relatively powerless. Indeed, it can be argued, as a number of other theorists have also done, that a controlling leadership style is a *result* rather than a *cause* of hostile, resistant, or noncompliant behavior on the part of subordinates.[22]

Thus, the relatively powerless in positions of organizational authority also have reason to be more controlling and coercive. If they have less call on the organization's resources, less backup and support from sponsors and managers, less cooperative subordinates, and less influence in the informal power structure, people can only use the strongest tools at their disposal: discipline or threats or maintaining tight control over all of the activities in their jurisdiction. If managers or supervisors who encounter resistance from those they are trying to direct tend to become more coercive in their power tactics, it is a vicious cycle: powerless authority figures who use coercive tactics provoke resistance and aggression, which prompts them to become even more coercive, controlling, and behaviorally restrictive.

At Indsco relatively powerless managers who were insecure about their organizational status tended to give the least freedom to subordinates and to personally control their department's activities much more tightly. (I used formal job characteristics, other people's perceptions, and my own observations to decide who was relatively powerless). These managers made all of the decisions, did an amount of operating work themselves that others in the organization would consider "excessive," and did not let subordinates represent them at meetings or on task forces. They tried to control the communication flow in and out of their department, so that all messages had to pass through them. One manager in a low-power situation, who was considered "tough to work for—too tight," jumped on a subordinate for calling a vice-president directly to ask a question, saying, "*I'm* the one who represents this function to v.p.'s." Another manager with good people working for him wanted to see that all the credit went to him. He wrote a report of his unit's activities that made it seem as though he, and not the salespeople involved, had generated an increase in sales: "By negotiating with the profit center, I saw to it that . . . ."

Sometimes low-power managers and supervisors took over the task and tried to do or direct closely the work of subordinates instead of giving them a free hand, because technical mastery of job content was one of the few arenas in which they *did* feel powerful. Often people get to first-line managerial jobs, for example, because they are good at the operating tasks. Trying to do the job themselves or watching over subordinates' shoulders to correct the slightest deviation from how the supervisors themselves would do it represents a comfortable retreat into expertise from the frustrations of trying to administer when organizational power is low. People can still feel good knowing that they could do the job well—or better than their subordinates. Thus, they are tempted to control their subordinates, keep them from learning or developing their own styles, jump in too quickly to solve problems, and "nitpick" over small things subordinates do differently. All of these things were considered characteristics of ineffective managers at Indsco. However, the temptation to take over the work of the next level down instead of engaging in more general leadership—a temptation that always existed, even for people at the very top, as one of them told me—was succumbed to especially by the powerless.

Conditions of work could intersect with low organizational power to reinforce a tendency toward closeness of supervision. Departments of women clerical workers run by powerless women managers were a case in point. The supervisors were, in turn, managed by men, who gave them detailed orders and little discretion, and the supervisors tended to be in a terminal job and poorly connected to informal power alliances. At the same time, the office setup encouraged a restrictive, controlled atmosphere. The clerical workers were confined to banks of desks in large offices virtually under the nose of the supervisor. These departments were considered among the most tightly run in the corporation. They had the least absenteeism and a decided "schoolroom" atmosphere. In contrast, the conditions of work in sales made it more difficult for even the most control-prone manager to supervise as tightly, since sales people under one manager were often scattered throughout several field offices, and sales workers were legitimately out of the office a great deal of the time. Field sales managers, similarly, operated away from the direct view of their own managers. So the greater freedom of the sales function was empowering all down the line. However, the setting for clerical workers and their bosses made it easier for them to remain powerless.

Rules-Mindedness

The powerless inside an authority structure often become rules-minded in response to the limited options for power in their situation, turning to "the rules" as a power tool. Rules are made in the first place to try to control the uncontrollable; invoking organization rules and insisting on careful adherence to them is a characteristic response of the powerless in authority positions. For one thing, "the rules" represent their only safe and sure legitimate authority, the place where higher-ups are guaranteed to give them backing, because higher-ups wrote or represent the rules. They have few other means to use in bargaining with subordinates for cooperation. As Crozier wrote, "If no difference can be introduced in the treatment given to subordinates, either in the present definition of the job or in the fulfillment of their career expectations, hierarchical superiors cannot keep power over them. Superiors' roles will be limited to controlling the application of rules."[23]

Second, powerlessness coupled with accountability, with responsibility for results dependent on the actions of others, provokes a cautious, low-risk, play-it-safe attitude. Getting everything right is the response of those who lack other ways to impress those above them or to secure their position; and in turn they demand this kind of ritualistic conformity from subordinates, like schoolteachers more concerned about neatness of a paper than its ideas. Secretarial supervisors at Indsco tended to be known for these traits: a concern with proper form rather than a good outcome. Or, as someone else said, "You don't give freedom or experiment with procedure when you're a first-liner. You try to cover your ass and not make a mistake they can catch you on."

Overconformity to the rules and ritual concern with formalities are characteristics of the "bureaucratic personality" identified in Robert Merton's classic essay. Bureaucratic organizations, by their very structures, exert constant pressures on employees to perform reliably within prescribed and predictable behavioral limits. At the same time, routinization of careers within a bureaucracy—the provision of planned, graded, incremental promotions and salary increases—offers incentives for disciplined action and conformity to official regulations. These features taken together, Merton concluded, produced the bureaucrat's substitution of means (the rules, the forms, the procedures) for ends (goals, purposes, underlying rationales).[24]

Melville Dalton also recognized that the powerless hang on to rules, contrasting the "strong" and the "weak" as models of managerial tendencies.

> The weak are fearful in conflict situations and absorb aggressions to avoid trouble. . . .They hesitate to act without consulting superiors and take refuge in clearly formulated rules, whether adequate or not for their footing at the moment. Following their fairy-tale image of the organization as a fixed thing, they suffer from their experience that it is not. This, of course, aggravates their difficulty in grasping the tacit expectations that associations do not want to spell out, when events are troublesome. . . . As they seek to escape dilemmas, their unfitness to act outside the haven of understood rules invites aggression from the strong who are searching for shortcuts in the network of official routes.[25]

Thus, it is those lower in power who become rules-minded, but it is a bit too simple to attribute the concern with rules only to a reactive stance—a general bureaucratic world view. For those with relatively little organizational power but who must lead or influence others, *their control of "the rules" can represent one of their few areas of personal discretion.* They can exchange a bending of the rules for compliance; they can reward their favorites with a lighter application of the rules. However, first the rules must be experienced and honored. Subordinates or clients or workers must know what the formalities are like before they can be grateful for a bit of special treatment. They must see that the manager or supervisor or official has the right to invoke the full measure of the rule. So the persons who concern themselves with the rules both have something that *must* command obedience and have the basis for a form of power through differential application of those same rules. Staff officials without the power or credibility to persuade people in other departments to carry out the *spirit* of new programs (like affirmative action or centralized secretarial hiring) could fall back on their *letter*, burying uncooperative departments in mounds of paperwork.

One Indsco manager who was particularly concerned about protocol, formalities, and proper procedure had come up the ranks the hard way and was still not in a very influential position. He was upset that perquisites and privileges that had taken him long to earn were now automatically given out to younger people. He felt that they took liberties and behaved much too casually. One time, a young person introduced himself to the manager at a company function and then called to make a lunch date. The manager turned him down and then phoned his boss to complain that the young person was trying to get into the executive dining room. However, there were hints of the true feelings behind the manager's complaints. The manager was someone whose only source of power and respect came through the organizational formalities. He counted on being able to control his subordinates by carefully doling out privileges or offering small deviations from the formal rules. If the rules did not mean much anymore, what did he have left?

Territoriality and Domain Control

Merton went on to argue that bureaucrats adopt a domineering manner because whenever they use the authority of their office with clients or subordinates, they are acting as representatives of the power and prestige of the entire structure.[26] Vicarious power—power through identification—Merton seemed to say, breeds bossiness. However, if we look more closely at the organizational structures he described, we can see that this aspect of the "bureaucratic personality" reflects a response to *powerlessness* rather than to power, delegated or otherwise. The organization's concern with regulations reduces administrators' spheres of autonomy, limits their influence and decision-making power. The very provision of graded careers stressing seniority, in which incremental advances are relatively small and all must wait their turn, fosters dependency on the organization, which always holds back some rewards until the next advance. It removes incentives for assertion and reduces people to a common denominator—one in which they did not participate in defining. Unless people can accumulate power through activities or alliances, they face a sense of helplessness and insignificance.

In response to organizational insignificance, officials turn to their own small territory, their own little piece of the system—their subordinates, their function, their expertise. They guard their domain jealously. They narrow their interests to focus exclusively on it. They try to insulate and protect it and to prevent anyone else from engaging in similar activities without their approval or participation as "the experts." Another organizational cycle is set in motion. As each manager protects his or her own domain, the sense of helplessness and powerlessness of other administrators in intersecting units increases. They, in turn, may respond by redoubling their domination over their territory and their workers. The result can be "sub-optimization": each subgroup optimizing only its own goals and forgetting about wider system interests. For example, a worker in Crozier's clerical agency described this territoriality of supervisors. Supervisors were squeezed by higher management, which blamed them for poor morale and delivered speeches and written instructions advising them to pay more attention to leadership. In the worker's view, "They worry too much about their career and the possibility of promotion. They are jealous and awfully competitive. They are also sectarian. Often there is a lot of hostility between sections. . . . Each one of them wants to have his little kingdom.''[27]

At Indsco, territoriality seemed more often a response of relatively powerless staff than of line officials. Line officials could turn to close supervision or rules application, but staff had only whatever advantage they could gain through specialized knowledge and jurisdiction over an area of expertise. This was especially clear around personnel functions. The organization was so large that personnel training, management development, and organization development responsibilities were divided up among many different units, some attached to divisions, some attached to the corporation, and some attached to specific functions. Such units often prevented each other from acting by claiming territorial encroachments. The result was that nearly all of them remained narrowly specialized and highly conservative. It was enough to kill a proposal with which other units would have to cooperate if the idea originated in one that was looking temporarily more powerful. There was a parallel problem on the wider system level, where one division was much larger and more powerful than others. Organizational and personnel innovations developed by the major division were rarely adopted by any of the others, even if they proved highly effective, because the other units were trying to protect their own territory as an independent domain.

There were also reflections of territoriality among low-power staff people on the individual level. The tendency was to hang on to a territory that provided legitimacy, even when inappropriate. One staff woman, hired to run affirmative action programs, tended to bring up the women's issue wherever she was, as though she would have no right to participate unless she dragged in her "expertise." Yet, on one occasion she had been invited to join a group of managers because of what she might contribute to general discussions of organizational issues. But she could not let go of her domain, and the managers were sorry they had included her. Similarly, sometimes staff people clung to whatever might help solve their future power issues, regardless of its relevance to present tasks. One manager asked a personnel staff official to send him an older, experienced woman for a position as his administrative assistant. Instead, the man in the personnel department insisted on sending him three ambitious, rather inexperienced younger women, making it clear that personnel matters, such as the decision about which candidates were appropriate, were his domain. However, perhaps there was something else underneath. The three women were ambitious and on the move. If he placed them fast, they owed him a favor, and because they were going to seek to move, they would have to keep coming back to him. Therefore, they were "his" candidates and represented possible future alliances.

Territorial control and domain concerns were also behind much of the treatment of secretaries at Indsco . . . ; but now it also becomes clear that relatively powerless bosses are likelier to be the ones who try to keep strong personal control over secretaries. Those secretaries who were encouraged by their bosses to seek promotions out of the secretarial ranks tended to work for the more powerful bosses.

The behavioral responses of powerless "leaders" to their situations, then, in controlling behavior, rules-mindedness, and territoriality, could make the conditions of work less satisfying for subordinates. To seek a more powerful leader could also be a way of seeking a more empowering, freedom-enhancing environment.

Cycles of Power and Powerlessness

Power rises and falls on the basis of complex exigencies: the organizational situation, environmental pressures, the simultaneous actions of others. However, in terms of individual behavior at least, power is likely to bring more power in ascending cycles, and powerlessness to generate powerlessness, in a descending cycle. The powerful have "credibility" behind their actions, so they have the capacity to get things done. Their alliances help them circumvent the more restricting aspects of the bureaucracy. They are able to be less coercive or rules-bound in their exercise of leadership, so their subordinates and clients are more likely to cooperate. They have the security of power, so they can be more generous in allowing subordinates power of their own, freedom of action. We come full circle. The powerful are not only given material and symbolic advantage but they are also provided with circumstances that can make them more effective mobilizers of other people. Thus they can accomplish and, through their accomplishments, generate more power. This means they can build alliances with other people as colleagues rather than threats, and through their alliances generate more power.

The powerless are caught in a downward spiral. The coping mechanisms of low power are also those most likely to provoke resistance and further restriction of power. The attitudes of powerlessness get translated downward, so that those under a low-power leader can also become ineffective. There was this vicious circle at Indsco: A young trainee was assigned to a "chronic complainer" of a manager, who had had organizational problems and had fallen well below the level of peers in his cohort. The trainee was talented but needed to be channeled. The manager's negativism began to transfer down to the trainee, and the young man started to lose his motivation. Nothing was done to correct the atmosphere. He became less motivated and more critical of the organization. He vented his hostility in nonconformist ways (long hair, torn clothes, general disrespect for people and things). Then people began to reinforce his negativity by focusing on what they observed: he's a "wise guy." They observed the symptoms but never looked at the real problem: the manager's situation. Finally, the trainee resigned just before he would have been terminated. Everyone breathed a sign of relief that the "problem" was gone. The manager lost even more credibility. This just reinforced his negativity and his coerciveness.

Since the behavioral responses of the powerless tend to be so ineffective as leadership styles, it would be the last rather than the first solution of most organizations to give such ineffective people more power or more responsibility. Yet all the indicators point to the negative effects of behavior that come from too little power, such as rules-mindedness and close supervision. Chris Argyris has noted that alienation and low morale accompany management's praise for the reliable (rules-obedient) rather than the enterprising (risk-taking) worker. Studies have shown that turnover varies with the degree to which supervisors structure tasks in advance and demand compliance, absenteeism with the tendency of supervisors to be "directive" and maintain close and detailed control. Yet when supervisors at Sears, Roebuck had responsibility for so many people that they could not watch any one person closely, employees responded to this greater latitude with greater job satisfaction.[28] So perhaps it is meaningful to suggest interrupting the cycle of powerlessness: to empower those in low-power situations by increasing their opportunities and their latitude rather than to continue to punish them for their ineffectiveness, reinforcing their powerless state of mind.

"Power" in organizations, as I am using the term, is synonymous with autonomy and freedom of action. The powerful can afford to risk more, and they can afford to allow others their freedom. The bureaucratic machinery of modern organizations means that there are rather few people who are really powerful. Power has become a scarce resource that most people feel they lack. Although the scramble for political advantage still distinguishes relative degrees of power, the organization places severe limits on everyone's freedom of action. The powerful get more, but they still share some of the mentality of powerlessness.

And women, in large hierarchical organizations, are especially often caught in the cycles of powerlessness.

Women and Power in Organizations

My analysis of the importance of power in large organizations and the behavioral consequences of powerlessness for management styles can help to explain some familiar clichés about women's lack of potential for organizational leadership: "No one wants to work for a woman"; and "Women are too rigid and controlling to make good bosses anyway."

Preference for Men = Preference for Power
There is considerable evidence for a general cultural attitude that men make better leaders. A large number of studies have concluded that

neither men nor women want to work for a woman (although women are readier to do so than men). In a 1965 survey of 1,000 male and 900 female executives, among *Harvard Business Review* readers, over two-thirds of the men and nearly one-fifth of the women reported that they themselves would not feel comfortable working for a woman. Very few of either sex (9 percent of the men and 15 percent of the women) thought that *men* felt comfortable working for a woman, and a proportion of the male respondents said that women did not belong in executive positions at all. A total of 51 percent of the men responded that women were "temperamentally unfit" for management, writing in gratuitous comments such as, "They scare male executives half to death. . . . As for an efficient woman manager, this is cultural blasphemy. . . ."[29] In the survey of nonexempts at Indsco, these workers, too, overwhelmingly agreed with the statement that "men make better supervisors." And they did so while also rejecting the idea that it was "unacceptable" or "unfeminine" for a woman to be a manager, as Table 17–1 indicates. Women managers were aware of this attitude. One woman at Indsco showed me a poster which she considered indicative; it was large and painted in dark, rather foreboding tones. Most of the poster was taken up by the head of a man wearing a workman's cap; he was saying furtively into a telephone, "I just quit. The new boss is a woman."

Yet when it comes to evaluating concrete leadership styles, as used by men or by women outside of organizations, research has found that there is no strong preference for men or general tendency to perceive men and women differently. In one study, subjects were asked to make judgments about male and female leaders exhibiting a variety of styles. The evalua-

Table 17–1
Attitudes of Nonexempt Employees at Indsco about Women as Supervisors†

	Mean rating of agreement with statement on 9-point scale, with 1 = strongly disagree 9 = strongly agree	
	Men (N = 23)	Women (N = 88)
1. "Men make better supervisors."	7.92	6.50*
2. "It is acceptable for a man to be competitive, but not a woman."	3.51	3.22
3. "A woman cannot be a supervisor and feminine as well."	3.30	3.10

*The difference between the ratings of men and women on this statement was statistically significant (p < .05).

†Figures reported by permission of G. Homall from "The Motivation to be Promoted among Non-Exempt Employees: An Expectancy Theory Approach," Masters Thesis, Cornell University, 1974.

tions of men and women did not differ significantly on most variables, including such critical ones as "production emphasis," but there was a tendency to give higher ratings to men than to women when they "initiated structure" and higher ratings to women than men when they showed "consideration," demonstrating some propensity for raters to "reward" people for sex-stereotypical behavior. Another study used a different set of categories but had nearly identical results.

Students and bank supervisors judged stories involving male and female leaders using four different styles. The "reward" style was rated somewhat more effective when used by men, but the "friendly-dependent" style (which the researchers hoped would capture a female stereotype) was rated high for *either* sex when used with the opposite sex. The use of "threat" was considered ineffective for both sexes, though there was a slight but not significant tendency to let men get away with it more than women. It has also been found that people who have once worked for a woman boss are more likely than those who never have to be favorably disposed toward women leaders.[30] And women, as Table 17–1 above showed, are slightly more accepting of the idea of women supervisors and managers than are men. Thus, sex preferences in general seem to play only a very small role, if any, in responding to the style of any specific leader.

Theories saying that women handle power differently from men, that men are the instrumental leaders, oriented toward competition and domination through nature or childhood training, also do not match the realities of adult life in organizations. By the age of ten, for example, leadership in groups does not reflect the use of different strategies of persuasion by females and males. Nor does either sex seem more naturally cooperative or susceptible to social influence from peers.[31] There is as yet no research evidence that makes a case for sex differences in either leadership aptitude or style. A wide variety of investigations, from field studies of organizations to paper-and-pencil tests, indicates that the styles of men and women vary over the same range and that there are no conclusive sex-related strategies.[32] . . . In an organizational simulation using college students, Kay Bartol found that sex of the leader did not by itself affect follower satisfaction, even when female leaders were characterized by high dominance, a trait most likely to "offend" male subordinates.[33] In fact, if sex stereotypes were true, then an argument could be made for the greater capacity of women for leadership roles in organizations, given socialization experiences emphasizing "people-handling" skills. One study showed that members of a business school class ranking high on "masculine" interests, power seeking, and aggressiveness met with less success in large organizations than those with more "feminine" interests in interpersonal relations.

If the much greater desire for men as leaders in organizations does not reflect real sex differences in style and strategy, what does it reflect? As we have seen, people often prefer the *powerful* as leaders. As the Pelz studies at Detroit Edison showed, good human relations skills and sensitivity but low power (a likely combination for women leaders in sexist organizations) could have negative effects on morale.[34] Thus, a *preference for men is a preference for power*, in the context of organizations where women do not have access to the same opportunities for power and efficacy through activities or alliances.

As in the old cliché, everyone likes a winner; in large organizations at least, people would rather work for winners than losers. Perhaps a preference for male managers reflects a "bet" that men are more likely to emerge as winners and power-holders than women. One clever social psychological experiment offers suggestive evidence. Judges were asked to rate paintings supposedly produced by either a man or a woman, with sex of artist varied for different judges. In one condition the paintings were presented as entries in a contest; in a second they were the winning paintings. The women presented as attempting to accomplish were judged less favorably than the men, but those whose paintings had succeeded were evaluated just as favorably.[35] In the great corporate contest, then, subordinates may be "betting" on who is going to be a winner when they respond differently to the idea of women or men as bosses. It is as though followers extend "credit" in the present for imagined future payoffs. This is reminiscent of the Mark Twain tale of the Englishman with the million-pound note. He made a bet with a wealthy man that he could live well forever just on the strength of the note and without using it. Credit was given to him; people vied with each other to supply his wants; and they graciously picked up the bills. He became wealthy and successful—and he never had to cash in the million-pound note. The power that devolved on star performers backed by sponsors at Indsco worked in much the same way. The problem with women was that, first, there were doubts about how far they could go in the corporation, and second, a widespread belief that women could only be individual "movers"—i.e., even if they moved, they could not take anyone else with them.

But power wipes out sex. A woman who does acquire power stops arousing the same level of concern about whether or not she will be wanted as a leader. People who want to attach themselves to power may not even notice sex. On one occasion, a senior Indsco salesman told a long story to colleagues about a problem with a "very, very smart, tough-minded" president of a small company. The president had made good friends among a number of senior Indsco people and therefore managed to get all kinds of concessions. The salesman had to bring this to an end, as well as tell this very powerful client that there would be no credit for the material that had failed when her customers, in turn, used it. . . . It look a long time for the audience to this story to realize that the salesman was saying "she." Some even interjected comments using "he."

The salesman presented the story with such awe of the powerful customer that sex made no difference. He said later that she was someone he would eagerly work for.

The "Mean and Bossy Woman Boss" Stereotype

The other issue around women as organizational leaders also turns out to be a power issue. Perhaps the most blatant picture of the negative American stereotype of a woman boss appeared on the cover of *MBA* magazine in March 1972. *MBA*, distributed to business school students and faculty, devoted this issue, as its blurb indicated, to "Women in Business!" Shown on the cover is a Roy Lichtenstein-style comic-cartoon head of a sultry blond woman with blue eyes, bright red lips, and a low-cut, cleavage-revealing dress. Head thrown back snottily, she is saying, "You're fired!"[36]

And that's what women bosses supposedly do with their authority. No wonder no one wants one.

Abuse of power is only the first in a long list of negative characteristics attributed to women managers over the last few decades by those who don't want them. One survey of 521 young working women just before World War II uncovered so much hostility toward women bosses that even the author, Donald Laird (who thought women belonged behind a typewriter), had to conclude that there was overreaction.[37] Of the women workers, 99.81 percent said they preferred a male boss for reasons such as the following:

1. Women bosses are too jealous. Their positions go to their heads. They boss for the mere sake of bossing, to remind you they are in charge.
2. Women bosses take things too personally. They are not businesslike.
3. Women bosses are overly concerned with efficiency and routine details. They are slaves to the system. They bother about small, petty things.
4. Women bosses supervise too closely. They delegate only superficially.
5. Women bosses find more fault. They are too critical.
6. Women bosses scream to impress people with their importance.

One less prejudiced woman, who had worked for both men and women, reflected on her experiences:

> The two women bosses I've had were very lovely people and were good bosses so far as women bosses go . . . but most women bosses have [this fault, which I call] "old-maid thinking." It is eternally thinking in terms of details, not in terms of the big thing—more interested in the details of the means than in the general significance of the results. A man [gives] me a job to do, and he'll let me do it and not ask how and why and did I check with an "x" or a "v"—which is wasting time and makes me want to yell. Further, a woman boss is so everlastingly curious about my personal business: "when, how many, how late, and who" about my own social affairs. A man doesn't give a hoot just as long as I'm on the job and on my toes when I'm on it.[38]

Laird himself concluded that women make poor supervisors in factories, offices, and even at home because of their tendency to "henpeck" and become too bossy. For evidence he cited, without specific reference, a study showing that being "too dictatorial" was a fault in twice as many women as men in the general population.

Burleigh Gardner, a human relations expert also writing during the war, when women entered formerly closed jobs, found similar complaints by both men and women about women bosses, although he felt that the system forced women into positions where they were likely to fail. His respondents said that women were too emotional, unfriendly, critical, strict, and petty. The National Manpower Council's report on "Woman-power" in the 1950s concluded that women supervisors were said to be more demanding and controlling of subordinates as well as guilty of partiality and discrimination. British surveys show the same thing.[39] And this refrain echoed through my interviews at Indsco.

Stereotypes persist even in the face of evidence negating them. The *real* extent of bossiness among women in authority in organizations may have little to do with the persistence of the stereotype, but this particular portrait has one very important characteristic. *It is a perfect picture of people who are powerless. Powerlessness tends to produce those very characteristics attributed to women bosses.*

A careful look at comparisons between men and women supposedly in the same position shows that what looks like sex differences may really be power differences. It has been hard to test this directly, partly because there are so few women managers, especially in the same organizational positions as men. (Rarity itself, as we see in the next chapter, creates a very different situation for the person who is rare.) One recent investigation, however, did find an organizational setting in which women leaders were more common: high school departments in Florida public schools. The research covered 205 teachers and 40 department heads (25 male and 15 female) in small departments with a roughly equal sex distribution. The first interesting finding was that on the usual measures of leadership style (like taking action, providing emotional support, and so forth), operating styles could not be distinguished by sex. However, there was one statistically significant sex-linked difference in group climate: there was a slightly greater tendency for women leaders to be perceived as generating a tight and controlled atmosphere. Departments headed by men were perceived as slightly higher in "esprit and intimacy"—a good indicator of morale; those headed by women, in "hindrance"—an indicator that the leader was thought to get in the way, to intrude too much, rather than to promote subordinates' autonomy and flexibility.[40] In short, the research uncovered a watered-down version of the bossiness complaint. Where could it have come from?

The difference in atmosphere in the woman-run departments can be traced directly to differences in organizational power of the men and women leaders, although the author of the research did not see this. Mobility prospects, the likelihood that department heads would be moving up in the system, were strikingly different for the men and women in this set of high schools. For one thing, there were no women *above* the level of department head in the whole county. Second, the women seemed to have moved to their last position. They had risen into the headship more slowly than the men; they were older, had put in more time teaching, and had spent a longer time in their previous jobs. At the same time, they had more limited aspirations; one-seventh of the women, in contrast to half of the men, expressed a desire for further promotions. Thus, the men and the women managers were not really in comparable positions. The women were much less mobile and much more powerless. And the powerless are handicapped in leadership.

Women at Indsco in exempt positions where they had organizational accountability or leadership responsibilities were differentially in the most powerless situations. They were primarily first-line supervisors of secretaries or clerical workers or they held staff jobs in personnel or public relations functions. There were no other women with line responsibilities and no women above grade 14, with the exception of a senior researcher. They were more likely to lack powerful alliances, and they reported constantly having to fight off the tendency for the organization to "protect" them by encapsulating them in safe situations. Statistics on the distributions of men and women in organizational functions . . . make clear how common this situation is. Women, when they do achieve managerial or leadership positions, are clustered in the low-power situations. It should not be surprising if they adopt the behavior of the powerless.

It is not only their own relative power that determines the behavior of managers but also the behavior and feeling of powerlessness of those above and below. The relationship with their own superiors is important in shaping the responses of those who supervise too closely. One such generalization about where most women bosses are found is that they are located in tightly supervised and rules-conscious hierarchies. The "female" professions, like nursing, social work, and primary school teaching, all feature close supervisory hierarchies and concern with detail. Government agencies, where more women managers are found than in private business, epitomize bureaucracy in civil service structure, endless red tape, and concern with rules and regulations. Women managers in these settings are likely to themselves be subject to bossy bosses and may take this restriction of their power out on their own subordinates, perpetuating the style downward. Simultaneously, they learn bossiness as a leadership style from their own role models. In corporations like Indsco, where women managers are so rare as to be tokens . . . they themselves may be watched more closely, so that again the restriction of their own latitude of conduct may be transmitted to subordinates.

Simultaneously, powerless feelings of subordinates are translated upward to leaders. Most women managers are likely to manage relatively powerless subordinates: clerical workers, women factory workers, low-level personnel. Powerless subordinates may take out their own frustration in resistance to their managers, provoking them to adopt more coercive styles. The powerless may also resent a boss's advantage, particularly if they think that they could just as easily be the boss. One woman at Indsco who had not attended college was forthright about her hostility toward "credentialed" women brought in to manage her department as a result of affirmative action efforts, while she was still held back. She resented the special treatment they were getting. Women who are jealous of another woman's promotion and try to let her know she's really no better than they may instead provoke her to try to demonstrate her superiority and her control. This is the "lording it over us" behavior some women have complained of in women bosses. From the subordinate's perspective, it is hard to be generously happy about the success of someone getting a chance denied to you. From the boss's perspective, it is hard to share power with people who resent you. The combination of these two viewpoints produces controlling, directive bosses.

Futhermore, people who feel vulnerable and unsure of themselves, who are plunged into jobs without sufficient training or experience, regardless of the official authority they are given, are more likely to first adopt authoritarian-controlling leadership styles. The behavior attributed to women supervisors is likely to be characteristic of new and insecure supervisors generally. Gardner saw this in his World War II studies, when the demands of war production brought inexperienced women into formerly all-male positions. He observed that many people complained about the bossiness of women supervisors but concluded that newly promoted men given supervisory jobs without sufficient training also showed these tendencies.

> Any new supervisor who feels unsure of himself, who feels that his boss is watching him critically, is likely to demand perfect behavior and performance from his people, to be critical of minor mistakes, and to try too hard to please his boss. A woman supervisor, responding to the insecurity and uncertainty of her position as a woman, knowing that she is being watched both critically and doubtfully, feels obliged to try even harder. And for doing this she is said to be "acting just like a woman."[41]

Without the experience or confidence to permit the minor deviations from the rules that in fact make the system work and without enough knowledge and faith in outcomes to loosen control, new managers may be prone to be too directive, controlling, and details-oriented.

In a variety of ways, then, powerlessness stemming from organizational circumstance breeds a particular leadership style caricatured in the stereotype of the bossy woman. This style reflects the situation more than sex, however—if the stereotype carries even a grain of truth—for men who are powerless behave in just the same ways. As Elizabeth Janeway pointed out, "The *weak* are the second sex."[42]

The problem of power thus is critical to the effective behavior of people in organizations. Power issues occupy center stage not because individuals are greedy for more, but because some people are incapacitated without it.

Notes

1. Donald C. Pelz, "Influence: A Key to Effective Leadership in the First-Line Supervisor," *Personnel* 29 (1952), pp. 3–11.

2. Joan E. Crowley, Teresa E. Levitan, and Robert P. Quinn, "Seven Deadly Half-Truths About Women," *Psychology Today* 7 (March 1973); William F. Whyte and Burleigh Gardner, "The Man in the Middle," *Applied Anthropology* 4 (Spring 1945), pp. 1–28.

3. The study of negativity: John W. Thibaut and Henry W. Riecken, "Authoritarianism, Status, and the Communication of Aggression," *Human Relations* 8 (1955), pp. 95–120. The study of professionals: Jacob I. Hurwitz, Alvin F. Zander, and Bernard Hymovitch, "Some Effects of Power on the Relations Among Group Members," in *Group Dynamics*, D. Cartwright and A. Zander, eds. (New York: Harper & Row, 1968). See also R. Lippit, N. Polansky, and S. Rosen, "The Dynamics of Power," *Human Relations* 5 (1952), pp. 44–50; this is a classic study.

4. Michel Crozier, *The Bureaucratic Phenomenon* (Chicago: University of Chicago Press, 1964), p. 164.

5. Charles Perrow has also analyzed the ways in which changing technical requirements affect organizational authority structures in his studies of hospitals. See Perrow, "Hospitals: Technology, Structures, and Goals," in *Handbook of Organizations*, J. G. March, ed. (Chicago: Rand McNally, 1965); and Perrow, "The Analysis of Goals in Complex Organizations," *American Sociological Review* 26 (1961), pp. 854–66. James Thompson made a similar point with respect to business in *Organizations in Action* (New York: McGraw-Hill, 1967).

6. In a system of sponsored mobility, elites or their agents choose recruits early and then carefully induct them into elite status. Ralph H. Turner, "Sponsored and Contest Mobility in the School System," *American Sociological Review* 25 (December 1960), pp. 855–67.

7. Margaret Cussler, *The Woman Executive* (New York: Harcourt, Brace, 1958); Margaret Hennig, *Career Development for Women Executives*, Unpublished Doctoral Dissertation, Harvard Business School, 1970; Michael Fogarty, A. I. Allen, Isobel Allen, and Patricia Walters, *Women in Top Jobs: Four Studies in Achievement* (London: George Allen and Unwin, 1971).

8. Paul Cowan, "Connecticut's Governor Grasso Remembers How She Made It," *New York Times*, May 4, 1975.

9. The evidence that social similarity and compatibility affects a leader's evaluation of followers or subordinates comes from a variety of situations. Borgatta found that high acceptability to a supervisor at the social level was associated with receiving high ratings from him in an all-male sample; Edgar Borgatta, "Analysis of Social Interaction and Socio-metric Perception," *Sociometry* 17 (February 1954), pp. 7–32. A study of staff nurses and their supervisors in three hospitals discovered that friendship with supervisors was a greater determinant of high evaluations than shared work attitudes and values. Ronald Corwin, Marvin J. Taves, and J. Eugene Haas, "Social Requirements for Occupational

Success: Internalized Norms and Friendships," *Social Forces* 39 (1961), pp. 135–40. The cause-effect relationship is not clear in these studies, of course.

10. Stein, "Getting There: Patterns in Managerial Success," Working Paper, Center for Research on Women, Wellesley College, 1976.

11. Stein, "Getting There: Patterns in Managerial Success."

12. Whyte and Gardner, "Man in the Middle." See also Donald R. Wray, "Marginal Men of Industry, the Foremen," *American Journal of Sociology* 54 (January 1949), pp. 298–301.

13. See Melville Dalton, "Conflicts between Staff and Line Managerial Officers," *American Sociological Review* 21 (June 1950), pp. 342–51.

14. Sidney Reynolds, "Women on the Line," *MBA* 9 (February 1975), pp. 27–30.

15. Robert Presthus, *The Organizational Society* (New York: Knopf, 1962), p. 35.

16. Karen Horney, *The Neurotic Personality of Our Time* (New York: Norton, 1937), pp. 163–70.

17. Rollo May, *Power and Innocence* (New York: Norton, 1972).

18. Stanley A. Hetzler, "Variations in Role-Playing Patterns Among Different Echelons of Bureaucratic Leaders," *American Sociological Review* 20 (December 1955), pp. 700–706.

19. Crozier, *Bureaucratic Phenomenon*, pp. 122–23.

20. Franz Fanon, *The Wretched of the Earth* (New York: Grove Press, 1965).

21. B. Goodstadt and D. Kipnis, "Situational Influences on the Use of Power," *Journal of Applied Psychology* 54 (1970), pp. 201–207; B. Goodstadt and L. Hjelle, "Power to the Powerless: Locus of Control and the Use of Power," *Journal of Personality and Social Psychology* 27 (July 1973), pp. 190–96.

22. Thibaut and Riecken, "Authoritarianism, Status, and the Communication of Aggression." Chow and Grusky, in a laboratory simulation with complicated results, found that worker compliance (the degree of productivity and the degree of aggressiveness) shaped supervisory style, especially closeness of supervision and adoption of a punitive style; there were complex interaction phenomena in the data. Esther Chow and Oscar Grusky, "Worker Compliance and Supervisory Style: An Experimental Study of Female Superior-Subordinate Relationships," Paper presented at the 1973 Meetings of the American Sociological Association. Blau and Scott also pointed out that a group's low productivity may be a cause of supervisory style, as well as a result. Peter M. Blau and W. Richard Scott, *Formal Organizations* (San Francisco: Chandler, 1962), p. 50.

23. Crozier, *Bureaucratic Phenomenon*, p. 188.

24. Robert K. Merton, "Bureaucratic Structure and Personality," in *Social Theory and Social Structure*, rev. ed. (Glencoe, Illinois: Free Press, 1957).

25. Melville Dalton, *Men Who Manage* (New York: Wiley, 1959), p. 247.

26. Merton, "Bureaucratic Structure and Personality."

27. Crozier, *Bureaucratic Phenomenon*, pp. 40–42.

28. Chris Argyris, *Integrating the Individual and the Organization* (New York: Wiley, 1964); M. Argyle, G. Gardner, and I. Cioffi, "Supervisory Methods Related to Productivity, Absenteeism, and Labor Turnover," *Human Relations* 11 (1958), pp. 23–40; study by E. Fleishman and E. Harris cited in Charles Hampden-Turner, "The Factory as an Oppressive Environment," in *Workers' Control: A Reader on Labor and Social Change*, G. Hunnius, G. D. Garson, and J. Case, eds. (New York: Vintage, 1973), pp. 30–44. The Sears study was James Worthy, "Organizational Structure and Employee Morale," *American Sociological Review* 15 (1950), pp. 169–79.

29. G. W. Bowman, N. B. Worthy, and S. A. Greyser, "Are Women Executives People?," *Harvard Business Review* 43 (July–August 1965), pp. 14–30. The preference for male bosses was also a finding of National Manpower Council, *Womanpower* (New York: Columbia University Press, 1957), pp. 104–6.

30. The first study is Kathryn M. Bartol and D. Anthony Butterfield, "Sex Effects in Evaluating Leaders," Working Paper No. 74–10, University of Massachusetts School of Business Administration, 1974. The second is Benson Rosen and Thomas H. Jerdee, "The

Influence of Sex-Role Stereotypes on Evaluations of Male and Female Supervisory Behavior," *Journal of Applied Psychology* 57 (1973), pp. 44–48.

31. Eleanor Emmons Maccoby and Carol Nagy Jacklin, *The Psychology of Sex Differences* (Stanford, California: Stanford University Press, 1974), pp. 261, 361.

32. Michel Crozier, *The World of the Office Worker*, trans. David Landau (Chicago: University of Chicago Press, 1971); D. R. Day and R. M. Stogdill, "Leader Behavior of Male and Female Supervisors: A Comparative Study," *Personal Psychology* 25 (1972), pp. 353–60; Cecile Roussell, "Relationship of Sex of Department Head to Department Climate," *Administrative Science Quarterly* 19 (June 1974), pp. 211–20.

33. Kathryn M. Bartol, "Male Versus Female Leaders: The Effect of Leader Need for Dominance on Follower Satisfaction," *Academy of Management Journal* 17 (June 1974), pp. 225–33; and "The Effect of Male Versus Female Leaders on Follower Satisfaction and Performance," *Journal of Business Research* 3 (January 1975), pp. 33–42.

34. Pelz, "Influence."

35. Gail I. Pheterson, Sara B. Kiesler, and Philip A. Goldberg, "Evaluation of the Performance of Women as a Function of Their Sex, Achievement, and Personal History," *Journal of Personality and Social Psychology* 19 (September 1971), pp. 114–18.

36. *MBA* 6 (March 1972).

37. Donald A. Laird, with Eleanor C. Laird, *The Psychology of Supervising the Working Woman* (New York: McGraw-Hill, 1942), pp. 175–79.

38. Laird, *The Psychology of Supervising the Working Woman*, p. 31.

39. Burleigh B. Gardner, *Human Relations in Industry* (Chicago: Richard D. Irwin, 1945), pp. 269–71; National Manpower Council, *Womanpower* (New York: Columbia University Press, 1957), p. 106; and the British reference is Fogarty et al., *Women in Top Jobs*, p. 15.

40. Roussell, "Relationship of Sex of Department Head to Department Climate."

41. Gardner, *Human Relations*, pp. 270–71.

42. Elizabeth Janeway, "The Weak are the Second Sex," *Atlantic Monthly* (December 1973), and *In Between Myth and Morning* (New York: William Morrow, 1974).

18
Mentoring and Irrationality: The Role of Racial Taboos

David Thomas

Introduction: Racial Taboos and Irrationality

We can create a partial picture of organizations if we consider them, for a moment, as instruments of rational action. Managers, leaders, and workers collaborate to achieve specific ends with limited means. Using technical logics that link cause and effect in a range of domains (marketing, engineering, production), organizations make decisions on how and when to act. But this is only a partial picture. An organization is also the seat of irrational life. People's unconscious hopes and fears, the dreams and myths they live by, and the history embedded in them—all influence their actions as well.

People experience or suppress the irrational at work when relating to others. Working in and through these relationships, people serve their conscious as well as their unconscious purposes. Researchers have highlighted how the mentor-protégé relationship between members of an organization, or profession, helps the organization reach its goals while facilitating the career and personal development of both parties (Kram, 1985; Clawson, 1980; Phillips, 1982; Dalton and Thompson, 1986). Shaped by broader social and cultural processes, these relationships reflect the ongoing tension between the rational and irrational levels of experience. Thus, for example, mentors and protégés are frequently pulled between two opposing archetypal images of the relationship itself. On the one side, the protégé feels like the child, and the mentor like the parent. On the other side, nourished by the myth of Mentor, the servant who raised the son of his master Oedipus to manhood, mentors feel obliged to educate the "young" so that the corporation can thrive. In the first case the protégé is the apprentice; in the second the mentor is the

Reprinted from David A. Thomas, *Human Resource Management,* vol. 28, number 2 (Summer 1989), pp. 279–290. © 1989 by John Wiley & Sons, Inc. Reprinted by permission of John Wiley & Sons, Inc. Also reprinted from Larry Hirschhorn and Carole K. Barnett, *The Psychodynamics of Organizations* (Philadelphia: Temple University Press, 1993), pp. 191–202.

servant. The lines between mentor as father or servant and protégé as apprentice or son constantly blur and re-form. Yet this fluidity is experienced largely unconsciously.

As research shows, these relationships have dramatic impacts on a person's career (Roche, 1977; Cox and Nkomo, 1986). By understanding how mentoring's irrational core inhibits certain relationships while facilitating others, we can understand how the irrational and unconscious shape upward mobility in the modern corporation.

In the United States feelings of racial identity shape unconscious fantasies and fears very powerfully. Just as a superior and subordinate can enact the unconsciously experienced dynamics of a parent and child, whites and blacks can enact the history of race relations, with all its difficulty and promise, in their everyday interaction, in the microdynamics of supervision and mentoring, and in career planning. Good Equal Employment Opportunity (EEO) practices will not eliminate these inner experiences. Indeed, as EEO opens doors to black managers, it engenders the deeper difficulties we face in creating a climate of authentic collaboration among blacks and whites.

Consider a white professional engineer's description of his encounter with a black female subordinate who recently joined his group.

> I was told that Kathy shared my special interests in product design, but I also found that I was staying away from her. I hooked up with all the other new junior people, but not with her. Finally, I approached her to join me on a project. I knew I was attracted to her. When I spoke she responded warmly, but I was also aware of a hesitancy in me, that I wanted to withdraw. It was as if a taboo was operating.

The word *taboo* is suggestive here. Taboos operate on two levels. They forbid action, but they also forbid *reflecting* on what is forbidden. As an injunction not to notice what is forbidden, a taboo operates out of awareness. That is why people find it difficult to discuss a taboo. It is not that they will perform the forbidden act, but that they will violate the unconsciously experienced injunction to ignore what they are ignoring. The racial taboo described above—the creation of a liaison between a white man and a black woman—links wider cultural processes to organizational reality while operating to suppress this linkage. It thus becomes the source of an experiential underground—a set of experiences often unconsciously enacted and rarely acknowledged which nonetheless shapes the relationships between blacks and whites in significant ways.

Based on a sample of interview results I obtained when studying mentoring relationships between black and white managers in WRL, a large corporation, this chapter suggests that race relations are embedded in taboos that both highlight and suppress the links between race and sex. I begin by examining how these taboos are experienced and then explore the links between these experiences and the process of mentoring. Finally, I suggest some implications for human-resource practice.

Of course, this chapter violates the very taboos it describes. My own experience suggests that the reader, like the engineer, will want to withdraw and deny the validity or plausibility of the experiences reported here. They may seem too primitive. Indeed, it is their primitiveness that leads us to question their validity. How can such feelings really exist or persist? This is the lesson of psychoanalysis, however. The primitive layer, whether based on sexual feelings or on early experiences of being judged unworthy, continues to shape an adult's unconscious life and ongoing actions. I ask the reader to suspend disbelief as a first step in examining and assessing these taboos rationally. As in psychoanalysis, irrationality must be acknowledged if it is to be overcome.

Sex and Race

Cross-Sex Relationships

Listen to Louise, a black woman manager, describe her experience of race relations at WRL.

> Being seen with white men presents problems. . . . White men are kind of funny around black women and if one knows about history. . . . Actually, I should own [the problem] myself. My being seen with white men, I have a problem with it. You know, being a white man's slut and all the connotations that go with it. So when I'm away on training, I isolate myself after hours. So, I have to own a piece of not feeling extremely comfortable.
>
> I remember all the negative things people used to say about Ann, a black woman manager, when she was out in the field and moving up. People thought she must have been sleeping her way up. Now those of us who know her realize how full of —— that was.

Louise's reference to "being a white man's slut and all the connotations that go with it" evokes a charged domain of feelings affecting the relationships between blacks and whites. But where do such feelings come from? What are their roots? Scholars of race relations agree that the history of slavery and its chronic aftershocks undergird these feelings. We are still living in the aftermath of a social earthquake—slavery and its sequelae's long-term effects on racial identity, black self-esteem, and white prejudice lie deep within our culture.

While racial dynamics are enacted in many ways, the social psychology of slavery and its later nonslave manifestations, as Grier and Cobbs (1968) and Kovel (1970) point out, typically pit the white man against the black man. At the economic level, of course, the white man owned the black's labor power. But at the intimate and primitive levels of social life, white men dominated because black men could not adequately protect their families, especially black women, from white men's whimsical and most often violent intrusion. In contrast, black men could be lynched simply for speaking to white women. Women became pawns in an unequal struggle that not only undermined the black male's status but distorted the relationship between the men and women of both races. *Thus from slavery's beginnings racial dynamics have been inextricably tied to gender relationships. Indeed, the former, I suggest, are not conceivable without the latter.* This is part of what gives race relationships their irrational character, their primitiveness, and their durability.

Consider, for example, the case that Davis and Watson (1982) relate in a study on black experience in a largely white corporation. A black woman, Joanne, described the pressures and dubious attributions placed on black women who are thought to be involved in career-enhancing relationships with white men. Talking about a black woman who rose up in the hierarchy, she notes:

> You had a lot of black males saying that she was aligning herself with the white boys to help her. Then you had a lot of black men saying that she was aligning herself with the white man against him, saying the white man promoted her and favored her because she could be counted twice on the EEO report. . . . If she hung out with the white boys they accused her of sleeping with white dudes. . . . See, this is history repeating itself.

In short, Joanne is saying that modern-day corporate relationships reproduce the feelings associated with the primitive dynamics of race relations. White men appropriate black women, black women can rise up by going along with this, and black men are angry and suspicious.

Similarly, consider the complex case of Bob, a black manager, and his white superior, Mary. They started out as peers in the same division but Mary was quickly promoted, while Bob, highly regarded for his technical skills, was not. Several years later Mary returned as the supervisor of Bob's unit, the two became friends, and Mary worked successfully to get Bob on the fast track.

Mary learned much from her experience. She reported that at committee meetings where promotions were decided, whites could be promoted upon the say-so of their supervisors. By contrast, black candidates faced a tough time. "Unless you sold the black person ahead of time," she noted, "they could get shot down." Reflecting on the struggle she faced in sponsoring Bob, she said that her peers wondered if Bob was "tough enough," ironically punishing him for behaving as blacks are supposed to—not pushy, not uppity.

Bob discussed his own career, and reflecting on his eventual promotion, he said that white men told him that he was considered one of the "good" black guys. There are black guys, he was told, that "vamp" on white women, but he was not one of them. In other words, it was safe to promote him.

Nonetheless, while he could be sponsored by a powerful white woman, it was difficult for him to sponsor a subordinate white woman. Thus he reports that later he began helping a white woman who shortly afterward withdrew emotionally from him.

> I can be the mentor and I tried that and did it OK. And it happened to be that the person was a white woman. Someone came to her and said, "You're hanging around with this black man too much; it will damage your career." She came back to tell me what the other one told her. I was the project leader. I am, like, "What can I do?"

Another black male described the dangers black men faced in associating with white females:

> I don't want to be seen too often talking with white females; . . . there is a lot of history that says that black men being somewhat familiar with white women isn't healthy. Maybe that is changing but there is enough history to say that it is something you should have some care around.

Interviewing whites and blacks, I found that none of the white male mentors, including the most enlightened about race relations, seemed aware of, or were willing to discuss, this history of race relations and sexual taboos. Yet this history was salient in the minds of black men and women and, to some degree, white women. This does not mean that the latter were exaggerating. Rather, just as white males once dominated the sexist pigmentocracy of slavery, current organizational and cultural norms support their long-standing tastes and interests. Secure and powerful in ways that women and minorities frequently are not, they can deny the anxieties created by the relationships between blacks and whites. Experiencing it only unconsciously, as a vague sense of uneasiness, they let blacks bear the burden of awareness. The power imbalance is reinforced, as blacks tread lightly, carefully, and whites comfortably go about their business. The powerful can choose what they wish to ignore.

Same-Sex Relationships

As these examples suggest, cross-race/cross-gender relationships pose special difficulties by activating a *triangle* of relationships. A black man mentoring a white female may upset white men. A black female's supportive alliance with a white man can upset black men.

Same-sex/cross-race relationships pose different and somewhat less volatile dynamics. For example, Frances, a white woman superior, and Harriet, a black woman subordinate, developed a close mentoring relationship. Frances was Harriet's first female supervisor. The two came to be friends; they socialized together after work, sharing details about one another's private nonwork lives.

Harriet credits Frances with opening up their relationship. As a black woman wary of being unfairly judged, Harriet put herself in a position of never making a mistake. This limited her development. Asking Harriet about this, Frances saw how Harriet's behavior was rooted in the simple reality that blacks' performance was more carefully scrutinized than whites' and their mistakes were more severely penalized. Harriet believed that this conversation was a breakthrough for them. She felt that Frances was the first white person she really trusted.

By contrast, in my study of cross-race couples at WRL, I found that black and white men rarely reported bonding around shared male interests. Men at work form close relationships by participating together in typical male activities after work. They join the same softball team, for example. But while white men could sponsor black men at WRL, they rarely formed close *mentoring* relationships that facilitated such extrawork relationships.

I suggest that female-female cross-race relationships differ radically from their male-male counterparts, because their histories differ. The relationship between Frances and Harriet evokes the earlier history of the frequently warm and congenial relationship between the black woman house slave and the white woman mistress (a relationship reproduced well beyond slavery as black women continued to function as "nannies" for white children). The white woman relied on the black woman to protect her children and care for her household. The two thereby developed a way of being with each other that suppressed their racial difference and drew upon the vein of commonality represented in their womanhood. By contrast, black and white men had few opportunities to develop such non-race-based relationships. They remained combatants.

In Sum

My interviews at WRL thus suggest that race relationships are embedded in a complex set of race-gender dynamics. Table 18–1 presents a way of ordering the different pairwise relationships in terms of their complexity, volatility, and the degree to which they evoke taboos.

The Impact of Mentoring and Careers

Mentoring and Identification

Sex and race taboos critically shape the dynamics of cross-race relationships. While linked to the overt process of career development and mobility, mentoring is grounded in the psychodynamics of identification. The mentor sees parts of himself or herself in the subordinate, and the subordinate wants to become like the mentor, to take up his or her voice, manner of dress, way of thinking. The two psychologically identify with each other, bringing their unconscious fantasies of who they are or might be to the relationship. As Kaplan (1984) described it, by identifying with each other, individuals come to know themselves, to discover themselves through their relationships with others.

Table 18-1
Relationships (Ranked by Power to Evoke Taboos)

Rank Order	Relationship	Tabooed Feeling
1	WM superior BF subordinate	White man having unlimited sexual access to black women
1	BM superior WF subordinate	Black man sexually approaching a white woman
2	WM superior BM subordinate	White man "freeing a slave," threatening other white men*
3	WF superior BF subordinate	Black woman abandoning her men, counterbalanced by shared experience of womanhood

*Wells and Jennings (1983) have described the psychodynamics of this relationship using the paradigm of the scandalous paradox. In this scenario, whites respond to black peers as though they were the illegitimate children of the father—in this instance, white elites who support EEO and black advancement. This relationship is viewed by white subordinates as scandalous and a threat to their inherited privileges and rights.

Racial difference and sex and race taboos can block blacks and whites from feeling close to each other, from identifying with each other. If they emotionally identify with their counterpart, they grow dangerously close to experiencing forbidden feelings and encountering unknown parts of themselves. One white manager talked about these feelings while describing the problem of selecting black managers to mentor.

> The first thing that you have to do is to accept that there is a difference, even though you don't always know what it is. For me a very important part of mentoring is identifying and knowing they'll be good. There has to be something in the person that you have identified. That is difficult in some cases to do with blacks. You have to pick out some dimensions that let you know this person will be good. You also have to realize that there are some things that you will never know. Things that come from growing up black that you may never understand. But if you believe in the person, in some way you have to get around that and work with them.

This is a complex statement. The white manager notes that because blacks and whites are different she finds it difficult to find parts or features of blacks that assure her of their goodness. She notes that her difficulty is linked to things "she may never understand." At first blush one might interpret the comment as strictly a racist one and leave it at that. But this manager has worked to overcome her felt inhibitions. I suggest that the statement describes how people unconsciously respond to the unknown, and how racism shapes this response. Just as children disappoint parents, a mentor can never predict for certain how his or her protégé will perform. The mentor overcomes this uncertainty emotionally, by identifying with the protégé, by locating what she trusts in herself and seeing this same characteristic in the protégé. Identification reduces the felt sense of risk and danger. But in the face of racial difference, the sense of what is not known expands, and the resulting anxieties are then unconsciously rationalized with the racist image of the dangerous and inferior black. The core anxiety of mentoring—the dread of what cannot be predicted—is filled out by the culture of racism. It is this set of feelings that obscures the white manager's vision of the goodness in blacks.

Cooling Out

Whites and blacks respond frequently to these difficulties by "cooling out" their relationships, by transforming potentially intimate mentoring relationships into more instrumental relationships of sponsorship. Consider the case of Ken and Karen. Ken was a powerful up-and-coming white manager at WRL. Placed on the fast track, he was told that he would shortly become treasurer of the corporation. Well connected to the dominant coalition, he was in fact advised to forgo an immediate promotion because his next would vault him into the power elite.

Karen, a black female, was one of his protégés. Describing her career, she noted that she spent the first four years working through and past her "naive" belief that good work begets recognition. Now she knew that she had to be careful, to stay at a distance from other people and not get hooked into the informal processes of the organization. She valued Ken as a model manager, as fair and competent, but she kept her distance.

Talking about race relations, she noted that at one point she was having some trouble getting good work out of a department that supported her unit. Ken suggested that it might have something to do with the fact that she was black and the other unit head was an older white male. She denied it—there was just a "bunch of old codgers" in that unit—but she confided later in the research interview that she was pleased that Ken could talk about racism openly with her.

Ken described his relationship to Karen in similarly "cool" terms, linking it to the company's strategic needs. He saw that minorities would soon constitute 70 percent of his workforce and that the company needed such people as Karen to become leaders. He was sponsoring Karen, helping her develop to further the organization's leadership needs.

Yet while each kept emotional distance from the other, he seeing her as an instrument of the organization's development and she seeing him as a model of the fair manager, in interviewing them I experienced both as vital people, in touch with their power and sexuality. They denied that they were attracted to each other (though what could they tell a black male researcher?), but I left the interviews with the feeling that while developing a workable relationship together, they had also depersonalized one another.

Instrumental relationships that provide career support can benefit upwardly mobile managers. Today, many blacks can hope for no more. However, both mentors and protégés lose out when, unable to identify with each other, they fail to connect emotionally. Facing penalties for poor decisions, a white executive will not advocate that a protégé be given risky assignments that can lead to the "top" unless he can see and identify with the protégé's "goodness." This perhaps explains why black high-potential managers in corporations plateau so early (Jones, 1986; Davis and Watson, 1982). By cooling their relationships out, blacks and whites protect themselves from jointly confronting the anxieties and paradoxes of their alliances, but they also limit their impact and significance.

The Limits of EEO

EEO as a Social Defense

Companies introducing and implementing EEO policies can help minority-group members have the careers and jobs they deserve. It has been an important first step in overcoming discrimination. But paradoxically EEO can also function as what Hirschhorn (1988) calls a social defense, as a system of procedures that detach people from their experiences so that they will not feel anxious. Situated squarely in the liberal tradition of the "melting pot," EEO is based on the assumption and hope that legislation and rules will make institutions color blind. But as I have argued, the taboos of race and sex are deeply embedded in feelings and practice, and people consciously hoping to treat one another fairly may nonetheless enact the system of suspicion, mistrust, and devaluation that shapes basic relations between the races in the United States. Ironically, because it posits the goal of a color-blind society, EEO may reinforce the very taboos that stop us from looking at the impact of color on our relationships to each other. Announcing that "here in this company, color doesn't matter" may unconsciously affirm the fantasy that color is unimportant, that its impact need not be confronted.

We need to complement the political model of using legislation and rules to reshape behavior with the psychoanalytic model for changing behavior. The latter is based on the assumption that irrationality can be overcome only when it is acknowledged. People must "work through" their feelings and experiences, even if this work is painful and difficult. While EEO has legitimized racism as a problem, we now need to build on this base of experience. We need to help people approach the taboos themselves, by working with them at retreats, workshops, and department meetings where unspoken thoughts can be safely expressed. This is a complex design and facilitation task, and in my experience such encounters work only when black and white people participate in them together. We have only begun to develop a social technology for confronting the racial taboos. But to be true to our pluralist values and to be socially responsible executives, we have no choice.

In Sum

While linking means and ends in rational ways, companies are also the seat of much irrationality. In the United States, racial taboos are at the source of many unspoken feelings and irrational acts. Rooted in the history of slavery, racial feelings are inextricably linked to dynamics of gender relationships. The explosive mix of race and sex makes racism particularly volatile and durable. Research highlights the nature of these taboos and suggests that cross-sex/cross-race relationships are the most difficult to sustain. Facing the taboos these relationships create, blacks and whites retreat to less intense ways of being together. Protégés are deprived of the mentoring relationship they need to develop and get ahead, and mentors are denied the experience of creativity, of generation, that they need in order to feel able to shape an institution's future and to create a personal legacy.

EEO has been an important tool in legitimizing the problem of racism, but it is insufficient. Based on the concept of the color-blind institution, it may paradoxically reinforce the power of the original taboo to silence reflection and inhibit thinking. We need to go beyond EEO and develop a social technology that will help blacks and whites more directly confront their history and the present. Only in this way can we create the corporation that truly supports and values pluralism.

Appendix: Description of the Research Project

The research result was based upon interviews with senior and junior parties to 22 cross-racial pairs. Three of these relationships took place outside the WRL Corporation. Through these interviews, data were yielded about 18 other cross-racial relationships. The interview study was part of a larger research project that included statistical analysis on survey data obtained for 486 mentoring pairs, 125 of which were cross-racial. Of these, all but 6 involved black protégés and white mentors or sponsors. Table 18–2 gives a breakdown of the focal interview pairs.

Table 18-2
Interview Pairs

Mentor/Sponsor	Protégé	Number
White Male	Black Female	3
White Female	Black Female	6
White Male	Black Male	9
White Female	Black Male	1
Black Male	White Female	2

Note

Acknowledgment: This discussion of taboos has benefited from several conversations with Larry Hirschhorn, who influenced me to use this term rather than a less provocative and, perhaps, less meaningful framing. For an extensive treatment of racial taboos, see Beth Day, *The Sexual Life between Blacks and Whites* (1974); Joel Kovel, *White Racism: A Psychohistory* (1970); and Angela Davis, *Women, Race, and Class* (1983).

References

Clawson, J. G. 1980. "Mentoring in Managerial Careers." In Brooklyn Derr, ed., *Work, Family, and Careers*. New York: Praeger.

Cox, T., and S. Nkomo. 1986. "Differential Performance Appraisal Criteria: A Field Study of Black and White Managers." *Group and Organization Studies* 11, no.2: 101–19.

Dalton, G., and P. M. Thompson. 1986. *Novations*. Glenville, Ill.: Scott, Foresman.

Davis, Angela. 1983. *Women, Race, and Class*. New York: Random House.

Davis, G., and G. Watson. 1982. *Black Life in Corporate America*. New York: Random House.

Day, Beth. 1974. *The Sexual Life between Blacks and Whites*. New York: Crowell, Apollo Editions.

Grier, W., and P. Cobbs. 1968. *Black Rage*. New York: Bantam.

Hirschhorn, L. 1988. *The Workplace Within: Psychodynamics of Organizational Life*. Cambridge, Mass.: MIT Press.

Jones, E. W., Jr. 1986. "Black Managers: The Dream Deferred." *Harvard Business Review*, May–June, pp. 84–93.

Kaplan, L. 1984. *Adolescence: A Farewell to Childhood*. New York: Simon and Schuster.

Kovel, Joel. 1970. *White Racism: A Psychohistory*. New York: Pantheon Press.

Kram, K. 1985. *Mentoring at Work*. Glenville, Ill.: Scott, Foresman.

Phillips, L. L. 1982. *Mentors and Protégés*. New York: Arden House.

Roche, G. R. 1977. "Much Ado about Mentors." *Harvard Business Review*, January, pp. 14–28.

Wells, L., and C. Jennings. 1983. "Black Career Advancement and White Reactions: Remnants of Herrenvolk Democracy and the Scandalous Paradox." In D. Vails-Webber and W. J. Potts, eds., *NTL Sunrise Seminars*. Arlington, Va.: NTL Institute.

19

Normal Accident at Three Mile Island

Charles Perrow

Accidents will happen, including ones in nuclear plants. But by and large, we believe accidents can be prevented through better training, equipment, or design, or their effects can be localized and minimized through safety systems. The accident at Three Mile Island (TMI) is being assessed in this fashion. The industry started a new training program, the equipment at the Babcock and Wilcox plants is being improved, the design has been modified, the utility chastised—all useful, if minor, steps. Furthermore, to nuclear proponents, such as Edward Teller, the accident proved that the effects can be localized and minimized. It is safe. No one has died as a direct result of radiation injuries in all the years of commercial nuclear plant operation.

But the accident at TMI was not a preventable one, and the amount of radiation vented into the atmosphere could easily have been much larger, and the core might have melted, rather than just being damaged. TMI was a "normal accident"; these are bound to occur at some plant at some time, and bound to occur again, even in the best of plants. It was preceded by at least sixteen other serious accidents or near accidents in the short life of nuclear energy in the United States, and we should expect about sixteen more in the next five years of operation—that is, in industry time, the next four hundred years of operation of the plants existing now and scheduled to come on stream.

Normal accidents emerge from the characteristics of the systems themselves. They cannot be prevented. They are unanticipated. It is not feasible to train, design, or build in such a way as to anticipate all eventualities in complex systems where the parts are tightly coupled. They are incomprehensible when they occur. That is why operators usually assume something else is happening, something that they understand, and act accordingly. Being incomprehensible, they are partially uncontrollable. That is why operator intervention is often irrelevant. Safety systems, backup systems, quality equipment, and good training all help prevent accidents and minimize catastrophe, but the complexity of systems outruns all controls.

Reprinted from *Society* 18, no. 5 (July–August 1981): 17–26, by permission of Transaction Publishers. Copyright © 1981 Transaction Publishers.

The normal accident has four noteworthy characteristics: signals, which provide warnings only in retrospect, making prevention difficult; multiple design and equipment failures, which are unavoidable since nothing is perfect; some operator error, which may be gross since operators are not perfect either, but generally is not even considered error until the logic of the accident is finally understood; and "negative synergy," wherein the sum of equipment, design, and operator errors is far greater than the consequences of each singly. The normal accident generally occurs in systems where the parts are highly interactive, or "tightly coupled," and the interaction amplifies the effects in incomprehensible, unpredictable, unanticipated, and unpreventable ways. When it occurs in high-risk systems, such as those dealing with toxic chemicals, radioactive materials, microwaves, recombinent DNA, transportation systems, and military adventures, the consequences can be catastrophic. Even a fairly benign system, such as electrical power distribution, can cause considerable harm.

No one who owns or runs a high-risk system wants to consider a classification scheme for accidents that includes a normal accident category. It would be an admission of liability, and for some unknown but finite period of time, an admission of inevitable disaster. The category takes on more meaning when contrasted to preferred ones. I will consider three major categories, although there are others. The best type of accident, for owners and managers, is the "unique" accident, such as the collapse of a building in a giant earthquake, or simultaneous heart attacks for the pilot and co-pilot of an airliner or bomber near a city. No reasonable protection is possible against freak accidents or Acts of God, so no liability can be assigned. They are so rare we need not fear them, and more important, even unreasonable expenditures will not produce a significant reduction in risk. Otherwise, we would build no dams, buildings, airplanes, or armies.

Nevertheless, the unique accident is sometimes contemplated for high-risk, long-lived systems. About halfway into the nuclear power age, it was required that the new plants be built to withstand large earthquakes and the impact of a jet airliner. But even here it was only the reactor building that was so guarded; the auxiliary buildings and the pipelines to it from the reactor building, essential for using radioactive liquids to cool the reactor core in an emergency, are generally not protected. It is easy to imagine the loss of both the main power and backup systems during an earthquake or even a storm. The designs, of course, have not been given destructive testing by actual earthquakes or falling planes. We missed a chance a few years ago when a Strategic Air Command Bomber, flying directly at a nuclear power plant in Michigan, crashed in a stupendous explosion just two miles short of the plant. The pilots at the nearby SAC base were routinely warned not to fly near or over the plant, though they routinely did, at 1000 feet, suggesting it would not have been a unique accident, after all, had it occurred two seconds later.

Because liability cannot be assigned, owners and managers cry "unique" when they can. Failing that, they move to the next most desirable category. This is the "discrete" accident—there was an equipment failure, but it could be corrected and it won't happen again. Generally, discrete accidents—which do occur, indeed are very plentiful in all human-machine systems, and nature itself—involve the failure of one piece of equipment, a limited design error, or an operator error. In a discrete accident, the system responds to that source of error without any significant synergistic developments. Backup systems and isolation devices come into play. While liability can be assigned (nothing should fail, no matter how complex the system), it is generally limited (things will fail, nothing is perfect). More important, the label of a discrete accident is comforting because the system will not be abandoned; it can easily or conceivably be fixed. It will even be "safer" afterwards than before, as with the nuclear power industry after each publicized accident.

At the press conference two months after TMI, Babcock and Wilcox, which built the reactor, argued that this was a discrete accident. There had been an instance of equipment failure, the pilot-operated relief valve, but it was the only instance of this and the system contained planned means to rectify the failure. The actual cause of the accident was the failure of the operators to follow correct procedures after the failure, they argued. If the operators had been on their toes it would have been a trivial event. As we shall see, there were multiple equipment failures, a major design error, and the operators did just what at least some of the experts, some months before, had said they should do. And the event was "mysterious" and "incomprehensible" even to Babcock and Wilcox experts at the site. But management prefers the discrete label to the one that suggests the complexity of the system is at fault.

Discrete accidents allow for operator intervention; the accident itself is comprehensible—someone made a mistake; the equipment failed; the design did not allow for this eventuality—so something can be done. They can also be prevented (to the extent that accidents ever can) by noting warning signals, by using backup or safety systems, and, of course, by rectifying the problem after the accident. Liability can be assessed, but our system of governance and our judicial system is lenient in this regard; "it won't happen again, sir."

The most troublesome category of accidents, both for owners and managers and for the theorist, is the "calculated risk" accident. Liability, where risk is calculated, could easily be assigned, so owners and managers avoid any admissions of calculation, and prefer the categories of unique or, failing that, discrete accidents. Theorists have troubles, too, since on the one hand there is a sense in which a calculation is made of every known risk, making the category vacuous, and on the other hand, there are presumably many unknown risks in complex systems, so calculations are not possible, again rendering the category vacuous. Between these two extremes (more could be done to prevent it since calculations are made, and nothing could be done to prevent it since some things will be incalculable) is a messy but useful area.

Reportedly, the fire that killed the astronauts on the launch pad was considered to be possible, but the level of safety deemed acceptable was below the level of this possibility, so the risk was run. Once it happened, the system was redesigned, perhaps because of the unfortunate publicity rather than a reassessment of the risk calculations, just as the still unburned Pintos were recalled once the government intervened in the private calculation of risk. However, our country was built on risk, as we are hearing lately.

Nuclear proponents are fond of saying that all imaginable risks have been calculated; indeed, they cite this as a major reason for the escalation in plant costs. However, substantial risks that are considered too high to run in new nuclear plants, and thus must be designed out of them, are left to simmer in old plants. In an important decision in 1973, the Atomic Energy Commission ruled that it would not be necessary to "retrofit" existing plants and those to be licensed for the next four years with a backup SCRAM system (an emergency system to halt reactivity). It was economically prohibitive. The Three Mile Island plant lacked a backup emergency core cooling system (ECCS) that is required of newer plants, just as the early ones, such as at Indian Point, New York, require *none*. As we shall see, however, it probably would not have made any difference in the TMI accident.

As suggested, this category is a messy one, open to debate after the fact and hidden from view before it. In any case, the tendency is to classify accidents as unique events, or discrete accidents, rather than calculated risks. Calculated risk accidents that we are able to learn about are generally cataclysmic (that is why we know of them), and thus, like unique accidents, operator intervention is negligible and synergistic effects are irrelevant, though probably present in those few seconds of disaster.

Warnings

Complex human-machine systems abound in warnings—signs in red letters, flashing lights, horns sounding, italicized passages in training manuals and operating instructions, decals on equipment, analyses of faults in technical reports, and a light snowfall of circulars and alerts. Warnings are embedded in construction codes, testing apparatus, maintenance checks, and, of course, fire drills. All personnel are expected to be only indifferently attentive and concerned, so training, drills, reports, and alarms are repetitive, numbing, essential parts of these systems.

Warnings work; but not all the time. We should not be surprised; the very volume of warning devices testifies to this likelihood. If warnings were heeded, we would need only a few modest and tasteful ones rather than a steady drill of admonitions punctuated by alarms and lights.

Yet we stand incredulous when confronted with, for example, the same engine on the same DC-10 aircraft failing twice within a few months (one fatality—a passenger sucked out of the plane); or the cargo doors of DC-10s, after repeated warnings, blowing open three times (the third time a fully loaded plane crashed and all died); or an accident at Three Mile Island that seemed to be almost a simulation of two previous accidents at other plants and fulfilled the predictions of an engineer's hypothetical analysis. Why are warnings not always heeded? There are many reasons, and when we consider the overpopulation of complex, high-risk systems that someone has decided we cannot live without, they are disturbing.

Consider three categories of warnings. First, there are deviations from steady-state conditions that do not activate significant alarms. There was rather a long list of these at Three Mile Island, to be considered later. Each one individually is considered trivial or interpreted in a routine framework. Only hindsight discloses the meaning of these deviations. Second, there are alarms, such as flashing lights or circuit breaker trips or dials reading in the red zone. But operators are accustomed to reinterpreting these alarms as insignificant when they have a conception of the problem which triggered them. Or if the operators have no conception of the problem, the alarm may be attributed to faulty alarm equipment. Since dials sometimes give faulty readings or breakers trip for no good reason even under routine conditions, and since disturbed conditions can create misleading alarms through malfunctioning or complex interactions, the operators may be correct. Alarms, like deviations, always outnumber actual accidents; warnings are in greater supply than actual malfunctions. "If we shut down for every little thing . . . ," the reasoning goes.

Past accidents, mute predictors of future ones, form the third category of warnings. But history is no guide for highly infrequent events. They are not expected to occur again; generally, they don't. Or, there may be compelling economic reasons for continuing to run the risk—as with the DC-10 cargo doors prior to the fatal crash near Paris. Past accidents also fail as warnings if the warning is available to only one part of the system, and that part is only loosely connected to the other parts. This was a major problem at TMI.

Any single plant with a complex technology is likely to be tightly coupled; a disturbance in one part will reverberate quickly to the other parts. But the plant may be only loosely coupled with other parts of its system. Warnings from another plant may not reach it; the mechanisms for transmitting such warnings in the case of nuclear power plants are reasonably redundant and plentiful—the Nuclear Regulatory Commission, the reactor builders, numerous institutes, university centers, and industry bodies all function in this capacity. Indeed, in a crisis, the system comes together tightly; it responded exceptionally well to the TMI accident. They knew that the future of nuclear power was at stake. But under normal conditions they have an interest in minimizing the dangers that exist, avoiding costly shut-downs, and carrying out their separate organizational concerns. These interests buffer the part of the system that experiences a disturbance from the other parts, unless the disturbance is very large and widely publicized. In such a manner TMI was buffered from a technical report prepared by an engineer at another utility, a somewhat similar accident in Europe, and a very similar accident in an adjacent state. All constituted unheeded warnings.

The technical report was prepared by Caryle Michelson, an engineer with the Tennessee Valley Authority, which was considering the purchase of a reactor from Babcock and Wilcox, one quite similar to the two reactors at TMI. Michelson wrote a long memo raising a number of concerns, including a remarkably prescient description of the dynamics of the TMI accident; a LOCA occurs (a loss of coolant accident), a high-pressure injection system (HPI) goes on to maintain pressure in one part of the system, the pressurizer. The pressure rises there, but falls in the reactor core for complex reasons. The operators fear over-pressurizing the pressurizer, because it might "go solid" (become saturated with water and/or steam). Going solid is to be avoided, since it means the reactor must be shut down if it isn't already (SCRAM, or inserting graphite control rods to stop the fission process), and even if it is already, it takes a long time to get it back in operation after going solid, and the utility loses money because it must buy electricity rather than make it. So they "throttle back" on the HPI, but this means less cooling of the reactor core and could lead, in minutes, to damage to the core and even a meltdown.

Michelson's report was sent to the NRC in November 1977; a reply acknowledged they understood the problem, but they kept it to themselves. In April 1978, eleven months before the accident, it was sent to the vendors, Babcock and Wilcox (B&W). There it received normal handling. The engineers read it, considered it, and wrote a reply nine months later, two months before TMI, stating that these matters had all been considered. We do not know what happened to it at the NRC; it seems to have disappeared in their vast files.

Meanwhile, on September 24, 1977, a LOCA occurred at the Davis-Besse plant near Toledo, Ohio. The operators throttled back on the HPI when they saw the pressure in the pressurizer rising, even though it was falling in the core. Fortunately, the plant was operating at only about nine percent capacity, and in a short time they discovered the cause of the accident—a faulty Pilot Operated Relief Valve (PORV)—and bypassed it before any damage to the core occurred. An engineer from B&W, Mr. Kelley, was sent to the plant to investigate the accident. Returning to B&W he gave a seminar on the accident, warning about the improper operator action of throttling the HPI system prematurely, and then wrote a memo suggesting that all units using this kind of equipment be warned about this improper action.

Mr. Kelley's superior, Mr. Dunn, took up the matter and had his memo sent around B&W. Only one engineer responded, and he misunderstood it and dismissed it. Dunn persisted, and the memo, now fathered by a Mr. Novack, made a slow ascent. It was sent over to that division of B&W concerned with customer services, to Mr. Karrasch. He said he gave it to two subordinates, but they do not recall ever seeing it. It was sent there because customer service is traditionally concerned about anything that might unduly interrupt service, and since going solid would, they should review it. (Kelley-Dunn-Novack were concerned about the far more dangerous matter of core damage and meltdown.) No word came from Karrasch, so Novack kept calling. Months went by, and still no answer as to whether they should alert all utilities to this danger. Meanwhile the training department had assured Kelley-Dunn-Novack the operators were, indeed, instructed to not throttle back on HPI in a LOCA, even though they had at Davis-Besse.

Finally, a Mr. Walters met Karrasch at the water cooler and asked about the memo from his people on the engineering side. Karrasch replied, off-handedly, something to the effect that "it's okay, no problem." Mr. Walters pondered the reply as Mr. Karrasch hurried off to a meeting—did it mean there was no problem of going solid, or no problem of uncovering the core, or what? He left the matter hanging. It all came out after the operators at TMI throttled back on the HPI and made a serious accident even more serious. Nineteen months had transpired since Kelly first wrote his memo. B&W then quickly sent out the Kelley-Dunn-Novack memo to all units using this equipment.

To the members of the President's Commission on the Accident at Three Mile Island, this was the familiar curse of a failure in communication, the phlogiston of organizational problems and of many disasters. Warnings were not made available to the proper people; Karrasch, at the least, had failed to communicate with the engineers. Karrasch was more perceptive, if aggressively defensive. There was no failure in communication he insisted; the matter was simply one of low priority. He then went on to suggest the several obvious high-priority matters his office was dealing with, ones forced upon them, the implication runs, by new and pressing NRC safety standards. He was right. Everyone at B&W did what they were supposed to do, with both the Michelson and Kelley memos. Only in retrospect had they assigned the wrong priority. In retrospect we often do.

How many warnings can one heed? The best set of warnings lie among the 2000 Licensee Event Reports (LERs) that are sent by the utilities to the NRC every year. These are required by law, and report significant events that might affect safety. The NRC has gagged on them; no reasonable system for analyzing them exists. The utilities dutifully report these and they sink into the enormous file. What would the operators, even if they were college-trained engineers, do with a steady stream of reports, memos, instructions, analyses that they would be required to remember for years on end, use rarely, and recall instantly in a complex emergency? Only if it had been remembered, along with all the other instructions that continually change, and more important, only if the operators had known it was this type of accident they were experiencing. As we shall see, they did not. Even the experts who were quickly at the scene did not know soon enough.

It is not clear that the system should be more tightly coupled so that warnings, for one thing, should travel faster and create their intended "perturbances." Were the TVA, NRC, Battelle Institute, Brookhaven Labs, university departments, Electric Power Research Institute, Oak Ridge Laboratories, Westinghouse, Combustion Engineering, Babcock and Wilcox, Davis-Besse and TMI and some seventy other plants all wired together into one low resistance circuit, the number of untoward events and immense complexities lying in the nuclear industry would drown them all in signals. Loosely coupled systems have slack, reserve time, and resources. One part of a system can be made to withstand the brunt of a disturbance and protect the others from incessant shocks. Parts can be isolated and even left to fend for themselves. Information is absorbed, summarized, compacted into bits of information in one part that can be sent to the others without inundating them. Centralization is avoided, innovation encouraged.

Such loosely coupled systems are resistant to change from the outside, however. By focusing upon TMI, the President's Commission unwittingly reinforced the survival values of loosely coupled systems—the utility was segregated from the industry, and reprimanded. Indian Point, with its old equipment grandfathered from safety requirements, perched upwind of the millions in the New York metropolitan area, is buffered. Better equipment and training and management at TMI will supposedly take care of the problem, along with a single-headed rather than hydra-headed NRC and some "new attitudes" there. Operators will be flooded with new warnings. But it is normal for the systems to have accidents; warnings cannot affect the normal accident. Tight coupling encourages normal accidents, with their highly interdependent synergistic aspects, but loose coupling muffles warnings.

Whether systems are loosely or tightly coupled, they all face another problem with warnings—the signal to noise ratio. Only after the event, when we construct imaginative (and frequently dubious) explanations of what went wrong, does some of the noise reveal itself as a signal. The operators at TMI had literally to turn off alarms; so many of them were sounding and blinking that signals passed into noise. The extremely detailed log of the accident (accurate to the tenth of a second) put out by B&W performs this merciful winnowing task for us now, selecting out the noise and giving us the signal, with the unspoken admonition "see this reading; *that* was significant." Noisy systems illustrate the banality of the normal accident.

Complex systems are simply not responsive to warnings of unimaginable or highly unlikely accidents. Because they are complex, organizational routines must be carefully followed and off-standard events reinterpreted in routine frameworks. Fortuitous events are always more plentiful than unfortuitous ones, Murphy's law notwithstanding. Most things that go wrong do not matter; the redundancies are plentiful. The "mind-set" that the commissioners referred to so often in their discussions with witnesses allows organizations to go forth without an agony of choice over every contingency. The phrase "I'll believe it when I see it" is misleading, an organizational theorist, Karl Weick notes; it is equally true that "I'll see it when I believe it." The warning of an incomprehensible and unimaginable event cannot be seen, because it cannot be believed. But since it is inconceivable that there were not warnings, investigators, congressional committees, and the superiors of hapless operators dig among the wreckage until they find what can pass for an unheeded warning. But the normal accident is unforeseeable; its "warnings" are socially constructed.

Design and Equipment Failure

It is obvious that designs cannot be perfect or fail-safe, nor can equipment. Everything dangerous would be far too expensive to build and maintain if we required maximum state-of-the-art efforts in equipment and design. Some risk must be run if we wish to have nuclear plants, rail and air transportation, chemical fertilizers, large buildings, military raids, and so on. Even nearly fanatic efforts to reduce risks are insufficient. Given the robustness of most industrial systems, equipment and design failures are not likely to be catastrophic; though they are obviously heavily involved in the 5000 or so industrial-accident deaths we produce in the United States each year. Failures might be catastrophic in high-risk industries, such as the nuclear power industry, especially when the failures are multiple and interacting. Multiple and interacting equipment and design failures abounded in the case of the TMI incident, and several other nuclear accidents or near accidents.

The major piece of equipment failure at TMI was the pilot operated relief valve (PORV). It stuck open. The event was not without prior warnings. There were at least eleven other failures of this key valve at other plants before TMI, including Davis-Besse. The valve had failed once before in TMI Unit 2, and some corrections had been made, but they were obviously insufficient. Furthermore, prior to that failure, it was not possible for the control room operator easily to determine whether the valve was open or closed. After the initial failure, a parsimonious step was taken. A signal was installed, but it only indicated whether a signal was sent to the valve to open or close it, not whether it was actually open or closed. In the March 1979 accident, the indicator said it was closed, while in actuality it was open. Furthermore, the valve had been leaking for some weeks, making check readings from the drain pipe attached to the valve unreliable.

The valve is a particularly crucial one in the pressurized water reactor design of B&W, since the steam generators may boil dry very rapidly—in two or three minutes—rather than slowly, as in the boiling water reactor design built by other firms (15 minutes in one design, and 30 in another). This instance of tight coupling makes core uncovery more likely, though B&W officials argue that it also provides advantages in other kinds of accidents. It also has the distinct commercial advantage of allowing the reactor to continue operating even if the turbine shuts down, thus minimizing expensive down-time.

This advantage was removed after TMI when B&W, following discussions with the NRC, reduced dependence upon this critical valve by having the reactor shut down whenever the turbine tripped. In testimony, a B&W official was reluctant to say that this corrective action signified a design problem in the original B&W equipment, but it would appear to indicate quite a significant one. Thus, there were several warnings, insufficient corrective action, a major failure, and only then, a design change in the system (not the valve).

There were other equipment failures during the accident. Paper jammed in the computer printout, and to get the printout operating, considerable data logging had to be sacrificed. The computer was presumably not designed to handle the volume of a major accident and was one and half hours behind in its printout at one point. There was an error in the instrumentation for the level indicator in the miscellaneous waste holding tank. A check valve was faulty and it let water into the condensate polisher system; this had been noticed before, but the attempt at correcting it had not succeeded. This particular failure probably started the whole accident, but in normal accidents the particular trigger is relatively insignificant; the interaction is significant.

There were serious leaks—the source of which was still unknown some weeks after the accident—in the venting system, allowing unintended radioactive releases to the atmosphere. A safety system was not used because it was not safe; it could easily leak. This was the normal backup system for cooling the reactor by returning liquid from the auxiliary building. Because it could not be trusted, poisonous gas was vented directly into the auxiliary building (and then went to the atmosphere) in a controversial decision, which produced the large radioactive puff. Several people (including a utility official from Metropolitan Edison) testified that leaks in this "safety" system made it a dangerous procedure. That a safety system would be too dangerous to use suggests both a design and equipment failure of some magnitude.

Numerous items were not working at the time of the accident or had failed in the recent weeks. The auxiliary building sump tank had blown a rupture disc some weeks prior to the accident; operators were bypassing the tank (there are no regulations that prohibit this). It complicated the intervention efforts. One operator testified that the plant had tripped twice before in connection with the condensate polishers. In addition, two weeks before the accident there had been a "sizable leak" in the air lines going to the polisher. A pump came on "inadvertently" about a month before the accident, was bypassed, and was still awaiting repair at the time of the accident. Three auxiliary feedwater pumps had been taken out of commission two weeks before the accident and left out, in violation of federal regulations.

There was not just a single piece of equipment failure that might have been bypassed, but equipment failure (and design problems) on a level that should cause concern even in a less deadly, non-nuclear plant, and the presence of warning signals that were not heeded. But the important point is not that Metropolitan Edison was particularly derelict, but that such a state of affairs is fairly normal in complex industrial and military systems. Ammonia plants, a mature part of the chemical industry, had an average failure rate of 10 to 11 shutdowns per year; 50 days of down-time per year; 1 fire per plant every 11 months. The nuclear power industry is extremely safety conscious, compared to most industrial concerns, but it will still have problems such as these, as the large number of accidents indicate. Equipment failures, like accidents, are normal, though not frequent.

Operator Error

From the beginning it was widely believed that operator error was the fundamental cause of the TMI accident. B&W flatly stated this, as did the British Secretary of State of Energy, who cited the cause of the accident as "stupid errors." The conclusion was attributed to the Nuclear Regulatory Commission by the press. The President's Commission on Three Mile Island, in their final report, blamed everyone, but most particularly the operators. They twice note that "the major cause of the accident was due to inappropriate actions by those who were operating the plant and supervising that operation," though problems of design, training, and procedures contributed to operator failure. But they also feel "they should have known" that they were in a Loss of Coolant Accident, "failed to realize" that various problems were due to a LOCA, and were "oblivious" for over four hours to the threat of uncovering the core. (A report prepared by outside consultants, the Essex Corporation, for the Nuclear Regulatory Commission, came to a different conclusion, one that deliberately distinguished the causes of human errors themselves: "The primary conclusion reached on the basis of this investigation was that the human errors experienced during the TMI incident were not due to operator deficiencies, but rather to inadequacies in equipment design, information presentation, emergency procedures and training."

It is not comforting that the most blatant operator error at TMI (though not, it is said, an important cause of the accident) is the one least susceptible to remedial action by educational requirements or training programs. After a routine testing procedure, two valves which were closed for the check were left closed rather than opened. Perhaps some people are more likely to lock themselves out of their houses or cars than others, but educational degrees and training would hardly seem to account for the variations. Such things simply happen. Operating personnel testified that with one or two thousand valves in the plant (making checks on every valve every shift unrealistic) one will expect to find one or two out of position for no good reason at times. One operator testified to personal knowledge of two in the previous year, and about five in the short history of TMI Unit 2.

Some valves are so important that they are locked, and a locked valve book is maintained; but an operator testified that it is "sometimes" not kept up to date. A valve that is checked every shift was once found open despite the check at the beginning of the shift. The problem is aggravated by engineering design where, presumably to save money, indicators do not tell whether the valve is actually open or closed, but only the position of the switch that is supposed to open or close it. Such designs create opportunities for operator error. One minor accident at TMI was caused by an operator inadvertently bumping into some switches while investigating a problem. Not only are there a large number of valves, but frequent testing and maintenance routines require them to be placed in non-normal positions for varying periods of time. Valves in wrong positions have caused and contributed to accidents in other nuclear plants. As long as eternal vigilance is a desideratum rather than a reality, the valve position will continue to cause or greatly complicate nuclear plant accidents.

Errors of judgment by operators are more difficult to analyze (and thus more easy to attribute) because the judgment becomes an error only after the fact. Most cases of operator error in normal accidents are "retrospective errors." Presumably many decisions are made that would be classified as errors according to the books or the training programs, but if they work or cause no problem they will be unnoticed, and thus not lead to a revision of standard procedures. If they work, they are in effect being misclassified as errors by virtue of erroneous procedures in the manuals. The cards are stacked in favor of a declaration of operator error, for operators will not be credited with successful actions which violate procedures, but only charged with those that result in investigated accidents. To aggravate the problem, the system and its procedures are not generally under review, only the operators.

More important, though, is the context of judgment errors. A high pressure spike in the reactor was noted because it automatically brought on a safeguard system. But the operator testified, regarding the spike, that "we kind of wrote it off at the time as possibly instrument malfunction of some sort." This was not an unreasonable conclusion, since instruments *were* malfunctioning. "We did not have a firm conclusion" regarding the spike, he went on, since it appeared and went away with such rapidity. Information about the spike was not widely disseminated at this time because it was neither believed nor understood (though a Senate investigation revealed that at least one person drew the correct conclusion at the time). Such is the common fate of novel signals in normal accidents.

The most significant error, by all accounts, was the failure to maintain the high pressure injection (HPI) system. But consider the context, and the matter of organizational routines and goals. Available readings indicated no problem with the level of coolant in the core; at the time it was not even clear what kind of a Loss of Coolant Action (LOCA) this was. These readings were misleading because of vaporization in the core, but that information was not available. There was no direct way to read the water level in the core, and one B&W official was reluctant to encourage having such an indicator because it would increase other problems (a typical interdependency problem in complex systems). Unaware that there was a danger of uncovering the core, the key danger in nuclear plants, the operators focused upon another danger of considerable magnitude—going "solid" in the pressurizer. They were faced with contradictory indicators. (Even a B&W officer, who blamed the accident upon the operator error of cutting back on the HPI system, said the indicators put on "a mysterious performance.") Pressure was low in the core, but it was thought to be adequately covered, while pressure in the pressurizing vessel was high and getting higher. As the B&W official put it, the pressurizer level should have been going down, but it was coming up, and high pressure injection only *aggravated* it, he added.

The operators did what the Davis-Besse operators had done in a similar accident; they throttled the HPI system back to about half level to prevent going solid. Going solid can cause serious damage to parts of the system, and can easily be avoided by manually overriding the HPI system, and cutting it back. The fear of the operators was shared by some experts at B&W and at least one in the NRC. The reason the Kelley-Dunn-Novack memo was held up and debated so many months was that B&W experts feared that keeping the HPI system on in almost identical circumstances would result in going solid. Subsequent to the accident, experts changed their mind and released the new instructions.

The key problem remains, however. It is not always possible to know just what kind of a LOCA one is in, and when the memo will apply. As one commission member noted, the decision to cut back on HPI has to be taken *before* one can know that it would be the wrong decision, and the B&W engineer testifying agreed. The new instructions may not solve the problem at all, except that they weigh heavily in favor of a more conservative course of action, risking going solid rather than uncovering the core. (In fact, the new instructions proved to be dangerous when followed at another plant several months later, and were revised back to something closer to pre-TMI instructions.)

There were other errors. Operators thought the complex pathways for radioactive wastes led to one tank, but they in fact led to another, which overflowed. The plumbing is so complex that scientists on the President's Commission could not read the tiny details in the chart when trying to trace out parts of the system. A technician was taking a sample to test for radioactivity. The reason they knew the liquid was not radioactive was that he got some of it on his hands, and then they checked *him* for exposure! The operators read on-line display indications of temperatures of 230°, whereas the computer printout (delayed an hour or so) indicated a much more serious 285°, which would have led to a different course of action. (It seems likely here that the operators misread the indicator because a higher figure was not congruent with the interpretation they were working under and which made most "sense"—a common attribute of normal accident behavior.) A supervisor testified he believed there was significant core damage the morning of the accident (Wednesday), but he did not mention this to anyone else at the plant when he talked by phone or when he came in the next day; other plant personnel (and the arriving experts) reportedly did not reach this conclusion until late Thursday, early Friday, or even the next week in the case of some Metropolitan Edison officials. The supervisor testified it would not have made any difference if people had been aware of significant damage, but this is hard to believe. Significant events such as the pressure spike and extreme thermocouple readings of core temperatures were not communicated to key personnel—because they were simply not believed.

The most serious case of possible operator error was the decision to vent radioactive gases (producing the puff and plume over the plant that almost triggered evacuation orders). An NRC officer in the control room at the time believed the venting was the automatic result of excess pressure; the supervisor who ordered it said it was an intended venting, with the concurrence of the NRC officer and prior warnings to civil defense personnel. Most people, including some officials of Met. Ed. and B&W and the NRC, believe that after the "puff" the valve was closed—the pressure having been relieved. But the supervisor testified that after the puff the valve was left open for days, since the level of radioactivity fell off rapidly in the next few minutes.

Defending the venting, the supervisor claimed that he was running low on water being used to cool the system. (A B&W official testified there was plenty of water.) He wanted that water in case the core heated up. (This is puzzling, since he was also sure that the core was stable two days before and had remained stable; indeed, everyone was sure.) He did not trust the backup safety system since its packing and valves might leak if it had to be used to cool the core should the core happen to become unstable. The pressure in the tank had been relieved several times by the previous shift supervisor by brief ventings, and by the present supervisor himself in his shift. Worried about his water reserve, and about the safety system, he decided to try what can only be called a large vent, and when the radioactivity did not continue at a high rate, it became a permanent vent. (Since there are some ambiguities in the published Staff Reports of the Commission, it seems possible that much more radioactive material was released than has been acknowledged. But this is only a possibility.)

Negative Synergy

Of such complexities are normal accidents made. Even in this most studied and documented piece of complex organizational behavior, the testimony is contradictory and the reasoning, elusive. Safety systems are not considered safe; cores are stable but are not considered stable so radioactive venting is risked in a large dose; the supervisor calls civil defense to alert them to the venting and they think he has said that the island is being evacuated, and so on. The closer normal accidents are studied, the more they reveal their potentials for even greater disasters. This is why, after close scrutiny, one can always say, no matter how serious the accident, "it was just luck that saved it from being worse."

Synergy is a buzz word in business management circles, indicating that the whole is more than the sum of its parts, or in their congenial familiarity, two plus two equals five. But minus two plus minus two can equal minus five thousand in tightly coupled, complex, high-risk military and industrial systems. This article has given repeated examples of negative synergy where complex, unanticipated, unperceived, and incomprehensible interactions of off-standard components (equipment, design, and operator actions) threaten disaster.

The observation is hardly novel; engineers frequently test for multiple failures and design against them. But it is significant that in possibly the most dangerous of all our industries, nuclear power generation, there are just two official categories of accidents, simple and complex, and only the first is used in training, since it is impossible to train for the second.

Operator training for accidents is based upon "design-based accidents," that is, those accidents that are anticipated and guarded against through plant design. If one part of the system fails—emergency feedwater, power outage, etc.—a backup system or a means of isolating faulty equipment and bringing other equipment into service is provided for. (This is akin to a "discrete" accident.) What the industry calls a "worst case" accident is one where there are failures not anticipated in the design, and no obvious or tested emergency procedures are available. (This is akin to normal accident.) Multiple-failure accidents are generally "worst case" accidents, because design-based accidents generally anticipate only one major cause. One author notes that "practically all of the reactor accidents that have occurred in the past have been multiple-failure accidents." Multiple-failure accidents are not simulated in training. The number of possible multiple-cause accidents is nearly limitless.

"Normal" accidents, in my terminology, are largely multiple failure accidents, or "worst case" accidents. They are infrequent, but far from rare. The more complex the system, the more likely they are to occur. They may, of course, have a single source; it is not the case that there have to be two or more *simultaneous* equipment or operator failures. But the single source leads to further events which are unanticipated and often unimaginable.

An indication of complexity at TMI is provided by this quote from one supervisor: "I think we knew we were experiencing something different, but I think each time we made a decision it was based on something we knew about. For instance: pressure was low, but they had opened the feed valves quickly in the steam generator, and they thought that might have been 'shrink.' There was logic at that time for most of the actions, even though today you can look back and say, well, that wasn't the cause of that, or, that shouldn't have been that long."

All operators and supervisors testified to experiencing a very unusual situation, and there are repeated indications that an attempt was made to force these situations into normal, routine explanations—the kind called for by the emphasis upon "design-based accidents." This is the significance of the widely reported comment by the NRC commissioners that if only they had a simple, understandable thing like a pipe break they would know what to do, and the (presumably joking) remark that perhaps they should arrange for one since there were standard procedures for handling it.

Testimony from operators as to why discharges were in one tank rather than another, involving back flows, spillovers, a previously ruptured and unrepaired disc, speculation as to the source of water in the sumps, concerns about whether to keep it in the containment building or the auxiliary building, and so on indicate just one part of the system that was difficult to visualize or conceptualize. This was only one of several parts of the system the operators were attempting to deal with and coordinate.

There is unfortunately a good reason for limiting training to design-based accidents rather than normal ones. As the power and size and complexity of plants increase, the permutations will increase geometrically, and so will the perturbations making protection humanly impossible. The recommendation (by Hans Bethe, for one) to marry fusion processes with fission processes in order to extend the life of current fission plants will extend the possible perturbations unimaginably.

The confluence of events is not limited to multiple equipment failures, of course. These will interact with expected operator errors. Equipment or design failures are likely to *elicit* operator errors because they are responding to expected, or routine scenarios, and will misinterpret the unexpected signals. There are several instances of not believing the signals in the TMI accident, and given the occasional unreliability of instrumentation, this is to be expected. When faced with ambiguous events and signals, operators can be expected to construct interpretations around familiar readings, dynamics, and routines, and will have the latitude to discount signals and construct interpretations. But of course, it is the novel interactions, the unexpected, the unimagined, that form the basis of a normal accident. Operators, then, are not conditioned to look for the novel explanation, and training in design failures reinforces the tendency to avert a glance into the unknown. The permutations referred to above make training for novelty, for the normal accident, exceedingly difficult. Prosaic failures—valves left closed, a valve failing to close though the indicator says it has, water in the condensate polisher system—quickly interact to produce the fourth and final characteristic of normal accidents: synergistic effects which are negative for the system and beyond the reach of training and experience.

Future Alternatives

All sorts of things will reduce the risk of discrete and calculated-risk nuclear accidents—revamping the NRC; better operator training, testing, and qualifications; closing of plants near large cities. A meaningful liability system would help. Financial risks from accidents need not be passed on to the rate payer in higher rates, or the public in general through the Price-Anderson Act, which limits the liability of the utility and passes it on to the taxpayer. In addition, warnings help. Some designs are demonstrably safer than others. The Navy may pay more attention to quality control than the private businesses that run most of our utility plants.

But normal accidents, whose origins lie fallow and simmer in the very complexity of the interactive system, waiting upon some failure of equipment, design, or operator action to give them their brief, fierce life, cannot be eliminated. Indeed, they grow with the complexity of the system, including the complexity added by the safety features.

Normal accidents are more likely to be perceived in folk expressions than they are in the technical studies of the labs, the NRC journal *Nuclear Safety,* or the literature on the regulatory process and the sins of the old Atomic Energy Commission. The average person, when she resignedly invokes Murphy's law (if anything can go wrong it will), or notes that "for want of a nail the shoe was lost, for want of a shoe the horse was lost . . . ," or mutters the ubiquitous blanket phrase "accidents will happen," is closer to the truth than the experts. The dominant theme for the experts is the accident that can be prevented by design—"design-based accidents" as they are perversely called. This is what the literature covers. A newer, subdominant theme, popularized by the President's Commission, is the "man-machine" interface, and the lack of attention to the "man." But neither theme is responsive to the key characteristic of tightly coupled, complex, high-risk systems that we pride ourselves on. Synergistic effects of a negative nature are bound to occur. Warnings will not prevent them, nor training, nor equipment and design changes, and intervention is limited.

The defenders of nuclear power are correct that "no energy source can be completely safe." The President's Commission agreed; the only thing to do is to make the risk tolerable. But the degree of risk and the level of toleration have not been tested. The industry is young. The catastrophic potentials—e.g., 100,000 immediate deaths, a poisoned land—have not been given a fair chance to be realized. Unanticipated, unpreventable, incomprehensible, uncontrollable accidents in high-risk systems are sufficiently rare to give us another five or ten years of grace. Then we shall see what is tolerable.

There are always alternatives to systems with catastrophic potential. Periodic, low-cost flooding of sparsely settled flood plains adjacent to rivers is less costly and dangerous than huge dams that tower over densely settled flood plains that people come to consider safe. The argument that "we must have dams" is insubstantial; we can live elsewhere. Our energy crisis does not require building Liquified Natural Gas ships that are the length of three football fields, with control panels that have to be as complicated as those in a nuclear plant. Most of the toxic substances we inevitably spew about are not essential to our lives, but only to private profits or war machines. At the very least let us consider including the externalities, real and potential, in the costs of these goods and services. Thus, for example, each propane gas truck in a city should pay insurance to cover the cost of blowing up a few office and apartment buildings when the truck crashes, the gas flows into the sewers for two or three minutes and spreads, and then is ignited by someone's cigarette near the scene of the accident.

Nuclear plants produce about twelve percent of the United States electrical power now, but we have over twice as much excess peak-demand power standing by in non-nuclear facilities that could be put to use instead. The potential of both conservation and the various forms of solar energy was completely unexpected by most experts and officials.

Decentralized, loosely coupled, low-risk alternatives abound. In these, a serious normal accident does not lie incubating. We get only the irritating but tolerable foul-ups that plague our daily life and our organizations.

20

The Department of Defense and the Military-Industrial Establishment: The Politics of the Iron Triangle

Gordon Adams

Introduction

Since World War II, the United States has maintained large, permanent military forces and a global network of security commitments. Despite occasional criticism of national commitments and the level of defense spending—for example, the disarmament movement of the 1960s and the opposition to the Vietnam War—a large military-industrial/national security establishment remains a constant feature of the American political landscape. This establishment, cloaked in national security, seems impervious to criticism and change.

The advent of the Reagan administration brought a dramatic increase in the size and scope of American national security policy. The sudden rapid growth in defense spending caused vocal criticism of defense policies and spending practices. The national debate over defense spending has provided a new opportunity to examine the defense policy process, to view its resistance to outside interference and change, and to explore new directions for American national security policy.

The size and rapid growth of defense spending since 1980 is clear. Between fiscal years 1980 and 1984, the defense budget will have doubled in current dollars and increased 40 percent in constant dollars. In 1984 alone, the defense budget of $270 billion will cost the average American household over $3,000, while the administration's five-year spending plan of $1.6 trillion will cost each household $20,000. By 1988, under current plans, the defense budget will have virtually tripled in current dollars in only eight years.

This rapid growth in spending is unprecedented since 1945. The Reagan military buildup has been the most dramatic peacetime increase in defense spending this nation has experienced. By 1985, defense spending will be at a higher constant dollar level than at any point since the Second World War.

Moreover, defense has become the largest single commitment of taxpayer funds. Roughly 50 percent of each income tax dollar funds military programs: the Defense Department, nuclear warhead programs in the Department of Energy, a part of the National Aeronautics and Space Administration (NASA) spending that serves military purposes, the Veterans Administration, and some proportion of the interest on the national debt incurred as a result of past military spending.[1] In addition, defense spending is a significant portion of federal purchases and research spending. The Defense Department buys 75 percent of all goods and services purchased by the federal government. Moreover, of the roughly $45 billion the federal government spends annually on research and development, 70 percent goes to military-related research and development.

The Reagan administration's commitment to unprecedented peacetime growth in defense spending also encountered widespread domestic and international criticism, opening up the debate about national security. The call for a bilateral nuclear weapons freeze, once a fringe appeal, was supported by as much as 75 percent of the American people, was approved by popular referenda in nine states and many cities, and was endorsed by the United States House of Representatives and by many Democratic politicians. Specific weapons such as the MX missile, mainstay of the Defense Department's effort to build a new generation of nuclear weapons, have been a target of vocal criticism.

This growing critique of defense policy forced the administration, deeply skeptical of arms control, into new arms control talks with the Soviet Union and brought new conflict to an Atlantic Alliance severely divided over the wisdom of deploying new intermediate-range nuclear weapons on European soil. In addition, Americans have grown concerned about the continuing crisis in Central America, persistent problems in the Middle East, and upheavals in the rest of the developing world that could lead to commitment of American troops to overseas combat.

Criticism also has focused on the efficiency of military spending and its impact on the American economy. Repeated investigations of defense spending have exposed flagrant wastefulness and problems with weapon performance—from the M-1 tank that won't drive, to the Bradley amphibious infantry fighting vehicle that can't float, to the four-cent diodes for F-18 simulators that are being bought for $110.[2] These criticisms are heard from conservative (Heritage Foundation), bureaucratic (Defense Department), and liberal (Brookings Institution) voices. They warn that the cost of weapons and the defense budget are out of control and that a crushing bill is mounting—with fearsome consequences for the budget and the economy.[3] The dramatic growth in new weapons purchases, for example, is putting pressure on the federal budget and could actually reduce military readiness; paying for weapons could force cuts in spending for operations, maintenance, and personnel.[4] Moreover, the defense budget may be exacerbating federal budget deficits, high interest rates, and low capital supplies while impeding future industrial investment and the creation of new jobs in the American economy.[5]

The debate over national security and defense spending is more widespread and vociferous than at any time in American political history since 1945. In the past, national security and defense spending issues were left to the experts; now, religious denominations, school children and teachers, civic groups, professional societies, and citizens have entered the debate over nuclear policy, defense budgets, and foreign policy.

The debate, however, has not dramatically changed the defense policy process in Washington. The Scowcroft Commission, appointed in 1983 by President Reagan to examine strategic policy, split the difference in the strategic arms debate, calling for the MX missile to be produced and deployed and, at the same time, for the production and deployment of a missile dubbed "Midgetman," which would substitute for the MX and make its construction unnecessary.[6] Liberal members of Congress known as critics of the administration's strategic policies, such as Representatives Les Aspin (D., Wis.) and Albert Gore, Jr. (D., Tenn.), endorsed this MX decision and urged its approval by Congress. Most dramatically, the call for a bilateral nuclear weapons freeze, passed by the House of Representatives after exhausting debate in spring 1983, was followed by a crucial vote on the MX missile, which would be halted by a freeze. Of the members of the House who endorsed a freeze, ninety-seven also voted *for* the MX program.

In the face of massive spending on new weapons and suggestions that the defense buying process might be out of control, Congress had continued to fund all the administration's requests for weapons procurement. Although Congress reduced the president's request in 1983 and cut the rate of real growth in defense spending from 10 percent to 5 percent, this action proved to be largely a paper exercise. Although the level of budget authority (the right to begin spending money) in 1984 was reduced by over $12 billion from the administration's request, actual outlays (the money to be spent in 1984) were only $5 billion less than what the administration had sought.

Defense policy alternatives offered in Washington stray very little from the administration's program. Despite public criticism of the direction of national security policy and the general sense that greater accountability is needed for defense spending, the policy process has continued to function with little change, operating in virtual isolation from the political process around it.

In order to render defense spending accountable, one needs to understand why it seems so impervious to the normal accountability process of American politics. Three different models can be used to explain the defense policy process; each provides an element that helps to clarify the closed nature of this part of American government.

The National Security Model

From the "national security" perspective, defense policies and budgets are designed through a rational process. A clear, precise definition of the "threats" to the United States (principally the Soviet "threat") leads directly to a rational definition of American military missions as the forces and weapons required to fulfill those missions.[7]

For many analysts of defense policy, the national security model is the only acceptable arena of debate. Commitments, forces, and weapons are subject to some discussion, but the terms of agreement are set in the logic of "threat," world events, and the capabilities of potential adversaries. Debate at this level has provided some isolation for the defense policy process. Cloaked in secrecy, national security arguments provide legitimacy for policy makers who have exclusive access to the secrets. Members of Congress and the public, less privy to the secrets, find they lack expertise and credibility—they are excluded from the policy process.

The nationwide debate over American national security in the 1980s began to strip away the veil of secrecy. Critics of the administration suggested, with growing legitimacy, that the "threats" to the United States were exaggerated and that the defense buildup was based on a series of myths about America's security. The myths purported that (1) the Soviet Union has outspent the United States on defense since 1970, (2) the USSR has a definite "margin of superiority" over American strategic forces, (3) these forces are, as a result, "vulnerable," and (4) the Warsaw Pact dramatically dominates the forces of the North Atlantic Treaty Organization (NATO).[8]

Moreover, it is not clear that a major expansion of weapons spending is actually designed to meet threats to national security. Strategic weapons expansion may fuel an arms race; the expansion of intervention capabilities may lead to war; weapons purchases could cut into funds for military readiness. The "security" model may explain some parts of defense policies and budgets; it may also conceal other sources of policy.

The Bureaucratic Model

A second model of defense policy enriches our understanding of the roots of national security spending and also helps to clarify the imperviousness of the policy process itself. This model focuses on defense policy making as a "bureaucratic" process.[9] Defense budgets and weapons programs, which emerge from bureaucratic self-promotion, inventiveness, and interservice rivalry in the Defense Department, are linked only loosely, if at all, to perceptions of "threat."

In the Defense Department, for example, interservice rivalry among the Army, Navy, and Air Force, leads to competition for funds and, frequently, duplication of weapons systems. The Air Force and the Navy, for example, each purchase several different types of fighter aircraft. Joint fighter programs do not exist.

Inside one service, officials can become attached to a weapon program less for its contribution to security than for its role in ensuring a continued mission for that service. For example, Air Force testimony in the 1970s suggested that the B–52 bomber could survive until the year 2000 as a cruise-missile carrier.[10] Strategic bombers, even those provided with new "stealth" characteristics that would make them less visible on radar, have an uncertain future, given the quality of Soviet air defenses. However, the B–1 bomber is the sole major aircraft program of the Strategic Air Command (SAC). Without the B–1 bomber, SAC's primary mission is the management of land-based strategic missiles. In the 1970s, the SAC was unified in promoting the B–1 over opposition from other parts of the Air Force, from other services, and even from within the office of the secretary of defense.[11]

The contracting practices of the defense bureaucracy also have a direct impact on the cost, size, and contents of the defense budget. David Stockman, director of the Office of Management and Budget, described the Department of Defense as a "swamp of waste" containing some $10 to $30 billion in excessive spending that could be eliminated with no risks for American national security.[12] In 1983 the Grace Commission, appointed by President Reagan to explore waste and savings in federal spending, pointed to roughly $30 billion a year in wasteful Pentagon spending that could be eliminated.[13]

There are many examples of such waste. For instance, 90 percent of all Defense Department prime contracts (in dollar value) are negotiated, not publicly advertised and competitively bid; two-thirds of these are negotiated with just one supplier—"a sole course." After contracts are signed cost control problems plague the Defense Department. Constant renegotiations with contractors change the price, performance, or schedule requirements of most weapons, thus increasing their cost and turning even "fixed price" contracts into "cost plus" contracts. Both the Defense Department and the defense industry lack incentives to keep costs down. Independent testing and cost analysis capabilities in the Pentagon are weak; auditing capabilities are inadequate.

Bureaucratic infighting, self-protection, and inefficiency keep defense spending levels high and directly affect procurement choices.[14] Moreover, the federal government's largest "buying" bureaucracy is committed to defending itself from outside criticism and penetration.[15] The bureaucratic model helps to explain the defense establishment's imperviousness to its critics. The model does not, however, explain why Congress fails to cut back on the rapid expansion of defense spending.

Defense budget and spending decisions cannot be explained solely by "rational" or "bureaucratic" models. The defense policy process is, finally, a "political" process.

The Political Model

This model for defense policies and budgets can be drawn from a more general discussion of the relationship between business and government in American society. The relationship between large corporations and American government has often been described as an antagonistic one, especially from the perspective of business. Business is frequently described as another "pressure" or "interest group" seeking government favors and engaging in a continuous battle to fend off government efforts to control its behavior and activities.[16]

The relationships between these two supposed antagonists in the twentieth century suggests, however, that a more cooperative set of relations has developed. Nowhere is this cooperative connection more apparent than in the defense sector. During World War I, business executives entered the federal government as policy makers, planning virtually all sectors of United States industrial production for the war effort. In addition, the war brought a fledgling aircraft industry into existence. With the end of the war, contractor dependence on government orders became clear.[17] Defense suppliers undertook strenuous efforts to ensure a steady flow of government orders for their products, federal subsidy of their research and development costs, and federal regulation of their behavior.

The emergence of a permanent relationship between the two followed World War II; once again, a surge of orders had expanded the defense industry, and business personnel had played a vital role in war production planning. Since the late 1940s, the Defense Department, which had subsidized construction of a vast military production base, has had a clear policy of maintaining that base in the private sector.[18] The role of the United States as the leading world power provided an apparent justification and focus for continuous defense planning, a large military force, and massive arms procurement. Moreover, the American economy seemed able to contain the expense, absorbing guns and butter in a constant expansion. Within this framework, service bureaucracies and industry officials interacted regularly, and the industry self-consciously developed the capacity to penetrate and influence the policy process.

This constant interaction meets the needs of both participants. Defense Department officials, engaged in self-protection, find useful allies among contractors committed to remaining in the business of defense production. Neither side of this relationship could continue, however, without the active participation of a third player, Congress. Through Congress, the Defense Department acquires the funding that enables the relationship to continue; therefore, Congress must be brought into the relationship as an active participant. The resulting political configuration is a familiar one in American politics: a closeness shared by a federal agency (the Pentagon), its client group in American society (the defense industry), and those in Congress with a special interest in that part of the federal budget (members of armed services committees and defense appropriations subcommittees, and members from congressional districts and states with concentrations of defense spending).

This relationship can be described as an "iron triangle," or "subgovernment," a part of American government that links major interested parties and is isolated from other areas of government policy making.[19] Such triangles exist in other arenas of federal policy making and share four characteristics.

First, a close working relationship in a specific area of policy is shared among three key participants: the bureaucracy, key committees and members of Congress, and a specific sector of American society.

Second, each triangle features an intimate interpenetration between the societal interest and the federal bureaucracy in question. Policy makers and administrators move freely between the two arenas, and policy issues tend to be discussed and resolved among participants who develop and share common values, interests, and perceptions.[20] As the groups in society and the government agency interact, they begin to share policy-making authority; often private sector parties become policy makers and administrators without ever entering public service. Government power and private power become indistinguishable and grow to resemble each other.[21]

Third, such a subgovernment emerges slowly. It is not willfully created in a single moment, but comes into being as a result of constant interaction among its participants. Government bureaucrats help create and maintain a subgovernment. Private industry pursues policies and procedures it desires from the government, and works to maintain the triangle as circumstances change. Shared interests develop between bureaucrats and industry, and disagreements are reconciled through constant interaction.

Fourth, the triangle has a strong tendency to become "iron." Eventually, it becomes isolated from other policy arenas, from Congress, and from the public. The participants exert strenuous efforts to keep it protected.[22] As a result of this gradual isolation, perspectives on policy alternatives narrow, and proposals from outside the subgovernment have no credibility inside. Policy makers and private participants begin to share the assumption that they are acting not only in their own interests, but also in the general "public interest." Ziegler and Peake describe the result:

> In the day-to-day performance of their tasks, administrators see very little of the more general public support which accompanied the establishment of the agency. The only people who are likely to come to the attention of administrators are those whose problems are uniquely a part of the administrative environment. . . . Under such circumstance it is not surprising that the administrator's perception of the public interest is in reality defined by the interests of the regulated parties.[23]

Decisions made for a variety of reasons can be routinely justified in terms of "national security." Behind the veil of national security, the defense iron triangle has unusual power. As Philip Hughes, former deputy director of the Budget Bureau, has described:

> The most relevant consideration is, in blunt terms, sheer power—where the muscle is—and this is a very power-conscious town, and the Secretary of Defense and the defense establishment are a different group to deal with, whether Congress is dealing with them or whether the Budget Bureau is dealing with them.[24]

The continued existence and success of the defense iron triangle depends on a steady flow of information, access, influence, and money. The most crucial actor in this process is the defense industry. Defense contractors are extremely self-conscious about the importance of the political arena to their business success. Defense is big business: The Defense Department contract market amounts to over $100 billion per year. It is also a concentrated and stable business: Most of the top 25 contractors to the Defense Department have been in the business for over 30 years and receive 50 percent of all the contract dollars the Defense Department awards. Finally, it is important business: Many of the leading contracting companies do over 50 percent of their sales with the federal government.[25]

As a result, defense contractors are among the most innovative corporations in finding ways to strengthen their relations with the federal government; they exercise an unusually strong influence over military policy—strategic and conventional alike. Contractor influence, which is unusually difficult to detect, frequently begins at the most invisible level of the weapons planning process: early research and development. The nation's eight leading military research and development contractors—Boeing, General Dynamics, Grumman, Lockheed, McDonnell-Douglas, Northrop, Rockwell International, and United Technologies—received a total of over $20 billion in research and development contracts alone in the 1970s.[26] In addition, these same companies were reimbursed roughly $2 billion for direct corporate investment in research work through the "Independent Research and Development Bids and Proposals" program.[27]

At this crucial early stage, ideas move freely between industry and government, thus giving contractors ample opportunity to influence future decisions. Major contractors are well represented on roughly fifty advisory committees (and hundreds of subcommittees) to the Defense Department and NASA—most notably, the Defense Science Board and the scientific advisory groups of each branch of the military. Membership on key committees gives contractors an opportunity to affect new weapons policies long before the public or Congress is aware of them.[28]

The constant interaction of government and contractor personnel at the research level means that new weapons ultimately bought by the Department of Defense are often created by the firms that stand to gain if these weapons are produced. The *Wall Street Journal* reported, for example, that Boeing was seeking very secret information about plans for land-based missiles from inside contacts at the Pentagon.[29] Early access enables a company to influence future weapons planning at the first possible stage. As one defense industry official described in the late 1960s: "Your ultimate goal is actually to write the R.F.P. [Request for Proposal], and this happens more often than you might think."[30]

Close ties between industry and government are reinforced by a steady flow of employees between the two sectors. In the 1950s, congressional studies showed that more than 1,000 retired military personnel had taken jobs in the defense industry. In the 1960s, this number rose to about 2,000. Between 1969 and 1974, the figure reached 2,000 for the top 100 contractors alone. An examination of the eight leading defense contractors noted above showed that, during the 1970s, 2,000 of their employees transferred either from industry to government or from government to industry. Of the nearly 500 civilians in this group, 34 percent had either worked in or moved to the key research and development offices of the Army, Navy, Air Force, and the office of the secretary of defense.[31]

Examples of the revolving door are numerous. General Alexander Haig, for example, moved from the Army to the presidency of United

Technologies, to secretary of state, and back to an advisory committee with United Technologies. United Technologies employs other government alumni. Clark MacGregor, head of the company's Washington, D.C. office, is a former member of Congress. Hugh Witt, a government relations specialist in the same office, previously worked in the office of the secretary of the Air Force as director of Federal Procurement Policy in the Office of Management and Budget.[32]

T. K. Jones, a former deputy program manager for Boeing, became staff assistant to the Defense Department delegation to the Strategic Arms Limitations Talks (SALT) in 1971, went back to Boeing in 1974 as program and products evaluation manager, and subsequently returned to the Defense Department to work on strategic policy in the Reagan administration. Seymour Zieberg, appointed deputy undersecretary of defense for Strategic and Space Systems in 1977, joined Martin Marietta in 1981 as vice president for research.[33]

The revolving door provides unique access to the defense policy-making process. The *Wall Street Journal* story about Boeing's MX involvement noted that Boeing had obtained its information from a Boeing employee "on leave to work in the Pentagon's Weapons Research and Development Office." Once this employee had read the relevant report, he telexed its substance to a former Defense Department employee working at Boeing's headquarters in Seattle. The newspaper concluded: "The movement of weaponry experts between industry and government jobs, frequently on the same project, facilitates the easy flow of information and tends to blur the distinction between national security and corporate goals."[34]

Research and development access and the revolving door help weapons projects get started. Once underway, a committed constituency grows, and the weapon becomes hard to cancel. Defense contractors use the lobbying resources of their government relations departments to keep the process moving. The contractors' Washington offices are frequently the nerve centers for this effort. From 1977 through 1979, the same eight leading defense companies employed 200 people in their Washington offices and 48 registered lobbyists. According to audits by the Defense Contract Audit Agency, Boeing, General Dynamics, Grumman, Lockheed, and Rockwell International together spent $16.8 million on their Washington offices in 1974 and 1975, an average of $1.6 million each per year. Rockwell alone spent $7 million from 1973 through 1975.[35]

These Washington offices keep track of program developments in the Pentagon and NASA, follow the process of legislation, lobby on Capitol Hill, handle public relations, funnel information back to the company, and negotiate with foreign weapons buyers. Virtually all of the nonentertainment expenditures of these offices, including lobbying activities, have been billed to the government as administrative expenses related to defense contracting.[36]

Congress is an active participant in the defense iron triangle. In principle, Congress's role in the policy process can be extensive.[37] Congress has the capability to conduct oversight on Defense Department activities, and Congress votes on the budget that provides the funding for the Defense Department and its contractors. Because of its critical role, Congress has been the target of lobbying activity, both by the Defense Department and by the contracting industry. Curiously, despite its potential for influence in the policy process, Congress has come to play a highly visible but secondary role. Weapons budgets and the information justifying them are produced by the Defense Department, not by Congress. Congress must react with less information.[38] Moreover, with many weapons contracts already underway, strong bureaucratic commitment, and corporate involvement, Congress has even less room to maneuver.

The net result is that congressional oversight activity, though extensive, seems to have little real impact on the policy process. Hearings on defense procurement waste in the late 1960s, for example, did little to change Defense Department procedure. The same issues are being raised in the 1980s; their effect on the Pentagon procurement process is not yet known. Nevertheless, because of its budgetary role, Congress remains an important focus of activity in the iron triangle.

From the industry's point of view, influence in Congress is crucial. Members of armed services and defense appropriations committees and members who represent defense contracting districts are most important. Committee members jealously guard their jurisdictions, and members from key districts must protect their turf; thus both are appropriate targets for contractor lobbying.

Beyond direct lobbying, contractors also reach members of Congress through campaign contributions.[39] Defense contractor political action committees (PACs) are among the largest corporate PACs in the country. Their contributions are concentrated on members of key congressional committees or members from districts with defense facilities or plants. While a campaign contribution does not mean the member will always vote with the company, it does bring access. Access, in turn, speeds the flow of information and influence in the policy process. Rockwell, for example, carried on a four-year battle to revive the B–1 bomber after President Carter cancelled it in 1977. Among other elements in this campaign, Rockwell's PAC focused its campaign contributions on members of defense appropriations and armed services committees in the House and Senate; nearly all of them voted for the program when the Reagan administration revived it.[40]

Defense contractors also organize grass-roots lobbying campaigns to influence Congress. Because company employees, the communities in which they are located, stockholders, and subcontractors depend on defense contracting for their survival, they are all part of a contractor's grass-roots network. Trade unions such as the United Auto Workers and the International Association of Machinists have many members in defense industries, and their locals often follow a company's call to support its weapons in Washington.

In the mid-1970s, for example, Rockwell International mounted a grass-roots effort on behalf of the B–1 bomber program, then on the brink of cancellation. The company urged its 115,000 employees and the holders of its 35 million shares of stock to write to their Congressmen. The company also asked more than 3,000 subcontractors and suppliers in 48 states to tell their Congressmen that scrapping the B–1 would adversely affect their districts. Rockwell spent $1.35 million on such efforts from 1975 through 1977, an amount that opponents of the B–1 could not have hoped to match.[41]

Conclusion

The political model of defense policy making fills many of the gaps in the explanation left by the national security and bureaucratic models. Through the political model, one can see the policy process in operation over a period of time. National security decisions establish the language, the rationale, and sometimes the screen behind which defense policy and spending decisions are made. While national security is indeed an important policy consideration, it cannot explain the size, scope, and political power of the defense policy apparatus. Bureaucratic explanations add to our understanding of the policy process, but provide only a partial understanding of where and how weapons originate, why they are so hard to stop, and why Congress remains a fairly passive ratifier of funding requests submitted by the Defense Department.

The political model helps answer these questions and displays how the process actually functions. The flow of information, the opening of doors of access, and the opportunities for influence all focus on the single largest piece of federal government buying. Much is at stake; thus, warding off external intervention and public criticism is an important part of the policy process itself. The debate over national security opened up the debate over this policy process. Whether massive public spending for defense actually provides security is dubious. The impact of such spending on the American economy and the substantial sums being wasted are growing concerns. The debate provides the opportunity to institute changes in the way the defense iron triangle functions—to join concerns about the accountability of the policy process with the need for legitimate debate about the requirements of American national security.[42] The defense debate helps one understand how the policy process functions. This understanding may well lead to significant changes in the way national security planning and defense spending will be conducted in the future.

Notes

1. David Gold and Paul Murphy, "Total Military Spending Budget," in *Military Expansion, Economic Decline*, ed. Robert W. DeGrasse, Jr. (New York: Council on Economic Priorities, 1983), 211–37.

2. On the M–1 tank, see contributions by Patrick Oster, Bruce Ingersoll, and John Fialka, in *More Bucks, Less Bang: How the Pentagon Buys Ineffective Weapons*, ed. Dina Rasor (Washington, D.C.: Fund for Constitutional Government, 1983), 34–50. On the Bradley Infantry Fighting Vehicle, see William Boly, "The $13 Billion Dud," in Rasor, *More Bucks, Less Bang*, 13–28. On the diode, see "Millions Found Wasted in Buying Military Spare Parts," *Chicago Tribune*, 11 July 1983, p. 4.

3. George Kuhn, "Department of Defense: Ending Defense Stagnation," in *Agenda '83*, Heritage Foundation, 69–114; Franklin C. Spinney, "The Plans/Reality Mismatch and Why We Need Realistic Budgeting," Defense Department briefing paper (Washington, D.C.: December 1982); U.S. Air Force Systems Command, "The Affordable Acquisition Approach Study" (Washington, D.C., U.S.A.F. Briefing, February 1983); William Kaufmann, "The Defense Budget," in *Setting National Priorities*, ed. Joseph A. Pechman (Washington, D.C.: Brookings Institution, 1983), 39–79.

4. House Armed Services Committee, "Staff Briefing on the FY 1984 DoD O&M Request" (Washington, D.C.: March 1983); Walter F. Mondale to the American Newspaper Publishers Association, New York, N.Y., 26 April 1983, p. 4.

5. See, for example, the appeal from The Bipartisan Appeal to Resolve the Budget Crisis, a business group, for slower growth in defense spending in a letter to William C. Clark, 25 March 1983.

6. *Report of the President's Commission on Strategic Forces* (Washington, D.C.: White House, April 1983).

7. This is, in general, the tone of the introduction to each annual report from Secretary of Defense Caspar Weinberger since the Reagan administration took office. See Department of Defense: *Annual Report of the Secretary of Defense to the Congress, Fiscal Year 1983* (Washington, D.C.: Department of Defense, 1982) and *Annual Report of the Secretary of Defense to the Congress, Fiscal Year 1984* (Washington, D.C.: Department of Defense, 1983).

8. See, for example: Franklyn Holzman, "Are the Soviets Really Outspending the U.S. on Defense?" *International Security* 4, no. 4 (Spring 1980): 86–104; Holzman, "Soviet Military Spending: Assessing the Numbers Game," *International Security* 6, no. 4 (Spring 1982): 78–101; Holzman, "Are We Falling Behind the Soviets?" *Atlantic* (July 1983): 10–18; Richard Stubbing, "The Imaginary Defense Gap: We Already Outspend Them," *Washington Post*, 14 February 1982, p. C-1; Federation of American Scientists, *Public Interest Report* (September 1982); John Collins, *U.S.-Soviet Military Balance: Concepts and Capabilities, 1960–1980* (New York: McGraw-Hill, 1980); and Senator Carl Levin, "The Other Side of the Story" (unpublished monograph, Washington, D.C., May 1983).

9. For examples of this model, see: Morton J. Peck and Frederick M. Scherer, *The Weapons Acquisition Process; An Economic Analysis* (Boston: Harvard School of Business Administration, 1962); J. Ronald Fox, *Arming America: How the U.S. Buys Weapons* (Boston: Harvard Graduate School of Business Administration, 1974); Harvey M. Sapolsky, *The Polaris System Development: Bureaucratic and Programmatic Success in Government* (Cambridge: Harvard University Press, 1972); A. Ernest Fitzgerald, *The High Priests of Waste*, (New York: Norton, 1972).

10. Gordon Adams, "A Bomber for All Seasons," *Council on Economic Priorities Newsletter*, New York, February 1982.

11. Gordon Adams, *The B-1 Bomber: An Analysis of Its Strategic Utility, Cost, Constituency and Economic Impact* (New York: Council on Economic Priorities, 1976).

12. William Grieder, "The Education of David Stockman," *Atlantic* (December 1981): 27–54.

13. U.S. Department of Commerce, President's Private Sector Survey on Cost Control ("Grace Commission"): *Task Force Report on the Office of the Secretary of Defense, Task Force Report on the Department of the Army, Task Force Report on the Department of the Navy, Task Force Report on the Department of the Air Force* (Washington, D.C., July 1983).

14. Fox, *Arming America*; Fitzgerald, *High Priests of Waste*; Peck and Scherer, *Weapons Acquisition Process*; and Richard Kaufmann, *The War Profiteers* (Garden City, N.Y.: Doubleday/Anchor Books, 1972).

15. See, for example, the major effort mounted by the Defense Department and the defense industry to avoid a redefinition of the defense acquisition regulations to make contractor lobbying costs unallowable against defense contracts, as shown in documents released by Common Cause in Spring 1981, and held by Common Cause, 2030 M St., NW, Washington, D.C. 20036.

16. Arthur Bentley, *The Process of Government: A Study of Social Pressure*, 2nd ed (Evanston, Ill.: Principia Press, 1945); E. E. Schattschneider, *The Semi-Sovereign People*, 2nd ed. (Hinsdale, Ill.: Dryden Press, 1975); David Truman, *The Governmental Process: Political Interests and Public Opinion* (New York: Knopf, 1975); and E. Pendleton Herring, *Group Representation Before Congress* (Baltimore: Johns Hopkins Press, 1929).

17. Robert D. Cuff, *The War Industries Board: Business-Government Relations During World War I* (Baltimore: Johns Hopkins Press, 1973); Paul A. C. Koistinen, *The Military-Industrial Complex: A Historical Perspective* (New York: Praeger Publishers, 1980); and Gordon Adams, "Defense Policy-Making, Weapons Procurement, and the Reproduction of State-Industry Relations" (paper presented to the American Political Science Association, Washington, D.C., 28 August 1980).

18. Kaufman, *The War Profiteers*; Fox, *Arming America*; Peck and Scherer, *Weapons Acquisition Process*; James Kurth, "The Political Economy of Weapons Procurement: The Follow-On Imperative," *American Economic Review* 62, no. 2 (May 1972): 304–11; Seymour Melman, *Pentagon Capitalism* (New York: McGraw-Hill, 1970); and Melman, *The Permanent War Economy* (New York: Simon and Schuster, 1974).

19. Among other writers who have explored the concept of such subgovernments, see: Gordon Adams, "Disarming the Military Subgovernment," *Harvard Journal on Legislation* 14, no. 3 (April 1977): 459–503; Lester Salamon and John Siegfried, "Economic Power and Political Influence: The Impact of Industry Structure on Public Policy," *American Political Science Review* 71, no. 3 (September 1977): 1026–43; Joel D. Auerbach and Burt Rockmen, "Bureaucrats and Clientele Groups: A View from Capitol Hill," *American Journal of Political Science* 22, no. 4 (November 1978); Grant McConnell, *Private Power and American Democracy* (New York: Knopf, 1967); John Lieper Freeman, *The Political Process* (Garden City, N.Y.: Doubleday, 1955); Douglas Cater, *Power in Washington* (New York: Random House, 1964); and Michael T. Hayes, "The Semi-Sovereign Pressure Groups: A Critique of Current Theory and Alternative Typology," *Journal of Politics* 40, no. 1 (1978): 134–61.

20. Harmon Zeigler and Wayne G. Peak, *Interest Groups in American Society*, 2nd ed. (Englewood Cliffs, N.J.: Prentice Hall, 1972), 180. The authors point out that in such a relationship "agencies and their clientele tend to develop coincident values and perceptions to the point where neither needs to manipulate the other overtly. The confident relationships that develop uniquely favor the interest groups involved. They need only exchange persuasive resources for instrumental policy benefits within administrative markets to satisfy many of their material demands."

21. Harold Seidman, *Politics, Position and Power* (New York: Oxford University Press, 1970), 18. The author points out that "private bureaucracies in Washington now almost completely parallel the public bureaucracies in those program areas where the federal government contracts for services, regulates private enterprise, or provides some form of financial assistance." McConnell, *Private Power and American Democracy*, 244, describes this interpenetration as the process of "privatizing" the state. James O'Connor, *The Fiscal Crisis of the State* (New York: St. Martin's Press, 1973), 66, uses the term "appropriation of a sector of state power by private interests" to describe the same phenomenon.

22. Adams, "Disarming the Military Subgovernment"; Schattschneider, *Semi-Sovereign People*; Hayes, "Semi-Sovereign Pressure Groups"; and Richard Neustadt, *Presidential Power* (New York: Wiley, 1976).

23. Zeigler and Peak, *Interest Groups*, p. 172.

24. Kaufmann, *The War Profiteers*, 248.

25. This is particularly true of General Dynamics, Grumman, Lockheed, McDonnell-Douglass, and Northrop, who are usually among the top ten contractors with the Defense Department.

26. Gordon Adams, *The Politics of Defense Contracting: The Iron Triangle* (New Brunswick, N.J.: Transaction Press, 1982).

27. Christopher Paine and Gordon Adams, "The R&D Slush Fund," *Nation* (26 January 1980); and Adams, *The Politics of Defense Contracting*, chap. 7.

28. Adams, *The Politics of Defense Contracting*, chap. 11. See also, the report of the Defense Department inspector general's office in 1983 on the interrelationship of industry and the Defense Department in the Defense Science Board, as reprinted in the *Congressional Record*, 22 July 1983, pp. S10663–S10677.

29. Kenneth Bacon, "Pentagon Studies How Boeing Got Secret Information," *Wall Street Journal*, 29 February 1980.

30. A North American Aviation official quoted in David Sims, "Spoon-Feeding the Military: How New Weapons Come to Be," in *The Pentagon Watchers* ed. Leonard Rodberg and Derek Sherer (Garden City, N.Y.: Doubleday, 1970), 249.

31. Adams, *The Politics of Defense Contracting*, chap. 6.

32. Ibid., chap. 6 and company profiles.

33. Ibid.

34. *Wall Street Journal*, 29 February 1980.

35. Adams, *The Politics of Defense Contracting*, chap. 9.

36. Ibid.

37. Adams, "Disarming the Military Subgovernment."

38. Now retired Senator Thomas McIntyre (D., N.H.) described the problem he faced as chair of the Senate Armed Services subcommittee on research and development in the face of thousands of Defense Department projects for research and development: "We spend an awful lot of time, but we are lucky if we can take a look at or have a briefing or hearing on, say, 15 percent of those projects." Quoted in Louis Fischer, "Senate Procedures for Authorizing Military Research and Development," in Joint Economic Committee, Subcommittee on Priorities and Economy in Government, *Priorities and Efficiency in Federal Research and Development: A Compendium of Papers*, 94th Cong., 2d sess., 29 October 1976, 26.

39. Adams, *The Politics of Defense Contracting*, chap. 13.

40. Adams, "A Bomber for All Seasons."

41. Adams, *The Politics of Defense Contracting*, chap. 13.

42. Gordon Adams, "Creating Real National Security," in *Alternatives*, ed. Irving Howe, forthcoming.

21

Bureaucracy and the Regulation of Health and Safety at Work: A Comparison of the U.S. and Sweden

Steven Kelman

The differences between the United States and Sweden in the extent to which fines are used to induce compliance with occupational safety and health regulations and in the extent to which superiors within the agencies supervise subordinates reveal different attitudes toward the kinds of controls that systems ought to use to induce desirable behavior by others.

Control Systems and Societies

Before occupational safety and health became a more important issue at the beginning of the 1970s, inspectors in both countries proceeded similarly. They encouraged compliance by offering employers normative rewards (praise for doing as they should). Fines were almost never used. One problem with this method was that real friendship ties could hardly be expected to grow on the basis of contact as infrequent as that between inspector and employer. In both Sweden and America, inspectors would find the same violations on later visits. Policy makers drew lessons from past failures in developing new strategies.

A classic debate that spans several of the social sciences concerns what kinds of inducements—in particular, rewards or punishments—are more likely to produce desired changes in behavior. Clearly no generalizations can be made across different types of people and situations; what works under some circumstances may fail in others. For normative inducements to function successfully, for instance, the individual whose behavior one seeks to change must regard those seeking to change his behavior as people whose good opinion is valued. In a classic study, Richard Schwartz compared two kinds of Israeli cooperative agricultural settlements, the *kvutza* and the *moshav*.[1] The kvutza was "a large primary

Reprinted from *Regulating America, Regulating Sweden*, by Steven Kelman (Cambridge, Mass.: MIT Press, 1981), 195–215, by permission of the publisher.

group whose members engage in continuous face-to-face interaction," where people worked and ate together. In the moshav, people owned land privately and performed only a few tasks together. And in the kvutza, there was no punishment through legal coercion; normative inducements were sufficient to achieve satisfactory compliance with group rules. This system was tried in the moshav, but it did not work. Instead the moshav had to introduce legal coercion to punish transgressors.

When policy makers choose among alternative control systems, they do so in the context of assumptions and experiences they have as members of their society. They begin with assumptions about how likely it is that individuals subject to a law will comply simply because the law expresses the authority of government. In neither America nor Sweden were occupational safety and health policy makers content with existing levels of compliance. There are, nonetheless, degrees of pessimism about baseline levels of obedience to the law. Out of the Swedish *overhet* tradition grows the notion that people ought to defer to the wishes of those in authority. Out of the American liberal tradition grows the notion that it is legitimate for people to define and pursue their own goals, independent of what the state thinks is best for them. But the forces of individual interest, once legitimized, are not easily controlled; there always exists the danger that people encouraged to be self-assertive will fail to see the distinction between doing so when this does no impermissible harm to others and doing so when such harm is done. The traditional problem of European states with established rulers has been to tame those rulers and let people breathe; that of America with its liberal tradition has been to tame the unruly so that other people can breathe.

The Lockean solution was to have people obey decisions made by impartial elected officials or judges, but even under the best of circumstances, obedience on the basis of such an abstract principle was likely to be imperfect. Thus the failure of government to act impartially creates a legitimacy problem for government commands in America. Self-assertive values therefore not only discourage agreement before decisions are made, but also—as comparative crime statistics in America and Europe testify—make it relatively more difficult to get people to comply with decisions once made.

A question was asked in the national inspectors' survey, where at one end of a seven-point scale was placed the statement, "Most employers are law abiding, and try to follow the standards simply because a government agency has issued them," and at the other was the statement, "Without the penalty-imposing powers we have, many employers would simply ignore the standards." The results (Table 21–1) indicate that American inspectors have little faith in the automatic acceptance of the law, while Swedish ones are more sanguine. The Swedish results do not show inspectors to be certain of automatic compliance; over half rated most employers at the middle of the scale or worse. But it is the overwhelming

Table 21–1
Evaluation by U.S. and Swedish Inspectors of Employer Compliance

	Scale	U.S. Inspectors (N = 78)	Swedish Inspectors (N = 74)
Most employers are	1–2	9%	18%
law abiding	3	6	26
	4	8	22
Many employers would	5	21	20
ignore standards	6–7	56	15

vote of no confidence American inspectors give employers that stands out.

If policy makers are pessimistic about predispositions to compliance, they are more likely to use punishments than rewards to induce compliance, since those not predisposed to obey the law will generally not be considered deserving of reward. Such assumptions also make the use of normative inducements of any kind less likely since those predisposed to noncompliance will probably be regarded as unlikely participants in a group that may induce compliance. Edmund Burke saw the destruction of deference and other normative means of compliance as the essential evil of liberalism. The use of coercive legal punishment becomes required because other institutions of control can no longer be mobilized. Without deference or other normative means, "laws are to be supported only by their own terrors," Burke warned. "In the groves of their academy," he wrote of the liberal philosophers, "at the end of every vista, you see nothing but the gallows."[2] Foreign observers visiting England during the eighteenth century were struck by the paradox of great concern shown for the rights of the accused and severe punishment for convicted criminals.[3] If this argument is correct, both have a common cause in liberal values. (While attention to rights of the accused is less in Sweden than the United States, punishment for criminal offenses tends to be much lower.)

Out of the overhet tradition in Sweden grew a tendency to deal with conflict by establishing small groups of representatives for the various parties to work out agreements. Another result of this tradition was a belief among modern organizational leaders that they ought to educate members to the beliefs of their leaders. In America it became common to arrange proceedings modeled on adversary trials. American policy makers, when they look at the society around them, not only start off with more pessimistic assumptions about predispositions to compliance but also see a greater tendency to use the legal system to regulate human interactions. Swedish policy makers, on the other hand, not only start off with less pessimistic assumptions about predispositions to compliance but also see a society making far greater use of small groups to regulate human interactions. Thus it is not surprising (though it is obviously not foreordained) that American policy makers chose an occupational safety and health compliance system based on punishments meted out through the legal system when they were dissatisfied with existing levels of compliance. Nor is it surprising that Swedish policy makers chose to use normative inducements, with legal punishments only as a backup. American policy makers don't always choose the means chosen in the case of occupational safety and health enforcement, nor do the Swedes universally choose the methods they chose here either. There are criminal laws in Sweden and areas where social control is achieved primarily through lawabidingness or small group normative inducements in the United States. This is both because dominant values are not universally held and because success or failure at establishing small group-based systems does not follow directly from a general Swedish relative preference for accommodationist institutions and an American relative preference for adversary institutions. Furthermore reliance on punishments through the legal system carries many costs, and for this reason as well, policy makers in America no less than in Sweden have hesitated before using it. But American policy makers may feel they have little choice if they are going to be serious about achieving compliance. In the one other instance of an area of earlier legislative concern that became more important in the late 1960s and where policy makers were dissatisfied with existing compliance levels—environmental protection—there has emerged a similar difference between America and Sweden on the tendency to rely on legal punishments.[4] But again, it is a question of tendencies and predisposition rather than of outcomes that can be predicted deterministically.

The overwhelming majority of the OSHA [Occupational Safety and Health Administration] inspectors questioned in the in-depth survey felt that first-instance sanctions were necessary. Responding to an open-ended question about their attitude toward "the penalty-imposing side of your job," 63 percent of respondents (N = 38) answered that such sanctions were a necessary part of OSHA compliance activities. Those favoring these sanctions did so overwhelmingly because they thought there would be little compliance otherwise. "Teeth are the only way to impress management with the seriousness of the situation," one inspector said. If first-instance sanctions disappeared, replied another, "OSHA would flop—we might as well write it off the books." If the inspector had no power to impose penalties, "they'd laugh at you when you came into the plant," a third stated. Two of the respondents replied with statements paralleling the argument made here. "It's the only means of enforcing the law," said one. "It's the only arm that we have," replied another.

Normative Inducements in Sweden

Deferent values and accommodationist institutions make available various normative inducements for compliance with regulations by employers. The operation of these processes during rule making helps produce a situation where, in contrast to the United States, employer leaders accept the regulations. Employer organizations then help seek compliance by member firms, using either the normative inducement of membership deference to leaders or opinion-formation activities. These are likely to aid compliance, though not to make it complete.

Normative inducements may also be exercised in small groups. The primary feature of the new compliance strategy in Sweden and the main substitute for legal punishments was replication at the plant level of the labor-management small groups used at the national level during rule making and the use of those groups both to monitor performance and to exert normative inducements for compliance. The vehicle was already there, half alive, in the form of existing plant-level worker safety stewards and labor-management safety committees.

The appointment of plant-level safety stewards and safety committees was first encouraged through a 1942 agreement between LO [Swedish Confederation of Labor] and SAF [Swedish Employers' Confederation] on occupational safety and health. Safety committees had by no means been unique to Sweden. Many large American firms have had safety committees. In Sweden unions had also sometimes selected a safety steward, frequently a shop-level union official who also held other union positions, to represent employees in making demands to management. The 1942 agreement required that safety stewards be appointed at all workplaces with ten or more employees and that safety committees be appointed at workplaces with more than one hundred employees.

Initial employer acceptance of the requirement is not hard to explain since the steward's function as it originally appeared was largely to reduce unsafe acts by workers through promoting employee safety consciousness. In the *Instruction for Safety Stewards*, the steward was called on to promote safety and health by becoming "knowledgeable about the safety rules established by the Factory Inspectorate and the employer which apply in the area under his responsibility" and by observing "to what extent these rules are being followed." The steward was "to inform workers about the dangers existing in the particular line of work" and "to emphasize to the workers the importance of having a clean and well-kept workplace, as well as to sharpen consciousness among the workers of how important it is to follow applicable safety rules."[5] Nothing suggested that safety stewards should be doing anything to get new safety devices installed or to increase safety consciousness among employers.

Following the 1942 agreement, safety stewards and safety committees were appointed around the land, but for the next twenty-five years, they maintained what one today might call a "low profile." (In the less discrete vernacular of the time, "nobody seemed to care" about them.) One problem was that most safety stewards did not know much about what made workplaces unsafe or unhealthy. The 1942 LO-SAF agreement had established the Joint Industrial Safety Council designed to educate safety stewards, but its efforts reached only a modest proportion of the target group.

When it was concluded in America that previous occupational safety and health enforcement methods were not working well enough, enforcement was made more punitive. In Sweden, in contrast, the role of the safety steward was revitalized. The first document of the new concern with occupational safety and health in Sweden, the joint LO-Social Democratic program *A Better Work Environment* (1969), made no mention of new legal sanctions for violation of safety and health regulations. Instead the document talked exclusively about giving safety stewards new responsibilities and establishing a special fund to support their education.[6] And the very first piece of legislation passed in 1971 was a law adding a surcharge to employer workmen's compensation premiums to set up a work environment fund that would arrange for such training.

Safety stewards were now going to be the entering wedge at the plant level for the concern with safety and health among national leaders and placed at the center of efforts to achieve compliance. According to the authors of a 1973 Work Environment Fund report, "Even though the work environment is a central issue for labor market organizations, government agencies, and researchers, and even though the mass media now gives the subject extensive coverage, it is doubtful whether occupational safety and health questions have gained a real foothold among workers at the plant level and among the general public. . . . What we must try to do is, by various means, to create an attitudinal and behavioral change."[7] Safety stewards, armed with an education reflecting the values of national leaders, would carry those values to the local level.

This role as entering wedge applied both to employers and to fellow workers. The old view of the safety steward as a person encouraging safety consciousness among workers did not completely die, but in the new view this role extended beyond encouraging the avoidance of unsafe acts to increasing the salience of safety and health such that workers would be unhappy about unsafe conditions. If many complained or even quit, a new inducement, originating in changed worker preferences, would be created for employers to comply with regulations.

Safety stewards would also be able to monitor compliance on an ongoing basis. This new role for stewards in relationship to employers was underscored dramatically when representatives for LO, SAF, and the Joint Industrial Safety Council discussed the planned education drive for safety stewards. At the meeting, LO surprised participants with a clearly articulated insistence that training take place at the plant level with study circles rather than having lectures by company safety engineers or courses away from the plant. The unions wanted course material to include exercises where participants could discuss problems at their own plants and even make inspections of plant conditions as part of the course. (The study circle leaders would be educated centrally.)

A joint committee developed the course material, which was written centrally and used as a basis for local study circles.[8] At the end of each lesson in the material, participants were instructed to tour their own plant to look for troublesome conditions. It was established that the study circles would take place during work time and that employers would pay participants normal wages during time spent on the course.[9] The Work Environment Fund paid for printing the course material and the central education of study circle leaders. From late 1974 through late 1976, the tremendous task of organizing courses for safety stewards at all but the tiniest workplaces was undertaken.

The most dramatic expression of the new role of the safety steward appeared in the revision to the Worker Protection Act in 1974. It allowed safety stewards to stop work temporarily until an inspector could arrive in situations with an "imminent and serious danger for employee life or health."[10] Since its inception, this provision of the law has been used around a hundred times per year.[11] Its significance is largely symbolic, since few employers want to see work continued if an imminent danger exists. But the symbolism is significant: it proclaims the safety steward a person with an important monitoring role.

The revised *Instruction for Safety Stewards* issued as part of a new LO-SAF agreement in 1976 codified the new conception of the steward's role. Although the old instruction from 1942 had referred to the task of the safety steward as being to learn about the functioning safety devices already installed, the new instruction stated that safety stewards should "*monitor* whether safety devices and other hygienic features *are present*, are in good condition, and are being used." Safety stewards should not only request that safety and health regulations be complied with but they should "participate in following up whether measures have led to the desired result."[12]

The safety committee would be used for providing normative inducements for employers. This required that management sit on the committee. The commentary to the 1967 LO-SAF occupational safety and health agreement stated that it was important that "the very top management of the firm" sit on the safety committee.[13] The 1976 agreement was even more specific and also provided that foremen join the committee.[14] A risk was that safety stewards on the committee would be influenced by employers not to press for compliance, rather than the influence going in the opposite direction. Although that probably happens to some extent, the increased salience in the small group setting of common standards, obedience to the law, and the right to equal treatment, which aid the stewards, works against this.

Enforcement Systems and the Inspection Process

Differences in the enforcement systems in the two countries influence both inspectors and the tenor of their inspections. American inspections are designed more as formal searches for violations of regulations; Swedish inspections are designed more as informal, personal missions to give advice and information, establish friendship ties between inspector and inspected, and promote local labor-management cooperation. Since OSHA inspections are intended as searches for violations, their purpose could be defeated were advance notice given. The *Field Operations Manual* underlines the importance of this point.[15] OSHA's first-instance sanctions system means that even if an employer corrects a violation in front of the inspector, this act cannot influence whether a fine is imposed, a method that contributes to a hostile atmosphere.

In Sweden, whether to give advance notice is left up to the inspector. The course material used to training inspectors says that "there are advantages to giving advance notice of your visit. Then the employer can prepare himself, and the union representative can have time to talk with fellow workers." The material also emphasizes that inspectors should try to create a relaxed attitude during the inspection. During the walk-around, the inspector is instructed, "You can talk about things that don't directly have to do with your mission, in order to create good rapport. Be sure to avoid controversial subjects." Unlike OSHA inspectors who are instructed to take notes constantly during an inspection to record violations, Swedish inspectors are warned that "to write too much during the walkaround can be impractical and irritating. While you're writing, the others will perhaps have nothing to do, or, even worse, will begin discussing some problem, leaving you outside the discussion."[16]

OSHA citations state what sections of the regulations had been violated. A violation might read something like,

> 29 CFS 1926.500(9)(c). Failure to guard wall openings, from which there is a drop of more than 4 feet—openings 2 through 6 not guarded.

Swedish inspectors, in their written inspection notices, are not supposed to refer to violations of regulations but to what steps should be taken. Instead of talking about failure to guard a machine, a written inspection notice would say something like, "A fixed guard should be installed to cover the unguarded transmission."

One of the questions in the in-depth and national surveys was designed to tap inspector enforcement attitudes. At one pole of a seven-point scale was the statement, "It's better for OSHA to be a tough enforcer of the regulations, even at the risk of being considered punitive," and at the other end the statement, "It's better for OSHA to seek to persuade

Table 21–2
U.S. and Swedish Inspectors' Enforcement Attitudes

In-depth survey	
American inspectors	3.4 (N = 40)
Swedish inspectors	5.1 (N = 18)
National survey	
American inspectors	4.2 (N = 78)
Swedish inspectors	4.8 (N = 73)

Note: Responses are on a seven-point scale. Scores less than 4 reveal that inspectors believe that enforcement should be tough—greater than 4, that it is better to persuade.

employers to comply with regulations voluntarily, even at the risk of being considered soft." The mean replies (Table 21–2) suggest that American inspectors tend to emphasize enforcement and Swedish inspectors, cooperation.[17] Comments by Swedish inspectors made during in-depth interviews illustrate this point. One said, "I'm not one of those who likes to write too many written inspection notices. I would rather reason together with the employer and the safety steward, and come up with a solution everyone accepts. Writing is so impersonal." Another, "I try to reconcile the parties during the inspection. The first time around I don't try to enforce every point, so as to get our relationship functioning as smoothly as possible." A third said, "I think we can give in on an issue, even if it makes the workplace more hazardous, in order to preserve cooperation. I don't want to destroy cooperation for good."

The Problems with Punishment

The American decision to rely on enforcement based on legal punishment created two major problems: punishment causes resentment, and the use of the legal system increases the transaction costs of achieving a given purpose.

Punishment (in this case, fines) tends to cause resentment because in exchange for the change in behavior, there is no improvement in one's original state but merely an avoidance of worsening. This tends to be perceived as an unfair exchange. To change behavior for a reward, however, means that both the person changing and the agent seeking the changed behavior are better off: the agent because the behavior has been changed as he wishes, and the person changing because an improvement in the original state has been achieved. Elements of OSHA inspections that grow out of the enforcement system described in the previous sections increase resentment further.

Resentment creates two problems. In a democracy, the resentful may

Table 21–3

Inspectors' Perceptions of Employer Attitudes during OSHA Inspections

How Often Do the Employer Representatives:	Most of the Time	Sometimes	Seldom	Almost Never
Seem to be afraid of you when you come in?*	36%	38%	15%	10%
Try to intimidate you?†	0	23	28	50
Try to be overly flattering, just to get on your good side?*	28	26	28	18

Note: Percentages may add up to more than 100 percent because of rounding.
*N = 39.
†N = 40.

act politically against the object of resentment, thus threatening the political future of a program. It also works against voluntary compliance. No sooner did OSHA inspectors move into the field and begin fining employers than the latter began displaying resentment over the treatment they were being subjected to. Table 21–3 displays results from the American in-depth inspectors' survey showing the tense atmosphere surrounding OSHA inspections. Within one year of the effective date of the OSHAct, members of Congress, inundated by protest mail, had introduced some one hundred bills to amend or even repeal the law. In 1972, only a year after the act had gone into effect, the House Select Committee on Small Business held hearings on the effects of OSHA on small business. Later that same year the House Education and Labor Committee and the Senate Labor and Public Welfare Committee held oversight hearings. In 1974 two more hearings in the House and one in the Senate were held. The testimony produced scattered complaints about costs of complying with OSHA regulations, but much of it, and a large proportion of the bitterness, related to how OSHA regulations were enforced. Congressmen presented letters from constituents who complained of the treatment they received.[18]

> A few years ago this type of harassment by the mobsters was considered illegal. Today the U.S. government does it, and it is legal. Please compare the penalty of up to $10,000 fine PER violation of the act with those extended to draft card burners, flag defilers, establishment vandals and other gross disrespectors of property rights and government. As a small business man, my fate is much worse than theirs.

> A criminal guilty of drug, robbery or murder charges is shown more consideration for his Constitutional rights than the owner of a business. For example, an OSHA inspector can enter your place of business without a search warrant. Try that on a drug pusher and the whole thing is thrown out of court.

If we allow tactics such as we experienced with this U.S. Department of Labor group from Billings, all the lives that were lost fighting Adolf Hitler and his henchmen were lost in vain. . . . We do not expect any special favors or attempts to bend the Laws for us, but we do expect this type of Gestapoism by Government employees to be stopped at once. It violates everything that our country is founded on. The Law Abiding Citizen is afraid to walk the streets of our larger cities day or night because of the Criminal element in our country. Why don't we use this misdirected energy to Restore Law and Order in our country?

The hearings also produced statements lamenting that employers were fined even though they complied with changes that the inspector required. One congressman told the following story:

[OSHA] came in on Monday, gave them an inspection. The OSHA inspector went through and cited him on 12 minor violations and 2 majors.

He said, "Mr. OSHA officer, are you going to be in town this week? . . . Will you come back before you leave town and check me out and see if I am up to snuff?"

The guy comes back on Thursday. . . . He had all the discrepancies corrected. The OSHA inspectors said, "I am really impressed with your attitude. You are really in there pitching. We really appreciate having someone like you. Here is your citation." He got fined $500.[19]

When OSHA asked a small business group to give it the names of members who had protested against heavy-handed inspectors so that the charges could be investigated, not a single complainant was willing to authorize the release of his name. One explained, "I am of the opinion, sadly, that the United States government is not to be trusted. It would not surprise me in the least if the remedial action they speak of would be directed at the source . . . of information, and not at themselves." The response of another employer was similar: "I have little doubt that the Labor Department would use this information in order to seek out our business, discover many violations and close us down. We have worked hard over the past six and a half years to establish our business, and, being in partnership with my parents, I do not feel I could fairly ask them also to risk being put out of business with OSHA officials as judge and jury. Isn't it too bad we have come to this in America."[20]

Resentment at punishment was also expressed through challenges in court to OSHA compliance activities. Violations found by inspectors may be appealed to the Occupational Safety and Health Review Commission, a quasijudicial panel independent of OSHA. When the commission was first formed, its staff estimated that its caseload would be one hundred to two hundred cases a year. Instead it ran about three hundred to four hundred a month.[21] Business also used the courts to display their resentment at OSHA's enforcement system by appeals alleging that key aspects of OSHA's enforcement procedures violated the Bill of Rights. One citation was appealed on the grounds that the provision in the OSHAct allowing the imposition of fines without a jury trial was unconstitutional, and the case went to the Supreme Court, which rejected the argument. The second case to reach the Supreme Court involved a businessman who refused an OSHA inspector entry to his premises, alleging warrantless inspections to be a violation of the protection against unreasonable search. The Supreme Court ruled that warrants were indeed required but established liberal procedures for OSHA to obtain them.[22]

OSHA's political problems resulting from its failure to achieve agreement at the rule-making stage were thus compounded by employers' resentment over its enforcement methods, a combination that spelled serious political trouble. Although outsiders have difficulty influencing bureaucratic behavior during rule making, the use of fines is established by statute, not by OSHA, and it is easier for Congress to intervene here.

Complaints about OSHA's enforcement methods led Congress to try to pass amendments to change these methods. As early as 1972 the House passed an amendment removing firms with fewer than fifteen employees from OSHA coverage entirely, but it did not pass the Senate. In 1973 a similar amendment passed both houses and did not become law only because President Nixon vetoed the appropriations bill to which the amendment was attached. In 1974 an amendment exempting firms with fewer than twenty-five employers was again passed by the House but rejected in the Senate.

Until 1976 OSHA had thus narrowly avoided changes in its enforcement methods. But the precariousness of OSHA's perch was demonstrated by the results of a seemingly small event in the summer of 1976 involving a pamphlet that OSHA had just issued, *Safety with Beef Cattle*. As part of a program to prepare booklets on job hazards for distribution to workers, OSHA had contracted to prepare a series of booklets for farmworkers. Some brochures were designed for workers whose native language was not English; there was no intention to distribute them to, say, Kansas wheat farmers. The first booklet in the series was one of those so written. However, this was nowhere stated on the brochure itself, so as not to offend recipients. Instead, it ended up offending everyone else. To someone not aware of the background, the booklet appeared paternalistic and patronizing; one passage warned farmworkers to be careful lest they slip on cowdung. Outraged newspaper editorials followed.

The booklet was withdrawn, but the damage was done. The uproar occurred just as Congress was debating the year's Labor-HEW appropriation. The coincidence proved to be more than OSHA's standing on Capitol Hill could bear. Amid floor attacks on the agency, the House passed a series of amendments aimed at OSHA enforcement effort. Assessing the situation, OSHA supporters decided some concessions would have to be made. They accepted an amendment exempting from coverage farms with fewer than ten employees and another, hitting at OSHA's fine system in a way no amendment had previously been able to do, prohibiting imposing fines for nonserious violations if there were fewer than ten such violations in a citation.[23]

Supporters of OSHA are unhappy that its enforcement methods have caused resentment among employers, but they have been caught in the American dilemma captured by Edmund Burke: in the absence of other inducements to change behavior, the alternative to punishment is perceived as a massive flouting of the regulations. The dilemma is illustrated by union reactions to proposals that OSHA inspectors be allowed to give employers penalty-free consultation. In order to preserve the principle of first-instance sanctions, whenever an OSHA inspector enters a workplace, it must be to make an inspection. (OSHA personnel may answer questions over the telephone, and many states offer consultation services.) Early on, proposals were made to amend the OSHAct to allow the agency to set up a service to give advice to business. This suggestion appears uncontroversial, yet union spokesmen were so afraid that any dilution of existing policy would destroy compliance that they successfully opposed on-site consultation.[24]

The second problem that resentment causes is that it works against voluntary compliance. Increasing the population of voluntary compliers relative to those who do not comply voluntarily is important for any enforcement system. "The sociological mind reels," John Scott notes, "at the cost of social controls which would have to cope with the unrestrained exercise of amoral human interest."[25] A number of psychological experiments show that people performing a behavior in exchange for some inducement continue spontaneously to engage in the behavior a shorter time after the inducement has ceased being offered than groups performing without benefit of the inducement.[26] Rewards encourage the development of attitudes favorable to voluntary compliance, but the resentment produced by punishment discourages the development of such attitudes. Indeed the dilemma of deterrence is that punishment can actually decrease the sum of compliance by increasing resentment. The evidence from psychological experiments, though not entirely consistent, tends to show that behavior change that punishment brings about ceases as soon as the direct application of the punishment stops unless the punishment of undesired behavior is accompanied by rewarding the behavior one wishes to promote.[27] Alvin Gouldner's *Patterns of Industrial Bureaucracy* is a classic study of the effects of the introduction of a system of formal rules and punishments in a plant where there had previously been few rules. The new system created resentment and produced a situation where employees worked only when someone was watching them.[28]

The greater likelihood that rewards will produce attitude change with respect to the behavior one seeks to encourage than will punishment may be explained in terms of a cognitive dissonance perspective used by some psychologists. Cognitive dissonance occurs whenever there is an imbalance between positive feelings about one object and negative feelings about another object associated with the first one. It is argued that people tend to reduce cognitive dissonance either by becoming less positive to the first object or more positive to the second.[29] For instance, if the Democratic party is associated with support for an increased minimum wage, a Democratic opponent of such a measure will tend to change either his feelings toward it or toward the Democrats. Thus if a person feels positive about a reward he is receiving for a given behavior but initially is indifferent or negative toward the behavior itself, he will experience cognitive dissonance. The dissonance may be reduced by changing his attitude toward the behavior in a positive direction. If a person is being punished for not doing something he does not want to do, there will be a cognitive dissonance; his attitude will remain negative. And if the person is initially indifferent to or only mildly negative toward the behavior, he may become more negative toward it to reduce cognitive dissonance.

The Swedish enforcement system, which uses predominantly normative inducements, has not produced the same resentment among employers. Although it is not true that the use of normative inducements always causes less resentment than use of economic or coercive ones, they do tend in this direction, perhaps because of their propensity to be associated with participation in small groups that provide members with an excess of rewards over punishments. If the safety committee has succeeded in its purpose, employer participants will be receiving more psychological benefits than they are paying costs. In this context, any normative punishment from employee representatives is less resented because its source is a group that bestows, on balance, benefits. Also given the normal conflict of interest between labor and management, it is unlikely that employers would be as stung by criticism as they are pleasantly surprised by praise. Given the status gap between workers and employers, safety stewards will likely seldom give employers a scolding to their face. The main inducements safety stewards probably use, then, are normative rewards.

Certainly there are other reasons beside the Swedish enforcement system for this lack of resentment, but the system is important. The relative lack of resentment could probably not survive its replacement by the American reliance on legal punishment, although any new resentment would probably not attain American levels. In one question on the Swedish in-depth inspectors' survey, inspectors were presented with a brief description of the American enforcement system and asked their reaction to it. Eleven of seventeen respondents thought it a bad one, two were ambivalent, and only three considered it was a good idea. Six of the eleven critical inspectors spontaneously stated that the introduction of such a system in Sweden would lead to increased employer resentment. Responded one inspector plaintively, "If we did that, an inspector could never feel himself welcome at a firm."

The Swedish manual used for training new inspectors warns them to "count on the fact that setting sanctions in motion can create a harder climate for you at the workplace."[30] In 1974 the Worker Protection Act was changed to allow imposition of conditional fines together with orders and prohibitions, and although a significant rise in the number of orders and prohibitions issued occurred, these still constituted a small fraction of 1 percent of the total number of inspections. This increase was accompanied by the appearance, for the first time, of contests of inspections. (Inspector decisions in Sweden may be appealed to agency headquarters and then, as an ultimate step, to the cabinet.) The number of contests has increased steadily from two in a six-month period in 1974 to fifteen in the same-length period in 1976. In Sweden, too, punishment increases resentment.

Another problem created by OSHA enforcement is that the use of the legal system increases transaction costs. Violations must be proven and the accused afforded an opportunity to appeal rulings. This is *a fortiori* so in America, with the great concern for individual rights in proceedings.

In Sweden appeals involve one submission of a letter by the appealing party and a reply by the district. There is no hearing or opportunity for oral examination, and no rules exist for where the burden of proof lies in deciding appeals. Lawyers are almost never involved.[31] In America appeals are first heard by an administrative law judge in the area where the business is located. Proceedings are oral and include cross-examination. OSHA is always represented by a lawyer, and the employer is usually represented by counsel. Burden of proof is on OSHA. A three-member review commission panel in Washington is the next step. It relies on the record developed earlier and on new briefs filed by the parties. Its decisions may in turn be appealed to the court of appeals and from there to the Supreme Court.

Since violations must be proved in order to mete out punishment, OSHA inspectors must be scrupulous about documentation. Inspectors in the in-depth inspectors' survey reported that their supervisors' most common request after reviewing their last ten inspection reports was for documentation. This means taking photos ("I try to get the employer or an employee representative so the employer can't say it was taken at another plant," one inspector noted) and employee statements. For a violation to exist, there must be worker exposure to the hazard, so if a particular machine is not running when the inspector comes through, the inspector must get a worker to say he normally uses it. Consideration of court challenge is the main explanation for a number of policies followed by many area offices. For example, most threshold limit values are expressed as eight-hour averages because often exposure varies widely over different phases of the process cycle, while other times a process is in operation only for a short period each day. Sometimes the inspector sees that exposure is relatively constant or observes that a process cycle is short enough to provide measurements of exposure peaks and troughs without sampling for a full eight hours. In such cases, eight-hour sampling merely increases the time an inspector must spend.

The problem is that if the regulations express a threshold limit value as an eight-hour average, an inspector who has not sampled the full period is open to legal challenge. Thus many area directors are wary about letting inspectors use their judgment on whether a full eight hours is necessary in a particular case, afraid of what will happen when lawyers question OSHA relentlessly about some 18½ minute sampling gap. Four of the fourteen area directors in the area directors' course survey responded that if an inspector had sampled for only six hours, they would insist that zero values be entered for the remaining two hours for the purpose of computing whether the threshold limit value had been exceeded. This means that in some cases where a threshold limit value has been exceeded, legal requirements prevent citation. In contrast, responses to the Swedish national district chiefs' survey showed that in half of the districts, inspectors issued written inspection notices in health cases without doing any sampling at all. (This is not as arbitrary as it may sound. Frequently an experienced person can tell that for a certain type of operation, a threshold limit value will be exceeded where control measures are absent.)

In situations such as these, the issue in any citation appeal may be not whether a hazard exists but whether legal requirements have been followed. To take a bizarre catch-22 type of situation, determining noncompliance with threshold limit values requires sampling, often using devices attached to the employee's body, but such devices may hinder employee movement, leading an employer to claim that the sample was not representative of worker exposure.

Perhaps the most unfortunate results come when legal requirements actually interfere with compliance because they make regulations so hard to understand.

There have been numerous complaints about the incomprehensibility of OSHA regulations, but Assistant Secretary Guenther pointed out that "there is a limit as to how far we can go in paraphrasing or simplifying the language of the standards, because, as you well know, the standards are a legal document in addition to an engineering document."[32]

Although OSHA inspectors may not give on-site consultation, there is no logical reason to believe that during an inspection they should not give employers advice, to the extent of their expertise, on how to correct violations. Yet in 1971 the OSHA legal office stated that if inspectors gave advice and an employer following the recommendations had not succeeded in correcting the problem, the citation could be thrown out in court. By contrast, most Swedish inspectors in the in-depth inspectors' survey responded that they considered giving employers advice as an important part of their job. "An inspector should give examples about how problems can be solved," one said. "Otherwise he's a bad inspector."

The cross-cultural validity of these generalizations about consequences of formalization is illustrated by the infrequent experience in Sweden with orders and prohibitions. The ASV [Worker Protection Board] training manual points out that "an order or prohibition demands more exact documentation. As soon as you suggest that sanctions may be used, you must be more careful about assembling documentation."[33]

The Problem with Normative Inducements

If the problem with using fines to induce compliance is that they produce resentment, the problem with normative inducements is that their success depends on placing the person whose behavior one seeks to influence into a group of relevant others who can influence him. The Swedes have set up institutions to achieve that aim, but success is not assured in any individual case. If this method does not work, compliance based on normative inducements exerts no inducements at all. Hence there arose in Sweden at the end of the period under investigation some criticism against the compliance system. The criticism, not nearly as strong as that in the United States, took an opposite tack. The report on occupational safety and health to the 1976 LO Congress stated that "consequences of violations of the Worker Protection Act are not severe enough."[34] One article in the LO journal was even headlined "Safety and Health Inspectors in the U.S. Have More Power than in Sweden"![35]

The 1976 final report of the State Commission on the Work Environment dealt at some length with sanctions under the new law but proposed no major revisions because "a strong local safety organization is doubtless a much more effective guarantee for compliance with the law than any general criminalization of actions violating the law or the regulations."[36] The committee did recommend, however, that ASV could, at its discretion, issue certain kinds of regulations with first-instance criminal sanctions after a guilty verdict in a trial. But Gunnar Danielsson, ASV director-general, believed that "it is not the idea that most regulations are going to be associated with first-instance sanctions. We must avoid making this law into a criminal law."[37]

Dissatisfaction from unions about primary reliance on normative inducements was expressed through demands to give safety stewards, or safety committees with union majorities, the right to make safety and health decisions. Were these demands realized, the role of safety stewards would no longer be simply to influence employers but to determine factory conditions themselves. LO raised such demands during negotiations for the 1976 LO-SAF safety and health agreement. They were successful in getting the composition of the safety committee changed to give union representatives a one-vote majority (the white-collar union at the plant would be included on the union side as well as the LO union). However, they failed in their central demand. The agreement provided that safety committee decisions involving spending money could be binding only were the vote unanimous, unless the committee was given a certain budget by the firm, in which case the committee could decide on the disposition of the budget by majority vote.[38]

Notes

1. Richard D. Schwartz, "Social Factors in the Development of Legal Control," *Yale Law Journal* 63 (February 1954).

2. Edmund Burke, *Reflections on the Revolution in France*, in *Selected Writings of Edmund Burke*, ed. Walter J. Bate (New York: Modern Library, 1960), 388.

3. Leon Radzionwicz, *A History of English Law and Its Administration* (New York: Macmillan, 1948), 25. The same phenomenon is observable in contemporary America.

4. On this difference, see Lennart Lundquist, *The Hare and the Tortoise* (Ann Arbor: University of Michigan Press, 1979).

5. Arbetarskyddsnamnden, *Allmanna regler for den lokala sakerhetstjanstens organisation* (Stockholm: Tiden, 1948), 50.

6. LO-SAF, *En Battre arbetsmiljo* (Stockholm: Prisma, 1969).

7. *Utbildning och upplysning inom arbetsmiljon* (Stockholm: Rotobeckman, 1973), 42–43.

8. Arbetarskyddsnamnden, *Battre Arbetsmiljo* (Stockholm: Tiden, 1975).

9. LO-SAF, *Overenskommelse om utbildning i arbetsmiljofragor* (Stockholm, 1976).

10. Arbetarskyddslagen, sec. 40(b).

11. "Hundra stopp 1975—och paragrafen anvands mycket mer," *Arbetarskydd* (May 1976): 2.

12. LO-SAF, *Arbetsmiljoavtalet* (Stockholm: Tiden, 1976), 42 (emphasis added).

13. LO-SAF, *Arbetarskydd och foretagshalsovard* (Stockholm: Arbetarskyddnamnden, 1967), 38–39.

14. LO-SAF, *Arbetsmiljoavtalet*, 26.

15. OSHA, *Field Operations Reporting Manual* (Washington, D.C., 1975), chap. V-1.

16. Ture Lindstrom, et al., *Inspektionsmetodik och yrkesskadeutredning* (Stockholm: Stencil, 1975), 7, 9, 11.

17. Differences for the in-depth inspectors' survey are far more dramatic, although the difference between the mean answers for the national inspectors' surveys is statistically significant to the 0.01 level. It is hard to know whether the in-depth or national results should be considered more indicative of inspectors' feelings. Respondents in mail-administered questionnaires may tend to give intermediate, indeterminate responses—that is, to circle "4"—because they had not given the questionnaire as much thought as did the respondents in interviews.

18. These quotations appear in U.S. House of Representatives, Hearings before the Select Subcommittee on Labor of the Committee on Education and Labor, *Occupational Safety and Health Act of 1970 Oversight and Proposed Amendments*, 93d Cong., 2d sess., March–November 1974; and U.S., House of Representatives, Hearings before the Select Subcommittee on Labor of the Committee on Education and Labor, *Occupational Safety and Health Act of 1970 Oversight and Proposed Amendments*, 92d cong., 2d sess., March 1972, pp. 43–44, 173, 399, 1488–1489.

19. *House Labor Hearings* (1974), p. 107.

20. Quoted from Neal Heard, "Undue Process of Law," *Trial* (September 1975): 26.

21. Nicholas A. Ashford, *Crisis in the Workplace* (Cambridge: MIT Press, 1976), 284, 286.

22. *Atlas Roofing Co. v. Occupational Safety and Health Review Commission*, 430 U.S. 442 (1977); *Marshall v. Barlow's, Inc.*, 436 U.S. 307 (1978).

23. Since these were amendments to the year's appropriations bill and not to the OSHAct itself, they applied only for one year and not permanently.

24. See, for instance, the testimony of Jack Sheehan and George Taylor in *House Labor Hearings* (1972), pp. 440–448, 607.

25. John F. Scott, *Internalization of Norms* (Englewood Cliffs, N.J.: Prentice-Hall, 1971), 114.

26. Edward L. Deci, *Intrinsic Motivation* (New York: Plenum Press, 1975), 133–134.

27. Albert Bandura, *Handbook of Behavior Modification* (New York: Holt, 1969), 316–317.

28. Alvin Gouldner, *Patterns of Industrial Bureaucracy* (New York: Free Press, 1954).

29. Leon Festinger, *A Theory of Cognitive Dissonance* (Evanston: Row, Peterson, 1957).

30. Lindstrom, et. al., *Inspektionsmetodik*, 14.

31. Interview with Goran Lindh, ASV.

32. *1972 House Labor Hearings*, 1972, p. 351.

33. Lindstrom, et. al., *Inspektionsmetodik*, 14.

34. LO, *Arbetsmiljo* (Stockholm: Prisma, 1976), 59.

35. Birger Viklund, "Yrkesinspektionen i USA har mera makt an i Sverige," *LO-Tidningen* 57 (February 10, 1977): 13.

36. *Arbetsmiljolag*, 304–305.

37. Interview with Gunnar Danielsson.

38. LO-SAF, *Arbetsmiljoavtalet*, sec. 19, 22.

22

Class and Politics in the Organization of Public Administration: The U.S. Department of Labor

Nancy DiTomaso

I. Introduction

Most analyses of public agencies take their existence for granted and focus instead on the politics of programs and policies. In other words, they have a theory of politics, but not a theory of the state itself. Yet such a theory is necessary if we are to understand the how, as well as the who and when, in studies of public administration. In this article, I address the how of public administration by a case study of the U.S. Department of Labor at two periods in its history. There are two basic points to the analysis: (1) decisions must be made about how public agencies will be organized, and these decisions are subject to a great deal of conflict among those groups that each think they will win or lose critical access to state power, and (2) because early decisions about organizational structure become institutionalized in the political process that follows the development of a new agency, subsequent political battles will be fought over attempts to reorganize.

An ancillary part of the argument is to interpret the meaning of various kinds of decisions about structure. Too often in organizational theory, the principles of administration have been developed in the absence of a particular case, thus leaving the meaning of certain conditional structures ambiguous. For example, within the Weberian model of organizations, hierarchy or centralization of decision making has been taken as the best means to maintain managerial control of subordinates, and alternatively, decentralization has been assumed to be a sharing of power. I will argue in part of this analysis that that is not necessarily so. Indeed, centralization or decentralization are—like many other aspects of organizational structure—subject to contingencies and constraints in both their purpose and their effect.

One of the basic premises on which this argument is built is that if conflict exists between groups within a democratic society, they will be just as concerned about the form of state administration as with its substance. This was certainly true in the U.S. Department of Labor, which was created during a period of intense conflict between management and workers over both the development of trade unions and the organizational control of industry and commerce in the country. Importantly, it continued to be true through other periods of the department's history when working-class and other subordinate groups were making demands on the state that would affect the resources of business and industry.

A second basic premise from which this analysis follows is that state managers do not have blueprints that enable them to know in advance the consequences of particular administrative struggles. Rather, they, like all managers, respond successively to crises as they occur, sometimes reinstituting a program, policy, or structure that had previously been abandoned or sometimes adopting those that had previously been rejected. In other words, they do whatever is necessary to meet the challenges of the day.

II. The Hypotheses

Based on my study of the U.S. Department of Labor, I can offer the following hypotheses about how power is exercised through bureaucratic structures within the state. Because state administration within the United States is part of a democratic governing process, it is subject to demands and constraints from any group that feels it has an interest in what the agency is likely to do. If several such groups are in conflict with each other, the agency itself is likely to be the subject of conflict, and in the playing out of their conflict, they are likely to seek allies to support their claims on the state, thus expanding the constraints with which the agency is confronted. In the formative period of the U.S. Department of Labor, the conflict was primarily between capital and labor, but farmers also were occasionally involved. In the later reorganization of the Labor Department, the conflicting groups were more differentiated: big and small business, craft and industrial unions, and minority groups and their supporters. Conflict erupted over each of the following decision points: who would get to define legitimate goals, the range of legal authority, the size and composition of the budget, the pattern of authority and decision making, and how the recruitment and screening of personnel would be carried out. As each of these decisions was affected by the general structure of control within the agency, a major focus of conflict was the relative centralization or decentralization of the agency at various times and for various purposes, but especially in the later period of reorganization.

Important to our understanding of how conflict over organizational structure shifts to meet new crises or circumstances is that the structure preferred by those in dominant positions was not always centralization and by those in subordinate positions was not always decentralization. Indeed, it depended on what was at stake and who else could make claims to it. Precisely because centralization concentrates power, it also makes it more visible, and when the locus of power is more visible, then the "point of change" is more easily identified. Therefore, centralization is an option preferred by dominant coalitions within organizations only when subordinates are acquiescent. However, when subordinates are pressuring for change, and especially if they have some hopes of succeeding in their demands, decentralization may be seen as a means to fragment power and make it more difficult to change. If pressure for change comes from outside pressure groups instead of subordinates, then a centralized structure that is insulated or buffered from its environment may be the preferred structure. And, within a democratic structure, when a new administration comes to power, the old administration may pressure for decentralization in order to insure its own access and to make reform of the agency more unwieldy. Of course, those who are excluded from the dominant coalition, inside or outside the agency, will pressure for the opposite in each case.

The creation of a Department of Labor was supported by industrial workers and tradespeople, especially those involved in the incipient union movement. It was, at first, opposed by politicians whose primary ties were to business. Opposition was redirected to setting the limits for organizational form and mission and to involvement in selection of personnel and control of the budget. In later years, conflict over reorganization reopened many of the same issues with strong consciousness of the alternative consequences of decisions regarding organizational structure.

III. Formation of the U.S. Department of Labor

The National Labor Union, a short-lived national organization of workers, was the first to demand an "executive department of government in Washington" to protect the interests of labor "above all others." Although "labor," it claimed, "was the foundation and cause of national prosperity," workers had no government agency to represent them (Sylvis, 1872:293). The demand for a department of labor was part of the more general struggle for workers' rights, which was critically shaped in the years from the Civil War to World War I. The major reason workers wanted their own government agency was to identify the sources and the distribution of wealth, as Terence Powderly argued:

> The legitimate aim of the labor bureau is to ascertain beyond the shadow of a doubt what the earnings of labor and capital are in order that justice may be done to both, in order that unscrupulous employers will not have it in their power to rob labor of its just dues, and take all of the profits of the combination of labor and capital for their own aggrandizement. (Powderly, 1890:306)

Workers resisted wage cuts, demanded higher wages and shorter hours, and insisted on their right to know how much wealth their employers made on their labor power.

The state of Massachusetts was the first government to respond to the demands of workers for a department of labor. Massachusetts workers were more organized than any others in the country at the time (perhaps because of the concentration of craftworkers in the state), and they were translating their union activities into the formation of producer cooperatives and into political strength at the polls. After a particularly bitter strike by shoemakers, who were called by one account the "most powerful labor organization in the world" (Lescohier, 1969:8), the political leadership in Massachusetts feared the disaffection of workers. To appease them, the state established the Bureau of Statistics of Labor, whose function was to "collect statistical details relating to all departments of labor in the Commonwealth, especially in its relations to the commercial, industrial, social, educational, and sanitary conditions of the laboring classes" (Wright, 1892 and Pidgin, 1904:7).

General Henry K. Oliver, former state legislator who was involved in the active reform movement in Massachusetts at the time, was appointed to head the new agency. Oliver assumed that a primary goal of the agency was the advocacy for workers. As one of their primary interests was to determine how much wealth employers had so they could know whether they were being paid a fair day's wage, he used the summons power of the agency to study deposits in savings banks. Regarding the incident, the Boston *Commonwealth* reported in 1872, "So the effort now is to abolish the bureau of labor. The struggle between capital and labor is growing bitter—bitter even now on the side of capital. It objects to investigation of its methods" (Reported in Congressional Record, House, April 19, 1884:3141). The enraged employers were unable to get the bureau abolished, but they were successful in their efforts to have Oliver replaced. The government appointed instead Carroll Davidson Wright, a man from a prominent family who had no ties to any labor organization and who had promised to maintain the "neutrality" of the agency.

Wright was to become prominent within the government for his "responsible" role in the collection of statistics on workers. The Massachusetts bureau, under his leadership, became the model for other states. Bureaus were established in Pennsylvania in 1872; Ohio in 1877; New Jersey in 1878; Indiana, Illinois, and Missouri in 1879; and New York, California, Michigan, and Wisconsin in 1883. Wright took the initiative to form a national organization of chiefs of state bureaus of labor, and he used his influence "to frustrate every effort to commit the chiefs to a program of labor reform" (Lombardi, 1942:39). Nevertheless, following the severe depression of 1873 to 1877, which culminated in the most violent and extensive strike the country had ever experienced, he joined with various labor leaders to promote a national bureau of labor statistics.

Legislation to establish such a bureau was modeled on the Massachusetts law and introduced in the U.S. Congress in 1884. A number of issues were discussed in both the Senate and the House; a checklist of some of these is provided in the following remark given in testimony regarding the proposed bureau:

> This is not a question of an eight-hour law; it is not a question of checking the accumulation of great estates in single hands; it is not a question of dividing the products of labor between labor and capital; it is a simple question of having information furnished by public methods and by public instrumentalities to legislators and to other persons interested in these public questions. (Congressional Record, Senate, March 7, 1884:1676)

It was pointed out in the discussions on the bill that each important labor organization in the country demanded a department of labor among its other requests. In the context of the discussion, it was noted also that the secretary of state had requested information on wages, living costs, and production costs from Great Britain, France, Germany, Belgium, Italy, Spain, the Netherlands, Sweden, Norway, and Denmark. The intent was to show that conditions of workers were far better in the United States than in Europe, but similar information did not exist for the United States. In addition, the information was desired to influence the bitterly debated tariff legislation of the time, "in consequence of the agitation in regard to the relations between capital and labor, which has signally marked the last decade" (Congressional Record, House, April 19, 1884:3142). Just as important was the fear among the legislators of what would occur if something were not done to solve "the labor question":

> If the existing rate of wages paid to workingmen in this country can not be maintained, and increased if possible, I despair of the maintenance of the Republic for many generations. (Senator George F. Hoar, of Massachusetts, in Congressional Record, Senate, March 7, 1884:1676)

Much of the discussion on the legislation revolved around where to place the national bureau of labor statistics. Those who assumed there was harmony of interests between capital and labor suggested the functions of the proposed bureau be added to the already existing Bureau of Statistics in the Department of Treasury, which, as the head of the agency noted, was really a department of commerce. (This bureau was the core for the later creation of a Department of Commerce.) Some suggested that it be included in the independent (noncabinet) Department of Agriculture, but this was never taken as a viable suggestion. Wright recommended that the bureau be placed in the Department of Interior, which already housed a bureau for the collection of education statistics. Because there were already committees on education and labor in both the House and the Senate, Wright's suggestion followed the already existing definitions of the proper location of labor matters in the federal government, namely, as social and not as economic issues.

Wright's major concern, then as earlier, was to prevent the agency from becoming "political" in the sense of becoming an advocate for the demands of organized labor. He assumed, like many of the congressional supporters of the legislation, that information on the conditions of workers would neutralize the political demands of workers: "to harmonize and unify existing divergencies between capital and labor" (Grossman and MacLaury, 1975:26). In contrast, a common theme among leaders of organized labor was that the agency would rigidly scrutinize "the means by which employers or moneyed men acquire wealth" and "put a stop to illegitimate profit-taking" (Powderly, 1890:158–160). Despite several forms of reorganization, the Department of Labor was never to take on the major task that workers had envisioned for it. Wright's recommendations, both for the organization and function of the national bureau, prevailed.

After the legislation was passed, labor leaders lobbied for seven months, without success, to get a union person appointed as head of the bureau. Instead, after delaying for many months, President Arthur appointed Wright to the position, while he simultaneously retained his position in Massachusetts. Wright gained increasing favor among government leaders, although he never developed strong ties with organized labor. Among other tasks, he was given responsibility for conducting the national census. In a short time, he became, for all intents and purposes, the adviser to the president on labor matters.

In 1888, his responsibility, along with the structure of the Bureau of Labor Statistics, was expanded again. The primary goal was for Wright to hire assistants to collect information on wages and working conditions in Europe, again within the context of the growing concern over tariffs. According to one congressman, the new legislation made "in other words, a department of industrial statistics" (Congressional Record, House, March 21, 1888:2318) of the bureau. The largest labor organization in the country at the time, the Knights of Labor, continued to lobby in local, state, and federal forums for a cabinet-level department of labor, but to no avail. Wright continued to argue, and continued to be supported by Congress, that the only way to prevent the agency from becoming "political" was to deny it cabinet status and to keep it removed from too close an association with organized labor. The "labor question" itself was a major part of the political agenda of the Congress for years, with many commissions reporting on the causes of strikes and lockouts. Following recommendations of the hearings after the extensive 1886 strikes for the eight-hour day, the Bureau of Labor Statistics was made into an independent, noncabinet Department of Labor, with Wright again at its head. Wright continued in the position for another fifteen years, but his impending retirement worried some of the conservative members of Congress and the business community. Data of central importance to business was collected by the Bureau of Statistics in the Department of Treasury, but major corporate leaders increasingly argued for more extensive information in order to expand markets abroad.

In 1900, the Republican party included a demand for a cabinet-level Department of Commerce in its party platform. The proposed department was to incorporate all of the separate statistical bureaus of interest to business, including as a subordinate bureau the previously created, independent Department of Labor. The legislation was quickly introduced in the Republican-controlled Congress, and hearings began in 1901. In the Senate, support for the legislation was orchestrated by people like Senator Mark Hanna of Ohio, one of the major capitalists in the country. Hanna is noted, among other things, for controlling the political machine in Cleveland, Ohio, and for organizing William McKinley's notorious front-porch presidential campaign against William Jennings Bryan.

The overwhelming concern among business leaders at the time for expanding foreign commerce explains the timing of the proposal for a cabinet-level Department of Commerce, but this only explains in part why the Department of Labor was to be subordinated within the new agency as a bureau. Wright's administration of the Department of Labor was characterized in the hearings on the legislation as "beyond praise," and "perfect." Senator Knute Nelson of Minnesota, who introduced the legislation for the Department of Commerce, also praised Wright, but added, "He is a very able man, but he will not always be with us." Because, Nelson argued, the future head of the Department of Labor may not be "so able and so good as he . . . it is altogether safer for the public service to have a division or a bureau of this kind under some responsible executive department" (U.S. Department of Commerce and Labor, 1904:491).

Hanna was one of several Republicans to argue that the interests of labor and capital are "identical and mutual." To this end, Hanna also argued, contrary to testimony offered by Samuel Gompers, the head of the American Federation of Labor, that organized labor had no objections to the legislation. Hanna argued that the proposed Department of Commerce should incorporate Labor because "a close, effective organization, with one able executive head, is always the best way to accomplish a result" (U.S. Department of Commerce and Labor, 1904:499).

His motivations were not only administrative efficiency, however. He also argued that "there is no interest in the United States today that demands the attention of Congress . . . more" than establishing a Department of Commerce, because "[we] must either find a market for [our] surplus or we must restrict our production . . ." (U.S. Department of Commerce and Labor, 1904:498, 500). Senator Joseph Quarles of Wisconsin, in a magnanimous statement, even suggested that the legislation would move "labor" out of a "tent on the outside . . . right into the mansion alongside of commerce, alongside of capital," so that "the Labor Bureau shall not be an orphan, entirely discredited and unaffiliated" (Congressional Record, Senate, January 28, 1902:1050).

At least some of the members of Congress questioned the motivations of the legislation toward workers. Congressman Dudley Wooten of Texas summarized the intent of the legislation as follows:

> . . . Such men as Morgan and Frick and Baer and . . . represent today the organized greed and tyranny and oppression of corporations and capital in this country. This is the kind of a department that the Republican party asked to be created, and this is the kind of department that the gentlem[e]n are now seeking to create by this bill. . . . (Congressional Record, House, January 17, 1903:908)

He further argued that the proposed legislation was "a deliberate attempt to deny the American laborer his just participation and protection in the organization of the Government" (Congressional Record, House, January 17, 1903:908). At least three attempts were made to simultaneously create a separate, cabinet-level Department of Labor, as well as follow through on the creation of the proposed Department of Commerce to which workers had no objection in principle. The legislation was also a forum for a number of issues regarding the conflicts between labor and capital of the time: immigration, tariffs, regional antagonisms between the North and the South, antitrust proposals, and others. Despite the frank discussions of the interests underlying the legislation, it was finally passed with one symbolic amendment. The new department was called "The Department of Commerce and Labor," but the labor portion of the department was allocated only $184,020 of a total department budget of $8,363,032. Wright continued for a short time as head of what again became the Bureau of Labor Statistics, but all of the secretaries of Commerce and Labor were affiliated with business interests.

For all the previous years, the Department of Labor had been denied cabinet status so that it would not become a "political" agency. What was really implied by this reasoning was to prevent it from becoming an advocate for organized labor. Wright joined with the others who opposed the Department of Labor's being allowed to perform that role. He argued that advocacy for organized labor would make the department an "instrument of propagandism," and "such a course would result in its immediate abolition" (Congressional Record, House, January 17, 1903:905). As business leaders began to recognize their own needs for the information collected by the Department of Labor and as they became increasingly concerned about their ability to control the work of the department following Wright's retirement, exactly opposite logic was used. Administrative efficiency, responsibility, and "dignity" were invoked to explain why the Department of Labor should be made a subordinate part of, but not itself become, a cabinet agency. In other words, as long as the business leaders perceived the agency as primarily symbolic appeasement for the demands of labor, it was isolated from the central operations of the government, although controlled through the screening of personnel, the limitations of its fundings, and restrictions on its legal authority to collect certain kinds of information. In the context of the growing strength of organized labor, when business leaders feared they would lose their control over the agency and when they saw the usefulness of the information that it collected for their own purposes, they proposed to incorporate the department into a centralized cabinet agency, which would predictably be controlled by business representatives. And, of course, they did so on the pretense of representing labor's best interests.

After a decade of political turmoil in which organized labor increasingly gained strength, the joint Department of Commerce and Labor was finally separated into two independent cabinet offices. The Progressive reform movement; the growth of a socialist consciousness among workers that led to the strength of the Socialist party; and the entry of organized labor into party politics all contributed in some important way to the creation of the new cabinet-level Department of Labor in 1913. The legislation creating the department said it would:

> . . . go far to allay jealousy, establish harmony, promote the general welfare, make the employer and employee better friends, prevent strikes and lockouts, stop boycotts and business paralysis, and every year save millions and millions of dollars of losses which result necessarily therefrom. (U.S. House of Representatives, Hearing before Committee on Labor, 1912:5)

Nevertheless, once the department was separated from the control of business leaders, it was again isolated from power. Its jurisdiction was limited, its budget severely restricted, and it was continually treated with suspicion by most administrations. For fifty years after, it remained one of the smallest of cabinet offices, and in the 1940s, there were even attempts to have it abolished.

There is an important difference in the operations of the Department of Labor before and after its incorporation into the joint Department of Commerce and Labor. Organized labor had wanted the agency to investigate the source and distribution of wealth, but as long as the agency had the appearance of being "labor's agency," it only collected information on workers themselves. Within the proposed Department of Commerce, the proposed Bureau of Labor Statistics was to "compile . . . statistics of cities," to report "the general condition . . . of the leading industries," and to collect other "facts as may be deemed of value to the industrial interests of the country" (Congressional Record, House, January 17, 1903:913). After the Department of Labor was made a separate cabinet agency, it became a highly decentralized, fragmented, and ineffectual agency. The few powerful bureaus within it by the late 1950s would not even allow their telephone calls to be handled through a central switchboard (Ruttenberg, 1970). Furthermore, this form of organization for the Department of Labor was strongly supported by conservative politicians and their business allies; various attempts to reorganize the Department of Labor into a more centralized form became a serious issue of conflict, as we shall see in the next section of this paper.

IV. Reorganization of the Department of Labor, 1962 to 1974

Although the identification of "capital" and "labor" as distinct social classes was common around the turn of the century, by the 1960s such terminology had disappeared from government deliberations. Instead, the common language had become "business" and "labor," and in the 1960s, a third group became centrally important in the reorganization struggles within the Department of Labor as well, namely, the "poor." In the 1960s, "poor" was often a euphemism for "black." A number of conflicts among and within these three groups were played out through the Department of Labor. Although "labor" and the "poor" are undoubtedly both part of the working class in the most general sense of the term, various organizations representing the two identified their interests in antagonism to each other during the decade of the War on Poverty.

Conflicts existed between business and organized labor, between organized labor and the poor, between business and the poor, within business (small versus large), and within organized labor (craft versus industrial unions). Although there may also have been conflicts among the poor, these were not an issue for the reorganization of the Department of Labor. The event that brought these conflicts to the Department of Labor was the development of federal manpower training programs. How these programs were organized within federal agencies was understood by all three parties to be an issue of the distribution of power in the country.

The Origin of Federal Manpower Training Programs
At the end of the 1950s and the beginning of the 1960s, workers and employers had distinctive but convergent concerns over employment

problems. A plethora of books and articles on automation and the supposed effects of technological change appeared at that time. One account suggests that "anxiety almost amounting to panic" developed "over the reported loss of jobs and escalation of skill demands due to automation" (Crossman and Larner, 1969:176). Workers feared the effects of automation on the elimination of jobs (termed "structural unemployment" by policymakers). Business leaders worried that the skill level of the U.S. labor force prevented the technological changes necessary to compensate for their competitive disadvantage with European economic organizations. These competing concerns were complicated by a close presidential election, a changing administration that had made elaborate campaign promises, and a growing and militant civil rights movement, which was yet to blossom to its full potential. This combination of factors induced policy makers to define federal manpower training programs as a solution to a crisis.

Despite the demands by organized labor that business compensate workers displaced by automation—including guaranteed income proposals—existing economic problems probably had more direct influence on the selection of manpower training programs as a solution to the crisis: an unprecented high unemployment rate during a period of expansion, a second recession closely following the first one (1960 to 1961 and 1957 to 1958), pockets of depression in the midst of overall prosperity, increasing mobility of both plants and workers, as well as the declining competitive position with Western Europe. In this context, a controversy among factions developed within the Kennedy and, later, the Johnson administrations. William McChesney Martin, head of the U.S. Federal Reserve Board under Kennedy, supported the use of more traditional and conservative economic policies, but Walter Heller, Kennedy's chairman of the Council of Economic Advisors, supported the use of Keynesian fiscal and monetary policies. The two positions were reconciled by the Manpower Development and Training Act of 1962 (MDTA), as explained by Sundquist:

> Those who favored an expansionary fiscal policy looked upon retraining as a necessary *supplement.* Those who opposed strong fiscal measures tended to seize upon retraining as a *substitute*. If the economy did not need stimulation to absorb the unemployed, they found themselves reasoning, then jobs for all must in fact exist or would exist if only the unemployed were competent to fill them. If the shortcomings were not in the economy, they could only be in the people. (1968:85–86)

The representatives of organized labor, however, were dismayed with their initial experience with federal manpower training programs. President Kennedy delegated responsibility for the first programs under the Area Redevelopment Act of 1961 to the Department of Commerce. At first Commerce did not implement them at all, and when it did, money was given to nonunion, runaway shops in the South. Despite their strong support for the idea of federal manpower training programs, organized labor was not much more successful in controlling the implementation of programs under MDTA.

Organized labor wanted the training programs to be administered by the Department of Labor, but there was no bureau within the department that could have served their purposes. Each of the three likely possibilities operated as a separate fiefdom within the department. The Bureau of Employment Security (BES) administered the critical unemployment insurance program in coordination with the state employment agencies, but BES was "business's" agency within the Department of Labor (Johnson, 1973:14). The Bureau of Employment Security is an example of centralization within decentralization; all of the major decisions regarding unemployment insurance are made at the state level of government, in close conjunction with employers. Business's interests are protected within the bureau by the Interstate Conference of Employment Security Agencies (ICESA), a government-funded, lobby group for BES. Although BES has field offices in every state and most large cities, organized labor had no desire to expand BES by giving it administrative responsibility for MDTA programs.

Organized labor's strongest ties in the Department of Labor were to the Bureau of Apprenticeship and Training (BAT), which oversees on-the-job training programs in the skilled trades. In that the high salaries of these occupations (especially building and metal trades) depend on limited recruitment, organized labor did not want BAT to administer MDTA because it would have necessitated a major expansion of their programs. A third agency, the Office of Manpower, Automation, and Training (OMAT), was newly created in the advent of MDTA, but it did not have any regional field offices, and its commitments were not well defined at that point. In lieu of any of these three bureaus, organized labor lobbied for the creation of an independent agency to administer MDTA, but was not successful.

Administration of MDTA was eventually shared between BES (for case finding) and another agency over which business had strong influence, the Bureau of Vocational Education (BVE), located in the Department of Health, Education, and Welfare. BVE was another centralized bureau within a decentralized agency; all decisions regarding vocational education, like those in BES, are made at the state level, as part of the "education" responsibilities of each state. BVE implemented the training for the cases found by BES. Despite the continued dismay of organized labor at the administrative arrangement for MDTA, the most immediate cause for their interest in government training programs—high (white male) unemployment—disappeared, so they turned their attention elsewhere for a while.

Manpower training programs, however, offered a solution to another emerging crisis, the civil rights movement, the two major goals of which were "jobs and freedom." The marches in Birmingham in the spring and the "March on Washington" in August of 1963 marked a turning point for the movement. By the end of the year "urban riots" began in a number of cities, and then expanded with fury in the several years to come. The Johnson administration responded with several critical pieces of legislation in 1964, the Civil Rights Act and the Economic Opportunity Act. Job training played a prominent role in both.

The Conflicts of Interest

The administrative arrangement preferred by business leaders when the working class has potential access to critical programs that affect business interests is decentralization. The Bureau of Employment Security and the Bureau of Vocational Education both fit this model, and each is one of the strongest bureaus in its parent agency. In other words, the parent agencies are decentralized, while the purportedly subordinate bureaus are insulated from upper-level administrative control. For this reason, each has also been the subject of conflict between business and labor. Business leaders have always lobbied for various kinds of labor programs to be administered by these bureaus (whenever they could not get them placed in "business" agencies, like the Department of Commerce), while organized labor has always objected. Because the decentralization of BES is understood by organized labor to be advantageous to business, the "federalization" of the bureau has been one of organized labor's continual demands since the inception of the program. Nevertheless, the locus of decision making at the state government level also means that "big" business shares these bureaus with "small" business. At various points in the 1960s, big business withdrew its support for each agency— when its own problems could better be solved nationally—over the objections of small business. Thus, no particular form of organization is as important as whose interests it serves in what context.

Industrial unions, however, seemed more concerned about BES and BVE than craft unions were. The craft unions were happily lodged in the Bureau of Apprenticeship and Training and had made an uneasy peace with BES. During the 1960s, the interests of industrial unions in gaining control over unemployment insurance (and thus over BES) led to a strategy among some unionists to trade off some of BAT's control over on-the-job training for the opportunity for greater union control of BES. This strategy turned out to be ill fated. BAT lost ground over on-the-job training without improving labor's input into the unemployment insurance program.

The conflicts that existed between and within business and labor were complicated in the 1960s by conflicts among . . . business and labor and the poor. For business leaders, when the demands of the poor appeared more threatening than the demands of organized labor and when the skill shortages created by the Vietnam War were of more concern than unemployment insurance (in a tight labor market), they supported a centralized Department of Labor, as long as they themselves controlled it. To solve business's problems with the poor, the Department of Labor was drawn into competition with the Office of Economic Opportunity (OEO), the agency of the poor. The conflict, however, affected the Bureau of Apprenticeship and Training, so the business leaders supporting the new policies solved two objectives by proposing to reorganize the Department of Labor. It was possible for them to do so because of the uneasy relationship that has always existed between unions and minority workers, and hence between unions and the poor. It appears that the business leaders used organized labor's desire to gain control over the Bureau of Employment Security to encourage a conflict between the Department of Labor and OEO's Community Action Agencies (CAAs), and they used minority group suspicion of craft unions to weaken BAT's control of on-the-job training programs. These various conflicts constitute the background against which proposals to reorganize the Department of Labor were made.

The Reorganizations

Conflict among the Bureau of Employment Security, the Bureau of Apprenticeship and Training, and the Office of Manpower, Automation, and Training developed immediately after the passage of the 1962 Manpower Act. The first attempt to reorganize the responsibilities among the bureaus occurred soon after the Birmingham riot in 1963. Secretary of Labor Wirtz appointed a Manpower administrator, John C. Donovan, to coordinate the activities of the three bureaus, and Donovan hired an outside consulting agency, whose recommendations were unsatisfactory to both BAT and BES. The consultant had recommended the dissolution of the field offices of both BES and BAT with a reintegration of their functions into a new, centralized agency called the Manpower Administration, the core of which was to be OMAT. The centralization proposed by this report would have placed the unemployment insurance program under the direct authority of the secretary of labor, and it would have placed the activities of the conservative craft unions under the closer scrutiny of the federal administrators at a time when new demands were being made on federally supported training programs. As the director of Employment Security at the time remarked, "The proposed reorganization would disrupt [existing] relationships and require the development of an entirely new fabric. . . ." (memo from Director Robert C. Goodwin, BES, to Secretary of Labor Wirtz, February 1, 1965). In other words, a centralization of authority within the Department of Labor at this time would have decreased the power of those groups that had purposely created decentralization in order to enhance their power. In this situation, the conservative building trades department of the American Federation of Labor and Congress of Industrial Organization (AFL-CIO) joined with the ICESA, the government-funded, business-controlled lobby, to prevent any reorganization of either BES or BAT. Donovan consequently resigned and a former AFL-CIO research director, Stanley Ruttenberg, took his place—under the condition that he would not support any reorganization of the Department of Labor (see Ruttenberg, 1970:76–78).

As urban riots increased, the Office of Economic Opportunity, which President Johnson had created to solve the problems of unrest, began to create problems of its own. The OEO activities that people in positions of power found most threatening were the organization of voter registration and other forms of political mobilization of the poor. As early as 1965, OEO was charged with "trying to wreck local government by setting the poor against city hall" and with being a "nightmare of bureaucratic bungling" (U.S. Code, Congressional and Administrative News, 1st sess., 89th Cong., 1965:3525–26). The Hatch Act, which restricts political activities of public employees, was extended to OEO, but this did not end the social movement to which OEO was providing an organizational base. Johnson had made OEO a "staff agency" in the White House, purportedly to protect it from congressional interference, but the real intent was probably so he could better control it. When it was evident that even direct White House control was not enough to curtail OEO's political effects, other means were sought. The proliferation of riots made it politically impossible to simply eliminate the War on Poverty, which OEO administered; instead, conservative politicians and their business advisers began taking steps to transfer OEO's programs into the more predictable and more easily controlled cabinet offices. In order to maintain the legitimacy of such an action, those agencies with liberal images, like the Department of Labor and the Department of Health, Education, and Welfare, were targeted to receive the programs. On the one hand, each of the programs and bureaus within them already had defined constituencies and, therefore, constraints on their actions; on the other hand, precisely because they had liberal images, representatives of surbordinate groups had more participation in them. This strategy, therefore, was a risky one for conservative politicians in a precarious political climate.

The President's administrative agency, the Bureau of the Budget, began working behind-the-scenes with the Labor Department to this end, and President Johnson himself began making statements favorable to an expanded Department of Labor. With the prospect of the Department of Labor gaining more power in the federal government, organized labor (especially AFL-CIO) then renewed its efforts to gain control over "its" agency. They supported attempts to centralize control over the various bureaus at the federal level, reinforcing their continual demands to federalize the Bureau of Employment Security.

Two reorganization plans were on the agenda for the Department; the two would have had opposite effects. One was supported by Secretary of Labor Wirtz and Assistant Secretary Ruttenberg. It would have centralized all the manpower training programs from OEO, HEW, and from various parts of the Department of Labor (including the on-the-job training programs of BAT) into a reorganized Manpower administration. This proposal was similar to Donovan's earlier aborted reorganization plan. It was strongly supported by organized labor, even though the craft unions were not anxious to jeopardize their control over on-the-job training. The second proposal was articulated by a 1965 task force headed by George Shultz, dean of the School of Business at the University of Chicago, later to become President Nixon's secretary of labor and President Reagan's secretary of state. This task force proposal recommended separating the U.S. Employment Service (the state employment agencies) from the unemployment insurance program in the Bureau of Employment Security, and increasing the funding from the Department of Labor's general budget for the employment service administrative costs, previously paid for by the tax on employers. The effects of this proposal would have been to insulate unemployment insurance even further from the access of organized labor and to prevent business-provided funds from being tapped for War on Poverty Manpower programs.

Wirtz and Ruttenberg were encouraged behind-the-scenes by the Bureau of Budget staff to pursue their own goals for reorganization in spring 1967. Ruttenberg held secret meetings in which he was assured White House support for the proposal, and Wirtz announced a "realignment" of the Department of Labor later in the year. The primary change in the department was to expand the on-the-job training program and to remove the administration of the new positions from the Bureau of Apprenticeship and Training (and consequently from the craft unions). Although the Interstate Conference on Employment Security Agencies and some unions opposed the change, their opposition was to no avail with the support of President Johnson (and therefore, also by those big businesses who were facing manpower shortages in the skilled trades).

By removing the Bureau of Apprenticeship and Training's control over on-the-job training, the programs could be used to channel unemployed blacks into "accelerated" (meaning shorter time and less training) apprenticeship programs with major corporations who were facing tremendous pressure from the urban riots (symbolized by the summer 1967 riot in Detroit) and who were experiencing shortages of skilled labor during the Vietnam War. The realignment prepared the way for President Johnson's launching of the $350 million on-the-job training program, sponsored by the newly formed National Alliance of Businessmen–Job Opportunities in the Business Sector (NAB-JOBS). The NAB-JOBS program benefited big business at government expense because the federal funds subsidized the training costs for industry to hire the disadvantaged (see U.S. Code, 1st sess., 1967:2576; Ball, 1972:175; and Perry, et al., 1975:187).

Just as important, however, this realignment was another step toward the Department of Labor's taking over the programs of OEO. Three "job creation" programs had already been moved from OEO and transferred to the Department of Labor in 1966, and the placement of the NAB-JOBS program in labor instead of OEO was significant. The Community Action agencies in OEO fought Labor's claims to the War on Poverty jobs programs, but their only support in the late 1960s was "public opinion" and some of the "pro-poverty" legislators. It appeared that the cooperation of organized labor in expanding on-the-job training outside of BAT's control was a means to demonstrate their commitment to minorities and to quell the suspicions of the "poverty" people. In return, they thought they would win approval to centralize unemployment insurance at the federal level.

Wirtz and Ruttenberg interpreted their success in the 1967 realignment as a coup and began to make plans for a more extensive reorganization soon thereafter. They were especially encouraged by the preferential support the Department of Labor was getting—in contrast to OEO, which was coming under increasingly hostile attacks—from the Bureau of the Budget and the White House staff (Ball, 1972:146). They began another series of secret meetings in 1968 with the same people who had planned the 1967 realignment. Their intent was to implement a reorganization plan similar to the one that had led to Donovan's resignation earlier. Assuming that the Interstate Conference of Employment Security Agencies was the primary obstacle to implementing the reorganization (in that the realignment had already neutralized opposition from BAT), Wirtz and Ruttenberg felt confident because they were assured of White House support. Much to their surprise, though, President Johnson rejected their plan to centralize the Department of Labor. In fact, Johnson threatened to fire Wirtz when he announced the reorganization over Johnson's objections, even though the incident occurred only two weeks before the 1968 presidential election. A compromise was finally reached between Wirtz and Johnson: Wirtz's reorganization order would remain in effect, but it would not be implemented until after the election.

When newly elected President Richard Nixon appointed George Schultz, the former task force head, as secretary of labor, Shultz recommended implementing the Wirtz-Ruttenberg reorganization plan on an interim basis. The reorganization that was carried out, however, was actually Shultz's own earlier plan. The effects of the 1969 reorganization were to further decentralize the Department of Labor, which meant greater input from business and less from organized labor. In addition, Nixon moved the Job Corps, the last of the War on Poverty jobs programs, from OEO to Labor. Nixon gave his full support to the NAB-JOBS program and to the Job Corps, both of which had become "for-profit" service delivery programs; all other programs were cut back. Within six months, George Shultz had left the Department of Labor to become head of the Office of Management and Budget (formerly the Bureau of the Budget).

Following the Shultz reorganization, the Department of Labor was said to have "fresh appeal" to employers. The president of the National Association of Manufacturers said that it was "one of the most accessible agencies in this town" (Cooney and Silverman, 1970:140), and a representative of the Chamber of Commerce said, ". . . the business community is pleased with the change of administrations in the Labor Department" (Cooney and Silverman, 1970:140). Nixon then embarked on his revenue-sharing campaign, in which the Manpower Revenue Sharing Bill was to be the first implemented. Organizationally, this legislation meant complete decentralization of all federal programs of interest to organized labor and the poor, because manpower was to be only the first of the revenue sharing bills. Nixon's own director of OEO said, "I know of no way in which the Comprehensive Manpower Bill can be proposed by the President without it being viewed by large segments of the public as a conscious and systematic diminution of the role of OEO . . ." (letter from Donald Rumsfeld, Secretary of OEO, to Robert Mayo, Director of the Bureau of the Budget, August 7, 1969). Despite opposition from organized labor and from "pro-poverty" legislators, the Comprehensive Employment and Training Act (CETA) was passed in 1973, with precisely the effects that organized labor and the poor feared. On the one hand, fewer minority and poor clients were enrolled in the training programs than had been during the War on Poverty days. On the other hand, organized labor ended up with even less access to the administration of the unemployment insurance program and less control over apprenticeship training in the skilled trades. In effect, what was a "double-cross" of the Office of Economic Opportunity by organized labor, turned out to be a "double-double-cross" of organized labor by the conservative politicians and their business allies.

The Department of Labor has remained decentralized and relatively unimportant in the family of federal agencies. Only after the demands of organized labor, in the context of controversy within the business community over the use of economic policies, led to the first federal training programs did the organizational structure of the Department of Labor again become a central concern to business leaders. These programs were first placed in business's agency (the Department of Commerce), and later in "business's bureau" (the Bureau of Employment Security). Within the Department of Labor, the administration of the programs was treated as a separate function from the department's other responsibilities. That the Manpower Administration remained in a separate building, even after the Department of Labor was given a new building during the Nixon administration, is an unobtrusive indicator of the special interest business leaders have in controlling these programs. The Department of Labor became a vehicle for confronting OEO when the demands of the poor posed a more immediate threat than the bargaining table demands of organized labor. At that point, business leaders supported some reorganization of the Department of Labor for their own purposes—which had the appearance of centralization—but organized labor never gained more access to unemployment insurance.

Representatives of organized labor tried at various times to effect organizational changes in the Department of Labor, both to increase their influence in the agency and to increase the agency's power in the government. The intensity of organized labor's concern with unemployment insurance made it possible for conservative politicians and their business advisers to use labor's own motivations against them. The charade of behind-the-scenes negotiations and end-run tactics were convincing. One political scientist concluded that the superior administrative skill of the Department of Labor was too much competition for a poorly managed agency like the Office of Economic Opportunity (Ball, 1972)—just one year before the Department of Labor was itself "internally dismantled." The business community's renewed interest, not the administrative skill of the Department of Labor, gave it the illusion of power in the 1960s.

V. Conclusions

This brief account of two periods in the history of the Department of Labor is intended to indicate the political character of decisions about organizational structure in the public sector. In addition, it has shown that almost all of the decisions about the structure of organizations in the public sector are linked to major social conflict in the society at large. In other words, public organizations are not only shaped by their environments, they are inherently part of their environments and vice versa. Even so, organizations, in the state and elsewhere, are not completely permeable. Once decisions are made and carried out, standard ways of operating are adopted and taken for granted by various constituencies in and out of the organization. Subsequent changes, therefore, also have to be "fought out," in the sense that they raise and are only resolved through conflict. What appear to be obvious alliances and obvious preferences are not always followed. Instead, strategies tend to address the needs of the moment, as long as the group proposing the strategy feels it has the allies and the resources to shape for its own purposes the consequences of whatever actions are taken. No single organizational model is preferred over others. The preferences change with the circumstances.

The issues that most concern the parties to organizational conflict are those that place constraints on or provide opportunities for organizational actors: the definition of goals, budgets, recruitment, and training and the pattern of authority in the organization and in its place within a general organizational network. Politics is always at the core of such decisions, while rationality is always defined by those who benefit most from one alternative or another.

References

Andersen, Gosta, Roger Friedland, and Erik Olin Wright. 1976. "Modes of class struggle and the capitalist state." *Kapitalistate* 4–5:186–220.

Babson, Robert W. 1919. *W. B. Wilson and the Department of Labor*. New York: Brentano's.

Ball, Joseph H. 1972. "The implementation of federal manpower policy, 1961–1971." Ph.D. dissertation, Columbia University.

Cooney, Robert, and Marcia Silverman. 1970. "CPR department study/the Labor Department." *National Journal* 2: 130–41.

Culhane, Charles. 1974. "Manpower report/revenue sharing shift set for worker training programs." *National Journal* 6: 5158.

DiTomaso, Nancy. 1978. "The organization of authority in the capitalist state." *Journal of Political and Military Sociology* 6 (Fall): 189–204.

Dulles, Foster Rhea. 1966. *Labor in America*. 3rd ed. New York: Crowell.

Feagin, Joe R., and Harlan Hahn. 1973. *Ghetto Revolts: The Politics of Violence in American Cities*. New York: Macmillan.

Goldberg, Arthur J. 1961–1962. Correspondence. National Archives.

Greenstone, J. David. 1969. *Labor in American Politics*. New York: Vintage.

Grossman, Jonathan. 1945. *William Sylvis, Pioneer of American Labor*. New York: Columbia University Press.

———. 1973. *The Department of Labor*. New York: Praeger.

Hodgson, James D. 1970–1973. Correspondence. National Archives.

Johnson, Miriam. 1973. *Counter Point: The Changing Employment Service*. Salt Lake City: Olympus.

Kipnis, Ira. 1968. *The American Socialist Movement, 1897–1912*. New York: Greenwood.

Lescohier, Don D. 1969. *The Knights of St. Crispin, 1867–1874*. New York: Anno, and the *New York Times*.

Levitan, Sar A. 1964. *Federal Aid to Depressed Areas*. Baltimore: Johns Hopkins University Press.

———. 1969. *Program in Aid of the Poor for the 1970s*. Baltimore: Johns Hopkins University Press.

Levitan, Sar A., and Garth L. Mangum. 1967. *Making Sense of Federal Manpower Policy*. Washington D.C.: National Manpower Policy Task Force.

Lombardi, John. 1942. *Labor's Voice in the Cabinet*. New York: Columbia University Press.

MacLaury, Judson. 1975. "The selection of the first U.S. Commissioner of Labor." *Monthly Labor Review* 98, no. 4 (April): 16–19.

Mangum, Garth L. 1968. *MDTA: Foundation of Federal Manpower Policy*. Baltimore: Johns Hopkins University Press.

Metcalf, Evan B. 1972. "Economic stabilization by American business in the twentieth century." Ph.D. dissertation, University of Wisconsin.

Mitchell, James P. 1953–1961. Correspondence. National Archives.

Perry, Charles R., Bernard E. Anderson, Richard L. Rowan, and Herbert T. Northrup. 1975. *The Impact of Government Manpower Programs in General and on Minorities and Women*. Philadelphia: Wharton School of Finance.

Philipson, Morris, ed. 1962. *Automation: Implications for the Future*. New York: Vintage.

Pidgin, Charles F. 1904. *Massachusetts Bureau of Statistics of Labor*. Boston: Wright and Potter.

Powderly, Terence V. 1890. *Thirty Years of Labor, 1859–1889*. Rev. ed. Philadelphia: T. V. Powderly.

Ruttenberg, Stanley. 1970. *Manpower Challenge of the 1970s*. Baltimore: Johns Hopkins University Press.

Shultz, George P. 1969–1970. Correspondence. National Archives.

Sundquist, James L. 1968. *Politics and Policy*. Washington, D. C.: Brookings Institution.

Sylvis, James C. 1872. *The Life, Speeches, Labors, and Essays of William H. Sylvis*. Philadelphia: Claxton, Remsen, and Haffelfinger.

Therborn, Goran. 1978. *What Does the Ruling Class Do When It Rules?* London: New Left Books.

Todes, Charlotte. 1942. *William H. Sylvis and the National Labor Union*. New York: International Publishers.

U.S. Code. *Congressional and Administrative News*. 87th through 93rd Congress, Legislative History, Manpower Development and Training Act, Vocational Education Act, Revenue Act, Civil Rights Act, Economic Opportunity Act, Social Security Act, Emergency Employment Act, and Comprehensive Employment and Training Act. St. Paul, Minn.: West Publishing Co.

U.S. Congress, House of Representatives, Committee on Education and Labor. 1912. *Hearings on H.R. 22913 To Establish a Department of Labor*. Washington, D.C.: Government Printing Office, 1912.

U.S. Department of Commerce and Labor. 1904. *Organization and Law of the Department of Commerce and Labor*. Washington, D.C. Government Printing Office.

Wilson, William B. 1913–1921. Correspondence. National Archives.

Wirtz, W. Willard. 1962–1969. Correspondence. National Archives.

Wright, Carroll D. 1892. "The workings of the Department of Labor." *The Cosmopolitan* 13, no. 2 (June): 229–236.

23
The AIDS Crisis and Organizational Failure

Charles Perrow and Mauro Guillén

We have argued that the federal government failed to fund education, research, and care; that the gay male community failed to warn and educate and change behavior quickly; that state and local governments failed to respond quickly; and that the blood industry failed to ensure the safety of their product. How might this record be accounted for? The initial failure of the gay community could be readily explained in terms of their fear and panic, defensiveness in the face of hostility and stigma, and political marginality. In any case, the gay community soon responded with warnings, education, care, and behavioral changes.

The failure of government agencies and of the health sector in general, however, is more surprising. Their poor record could be a matter of normal organizational failure—that is, of bureaucracy, the first of three explanations considered herein. A second is economics. The inadequate response of the political and health sectors might be attributed to the heavy costs to be borne by the blood industry, bathhouse owners, and city governments, and more generally as an unacceptable challenge to the fiscal policies and philosophy of the Reagan administration, which was unwilling to institute or to spend money for a new federal health program. There is a third possible explanation: the influence of a vigorous "moral majority" lobby that opposed action by the administration with which it was allied, though it could not affect the gay male groups or the blood industry so directly. All these explanations are important and are explored first. Finally, we argue that what made them more effective than usual was the unique nature of the disease itself. The specific characteristics of AIDS gave more force to these three explanations and added "synergy," the unexpected interaction of multiple failures, and increased the vulnerability of organizations to failure.

The Normal Failure of Organizations

Organizations are always failing to some degree, for they are imperfect and refractory tools.[1] The American health sector is particularly prone to failure. The United States spends more money per capita on health care and gets less results in aggregate good health statistics than any other industrialized nation. The public health system is highly fragmented, and the division of funding and services into a public and a private sphere is recognized as counterproductive by virtually all experts. In 1988 the Institute of Medicine issued a report, *The Future of Public Health,* painting a bleak portrait of a system in disarray, a system characterized by fragmented services, poor national leadership, and a complacent public. The slow response to the AIDS crisis is a symptom of a sickly health sector. "Who knows what crisis will be next?" asked the chairman of the committee that produced this report.[2]

AIDS fell upon a "system" that could tolerate only small-scale disturbances, such as Legionnaires' disease or toxic shock syndrome, and that bungled its response to the epidemic that never was, swine flu.[3] Moreover, AIDS appeared after a time of high inflation and during a period of large federal cutbacks in poverty programs, housing, health care, and social services. Federal attempts to stem Medicare costs resulted in the DRG (diagnosis-related groups) program, which cut payments to hospitals. With reduced revenues, the hospitals had less slack to draw on when a surge of both mental patients and AIDS patients arrived in the mid-1980s. The fragile and inefficient health care system of the nation was thus subjected to multiple assaults. Even without the stigma and other unusual aspects of AIDS, there would probably have been a number of sizable organizational failures. Even if the blood industry or organized gay men's groups or city politicians had responded quickly and effectively, the failing health sector, and especially the hospitals responsible for acute care, might have ensured a disastrous overall response to the epidemic.

In the United States, in contrast to other industrialized nations, the hospitals are the focal point of the health care system. They are so important because we do so little in the way of preventive care; because physicians prefer to work out of hospitals rather than from their offices when possible; because we are more likely than other nations to use hospitals for routine procedures; and because the poor do not have physicians and so use the emergency facilities of hospitals. But the hospitals have been hit badly by the AIDS epidemic.

First, it has been estimated that private and public teaching hospitals, where many of the AIDS patients go, are reimbursed for just 76 percent of the hospitalization costs of an AIDS patient who has some private or government insurance. Two authorities, Lawrence Shulman and Joanne Mantell, argue that "hospitals have borne this burden and are losing significant amounts of money because of unreimbursed costs" (1988).[4] They call for alternative locations for acute PWA (persons with AIDS) and alternative means of financing that spread the burden. Hospitals, they argue, cannot be blamed for the inadequate response to the AIDS crisis because their financial problems prevent an adequate response. Furthermore, they note, AIDS has affected hospitals in other negative ways. Hospitals with a specialized AIDS unit may experience "mass defection of nonAIDS patients who go elsewhere for medical care" (1988).[5] In addition, inner-city areas have experienced cutbacks in hospital beds because of an "overbedding crisis" that occurred as the suburbs built their own community and for-profit hospitals. The bed crisis in New York City is severe.

Thus, it might be argued that even a major epidemic of the nonpoor, nonstigmatized mainstream—for example, one that stemmed from widespread groundwater pollution and particularly affected the affluent suburbs—would have produced a number of organizational failures in the health care sector. We would have had instant hospital overcrowding, aggravating an existing shortage of nurses and prompting a financing crisis; an underfunded research establishment would have fumbled the research efforts; an image-conscious bloody industry would have resisted testing the blood supply; and there would certainly be a shortage of nursing homes and hospices.

Timing is also crucial. The American health care sector has been undergoing major changes in recent decades, and AIDS joined and contributed to an ongoing crisis. Daniel Fox, a medical historian, discusses a number of important changes in recent decades that prevent effective management of an epidemic the size of AIDS. He notes the following relevant issues: changes in the causes of sickness and death that have required changes in facilities (for example, the increase in chronic diseases and the decline in infectious diseases); ambivalence about the recent progress of medical research and expensive life-extending procedures; a growing belief that people should take more responsibility for their own health (the "life-style" issue); a concern with uncontrollable rising costs; a policy that links health insurance "to employment rather than to membership in society"; and an increase in the power of for-profit health institutions, in the role of corporations in health benefits, and in the role of states as the federal government withdrew, all three contributing to a crisis of authority. As a consequence, Fox believes, conventional responses to any epidemic will be inadequate. He writes:

> A policy that is focused on chronic degenerative disease, that embraces cost control as the chief goal of health policy, and in which central authority is diminishing cannot address this epidemic as it has others of the recent past. . . . If the policy responds to AIDS as it has done since 1981, it

is likely that the epidemic will be another incident in the gradual decline of collective responsibility for the human condition in the United States. (1986: 18, 26, 29)

It is difficult to evaluate this forceful argument, since historical experience is of limited applicability. Past epidemics, such as the influenza epidemic after World War I that killed 500,000 in the United States in one year, occurred in a society with many fewer resources. The response to the outbreak of Legionnaires' disease that took twenty-nine lives in 1976 was prompt, despite interagency fumbling and infighting (Culliton, 1976). Had the cases begun doubling every six months, as was true of AIDS in the early stages, we believe that funds for research, prevention, and treatment would have poured forth for this new disease that affected middle-class visitors of convention centers, despite the state of the public health system. The response to the toxic shock syndrome was slow and barely adequate but much better, it seems to us, than the response to the AIDS epidemic.

The response of President Gerald R. Ford, the federal bureaucracy, and the drug industry to the swine flu epidemic bordered on the comical (had it not been for loss of life), but the comedy was partly the overresponse, not an underresponse. On the basis of only three cases of swine flu in a military camp, we proceeded to inoculate millions. The drug industry was late in producing the vaccine and demanded immunity from any suits claiming faulty vaccine quality. Dr. David Sencer was head of the Centers for Disease Control (CDC) at the time. In contrast to his behavior much later when he was the New York City health commissioner denying an AIDS epidemic, at this time he ignored warnings that three cases do not an epidemic make and convinced President Ford that a supreme national effort was necessary. Twenty or more deaths resulted from the vaccination program (Dutton, 1988).

The record, then, is mixed; we have done better in some cases, though the cases are hardly comparable; we have many more resources to do much better than we have had in the past, but in many respects, as noted by Fox, we are more vulnerable now than before. Even though organizations in general and health care agencies in particular were prone to failure, we argue that more than a bureaucratic bungle was involved in the case of AIDS.

The Reagan Administration: Reducing Public Spending

A second reason for organizational failure in the AIDS crisis is the Reagan administration's aversion to any increase in spending for human services—or most governmental activities other than defense. We count this as important because this resistance to what was called "big government" occasionally overrode ideological considerations and even interfered with life-saving efforts directed toward people for whom there was widespread sympathy. For example, stopping the drug trade would appear to be a natural endeavor for an administration that embraces the moral majority groups, and domestic spending for apprehending drug dealers would seem to be a top priority. Yet funds for the "war on drugs" were frequently cut on budgetary grounds. Similarly, the race to develop superconductors following the breakthrough in high-temperature super-conductivity would appear to serve virtually every legitimate goal of the administration, including increasing business profits, increasing our defense, and improving economic growth and competitiveness. The "crisis" had some of the overtones of the AIDS crisis: researchers were raiding other programs in materials science to work on the new developments for funds, few graduate students had been attracted to the area before, and publicity was considerable. A large conference was held to announce the heavy commitment of the federal government, and many promises were made. One year later funding for the general area of materials science had not only not been increased but was cut by 20 percent. Graduate students stayed away for lack of funds, and the raids on other projects continued (Crawford, 1988). Japan and Europe surged ahead.

One final, deadly example from the AIDS experience. When an antibody blood test was finally available for screening the blood supply, Congress approved $8.4 million to make the test available to the blood banks. But the administration would not release the funds, though presumably it did not harbor any enmity toward hemophiliacs and the countless middle- and upper-class patients requiring transfusions, all at the risk of infection and death. Asked about the delay after several months, the administration would say only that the matter was "still under discussion" (Shilts, 1987: 502).

Thus, budget considerations may have played a sizable role in the response of the federal administration independent of the ideological and community pressures to "punish" HIV carriers. Shilts reports that the Office of Management and the Budget had no objections to the Secretary of Health and Human Services spending as much of the department's $6 billion budget on AIDS as she wished (1987: 288); she just could not have extra money for AIDS, so something else would have to be cut. Panem makes a similar observation (1988: 80–81, 90–91). In an administration that attempted each year to cut expenditures on health and human services, AIDS was not likely to get new money and would have a hard time displacing old programs. There was "tension among individual PHS agencies, the DHHS [Department of Health and Human Services], and Congress" (Office of Technology Assessment, 1985). Financial considerations could have kept the blood industry from screening for hepatitis B (for the profit-making companies a 10-percent increase in cost could be important if it led to lower sales) and from jeopardizing the blood supply by asking high-risk persons not to donate. And, of course, the bathhouse owners would have ample reason not to post strong warnings in the houses or to close them. But we expect that had an epidemic broken out that affected, say, middle- and upper-class consumers of fine wine and liquor, congressional appropriations two or three times those made for AIDS would have been welcomed and quickly spent by the administration.[6]

The Ideology of the Moral Majority

A third reason commonly cited to explain why government mishandled the AIDS epidemic is the alliance of the Reagan administration with those groups loosely labeled the "moral majority." AIDS victims are highly stigmatized; any administration would face obstacles in mobilizing government and private groups. But the administration was particularly beholden to the moral majority and thus particularly unenthusiastic about taking action. Conservative groups reportedly were successful in blocking educational programs and limiting counseling services; it is possible that they even blocked appropriations for research, education, and treatment programs.

Congress is less beholden to the conservative groups than the administration and was more responsive. The House and Senate consistently voted far more funds than the administration sought and threatened to go to court when the administration refused to spend the allocations. A few members of Congress went to considerable lengths to increase funding for research, treatment, and education. Although some of these were from northern California, where the gay vote is significant, others were not, and, most important, large majorities in both houses of Congress went along. Congressional appropriations have exceeded administration requests by 76 to 115 percent every year from 1983 to 1988 (General Accounting Office, 1987). But the response of state and local authorities (except in California and San Francisco) was far less positive. Indeed, one of the ironies of New York State politics is that liberal Democrat Governor Mario Cuomo, hardly beholden to the moral majority, threatened to veto AIDS bills that were overwhelmingly supported by the Republicans. Democratic Governor Michael Dukakis of Massachusetts was also quite reluctant to spend the monies the elected representatives offered (Shilts, 1987: 559).

On the one hand, the influence of the moral majority, while undeniable, failed to stop Congress; on the other hand, some of those who were not subject to the moral majority in any substantial way held back their support. Government was not of a piece, even at the federal level, and funds, though inadequate according to the health agencies dealing with the epidemic, did appear. We can include this argument for failure by ideology with those of financial stringency and typical organizational failure: true but not sufficient.

It remains possible that the crisis in the health care sector is a true and sufficient reason for the weak response to the epidemic. The severely weakened state of the health care "system" in cities such as New York was sufficient to disable care and prevention programs. AIDS may have overloaded a precarious system to such an extent that unprecedented failures at the institutional and organizational level were assured. We have no way of testing this "breakdown" thesis against the argument that AIDS is unique among health problems. To some degree they are not in conflict. But we believe that a crisis on the order of AIDS that affected nonstigmatized citizens would have been fought with more resources and less organizational denial, regardless of the state of the health system. In any case, our main concern is to explore the organizational response to AIDS; demonstrating that AIDS is a unique disease, as we shall try to do next, completes the picture but is not essential to documenting the breakdown.

The Unique Features of AIDS

AIDS in America has two primary sources at present: unprotected anal intercourse, which is associated with gay male behavior and which probably accounts for the bulk of the existing cases nationwide; and intravenous drug injection with virus-contaminated needles, which is currently the major source of new cases and is likely to be the source of most cases within a few years.[7] Table 23–1 gives some of the recent statistics for the world, the United States, and New York City.

The characteristics of AIDS that make it unique among public health problems are best seen by contrasting AIDS with other health problems. Since it has appeared in epidemic form, it is appropriate to contrast it with potentially damaging *conditions,* such as infection by the polio virus; but since it involves activity patterns that can be deliberately changed, it can also be contrasted with the results of potentially damaging *behaviors,* such as compulsive eating or drinking. And since it involves sexual and drug habits, it can be contrasted with the problems caused by these potentially damaging behaviors *as they existed before AIDS.*

Intentional Behavior

The important contrast with infectious diseases of the past, such as polio, swine flu, Legionnaires' disease, and the more distant ones such as cholera, is that for these diseases changing one's behavior did not protect one from the disease. The 20 million worldwide victims of the influenza epidemic of 1918–19 (500,000 in the United States) could have done nothing to protect themselves. Even in the polio epidemic during the first half of this century, protective measures were limited to such things as

Table 23-1

Some Basic Statistics on the AIDS Epidemic

Persons with HIV	World: 5–10 million Africa: 3–4 million United States: 1–1.5 million[a]
AIDS cases in the United States	Cumulative, as of November 1989: 115,158[b]
Transmission categories (U.S.)	60% homosexual or bisexual male 21% intravenous drug user 7% both homosexual or bisexual male and intravenous drug user 5% heterosexual contact 2% recipient of blood transfusion 1% pediatric 1% hemophiliac 3% other
New cases (U.S.)	About 686 new cases were reported every week during 1989, as opposed to 618/week during 1988[c]
Deaths (U.S.)	As of November 1989: 68,441, or 60% of all cases[b]
Cases in New York City	Cumulative, as of November 1989: 23,066; active: 10,263[d]
Deaths (N.Y.C.)	As of November 1989: 12,803, or 56% of all cases[d]
Persons with HIV (N.Y.C.)	200,000[e]
Living situations for persons with AIDS (N.Y.C.)	Hospitals: 1,531[f] Homeless in shelters: 1,000–2,000[g] City-subsidized apartments: 777[g] Municipal beds: 600[h] Other and unaccounted for: 1,479–2,479[i]
In New York and San Francisco	Over 50% of gay men have AIDS or HIV[j]

[a]Chin, 1989:26. CDC estimates for the end of 1987 range from 945,000 to 1.4 million in the United States, whereas Hudson Institute estimates range from 1.9 to 3.0 million. See "AIDS Virus Test," 1988; Boffey, 1988a. The Hudson Institute reports that 200,000 to 500,000 non-IVDU heterosexuals are infected with the virus; CDC's estimate is 80,000 to 165,000.

[b]Centers for Disease Control, 1989: 1–16.

[c]Based on reported cases between December 1988 and November 1989 (for 1989), and December 1987 and November 1988 (for 1988).

[d]New York City, 1989.

[e]Estimate down from a previous figure of 400,000; Lambert, 1988a.

[f]Lambert, 1988b. Others estimates go up to 2,800 beds occupied by PWAs.

[g]Kolata, 1988.

[h]Figure is an estimate.

[i]Number of New York City active cases as of April 1988 (6,387), less cases accounted for in the four preceding categories.

[j]Boffey, 1988b.

public laws requiring children to remain indoors during the hottest days of the summer. (For a disease like tuberculosis, avoiding others with the disease is sufficient protection, but this is not possible for city dwellers, and especially the poor among them.)

We believe that the possibility of changing one's behavior to avoid infection is fundamental to understanding the response to AIDS. Once the information on AIDS is available, supermarket remedies will prevent infection for the great majority of those whose behavior puts them at risk of being exposed to HIV (that is, excluding cases of blood transfusion, use of blood products by hemophiliacs, and pediatric cases). It may be very difficult in some subcultures for a female partner to leave a man at risk of AIDS who refuses to use a condom, but it is possible. Because PWAs are seen as willing participants in the acts by which they became infected, they are held responsible for their infection, and concern over their civil liberties and care has been less compassionate than the concern shown for "the innocent." This has important consequences for charges of antihomosexual reactions to the AIDS crisis: even among people who are *not* antihomosexual, there are those who have been critical of the minority of gay men who continued to have unprotected anal sex with multiple partners after the risk was publicized.

Degrees of Cultural Tolerance or Help

There is a host of potentially damaging behaviors for which the damaged person is held accountable, so that in itself does not make AIDS unique. But we have widespread cultural tolerance for the most prevalent of these damaging behaviors, in contrast to the intolerance shown persons who have AIDS. Our society has evolved a culture of reasonable tolerance for, and offered some assistance in making behavioral changes to, those suffering from the widespread compulsions of smoking, overeating, gambling, and alcoholism. Despite the fact that these behaviors are seen as avoidable and self-inflicted, we have medical programs to deal with the symptoms and associated disabilities (such as cirrhosis of the liver caused by alcoholism or lung cancer caused by smoking) as well as programs to help change the (voluntary) behavior that caused the disorder. Public funds are available for these purposes, and their use is not considered controversial. We also find routine and substantial research on the etiology of many offending behaviors. And we find the disorders incorporated into a mildly stigmatizing but still tolerant and generally humorous folklore.

Most citizens, therefore, partake of the offending behaviors in mild degrees or have done so at some point in time. These people understand, and thus are more tolerant of, the problems of excess eating, alcohol, smoking, prescription drug abuse, and even gambling. The offending behavior is not strongly linked to class or minority status. The social costs—or externalities, as they are called—are tolerated even though they are borne by society at large or by persons who do not indulge in the behavior, through tax-supported medical costs, unemployment, early death, and in some cases the death of others (as in auto accidents) or the support of families that have been abandoned. This degree of tolerance is not extended to PWAs (Kagay, 1988).

It should be noted that there is nothing immutable or enduring about intolerance. Over time these behaviors may become more or less tolerated, associated more or less with stigmatized groups, seen as more or less involuntary. Marijuana smoking is not on our list because it is changing in status. It may achieve the social and legal tolerance that alcohol addiction has achieved, especially as society realizes that it is far less physically damaging than drinking or smoking legal substances and causes fewer deaths. It is possible that in time the lack of tolerance associated with AIDS will subside.

But tolerance is not extended to two other behaviorally related groups: users of illegal drugs and those who have contracted sexually transmitted diseases other than AIDS and prior to the appearance of AIDS. Both of these groups, however, can be distinguished from PWAs.

The Possibility of Unwitting Transmission

Before AIDS, users of cocaine, heroin, and crack (though the last was not widespread until well after the appearance of AIDS) differed from today's IVDUs in that they could not transmit a fatal disease to others unwittingly or unknowingly. Hepatitis B and other nonfatal disorders might be transmitted through shared needles, but they are treatable diseases. Furthermore, the general public and public service workers did not fear picking up diseases from drug users unknowingly. (There was some fear among health care workers, especially surgeons, of getting hepatitis B from drug addicts, but there is now a vaccine). This dimension of the disease of AIDS is particularly menacing as the latency period of the disease—the time it takes for it to manifest itself in disorders—is discovered to be longer and longer, up to eight to ten years at the present. Surveys indicate that 25 percent of the population think the disease can be spread by coughing (Blendon and Donelan, 1988). Health care workers fear that a seropositive patient who is not diagnosed as having AIDS may transmit it in fairly casual ways. Both beliefs are unfounded, of course, but AIDS is unusual in this respect. Unwittingly transmission of the virus can occur, however, through the sharing of unsterilized needles, through homosexual or heterosexual contacts, and through the use of contaminated blood.

If a threatening condition can be transmitted unknowingly and unwittingly from a human carrier to another human, it will be treated differently than if the source were a virus generated by swine, mold, or other nonhuman agents. There is an element of menace or threat in person-to-person transmission. If, in addition, there is a long latency period during which carriers may not even know that they can transmit the disease, and still worse, if they do know but wish to disguise the fact, the potentially damaging condition is feared even more. We would view alcoholism or coke sniffing with far more alarm if the damaging physical consequences of cirrhosis or immune-system suppression could be transmitted to anther person by the alcoholic or coke user. The tentative findings about passive smoking probably had a great deal to do with anti-smoking legislation; when it was demonstrated that breathing another's smoke was a health danger, smoking was seen as a greater menace.

The transmission problem becomes a civil liberties issue. Though we have legislation restricting the freedom of those with active tuberculosis and those with syphilis to infect others, and some seek similar laws regarding those with HIV infection, the enforcement of such legislation jeopardizes civil rights. By avoiding detection, the HIV-seropositive person can enjoy normal civil rights (and thus not be fired, lose insurance coverage, be denied access to housing or public schools); these rights could easily disappear if the seropositive condition is detected. Thus many in high-risk groups resist taking the HIV-antibody test lest they lose their jobs, insurance, housing, and freedom of movement.[8]

Sexual and Other Stigmas

Sexually transmitted diseases that result from casual or commercial sex, and especially from unprotected anal sex, partake of all the characteristics we have mentioned. They are due to changeable behavior, there is little or no culture tolerance available for them, and they can be transmitted unknowingly. But unprotected anal sex is further characterized by the special sexual stigma attached to it, either as an "unnatural act" among heterosexuals or as a homosexual act. We know almost nothing about the prevalence of anal intercourse among heterosexuals; it is a very private behavior that leaves no "markers." It is the category of male homosexual acts that is the most relevant to AIDS. It was stigmatizing even before AIDS and probably has become even more so since AIDS. Though the stigma is different from that associated with the unsterilized injection of drugs once AIDS appeared upon the scene, we will treat both stigmas together.

Once AIDS came on the scene, male homosexuals and IVDUs experienced a societal reaction that goes beyond the absence of cultural tolerance or help and the fear of transmission: gay men faced a homophobia grown more intense, and IVDUs met with a disapproval now mixed with fear and, often, racism. Prior to the appearance of AIDS, there were many middle-class and working-class IVDUs who, as long as they were not gay men or black or Hispanic, were not stigmatized. With the appearance of AIDS, we would argue, white heterosexual drug abusers are stigmatized; they leave a category with only two strikes against it—disapproval of the act itself, and the fact that the act is seen as voluntary—and move to one with two additional strikes: the fear that the disease may unknowingly or secretly be transmitted, and the association of the disease with two stigmatized groups—homosexual men and impoverished blacks and Hispanics.

Stigmatization involves social isolation, such that people have to leave their normal living situation and live alone or with others in the same plight; isolation at the workplace or other public places; fear of job loss even if the condition does not affect job performance; possible loss of social entitlements such as health care, Social Security, unemployment insurance, commercial insurance, and access to public housing; a low priority in terms of government funding for research, treatment, and education and, also important, extensive controversy over that funding; and lack of normal access to resources for coping with problems (private charity, churches, short-term credit, social clubs, and so on).

Some of the stigma associated with AIDS is transferred to another group: hemophiliacs. The fact that hemophiliacs were dying of AIDS in large numbers as a result of contaminated blood products that they needed meant that the New York Chapter of the National Hemophilia Foundation began to lose volunteer fund raisers and board members, who did not want to be associated with the stigmatized condition. Hemophiliacs with AIDS do not share all the other negative factors we have been considering. Their illness was not due to any behavior that they could change. By and large, cultural tolerance and help was still available, though they were diminished, even though unwitting transmission was possible. (It is also possible that some of the stigma associated with AIDS is being transferred to those heterosexuals who have multiple casual sexual encounters, though there is no documented evidence of this.)

The interaction of mysterious diseases and stigmatized populations is dramatically drawn by Zachary Gussow (1989) in his examination of leprosy and racism. Leprosy is a very old disease, but its association with stigma has been neither continuous nor universal. Westerners in the nineteenth century often associated the disease with inferior peoples as they came across it in their colonial empires, and fear of leprosy was used to limit immigration to the United States in the late nineteenth and early twentieth centuries. Many Americans, already persuaded of racist beliefs, found it easy to link the disease with hated foreign groups, especially the Chinese (who were called the "Yellow Peril" because of the disease). The handful of lepers in the United States were isolated and contained in Louisiana.

In Norway, however, where the disease was hyperendemic among the rural poor, there was little racism in the nation and no racial categories with which to link the disease. The government established clinics and treatment centers and sponsored the basic research that led to identification of the infectious agent by Armauer Hansen. Even though Hansen called for isolation of lepers, because it was still unclear how infectious the disease was, the Norwegian government resisted; it continued to sponsor research and emphasize a strictly medical approach. In our terms, the fact that Norwegians, rather than people of another race or ethnicity, had the disease, even though they were poor, meant that there was only a low hurdle in the way of "medicalizing" the disease for the government to overcome. This hurdle was readily overcome because there was, in so homogeneous a culture, more tolerance of poverty. In the United States and other nations, the presence of racism in general and the concentration of leprosy (Hansen's disease, it is now called) among racial groups meant that the government and private health authorities had a high hurdle to overcome. They did not succeed, and the disease was, in contrast, "moralized." It seems to be so with AIDS in the United States as compared with AIDS in some European countries.

Unusual Social and Medical Disabilities

Finally, persons with AIDS are subject to a long list of unusual social and medical disabilities. Although a few of these may be shared with the other groups we have been considering—victims of other infectious diseases, of compulsions, drug abuse before AIDS, and sexually transmitted diseases—AIDS appears to be unique in exhibiting them all.

The virus is still changing and is deceptive in its invasion of the body; no vaccines or cures are currently available, and palliatives are limited to a few drugs, especially AZT; the care is very expensive; the course of the disease is long and painful and disfiguring; there is a potential risk to health care workers; there is an unfounded but widespread fear of contamination through casual contact, such as sharing tools or kitchen or toilet facilities; the hospital system is being overwhelmed by AIDS patients, and there is an acute shortage of nurses, orderlies, and other care personnel; and death appears to be certain (though we have not been into the epidemic long enough to know for sure).

The Peril, the Stigma, and the Cost

Table 23–2 summarizes our discussion and highlights the special character of AIDS. It emphasizes that PWAs suffer from *all* of the problems that may complicate effective social response to a disease. Our scale is cumulative for the most part. In the public view, the infection is caused by behavior that could have been avoided, thus making PWAs responsible for their plight even if they were uninformed of the consequences of the behavior. Even if the behavior that led to AIDS is thought to be compulsive, as in the case of drug addiction, it is not given the tolerance of compulsive smoking, drinking, eating, or gambling. Because HIV may be carried by a person for a long time before it is discovered, the person may infect others unwittingly; when infected persons learn of their condition, they are reluctant to disclose it or even seek help because their

Table 23–2
Features of a Disease or Behavior That Lessen Tolerance or Increase Fear of It

Potentially damaging conditions or behavior	Due to changeable behavior	Little or no cultural tolerance or help	Possibility of unwitting transmission	Sexual or other stigma	Unusual social or medical aspects*
Before AIDS					
Infectious diseases (polio, swine flu, Legionnaires' disease)	no	no	no	no	no
Widespread compulsions (smoking, overeating, gambling, alcoholism)	yes	no	no	no	no
Drugs (IV injection, cocaine or crack use)	yes	yes	no	no	no
Sexually transmitted diseases					
Casual/commercial sex	yes	yes	yes	no	no
Unprotected anal sex	yes	yes	yes	yes	no
Coupled with AIDS					
Hemophilia	no	partial	yes	partial	yes
Heterosexual casual contact	yes	no	yes	partial	yes
IV unsterilized injection	yes	yes	yes	yes	yes
Unprotected homosexual sex (anal intercourse, semen injection)	yes	yes	yes	yes	yes

*Social: civil liberties dilemmas; screening; quarantine. Medical: changing virus; no vaccines or cures or palliative; expensive care; bed and nurse shortage; long, painful dying; fatal.

civil liberties will be curtailed when they most need them. IVDUs are violating the law, and conservative elements of our society are seeking to make homosexual behavior illegal (it already is in about half of the states, and there have been a few prosecutions) and to criminalize some behaviors of PWAs. The stigmas are very pronounced. Finally, the medical aspects are extreme; treatment is expensive and prolonged, and the disease is debilitating and fatal.

These elements are not only cumulative but are interactive for PWAs and the risk groups they come from. There is a "system effect" in that failures in one part of the social system interact with failures in another. For example, the possibility of changing a risky behavior aggravates the stigma attached to that behavior. Even if homosexuality is accepted, the changeable-behavior dimension places gay men in the IVDU category—people may be accepting of the sexual preference but still hold gay men accountable for not taking precautions. Medical aspects such as fear of contamination reinforce the cultural isolation and intolerance. The minority status of many PWAs means that few resources are allotted in the community for care and prevention.

In contrast to the blacks and Hispanics, the white homosexual population is fairly affluent and politically sophisticated, and it has its own community. The gay male population has been very effective, especially in San Francisco, in developing resources, securing an immense amount of volunteer labor, and gaining civil liberties protection. In New York City it has organized an extremely effective education and self-help group, the Gay Men's Health Crisis, which constituted the only substantial response to the epidemic for four years. Affluence and political sophistication, however, have not been able to make up for the deficits of cultural intolerance and sexual stigmatization and the debilitating medical aspects of AIDS.

If we add to the characteristics of the AIDS epidemic shown in Table 23–2 the other conditions we have detailed—organizational ineffectiveness and weakness of the public health sector, the economic concerns of the Reagan administration, and the administration's alliance with the moral majority—we can begin to see why the AIDS epidemic is overwhelming the normal defenses of organizations.

The problems might be summarized as threefold: peril, stigma, and cost. The *peril,* or threat, is to the rest of the population as the disease spreads beyond IVDUs and gay men. (As it is checked by drugs such as AZT and as the more privileged classes are better educated, the disease will be "redlined" and the peril for the general public will decrease.) The *stigma* is attached to the disease because it affects primarily gay men and IVDUs. The *financial* burden is on government, private care providers, and insurance companies. A fourth problem, that of *system effects,* concerns the unexpected interaction of failures. Each individual failure in housing, employment discrimination, hospital bed shortages, rise in syphilis, and so on might be considered the particular problem of the appropriate authority (housing authority, employment agency, hospital commission, public health agencies). But if the bed shortage means that some patients without housing will be discharged with a false diagnosis in order to free up a bed, and then are sexually assaulted in a poorly supervised shelter, possibly spreading the virus to the aggressor, we have an unanticipated "systems effect."

Notes

1. For a "refractory tool" view of organizations and their proneness to failure, see Perrow, 1986; see also Perrow, 1984.

2. On the performance of national health care sectors, see Schieber, 1987. For an analysis of the health care sector in New York City, see Paine, 1978, and Piore, Lieberman, and Linnane, 1977. See also Institute of Medicine, 1988.

3. For a particularly good account of the swine flu scare and the government's fumbling response, see Dutton, 1988.

4. Shulman and Mantell (1988) emphasize the need to find and implement alternatives to hospitalization of PWAs for acute care and to involve communities and government at all levels in order to share the soaring hospital costs for AIDS patients.

5. For another expression of concern over this issue, see Fineberg, 1988.

6. Consider this fantasy: A rare mold appears in church organs and contaminates the congregations. Despite repeated warnings from church leaders and government officials, many churches insist upon staying open to accommodate their members, who prefer to risk the deadly mold infection than to risk damnation. The federal government commits $10 billion to research and organ sterilization despite the huge federal deficit, and the most talented researchers, sensing a Nobel prize, drop their other work to deal with this problem. The electronics industry institutes a crash program to create synthesizers that will mimic a wheezy organ. Passages are discovered in sacred texts that justify staying away from church, and the public schools are opened up for Saturday and Sunday services, thus persuading the faithful to give up their near-compulsive pattern and modify their risky behavior.

We have no doubt that despite the tendency to organizational failure, organizations and individuals will respond when certain majority values are in jeopardy.

7. The other pathways for AIDS known today are transfusions with contaminated blood or blood products used by hemophiliacs, perinatal transmission from mother to fetus, heterosexual transmissions, and, extremely rare, unusual contact with the virus by health care or child care personnel. Though still small, the fastest growing group of AIDS cases is female partners of intravenous drug users (IVDUs) and their babies.

8. For a good, brief discussion of the dangers of compulsory testing, see Weiss and Thier, 1988. The authors are from the Institute of Medicine of the National Academy of Sciences.

References

"AIDS Virus Test in Midwest Indicated Low Infection Rate." 1988. *New York Times,* 16 April.

Blendon, Robert J., and Karen Donelan. 1988. "Discrimination against People with AIDS." *New England Journal of Medicine* 319: 1022–26.

Boffey, Philip M. 1988a. "Research Group Says AIDS Cases May Be Twice the U.S. Estimate." *New York Times,* 20 August.

―――. 1988b. "Spread of AIDS Abaiting, But Deaths Will Still Soar." *New York Times,* 14 February.

Centers for Disease Control. 1989. *HIV/AIDS Surveillance Report,* December.

Chin, James. 1989. "Current and Future Dimensions of the HIV/AIDS Pandemic." Paper presented at the International Institute for Applied Systems Analysis (IIASA) Workshop, Budapest, Hungary, 23–24 November.

Conrad, Peter. 1986. "The Social Meaning of AIDS." *Social Policy,* Summer, pp. 51–56.

Crawford, Mark. 1988. "Superconductor Funds Flat." *Science* 239: 1089; see also 1987: 593.

Culliton, Barbara J. 1976. "Legion Fever: Postmortem on an Investigation That Failed." *Science* 194: 1025–27.

Dutton, Diane. 1988. *Worse Than the Disease: Pitfalls of Medical Progress.* New York: Cambridge University Press.

Fineberg, Harvey V. 1988. "The Social Dimensions of AIDS." *Scientific American* 258: 128–34.

Fox, Daniel M. 1986. "AIDS and the American Health Policy: The History and Prospects of a Crisis of Authority." *Milbank Quarterly* suppl. 1: 7–33. Reprinted in *AIDS: The Burdens of History,* ed. Elizabeth Fee and Daniel Fox, pp. 316–43. Berkeley: University of California Press, 1988.

General Accounting Office. 1987. *AIDS Prevention: Views on the Administration's Budget Proposals,* August. Washington, D.C.: Government Printing Office.

Gussow, Zachary. 1989. "Social Policy and Chronic Disease Control." In *Leprosy, Racism, and Public Health.* Boulder, Colo.: Westview Press.

Institute of Medicine, 1988. *The Future of Public Health.* Washington, D.C.: National Academy Press.

Kagay, Michael. 1988. "Poll Finds Antipathy towards AIDS Victims." *New York Times,* 12 October.

Kolata, Gina. 1988. "New York Shelters, A Last Stop for Hundreds of AIDS Patients." *New York Times,* 4 April.

Lambert, Bruce. 1988a. "AIDS Count: Is the Quest for Precision on the Right Track?" *New York Times,* 24 July.

―――. 1988b. "Outlook Dim for Expanding Health Care." *New York Times,* 5 April.

New York City, Department of Health AIDS Surveillance Unit. *AIDS Surveillance Update,* 29 November. New York: Department of Health.

Office of Technology Assessment. June 1988. *How Effective is AIDS Education?* Staff Paper No. 3. Washington, D.C.: Office of Technology Assessment.

―――. 1985. *Review of the Public Health Service's Response.* Washington, D.C.: Office of Technology Assessment.

Paine, Leslie H. W., ed. 1978. *Health Care in Big Cities.* New York: St. Martin's.

Panem, Sandra. 1988. *The AIDS Bureaucracy.* Cambridge, Mass.: Harvard University Press.

Perrow, Charles. 1986. *Complex Organizations: A Critical Essay,* 3rd ed. New York: Random House.

―――. 1984. *Normal Accidents: Living with High Risk Technologies.* New York: Basic Books.

Piore, Nora, Parlaine Lieberman, and James Linnane. 1977. "Public Expenditures and Private Control? Health Case Dilemmas in New York City." *Milbank Memorial Fund Quarterly* 55: 79–116.

Schieber, George J. 1987. *Financing and Delivering Health Care: A Comparative Study of OECD Countries.* Paris: OECD.

Shilts, Randy M. 1987. *And the Band Played On: Politics, People, and the AIDS Epidemic.* New York: St. Martin's.

Shulman, Lawrence C., and Joanne E. Mantell. 1988. "The AIDS Crisis: A United States Health Care Perspective." *Social Science and Medicine* 26, no. 10: 979–88.

Weiss, Robin, and Samuel O. Thier. 1988. "HIV Testing Is the Answer—What's the Question?" *New England Journal of Medicine* 319: 1010–12.

PART IV

Organizational Alternatives and Social Change

The essays in this section focus on strategies of empowerment that promise to reverse some of the dominant tendencies of bureaucratic organization. They range across public, private, and nonprofit sectors, examine possibilities in organizations large and small, and explore the problems and paradoxes of democracy among those committed to community, gender equity, and diversity of racial and ethnic identity and sexual preference. Examples are drawn from urban public-school systems and federal bureaucracies such as the Department of Housing and Urban Development (HUD), industrial and service-sector firms using advanced technologies, community organizations and democratic collectives, feminist social movement and service organizations, and environmental programs with extensive public participation in resource and waste management and planning. While inspired by alternative visions and practical experiences of transforming the way organizations work, the essays remain self-critical and sober about many of the problems, limits, and continuing challenges of democratic strategies of empowerment.

Joyce Rothschild's essay compares two ideal types of organization, the Weberian rational-bureaucratic model and the collectivist-democratic one. The latter reemerged in many innovative service and social-movement organizations in recent decades and challenged many of the claims of the former. Basing her essay on case studies of five democratic collectives (a free clinic, law collective, food coop, alternative newspaper, and free school), Rothschild examines the conditions facilitating a highly democratic and egalitarian model, as well as the constraints and costs of such (time, emotional intensity, organizational environments, individual and skill differences, and the like), that might lead actors to exit or revise structures along various dimensions. Her analysis permits us not only to compare alternative models at the extremes of the organizational spectrum, but to understand many of the reasons why change occurs within organizations committed to democratic ideals.   **443**

David Osborne and Ted Gaebler's essay examines the idea of community-owned programs as one of a variety of ways for "reinventing government" to make it more responsive, entrepreneurial, and empowering. Arguing that communities are much more effective, caring, and empowering of citizens than are professional bureaucracies that see themselves as serving clients, they survey a range of innovations occurring across the United States today, from community-oriented policing, community development corporations, Head Start centers, and parent councils in school reform programs to community-based health care for the elderly, infirm, and those infected with the AIDS virus. An extended case study of tenant management in a drug- and crime-ridden public housing project in Washington, D.C., portrays a successful collaborative effort between HUD and local residents who mobilized to take back control of their community, to develop a range of services to attack problems in a coordinated fashion and reduce welfare and drug dependency, and eventually to completely renovate and gain legal ownership of the entire housing project.

Robert Moses, Mieko Kamii, Susan McAllister Swap, and Jeffrey Howard examine the Mississippi tradition of community organizing within the civil rights movement that was inspired by African American organizer and *fundi* Ella Baker, and show how that tradition informed an innovative program of math-science pedagogy in the Cambridge public schools and might become part of broader school reform efforts elsewhere. Bob Moses had been a youthful leader of the Student Nonviolent Coordinating Committee in the early 1960s and was now a parent of children in the Martin Luther King, Jr., Open School in Cambridge, Massachusetts, where public-school choice and innovation had recently been instituted. The Algebra Project adopted three key principles from the organizing tradition Moses had known in Mississippi: (1) the centrality of families to the work of organizing; (2) the empowerment of grass-roots people and the development of their leadership capacities; and (3) "casting down your bucket where you are," or organizing in the context in which one lives and works. Moses's personal involvement in the project, triggered by his own daughter's resistance to algebra, elicited a subtle empowerment strategy among other parents, teachers, and students, which in turn mobilized voluntary resources and commitments to public service among black college students and graduates from nearby colleges. Community empowerment led to reframing the discourse about ability groupings and effective teaching for children of color, and led to a highly innovative algebra program that draws upon students' everyday competences, such as riding the Boston subway system. The authors compare their own project with other school reform efforts, such as those of James Comer in New Haven.

Robert Howard and Leslie Schneider's essay examines a spectrum of approaches to managing workplace technological change and the possibilities and constraints they pose for worker participation in this process.

The technocentric approach sees technology driving the process and excludes participation as disruptive. The organization-centered approach recognizes the need to look at organizational factors that promote or hinder technical rationality and business effectiveness in developing and adopting new technologies, and has been sensitive to the kinds of questions posed by Shoshana Zuboff about informating potentials and by Michael Piore and Charles Sabel about flexible specialization. It opens up space for a variety of perspectives to be given voice in the work redesign process, such as the ETHICS methodology of Enid Mumford and the Digital Equipment Corporation. But, as the case study from the American telecommunications industry shows, limited job redesign and autonomous work groups do not create a self-sustaining dynamic of empowerment in the absence of a broader view of worker and consumer interests, and more effective ways of engaging managers, engineers, systems designers, and union officials together in proactive strategies of technology and workplace design. The third model of negotiation, which has been developed most extensively in Scandinavia, recognizes that workers have legitimate interests separate from, and often in conflict with, allegedly neutral organizational interests in effectiveness, and that consensual frameworks and labor management committees are often not adequate to articulate and represent these effectively. Building upon nationally legislated rights to participate, as well as relatively strong union organizational resources, workers and unions have negotiated a range of new ways of engaging in participatory workplace and technology design, including data stewards, local study circles, and the use of their own technology consultants and design laboratories. These reforms have been won by framing the question more broadly than simple organizational effectiveness to include social interests in industrial democracy, gender equity, rights to continued skill development and adult learning, and the quality of working life as well as consumer service. Case studies from the Norwegian postal service and savings bank industries illustrate how such broad social interests can complement and enhance organizational effectiveness as traditionally conceived. Howard and Schneider also analyze factors in the larger market, regulatory, technological, and political-organizational environment that constrain such ambitious participatory strategies, and they explore how these might be changed.

Jane Mansbridge analyzes some of the organizational forms that have been developed by the feminist movement over the past two decades in the United States. She pays particular attention to the consciousness raising group and the face-to-face consensual form of participatory democracy, since these have had special relevance to feminist goals of personal transformation. Yet her own research on small-scale democratic organizations shows that this form, while important, is of only limited value to disadvantaged groups, including women, and that feminism ought not inscribe any single "form of freedom," but choose from a range of plural forms. Such choices will depend on many things, including specific goals and contexts, and particularly on whether participants' interests tend to converge or conflict.

Carmen Sirianni's essay, drawing upon the pluralist insights of Mansbridge's analysis and other democratic and feminist theorists, analyzes organizational and historical learning processes in feminist organizations from the 1960s to the 1990s. Examining a broad range of cases among movement and political organizations, as well as educational and service ones (consciousness-raising groups, socialist-feminist unions, the National Organization for Women (NOW), the National Women's Studies Association, shelters for battered women, rape crisis centers, and the like), he argues that feminists have deepened and enriched the ideals and practices of participatory democracy, and yet that this process has compelled them from the beginning to continually rethink and revise their notions of what constitutes democratic process, pluralist citizenship, and effective empowerment. Analyzing not only earlier problems with structurelessness and institutionalization but more recent questions of the ethics of care and the politics of diversity in multicultural feminist organizations, Sirianni argues that there has been an often very difficult and problematic, yet nonetheless innovative and dynamic process of learning pluralism, and that the continuing paradoxes and tensions in feminist organizational practice have much to say to a participatory and postmodern pluralist democracy.

Gary Delgado's essay explores the organizational dynamics within the low-income multiracial network of community organizations known as ACORN (Association of Community Organizations for Reform Now), which extends throughout the majority of states in the United States today and has had important impacts not just in local communities but in broader political and regulatory arenas. He examines how indigenous leadership is recruited and developed by organizing staff, as well as some of the tensions that develop between outside organizers and local leaders, especially where these overlap with differences in class, race, and gender composition. The problem of oligarchy that Michels identifies (see Part I, Chapter 3) thus presents some peculiar twists and particular challenges for today. Delgado also explores the ways the organizing model shapes issue choice, ideology, internal solidarity, and the mobilization of resources. Although ACORN represents only one among a variety of community organizing models practiced today, it is engaged in a dynamic internal learning process that Delgado's own critical analysis has itself helped to spur.

Daniel Mazmanian and Jeanne Nienaber's essay analyzes one of the most innovative efforts to introduce highly visible democratic techniques into water and resource management, and presents the challenge of how we might introduce community-based democratic discourse and organizing into a regulatory and development arena dominated by bureaucratic and commodity values, interest group intermediation, or—at best—

procedural democracy and public-interest regulation insulated from a broader public debate. Fishbowl planning emerged in the Seattle District of the Army Corps of Engineers in the early 1970s in response to a controversy among environmentalists, valley farmers, and others over a planned dam on the middle fork of the Snoqualmie. The procedure used an innovative combination of democratic techniques to make the planning process as visible as if it were occurring in a fishbowl. These included: (1) public meetings to discuss and develop alternative plans for water and land management; (2) mini-workshops convened by various interested parties, from the Sierra Club and other environmental groups to valley farmers and others interested in flood control and economic development, with Army Corps experts playing a largely facilitative role; (3) a citizen's committee composed of community and organization leaders to inform and mobilize people to participate in various meetings and workshops; and (4) an evolving study brochure that guided public debate through some half-dozen revisions and contained all proposals generated, with summaries of arguments for and against. Although the planning process required mediation before a workable consensus was reached, it demonstrated ways of opening up even the most bureaucratic of regulatory and development agencies, and it pointed to ways in which public interest and environmental organizations like the Sierra Club and the League of Women Voters might help facilitate community-based organizing and discourse, and thus promise to enrich the public interest regulatory model with elements of civic republicanism and discursive democracy.

Barry Rabe's essay addresses the problem of NIMBY (not in my back yard) that arises in the management of hazardous waste and the siting of facilities—a problem of enormous proportions in Canada and the United States that traditional top-down regulatory and market approaches only exacerbate. He explores the singularly successful case of siting in Alberta in the 1980s, which used a variety of participatory forms: some 120 educational meetings convened by officials across the province, community plebescites in five applicant communities, intensive public meetings in the community that was chosen, negotiation of compensation packages, including resources that support the community's capacity to monitor the ongoing management of the facility. Rabe also analyzes attempts to transplant this model to the United States, particularly in Minnesota. The Minnesota case differs from the Alberta one in having had less extensive public participation, the absence of a public or crown corporation as a partner of the private waste management firm, and less comprehensive compensation packages. But the comparison raises more general questions about the possibilities of moving beyond NIMBY in a U.S. context where political culture is more adversarial, the environmental regulatory regime is less prone to industry capture, and environmental groups are more highly organized and mobilized on local and national levels.

24

The Collectivist Organization: An Alternative to Rational- Bureaucratic Models

Joyce Rothschild

This article represents a first approach to a model of collectivist organization, a model that is premised on the logic of substantive rationality rather than formal rationality. To date, theories of organizational action have assumed, explicitly or implicitly, that norms of formal rationality prevail (Thompson, 1967). Indeed, in a modern society they almost always do. This decade, however, has given rise to a wide array of work organizations that self-consciously reject the norms of rational bureaucracy and identify themselves as "alternative institutions." The emergence of these contrabureaucratic organizations calls for a new model of organization that can encompass their alternative practices and aspirations.

Max Weber delineated four types of social action: traditional, affectual, instrumentally rational, and value rational. The first three forms of social action correspond respectively to traditional, charismatic, and legal-rational bases of authority, with each type of authority implying a particular type of organization to implement its aims. But the last type of social action, value rationality, has no counterpart in his typology of authority and organization. Some recent scholars have begun to look to Weber's missing type, value-rational authority, to understand certain kinds of professional and church organizations (Satow, 1975; Wood, 1978).

A value-rational orientation to social action is marked by a "belief in the value for its own sake . . . independent of its prospects of success" (Weber, 1968:24). It is evidenced by actions that put into practice people's convictions. For Weber (1968:37) natural law is one of the purest instances of value-rational legitimacy.

The tension between substantive or value-rational action, on the one hand, and formal or instrumentally rational action, on the other, was

Reprinted from Joyce Rothschild-Whitt, *American Sociological Review* 44 (August 1979): 509–27, by permission of the American Sociological Association and of the author.

well recognized by Max Weber. For Weber, formal rationality and its main locus of expression in bureaucracy would come to dominate modern society, but it would be continually "confronted by the inevitable conflict between an abstract formalism of legal certainty and [the] desire to realize substantive goals" (Weber, 1954:226). The modern legal order could not exclude a substantive theory of natural law any more than the modern bureaucracy could eliminate all moral values. In Weber's view, the conflict between formal and substantive justice has no ultimate solution (Bendix, 1962:391–438). Nevertheless, in his classic statement on bureaucracy, Weber (1946:196–244) sets forth the characteristics of this mode of organization as if it could eliminate all substantive, nonformal considerations, and contrasts this ideal-type conception of bureaucracy with patrimonial administration. The polar opposite of the monocratic, formal bureaucracy drawn by Weber would be a fully collectivized democracy that turned on principles of substantive rationality.

Just as the ideal of bureaucracy, in its monocratic pure type, is probably not attainable (Mouzelis, 1968), so the ideal of democracy, in its pure and complete form, is probably never achieved. In practice, organizations are hybrids.

This paper aims to develop an ideal-type model of collectivist-democratic organization. It is an attempt to delineate the form of authority and the corresponding mode of organization that follows from value-rational premises. As such, it is grounded in observations of counterbureaucratic organizations that aspire to being "collectives," or in Weberian terms, that have explicitly rejected instrumentally rational social action in favor of value-rational behavior. The ideal-type approach allows us to understand these new forms of organization, not only in terms of bureaucratic standards they do not share, but in terms of the alternative values they do hold (cf. Kanter and Zurcher, 1973). Further, the use of an ideal type permits us to locate actual organizations along a continuum.

Constraints and social costs that inhibit the realization of organizational democracy are addressed in the latter half of this paper.

Research Settings and Methods

During the 1970s the United States has witnessed an impressive proliferation what have popularly come to be termed *alternative institutions*. Alternative institutions may be defined in terms of their members' resolve to build organizations that are parallel to, but outside of, established institutions and that fulfill social needs (for education, food, medical aid, and the like) without recourse to bureaucratic authority.

Parallel, oppositional organizations have been created in many service domains—e.g., free medical clinics, free schools, legal collectives, alternative media collectives, food cooperatives, research collectives, communes. Grass-roots cooperative businesses are proliferating as well, especially in fields with relatively low capitalization needs such as restaurants, bookstores, clothing manufacture and retail, auto repair, housing construction, alternative energy installation, newspapers, and so forth. They are burgeoning at a remarkable rate. For instance, in 1967 there were about 30 free schools in the United States. By 1973 there were over 800 documented free schools (New Schools Exchange Directory, 1967; 1973). A 1976 directory locates some 5,000 alternative organizations nationwide and does not even claim to be exhaustive (Gardner, 1976). These collectively owned and managed work enterprises represent one of the enduring legacies of the antiauthority movements of the 1960s.[1]

Little social scientific research has been devoted to this social development. Some research studies describe one or another of these alternative work organizations, but few point to commonalities that link them. This paper identifies some of the structural commonalities and attempts to develop a general organizational framework of collectivist democracy in which specific cases may be understood.

The organizational properties formulated in this paper are grounded in comparative data from different types of collectivist organizations. Glaser and Strauss (1967) have argued that theory generated from data, namely, grounded theory, will have more power to predict and explain the subject at hand than will theory arrived at through speculation or logical deduction.

Following the comparative research strategy of Glaser and Strauss (1967), I selected for study five collectivist work organizations that were as varied as possible: a free medical clinic, a legal collective, a food cooperative, a free school, and an alternative newspaper.[2] All are located in a medium-sized city in California. Although they differ greatly as to the type of product or service they provide, organizational size, funding sources, technology utilized, and so forth, they are unified by the primacy each gives to developing a collectivist-democratic form of organization.

Participant observation was conducted in each of the research settings, ranging in duration from six months to two years per organization. Observational material was amplified by structured interviews with selected members of each of the organizations, with a mean interview time of 2¼ hours. This was followed by questionnaire surveys to the membership of three of the organizations under study.

Each theoretical point in the paper is grounded in numerous instances from the empirical material. I have tried to select those few that seem most characteristic of the data. Of course, no number of illustrations can ever constitute a "proof." The theoretical formulations in this work should be assessed for their logical consistency, clarity, integration, and especially for the extent to which they are found to be generic properties of collectivist organizations.

The Collectivist Organization:

Characteristics

Collectivist-democratic organizations can be distinguished from bureaucratic organizations along at least eight dimensions. Each of these characteristics will be taken up in turn, and a summarizing chart will follow.

Authority

> When we're talking about collectives, we're talking about an embryonic creation of a new society. . . . Collectives are growing at a phenomenal rate all over this country. The new structures have outgrown the science of analyzing them. Sociology has to catch up with reality. . . . Collectivism is an attempt to supplant old structures of society with new and better structures. And what makes our's [*sic*] superior is that the basis of authority is radically different. (Staff member, Alternative Paper)

The words of this activist get right to the heart of the matter: authority. Perhaps more than anything else, it is the basis of authority that distinguishes the collectivist organization from any variant of bureaucracy. The collectivist-democratic organization rejects rational-bureaucratic justifications for authority. Here authority resides not in the individual, whether on the basis of incumbency in office *or* expertise, but in the collectivity as a whole.

This notion stems from the ancient anarchist ideal of "no authority." It is premised on the belief that social order can be achieved without recourse to authority relations (Guerin, 1970). Thus it presupposes the capacity of individuals for self-disciplined, cooperative behavior. Indeed, collectivist organizations routinely emphasize these aspects of human beings. Like the anarchists, their aim is not the transference of power from one official to another, but the abolition of the pyramid in toto: organization without hierarchy.

An organization cannot be composed of a collection of autonomous wills, each pursuing its own personal ends. Some decisions must be binding on the group.

Decisions become authoritative in collectivist organizations to the extent that they derive from a process in which all members have the right to full and equal participation. This democratic ideal, however, differs significantly from conceptions of "democratic bureaucracy" (Lipset et al., 1962), "representative bureaucracy" (Gouldner, 1954), or even representative democracy. In its directly democratic form, it does not subscribe to the established rules of order and protocol. It does not take formal motions and amendments, it does not usually take votes, majorities do not rule, and there is no two-party system. Instead there is a "consensus process" in which all members participate in the *collective* formulation of problems and *negotiation of decisions*.[3] All major policy issues, such as hiring, firing, salaries, the division of labor, the distribution of surplus, and the shape of the final product or service, are decided by the collective as a whole. Only decisions that appear to carry the consensus of the group behind them, carry the weight of moral authority. Only these decisions, changing as they might with the ebb and flow of sentiments in the group, are taken as binding and legitimate. These organizations are collectively controlled by their members or workers: hence the name *collectivist* or *collectivist-democratic* organization.

In Weberian terms, we are concerned here with organizations that aspire and claim to be free of *Herrschaft*.[4] They are organizations without domination in that ultimate authority is based in the collectivity as a whole, not in the individual. Individuals, of course, may be delegated carefully circumscribed areas of authority, but authority is delegated and defined by the collectivity and subject to recall by the collectivity.

Rules

Collectivist organizations also challenge the bureaucratic conception that organizations should be bound by a formally established, written system of rules and regulations. Instead, they seek to minimize rule use. But, just as the most bureaucratic of organizations cannot anticipate, and therefore cannot circumscribe, *every* potential behavior in the organization, so the alternative organization cannot reach the theoretical limit of *zero* rules. Collectivist organizations, however, drastically can reduce the number of spheres of organizational activity that are subject to explicit rule governance.

In the most simple of the collectivist organizations in this study, the free high school, only one explicit organizational rule was formulated: no dope in school. This rule was agreed upon by a plenary meeting of the school's students and staff primarily because its violation was perceived to threaten the continued existence of the school. Other possible rules also were discussed at the Free School, rules that might seem self-evident in ordinary schools such as "each student should take X number of classes" or "students are required to attend the courses for which they are registered," but these did not receive the consensual backing of the school's members.

In place of the fixed and universalistic rule use that is the trademark of bureaucracy, operations and decisions in alternative organizations tend to be conducted in an ad hoc manner. Decisions generally are settled as the case arises, and are suited to the peculiarities of the individual case.

No written manual of rules and procedures exists in most collectives, though norms of participation clearly obtain. Although there is little attempt to account for decisions in terms of literal rules, concerted efforts are made to account for decisions in terms of substantive ethics. This is like Weber's (1968:976–8) *Kadi* justice and far removed from the formal justice that informs rational-bureaucratic action.

One of the chief virtues of extensive rule use in bureaucracy is that it permits predictability and appeal of decisions. The lack of universalistic standards in prebureaucratic modes of organization invited arbitrary and capricious rule. In bureaucracy decisions could be calculated and appealed on the basis of their correspondence to the written law. In collectivist organizations, however, decisions are not necessarily arbitrary. They are based on substantive values (e.g., equality) applied consistently, if not universally. This permits at least some calculability on the basis of knowing the substantive ethic that will be invoked in a particular situation.

Social Control

From a Weberian point of view, organizations are tools. They are instruments of power for those who head them. But what means does the bureaucracy have of ensuring that lower-level personnel, people who are quite distant from the centers of power, effectively will understand and implement the aims of those at the top? This issue of social control is critical in any bureaucracy. Perrow (1976) examines three types of social control mechanisms in bureaucracies: direct supervision, standardized rules, and selection for homogeneity. The first type of control, direct supervision, is the most obvious. The second is far less obtrusive, but no less effective: standardized rules, procedures, and sanctions. Gouldner (1954) showed that rules can substitute for direct supervision. This allows the organization considerable decentralization of everyday decision making, and even the appearance of participation, for the *premises* of those decisions have been carefully controlled from the top. Decentralized decision making, when decisional premises are set from the top via standardized rules, may be functionally equivalent to centralized authority (cf. Blau, 1970; Bates, 1970; Perrow, 1976).

Collectivist organizations generally refuse to legitimate the use of centralized authority *or* standardized rules to achieve social control. Instead, they rely upon personalistic and moralistic appeals to provide the primary means of control, as Swidler (1979) demonstrates in her examination of free schools. In Etzioni's (1961) terms, compliance here is chiefly normative. One person appeals to another, "do X *for me*," "do X in the interest of equality," and so forth.

The more homogeneous the group, the more such appeals can hold sway. Thus, where personal and moral appeals are the chief means of social control, it is important, perhaps necessary, that the group select members who share their basic values and worldview. All five of the alternative organizations in this study tried to do that. At the Law Collective, for instance, I asked how they decide whether to take in a new member:

> They have to have a certain amount of past experience in political work . . . [,] something really good and significant that checks out . . . . Secondly, they have to share the same basic assumptions as far as politics goes and they have to be willing to accept the collective way of doing things. . . .

Such recruitment criteria are not at all uncommon or hidden in alternative work organizations.

In Perrow's (1976) terms, alternative organizations eschew first- and second-level controls but accept third-level controls. Third-level controls are the most subtle and indirect of all: selection of personnel for homogeneity. On this level social control may be achieved by selecting for top managerial positions only people who "fit in"—people who read the right magazines, go to the right clubs, have the right style of life and worldview. This is also true in collectivist organizations. Where people are expected to participate in major decisions (and this means *everyone* in a collective and high-level managers in a bureaucracy) consensus is crucial, and people who are likely to challenge basic assumptions are avoided. A person who reads the *Wall Street Journal* would be as suspect in applying for a position at the Law Collective, as a person who reads the *New Left Review* would be at ITT. Both kinds of organizations use selection for homogeneity as a mechanism for social control.

Social Relations

Impersonality is a key feature of the bureaucratic model. Personal emotions are to be prevented from distorting rational judgements. Relationships between people are to be role-based, segmental, and instrumental. Collectivist organizations, on the other hand, strive toward the ideal of community. Relationships are to be holistic, affective, and of value in themselves. The search for community may even become an instance of goal displacement, as when, for example, a free school comes to value community so highly that it loses its identity as a school and becomes a commune (see, e.g., Kay, 1972).

Recruitment and Advancement

Bureaucratic criteria for recruitment and advancement are resisted in the collectivist organization. Here employment is not based on specialized training or certification, nor on any universalistic standard of competence. Instead, staff are generally recruited and selected by collectives on the basis of friendship and social-political values. Personality attributes that are seen as congruent with the collectivist mode of organization, such as self-direction and collaborative styles, also may be consciously sought in new staff (see, e.g., Torbert, 1973).

Employment does not constitute the beginning of a career in collectivist organizations in the usual sense, for the collective does not provide a life-long ladder to ever-higher positions. Work may be volunteer or paid, and it may be part time or full time or even 60 hours per week, but it is not conceptualized as a career. Bureaucratic career advancement (based on seniority or achievement or both) is not a meaningful concept in collective work organizations, for there is no hierarchy of offices. Therefore, there can be no individual *advancement* in positional rank (though there may be much change in positions).

Collectivist work organizations generally recruit competent and skilled personnel even though their selection criteria explicitly emphasize friendship networks, political values, and personality traits. To illustrate, during the year in which the Free Clinic was observed, four full-time staff positions were filled, and between nine and sixty-five applications were received for each position. Yet each of the four positions went to a friend of present staff members. The relevant attributes cited most frequently by the staff making these decisions were: articulation skills, ability to organize and mobilize people, political values, self-direction, ability to work under pressure, friendship, commitment to the organization's goals, cooperative style, and relevant experience. These selection criteria are typical of alternative organizations. In spite of their studied neglect of *formal* criteria of competence (e.g., certification), alternative organizations often attract highly qualified people.[5] In many ways, their selection criteria are well suited to their needs for multitalented and committed personnel who can serve a variety of administrative and task-oriented functions and who are capable of comanaging the organization in cooperation with others.

Incentive Structure

Organizations use different kinds of incentives to motivate participation. Most bureaucratic workplaces emphasize remunerative incentives, and few employees could be expected to donate their services if their paychecks were to stop. Collectivist organizations, on the other hand, rely primarily on purposive incentives (value fulfillment), secondarily on solidary incentives such as friendship, and only tertiarily on material incentives (Clark and Wilson, 1961). According to Etzioni (1961), this kind of normative compliance system tends to generate a high level of moral commitment to organization. Specific structural mechanisms that produce and sustain organizational commitment are identified by Kanter (1972a). Because collectivist work organizations require a high level of commitment, they tend to use some of these mechanisms as well as value-purposive incentives to generate it. Indeed, work in collectives is construed as a labor of love, and members may pay themselves very low salaries and may expect each other to continue to work during months when the organization is too poor to afford their salaries.

Alternative organizations often appeal to symbolic values to motivate people to join and to participate actively. The range of these values is considerable. At the Free Clinic, for instance, a member describes motivation: "Our volunteers are do-gooders. . . . They get satisfaction from giving direct and immediate help to people in need. This is why they work here." At the Alternative Newspaper, the following is more illustrative:

> Our motives were almost entirely political. We were moving away from a weathermen type position, toward the realization that the revolution will be a very gradual thing. . . . We wanted to create a base for a mass left. To activate liberals and open them up to left positions. To tell you the truth, the paper was conceived as a political organ.

At the Food Co-op it is the value of community that is most stressed, and the Co-op actively helps to create other community-owned and controlled institutions in its locale.

However, we should guard against an overly idealistic interpretation of participation in alternative organizations. In these organizations, as much as any, there exists an important *coalescence of material and ideal interests*. Even volunteers in these organizations, whose motives on the face of it would appear to be wholly idealist, also have material incentives for their participation.

For example, staff members at the Free Clinic suspect that some volunteers donate their time to the clinic "only to look good on their applications to medical school." Likewise, some of the college students who volunteered to teach at the Free School believed that in a tight market, this would improve their chances of getting a paid teaching job. And, for all the talk of community at the Food Co-op, many members undoubtedly joined simply because the food was cheaper. Because material gain is not part of the acceptable vocabulary of motives in these organizations, public discussion of such motives is suppressed.

Nonetheless, for staff members as well as for volunteers, material incentives coalesce with moral incentives. At the Law Collective, for instance, legal workers often used their experience there to pursue the bar, since California law allows eligibility for the bar through the alternative means of apprenticing under an attorney for three years. At the Alternative Newspaper, a few staff members confided that they had entered the paper to gain journalistic experience.

Yet members of alternative institutions often deny the existence of material considerations and accept only the idealistic motivations. In the opinion of one longtime staffer at the Alternative Paper:

> I don't think anyone came for purely journalistic purposes, unless they're masochists. I mean it doesn't pay, the hours are lousy, and the people are weird. If you want professional journalistic experience you go to a straight paper.

In many ways, she is right: Alternative institutions generally provide woefully inadequate levels of remuneration by the standards of our society. But, it does not impugn the motives of participants to recognize that these organizations must provide some material base for their members if they are to be alternative places of employment at all.

At the Free Clinic full-time staff were all paid $500 per month during 1974–1975, at the Law Collective they were paid a base of $250 per month plus a substantial supplement for dependents, and at the Alternative Paper they received between $150 and $300 per month, in accordance with individual "needs." These pay levels were negotiated in open discussion of the collectives as a whole, as were decisions regarding the entire labor process. If these wage levels appear exploitative, it is a case of self-exploitation. It is the subsistence wage levels that permit the young organization to accumulate capital and to reinvest this surplus in the organization rather than paying it out in wages. This facilitates the growth of the organization and hastens the day when it may be able to pay higher salaries.[6]

Many collectives have found ways to help compensate for the meager salaries they pay their members. The Law Collective stocked food so that members could eat at least a meal or two per day at the office for free. The collective also maintained a number of cars that its members could share, thereby eliminating the need for private automobile ownership. Free Clinic staff decided to allow themselves certain fringe benefits to compensate for what they regarded as underpaid work: two weeks of paid vacation time each year, plus two additional weeks of unpaid vacation (if desired); one day off every other week; and the revised expectation that staff would regularly work 28–30 hours rather than a 40-hour week. But these are compensations or supplements for a generally poor income, and like income, they do not motivate people to work in alternative organizations, they only make work there possible.

First and foremost, people come to work in an alternative organization because it offers them substantial control over their work. Collective control means that members can structure both the product of their work and the work process in congruence with their ideals. Hence, the work is purposeful to them. It is not infrequently contrasted with alienating jobs that they have had, or imagine, in bureaucracies:

> A straight paper would have spent a third of a million dollars getting to where we are now and still wouldn't be breaking even. We've gotten where we are on the sweat of our workers. They've taken next to no money when they could have had [$]8,000 to 15,000 in straight papers doing this sort of

job. . . . They do it so they can be their own boss. So they can own and control the organization they work in. So they can make the paper what *they* want it to be. . . . (interview, member of Alternative Newspaper)

Social Stratification

In the ideal-type bureaucracy, the dimensions of social stratification are consistent with one another. Specifically, social prestige and material privilege are to be commensurate with one's positional rank, and the latter is the basis of authority in the organization. Thus, a hierarchical arrangement of offices implies an isomorphic distribution of privilege and prestige. In this way, hierarchy institutionalizes (and justifies) inequality.

In contrast, egalitarianism is a central feature of the collectivist-democratic organization. Large differences in social prestige or privilege, even where they are commensurate with level of skill or authority in bureaucracy, would violate this sense of equity. At the Free Clinic, for instance, all full-time staff members were paid equally, no matter what skills or experience they brought to the clinic. At the Law Collective and Alternative Newspaper pay levels were set "to each according to his need." Here salaries took account of dependents and other special circumstances contributing to need but explicitly excluded considerations of the worth of the individual to the organization. In no case I observed was the ratio between the highest pay and the lowest pay greater than two to one.

In larger, more complex, democratic organizations wages are still set, and wage differentials strictly limited, by the collectivity. For example, in the sixty-five production cooperatives that constitute the Mondragón system in Spain pay differentials are limited to a ratio of three to one in each firm (Johnson and Whyte, 1977). In the worker-owned and managed refuse collection firms in San Francisco, the differential is only two to one, or less (Russell, 1979; Perry, 1978). Schumacher (1973:276) reports a seven-to-one ratio between the highest and the lowest paid at Scott Bader, a collectively owned firm in England. The cooperatively owned plywood mills in the Pacific Northwest pay their members an equal wage (Bernstein, 1976:20–21). By comparison, the wage differential tolerated today in Chinese work organizations is four to one; in the United States it is about a hundred to one.

Prestige, of course, is not as easily equalized as is pay. Nonetheless, collectivist organizations try in a variety of ways to indicate that they are a fraternity of peers. Through dress, informal relations, task sharing, job rotation, the physical structure of the workplace, equal pay, and the collective decision-making process itself—collectives convey an equality of status. As Mansbridge (1977) observes of collectives, reducing the sources of status inequality does not necessarily lead to the magnification of trivial differences. Likewise, decreasing the material differentials between individuals in a collectivist organization does not ordinarily produce a greater emphasis on status distinctions.

Differentiation

A complex network of specialized, segmental roles marks any bureaucracy. Where the rules of scientific management hold sway, the division of labor is maximized: jobs are subdivided as far as possible. Specialized jobs require technical expertise. Thus, bureaucracy ushers in the ideal of the specialist-expert and defeats the cultivated, renaissance man of an earlier era (Weber, 1946:240–44).

In contrast, differentiation is minimized in the collectivist organization. Work roles are purposefully kept as general and holistic as possible. They aim to eliminate the division of labor that separates intellectual workers from manual workers, administrative tasks from performance tasks. Three means are commonly used toward this end: role rotation, teamwork or task sharing, and the diffusion or demystification of specialized knowledge through internal education.

Ideally, universal competence (of the collective's members) would be achieved in the tasks of the organization. It is the *amateur-factotum* then who is ideally suited for the collectivist organization. In the completely democratized organization, everyone manages and everyone works. This may be the most fundamental way in which the collectivist mode of organization alters the social relations of production.[7]

This alteration in the division of labor is perhaps best illustrated by the Free School, an organization in which administrative functions were quite simple, and undifferentiated. The Free School had no separate set of managers to administer the school. Whenever administrative tasks were recognized, "coordination meetings" were called to attend to them; these were open to all interested teachers and students. Coordinators were those who were willing to take responsibility for a particular administrative task (e.g., planning curriculum, writing a press release, organizing a fund-raiser). A coordinator for one activity was not necessarily a coordinator for another project. Further, the taking on of administrative tasks was assumed to be a part-time commitment which could be done along side of one's other responsibilities. Coordinators, then, were *self-selected, rotated,* and *part time.* No one was allowed to do administration exclusively. By simplifying administration and opening it up to the membership-at-large, the basis and pretense of special expertise was eliminated.

The school even attempted to break down the basic differentiation between students and staff, regarding students not as clients but as members with decision-making rights and responsibilities. The Free Clinic also tried to integrate its clients into the organization. For instance, it created spaces on its board of directors for consumers of medical care and recruited many of its volunteers from the ranks of its patients.

Most alternative organizations are more complex than the Free School. They cannot assume that everyone in the organization knows how (or would want to know how) to do everything. Thus, they must develop explicit procedures to achieve universal competence. Such procedures, in effect, attack the conventional wisdom of specialized division of labor and seek to create more integrated, multifaceted work roles.

The Alternative Newspaper, for example, utilizes task sharing (or team work), apprenticeships, and job rotations toward this end. Instead of assigning one full-time person to a task requiring one person, they would be more likely to assign a couple of people to the task part time. Individuals' allocations of work often combine diverse tasks, such as fifteen hours writing, fifteen hours photography, and 10 hours production. In this way, the distribution of labor combines satisfying tasks with more tedious tasks and manual work with intellectual work. People do not enter the paper knowing how to do all of these jobs, but the emphasis on task sharing allows the less experienced to learn from the more experienced. Likewise, if a task has few people who know how to perform it well, a person may be allocated to apprentice with the incumbent. Internal education is further facilitated by occasional job rotations. Thus, while the Alternative Paper must perform the same tasks as any newspaper, it attempts to do so without permitting the usual division of labor into specialties or its concomitant monopolization of expertise.

Minimizing differentiation is difficult and time consuming. The Alternative Paper, for instance, spent a total of fifteen hours and forty minutes of formal meeting time and many hours of informal discussion in planning one systematic job rotation. Attendance at the planning meetings was 100 percent. The time and priority typically devoted to internal education in collectivist organizations makes sense only if it is understood as part of a struggle against the division of labor. The creation of an equitable distribution of labor and holistic work roles is an essential feature of the collectivist organization.

Table 24–1 summarizes the ideal-type differences between the collectivist mode of a organization and the bureaucratic.[8] Democratic control is the foremost characteristic of collectivist organization, just as hierarchical control is the defining characteristic of the smoothly running bureaucracy. Thus, collectivist-democratic organization would transform the social relations to production. Bureaucracy maximizes formal rationality precisely by centralizing the locus of control at the top of the organization; collectives decentralize control such that it may be organized around the alternative logic of substantive rationality.

Table 24–1
Comparisons of Two Ideal Types of Organization

Dimensions	Bureaucratic Organization	Collectivist-Democratic Organization
1. Authority	1. Authority resides in individuals by virtue of incumbency in office or expertise or both; hierarchical organization of offices. Compliance is to universal fixed rules as these are implemented by office incumbents.	1. Authority resides in the collectivity as a whole; delegated, if at all, only temporarily and subject to recall. Compliance is to the consensus of the collective, which is always fluid and open to negotiation.
2. Rules	2. Formalization of fixed and universalistic rules; calculability and appeal of decisions on the basis of correspondence to the formal, written law.	2. Minimal stipulated rules; primacy of ad hoc, individuated decisions; some calculability possible on the basis of knowing the substantive ethics involved in the situation.
3. Social Control	3. Organizational behavior is subject to social control, primarily through direct supervision or standardized rules and sanctions, tertiarily through the selection of homogeneous personnel especially at top levels.	3. Social controls are primarily based on personalistic or moralistic appeals and the selection of homogenous personnel.
4. Social Relations	4. Ideal of impersonality. Relations are to be role based, segmental, and instrumental.	4. Ideal of community. Relations are to be holistic, personal, of value in themselves.
5. Recruitment and Advancement	5.a. Employment based on specialized training and formal certification.	5.a. Employment based on friends, social-political values, personality attributes, and informally assessed knowledge and skills.
	5.b. Employment constitutes a career; advancement based on seniority or achievement.	5.b. Concept of career advancement not meaningful; no hierarchy of positions.
6. Incentive Structure	6. Remunerative incentives are primary.	6. Normative and solidarity incentives are primary; material incentives are secondary.

Table 24–1, continued

Dimensions	Bureaucratic Organization	Collectivist-Democratic Organization
7. Social Stratification	7. Isomorphic distribution of prestige, privilege, and power; i.e., differential rewards by office; hierarchy justifies inequality.	7. Egalitarian; reward differentials, if any, are strictly limited by the collectivity.
8. Differentiation	8.a. Maximal division of labor: dichotomy between intellectual work and manual work and between administrative tasks and performance tasks.	8.a. Minimal division of labor: administration is combined with performance tasks; division between intellectual and manual work is reduced.
	8.b. Maximal specialization of jobs and functions; segmental roles. Technical expertise is exclusively held: ideal of the specialist-expert.	8.b. Generalization of jobs and functions; holistic roles. Demystification of expertise: ideal of the amateur factotum.

Imperfect Democracy:
Constraints and Social Costs

Various constraints limit the actual attainment of democracy, and even to the extent that the collectivist-democratic ideal is achieved, it may produce social costs that were unanticipated. This section outlines some of the more important of these constraints and social costs.

Judgments about the relative importance of the listed social costs are intricately tied to cultural values. Alternative organizations may be mistakenly assessed when seen through the prism of the norms and values of the surrounding bureaucratic society.

Time

Democracy takes time. This is one of its major social costs. Two-way communication structures may produce higher morale, the consideration of more innovative ideas, and more adaptive solutions to complex problems, but they are undeniably slow (Leavitt, 1964:141–50). Quite simply, a boss can hand down a bureaucratic order in a fraction of the time it would take a group to decide the issue democratically.

The time absorbed by meetings can be extreme in democratic groups. During the early stages of the Alternative Newspaper, for instance, three days out of a week were taken up with meetings. Between business meetings, political meetings, and "people" meetings, very little time remained to do the tasks of the organization. Members quickly learn that this is unworkable. Meetings are streamlined. Tasks are given a higher priority. Even so, constructing an arrangement that both saves time and ensures effective collective control may prove difficult: Exactly which meetings are dispensable? What sorts of decisions can be safely delegated? How can individuals still be held accountable to the collectivity as a whole? These sorts of questions come with the realization that there are only twenty-four hours in a day.

There is a limit, however, to how streamlined collectivist meetings can get. In the end, commitment to decisions and their implementation can only be assured in collectives through the use of the democratic method. Unilateral decisions, albeit quicker, would not be seen as binding or legitimate. With practice, planning, and self-discipline, groups can learn to accomplish more during their meeting time. But once experience is gained in how to conduct meetings, time given to meetings appears to be directly correlated with level of democratic control. The Free Clinic, for instance, could keep its weekly staff meetings down to an average of one hour and fifteen minutes only by permitting individual decision making outside the meeting to a degree that would have been unacceptable to members of the Alternative Paper, where a mean of four hours was given over to the weekly staff meeting.

Homogeneity

Consensus, an essential component of collectivist decision making, may require from the outset substantial homogeneity. To people who would prefer diversity, this is a considerable social cost.

Bureaucracy may not require much homogeneity, partly because it does not need the moral commitment of its employees. Since it depends chiefly on remunerative incentives to motivate work and since in the end it can command obedience to authority, it is able to unite the energies of diverse people toward organizational goals. But, in collectives where the primary incentives for participation are value-purposive and the subordinate-superordinate relation has been delegitimated, moral commitment becomes necessary. Unified action is possible only if individuals substantially agree with the goals and processes of the collective. This implies a level of homogeneity (in terms of values) unaccustomed and unnecessary in bureaucracy.[9]

Consequently, collectivist organizations also tend to attract homogeneous population in terms of social origins. At the Alternative Paper full-time staff members came from families where the mean parental income was about $29,000. A random sampling of the general membership of the Food Co-op (consisting of 1,100 people) reveals an average parental income of $19,500, while the most active members of the Co-op, the staff and board, show a mean parental income of $46,000. In addition to being of financially privileged origins, people in alternative organizations tend to come from well-educated families. In both of the above organizations, over half of the mothers had at least some college; fathers on the average had acquired some graduate or professional training beyond the bachelor's degree. Thus, the need for substantial agreement on the values, goals, and processes of the collective, in effect, has limited their social base. This is an important constraint to members who would like to broaden the base of their social movement.

This is also an important constraint in organizations with heterogeneous populations of employees. For example, International Group Plans, a Washington, D.C., insurance company, is in the process of trying to democratize its ownership and governance structure (Zwerdling, 1977). To many of its employees who do not share collectivist values, democratization may only mean added time and responsibility, and they may wish to retain the traditional separation of managers and workers.

To guard against this problem and to ensure that all members profess collectivist values, alternative organizations tend to recruit very selectively. The Law Collective, for instance, instituted a probationary period of six months on top of its careful selection procedures.

In sum, cultural homogeneity makes reaching and abiding by a consensus easier, but it may constrain the social base of collectivist organization.

Emotional Intensity

The familial, face-to-face relationships in collectivist organizations may be more satisfying than the impersonal relations of bureaucracy, but they are also more emotionally threatening. The latter may be experienced as a social cost of participatory organization.

Interpersonal tension is probably endemic in the directly democratic situation, and members certainly perceive their workplaces to be emotionally intense. At the Law Collective a member warns that "plants die here from the heavy vibes." At the Alternative Newspaper I observed headaches and other signs of tension before meetings in which divisive issues would be raised. A study of the New England town meeting found citizens reporting headaches, trembling, and even fear for one's heart as a result of the meetings. Altogether, a quarter of the people in a random sample of the town spontaneously suggested that the conflictual character of the meetings disturbed them (Mansbridge, 1979; 1973).

To allay these fears of conflict, townspeople use a variety of protective devices: criticism is concealed or at least softened with praise, differences of opinion are minimized in the formulation of a consensus, private jokes and intimate communications are used to give personal support during the meetings. Such avoidance patterns have the unintended consequence of excluding the not fully integrated member, withholding information from the group, and violating the norms of open participation. Further, these same fears of conflict and avoidance patterns are in evidence even in groups that are highly sensitive to these issues and in which many members have been trained in group process (Mansbridge, 1979).

The constancy of such feelings in all of the groups I observed suggests that they are rooted in the structure of collectivist decision making. Although participants generally attribute conflict and avoidance to the stubborn, wrongheaded, or otherwise faulty character of others, it may be an inherent cost of participatory democracy.

Structural tensions inherent in collectivist organization render conflict difficult to absorb. First, the norm of consensual decision making in collectives makes the possibility of conflict all the more threatening because unanimity is required (where a majoritarian system can institutionalize and absorb conflicting opinions). Second, the intimacy of face-to-face decision making personalizes the ideas that people espouse and thereby makes the rejection of those ideas harder to bear (while a more formal bureaucratic system, to the extent that it disassociates an idea from its proponent, makes the criticism of ideas less interpersonally risky).

Nondemocratic Individuals

Because of prior experiences, many people are not very well suited for participatory democracy. This is an important constraint on its development.

The major institutions of our society, such as educational institutions, combine to reinforce ways of thinking, feeling, and acting that are congruent with capitalist bureaucratic life and incompatible with collectivist orientations. For example, Jules Henry (1965) has shown how the norms of capitalist culture become the hidden curriculum of the school system. Even at the preschool level, the qualities of the bureaucratic personality are unconsciously, but nevertheless consistently, conveyed to children (Kanter, 1972b). In fact, Bowles and Gintis (1976) argue that the chief function of the entire educational apparatus is to reproduce the division of labor and hierarchical authority of capitalism.

In the face of these behavior-shaping institutions, it is very difficult to sustain collectivist personalities. It is asking, in effect, that people in collectivist organizations constantly shift gears, that they learn to act one way inside their collectives and another way outside. In this sense, the difficulty of creating and sustaining collectivist attributes and behavior patterns results from a cultural disjuncture. It derives from the fact that alternative work organizations are as yet isolated examples of collectivism in an otherwise capitalist bureaucratic context. Where they are not isolated, that is, where they are part of an interlocking network of cooperative organizations, such as the Mondragón system in Spain (Johnson and Whyte, 1977), this problem is mitigated.

In their present context the experience of the alternative institutions has shown that selecting people with collectivist attitudes does not guarantee that these attitudes will be effectively translated into cooperative behavior (see, e.g., Swidler, 1976; Taylor, 1976; Torbert, 1973).

Nevertheless, a number of recent case studies of democratic workplaces, one of the worker-owned refuse collection companies (Russell 1979; Perry, 1978) and one of a women's health collective (Bart, 1979), reveal that the experience of democratic participation can alter peoples' values, the quality of their work, and ultimately, their identities. In a comparative examination of many cases of workers' participation, Bernstein (1976:91–107) finds democratic consciousness to be a necessary element for effective workers' control to take place.

Fortunately, the solution to this problem of creating democratic consciousness (and behavior) may be found in the democratic method itself. In this vein, Pateman has amassed a considerable body of evidence from research on political socialization in support of the classical arguments of Rousseau, Mill, and Cole. She concludes:

> We do learn to participate by participating and . . . feelings of political efficacy are more likely to be developed in a participatory environment.
> . . . The experience of a participatory authority structure might also be effective in diminishing tendencies toward non-democratic attitudes in the individual. (1970:105)

Elden (1976) provides further empirical support for Pateman's position that participation enhances feelings of political efficacy. If bureaucratic organizations thwart the sense of efficacy that would be needed for active participation in democracy (see Blumberg, 1973:70–138), then collectivist-democratic organizations must serve an important educative function, if they are to expand beyond their currently limited social base.[10]

Environmental Constraints

Alternative organizations, like all organizations, are subject to external pressures. Because they often occupy an adversary position vis-à-vis mainstream institutions, such pressures may be more intense. Extraorganizational constraints on the development of collectivist organizations may come from legal, economic, political, and cultural realm.

It is generally agreed among free schoolers, for instance, that building and fire codes are most strictly enforced for them (Kozol, 1972; Graubard, 1972). This is usually only a minor irritant, but in extreme cases it may involve a major disruption of the organization, requiring them to move or close down. One small, collectively run, solar power firm was forced to move its headquarters several times through this sort of legal harassment. At one site, the local authorities charged over a hundred building "violations" (Etzkowitz, 1978). An even more far-reaching legal obstacle is the lack of a suitable statute for incorporating employee-owned and controlled firms. The Alternative Newspaper, for example, had to ask an attorney to put together corporate law in novel ways in order to ensure collective control over the paper.[11]

The law can be changed, but the more ubiquitous forces against collectivism are social, cultural, and economic. In fact, alternative organizations often find that bureaucratic practices are thrust on them by established institutions. The Free School, for example, began with an emphatic policy of absolutely no evaluative records of students. In time, however, it found that in order to help its students transfer back into the public schools or gain entrance into college, it had to begin keeping or inventing records. The preoccupation of other organizations with records and documents may thus force record keeping on a reluctant free school. In another free school, the presence of a steady stream of government communications and inspectors (health, building, and the like) pushed the organization into creating a special job to handle correspondence and personal visits of officials (Lindenfeld, 1979).

Alternative organizations often strive to be economically self-sustaining, but without a federated network of other cooperative organizations to support them, they cannot. Often they must rely on established organizations for financial support. This acts as a constraint on the achievement of their collectivist principles. For instance, in order to provide free services, the Free Clinic needed and received financial backing from private foundations as well as from county revenue-sharing funds. This forced them to keep detailed records on expenditures and patient visits and to justify their activities in terms of outsiders' criteria of cost-effectiveness.

In less fortunate cases, fledging democratic enterprises may not even get off the ground for failure to raise sufficient capital. Two recent attempts by employee groups to purchase and collectively manage their firms reveal the reluctance of banks to loan money to collectivist enterprises, even where these loans would be guaranteed by the government. From the point of view of private investors, collective ownership and management may appear, at best, an unproven method of organizing production, and at worst, a dangerous method.[12]

For a consistent source of capital, collectivist enterprises may need to develop cooperative credit unions as the Mondragón system has done (Johnson and Whyte, 1977) or an alternative investment fund. In many collectives the unpaid (or poorly paid) labor of the founders forms the initial capital of the organization, enabling some measure of financial autonomy. In any case, the larger issue of organization-environment relations remains problematic, particularly when we are considering collectivist-democratized organizations in a capitalist bureaucratic context.[13]

Individual Differences

All organizations, democratic ones notwithstanding, contain persons with very different talents, skills, knowledge, and personality attributes.

Bureaucracies try to capitalize on these individual differences, so that ideally people with a particular expertise or personality type will be given a job, rewards, and authority commensurate with it. In collectives such individual differences may constrain the organization's ability to realize its egalitarian ideals.

Inequalities in influence persist in the most egalitarian of organizations. In bureaucracies the existence of inequality is taken for granted, and in fact, the exercise of power is built into the opportunity structure of positions themselves (Kanter, 1977). However, in collectivist organizations this may be less true. Here, precisely because authority resides in the collectivity as a unit, the exercise of influence depends less on positional opportunities and more on the personal attributes of the individual. Not surprisingly, members who are more articulate, responsible, energetic, glamorous, fair, or committed carry more weight in the group.[14] John Rice, a teacher and leader of Black Mountain (a group that "seceded" from the educational system and anticipated the free school movement) argued that Black Mountain came as close to democracy as possible: the economic status of the individual had nothing to do with community standing. But beyond that, "the differences show up . . . [;] the test is made all day and every day as to who is the person to listen to" (Duberman, 1972:37).

Some individual differences are accepted in the collectivist organization, but not all, particularly not differences in knowledge. In bureaucracy differences of skill and knowledge are honored. Specialized jobs accompany expertise. People are expected to protect their expertise. Indeed, this is a sign of professionalism, and it is well known that the monopolization of knowledge is an effective instrument of power in organizations (Weber, 1968; Crozier, 1964). For this very reason, collectivist organizations make every attempt to eliminate differentials in knowledge. Expertise is considered not the sacred property of the individual, but an organizational resource. In collectives, individually held skills and knowledge are demystified and redistributed through internal education, job rotation, task sharing, apprenticeships, or any plan they can devise toward this end.[15]

The diffusion or demystification of knowledge, while essential to help equalize patterns of influence, involves certain trade-offs. Allowing a new person to learn to do task X by rotating her or him to that job may be good for the development of that person but it may displace an experienced person who had received a sense of satisfaction and accomplishment in job X. Further, encouraging novices to learn by doing may be an effective form of pedagogy, but it may detract from the quality of goods or services that the organization provides, at least (theoretically) until universal competence in the tasks of the organization is reached.

Even in the collectivist organization that might achieve universal competence, other sources of unequal influence would persist (e.g., commitment level, verbal fluency, social skills).[16] The most a democratic organization can do is to remove the bureaucratic bases of authority: positional rank and expertise. The task of any collectivist-democratic workplace, and it is no easy task, is to eliminate all bases of individual power and authority, save those that individuals carry in their person.

Conclusion

The organizations in this study are admittedly rare and extreme cases. To the extent that they reject received forms of organization, they present an anomaly. For precisely this reason they are of great theoretical significance. By approaching the polar opposites of bureaucracy, they allow us to establish the limits of organizational reality. The parameters appear to be far wider than students of organizations have generally imagined. Once the parameters of the organizational field have been defined, concrete cases can be put into broader perspective. Professional organizations, for example, while considerably more horizontal than the strictly hierarchical bureaucracy (Litwak, 1961), are still far more hierarchical than the collectivist-democratic organization. Thus, we may conceive of the range of organizational possibilities illustrated in Figure 24–1.

By contrasting collectivist democracy and rational bureaucracy along eight continuous dimensions, this paper has emphasized the quantiative differences between the two. In many ways, this understates the difference. At some point differences of degree produce differences of kind. Fundamentally, bureaucracy and collectivism are oriented to qualitatively different principles. Where bureaucracy is organized around the calculus of formal rationality, collectivist democracy turns on the logic of substantive rationality.

If, in the Weberian tradition, we take the basis of authority as the central feature of any mode of organization, then organizations on the right half of Figure 24–1 empower the *individual* with authority (on the basis of office or expertise), while organizations on the left side grant

Figure 24-1
Range of Organizational Forms

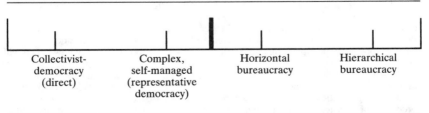

| Collectivist-democracy (direct) | Complex, self-managed (representative democracy) | Horizontal bureaucracy | Hierarchical bureaucracy |

ultimate authority only to the *collectivity* as a whole unit. Moreover, if, following Marx's lead, we take the division of labor as the key to the social relations of production, organizations on the right side of the diagram maintain a sharp division between managers and workers, while organizations on the left side are integrative: those who work also manage. Departures of this magnitude from established modes of organization may be considered a "social invention" (Coleman, 1970).

Organization theory has for the most part considered only the right half of this spectrum, and indeed, the vast majority of organizations in our society do fall on the right side of the continuum. Still, we gain perspective on these organizations by putting them into a broader frame of reference. With the proliferation of collectivist organizations both in this society and in others (e.g., China, Spain, Yugoslavia), we will need an alternative model of organization, one which they themselves aspire toward, by which to assess their impact and success. To wit, collectivist organizations should be assessed not as failures to achieve bureaucratic standards they do not share, but as efforts to realize wholly different values. It is in the conceptualization of alternative forms of organization that organizational theory has been weakest, and it is here that the experimentation of collectives will broaden our understanding.

Notes

Acknowledgements: I would like to thank William Foote Whyte, J. Allen Whitt, Robert Stern, Charles Perrow, Carole Pateman, Rosabeth Kanter, Howard Aldrich, and the anonymous reviewers of the *American Sociological Review* for valuable comments and suggestions on an earlier draft of this paper. In addition, I would like to acknowledge the support of the New Systems of Work and Participation Program at ILR, Cornell University (NIMH grant #MH 29259-03) during the completion of this work. A previous version of this paper was presented at the Ninth World Congress of Sociology in Uppsala, 1978.

1. Gardner (1976) estimates that about 1,000 new alternative institutions are being created annually in the United States. This is his best estimate, but the kind of evidence that would be needed to compute actual rates of creation and of dissolution is not yet available. However, the historical record is instructive. The nineteenth century and the first third of the twentieth century saw at least 700 cases of producers' cooperatives (Aldrich and Stern, 1978). These were in many ways the forerunners of the contemporary wave of collectives and cooperatives discussed in this paper. Historically, cooperatives have come in distinct waves—the 1840s, the 1860s, the 1880s and the 1920s–1930s. Their longevity has varied widely between industries (Aldrich and Stern, 1978). Those of the nineteenth century had a median duration of less than ten years, whereas more than half of the worker cooperatives of the 1920s and 1930s (particularly in the plywood industry and in the refuse collection industry) are still in operation today (Jones, 1979). Since the current wave of collectives is largely a post-1970 phenomenon and is still on the rise, it is too early to say how long it will last.

2. All persons and organizations have been given fictitious names in this paper. For a more detailed account of the research sites and methods see Rothschild-Whitt (1976; 1978).

3. As organizations grow beyond a certain size, they are likely to find purely consensual processes of decision making inadequate and may turn to direct voting systems. Other

complex, but nevertheless democratic, work organizations may sustain direct democracy at the shop-floor level, while relying upon elected representative systems at higher levels of the organization (cf. Edelstein and Warner, 1976).

4. Actually, Weber did recognize the possibility of directly democratic organization, but he dealt with this only incidentally as a marginal type case (Weber, 1968:958–52, 289–92). Although Weber's three types of legitimate domination were meant to be comprehensive, both in time and in substance, as Mommsen (1974:72–94) points out, it is difficult to find an appropriate place for modern plebiscitarian democracy in Weber's scheme. Weber did come to advocate the "plebiscitarian leader-democracy," but this was a special version of charismatic domination (Mommsen, 1974:113). He did not support "democracies without leadership" *(fuererlose Demokratien)* which try to minimize the domination of the few over the many because organization without *Herrschaft* appeared utopian to him (Mommsen, 1974:87). Thus it is difficult to identify the acephalous organizations of this study with any of Weber's three types of authority.

5. A dissertation conducted in the San Francisco area found that free-school teachers there have higher degrees from more prestigious universities than their public school counterparts (McCauley, 1971:148).

6. The self-exploitation common in collectivist organizations and the justifications for it (e.g., autonomy, control over the workplace, self-expression in work) are similar to that of the small entrepreneur. It may be that as economic concentration and oligopolistic control over markets renders traditional entrepreneurial activity obsolete, collectively owned enterprises may grow. For, in many ways, collectivist efforts evoke the old entrepreneurial spirit, but today, it may require the intense work and self-sacrifice of many people rather than just one to make a fledging enterprise viable.

7. Industrial organizations in China have implemented similar changes in the division of labor. These were considered an essential part of transforming the social relations of production. Their means for reducing the separation of intellectual work from manual work and administration from performance tasks were similar to those used by the alternative work organizations reported in this paper: team work, internal education, and role rotation. For specific points of comparison see Bettleheim (1974) and Whyte (1973).

8. The eight dimensions discussed here are clearly interrelated, a point not explored herein. However, there is evidence from bureaucracies that they are also somewhat independent (Hall, 1963). That is, an organization may be highly collectivist on one dimension but not so on another. The interrelationships between these variables may be elusive. For instance, of seven propositions offered by Hage (1965) in an axiomatic theory of organizations, six could be supported by the organization in this study. One, however, that higher complexity produces lower centralization, was contradicted by the evidence of this study, although it has received empirical support in studies of social-service bureaucracies (Hage, 1965; Hage and Aiken, 1970). Hage suggests that relationships in organizational theory may be curvilinear: when organizations approach extreme scores, the extant relationships may no longer hold or may actually be reversed. This is an important limitation to bear in mind, especially as we begin to consider organizations, such as the ones in this study, that are by design extreme on all eight continua proposed in this model.

9. Organizations that are homogeneous in this sense probably register substantial agreement over organizational goals (or what Thompson and Tuden [1959] call "preferences about outcomes"), but register considerable disagreement about how to get there ("beliefs about causation"). In such cases, Thompson and Tuden predict that organizations will reach decisions by majority judgment. A collegium type of organization, they maintain, is best suited for solving judgmental problems. This would require all members to participate in each decision, route pertinent information about causation to each member, give each member equal influence over the final choice, require fidelity to the group's preference structure, and designate as ultimate choice the judgment of the majority. On all but the last point they correctly describe collectivist work organizations. Further, as they point out, the social science literature does not contain models of this type of organization as it does for bureaucracy (Thompson and Tuden, 1959:200).

10. To Pateman (1970) the theory of participatory democracy rises or falls on this educative function. But other social scientists (see especially, Argyris, 1973) remain unconvinced that participation in collectivist democratic processes of organization can produce the desired changes in peoples' behavior. For Argyris, unilateral, defensive, closed, mutually protective, non-risk-taking behavior, what he calls Model I behavior, is nearly universal: it permeates not only western bureaucracies but also counterbureaucracies such as alternative schools as well as collectivist organizations in contemporary China and Yugoslavia. Change in organizational behavior cannot be expected to follow from fundamental change in the mode of production, for Model I behavior is rooted in the pyramidal values of industrial culture and in the finiteness of the human mind as an information-processing machine in the face of environmental complexity.

Contrarily, I am arguing that where people do not have participatory habits, it is because they generally have not been allowed any substantive control over important decisions. Nondemocratic (pyramidal) habits are indeed a problem for democratic groups, but they are not a problem that a redistribution of power could not resolve. Admittedly, the evidence is not yet conclusive on this issue, but much of it does indicate that the practice of democracy itself develops the capacity for democratic behavior among its participants (see especially, Blumberg, 1973; Pateman, 1970).

11. The result of this effort was a two-tiered structure: the paper was incorporated as a general corporation and a trust, which owns all the stock in the paper. Each six months of full-time work is worth one voting share in the trust. This grants ultimate control of the paper to the staff, past and present. Immediate control is exercised by the board of directors of the corporation, which consists of the currently working staff. As a member of the paper said, "the structure is neither graceful nor simple, but it . . . guarantees that the working staff will maintain editorial control, and makes it nearly impossible ever to sell the paper."

12. See the abortive attempts to raise capital for employee-ownership at Kasanof's Bakery, *The Boston Phoenix,* 26 April 1977, and at the Colonial Press in Clinton, Massachusetts.

13. Organization-environment relations are always reciprocal. In part, the low wages, hard work, and intense personal involvement that make collectivist organizations seem so costly may be due to costs imposed by the environment. Conversely, collectivist organizations rely upon goods and services produced by the surrounding bureaucratic organizations, e.g., light bulbs, fast-food chains.

14. Swidler (1976) vividly describes the extent to which members of a free school will literally ransack their private lives to locate sources of glamour that will enhance their sense of worth and influence in the group.

15. A case study of the demystification of skills in a collectivist work organization is provided by Bart (1979).

16. Mansbridge (1977) observes that even the most genuinely democratic organization will accept some measure of inequality of influence in order to retain individual liberties.

References

Aldrich, Howard, and Robert Stern. 1978. "Social Structure and the Creation of Producers' Cooperatives." Presented at the Ninth World Congress of Sociology, Uppsala.

Argyris, Chris. 1973. "Personality and Organization Theory Revisited." *Administrative Science Quarterly* 18:141–67.

Bart, Pauline, and Melinda Bart. 1979. "Collective Work and Self-identity: The Effect of Working in a Feminist Abortion Collective." In F. Lindenfeld and J. Rothschild-Whitt, eds., *Workplace Democracy and Social Change.* Boston: Porter Sargent.

Bates, F. L. 1970. "Power Behavior and Decentralization." Pp. 175–76 in M. Zald, ed., *Power and Organizations.* Nashville: Vanderbilt University Press.

Bendix, Reinhard. 1962. *Max Weber: An Intellectual Portrait*. Garden City: Anchor Books.

Bernstein, Paul. 1976. *Workplace Democratization: Its Internal Dynamics*. Kent: Kent State University Press.

Bettleheim, Charles. 1974. *Cultural Revolution and Industrial Organization in China*. New York: Monthly Review Press.

Blau, Peter. 1970. "Decentralization in Bureaucracies." Pp. 150–74 in M. Zald, ed. *Power and Organizations*. Nashville: Vanderbilt University Press.

Blumberg, Paul. 1973. *Industrial Democracy: The Sociology of Participation*. New York: Schocken.

Bowles, Samuel, and Herbert Gintis. 1976. *Schooling in Capitalist America*. New York: Basic Books.

Clark, Peter B., and James Q. Wilson. 1961. "Incentives Systems: A Theory of Organizations." *Administrative Science Quarterly* 6:129–66.

Coleman, James. 1970. "Social Inventions." *Social Forces* 49:163–73.

Crozier, Michael. 1964. *The Bureaucratic Phenomenon*. Chicago: University of Chicago Press.

Duberman, Martin. 1972. *Black Mountain: An Exploration in Community*. New York: Dutton.

Edelstein, J. David, and Malcolm Warner. 1976. *Comparative Union Democracy: Organization and Opposition in British and American Unions*. New York: Wiley.

Elden, J. Maxwell. 1976. "Democracy at Work for a More Participatory Politics: Worker Self-Management Leads to Political Efficacy." Ph.d. dissertation, Department of Political Science, University of California, Los Angeles.

Etzioni, Amitai. 1961. *A Comparative Analysis of Complex Organizations*. Glencoe: Free Press.

Etzkowitz, Henry. 1978. "The Liberation of Technology." *WIN Magazine* 14.

Gardner, Richard. 1976. *Alternative America*. Privately published.

Glaser, Barney, and Anselm Strauss. 1967. *The Discovery of Grounded Theory: Strategies for Qualitative Research*. Chicago: Aldine.

Gouldner, Alvin. 1954. *Patterns of Industrial Bureaucracy*. Glencoe: Free Press.

Graubard, Allen. 1972. *Free the Children*. New York: Pantheon Books.

Guerin, Daniel. 1970. *Anarchism: From Theory to Practice*. New York: Monthly Review Press.

Hage, Jerald. 1965. "An Axiomatic Theory of Organizations." *Administrative Science Quarterly* 10:289–320.

Hage, Jerald, and Michael Aiken. 1970. *Social Change in Complex Organizations*. New York: Random House.

Hall, Richard. 1963. "The Concept of Bureaucracy: An Empirical Assessment." *American Journal of Sociology* 69:32–40.

Henry, Jules. 1965. *Culture against Man*. New York: Vintage.

Johnson, Ana Gutierrez, and William Foote Whyte. 1977. "The Mondragón System of Worker Production Cooperatives." *Industrial and Labor Relations Review* 31:18–30.

Jones, Derek. 1979. "Producer Cooperatives in the U.S.: An Examination and Analysis of Socio-economic Performance." Unpublished paper. Department of Economics, Hamilton College.

Kanter, Rosabeth Moss. 1972a. *Commitment and Community*. Cambridge: Harvard University Press.

———. 1972b. "The Organization Child: Experience Management in a Nursery School." *Sociology of Education* 45:186–211.

———. 1977. *Men and Women of the Corporation*. New York: Basic Books.

Kanter, Rosabeth M., and Louis Zurcher, Jr. 1973. "Concluding Statement: Evaluating Alternatives and Alternative Valuing." *Alternative Institutions,* a special issue of the *Journal of Applied Behavioral Science* 9:381–97.

Kay, Michael. 1972. *The Teacher Was the Sea: The Story of Pacific High School*. New York: Links Books.

Kozol, Jonathon. 1972. *Free Schools*. Boston: Houghton-Mifflin.

Leavitt, H. J. 1964. *Managerial Psychology*. Chicago: University of Chicago Press.

Lindenfeld, Frank. 1979. "Problems of Power in a Free School." In F. Lindenfeld and J. Rothschild-Whitt, eds. *Workplace Democracy and Social Change*. Boston: Porter Sargent.

Lipset, S. M., Martin Trow, and James Coleman. 1962. *Union Democracy*. New York: Anchor.

Litwak, Eugene. 1961. "Models of Bureaucracy Which Permit Conflict." *American Journal of Sociology* 67:177–84.

McCauley, Brian. 1971. "Evaluation and Authority in Radical Alternative Schools and Public Schools." Ph.D. dissertation, Department of Education, Stanford University.

Mansbridge, Jane. 1973. "Town Meeting Democracy." *Working Papers for a New Society* 1:5–15.

———.1977. "Acceptable Inequalities." *British Journal of Political Science* 7:321–36.

———. 1979. "Fears of Conflict in Face-to-Face Democracies." In F. Lindenfeld and J. Rothschild-Whitt, eds. *Workplace Democracy and Social Change*. Boston: Porter Sargent.

Mommsen, Wolfgang. 1974. *The Age of Bureaucracy: Perspectives on the Political Sociology of Max Weber*. New York: Harper and Row.

Mouzelis, Nocos. 1968. *Organization and Bureaucracy: An Analysis of Modern Theories*. Chicago: Aldine.

Pateman, Carole. 1970. *Participation and Democratic Theory*. Cambridge, Eng.: Cambridge University Press.

Perrow, Charles. 1976. "Control in Organizations: The Centralized-Decentralized Bureaucracy." Presented at annual meeting of American Sociological Association, New York.

Perry, Stewart. 1978. *Dirty Work, Clean Jobs, Proud Men*. Berkeley: University of California Press.

Rothschild-Whitt, Joyce. 1976. "Conditions Facilitating Participatory-Democratic Organizations." *Sociological Inquiry* 46:75–86.

———. 1978. Organizations Without Hierarchy: A Comparative Study of Collectivist-Democratic Alternatives to Bureaucracy. Ph.D. dissertation, Department of Sociology, University of California, Santa Barbara.

Russell, Raymond. 1979. "Rewards of Participation on the Worker-Owned Firm." In F. Lindenfeld and J. Rothschild-Whitt, eds., *Workplace Democracy and Social Change*. Boston: Porter Sargent.

Satow, Roberta Lynn. 1975. "Value-Rational Authority and Professional Organizations: Weber's Missing Type." *Administrative Science Quarterly* 20:526–31.

Schumacher, E. F. 1973. *Small Is Beautiful: Economics As If People Mattered*. New York: Harper and Row.

Swidler, Ann. 1976. "Teaching in a Free School." *Working Papers for a New Society* 4:30–34.

———. 1979. *Organization Without Authority: Dilemmas of Social Control in Free Schools*. Cambridge, Mass.: Harvard University Press.

Taylor, Rosemary. 1976. "Free Medicine." *Working Papers for a New Society* 4:21–3, 83–94.

Thompson, James D. 1967. *Organizations in Action*. New York: McGraw-Hill.

Thompson, James D., and Arthur Tuden. 1959. "Strategies, Structures, and Processes of Organizational Decision." Chap. 12 in J. Thompson, ed., *Comparative Studies in Administration*. Pittsburgh: University of Pittsburgh Press.

Torbert, William. 1973. "An Experimental Selection Process for a Collaborative Organization." *Journal of Applied Behavioral Science* 9:331–50.

Weber, Max. 1946. *From Max Weber: Essays in Sociology*. Trans. and ed. by Hans Gerth and C. Wright Mills. New York: Oxford University Press.

————. 1954. *Max Weber on Law in Economy and Society*. Cambridge, Mass.: Harvard University Press.

————. 1968. *Economy and Society*. Ed. by Guenther Roth and Claus Wittich. New York: Bedminster Press.

Whyte, Martin King. 1973. "Bureaucracy and Modernization in China: The Maoist Critique." *American Sociological Review* 38:149–63.

Wood, James R. 1978. "Legitimate Leadership in Voluntary Organizations: The Controversy Over Social Action in Protestant Churches." Unpublished monograph. Department of Sociology, University of Indiana, Bloomington.

Zwerdling, Daniel. 1977. "At IGP, It's Not Business as Usual." *Working Papers for a New Society* 5:68–81.

25

Community-Owned Government: Empowering Rather than Serving

David Osborne and Ted Gaebler

The older I get, the more convinced I am that to really work, programs have to be owned by the people they're serving. That isn't just rhetoric, it's real. There's got to be ownership.
                                        —George Latimer,
                                        former mayor of St. Paul

In 1982, Lee Brown became chief of police in Houston, Texas. The Houston police force was beset by charges of racism and brutality. Brown, who is black, set out to transform it. The vehicle he chose was "neighborhood-oriented policing": the notion that the police should not simply respond to incidents of crime, but also help neighborhoods solve the problems that underlie crime.

Brown assigned most of his officers to neighborhood beats. He set up

---

From *Reinventing Government: How the Entrepreneurial Spirit Is Transforming the Public Sector* (Reading, Mass.: Addison-Wesley, 1992), pp. 49–75. Reprinted by permission of Addison-Wesley Publishing Company. © 1992, David Osborne and Ted Gaebler.

twenty storefront mini-stations in the neighborhoods. He instructed his officers to build strong relationships with churches, businesses, PTAs, and other community organizations. In one high-crime area, he had officers on the beat visit more than a third of all homes, to introduce themselves and ask about neighborhood problems.

"What we're doing is revolutionary in U.S. policing," Brown told one columnist. "We're redefining the role of the patrol officer—we want him to be a community organizer, community activist, a problem solver. . . . I want people as committed to neighborhoods as young Americans were to the Peace Corps."[1]

Now the police chief in New York City, Brown is a leader in what political scientist James Q. Wilson calls "the most significant redefinition of police work in the past half century."[2] Wilson and others call it community-oriented policing. The basic idea is to make public safety a *community* responsibility, rather than simply the responsibility of the professionals—the police. It transforms the police officer from an investigator and enforcer into a catalyst in a process of community self-help. Sometimes this means police officers help neighborhood members clear out vacant lots and rusting cars. Sometimes it means they help organize marches in front of crack houses. Sometimes it means they work with community leaders to keep neighborhood children in school.

"You can't rush in with the police car, handle the call, and leave," says Tulsa Police Chief Drew Diamond. "Then what you've done is reactive, a momentary solution to the problem, and you're going to be back."[3]

Under Chief Diamond's leadership, the Tulsa police studied arrest trends, school dropout statistics, drug treatment data, and the problems of the city's public housing developments. They concluded that teenagers from one section of town were creating most of the city's drug problems—so they began to work with the community to attack the problem at its roots. They organized the residents of one apartment complex, and with their backing prosecuted and evicted residents who were dealing or helping dealers. They created an antidrug education program in the housing projects. They set up job placement programs and mentoring initiatives for young men and women. They set up a youth camp for teenagers. And they worked with the schools to develop an antitruancy program.

Community-oriented policing is under way in more than 300 American cities, from Newark, New Jersey, to Dallas, Texas; Charleston, South Carolina, to Madison, Wisconsin. In addition some 18,000 "neighborhood watch" groups, with a million members, work with local police forces to help defend their communities against crime, according to the National Association of Town Watch.[4] To make a long-term impact, most experts have concluded, such groups need to focus on their community's underlying problems. Community-oriented policing turns the local police officer into their ally.

The real key, says Hubert Williams, president of a research institute called the Police Foundation, "is the ability of the police to act as a catalyst to draw together community resources, to provide resources, backup and training."[5]

In short, the police can be most effective if they help communities help themselves. This is really just common sense. We all know that people act more responsibly when they control their own environments than when they are under the control of others. We know that owners take better care of homes than renters. We know that workers who own a piece of the company are more committed than those who simply collect a paycheck. It stands to reason that when communities are empowered to solve their own problems, they function better than communities that depend on services provided by outsiders.

Empowerment is an American tradition, as old as the frontier. We are a nation of self-help organizations. We create our own day-care centers, our own babysitting cooperatives, our own Little Leagues, our own Girl Scout and Boy Scout troops, our own recycling programs, our own volunteer organizations of all kinds.

And yet, when we organize our public business, we forget these lessons. We let bureaucrats control our public services, not those they intend to help. We rely on professionals to solve problems, not families and communities. We let the police, the doctors, the teachers, and the social workers have all the control, while the people they are serving have none. "Too often," says George Latimer, "we create programs designed to collect clients rather than to empower communities of citizens."[6]

When we do this, we undermine the confidence and competence of our citizens and communities. We create *dependency*. It should come as no surprise that welfare dependency, alcohol dependency, and drug dependency are among our most severe problems.

Latimer likes to quote Tom Dewar, of the University of Minnesota's Humphrey Institute, about the dangers of "clienthood":

> Clients are people who are dependent upon and controlled by their helpers and leaders. Clients are people who understand themselves in terms of their deficiencies and people who wait for others to act on their behalf.
>
> Citizens, on the other hand, are people who understand their own problems in their own terms. Citizens perceive their relationship to one another and they believe in their capacity to act. Good clients make bad citizens. Good citizens make strong communities.[7]

Pulling Ownership Out of the Bureaucracy, Into the Community

Clienthood is a problem that emerged only as our industrial economy matured. Before 1900 what little control existed over neighborhoods, health, education, and the like lay primarily with local communities, because so many products and services, whether public or private, were produced or sold locally. It was only with the emergence of an industrial economy of mass production that we began to hire professionals and bureaucrats to do what families, neighborhoods, churches, and voluntary associations had done.

We started with the best of intentions, to heal the new wounds of an industrial, urban society. We moved ahead rapidly when the economic collapse of the Depression strained the capacities of families and communities to the breaking point. And we continued on after the Depression, as prosperity and mobility loosened the old bonds of geographic community, leaving the elderly far from their children, the employed uninvolved in their neighborhoods, and the churches increasingly empty. But along the way, we lost something precious. The Progressive confidence in "neutral administrators" and "professionalism" blinded us to the consequences of taking control out of the hands of families and communities.

The reaction was not long in coming. During the 1960s neighborhoods fought against the urban renewal schemes dreamed up by professional city planners. Minority communities fought for control over Great Society programs like Community Action and Model Cities. By 1970 a welfare rights movement had emerged to demand more control over the welfare system, a tenants' rights movement had emerged to demand more control over public housing, and a neighborhood movement had emerged to demand more control over urban development and public services. Soon middle-class America joined in, with a consumer movement, which sought to give consumers more control over the products made by private corporations; a holistic health movement, which sought to give individuals more control over their own health; a deinstitutionalization movement, which sought to give mental patients more control over their environments; and a general effort to force authorities of all kinds to share their power, through "sunshine" laws, freedom-of-information acts, right-to-know laws, open-meeting laws, and the like. These movements were animated by a common sense that real control over our lives had been lost to the mega-institutions of society: big business, big government, and big labor.

Slowly, government has begun to respond. Community-oriented policing is not an isolated phenomenon. The same themes of community ownership and empowerment appear in virtually every segment of American public life. Our governments are beginning to push ownership and control of public services out of the hands of bureaucrats and professionals, into communities.

During the huge refugee resettlement effort for those fleeing Southeast Asia, the federal government did not pay professionals or bureaucrats to help people find homes and jobs; it used churches.

As recycling became a priority, the city with the best track record,

Seattle, credited part of its success to voluntary block captains who helped their neighbors figure out how to make curbside recycling work.[8]

Most housing initiatives now use community development corporations, tenant cooperatives, and the like to develop low-income housing. Boston even let one community organization take over abandoned buildings and lots through eminent domain.

In education parents are beginning to assert control over the schools. According to John Chubb, coauthor of *Politics, Markets and America's Schools,* "The largest estimated influence on the effectiveness of school organization is the role of parents in the school. All other things being equal, schools in which parents are highly involved, cooperative, and well-informed are more likely to develop effective organizations than are schools in which parents do not possess these qualities."[9] And yet most public schools let parents handle little more than bake sales, fundraising, and PTA meetings.

In Chicago every public school is now run by a council of six parents, elected by parents; two community members, elected by community residents; two teachers, elected by the school staff; and the principal. This council acts as the board of directors: it hires the principal (on a four-year performance-based contract), prepares a school improvement plan, and prepares the school budget, in accordance with its improvement plan. Principals are now hired and fired on the basis of merit rather than seniority. After the first year 81 percent of parents and 62 percent of teachers said their schools were operating "better" than before the reform. Seventy-eight percent of parents reported improvements in safety and discipline, 61 percent saw improvements in the physical plant, and 83 percent reported progress in educational programs.[10]

"Lots of people told us we were making a terrific mistake, because we were turning power over to illiterate, underclass people, taking it away from those who had the professional knowledge," says Don Moore, whose advocacy organization, Designs for Change, spearheaded the reform effort:

> They said we wouldn't get people to run for the councils. But 17,000 people ran, and we had a higher turnout than they get in suburban school board elections. We see the councils as a new democratic unit in the community. We expect that the people who serve on councils will probably get involved in other issues, like housing, economic development, and adult education. These are real seedbeds for leadership development.[11]

New Haven, Connecticut, tried something similar back in 1968. At two failing, inner-city schools it set up Governance Management Teams made up of parents, teachers, other staff members, and the principal. By 1978 students at the two experimental schools had caught up to grade level. By 1984 they scored third and fourth highest in the system and had the best attendance records. By 1990 the specific model, called the

School Development Program, was used in all forty-two New Haven schools—and in more than sixty other schools in eight states. Professor James Comer of Yale, who initiated it, was even planning to introduce it in six Chicago schools.[12]

The same trends are evident in early childhood education. From its inception Head Start has "made an all-out attempt to use the parent as part of the teaching process," in the words of one expert. Even where parents do not teach, they work as aides, serve on boards, and help with field trips and other activities. "The best Head Start programs in this country learned a long time ago that when the parents really feel like they're in charge, like they've got ownership, you get a different performance out of that kid," says Curtis Johnson, a former college president who, as director of the Citizens League, has been a key force behind education reform in Minnesota. Today, Head Start is considered by many one of our most successful antipoverty programs.[13]

Several states have gone even further, developing programs that encourage parents to teach their own children. Arkansas imported its model—the Home Instruction Program for Preschool Youngsters (HIPPY)—from Israel. Every day 2,400 welfare mothers spend twenty minutes teaching their children at home, with simple workbooks. A trained HIPPY worker—often a former HIPPY mother—visits once a week to help plan the next week's work. In 1989 the percentage of children testing at or above national averages jumped from 6 percent going into the program to 74 percent at the end of the year. "In one project, 18 of the 39 participating welfare mothers enrolled in education courses for themselves after the first year," says Governor Bill Clinton. "The HIPPY program builds in its own follow-up by changing the parent into the child's first teacher, which is what every parent should be."[14]

Even job training agencies are beginning to empower workers. The Massachusetts Industrial Services Program, which provides training for dislocated workers, uses some of those very workers to help staff its thirty-odd centers around the state. When a plant announces a closing or major layoff, the state sets up a temporary center and hires a staff to provide counseling, training, help in finding another job, and related services. It hires several of the dislocated workers, then keeps those who excel to staff other centers. In some centers every staff member is a former dislocated worker.

These workers know firsthand the problems their colleagues face, and they are determined to do something about them. "I love these people in the plant, and I've worked with them for 25 years," says Richard Wisniewski, a former machinist who became a career counselor at one center. "I wish I could change and take away their hurt, but I can't do that. But maybe I ease the pain just a little bit by giving 110 percent to my job."[15]

The program is one of the most effective in the country. Over its first five years it served more than 37,000 dislocated workers, placing 80 percent in jobs that paid, on average, 92 percent of their former wages.

In criminal justice, community-oriented policing is just the beginning. San Francisco uses Community Boards, with voluntary mediators, to resolve the kinds of everyday conflicts that often erupt into violence. Pioneered in the late 1970s by neighborhood activists, these boards now handle and settle more cases than the San Francisco Municipal Court. They save a tremendous amount of money, but more important, they build a sense of empowerment, a sense that people working together in neighborhoods can solve their own problems. A third of their volunteers are people who have found themselves in a neighborhood dispute, used a Community Board to resolve it, and liked the process so much they volunteered.[16]

Some community organizations are even taking ownership of the justice process *after* a criminal is arrested. Florida paroles first-time convicted criminals into the care of the Salvation Army—25,000 of them at any one time. Massachusetts closed its traditional, prison-like juvenile corrections institutions and moved its juvenile offenders into small, community-based group homes. A 1989 study by the National Council on Crime and Delinquency found that this system not only led to lower re-arrest rates than most states and fewer violent crimes, but cost less than incarceration.[17]

David and Falakah Fattah opened their own home in Philadelphia to fifteen teenage gang members in 1969. Since then, they have "adopted" more than 500 former gang members, with such success that the juvenile courts have begun to send many of their worst cases to the Fattahs' House of Umoja. Those who stay abide by strict rules: they must rise by 6 A.M. every morning for a conference to set goals for the day; they must do chores; and they must attend a weekly meeting to review their behavior. In return, they get the support of a strong, dedicated family. In a study of recidivism, the Philadelphia Psychiatric Center found the rearrest rate of ex-offenders sent to the House of Umoja to be just 3 percent. At the city's far more expensive correctional facilities, rearrest rates ranged from 70 to 90 percent.[18]

Health care is a system thoroughly dominated by professionals, but even here a shift toward community is evident. Our health care system was set up to deal with acute care: life-threatening illnesses and injuries. It was so effective that today most people die of chronic, degenerative problems—of "old age." Yet we continue to respond with an acute-care system of high-technology hospitals and highly trained doctors. Ironically, it was our very success at acute, professional care that left us with an elderly population desperate for something more.

"Chronic care requires a fundamentally different response, one grounded in the meaning and familiarity of community, family, and friends," explains David Schulman, who runs the Los Angeles City Attorney's AIDS/HIV Discrimination Unit. "That explains the powerful growth of hospice—providing a homelike setting for supportive care of the terminally ill."

Between the late 1970s and the late 1980s, Schulman reports, the number of hospices in the United States swelled from a few dozen to a few thousand. The home health care industry also exploded. State governments developed extensive programs to help the elderly stay in their own homes rather than go into nursing homes. Most health insurance companies began covering home health care. One even began to pay family members, trained by nurses, to provide care at home. By 1989 home health care was a $7 billion industry.[19]

AIDS catalyzed perhaps the most profound shift from the old model to the new. "The San Francisco gay and lesbian community adopted the hospice model," explains Schulman. "They got teams of friends and volunteers together to care for people with AIDS at home—at a fraction of the cost of hospital care. It not only works better, it helped San Francisco soften a blow that may yet bankrupt it."

In a powerful article in the *Washington Monthly,* Katherine Boo described the process. It began when a gay nurse at San Francisco General Hospital, Cliff Morrison, convinced his superiors to let him suspend the normal hierarchical, bureaucratic rules on the AIDS ward. He let patients set visiting rules, recruited hundreds of volunteers to help AIDS patients—often just to sit with them—and set up a special kitchen and other facilities.

But "a comfortable hospital is still a hospital," as Boo put it. So Morrison and his staff "began suturing together a network of local clinics, hospices, welfare offices, and volunteers that would get patients out of the ward and back into the community." For two years Morrison spent much of his time "battling the higher-ups." But when San Francisco's average cost of AIDS treatment dropped to 40 percent of the national average, they finally understood.

The idea spread quickly to other cities. In some, the new communities of care even began helping AIDS patients do battle with Medicaid and welfare bureaucracies. "For the first time in recent history, AIDS brought members of the organized middle class into the ghetto of the human services bureaucracy," Boo wrote. "They found the system lacking, so they changed it. Outside the fragmented, assembly-line world of social services, with an army of volunteers, the gay community built a new way of caring for some of society's most vulnerable members."

"This is how effective social service programs work: intimately, aggressively, with feeling."[20]

Public Housing: A Case Study

To understand just how profound a force community ownership can be, let us take a close look at one example: the transformation that occurs when public housing tenants take control of their own environment.

Public housing began as transitional housing for working people who had come upon hard times, during the Depression. It was an inexpensive, safe, stable environment for families while they got back on their feet. Public housing authorities had rigid standards, and residents had clear responsibilities: they had to pay their full rent; they were generally not welcome if they were on welfare; if they had children, they had to be married; and if they found jobs and could afford better housing, they had to move.

Public housing worked well for two decades, even though it was a classic example of the centralized, top-down, bureaucratic model. Then, during the prosperity of the 1950s, a dramatic change took place. Working families moved out of public housing, and poor, illiterate blacks from the rural South poured in. Bureaucratic organizations are slow to respond when conditions change, and housing authorities were no exception. As this radically different population moved in—most of whom had never *seen* a high-rise building, let alone lived in one—few housing authorities changed anything.

Meanwhile, Congress decided to deny welfare to most families if the father was present—thus driving many fathers away. It also gave welfare mothers in public housing subsidized rent, which meant that their rent often tripled or quadrupled if they left welfare to work. These changes created powerful incentives to stay single and unemployed.

Before long, public housing developments were functioning as traps, not safe havens. In many cities they sank into a vicious cycle of drugs, crime, teenage pregnancy, and welfare dependency. Because all the control lay with a central bureaucracy—the local housing authority—residents were powerless to enforce standards of behavior or evict criminals. If someone dealt drugs out of the apartment next door, residents could complain—but the system rarely responded.

The Kenilworth-Parkside development, in northeast Washington, D.C., was a classic example. By 1980 its main street was an open-air drug market, and violence was so common that the management company put a bulletproof barrier around its office. Residents went without heat or hot water for months at a time. The roofs leaked, the grass died, and the fences were torn down. Rubbish was picked up so infrequently that rats infested the buildings.

Over the next ten years, however, Kenilworth-Parkside's residents transformed their community. By 1990 the drug dealers were gone, crime was negligible, and the buildings were under repair.[21]

The catalyst for this transformation was an extraordinary woman named Kimi Gray.

When she got her first apartment at Kenilworth-Parkside, in 1966, Kimi Gray personified the stereotype many people have of the welfare mother: twenty-one, black, divorced, on welfare, with five children.

Today she is an example not of dependency but of the mountains people can move when they decide to take control of their own lives.

In 1974, Gray remembers, "some students came to me and said, 'Miss Kimi, we want to go to college.' What the hell did I know about going to college? [But] I said, 'Let me check it out, let me see what I can do.' " Soon she and several recruits were tutoring students, helping them find summer jobs, enrolling them in Upward Bound, helping them fill out college applications, and drumming up scholarship money. The students called their project College Here We Come. They held bake sales and raffles, got part-time jobs, and opened bank accounts. After Kimi had hustled all the scholarships and loans and work-study jobs she could, and a student still needed $600 or $1,000, College Here We Come kicked in the rest.

Seventeen kids left for college the first August. Word spread quickly: "Man, this stuff is real! People really going to college! These children couldn't believe that," Kimi says. "Poor people, from public housing, their mothers on welfare, absent fathers, going to college?"

In the fifteen previous years two residents of Kenilworth-Parkside had attended college. Over the next fifteen years, 700 did—and three-fourths of those graduated, according to Gray. Today even sixteen-year-old boys on street corners look up to those who attend college.

The second phase of the transformation began in 1982. For several years Kenilworth-Parkside's residents had been pressuring the mayor to let them manage the property. Finally, grudgingly, he agreed. The tenants wrote their own constitution and bylaws, their own personnel and policy procedures, their own job descriptions.

The bureaucrats "*could not* believe it," Kimi says. "Public housing residents? I said, 'The worst it can do is have wrong grammar in it. But at least we would understand and we would know clearly what was in it, right? So therefore we could enforce what we knew we had written.' " Besides, if the Department of Housing and Urban Development (HUD) wrote it, there would be ten lawyers in the room, writing, "rules for things that don't even exist. I mean the crime hasn't been committed and they got a rule for it already."

The Kenilworth-Parkside Resident Management Corporation hired and trained residents to manage the property and do the maintenance. They held monthly meetings of all tenants. In their Bring the Fathers Out of the Closets campaign, they hired absentee fathers. Believing that peer pressure was the key to changing their environment, they set up fines for violating the rules—littering, loitering in hallways, sitting on fences, not cutting your grass. They created a system of elected building captains and court captains to enforce them. They started mandatory Sunday classes to teach housekeeping, budgeting, home repair, and parenting. And they required mothers who enrolled their children in the day-care center to work, attend school, or get job training.

On the basis of the results of a needs survey, the Resident Management Corporation created an after-school homework and tutorial program for kids whose mothers worked full time. They set up courses to help adults get their high school degrees; contracted with a doctor and a dentist to set up part-time office hours and make house calls at the development; set up an employment office to help people find training and jobs; and began to create their own businesses, to keep money and jobs within the community.

The first was a shop to replace windows, screens, and doors, owned by a young man who could neither read nor count. In return for a start-up loan from the residents council, he trained ten students, who went on to market their skills elsewhere in Washington. The board fired the garbage collection service and contracted with another young man, on condition that he hire Kenilworth-Parkside residents. Before long they had a cooperative store, a snack bar, two laundromats, a beauty salon, a barber shop, a clothes boutique, a thrift shop, a catering service, a moving company, and a construction company that helped renovate vacant apartments. All the businesses employed residents, and all were required to hire young people to work with the adults. At one point, 120 residents had jobs at Kenilworth.[22]

Gradually maintenance improved as well. The managers and maintenance men lived on the property; if the heat went out over the weekend, they got cold too. "It has to be someone who's there all the time, on the property," says Renee Sims, head teacher at Kenilworth's Learning Center. "Because of you have someone outside managing it, and a pipe bursts over the weekend, you're not going to get it done."

Kimi and her managers estimate that in 1982, when they began, less than half the residents were paying rent. Resident manager Gladys Roy and her assistants began going door to door, serving thirty-day eviction notices. They explained that if people did not pay the rent, they could not afford the repairs people needed. If people did not have the cash, they worked out payment plans or collected what they could. By 1987 rent collections were up to 75 percent.[23]

Perhaps the worst problem at Kenilworth-Parkside was drugs. Every evening hundreds of dealers lined Quarles Street. Many of the worst offenders lived at Kenilworth, but the police were reluctant to enter the neighborhood because residents were hostile. Mothers kept their children barricaded indoors.

Finally, Kimi called a meeting and invited the police. At first most residents stayed home, afraid to be seen as snitches. Kimi and the few who did attend asked for foot patrols at Kenilworth. Then they suggested a temporary station—a trailer—right on the grounds. The police agreed.

"By putting guys over there, on a regular basis, they began slowly to develop a sense of trust in us," says Sergeant Robert L. Prout, Jr. "And they began to give us information. . . . And now, it's got to the point where we have mothers that have sons that if they're wanted for something, they'll pick up the phone and call us."

Kimi remained the role model. She turned in anyone who was selling drugs—even members of her beloved College Here We Come. (Her own son was arrested for dealing in southwest Washington.) She made sure a thirty-day eviction notice went to every household in which someone was dealing. If nothing happened, the Resident Management Corporation started litigation.

"We got with the attorney down at the Housing Department and we wore 'em to death, 'til we got them to take our cases to court," Kimi explains. "Now once we got to court, we were alright, because we would take residents with us down to court to say, 'No, your honor, that fella cannot stay in our community any longer.' " Four families were evicted. "That's all it took. People seen, 'Hey, they serious.' "

Evictions did not stop the dealers who lived elsewhere, of course. Finally, in 1984 the residents decided to confront the dealers head on. "We got together and we marched," says Denise Yates, assistant manager of the Resident Management Corporation. "Day after day, and in the evening too. We marched up and down the street with our signs. We had the police back us. Maybe half the community would march. A lot of teenagers and little kids, in addition to mothers."

After several weeks of disrupted business, the dealers began to drift away. Some resisted, and for a time things got nasty. Someone cut the brake lines in Kimi's car, put sugar in her gas tank, slashed her tires. But she refused to bend, and her confidence rubbed off on the others.

"When she didn't show any fear of being seen with the police, or riding through the neighborhood with us, then they more or less followed suit," says Sergeant Prout. By 1989 the crime rate had fallen from between twelve to fifteen crimes a month—one of the highest levels in the city—to two.

The lesson is clear: the police can make raid after raid, but only if a community decides to take responsibility for its own safety can the police be truly effective. "We tell them, 'The police can't be here all the time,' " Prout explains. " 'You live here, you know more about what goes on, you know who does what. It's just a matter of whether you want your community, or whether you want them to have your community.' "[24]

In 1986 the accounting firm Coopers & Lybrand released an audit of Kenilworth-Parkside. During the first four years of tenant management, it reported, rent collections increased 77 percent—seven times the increase at public housing citywide. Vacancy rates fell from 18 percent—then the citywide average—to 5.4 percent. The Resident Management Corporation helped at least 132 residents get off welfare: it hired 10 as staff and 92 to run the businesses it started, while its employment office found training and jobs for 30 more. (Others received part-time jobs.)

Overall, Coopers & Lybrand concluded, four years of resident management had saved the city at least $785,000. If trends continued over the next six years, it would save $3.7 million more—and the federal government would reap additional savings.[25]

Since the Coopers & Lybrand audit, a complete renovation of Kenilworth has been done, under HUD's normal renovation program. In 1990 the residents bought the development—for a grand total of $1. A community of 3,000, once characterized largely by single-parent families on welfare, is now a community of homeowners, the majority of whom work.

Expectations are powerful. Before they took control of their own environment, people at Kenilworth-Parkside expected things to happen to them. They *expected* to lose their heat or hot water. They *expected* to be victimized by crime. They *expected* their roofs to leak. They *expected* their sons to get into drugs, their daughters to get pregnant. They expected to have no power to change any of this, because all the power in their environment lay with the housing authority, the police, or the criminals.

As they took control of their environment, their expectations began to change. "There is a conversion experience that people go through," says David Freed, a real estate consultant who specializes in low-income tenant buy-outs in Washington, D.C. "It happens when there is a process that renters go through together and there is a change in people's view of themselves and their neighbors. I see it again and again. It's what's exciting about my work: it's that conversion experience."

Today, more than fifteen tenant organizations around the country manage their own public housing projects, and more than 200 groups have received formal training for the management role. Several want to buy their developments, as Kenilworth-Parkside residents have.

"Development begins with a belief system," says Robert Woodson, whose National Center for Neighborhood Enterprise has functioned as an informal staff for the tenant management movement:

> What Kimi and other tenant leaders have done is just self-confidence, and they've passed that self-confidence on to others. Only when you overcome the crisis of self-confidence can opportunity make a difference in your life. But we act with programs as if opportunity carries with it elements of self-confidence. And it does not.

Professional Service Versus Community Care

The empowerment of communities like Kenilworth-Parkside not only changes expectations and instills confidence—it usually provides far better solutions to their problems than normal public services. John McKnight, director of community studies at Northwestern University's Center for Urban Affairs and Policy Research, spent several decades as a community organizer in Chicago. His experiences convinced him that by pulling ownership of services out of the community and into the hands of professionals and bureaucracies, we have actually weakened our communities and undermined our people. "There is a mistaken notion that our society has a problem in terms of effective human services," he says. "Our essential problem is weak communities."[26]

McKnight provides an illuminating series of contrasts between professional service delivery systems and what he calls "associations of community"—the family, the neighborhood, the church, and the voluntary organization.[27] For example:

Communities have more commitment to their members than service delivery systems have to their clients. Kimi Gray and her staff are more committed to their residents than any housing authority could be. Those who join Mothers Against Drunk Driving are more committed to their mission than any government agency could be. The nonprofit organizations CODAMA (Community Organization for Drug Abuse, Mental Health and Alcoholism Services, Inc.) contracts with in Arizona are more committed to their patients than any hospitals or psychiatrists could be. "In our organizations, bachelor-level counselors are working for around $15,000," says Alan Flory. "They tend to be very committed people. Some of them are recovered alcoholics, or people who've had alcohol or drug problems in their families."

Communities understand their problem better than service professionals do. No bureaucrat could know more about problems in a public housing development than the people who live there. No state employee can understand the problems of unemployed workers better than their coworkers. "I'm from manufacturing, and I speak their language," says Barbara Gillette, a former sugar refinery worker who joined the staff of a Worker Assistance Center in Massachusetts. "The key to what I do is to let people know I've experienced it. I had difficulty and I had losses too, but I came through it."[28]

Professionals and bureaucracies deliver services; communities solve problems. McKnight describes a neighborhood organization in Chicago that tried to forge a partnership with the local hospitals to improve health care. When the effort yielded few results, the organization gradually began to look "not at more professional service, but instead at the question of what brought their people to the hospital in the first place." The answers were predictable: automobile accidents, interpersonal violence, accidents, alcoholism, and dog bites.

> When this became clear, the people in the neighborhood immediately saw that what they needed was not really more and better medical/hospital

service, but to work down the volume of auto accidents, interpersonal violence, accidents, alcoholism, and dog bites. . . . They began with dog bites. It occurred to them to offer kids in the neighborhood a bounty for bringing in dogs running loose. They had been paying something like $185 for the treatment of a dog bite. They paid a $5 bounty for dogs. And they gradually began to be aware, as this went on, that though there is a market for professional service, there is not really a market for problem solving. Nobody puts up money to reduce dog bites; they put up money to stitch up dog bites. Most of the activity and the money nominally addressed at solving problems is, in fact, simply going to pay for services.[29]

As we write, the city of Boston is forcing its hospitals to expand their services for pregnant women in Boston's black neighborhoods, where infant mortality is on the rise. But anyone who reads the newspaper knows that the problem is not simply a lack of medical services. The problems are poverty, drug addiction, teenage sex, and the dissolution of the black family. More medical services will have very little impact.

Institutions and professionals offer "service"; communities offer "care." Care is different from service. Care is the human warmth of a genuine companion; care is the support of loved ones as a family copes with tragedy; care is the gentle hand of a helper when one is bedridden. Economist Steven E. Rhoads describes one example:

> Over 6,000 people in our community of 100,000 perform volunteer work. One hundred participate in the "Meals on Wheels" Program, donating a few hours a week and driving expenses to take hot meals to elderly people who cannot cook for themselves.
>
> This program is the perfect example of the kind of in-kind redistribution program economists typically attack. The charge would go something like this. "Why have a separate bureaucracy charged with one small thing—delivering hot meals to the elderly? What is so special about a hot meal anyway? Why not give the poor the money we spend on the program to do with as they wish?"
>
> This analysis misses something. The most important thing that the volunteers bring the elderly is not the hot meal, but the human contact and the sense that someone cares. Volunteers can do this more convincingly than bureaucrats.[30]

Communities are more flexible and creative than large service bureaucracies. Kenilworth-Parkside is a perfect example. An Illinois initiative called One Church, One Child provides another. A decade ago, the Illinois Department of Children and Family Services was having trouble placing black children for adoption; it had a backlog of 1,000. The problem, according to black leaders, was the bureaucracy. Its members brought the same middle-class standards to black adoptions that they used for white adoptions. They turned down black families because they lived in apartments rather than houses, they did not have enough formal education, they lacked middle-class incomes, or they had only one parent.

In 1980 the department turned to the black community for help. Working with black ministers, it asked each black church to find at least one family willing to adopt a child. The first person to volunteer was an unmarried black minister. The churches have since found homes for more than 3,000 black children, and the backlog of black children waiting for adoption has fallen below that for whites.

Communities are cheaper than service professionals. One Church, One Child saved Illinois an estimated $15 million in just three years.[31] Florida saves $180 million a year by financing home care and community care to keep people out of nursing homes.[32] The community mental health organizations with which Arizona contracts save the state millions of dollars every year. (In fact, the state makes them raise 25–50 percent of their budgets on their own; by 1989 this amounted to $12 million a year.)[33]

"The professional servicers take increasing proportions of public money, desperately needed by the poor, and consume it in the name of helping poor families," says McKnight.[34] His center at Northwestern University did a study of government spending on the poor in Cook County, which includes Chicago. They found that in 1984 federal, state, and local governments spent $6,209 per poor person in Cook County— enough to get everyone over the poverty line. Yet only 35 percent of this money reached the poor in the form of cash. Another 13 percent came as food stamps and rent vouchers. The majority, 52.6 percent, went to service providers: hospitals, doctors, nursing homes, social service agencies, job trainers, lawyers.[35] The Community Services Society of New York did a similar study, with similar results. Of the roughly $7,000 in public and private money expended per low-income person in New York City in 1983, only 37 percent reached the poor.[36]

Communities enforce standards of behavior more effectively than bureaucracies or service professionals. Several years ago a Catholic church in Brooklyn closed down a shelter for homeless men, which provided a bed, clothing, and help in finding a job. The church had run it successfully for ten years, but when the city opened a shelter nearby, most of the men left. Why? Because they preferred the city shelter—where no one forced them to give up alcohol and drugs, to wash up, or to look for a job.

Sister Connie Driscoll runs a nationally recognized shelter for homeless women and children in Chicago. Those who stay have to take classes, do chores, and save 70 percent of their welfare checks. In seven years 6,000 women have moved through the shelter, and according to Driscoll, only 6.5 percent have returned to the shelter system. Driscoll believes other shelters should start requiring things like education—"if you can get the liberal left to get off the bandwagon about 'You can't force people to do things because you think it's right.' Well, maybe they can't, in publicly operated shelters and publicly funded shelters. But, as a private shelter, we can make it a part of our contract—and we do."[37]

Like public bureaucracies, professionals are also reluctant to impose their values by telling clients how to behave. In fact, by treating problems as "diseases," professionals often avoid the question of values and behavior altogether. Family members, church members, and community members are not so reluctant.

"One of the things that this community has brought back is a kind of old-fashioned shunning," says Dr. Alice Murray, a psychologist who runs Kenilworth-Parkside's Substance Abuse Prevention project. "It's a way of saying, 'This is behavior we will not tolerate. Should it happen, then we put you through all the services, but we don't expect it to happen ever again.' It's done in a very kind and gentle and loving way, but there's shame when it occurs—which is not the case in the outside community."

Communities focus on capacities; service systems focus on deficiencies. Communities like Kenilworth-Parkside depend on the capacities of their members to get things done. Think of your church, your synagogue, your voluntary organization. It wants a contribution from you, in time, talent, or treasure. Hence its entire attention is on your *capacities*—on what you can bring to the task. In contrast, job training programs, social work agencies, police departments, and welfare programs focus on your deficiencies: what you do not know, what you cannot do, how you have been victimized. Most professionals "basically see the family as a client in need of treatment and therapy," says McKnight. This has "the increasing effect of convincing families that they are incompetent to know, care, teach, cure, make, or do. Only certified people can do that for you."[38]

Managing the Transition from Service to Empowerment

If community ownership is the goal, what role can government play? How can it empower stakeholders? Does it simply abandon services delivered by bureaucrats and professionals?

Of course not. Public housing again provides a useful illustration. In the mid-1980s Robert Woodson asked Kimi Gray and other tenant management leaders to draw up a list of policy changes that would remove barriers to their success. On the basis of that list, they developed seven amendments to the federal Housing Act. The resulting bill gave resident councils a clear right to manage their own developments; gave them priority for HUD renovation grants; set up procedures by which resident management corporations could buy their projects after three years of successful management; and appropriated $5 million to train residents in self-management at 50 projects. When Jack Kemp became secretary of housing and urban development, he made tenant management and ownership one of HUD's top priorities. By 1993 he hopes to have moved 250 public housing developments through training for tenant management.

Government cannot force people to take control of their housing or schools or neighborhoods. When HUD and the Ford Foundation tried to stimulate tenant management from the top down, during the 1970s, most of their attempts failed. But governments *can* structure things so that people can take control, if they want it. "I'm not suggesting that we're going to force it down people's throats, and I'm not suggesting that everybody might want to do it, and I'm not suggesting that everybody should be treated in exactly the same manner," says Kemp. "But I at least want the opportunity out there for everybody."

Kemp's strategy includes many of the specific steps government can take: it can remove the barriers to community control; encourage organized communities to take control of services; provide seed money, training, and technical assistance; and move the resources necessary to deal with problems into the control of community organizations.

Public organizations can create a spectrum of opportunities, which different communities can seize as they are ready. Many public housing authorities create resident advisory boards, give tenants seats on the board of directors, or encourage residents to form tenant councils at each development. Some encourage tenant councils to hire and fire private management firms. A few encourage tenants to form their own corporations and manage the property themselves. And a handful, including those in Washington and Louisville, have allowed tenants to buy developments.

None of this is easy, or automatic. In poor communities enormous leadership is necessary to make something like tenant management work. "The Kimi Grays are rare," says Andrea Duncan, who runs the Housing Authority of Louisville. "Most public housing residents are women who are very dependent, who don't have a lot of confidence, who have a long way to go just to deal with their own sense of wellness, their own life management." But it takes enormous leadership to create any successful enterprise—whether Kenilworth-Parkside Resident Management Corporation or IBM. So why not create more opportunities in poor communities and see how many leaders emerge?

It would be wrong to force people who have long been dependent to suddenly manage on their own, without some kind of transitional support. "You can't take residents of public housing who spent most of their lives in a colonial state and expect them to turn around and have the attitudes of entrepreneurs and the skills of private sector administrators," says Robert Stumberg, a housing expert with the National Center for Policy Alternatives, in Washington, D.C. One solution, he argues, is some form of "intermediary ownership structure, such as a mutual housing association—a corporation owned by its residents:

> People have a vested interest in how it's run, they have a direct democratic vote in management, they are encouraged and involved in policy making about such things as rent structures and resident obligations, and they get a financial cut in terms of personal tax benefits and the rewards of sweat equity in maintaining their own units. But they still have corporate accountability in terms of making the whole thing work. There are professional managers who are hired and fired by the residents.

Even in the best situations, there will be problems. Corruption has plagued some tenant management corporations. The Housing Authority of Louisville quit contracting with one of its resident management corporations because the corporation began to cheat. But Louisville's experience also demonstrates the answer: it discovered the corruption because it had strict, measurable performance standards in its contract. When performance began to fall off—because the corporation was engaging in nepotism and other self-dealing practices—the performance measures quickly showed it. The success of empowerment is thus directly dependent on the success of other concepts described here, including accountability for results.

When governments push ownership and control into the community, their responsibilities do not end. They may no longer produce services, but they are still responsible for making sure needs are met. When governments abdicate this steering responsibility, disaster often follows. The massive deinstitutionalization of mental patients in favor of community-based treatment during the 1970s was a perfect example. It worked in a few places, but most governments abdicated their steering responsibilities. They failed to make sure that community treatment centers and homes were in place, with adequate funding, and they failed to monitor what happened to patients who left their hospitals. As a result, many of the mentally ill ended up on the streets, homeless.

Empowering Citizens through Participatory Democracy

The ultimate form of ownership is not ownership simply of problem solving or of services, but of government. In theory, our representative system of democracy gives us that ownership. In reality, few Americans feel that they "own" or "control" their governments. By 1989 three out of four Americans surveyed agreed that "most members of Congress care more about special interests than they care about people like you." By 1990 efforts to take control back—through term limits, campaign finance reform, and a broader use of ballot initiatives—had begun to sweep the country.[39]

Campaign finance reform is obviously a precondition to recapturing our governments. Many people have recommended other forms of democratic participation, from neighborhood assemblies to a national initiative and referendum process.[40] Many cities and states have used "future projects" to generate widespread discussion of issues.[41]

Most of these ideas make eminent sense. We would no doubt be better off if they were adopted by every government in America. But there is a reason they have not been. Americans are not clamoring for more elections, more opinion polls, and more meetings to attend; most of us are far too busy making ends meet and raising our children. America already holds more elections than virtually any other country on earth—national elections, state elections, city elections, county elections, school board elections, water board elections, transit board elections. . . . We already have 504,404 elected officials, one for every 182 voters.[42] We all know the sinking feeling that comes in the voting booth, after we get through the national and state and city council races, when we see pages of names we do not know and contests for offices we know nothing about.

What Americans *do* hunger for is more control over matters that directly affect their lives: public safety, their children's schools, the developers who want to change their neighborhoods. They care so much about these things, in fact, that many of them devote precious hours every week to volunteer work in the schools, on neighborhood watches, or in community organizations. It is precisely here that participatory democracy is becoming real within American governments.

In St. Paul, for example, George Latimer pushed ownership of dozens of services into the community, from home energy audits and weatherization to the replacement of trees killed by Dutch elm disease. He was so intent on getting citizens to feel like they owned the city that he published an *Owner's Manual* listing all city services and departments. His principal instrument was a remarkable system of seventeen elected district councils. (Several other cities, including Dayton, Cincinnati, Birmingham, Seattle, and Portland, Oregon have similar systems.) The city subsidized an office and an organizer for each council, and the councils acted as sounding boards for city government, set priorities for half a billion dollars' worth of public works investments, initiated special projects founded by the city, and delivered services.

Some district councils remained essentially reactive, but others actively attacked problems in their neighborhoods. Many sponsored neighborhood watches. One managed the city park in its neighborhood. Another organized a Chore Service that paid neighborhood kids to do chores for the elderly. Still another organized a Block Nurse Program, through which neighborhood residents and nurses provided nursing care, companionship, and help with household chores to elderly residents, so they could stay out of nursing homes. Church groups trained the volunteers, church youth groups helped out with things like lawn care, Boy Scouts painted house, and local stores provided goods.

Kathy Tarnowski, the paid organizer for the District 14 Community Council, summed it up well: "The strength of our process is not in reactive governance. The strength is that we're solving our own problems. That's the kind of thing a politician—an alderman—can't do."[43]

Notes

1. Neal R. Peirce, "Police as Neighborhood Organizers: Chief Brown's Momentous Innovation," Washington Post Writer's Group, 13 March 1988. On community-oriented policing, see also James Q. Wilson and George L. Kelling, "Making Neighborhoods Safe," *Atlantic,* February 1989, pp. 46–52; several articles in the July 1990 issue of *Public Management* (published by the International City Management Association, Washington, D.C.); John F. Persinos, "The Return of Officer Friendly," *Governing,* August 1989, pp. 56–61; and Richard Lacayo, "Back to the Beat," *Time,* 1 April 1991, pp. 22–24.

2. Wilson and Kelling, "Making Neighborhoods Safe."

3. Persinos, "Return of Officer Friendly," 64–65.

4. "Neighbors Join to Roust the Criminals in the Streets," *Insight,* 28 November 1988, p. 9.

5. Ibid., 20.

6. *The Saint Paul Experiment: Initiatives of the Latimer Administration,* ed. David A. Lanegran, Cynthia Seelhammer, and Amy L. Walgrave (St. Paul: City of St. Paul, December 1989), xxii.

7. George Latimer, "1986 State of the City Address."

8. See Randolph B. Smith, "Aided by Volunteers, Seattle Shows How Recycling Can Work," *Wall Street Journal,* 19 July 1990, pp. 1, A5; and "Recycling Life's Debris," *Governing,* October 1990, p. 47. Two years after the program began, Seattle was recycling 38 percent of its waste stream.

9. John E. Chubb, "Why the Current Wave of School Reform Will Fail," *Public Interest* 90 (Winter 1988): 40.

10. *Closer Look* [published by Designs for Change, Chicago] 1 (February 1991): 5.

11. Ibid.

12. See Sharon Elder, "The Power of the Parent," *Yale* [alumni magazine], October 1990, pp. 50–54.

13. See Liza Mundy, "The Success Story of the War on Poverty," *Washington Monthly,* December 1989. As Mundy reports, a careful long-term study of one Head Start center in Ypsilanti, Michigan, found that children who attended were more likely than their counterparts in the community to finish high school, to go to college or vocational training, and to become self-supporting, and they were less likely to be detained or arrested or to become pregnant as teenagers. A cost-benefit analysis showed that every dollar spent on the center saved $6 in later special education, social service, court, and prison costs.

14. Bill Clinton, "Repairing the Family," *New Perspective Quarterly,* Fall 1990, pp. 12–15.

15. From Gregg McCutcheon, *In Their Own Words* (Boston: Industrial Services Program, 1990), 8.

16. *Rebuilding American Community* (New York: Project for Public Spaces, August 1988).

17. Peter Drucker, *The New Realities* (New York: Harper & Row, 1989), 200–203.

18. Stuart Butler and Anna Kondratas, *Out of the Poverty Trap* (New York: Free Press, 1987), 77, 124; and Lynn A. Curtis, "Neighborhood, Family and Employment," in *American Violence and Public Policy,* ed. Lynn A. Curtis (New Haven: Yale University Press, 1985), 208.

19. Mary Sit, "Lifetime Corp: House Calls with a Hug," *Boston Globe,* 13 June 1989, pp. 57, 58.

20. Katherine Boo, "What Mother Teresa Could Learn in a Leather Bar." *Washington Monthly,* June 1991, pp. 34–40.

21. For more on Kenilworth-Parkside, see David Osborne, "They Can't Stop Us Now," *Washington Post Magazine,* 30 July 1989, pp. 12–19, 27–31, from which this discussion is drawn.

22. *Cost Benefit Analysis of the Kenilworth-Parkside Public Housing Resident Management Corporation: Executive Summary* (Washington, D.C.: National Center for Neighborhood Enterprise, May 1986). This report was based on a cost-benefit analysis done by the consulting firm Coopers & Lybrand.

23. Dennis Eisen, interview with authors. Eisen is a real estate consultant hired to prepare a financial plan for resident ownership at Kenilworth-Parkside.

24. Sgt. Robert L. Prout, Jr., Washington, D.C., police department, interview with authors.

25. *Cost Benefit Analysis of the Kenilworth-Parkside Public Housing Resident Management Corporation.*

26. John L. McKnight, "Regenerating Community," *Social Policy,* Winter 1987, p. 58.

27. Ibid., 56–58.

28. From McCutcheon, *In Their Own Words,* 22, 45.

29. From "The Cleveland Conference on Fiscal Constraints/Constructive Responses/Action Steps," report on a conference held in Cleveland, 21–23 April 1982, sponsored by the Cleveland Foundation and the Hubert H. Humphrey Institute of Public Affairs.

30. Steven E. Rhoads, *The Economist's View of the World* (Cambridge: Cambridge University Press, 1985), 192.

31. John Herbers, "And a Little Child Shall Lead Them," *Governing,* October 1989, pp. 34–35.

32. Florida TaxWatch, *Cost Savings in Florida Government 1980–89* (Tallahassee: Florida TaxWatch, 1989), 20.

33. *Behavioral Health Service System Description* (Phoenix: Arizona Department of Health Services, February 1989), 3.

34. John L. McKnight, testimony before the U.S. Senate, Subcommittee on Aging, Family and Human Services, 17 September 1981.

35. Diane Kallenback and Arthur Lyons, *Government Spending for the Poor in Cook County, Illinois: Can We Do Better?* (Evanston, Ill.: Northwestern University Center for Urban Affairs and Policy Research and Center for Economic Policy Analysis, April 1989).

36. McKnight, "Regenerating Community," 55–56. The study was *New York City's Poverty Budget,* done by the Community Services Society of New York, 105 East 22nd Street, New York, N.Y. 10010.

37. Bryan Miller, "House of Hope," *Reasons,* May 1991, pp. 50–53.

38. McKnight, testimony, pp. 2–3.

39. Richard Morin and Dan Balz, "Majority in Poll Criticize Congress," *Washington Post,* 26 May 1989, p. A8.

40. In his book *Strong Democracy: Participatory Politics for a New Age* (Berkeley: University of California Press, 1984) Benjamin R. Barber outlined an ambitious set of proposals, including weekly or monthly neighborhood assemblies, town meetings using two-way televised communications, a national initiative and referendum process, and the use of interactive video communications to hold frequent straw polls and plebiscites as a way to spur discussion of important issues.

41. For more information on "futures projects," see Clement Bezold, ed., *Anticipatory Democracy* (New York: Vintage Books, 1978).

42. Richard Morin, "A Half a Million Choices for American Voters," *Washington Post National Weekly Edition,* 6–12 February 1989, p. 38. According to the *Statistical Abstract of the United States 1990* (Washington, D.C.: Bureau of the Census, 1990), 263 (table 440), 91,595,000 votes were cast in 1988. This works out to one elected official for every 182 voters.

43. For more on St. Paul's district councils, see *The Saint Paul Experiment,* 388–405.

26
The Algebra Project: Organizing in the Spirit of Ella

*Robert Moses, Mieko Kamii,
Susan McAllister Swap, Jeffrey Howard*

The United States is beginning to address, in a fundamental way, the teaching of mathematics in its middle schools. The National Science Foundation (1989), for instance, has issued a request for proposals to develop materials for middle-school mathematics instruction; the request sets out the technical elements of the problem in great detail. At the heart of math-science education issues, however, is a basic political question: If the current technological revolution demands new standards of mathematics and science literacy, will all citizens be given equal access to the new skills, or will some be left behind, denied participation in the unfolding economic and political era? Those who are concerned about the life chances for historically oppressed people in the United States must not allow math-science education to be addressed as if it were purely a matter of technical instruction.

The Algebra Project, a math-science program in Cambridge, Massachusetts, has organized local communities to help make algebra available to all seventh- and eighth-grade students, regardless of their prior level of skill development or academic achievement. The project's philosophy is that access to algebra will enable students to participate in advanced high-school math and science courses, which in turn are a gateway for college entrance. The project offers a new curriculum and a five-step curricular process for sixth graders, which provides the following: a smooth transition from the concepts of arithmetic to those of algebra, increasing the likelihood of mastery of seventh- and eighth-grade algebra; a home, community, and school culture involving teachers, parents, community volunteers, and school administrators in activities that support students' academic achievement; and a model of intellectual development that is based on motivation rather than ability.

The belief that ability is the essential ingredient driving intellectual

---

Reprinted from Robert P. Moses, Mieko Kamii, Susan McAllister Swap, and Jeffrey Howard, *Harvard Educational Review* 59, no. 4 (November 1989): 423–43. Copyright © 1989 by the President and Fellows of Harvard College. All rights reserved.

development and necessary for mastering advanced school mathematics is the basis for the differentiation in mathematics curricula at the eighth-grade level as well as the widespread practice of offering eighth-grade algebra only to students who are "mathematically inclined" or "gifted." The developers of the Algebra Project have called upon the traditions of the civil rights movement to assist communities in organizing a challenge to the ability model and its institutional expressions.

Traditions of the Civil Rights Movement in Mississippi

Through the Public Broadcasting System's "Eyes on the Prize" series, the American public has been given an opportunity to revisit the civil rights movement's "community mobilization tradition." Masses of people were mobilized to participate in large-scale events such as the Birmingham campaign, the march on Washington, and the Selma-to-Montgomery march, which were aimed at achieving equal access for southern blacks to public facilities and institutions. The tradition is epitomized by Dr. Martin Luther King, Jr., who lifted the movement by inspiring immense crowds in vast public spaces.

Within the civil rights movement was an older, yet less well known, "community organizing tradition." This tradition laid the foundation for Mississippi Freedom Summer (1964), which revolutionized race relations in Mississippi, and the Voting Rights Act of 1965, which altered politics throughout the South during the last quarter of this century. Its leader was Ella Baker, a community organizer and *fundi* whose wisdom and counsel guided the black veterans of the first wave of student sit-ins through the founding and establishment of the Student Nonviolent Coordinating Committee (SNCC).[1] She inspired in SNCC field secretaries a spiritual belief in human dignity, a faith in the capacity of blacks to produce leaders from the ranks of their people, and a perseverance when confronting overwhelming obstacles. Baker symbolizes the tradition in the civil rights movement of quiet places and the organizers who liked to work them.[2] Just as her spirit, consciousness, and teaching infused the Mississippi movement, they permeated the Algebra Project from its inception.

Three aspects of the Mississippi organizing tradition underlie the Algebra Project: the centrality of families to the work of organizing; the empowerment of grass-roots people and their recruitment for leadership; and the principle of "casting down your bucket where you are," or organizing in the context in which one lives and works, and working the issues found in that context.[3]

Families and Organizing

Of central importance to the Mississippi movement was the capacity of black families to adopt, nurture, love, and protect civil rights organizers as if they were family members. This practice, known in the literature as "informal absorption," allowed SNCC and CORE (Congress of Racial Equality) field secretaries and organizers to move from place to place in Mississippi with scarcely a dollar in their pockets, knowing full well that a family welcome awaited them at the end of their journeys. The absorption of civil rights organizers into black families was spiritual gold for the Mississippi movement, and it empowered movement organizers with the one credential that they could never earn: being one of the community's children. This credential contradicted the label of "outside agitator," used in Mississippi by the white power structure to negate the impact of the movement. By the same token, movement organizers empowered their adoptive families by reinforcing and enlarging the connections between them and the larger movement family, with its extensive networks across the land.

Grass-roots People and Grass-roots Leadership
The Mississippi movement's message of empowerment for grass-roots people was delivered to the entire country on national television at the 1964 Democratic National Convention by the black sharecroppers, domestic workers, and farmers who formed the rank and file of the Mississippi Freedom Democratic party (MFDP). Thereafter the message of empowerment was carried by black and white community organizers into many areas of community activity, including education, health, welfare, religion, and politics. However, neither the MFDP nor other grass-roots organizations took root and flourished into a strong national movement for empowering black people. The echoes heard from the Democratic party to the federal government and from the religious sector to public school systems were the same: institutionalizing empowerment in the hands of black "folk" is too risky a notion to attract lasting political support.

The issue of community empowerment in the public schools, first raised by black community organizers in Harlem in 1965, also found expression in white, liberal America. For example, in 1969 the Open Program of the Martin Luther King, Jr., School was established as a magnet program in the Cambridge public schools, in part because of the clamoring of Cambridge parents for more open education programs for their children, and in part because of the response to desegregation of the Cambridge schools.[4]

"Cast down your bucket where you are"
To master the art of organizing that strives to empower grass-roots people, one needs to learn to "cast down your bucket where you are." In 1976 Bob and Janet Moses, both former organizers for SNCC in Mississippi, cast down their bucket in Cambridge and looked to the Open Program of the King School as a place to educate their children.[5] What

would later become the Algebra Project began in 1982 when their eldest daughter, Maisha, entered the Open Program's eighth grade.

The Algebra Project

Before 1982, Moses, whose background included teaching secondary school mathematics in New York City and in Tanzania, had been teaching math to his children at home. Maisha, as a junior at Harvard University, recalled these lessons, conducted weekly during the school year and daily during the summer and vacations:

> Doing math at home was always a lot harder than math at school. It was somewhat like a chore. In our family, extra reading with my mom when we were much younger and math with my dad was part of our responsibility in the family, like taking out the garbage or doing the laundry.

Moses faced a familiar challenge: the resistance of adolescent children to performing what they regarded as a "household chore." Maisha explains:

> As we were getting older, it was a lot harder to get us to do math at home. We battled a lot more and complained. "Why do we have to do this? No one else has to do this." Dad would say, "It's important. I want you to do it. You need to do it." But we wouldn't be satisfied. I didn't really want to do it. Dad would have to sit there and force answers out of me. Finally he decided that the only way to get me to do algebra was to go into school.

In the fall of 1982 Mary Lou Mehrling, Maisha's eighth-grade teacher, invited Moses into her seventh/eighth-grade classroom to work with Maisha and three other eighth graders on algebra. That spring Maisha and two others took the Cambridge citywide algebra test, offered to students who wish to bypass Algebra I and go directly into Honors Algebra or Honors Geometry in ninth grade. All three passed, becoming the first students in the history of the King School to be eligible to pursue the honors math and science curriculum at Cambridge's only high school, Cambridge Rindge and Latin.[6]

With one eye on his eldest son, who was about to enter the Open Program's seventh grade, Moses decided to continue working the next year (1983–84) with Mehrling and another seventh/eighth-grade teacher. The number of eighth graders studying algebra with Moses was increased to nine. Partway through the year, the teachers selected seven seventh graders whom they thought likely to begin algebra the following year, creating the first group of "high ability" seventh graders for Moses to direct. In the spring all nine of Moses's eighth graders took the citywide algebra test, and six passed.

In the following year the program expanded again, but it was no longer quite the same. As early as 1983–84, it was evident that in spite of the commitment to meeting the educational needs of all its pupils, mathematics instruction in the Open Program was unwittingly skewed along racial lines.[7] Children in the two seventh/eighth-grade classrooms were clustered into separate "ability" groups: above–grade-level tracks primarily composed of middle-class whites; below–grade-level tracks made up almost exclusively of blacks and other children of color; and grade-level tracks that were racially mixed. The Open Program's system of ability groups effectively shunted most students of color onto the nonalgebra track, inbuing too many youngsters with the self-fulfilling notion that little was expected of them.

Additionally, Moses and Mehrling became aware that some high-achieving black males felt uncomfortable joining the algebra group, for it meant being separated from their friends, who were on other math tracks. On the whole, young people feel the need to be as similar to their peers as possible. Separating academically talented adolescents from their peers for the sake of participation in the academic "fast track" potentially aggravates the anxiety that accompanies adolescents' identity development.[8] Moreover, enduring attitudes toward math are shaped by math instruction at the seventh- and eighth-grade levels. Traditionally, very few new math principles are introduced in these two grades, when attention focuses instead on review (Usiskin, 1987). Moses and Mehrling hypothesized that using the seventh and eighth grades to lay a ground-work of competence in algebra might enhance students' general self-confidence and provide them with the mathematical background neces-sary for advanced high-school courses.

The Mississippi movement's organizing tradition used everyday issues of ordinary people and framed them for the maximum benefit of the community. In Mississippi the issue was the right to vote; technically: "What are the legal, judicial, political, and constitutional obstacles to the right to vote? How can we initiate court cases, introduce legislation, and mobilize political support to remove these obstacles?" SNCC and CORE workers pursued this by establishing beachheads, through black families, in the most resistant counties throughout the state. But the Mississippi organizers did something of even greater importance, and that was to conceive of the issue of voting in its broadest political sense. Midway through voter registration efforts, they began to ask themselves and the black community: "What is the vote for? Why do we want it in the first place? What must we do right now to ensure that when we have the vote, it will work for us to benefit our communities?" After the organizers and key community groups had worked and reworked these and other questions, they shifted the organizing strategy from increasing voter registration to laying the basis for a community-based political party, which eventually became the Mississippi Freedom Democratic party. Creating a new political party became the Mississippi movement's focus, because of its greater potential for involving community people in a substantive long-term effort. Participants would come to own the political questions and their responses to them.[9]

In the Open Program the everyday issue was teaching algebra in the seventh and eighth grades. Moses, the parent-as-organizer in the program, instinctively used the lesson he had learned in Mississippi, transforming the everyday issue into a broader political question for the Open Program community to consider: What is algebra for? Why do we want children to study it? What do we need to include in the mathematics education of every middle-school student, to provide each and every one of them with access to the college preparatory mathematics curriculum in high school? Why is it important to gain such access?

By linking the content of math education to the future prospects of inner-city children, Moses transformed what had previously been a purely curricular issue into a broader political question. Drawing on his experience as an organizer, educator, and parent, Moses transformed the dialogue in the Open Program among parents, teachers, and school administrators into one that centered on questions that would get at the heart of educational practice: How can a culture be created in the Open Program in which every child is expected to be as good as possible in his or her mathematical development? What should the content of middle-school mathematics be? What curricular processes make that content available to all students?

A cornerstone of the evolving Algebra Project thus became the expectation that every child in the Open Program could achieve math literacy, an ethos powerful enough to suffuse both the peer and adult culture. The components of this effort included changing the content and methods of teaching math, involving parents in activities that would enable them to better support their children's learning, teaching students to set goals and motivating them to achieve, and reaching out to black college graduates in the Boston area who would serve as tutors and role models of academic success.

Teachers as Learners

From the beginning, Mehrling and Moses modeled the notion that there is no shame in confessing ignorance—if it is the first step in learning. Mehrling, an ex-music teacher, took courses in mathematics, beginning with algebra, and eventually achieved state certification in math. But she did something more profound: she turned her inexperience with math content into a component of learning by adopting a position of mutual inquiry with her students, and by presenting herself to them as a learner. As she states, she "developed methods of responding to student's questions that helped both the students and me to think through the problem." As she had questions, she would ask Moses for help, on the spot.

> Presenting myself as a learner, in front of my students, helped me to understand what they were experiencing, and helped them to feel comfortable asking for help. Students no longer felt threatened if they did not understand a problem or a concept, for they saw that we all were learners and we all learn in different ways.

Because Mehrling presented herself openly and honestly as a student of the subject she was teaching, she was able to help build her students' confidence. She overtly transmitted the message, "if I [your teacher] can risk embarrassment to learn this subject, surely you can, too." But she also conveyed to them a powerful latent message:

> I am confident that people who don't know this subject can learn it; to learn it they have, at all times, to be ready not to pretend to understand what they do not truly understand; to learn it they must be comfortable asking for help and willing to risk embarrassment.

Mehrling's message recapitulated a memorable message that Fannie Lou Hamer and others conveyed at the height of the MFDP challenge to the Democratic National Convention of 1964—confidence that people who did not know the business of politics could learn it by asking direct questions and risking embarrassment. Each confronted their inexperience with honesty and integrity, turning potential liabilities into strengths.

Involving Parents

From its inception, the Open Program had evolved a set of policies and practices that encouraged parents' active involvement in staff hiring, curriculum development, observation and evaluation of teachers, and governance and administration of the school. Parental involvement in the Algebra Project grew naturally in this context.

Parents who served on the program's seventh/eighth-grade committee in 1984–85 concluded that decisions about studying algebra in the seventh and eighth grades could not be left up to individual sixth graders to make. These children were too young to fully understand the long-range implications of their decisions for college entrance. Nor should such decisions rest solely with the teachers, curriculum coordinators, or school or districtwide administrators, each of whom had their own ideas about who should study algebra and in which grade. Rather, parents needed to be involved in making educational choices for their children at both individual and policy-making levels. They also had to be better informed about details of the middle-school math curriculum, so that they would be able to make informed decisions and to protect the best interests of their children.

During the spring of 1985 a parent from the Open Program's seventh/eighth-grade committee collaborated with Moses to distribute a letter to the parents of all the sixth graders, asking whether they thought that every seventh grader should study algebra, and whether they thought their own child should study algebra in the seventh grade. In reply, a few parents thought that some seventh graders probably were not ready, but no parent thought his or her own child should be denied access to algebra in the seventh grade. Exposing the contradictions between parental assessments of their children's capabilities and curricular assumptions at the community level provided a means for building consensus around educational outcomes for all children.

This was the catalyst for inviting all Open Program children entering the seventh grade in the fall of 1985 to study algebra three times a week. With the exception of a few eighth graders who in their teacher's judgment "were not ready," the entire eighth grade was also invited to study algebra. The consensus statement from parents launched a change in school policy and culture. Currently, every Open Program student is expected to study algebra in the seventh and eighth grades.

As the project evolved, parental participation increased as parents volunteered in classrooms and participated in workshops on student self-esteem and achievement. Parents from throughout the King School were invited to attend "Honors Bound" parent groups, which prepared students of color to accept the challenge of taking honors courses in high school, and created a home-school culture that would nurture and support serious intellectual effort. A Saturday morning algebra course for parents was offered, teaching algebra in the same way that it was being taught to their children.

Parents who took algebra during the Saturday classes committed themselves to making the project "theirs" in a fundamental sense. A grateful parent captured the multiple dimensions of this experience in a 1987 letter to the Cambridge School Committee:

> this program exemplifies to me all that I hope most for in the education of my daughter and other young people in our community: a positive orientation to learning; a rich understanding of advanced mathematics; recognition of the relationship between what is learned in the classroom and what goes on in life, and a sense of personal empowerment.
>
> As a sixth grader in her first year in the program, my daughter began to overcome her fear of math and distorted perceptions of what she is capable of doing and why it is important. I believe this was due to several factors including the climate of learning in the classroom (in part, a sense that students, teachers and aides alike were learning *together*); the demystification of the subject by relating it to life experiences; and by the fact that her mother, along with other parents and community members, was simultaneously overcoming latent math panic by taking the course on Saturdays.
>
> This experience not only helped me understand the program (and learn math), it also greatly enhanced my comprehension of the life of the school and neighborhood community and of problems that as a citizen I can help to resolve . . . .

Parents were barraged with letters and opportunities to talk, to ask questions, and to join in planning, all as an acknowledgment of the centrality of parents in the construction of a home-school culture of high achievement.

Creating a New Teaching and Learning Environment for Math

As an adjunct to opening up algebra to all seventh and eighth graders in 1985, ability grouping was replaced with individual and small-group instruction. Students were taught skills for learning hard material "on their own." In conferences with teachers, students were asked to set their own short-term objectives (for example, deciding how many lesson sets they wished to complete each week) and longer-range goals (for example, deciding to prepare for the citywide test). Parents were informed about the goals and were asked to sign their child's goal statement each semester. The pace and scope of students' mathematical studies therefore came under student control. Mehrling tells a story that reflects the individual and group motivation that such goal-setting can foster:

> Andrea spoke up at one of our first meetings and said, "I'm going to do four lessons a week because I want to finish such-and-such by the end of seventh grade, so I can finish the book by the end of the eighth grade, so I can be in honors geometry in the ninth grade." This was a twelve-year-old. The others looked at her—this hadn't come from a teacher—and said, "Are you crazy?" She said, "That's what I'm going to do." Bob [Moses] was there, and he started to frame for them why what Andrea had just done was a very mature and farsighted act, and how maybe they weren't ready to do that yet. But it gave Andrea a lot of support and affirmation for having said that in the group. And it changed what the others were going to say next. Everything from then on was in terms of Andrea: "Well, I'm not going to do quite what Andrea is, but . . . ."

Students also learned to work harder than they had before. They were encouraged to develop habits of concentration, patience, and perseverance in approaching their daily math work. Students decided which of several resources to consult—the textbook, the instructor, or a peer—when they had a question or ran into difficulties in solving a problem. Teachers met with small groups for brief lessons on specific concepts and regularly held small-group review sessions. Reflecting on this decision, Mehrling recently explained:

> Adolescent learners can sometimes interrelate with materials, and it's not nearly as threatening as interacting with an adult. If they can go to an adult to ask a question about the materials, when they're ready to go to an adult it's wholly different from being in a group, being pinpointed and put on the spot, and feeling vulnerable about the pieces they don't have in place yet. Once they start to interact with materials, they get not only very possessive of them, but very reluctant to go back to any kind of teacher-directed

> lessons. They're empowered, in a curious way, around materials—something I would never have even thought about. The Open Program generally is a very teacher-intensive kind of program. We motivate, we bring in materials from everywhere, and our teaching is interpersonal. We discovered at the seventh and eight grade level that that was one of the problems with students who felt vulnerable. It put them on the spot.

As part of the new curricular, pedagogical, and social environment for studying math, the seventh- and eighth-grade teachers assumed the role of "coach" as opposed to "lecturer" in their relationship with students.

The project produced its first full graduating class in the spring of 1986. When they entered high school the following autumn, 39 percent of the graduates were placed in Honors Geometry or Honors Algebra. Not a single student in that cohort ended up at Cambridge Rindge and Latin School in lower-level math courses, such as Algebra I.

Curricular Expansion

By 1986 attention turned to the preparation of students for seventh-grade algebra. With all students in the seventh and eighth grades taking algebra, lower grade teachers began to question the adequacy of their own math curricula as preparation for algebra. To address this question systematically, the entire staff of the Open Program participated in a year-long institute centered on the question of math literacy.

After the institute, teachers at all levels (K-8) implemented new curricula in mathematics, appropriate for the age and grade levels that they taught. Some teachers found it unsettling to devise their own curricular practices around the needs of children and their own teaching styles. The results of the Algebra Project suggest that flexibility leads to better pedagogy. For example, when fifth/sixth-grade teachers tried a materials-centered approach with sixth graders that had worked very well at the seventh/eighth-grade level, they found that younger children, accustomed to more teacher-centered instruction, needed more teacher-child and small-group interaction in the sixth-grade transition curriculum. The teachers modified their classroom technique but retained the principle of encouraging greater self-reliance in finding answers to problems. Improved adaptation of curriculum was itself beneficial. But equally important, this process gave teachers the same sense of empowerment experienced by students. Teachers who participated in the innovation and trained themselves in how to present the curriculum were more likely to understand, appreciate, and foster the skill of self-education that was central to the Algebra Project. One teacher explained:

> Bob was affirming what we were doing while he was helping us change. He didn't come in and say, "We're throwing this out, it's junk." He came in and said, "You guys are great. Wanna try something different?" When we

asked, "How will it work?" he turned it around and asked, "Well, how do you think it should work? What do you want to have happen?" He didn't really give us a way, which admittedly was frustrating, but it also gave us ownership around it. Bob didn't have all of the answers. At first I was really annoyed that he was making me go through this process. I kept saying, "Bob has an agenda. Why doesn't he tell us? We're wasting so much time!" But he knew that it had to come from us. He knew he couldn't impose, because he didn't know what would work. He wasn't a classroom teacher. He just had the vision. If he could help us catch the vision, we would make it work.

A second outcome was that Moses agreed to develop a curriculum for the sixth grade that would provide a conceptual transition from arithmetic to algebra. The main features of what has come to be called the Algebra Project, and the philosophy that guided its construction, are discussed below.

What to Teach and How to Teach It

The opening of algebra to everyone in 1985–86 gave Moses the opportunity to work closely with several students who had great difficulty with the initial chapters of the algebra textbook. In particular, one black male student took many months to complete the first few lessons. Moses wondered precisely where the student's conceptual knot lay. Was it possible to lead the student from arithmetic to algebra by mapping a conceptual trail, beginning with concepts that were obvious, and proceeding by equally obvious steps?

After working with a number of students who were having difficulty, Moses came to the conclusion that the heart of the problem lay in their concept of number. In arithmetic, the distinctive feature of a number is magnitude or quantity. In algebra a number has two distinctive features: one is quantitative; the other is qualitative and must be explicitly taught. Students of arithmetic have in their minds one question that they associate with counting numbers: "How many?" Students of algebra need to have two: "How many?" and another question, such as "Which way?" as points of reference for the intuitive concept of opposites. Children understand the question, "Which way?" from their early years, but it is not a question that they associate with number. The number concept used in arithmetic must be generalized in algebra, and failure to make this generalization blocks students' understanding. Once students have generalized their concept of number, they must also generalize their knowledge of basic operations such as subtraction.

Moses gradually arrived at a five-step teaching and learning process that takes students from physical events to a symbolic representation of those events, thereby accelerating sixth graders' grasp of key concepts needed in the study of algebra.[10] The five steps are:

1. Physical event
2. Picture or model of this event
3. Intuitive (idiomatic) language description of this event
4. A description of this event in regimented English
5. Symbolic representation of the event

The purpose of the five steps is to avert student frustration in "the game of signs," or the misapprehension that mathematics is the manipulation of a collection of mysterious symbols and signs. Chad, a young black seventh grader, recently looked up from reading a page in the first chapter of a traditional algebra text and said to his mother, "It's all just words." For too many youngsters, mathematics is a game of signs they cannot play. They must be helped to understand what those signs *really* mean and construct for themselves a basis of evidence for mathematics. When middle-school students use the five-step process to construct symbolic representations of physical events (representations that they themselves make up), they forge, through direct experience, their own platform of mathematical truths. Their personally constructed symbolic representations enter into a system of mathematical truths that has content and meaning.

At the Open Program students initiate this process with a trip on the Red Line of Boston's subway system (the physical event). This experience provides the context in which a number of obvious questions may be asked: At what station do we start? Where are we going? How many stops will it take to get there? In what direction do we go? These questions have obvious answers, forming the basis for the mathematics of trips. When they return, students are asked to write about their trip, draw a mural or construct a three-dimensional model, make graphs for trips that they create, and collect statistical data about them. The purpose is to fuse in their minds the two questions "How many?" and "Which way?" and to anchor these questions to physical events.

Students then use this process to explore the concept of equivalence, in the broad cultural context of everyday events such as cooking, coaching, teaching, painting, and repairing. They explore any concept in which an object A is substituted for another object B to achieve a certain goal. They conclude the discussion of equivalence in subway travel with open-ended constructions of equivalent trips, leading to an introduction of displacements as "trips that have the same number of stops and go in the same direction."

Once displacements are introduced, they investigate the concept of "comparing" as a prelude to generalizing their concept of subtraction. Most algebra texts introduce subtraction as a transformed addition problem. Students are asked to think of subtraction $(3 - (-2) = + 5)$ as "adding the opposite" or "finding the missing addend" $(3 - ? = 5)$, which provides one group of signs as a reference for another. But students look for concrete experiences, pictures, or at least a concept, to link directly to algebraic subtraction. The problem is compounded because students have overlearned "take-away" as the concept underlying subtraction. In algebra, "take-away" no longer has a straightforward application to subtraction. Within a couple of months of beginning algebra, students confront subtraction statements that have no discernible content, have only indirect meaning in relation to an associated addition problem, and are not at all obvious.

To give additional content, meaning, and clarity to subtraction in beginning algebra, students begin with the physical event of comparing the heights of two students, Coastocoast who is six feet tall, and Watchme who is four feet tall. The class works with a picture of this event, generating questions that can be used to compare heights:

1. Which one is taller?
2. What is the difference in their heights?
3. How much shorter is Watchme than Coastocoast?
4. Who is shorter?
5. How much taller is Coastocoast than Watchme?

In arithmetic there are two subtraction concepts, the concept of "take-away" and the concept of "the difference between." The latter provides the appropriate entry into subtraction in algebra, as illustrated in the above set of questions. Students will readily identify an answer to the second question by subtracting to find the difference in the heights. This prepares them to accept subtraction as the best approach to answering comparative questions—questions that belong to algebra and not arithmetic.

The answers to these questions are carefully processed in three stages: intuitive language, regimented English, and symbolic representations. "How much taller is Coastocoast than Watchme?" is explored in the following way:

- *Intuitive language:* "Coastocoast is two feet taller than Watchme."
- *Regimented English:* "The height of Coastocoast compared to the height of Watchme is two feet taller."
- *Symbolic representations:*
  (5a) H(C) compared to H(W) is $2'$ ↑

  (5b) $H(C) - H(W) = 2'$ ↑

  (5c) $6'$ ↑ $- 4'$ ↑ $= 2'$ ↑
  (that is, $6'$ is $2'$ taller than $4'$)

"How much shorter is Watchme than Coastocoast?" proceeds along a similar track.

- *Intuitive language:* "Watchme is two feet shorter than Coastocoast."
- *Regimented English:* "The height of Watchme compared to the height of Coastocoast is two feet shorter."

- *Symbolic representations:*

  (3a) H(W) compared to H(C) is 2' ↓

  (3b) $H(W) - H(C) = 2'$ ↓

  (3c) $4' ↑ - 6' ↑ = 2'$ ↓

  (that is, a height of 4' is 2' shorter than a height of 6')

This way of comparing physical quantities is easily reinforced with work stations at which students compare weights, lengths, temperatures, and speeds. They may return to their experience on the subway to compare positions of stations on the Red Line, using the following model.

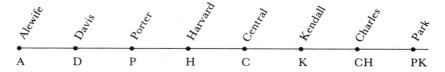

When asked, "What is the position of Harvard compared to Kendall?" students work through the following steps:

- *Intuitive language:* "Harvard is two stops outbound from Kendall."
- *Regimented English:* "The position of Harvard compared to the position of Kendall is two stops outbound."
- *Symbolic representations:*

  (a) P(H) compared to P(K) is $\overset{\leftarrow}{2}$

  (b) $P(H) - P(K) = \overset{\leftarrow}{2}$

In a similar way the question, "What is the position of Kendall relative to Harvard?" yields

$$P(K) - P(H) = \overset{\rightarrow}{2}$$

As soon as integers are introduced as a system of coordinates, students are ready to generate their own subtraction problems. The notion of an arbitrary point of reference having been introduced earlier, systems of coordinates are assigned to the stations, with the zero point alternately assigned to various stations. Each assignment generates a different subtraction problem for the question, "What is the position of Harvard relative to Kendall?"

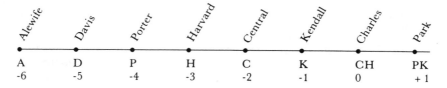

(a)   P(H) compared to P(K) is $\overset{\leftarrow}{2}$

(b)   P(H) − P(K) = $\overset{\leftarrow}{2}$

(c)   −3 − (−1) = −2

By similar reasoning, the question, "What is the position of Kendall relative to Harvard?" yields

$$P(K) - P(H) = \overset{\rightarrow}{2}$$
$$-1 - (-3) = +2$$

The opposite comparisons [P(H) compared to P(K), and P(K) compared to P(H)] lead to opposite expressions [(−3) − (−1), and (−1) − (−3)] as well as opposite integers [(−2) and (+2)], in a way that gives direct, intuitive meaning to subtraction of integers and provides students and teachers alike with control over the generation of simple subtraction problems and equations. The curriculum and curricular process used in the sixth grade have made algebra accessible for all middle-school students. The project has demonstrated that all seventh- and eighth-grade students in the King School's Open Program can study algebra, and that the entire school community expects them to do so.

Community Participation in Creating a Culture of Achievement

For youngsters who have felt excluded from the culture of academic achievement in school, the expectation that they, too, can learn is crucial. During the 1987–88 school year the project's response to children who did not think they were likely to succeed in math was to institute a series of measures designed to create a culture of mathematical and scientific literacy, not only in the Open Program but in other programs within the King School as well. The Seymour Institute for Advanced Christian Studies, a service organization conceived by black Harvard graduates to support community-based development in urban areas, provided black role models to go into classes to tutor students and to run before-school algebra study halls four mornings a week. The study halls were open to seventh and eighth graders from all of the King School's four programs. The tutors, who came from Harvard, MIT, Wentworth Institute, and Boston University, established relationships with individual children and became role models of academically successful young adults for seventh and eighth graders to emulate. A Harvard Law School student and tutor wrote:

> I have been impressed by the fact that these seventh and eighth graders are able to read and understand their math textbooks, already have some understanding of algebraic concepts, and are willing to come out at 7:30 A.M. in order to work on their mathematical skills. . . . The students in the Algebra Project are able to help themselves, and each other, by using their

believe that it is their friendships that keep them coming to early morning study halls; relationships that support educational achievement are being established outside the classroom.

As the Algebra Project developed, the message that each child could learn was more systematically articulated by the Efficacy Institute.[11] Emphasizing confidence and effective effort as key ingredients in the process of intellectual development, the Efficacy model provides educators, parents, and students with an explicit alternative to the ability model of learning. Efficacy assumes that children, who are well enough endowed to master the fundamentals of language at an early age, are fully capable of learning mathematics. In order to learn, children are required to marshal effective effort. They must learn to work with commitment, focused attention, and reliable strategies. When learning is perceived as a function of effective effort, one seeks factors inhibiting children when they are having difficulties learning or understanding a concept, rather than "disabilities" that disallow learning.

Many children of color learn from an early age that there are doubts concerning their capacity to develop intellectually. Messages communicated from school (low ability placements in the primary grades), from peers (pervasive anti-intellectualism within the peer group), and the media (expectations of inferiority) all serve to impress upon them that they may not be up to the task of advanced studies. The lack of confidence engendered by the internalization of these messages shapes the meaning of any failure ("I guess this proves I'm not smart") and undermines the capacity to work ("Why bang my head against the wall if I'm unable to learn the stuff anyway?").

To redress these circumstances, Efficacy works to plant an alternative idea in the child's mind: "If I work hard enough, I can get smart":

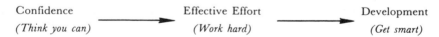

Confidence	Effective Effort	Development
(Think you can)	*(Work hard)*	*(Get smart)*

Emphasis is placed on the process of development and some measure of control is returned to the child.

Teachers are the carriers of Efficacy ideas, and it is to them that responsibility falls for building confidence and shaping strong effort in children. Teachers attend an intensive, five-day seminar to learn the Efficacy model of development and study its implications for their own teaching. They are then provided with formal curriculum to use with their students over the course of an academic year. The curriculum gives teachers and students a shared language and a conceptual framework for reworking questions, such as why a particular child has been unable to "do math" in the past. The teacher is able to impress upon the child that learning is a function of effort, not of innate ability. The curriculum helps the students to raise their consciousness, so they can affirm for themselves their own need for self-development. Such affirmation on their part is a critical prerequisite to confronting obstacles to their own development and acquiring attitudes and habits that will ensure success in many endeavors, including the algebra program.

In 1988 a sixth-grade teacher in the Open Program began teaching the Efficacy curriculum to all the sixth graders twice a week. She explains:

> We all consider ourselves to be good teachers, and yet we know that we are failing some students. Bob talked to us about a way that could help us to help those children achieve. We realized what that will mean not only to those students but to all of the children in our classrooms, and from there, what that will mean to the community at large.

The Project Continues
The Algebra Project continues at the Open Program. The Efficacy and Algebra curricula are taught to sixth graders, and algebra is studied by all seventh and eighth graders. The project is now challenging other schools to make the political decision to alter their own math curricula. For example, discussions are proceeding with administrators and teachers in Boston, where three schools have volunteered to experiment with both the Efficacy and Algebra Project curricula and receive training in their implementation. Moses has also begun to train selected middle-school teachers in Atlanta. Currently, the project is exploring relationships with school systems in other cities.

Conclusion

Community Organizing and Educational Innovation
The community organizing approach to educational innovation differs from traditional educational interventions in several important ways. The principle of "casting down your bucket where you are" stands in marked contrast to research programs originating in universities, where scholars design interventions they hypothesize will result in outcomes they articulate in advance and that are replicable. Researchers in universities and consulting firms must have well-designed, highly articulated interventions in order to convince funding agencies that their projects have promise. Depending upon the focus of the investigation, the researcher generally targets selected neighborhoods, schools, or organizations for participation because of their demographic or similarly quantifiable characteristics. Additionally, researchers have intellectual roots in their own disciplines and view problems through lenses that are consonant with their disciplines, rather than through the eyes of a community.

In contrast to the university-based researcher, the organizer working in the tradition of Ella gradually becomes recognized by community members as having a commitment to their overall well-being. The organizer immerses him- or herself in the life of the community, learning its strengths, resources, concerns, and ways of conducting business. The organizer does not have a comprehensive, detailed plan for remedying a perceived problem, but takes an "evolutionary" view of his or her own role in the construction of the solution. He or she understands that the community's everyday concerns can be transformed into broader political questions of general import. The form they will take is not always known in advance.

Once political questions are identified, the organizer's agenda must remain simultaneously focused and fluid—sharply focused on the long-range goal, but fluid with respect to how the goal will be attained. The organizer seeks out views of community participants who have strong interests in the issue and informally educates community members who are uninvolved but whose interests are at stake. It is the organizer's task to help community members air their opinions, question one another, and then build consensus, a process that usually takes a good deal of time to complete.

Improving the mathematics curriculum and curricular process in a middle school has gradually become the focus of the Algebra Project. At the outset Moses did not know that the project would become a vehicle for raising questions about ability grouping, effective teaching for children of color, or the community's roles in educational decision making. He did not imagine that it would trigger an interest in teaching algebra to inner-city middle-school students beyond his daughter's classroom.

As we have seen, the program's innovations relied on the involvement of the entire community: teachers, parents, school administrators, students, tutors, and consultants from the Greater Boston community. In her review of programs that have been helpful in breaking the cycle of disadvantage, Lisbeth Schorr (1988) highlights the importance of comprehensive, flexible, and intensive approaches to reform.[12]

> Many interventions have turned out to be ineffective not because seriously disadvantaged families are beyond help, but because we have tried to attack complex, deeply rooted tangles of troubles with isolated fragments of help, with help rendered grudgingly in one-shot forays, with help designed less to meet the needs of beneficiaries than to conform to professional or bureaucratic convenience, with help that may be useful to middle-class families but is often irrelevant to families struggling to survive. (pp. 263–64)

The work of discovering new solutions, building a broad base of support, and overcoming barriers takes time. Moses's effort to work with teachers, parents, and administrators to transform the middle-school mathematics curriculum and curricular process in the Open Program began seven years ago. We note that it took fifteen years for James Comer's efforts at comprehensive reform in two New Haven schools to yield striking improvements in test scores (Comer, 1988, 1980).[13] Durable reforms are possible, but there are no shortcuts in bottom-up implementation.

In the Open Program faculty volunteered to participate, committing themselves to working together to discover better ways to teach math and struggling to reach consensus. Parents were deeply involved as learners, supporters, contributors, and decision makers. Students voluntarily set goals for themselves and came to 7:30 A.M. study halls four mornings a week. School administrators supported teachers as they tried out new strategies, worked to secure funding, and acted as spokespersons for the project. Strengths of various contributors were recognized, and they were empowered to adapt, create, and evaluate their progress in attaining a shared vision.

Others have learned that it is through struggling with a problem and shaping the solutions that commitment to change really occurs. Schorr (1988) reports: "Dr. Comer wanted to make sure I understood that the essence of his intervention is a process, not a package of materials, instructional methods, or techniques. 'It is the creation of a sense of community and direction for parents, school staff, and students alike' " (p. 234). Comer is pointing to the fact that significant innovations must transform the culture, and transformation requires a broad base of voluntary support. It is crucial that participants have time to understand an idea, explore their commitment, and adapt the innovation to their needs.

Henry Levin (1988) also emphasizes the importance of process.[14] He states:

> Underlying the organizational approach are two major assumptions: First, the strategy must "empower" all of the major participants and raise their sense of efficacy and of responsibility for the outcomes of the school. Second, the approach must build on the considerable strengths of the participants rather than decrying their weaknesses. (p. 5)

Many will find it useful to follow the precept "cast down your bucket where you are," as Jamie Escalante did in Los Angeles when he began offering calculus to disadvantaged youth. The starting point for reform is less important than whether the issue is powerful and inspiring enough to generate enthusiasm, reveal broader political questions, compel devoted leadership, and serve as a vehicle for community commitment.

Funding to Support Innovation

The Algebra Project would not have developed as it did had it not been for the MacArthur "no strings attached" Fellowship that allowed Moses to work in the Open Program for five years, without having to account for the way he spent his time. Subsequent funding has been difficult. For eighteen months Wheelock College in Boston supported Moses as he looked for resources to provide release time for teachers, cover materials and reproduction costs, and secure consultation from the broader academic community. Moses is still spending an enormous amount of time trying to secure long-term funding to support the continuation and dissemination of the Algebra Project.

Finding support can be a depleting struggle for many innovative efforts. National funding sources are hesitant to fund projects with grass-roots leadership, a community focus, a long time-frame, and a philosophy that casts educational issues in political as well as technical terms. Declining state and local budgets also threaten commitment to comprehensive, long-term reforms. But only when major political questions are addressed (for instance, that *all* children can benefit from and should have access to algebra in their middle-school years) can we discover the most appropriate ways to organize knowledge, develop curriculum, and encourage home, school, and community participation.

Transforming School Culture

Teachers and parents in the Open Program came to believe that ability grouping in mathematics seriously impaired the capacity of middle-school students of color and females to learn as well as they might. Questioning the policy was the first step toward comprehensive change. Others concur that differentiating students harms those who are disadvantaged or placed in lower tracks.[15] After articulating a vision of high expectations in algebra for all students, participants worked to transform the culture of the school, so that policies, teaching strategies, and the Efficacy curriculum could together help students.

The project speaks to the importance of family as a link to school success. Henderson (1987) concludes her review of research concerning parental involvement in student achievement by categorically stating that "the evidence is beyond dispute: parent involvement improves student achievement" (p. 1). This finding holds for middle- as well as low-income families, at different grade levels, and in a broad spectrum of interventions. As the U.S. population becomes more diverse, it is absolutely fundamental that schools join with families to define and support school success. Continuity between home and school must be forged for all children, and we must draw on the strengths and resources that families can provide.

Curriculum and Curricular Process

Among the strengths of the faculty and volunteers in the Open Program was their curiosity about why some children were not succeeding in mathematics, and their willingness to explore the possibility that their own teaching strategies might be a factor. Moses and the teachers became classroom researchers—analyzing student errors, locating con-

became classroom researchers—analyzing student errors, locating conceptual knots, and experimenting with materials and teaching processes that might improve students' mathematical development. A sixth-grade transition curriculum that allows students to relate everyday experiences to mathematical concepts represented symbolically should be disseminated widely.

In 1964 national attention was focused on the disenfranchised citizens of the South. In 1989 another kind of disenfranchisement exists, as many poor, indigenous, and immigrant children of color are denied access to programs and teaching that support their success in school. The success of the Algebra Project stands as a challenge to public school teachers, administrators, scholars, and, most important, those individuals who have traditionally advocated for the democratization of the society and schools: Will you wage a campaign for mathematical literacy, which acknowledges that every middle-school student can and should learn algebra while simultaneously empowering the child's community and family? Will you organize in the spirit of Ella?

Notes

Acknowledgments: The authors wish to thank the following people for their contributions to this article: Theresa Perry, Daniel Cheever, Barney Brawer, Ceasar McDowell, and, finally, the teachers and administrators of the Open Program of the Martin Luther King, Jr., School.

1. *Fundi* is a Swahili term for a person who has an expertise valued by society, and who passes on his or her art to the young by example and instruction. Ella Baker was a *fundi* to the SNCC workers learning the art of community organizing.

2. One such quiet place was Amite County, in a remote corner of southwest Mississippi, where E. W. Steptoe's family welcomed Bob Moses, SNCC's first field secretary, into the community in the summer of 1961. Mr. Steptoe was president of Amite County's NAACP chapter in the late 1950s when the county sheriff raided a chapter meeting and confiscated the group's books, thus exposing the members to economic reprisals and physical danger. By the time the first wave of SNCC organizers spread out across the rural South, activities at places like the Steptoe farmhouses had ground to a halt.

3. "Cast down your bucket where you are" was used by Booker T. Washington in an address at the Atlanta Exposition, 18 September 1895.

4. The King School is a large, modern facility, built on the site of a school that had served Cambridge's black community for many years. By the late 1970s the King School housed four programs for grades K–8: a regular program composed of personnel from the former school; a magnet Open Program; and smaller bilingual and special needs programs.

5. Because some but not all authors of this article are also the subjects of discussion, we have chosen to use third-person references throughout to avoid confusion.

6. The fourth student opted to go to a private high school and did not take the test.

7. See Delpit (1986) for a discussion of the differences between the instructional needs of mainstream and minority children.

8. See Fordham (1988) for a discussion of the tensions high-achieving black students feel when they strive for academic success.

9. It was only in Mississippi, where the entire state was structured along a community organizing tradition, that the issue of the right to vote was perceived as a broad political question.

10. This model is a synthesis of ideas derived from three sources. The first was the Open Program itself. Moses observed teaching practices in the Open Program and attended workshops with teachers in which Virginia Chalmers and others explained the teaching and learning ideas that they had developed for primary grades. The second was Quine's (1981) notion of "mathematization in situ." "A progressive sharpening and regimenting of ordinary idioms: this is what led to arithmetic, symbolic logic, and set theory, and this is mathematization" (p. 150). Quine insisted that "set theory, arithmetic, and symbolic logic are all of them products of the straightforward mathematization of ordinary interpreted discourse" (p. 151). The third source was Dubinsky (1987), who shared his insight that in the future, mathematics education would center on a "fixed curricular process" rather than a "fixed curriculum."

11. The Efficacy model of intellectual development is based on motivation. The role of motivation in self-development was studied by Jeffrey Howard, director of the Efficacy Institute, who, in collaboration with educators, developed the model summarized here.

12. As a participant of the Harvard University Working Group on Early Life and Adolescence, Lisbeth Schorr believed that with the knowledge currently available, society could prevent the damaging outcomes for adolescents associated with disadvantage, such as teenage pregnancy, juvenile crime, school failure, and unemployment. She visited an array of health and education programs that were successful in interrupting the cycle of disadvantage and discovered that what the programs had in common was a comprehensive, flexible, and intensive approach to reform.

13. In 1968 James Comer, a psychiatrist at the Yale Child Study Center, began a program of reform in the two New Haven schools that had the lowest achievement scores and the worst attendance and behavior records in the system. Today, although the community is still impoverished, these demonstration schools now boast top achievement scores in the New Haven system (third and fourth), no serious behavior problems, and superior attendance records. The critical components of the reform, now disseminated to fourteen other sites, include a school planning and management team (composed of the principal, parents, and teachers), a mental health team that provides coordinated services to children in conflict, and extensive parent involvement.

14. Henry Levin is the director of the very successful Accelerated Schools Project in the San Francisco Bay Area, whose mission is "bringing children into the educational mainstream so that they can fully benefit from future schooling and their adult opportunities" (1988; 3).

15. Levin (1988) argued that the major reason for the failure of many disadvantaged children is low teacher expectation, which in turn leads to pull-out programs based on tedious drill-and-practice curricula. Peterson (1989) conducted a study in Utah, concluding that ability grouping is harmful to remedial students, and that participation in accelerated programs is a more effective route to higher achievement.

References

Comer, James 1988. *Maggie's American Dream*. New York: New American Library.
———. 1980. *School Power*. New York: Free Press.
Delpit, L. 1986. "Skills and Other Dilemmas of a Progressive Black Educator." *Harvard Educational Review* 56:379–85.
Dubinsky, E. 1987. "How Piaget's and Related Work Should Influence K–12 Curriculum Design." Unpublished manuscript.
Fordham, S. 1988. "Racelessness as a Factor in Black Students' School Success: Pragmatic Strategy or Pyrrhic Victory?" *Harvard Educational Review* 58:54–84.
Henderson, A. 1987. *The Evidence Continues to Grow: Parent Involvement Improves Student Achievement*. Columbia, Md.: National Committee for Citizens in Education.
Levin, Henry. 1988. "Don't Remediate: Accelerate." In *Proceedings of the Stanford*

University Centennial Conference, Accelerating the Education of At-Risk Students (available from the Center for Educational Research, CERAS Building, 402-South, Stanford University, Stanford, Calif. 94305.)

National Science Foundation. 1989. *Materials for Middle School Mathematics Instruction.* Catalog of Federal Domestic Assistance No. 47.067, Materials Development, Research, and Informal Science Education.

Peterson, J. 1989. "Remediation Is No Remedy." *Educational Leadership* 46(6):24–25.

Quine, W. V. 1981. *Theories and Things.* Cambridge: Harvard University Press.

Saxon, J. H., Jr. 1982. *Algebra I: An Incremental Development.* Norman, Okla.: Saxon Publishers.

Schorr, Lisbeth. 1988. *Within Our Reach: Breaking the Cycle of Disadvantage.* New York: Anchor Press/Doubleday.

Usiskin, Z. 1987. "Why Elementary Algebra Can, Should, and Must Be an Eighth-Grade Course for Average Students." *Mathematics Teacher* 80:428–37.

27
Worker Participation in Technological Change: Interests, Influence, and Scope

Robert Howard and Leslie Schneider

The concerns of this paper lie at the intersection of two highly visible trends in working life. The first is the technological transformation of work associated with the spread of computer-based systems throughout industry. The second is the proliferation of new organizational mechanisms for employee participation, designed to expand the scope of worker involvement in a variety of issues affecting the organization and performance of work.

During the past decade the idea of worker participation has attracted both increased attention and a multiplicity of meanings. In the early 1970s participation was championed as a way to counter what was

From *Worker Participation and the Politics of Reform,* ed. Carmen Sirianni (Philadelphia: Temple University Press, 1987), pp. 67–94.

perceived as a wave of increasing worker dissatisfaction in industrial societies and to improve the overall "quality of work life." By the end of the 1970s, as industrial economies faced growing international competition and declining productivity, participation became a means to improve productivity and product quality along the lines of the "quality circles" first popularized in Japan (Hayashi, 1983). More recently, some observers have begun to redefine participation once again—as a response to the unique demands of the computerized workplace and a useful (indeed, necessary) mechanism for effectively managing rapid workplace technological change (Walton and Vittori, 1983).

Thus, what began as a concept to improve the quality of work life and increase equity in the workplace has evolved into a technique to fulfill crucial business interests for efficiency—in particular, the effective exploitation of new workplace technology. A common assumption in much of the recent literature on worker participation in technological change is that participation offers managers and workers the best of both worlds: both a more equitable and a more efficient work environment.

The perspective of this paper is somewhat different. Although increased worker participation in technological change certainly has the potential to improve both job quality and efficiency, the precise path to these goals is rarely as simple or straightforward as some proponents of participation tend to suggest. Worker participation, like any innovation process, has its costs; the interests and goals that various social groups bring to the workplace can, and often do, conflict. Participation that is not only successful for the work organization but also meaningful for participants themselves may have to allow both for the possibility (indeed, the likelihood) of such conflicts and for the representation of conflicting interests in the participation process (Ciborra, 1985).

Put another way, worker participation in technological change may need to extend beyond the business interests of the individual firm to the myriad social interests at play in any technological change process: issues concerning technology and employment, technology and the organization of work, technology and the sexual division of labor—in short, the overall distribution of technology's social costs and benefits in the workplace and in society as a whole.

This paper describes a spectrum of approaches to managing workplace technological change and their implications for worker participation: The "technocentric" model conceives technological change as primarily a technical issue; participation is generally avoided as a potentially disruptive element. The "organization-centered" model conceives technological change, first and foremost, as an organizational issue; it sees participation as an effective mechanism for furthering business interests of increased efficiency and improved organizational effectiveness. Finally, the "negotiation" model conceives technological change as a social issue; and participation is the process by which the various social groups of the workplace negotiate tradeoffs, reconcile social interests and business goals, and equitably distribute the costs and benefits of technology in the work organization.

In the course of this discussion we shall also examine a few experiments at worker participation in technological change from the United States and Europe. Finally, we shall explore some of the most common obstacles to such participation and suggest a few ideas for overcoming them.

The Legacy of Traditional Industrial Organization: The Technocentric Model

British scientist Arnold Pacey (1983:4) has emphasized the importance of understanding technology "Not only as comprising machines, techniques, and crisply precise knowledge, but also as involving characteristic patterns of organization and imprecise values." What we think of as technological change is, in fact, a complex social process. And its impacts are the outcome of specific social choices and values.

Obviously, the capabilities of technology itself set the limits of the technically possible in any particular case. Within those limits, however, business firms can pursue a variety of organizational options that reflect everything from the markets in which they operate and the firms with which they compete to the prevailing ideas, traditions, and models of industrial organization that shape how business managers conceive of their responsibilities and their tasks.

The most important managerial model shaping the early stages of the computerization of work we call, following Peter Keen (1982), the "technocentric" approach. According to this model, the exploitation of new computer technology in the workplace is conceived primarily as a technical issue. The goal of workplace technological change is to increase efficiency by mechanizing production and reducing labor costs. And the design and implementation of new technical systems is the special responsibility of technical specialists, experts in "systems design" and often grouped in special electronic data processing (EDP) or information resources management (IRM) departments (Mathaissen, 1981; Lanzara, 1983).

This description is something of a caricature, but anyone with experience in contemporary work organizations will recognize it, for the roots of the technocentric approach run deep in the traditions of scientific management, the dominant form of work organization in industrial societies throughout much of the twentieth century. Scientific management defines a set of principles for managing mass production industrial work: the functional separation of execution and design; the systematic standardization, fragmentation, and mechanization of work tasks; and the imperative of increased managerial control. The principles of scientific management, particularly as embodied in the discipline of industrial engineering, provided a handy model for the first attempts at the computerization of work (Strassmann, 1985).

The technocentric approach also closely corresponded to the early limitations of computer technology. As long as computer systems were relatively complicated to use and difficult to apply to work tasks, computerization reinforced the dominance of technical personnel. The technical problems associated with getting the system in and functioning smoothly became the predominant concern of most managers, not only the engineers who designed the new workplace computer systems but the line managers who had to use them.

Implicit to the technocentric approach is the traditional concept of the industrial work organization as a kind of military hierarchy with clear-cut lines of authority and a top-down decision-making structure. For this reason, the idea of worker participation in technological change is the antithesis of sound management, something to be avoided rather than encouraged. Participation threatens to dilute lines of authority and disrupt managerial control. To the degree that workers and their points of view are taken into account at all, it is usually as a problem of human engineering—how to minimize human intervention in new systems and thus avoid human error.

Recently, there has been extensive business literature criticizing this technocentric model. Nevertheless, the overly technical approach to workplace technological change is anything but a relic of our industrial past. Substantial recent literature has amply demonstrated the remarkable persistence of technocentric managerial attitudes about computer technology in American industry—even in the face of substantial costs to social equity and organizational efficiency alike (Noble, 1984; Shaiken, 1984; Howard, 1985b). Nor are such attitudes found solely among technical personnel. Line managers and workers themselves often share many of the assumptions of the technocentric approach. These assumptions constitute a kind of unrecognized and unexamined professional common sense about how to use computer technology in the workplace today.

Participation in the Service of Business Interests:
The Organization-Centered Model

The recent managerial critique of the technocentric model is founded on a practical management problem: the tendency of early uses of computer technology in the workplace to create what Richard Walton and Wendy Vittori (1983) have called "unrealized gains" and "unanticipated costs." As computerization has spread to new industries and tasks (in particular, those of the rapidly expanding service sector), as computer technology itself has decreased in price and increased in versatility, managers have found that the assumptions of the technocentric model, far from ensuring the effective use of new technology, have become an obstacle to the successful implementation of the new technology itself.

For example, Paul Strassmann (1985:163) of the Xerox Corporation has recently estimated that, in the banking and insurance industry, where major investment in computerization has taken place, computerization has had "no discernible effect on labor productivity." Managers like Strassmann have located the source of this failure in the tendency of managers schooled in the technocentric approach to systematically underestimate the organizational dimensions of workplace technological change. This had led to a series of managerial misconceptions about work and technology that constitute a serious barrier to the efficient exploitation of workplace computer systems.

The words of one prominent management consultant capture the flavor of this, by now, quite common point of view: "The systems development Fiasco Hall of Fame," he writes, "is packed with examples of costly mistakes, costly in terms of disruption and morale, not just money, caused by the tenacious ignorance regarding users and their world. . . . The technocentric tradition has largely led to a naive view of the user, simplistic concepts of work, overmechanized and inflexible models of organizational and social processes, and, above all, a definition of 'productivity' in terms of the ethos of efficiency" (Keen, 1982).

Like the more general interest in employee participation during the past decade, the simplest versions of this critique of the technocentric approach have emphasized its human resources and labor relations costs—in particular, how ignoring the user can spark employee resistance to workplace technological change.

A more complex version emphasizes how industrial concepts of efficiency misunderstand both the nature of information work and the unique demands placed on workers by computer technology. On the one hand, much of the work done in offices is informal and unstructured, not amenable to conventional strategies of mechanization and standardization. Thus, the technocentric approach can end up creating rigid computer systems that violate the very logic of the work to be automated (Strassmann, 1985).

On the other hand, work with the new technology makes qualitatively new demands on workers. Work becomes more conceptual and abstract. Responsibilities are expanded and broadened. Workers become more interdependent, their individual tasks connected in a seamless web of integrated information systems (Zuboff, 1982; Adler, 1983; Hirschhorn, 1984). In such a work environment the fragmentation of work common to the technocentric approach tends to ensure that workers do not develop the requisite attitudes and skills for the effective use of the new technology.

Finally, some observers have argued that the transformation of world markets and the ongoing restructuring of the global economy have rendered increasingly obsolete the traditional model of efficiency on which the technocentric approach is based (Sabel, 1982; Piore and Sabel, 1984). In the new circumstances of the world economy market success is founded, not on mass production, but on "flexible specialization." And successful work organizations are those that dismantle rigid hierarchies and build flexible organizations based on a broad distribution of skill, decentralization of decision making, and increased worker initiative. In other words, sustained worker participation in work—including both the tasks at hand and the development of organization structures that are consistent with the demands of the new technology—becomes a key to efficiency in today's corporation.

For example, Japanese business school professor Masaki Hayashi (1983) has argued that Japanese quality circles, far from reflecting some intangible cultural predisposition toward collective decision making and consensus, are best understood as a managerial technique allowing Japanese manufacturers to meet the special challenges posed by work in a highly automated, computerized environment. The development of highly integrated computer-aided manufacturing systems, writes Hayashi, "has increased the necessity for cooperation between workers both in the plant and in the office as well as between engineers and management at their place of work and between the various departments of the firm." (1983:2). The idea of worker participation, embodied in quality circles and other forms of "small group activity" in the Japanese workplace, "has been introduced to cope with the demands coming from the [automation] of the production process." (1983:13).

All these arguments have contributed to the development of an emerging alternative model of technology management. Since it emphasizes the organizational dimensions of technological change, it can be called the "organization-centered" approach. If the model of industrial organization implicit in the technocentric approach is the military, the model of the information organization is, in Peter Drucker's apt metaphor, the orchestra, where each player has a different part to play, but where everyone plays the same score.

According to this perspective, technological change is one part of a much broader organizational change process. Its ultimate goal is not so much discrete gains in individual efficiency as the improvement of overall organizational effectiveness (Strassmann, 1985). And the role of the technology manager is not that of the technical specialist but of a "change agent" who knows how to address the complex organizational issues that new technology implementation can create and on which the successful use of the new technology depends (Keen, 1982).

Because the users of technology play such a central role in the organization-centered approach, both as a source of expertise and information about the work organization and as the ultimate arbiters of how best to use technology in order to better perform their jobs, participation is a key element of this approach to managing workplace technological change. Participation is the technique by which the effective use of the new technology is assured. At the same time it is a means to guarantee worker satisfaction and commitment to the technological change process itself. For this reason, user participation has become a standard element in vendor implementations.

One can think of the value of user participation in terms of three stages of the technology development process.[1] At the stage of design the people who actually do the work to be automated and who will operate the new technology once it is developed are a crucial source of information for systems designers. Without the involvement of these users, as informants or "local experts" during the design stage, designers run the risk of creating systems that do not accurately reflect the work tasks and work organization to be automated—what one designer has called "automating a fiction" (Suchman and Wynn, 1979; Suchman, 1980; Sheil, 1983).

Once a system is ready for implementation, user participation becomes especially important. If the views of users are not taken into account in the implementation process, technology managers run the risk of generating worker opposition to the new system and new work practices—what is known, in the parlance of the profession, as "resistance." Resistance can lead to the consistent underutilization of new technology or, worse, its outright rejection by users.

Finally, the absence of user involvement can have long-standing impacts even after systems are implemented. Effective use of new technology is intimately related to the quantity and quality of the training workers receive—a fact that the technocentric approach tends to overlook (Kelley, 1984; Schneider, 1984). Often, the best judges of how much and what kind of training workers need are the workers themselves. User participation can prove to be an effective way to organize worker training for new systems to ensure that users have the requisite skills for operating new technical systems.

One rather advanced model of user participation is a methodology, developed by Enid Mumford in conjunction with the Digital Equipment Corporation, known as ETHICS ("Effective Technical and Human Implementation of Computer-based Systems") (Bancroft, 1982; Bancroft et al., n.d.). From the moment an office or department is slated for automation, a "design group" consisting of workers from a broad cross-section of occupational categories is established. Advised by technical experts and in regular contact with a management steering committee that sets the boundaries of the design group's work, the members analyze their own workplace, propose alternative ways of organizing work tasks, and help select the technology best suited to the redesigned work organization.

The idea behind the ETHICS methodology is to include as many different perspectives as possible in the work redesign process. One

ETHICS report (Bancroft et al., n.d.:4) even encourages companies to include a few "good 'devil's advocates' " in the design group in order to stimulate the consideration of alternative organizational plans. In this way, user participation is designed both to meet the efficiency goals of the organization and to win worker support for technological change. As the Digital report on ETHICS puts it, "Groups which are passive recipients of major innovation may be afraid and resistant; whereas those who are involved will learn how to cope, exert control and mold the change to fit their own needs, and the needs of their departments and companies." Participation in technology design and implementation, the report continues, allows employees to "mold their own futures" and to "acquire confidence in their ability to contribute to the management of their own change" (Bancroft et al., n.d.: 11).

The Limitations of the Organization-Centered Model

The concept of participation common to the organization-centered model seems to rest on a number of assumptions: That workers and managers share a community of interests about the means and the ends of workplace technological change, and that participation in the service of business interests will also lead to better work quality and improved worker satisfaction. At times these assumptions take on the quality of "necessary conditions" without which participation becomes, at best, problematic and, at worst, impossible.

However, what happens when the interests of various social groups in the workplace conflict? When the claims of equity and of efficiency, instead of reinforcing each other, prove contradictory? Because the concept of participation implicit in the organization-centered approach to workplace technological change is founded on the idea of consensus, such conflicts tend to threaten the very idea of participation itself.

The possibility of such conflicts generally means that, in the organization-centered approach, managers are constantly trying to control participation in order to make sure that it stays within predetermined limits. Thus, while Walton and Vittori (1983:15) call for an organizational approach to technological change and for active user participation in the change process, they make clear that "the particular criteria and [organizational] preferences" on which participation is based "will depend upon management's philosophy and values, the nature of the business and past experience," in short, business concerns alone.

The recent history of user participation by technology vendors reflects this same management-oriented conception of participation. Eleanor Wynn (1983) has described how most technology vendors conceive of user participation in a highly superficial way—more as a matter of marketing (how to "sell" new systems to potential customers) than as a mechanism for fundamental organizational transformation. According to Wynn, what passes for user participation at many technology vendors does not involve the ultimate users of the technology at all. Rather, it is a term to describe vendors' efforts to communicate with and otherwise involve the line managers who manage the implementation of new systems.

Even relatively advanced forms of user participation, such as ETH-ICS, provide participants with little opportunity to actually influence the management decision-making process concerning technological change. Users are conceived exclusively as the performers of certain functions in the work organization, but not as bearers of social interests. And a management steering committee sets the parameters for the design group's activities and investigations. Crucial decisions about personnel requirements, layoffs, and other issues are often made beforehand, without worker influence or line-manager input.

Moreover, the organization-centered approach to participation tends to underestimate the considerable difficulties involved in moving an organization from one work system to another. The assumptions and attitudes of the technocentric model are deeply ingrained throughout most work organizations; these attitudes do not simply disappear when a change in policy is made at the top. It is one thing to create a participative, high-commitment work organization in a brand-new company in a brand-new industry (e.g., Silicon Valley). It is quite another to imagine radically changing an already existing work organization and a corporate culture that is based upon some version of scientific management.

Finally, the organization-centered model seems to imply that, to the degree that there are labor relations problems or conflicts of interest between stakeholders, they can be—and should be—resolved at the level of the individual firm. But this is not always possible and, again, the technology issue provides the best example. The impacts of technology are often of a scope extending far beyond the corporation itself. Companies buy ready-made technology from vendors; what are the mechanisms for its managers or workers to influence how those vendors design systems? And what about those workers who end up losing their jobs because of technological change? What are the mechanisms for addressing that impact? In short, this approach ignores the fact that addressing the social impacts of technology may require social regulation that transcends the individual work organization.

Such built-in limitations to the scope and content of worker participation in technological change may be relatively easy to ignore in a workplace where the degree of worker organization is weak. However, where workers are formally represented by a trade union, it is more difficult to contain participation within management-defined limits. In addition to the business interests and goals of management, unions bring their own collective and social interests and goals to the workplace. As independent user representatives, unions provide a mechanism where the very criteria of worker participation in technological change themselves become subject to participation and negotiation.

In recent years there have been a number of attempts at worker participation in technological change involving unionized workforces in the United States. Often, they have taken place in industries facing new competitive pressures, whether as a result of increased international competition, as in the case of the auto industry, or of the deregulation of quasi-monopoly markets, such as the airlines and telecommunications industries.

A common theme in many of these cases is the potential conflict between management and union over the scope of participatory programs. These conflicts suggest the limitations of participation conceived purely in terms of business interests. To the degree that the two parties have been able to define mutually acceptable goals, participation often works. But when both management and workers understand participation solely in terms of cooperation, they are generally ill-prepared to deal with the conflicts of power and interest that changes in technology inevitably stimulate.

Thus, on issues where goals or interests conflict, participation breaks down quickly and each side reverts back to traditional managerial principles. Though the new participatory mechanisms are certainly a necessary step for designing effective workplace systems, they are not sufficient for addressing the unequal distribution of the social costs of technology. And, often, they become an excuse to do nothing.

Perhaps the most revealing American example is that of the joint labor-management programs of AT&T, the Bell operating companies, and the three major unions of the telecommunications industry. Few industries have seen more technological change in the past decade than telecommunications, and few corporations have had more experience with viewing technology as an element in a far-ranging organizational change.[2]

Participation in the telecommunications industry was the product of both equity and efficiency concerns. Technological development in the Bell system had traditionally been a classic example of some of the worst features of the technocentric model, where system engineers and technicians from Bell labs set the technical standards and work organizations used throughout the entire Bell system. It had been highly centralized with engineers and systems designers at Bell Laboratories creating the systems used throughout the entire telecommunications network.

With the rapid computerization of telephone work in the 1970s, workers in the industry suffered the spectrum of social costs typically associated with the technocentric approach—including the erosion of job skills and autonomy, increased job pressures, and occupational stress (Howard, 1980, 1985b; Kohl, 1982). In addition to the negative impact of these changes on employee morale, Bell System managers were especially concerned that the workforce and work systems at the Bell operating companies were especially ill-suited to compete in the deregulated telecommunications environment that was rapidly taking shape. In response to these dual concerns of declining employee morale and growing worker protests, on the one hand, and managerial concerns about efficiency, on the other, the 1980 Bell System collective-bargaining negotiations established a network of joint labor-management committees designed to address some of the problems associated with rapid technological and organization change.

One was a National Committee on Joint Working Conditions and Service Quality Improvement, consisting of three company representatives and three union representatives. It was mandated to set up a systemwide QWL program consisting of shop-floor QWL committees. Although the letter of agreement establishing the program did not refer specifically to technology, for the unions this was clearly one of the many work-related issues that the Bell system QWL program would address.

The two sides also established joint Technology Change Committees where, according to the language of the formal letter of agreement, the unions could "discuss major technological changes with management before they are introduced" (AT&T-CWA, 1980). Unlike the shop-floor QWL committees, they exist on a much higher level of authority. Each AT&T division and Bell operating company has its own committee, usually consisting of three upper-level corporate managers and three full-time district union officials. As part of this provision, the corporation also agreed to provide the union with six months' advance notice of all major technological changes.[3]

Five years after the establishment of these joint labor-management participation programs, it seems clear that the Bell system QWL committees have been an important vehicle for building workers' informal participatory practice at the local level. According to a recent study sponsored by the U.S. Department of Labor (Communications Workers of America et al., 1984:1), the Bell system QWL effort is "one of the largest worker participation programs in the country." At the time of the Bell system divestiture in January 1984, there were more than 1,200 shop-floor QWL committees in operation throughout AT&T, involving nearly 15,000 unionized employees. And these QWL team members reported levels of job satisfaction 12 percent higher than those of the Bell system as a whole.

Though most of the committees have dealt primarily with environmental issues (improving the physical office environment, ameliorating local management practices and attitudes) in a few cases, they have gone further to touch upon issues of work organization and job redesign—for example, instituting flexitime programs or reorganizing office scheduling procedures in order to give workers some choice over their work hours. However, as the committees have moved closer to addressing issues that transcend the immediate workplace and involve company-wide policies about technology development, they have encountered some major obstacles. The choices and decisions about technology made by these technical personnel are largely beyond the capacity of local QWL groups to address (Howard, 1985b).

A case in point is what, for a time, was perhaps the most dramatic QWL success story, AT&T's new Hotel Office Business Information System (HOBIS) office in Tempe, Arizona. Under the guidance of a manager sympathetic to the QWL concept, the office was planned in close cooperation with a QWL team. The committee developed a new work organization consisting of autonomous work groups in which some 120 office workers scheduled and performed their jobs without any first-line supervision. The savings resulting from the group's reorganization plan (estimated at $250,000 in supervisors' salaries alone) were put aside in a discretionary fund controlled by the committee and used to finance workers' participation in company training programs.

However, in November 1985 executives at AT&T corporate headquarters decided for economic reasons to consolidate the Tempe facility with another HOBIS office in a different location. Despite the opposition of the local QWL committee and the Communications Workers of America (CWA) international, the Tempe office was closed and its promising experiment in worker autonomy cancelled. While some of the innovations developed in the Tempe HOBIS facility have been used in other AT&T offices, none has recreated the same degree of worker autonomy enjoyed by the Tempe workforce.

In theory, the Technology Change Committees, also established in the 1980 contract, are supposed to be the forum where these broader policy issues about technology can be addressed. Also, the six months' advance-notice provision, at least potentially, provides a way for workers' union representatives to be involved in company planning before systems reach the workplace. However, of the three joint committees established in 1980, the Technology Change Committees have been the least successful.

The formal union rights defined by the Technology Change Committees provision are extremely limited. The committees are primarily a vehicle for "notification" in which "the Company will advise the union of its plans with respect to the introduction of [technological] changes and will familiarize the union with the progress being made" (AT&T-CWA, 1980). The unions do not have the right to participate in the actual conception, design, or testing of new technical systems. Nor do the committees have any authority to make policy decisions or binding agreements about the technology development process. At best, the committees can only develop "facts and recommendations so that the company can make well-informed decisions regarding technological change" (AT&T-CWA, 1980).

The practice of the Technology Change Committees has reflected this narrow conception of participation. A Harvard Business School study[4] conducted in 1983 found that, in the first three years of the program, nearly two-thirds of the committees had yet to have a single meeting. Where they had, the management participants called the meetings, set the agenda, decided what issues would be discussed, and determined how much information about management plans would be provided to their union counterparts. In a survey of Technology Change Committee members, conducted as part of the Harvard study, over half of the union representatives who responded reported that management regularly failed to provide them with the mandatory six months' advance notice of major technological changes—a clear violation of the 1980 contract.

At times management involvement in the committees seems expressly designed to insulate management decision making about technology from effective influence on the part of the telecommunications unions. For example, the typical management representatives on the committees are labor relations personnel; their background and experience is in dealing with unions, not managing technological change. (In one case, management participants prepared their formal presentations beforehand with company lawyers, in order to avoid providing union officials with information that might prove useful in collective bargaining.) The engineers, systems designers, and other technical personnel who are responsible for determining how technology will be designed and used are rarely committee members. And those labor relations personnel who are on the committees often do not have basic information about new technical systems and their expected impacts—putting them in a position of ignorance not all that different from that of their union counterparts. (One point on which both management and union respondents to the Harvard Business School survey agree is that the prime obstacle to the effectiveness of the Technology Change Committees is their "lack of timely knowledge about the types of systems to be developed.") To the degree that line managers or engineers themselves try to make the innovation process more responsive to social concerns, they do so, not through the Technology Change Committee but independent of it. This means that the official participative structure is bypassed.

As for the idea that, through the committees, unionists might actually influence company planning and development of new technology, a full 75 percent of union participants said the discussion in their committee had never resulted in changes in the implementation of new technical systems or in their design.

Part of the problem is with the union representatives themselves. In general, they are full-time district officials who are usually quite removed from the new technological systems and their impacts on the shop floor. And their work on the committee is just one small part of their overall responsibilities. In general, the unions have barely begun to think through what it would take to make concrete their hopes for a substantial role in the development of new technology. They have not committed the necessary resources—in terms of personnel, training, time, or money—in order to effectively influence the technological change process.

Thus, despite considerable progress in developing informal practice through the shop-floor QWL committees, the lack of formal rights of participation in company decision making about technology has limited the impact of the telecommunications worker participation effort. A 1984 report from the CWA Development and Research Department (Straw and Hecksher, 1984) captured this ambiguous result: "Though the QWL process has led to improved relations and less burdensome supervision in many offices, it has not reached to the fundamental policies which shape the development of new technologies. It seems that for every improvement in individual locations, a dozen systems come from Bell Laboratories reinforcing the dehumanizing patterns we are battling." And the effectiveness of the Technology Change Committees, the report continued, "has been limited by the resistance of management . . . and by the lack of experience of union participants. As a result, membership attitude surveys over the past three years have shown, if anything, increasing levels of discontent with job pressures."

Participation in the Service of Social Interests

There is another concept of participation that transcends some of the limitations of the organization-centered approach. It is based on the premise that participation should include the possibility (indeed, the likelihood) of conflicting interests in the workplace. Such an approach might be termed the "negotiation" model.

According to this perspective, instead of depending on shared interests, participation would be the process by which interest groups balance their various concerns about efficiency and equity and negotiate trade-offs between those concerns when they differ. In economic terms, participation becomes a mechanism for "internalizing" the social costs of technological change and bargaining their distribution in a particular work organization (Ciborra, 1983a, 1983b).

In order for this to happen, however, participation must also include sharing power or influence. As Pacey (1983: 157) writes, "to engage in a genuinely open dialogue is inevitably to share power over the final decision." Such influence can take two basic forms: "formal rights" giving workers an explicit role to play in company decision making concerning new technology; and "informal practice" or the constantly evolving activities, knowledge, and expertise that workers can bring to bear on company technology policies in the workplace itself.

The relationship between these two forms of influence is especially important. Without formal rights, informal participatory practice, however elaborate, runs the risk of becoming unstable, particularly when workers' interests do conflict with those of technology designers or management. However, in the absence of active (and informed) informal practice, even the most explicit formal rights usually remain unrealized. It is precisely the interplay of strong formal rights and robust informal practice that makes for effective worker participation.

Finally, a concept of participation as negotiation would also expand the scope of worker participation in technological change. A broad participatory scope would, first, extend worker influence beyond merely discussing the impacts of technology (such as takes place in the U.S. telecommunications industry Technology Change Committees) to the very choices that shape how technology is developed and designed. In other words, it would involve a concept and method of "participatory systems design" (Nygaard, 1983). Second, it would extend worker influence beyond both technical and organizational issues to include the social goals of the entire work organization.

The negotiation model of worker participation in technological change is far more common in Europe than in the United States. Participatory experiments in European countries often have an explicit social component, and efforts in specific workplaces occur within a broad social context of formal collective-bargaining agreements and national work environment legislation. Often, this serves to create a social framework that influences the form and the content of worker participation at particular firms.

Perhaps the most advanced version of the negotiation model can be found in the Scandinavian countries, particularly Norway. For more than twenty years there has been a strong tradition of worker participation in Norway. In the early 1960s the Norwegian Industrial Democracy project spread joint labor-management participation experiments throughout industrial enterprises. Many of these early efforts at participation were similar in form to current American QWL initiatives (in fact, some of the recent U.S. initiatives are modeled on these early Scandinavian experiences).

However, in the late 1960s Norwegian unions began to grow dissatisfied with the limits of these joint labor-management projects, particularly in the area of workplace technological change. They found that technology often was the source of conflicts of interest between labor and management that made cooperation nearly impossible. Thus, unions began to search for ways to develop their own independent strategy to address workplace technology issues.

An important contribution to this goal was a unique social dialogue between the unions and a small but influential group of Norwegian computer scientists and systems designers. Often working at government research centers, these technical experts were sympathetic to the unions' goals and joined with them in a series of action research projects aimed to build local union expertise on technology issues. These projects stimulated union activism and eventually led to the negotiations of the first labor-management collective-bargaining agreements on technological change, known as the Technology Agreements, in the mid-1970s.

The first national Framework Agreement was negotiated and signed by the Norwegian Employers Confederation (NAF) and the Trades Union Congress (LO) in 1975. Since then, similar agreements have also been negotiated in the public sector. And some of the provisions of the

Technology Agreements have also been written into law in Norway's 1977 Work Environment Act (Hjort, 1983; Schneider, 1984).

Unlike initiatives in this country to encourage worker participation on technology issues, the Norwegian Technology Agreements establish a comprehensive array of formal worker and union rights. Unions not only have the right of access to company information about new technical systems, they also can participate in company decision making about technology and bargain over company plans. In other words, negotiation about technology has become a legitimate part of the collective-bargaining relationship between managements and unions.

Local unions can negotiate local technology agreements that elaborate on and occasionally expand the rights defined in the national agreements. They also have the right to elect a permanent local union representative responsible for technology issues—known as the "data shop steward"—and to hire outside "technology consultants" (at company expense) to help them research the impacts of technology and prepare their collective-bargaining demands (Nygaard and Fjalestad, 1979; Keul, 1983; Schneider, 1984).

But the Technology Agreements have not only articulated new worker rights. They have been designed to expressly encourage the development of informal participatory practice so that workers and their union representatives can successfully put these new rights into effect (Elden, 1981; Finne and Rasmussen, 1982). For example, according to the agreements, workers are guaranteed both job-related training on specific technical systems and general education about computer technology and its design. And, under the provisions of the Work Environment Act, some 150,000 Norwegian workers (nearly 10 percent of the entire workforce) have completed, on company time, a forty-hour basic training course in techniques for analyzing and improving their workplace (Gustavsen and Hunnius, 1981).

In the immediate aftermath of the Technology Agreements, there was a tendency on the part of many unions to assume that the very existence of their new rights was sufficient to increase worker influence over technological change. Union locals would pursue what might be termed an after-the-fact strategy. They would wait for new technical systems to be introduced in the workplace, then bargain with management over the details of work assignments, wage rates, and the like, much as they had in the past.

However, some unions soon realized that if they waited until new technology was appearing on the shop floor, it was already too late. They began to formulate a before-the-fact approach that extends union and worker participation into the planning stages of technology development and also into broader questions about the organization of work.

These two factors—an emphasis on both general formal rights and local informal practice, and the conviction that union involvement must take place before the fact and extend to broad issues of work organization—have allowed Norwegian workers to move beyond narrow function-based participation (such as management-directed participation programs that conceive users as performers of functions) and to experiment with participation based on social interests. It has also made possible the extension of worker participation from narrow technical issues and goals (which vendor to choose, how best to configure a specific system, and so forth) to the organizational and social criteria and choices that shape technology in the first place.

To grasp the extremely broad extent of participation in Norwegian industry, consider the example of the Norwegian post office.[5] In the late 1970s the Norwegian postal authorities inaugurated a large development project to automate the accounting functions in about 450 local post offices across the country. As is typical throughout Norwegian industry, the postal workers union negotiated representation on the formal project steering committee to oversee the development of this new system. Two experienced union members participated in three project subgroups— one developing system specifications, one analyzing training and work environment issues, and a third devoted to ergonomics.

The presence of these union workers on the steering committee proved very important in the early stages of the project, but not in the way that the union had hoped. The workers found that their role was primarily that of "end user informants" rather than as representatives of the union's interests. In other words, the technical team wanted their advice on various technical aspects of the system. This role was not unimportant. The workers' knowledge about work processes and organizational problems helped the systems designers to develop reasonably accurate specifications for the counter transactions to be automated. However, the unionists involved found that they were becoming preoccupied with planning the technical details of the new system—what they called becoming "hostage" to the technology—rather than examining what the impacts of the new system might be and whether they were desirable or not.

Convinced that it needed to broaden the scope of worker participation and union involvement in the project, the union requested that management commission a study of the work environment consequences of the new technology. An outside consultant from the Norwegian Computing Center, a public research institute, assembled two informal worker research teams consisting of sixteen postal employees drawn from a variety of occupational categories and from post offices all over the country.[6] These teams set out, not merely to analyze the prospective impacts of the new system, but to actually develop a set of social, organizational, and technical criteria which would guide the development of the system itself.

Instead of starting with the proposed system specifications already developed by the design team, the worker participation groups began by analyzing their own work organization. From this analysis, they developed criteria for the kind of work organization most desirable from a social point of view. Then they evaluated the systems specifications developed by the design team against these criteria, suggesting numerous changes.

For example, the specifications had originally foreseen the establishment of data-entry centers where data would be read into the new automated system. To avoid the creation of what they considered to be narrow and monotonous data-entry jobs, the groups recommended that optical character readers be installed in each local office.

The original specifications had also called for worker access to information by means of video display terminals (VDTs) placed to the side of each post office window. However, because the space at each window was so limited and because they worried that VDT operation could potentially disrupt contact with customers and become an obstacle to quality service, the groups recommended that the VDTs be replaced with a small movable "text window" adequate for the information that workers would need.

It should be emphasized that worker research teams had no formal status in the technology design process. However, they came to have a great deal of influence. Although the changes they recommended were controversial and, at times, expensive, they were able to influence major aspects of the system specifications. One reason is that they had union support. There were strong ties between the formal union representatives on the design team and the union members involved in the informal worker research effort. Another reason is that, in the course of their fifteen-month research effort, they made themselves into the resident experts on the relationship between technology and work organization at the post office. This new expertise was something to which the design team and management had to respond.

The effort at the Norwegian post office concerned the development of a specific technical system. Other Norwegian unions have tried to institutionalize broad participation across the spectrum of workplace technology issues. In the process, they have systematically included union social goals as one criterion in the technological change process.

An appropriate example is the work of the Norwegian Bank Employees Union (NBF).[7] One important aspect that has shaped this situation is that women make up approximately half of the union's 26,000 members. They hold the lowest-level jobs (usually those to be automated first), and nearly 70 percent work part time. According to a union-sponsored survey, 68 percent of these women have had no formal professional training.

These factors have shaped the union's technology policy. The NBF is especially concerned that, as new technology transforms jobs in the banking industry, requiring new kinds of skills and more formal work knowledge, many of the union's women members will become trapped in a progressively smaller low-wage ghetto and will be passed over for promotion to the skilled jobs that technology may create.

Therefore, the union has tried to design its technology policy so that it furthers social goals of equal opportunity in the banking industry. For example, as new technologies reorganize work, access to training becomes a determining factor of opportunity in the workplace. In the Norwegian banking industry, union and management have set aside a minimum of 40 percent of the places in their joint industry training center for women. This is an extremely important step because promotions and salary increases depend upon completing institute courses.

The union has also negotiated special access to training for worker mothers—including five hours per week of education study on company time for all women with children ten years old or younger.

Union technology policy also states that technology should be used not only to rationalize work but also to improve the quality of both workers' jobs and customer service. It sees participation in technology development as only one part of a broad participatory process. Union officials like to talk about the "three legs of the stool"—three areas of participation necessary in any effective work organization: technology development, organizational development, and personnel development. This way, technology does not become isolated from other factors, in particular, the organizational and social needs of the workforce.

The NBF has developed elaborate structures to guarantee its participation in technology development. The union has its own internal technology policy committee, which develops and implements the union action program for new technology (revised and updated every two years); the members of the committee are also the union representatives on the steering committees of major industry technology development projects.

Union representatives also participate actively in the design of new computer-based systems both nationally and locally. For example, in November 1982 Norway's twenty-one savings banks announced a joint project to design and implement a $70 million state-of-the-art computer system in 300 branch banks over a four-year period. Over eighty bank employees from a variety of jobs (expedition clerks, back office clerks, tellers, and others) were involved in developing the preliminary system specifications for the applications software. Ten working groups (each consisting of eight users and one technical specialist) met for three two-day sessions every month for a five-month period. Between meetings, the user participants returned to their workplaces to discuss and evaluate proposed recommendations with their coworkers. Once the recommendations were finalized, someone from the group was chosen to write up the findings as formal system specifications.

When systems designers at the banking industry's research and development center proposed the acquisition of an automated loan-processing system, a union-management team at the largest savings bank chain in eastern Norway evaluated it to determine whether the proposed system was consistent with organizational goals. The team, made up of managers and workers from local branches, suggested a number of changes. For example, whereas the systems designers had planned to build loan criteria directly into the system (this was also true for the loan limits of individual loan officers), the union wanted the individual bank worker to retain the decision-making power to grant or not to grant loans. They also suggested that the dialogue between user and the computer be flexible so that data could be entered in any order rather than in one specific way. The group argued that these recommendations would improve both the quality of workers' jobs and the services provided to customers.

It should be pointed out that, although the NBF counts on the formal rights of union participation as the foundation of this elaborate participatory process, the union realizes that these formal rights are not sufficient. For example, unlike other Norwegian unions, the NBF does not use the data shop steward system, in the belief that setting up worker technical experts can become an obstacle to broad worker participation on technology issues. Thus, the worker representatives in systems design projects are usually normal shop stewards or rank-and-file workers.

The union also emphasizes the importance of developing informal relationships or alliances with bank technical personnel, in an ongoing effort to educate them about the union's social goals for technology. This relationship has developed to the point where some designers at the bank industry's research and development center see union and worker participation as the preferred approach to creating new technical systems.[8]

One should emphasize that this kind of worker participation in technological change is always a balancing act. There is an ongoing effort, not always successful, both to use the formal rights provided by collective-bargaining agreements and legislation and, at the same time, to develop the informal practices which make those rights effective. From this perspective, participation is a kind of learning process, alternating between moments of cooperation and moments of negotiation over conflicting interests and goals. Workers are able to ask questions about changing fundamental aspects of their organizations (Argyris, 1983a; 1983b). What is more, informal cooperation becomes possible precisely because management recognizes the union's formal rights. And, where interests of union and management conflict, the existence of these formal rights can become especially important.[9]

The work of Norwegian unions with the Technology Agreements does not eliminate all obstacles to worker participation in technological change. Nor are the specific mechanisms of participation, part of the unique social, political, and labor relations climate of the Scandinavian countries, easily translated to other contexts. However, the Norwegian experience does constitute an intriguing example of participation as a true negotiating process, one that, far from being limited to discrete projects or experiments, represents a new model for the overall organization of working life.

Barriers to Worker Participation

The extensive worker participation in technological change reflected in Norwegian union work with the Technology Agreements does not take place in a vacuum. Any participatory project faces a number of obstacles or barriers that threaten to constrain either the interests subject to participation, the degree of influence that workers actually have, or the scope of issues open to participation. What follows is a brief list of the most common of these obstacles.

Obviously, firms with a disadvantageous market position can find participation based on social interests especially difficult to maintain. When near-term competitive pressures are overwhelming, the short-term costs that participation can entail become too expensive. Often, worker participation is relegated to the back burner of both managerial and union priorities.

For example, workers at the Norwegian conglomerate Viking Askim (a manufacturer of automobile tires and rubber boots) were among the first in the Norwegian labor movement to develop a local technology agreement, dating back to the late 1960s. However, during the past decade the firm has faced increased international competition, which has forced the closing of some of its Norwegian operations and the shifting of production abroad, primarily to Southeast Asia. Faced with economic crisis and declining jobs, both management and union at Viking Askim have tended to see participation in technological change as a secondary concern, far less important than the more immediate priorities of economic restructuring and saving jobs.

At the same time, other firms see participation as an important means to becoming more responsive to competitive markets. This is certainly the case both at AT&T and the Norwegian banks. In both cases, work organizations that previously enjoyed a quasi-monopoly position are now confronted with new kinds of competition. In both situations technology plays a crucial role in determining ultimate competitiveness. Participation has become a mechanism to improve the organization's ability to adapt to both changing technology and changing markets.

A second potential barrier to broad worker participation in technological change is the state of technology itself. Indeed, one can think of the opportunity for participation throughout the period of development of any particular technology as a kind of bell-shaped curve. Early applications of the technology often take place when both the technology and the uses to which it can be put are poorly understood. Technology experts dominate the situation and narrow technical concerns loom large. Broad participation in such a situation can prove extremely difficult if not impossible. As particular applications of the technology become better understood, however, organizational flexibility and, along with it, the possibility for participation expand. Finally, when the particular application becomes mature, the possibility for participation may decline once again as clearly defined package systems become the sensible option from an economic point of view.

Certainly, the development of computer-based technical systems reflect this trend. In the early phases the technocentric approach predominated. In the second phase, as the technology itself has increased in flexibility, the organization-centered approach and user participation has become more popular. But already-packaged systems are making any but the most superficial function-based participation difficult to put into effect. For example, in Norway, many unions have found that the increasing tendency of companies to rely on system packages (often designed in the United States, where the social concerns of the Norwegian unions are often less successfully articulated) has become an obstacle to their ability to influence how workplace technology is designed.

However, there is another argument that suggests that computer-based systems, unlike previous technologies, presents unique opportunities for participation. As the automation of discrete functions is increasingly replaced by the integration of entire computerized work systems, effective work will increasingly depend upon broad worker knowledge of both technology and the work organization itself. Participation may prove to be the most effective means for ensuring that that knowledge is widespread throughout the firm. In this respect, the evolution of workplace computer technology may actually require more worker participation, not less.

Another potential barrier is not so much technological as organizational—the ingrained practices and habits of thinking and working that influence (and, often, inhibit) what can be described as the organizational learning process. Using new technology effectively seems to require thinking about it in a new way. Instead of seeing technology management as merely a technical process (whether for the techniques of Taylorism or user participation), it conceives the design and development of new workplace technical systems as fundamentally social (or even political)—that is, as central to the realization of the goals and values of the organization as a social institution. From this perspective technology management is simply one facet of a much broader task—the overall organizational development of the firm. And precisely because technology is so important, it cannot be left to managers alone. Rather, it becomes the responsibility of both managers and workers, with company and union as equal partners.

But this still will not ensure that participation will extend to the social interests that various social groups bring to the workplace. One final barrier to the broad worker participation that we have described is the absence of formal institutions to represent worker interests in the workplace. When participation is managed entirely by management, there is a tendency in situations of conflict to revert to narrow business interests or to do away with participation altogether. This tendency to view participation as taking place entirely at the level of the individual firm ensures that participation will almost always remain hostage to the imperatives of efficiency and competitiveness. The idea of negotiating social tradeoffs between equity and efficiency will be weighted to the latter.

Part of the solution is similar to that developed in other areas of working life, such as occupational health and safety: to create a regulatory environment extending beyond the individual firm that, in effect, takes technology out of competition and sets certain standards or criteria for working life across the entire economy. This has been the impact, for example, of the Work Environment Act in Norway. This same mechanism is at work in occupational health and safety, equal opportunity, and minimum-wage legislation in this and other industrial countries.

Of course, this is no simple task, especially when long-term social interests come into conflict with the immediate demands of international competition. However, it may be that this broader conception of worker participation in technological change is one part of a long-term evolution of labor relations in industrial societies. And one step in the creation of new institutions more suitable to an economic world founded on innovation and change.

Notes

1. Of course, these three stages of the technology development process are abstractions. This is not to imply that the process has a discrete beginning, middle, and end. In fact, systems design is an ongoing, iterative process. Once particular systems are in place, they are constantly being updated, maintained, and adapted to new uses. This makes user participation all the more necessary.

2. There are three unions representing workers at AT&T and the Bell operating companies—the Communications Workers of America (CWA), the Telecommunications International Union (TIU), and the International Brotherhood of Electrical Workers (IBEW). In 1980 AT&T established Quality of Worklife (QWL) committees with each of the three unions. The examples used in these pages are drawn from the experience of the CWA and TIU.

3. When more than one union represented workers in a particular AT&T division or Bell operating company, a separate Technology Change Committee was established with each union. The 1980 Bell system collective-bargaining agreement also established a joint Occupational Job Evaluation Committee. The work of this group is not considered here.

4. Dr. Schneider conducted this study in conjunction with Professor Richard E. Walton. The following information is based upon as yet unpublished personal interviews and survey data from that research project.

5. The description of worker participation at the Norwegian post office is based, in large part, on internal reports from the Norwegian Computing Center to the Norwegian Postal Directorate and on personal interviews conducted by the authors.

6. The worker participants were jointly chosen by management and the union. Although involvement in the union was not a formal criterion for selection, most of the participants were in fact union activitists.

7. This example is based on personal interviews conducted by the authors.

8. According to the NBF official responsible for technology issues: "It used to be that there was always a big discussion about precisely when the union should be informed. The question was, 'When does a pre-project actually become a formal project?' Now, our attitude is, 'The moment an idea strikes you, that's the time to call the union and begin discussing it.' "

9. As the NBF official says, "You can cooperate on these issues, because management, by and large, has come to recognize the union as an equal partner. They have also recognized that technology has social costs. They may not consider it as much of a problem as we do, but at least they recognize that, when you implement technology, you have to deal with the social and organizational consequences. When they stop listening, the union can always bang our little green collective bargaining contract and data policy on the table. Usually, that is enough to begin the dialogue again."

References

Adler, Paul. 1983. "Rethinking the Skill Requirements of New Technologies." Working paper HBS 84–27, Harvard Business School, Harvard University.

Argyris, Chris. 1983a. *Reasoning, Learning and Action*. San Francisco: Jossey-Bass.

———. 1983b. *Strategy, Change and Defensive Routines*. Boston: Pitman.

AT&T-CWA. 1980. *National Bargaining Report*. Washington, D.C.: Communications Workers of America.

Bancroft, Nancy H. 1982. "Productivity in the Office." Prepared for the Manufacturing Distribution and Control Business Group, Digital Equipment Corporation. Westminster, Mass.: Office Systems Consulting.

Bancroft, Nancy H., Enid Mumford, and Bonnie Sontag. N.d. "Participative Design— Successes and Problems." Unpublished paper, Digital Equipment Corporation.

Bermann, Tamar. 1984. "Not Only Windmills: Female Service Workers and New Technologies." Published in the proceedings from the IFIP (International Federation for Information Processing, Work Group 9.1) Conference on "Women, Work and Computerization" held at Riva del Sole, Italy, 17–21 September 1984.

Brooks, Harvey et al. 1984. *Technology and the Need for New Labor Relations*. Discussion Paper 129D, John Fitzgerald Kennedy School of Government, Harvard University.

Ciborra, Claudio. 1983a. "The Social Costs of Information Technology and Participation in System Design." In U. Briefs, Claudio Ciborra, and Leslie Schneider, eds., *Systems Design for, with, and by the User*, 41–50. Amsterdam, New York, Oxford: North Holland.

———. 1983b. "Bargaining Over the Social Costs of Information Technology." In Daniel Marschall and Judith Gregory, eds., *Office Automation: Jekyll or Hyde?*, 22–29. Cleveland, Ohio: Working Women Education Fund.

———. 1985. "Reframing the Role of Computers in Organization: The Transaction Costs Approach." In Lynn Gallegos et al., eds., *Proceedings of the Sixth International Conference on Information Systems*, 57–69. Indianapolis: Society for Information Management and Association for Computing Machinery.

Communications Workers of America. 1984. "The Quality of Work Life Process of AT&T and the Communications Workers of America: A Research Study After Three Years." Condensed version of report on the Quality of Work Life research project submitted to U.S. Department of Labor. Washington, D.C.: Communication Workers of America.

Elden, Max. 1981. "Varieties of Workplace Participatory Research." Unpublished paper, Center for Effective Organizations, Graduate School of Business Administration, University of Southern California, Los Angeles.

Fellesdata, A. S. 1983. "Sammendrag Av Bankrettet Kravspesifikasjon for Ny Terminal." Unpublished paper. Prepared for the Bankrettet gruppe i NTG.

Finne, Hakon, and Bente Rasmussen. 1982. *Strategic Competence and Learning from Experience: A Course Model for Improving Local Trade Union Action*. Norway: Institute for Social Research in Industry (IFIM).

Fjalestad, Jostein. 1980. "Teknologi og Deltaking." Prepared for Norsk Regnesentral/ Norwegian Computing Center, Oslo, Norway.

Fossum, E., ed. 1983. *Computerization of Working Life.* New York, Brisbane, Chichester, Toronto: Halsted Press (division of John Wiley & Son).

Gustavsen, Bjorn, and Gerry Hunnius. 1981. *New Patterns of Work Reform: The Case of Norway.* Oslo, Bergen, Tromso: Universitetsforlaget.

Hayashi, Masaki. 1983. "The Japanese Style of Small Group QC–Circle Activity." Tokyo: The Institute of Business Research, Chuo University.

Hirschhorn, Larry. 1984. *Beyond Mechanization: Work and Technology in a Postindustrial Age.* Cambridge, Mass. and London, England: The MIT Press.

Hjort, Lisbet. 1983. "Labor Legislation in Norway: Its Applications to the Introduction of New Technology." In Daniel Marschall and Judith Gregory, eds., *Office Automation: Jekyll or Hyde?*, 143–49. Cleveland, Ohio: Working Women Education Fund.

Howard, Robert. 1980. "Brave New Workplace." *Working Papers for a New Society* 7(6):21–31.

———. 1985a. "Utopia: Where Workers Craft New Technology." *Technology Review* 88(3):43–49.

———. 1985b. *Brave New Workplace.* New York: Elisabeth Sifton Books, Viking Press.

Keen, Peter G. W. 1982. Editor's preface. *Office: Technology and People* 1(1):1-11.

Kelley, Maryellen R. 1984. "Computer-oriented Machines and the Disruption of Workplace Productivity: Establishing a New Labor-Management Relationship." In *Technology and the Need for New Labor Relations,* discussion paper 129D, John F. Kennedy School of Government, Harvard University.

Keul, Vidar. 1983. "Trade Union Planning and Control of New Technology." In U. Briefs, Claudio Ciborra, and Leslie Schneider, eds., *Sysems Design for, with, and by the User,* 207–18. Amsterdam, New York, Oxford: North Holland.

Kohl, George. 1982. "Changing Competitive and Technology Environments in Telecommunications." In Donald Kennedy, Charles Craypo, and Mary Lehman, eds., *Labor and Technology: Union Response to Changing Environments,* 53–76. University Park: Pennsylvania State University, Department of Labor Studies.

Lanzara, Giovan Francesco. 1983. "The Design Process: Frames, Metaphors, and Games." In U. Briefs, Claudio Ciborra, and Leslie Schneider, eds., *Systems Design for, with, and by the User,* 29–40. Amsterdam, New York, Oxford: North Holland.

Mathiassen, Lars. 1981. *Systemudvikling og systemudviklingsmetode* (Systems development and systems development method). Department of Computer Science, University of Arhus, Denmark.

Noble, David F. 1984. *Forces of Production: A Social History of Industrial Automation.* New York: Alfred A. Knopf.

Norske Bankfunksjonaerers Forbund. 1983. *Malsettings-og handlingsprogram.* Oslo, Norway.

Nygaard, Kristen. 1983. "Participation in System Development: The Tasks Ahead." In U. Briefs, Claudio Ciborra, and Leslie Schneider, eds., *Systems Design for, with, and by the User,* 19–25. Amsterdam, New York, Oxford: North Holland.

Nygaard, Kristen, and Jostein Fjalestad. 1979. "Group Interests and Participation in Information System Development." Paper presented to the Special Session on Microelectronics, Productivity, and Employment. Working party on Information, Computer and Communications Policy, OECD, Paris, 27–29 November 1979.

Pacey, Arnold. 1983. *The Culture of Technology.* Cambridge, Mass.: The MIT Press.

Piore, Michael J., and Charles F. Sabel. 1984. *The Second Industrial Divide: Possibilities for Prosperity.* New York: Basic Books.

Sabel, Charles. 1982. *Work and Politics: The Division of Labor in Industry.* Cambridge: Cambridge University Press.

Schneider, Leslie. 1984. "Technology Bargaining in Norway." In *Technology and the Need for New Labor Relations,* Discussion paper 129D, John F. Kennedy School of Government, Harvard University.

Shaiken, Harley. 1984. *Work Transformed: Automation and Labor in the Computer Age.* New York: Holt, Rinehart and Winston.

Sheil, B. A. 1983. "Coping with Complexity." *Office: Technology and People* 1:295–320.

Strassmann, Paul A. 1985. *Information Payoff: The Transformation of Work in the Electronic Age*. New York: The Free Press.

Straw, Ronnie J., and Charles Hecksher. 1984. U.S. Report. *QWL Focus: The News Journal of the Ontario Quality of Work Life Center* 4(1).

Suchman, Lucy A. 1980. "Office Procedures as Practical Action: Theories of Work and Software Design." Presented at the Workshop of Research in Office Semantics, 15–18 June 1980, Chatham, Mass.

Suchman, Lucy A., and Eleanor Wynn. 1979. "Procedures and Problems in the Office Environment." Unpublished paper, Xerox, Advanced Systems Department, Palo Alto, Calif.

Thoresen, Kari. 1980. *Skrankemaskiner og Arbeidsmiljø*. Oslo: Norsk Regnesentral.

Tranøy, Espen. 1983. *Sannsynlige Utviklingstrinn I Framtidens Bank*. Prepared for the Norske Bankfunksjonaerers Forbund.

van Beinum, Hans. 1981. "Organisational Choice and Micro-electronics." *QWL Focus: The News Journal of the Ontario Quality of Work Life Center* 1(3):1–6.

Walton, Richard E. 1982. "Social Choice in the Development of Advanced Information Technology." *Technology in Society* 4:41–49.

———. 1984. "From Control to Commitment: Transforming Work Force Management in the United States." Prepared for the Harvard Business School's 75th Anniversary Colloquium on Technology and Productivity, 27–29 March 1984.

Walton, Richard E., and Wendy Vittori. 1983. "New Information Technology: Organizational Problem or Opportunity?" *Office: Technology and People*, May 1983, 249–73.

Wynn, Eleanor H. 1983. "The User as a Representation Issue in the U.S." In U. Briefs, Claudio Ciborra, and Leslie Schneider, eds., *Systems Design for, with, and by the User*, 349-58. Amsterdam, New York, Oxford: North Holland.

Zuboff, Shoshanna. 1982. "New Worlds of Computer-mediated Work." *Harvard Business Review* 60(5):142–52.

28

Feminism and the Forms of Freedom

Jane Mansbridge

Early in the feminist movement of the late 1960s, it became clear that the forms of organization best adapted to the movement's needs were identical to the classic anarchist forms.

1. The consciousness-raising group and its sister, the action group, had the same role in the larger movement that the anarchist "affinity groups" had in Spain in the civil war. The larger radical feminist organizations adopted a federative form of organization, based on small collectives or cells. In Bread and Roses in Boston, in the Women's Liberation Union in Chicago, in Redstockings in New York, in almost every other

major city in the United States, and even in the Women's Liberation Workshop in London, radical feminists adopted the same form of organization: a voluntary federation of small (six to twelve person) collectives.

2. The radical women's movement consciously avoided creating "stars." Women whom *Time* and *Life* asked to pose for covers featuring the women's movement refused to do so. Other women, giving public speeches, spoke in groups and wore masks to emphasize their collectivity and anonymity. Boston's Bread and Roses had a rule that no woman should appear on television, radio, or in the news without at least one other woman with her. New York's Redstockings censured T. Grace Atkinson when she attracted too much personal attention. Even the National Organization for Women (NOW), traditionally and hierarchically organized, found itself under attack from its members for creating the position of president in which one woman became a formal leader. In the radical women's movement, the conscious avoidance of publicity and unequal status parallels similar concerns raised in the Spanish anarcho-syndicalist revolutionary union Confederación National del Trabajo (CNT), where, for example, certain assemblies decided not to applaud their speakers, on the ground that applause would direct attention to the individual rather than to the substance of the talk.

3. The small collectives and even some large assemblies in the women's movement took their decisions by consensus, not by majority vote. This ensured that each member would then act only on her own commitment. This mode of decision, too, is consonant with much anarchist theory, though not always with anarchist practice.[1]

4. Whenever federated women's collectives had to make joint decisions, they chose the format of a direct, face-to-face assembly attended by all the membership. Anarchist theory also has always inveighed against representation and promoted the face-to-face assembly. Murray Bookchin argues, for example, that the direct face-to-face assembly is the only governmental form that preserves individual liberty. For Bookchin, face-to-face assemblies are the "forms of freedom."[2]

These forms of organization represented a sharp break with the past for many, if not most, of the women who practiced them. The Students for a Democratic Society (SDS) had initiated decentralized, consensual forms in its organization, but the concept never acquired the strength in SDS that it did in the women's movement, and nowhere in SDS did affinity groups play the powerful and all-pervasive role that they played in the women's movement. Nor had most members of the women's movement any previous contact with anarchist theory. The great proliferation of books on anarchism in the paperback bookstores in the mid-1970s came after the women's movement, not before, and may well have been caused, at least in part, by the success of anarchist forms in feminist organization. In short, the theory came after the practice.

Why this strong resemblance, reaching almost to identity, between women's forms and anarchist forms? It is not as if all oppressed groups spontaneously choose anarchist forms. Black groups in the United States, for example, often choose hierarchical forms of organization. The importance to women of the small, egalitarian, consensual collective was, I believe, directly related to one of the major goals of the women's movement—changing women's perceptions of themselves.

The women's movement of the 1960s and 1970s had many goals, most of them aimed at changing the male-dominated institutions that excluded and oppressed women. But unlike most oppressed groups, which can concentrate primarily on external sources of oppression, women had a peculiar relation with their oppressors. Women often loved men, and were loved by them. Women and men often had the same class background. Women and men often worked together intimately in the family. As members of a family, women and men often had the same interests *vis à vis* the larger polity. While some of these characteristics also apply to other relations of domination and subordination, nowhere are the ties so strong as between men and women. This meant that a primary task of the women's movement—perhaps *the* primary task—was to help women change the character of their most intimate relations. Before they could try to seize political or economic power, they had to help one another see their relations with men in a new light, and this required changing their understanding of themselves. For this purpose, the small egalitarian collective provided the necessary high levels of intimacy and support. The antipathy to leaders and the stress on personal commitment rather than subjection to a majority also served to strengthen psyches—to teach women that they could and should respect themselves, that they could and should resist domination.[3]

During the height of the women's movement, several women questioned whether the forms the movement had chosen really promoted its ends.[4] My object here is to question whether those forms, if adopted into the larger society, would serve women's ends.

A movement based on small primary groups—whether Communist cells, anarchist affinity groups, or feminist consciousness-raising groups—can derive great strength from linking the goals of the larger movement to the personal loyalties, expressed commitments, and protection from external culture that a small "primary" group provides. The consciousness-raising (C–R) group allowed six to twelve women to come together informally once a week or so, to share their experiences of being a woman, and, as the Chinese say, to "speak bitterness." They discovered that problems they thought had arisen from the individual peculiarities of their own experience were in fact the same problems that others had, and that those problems were rooted in the systematic oppression of women as a class. In these discussions, each woman discovered that "the personal is political."

Some consciousness-raising groups evolved into action groups—putting out a newsletter, doing guerilla theater, or executing graffiti raids on pornography stores and Playboy clubs. Other groups evolved into personal support groups for the women members, who then did what they could for the women's movement either individually or in other action groups formed for specific purposes. Many C-R groups simply dissolved after a year or so, when their primary purpose of personal evolution was accomplished or when their members moved to other parts of the country.

The radical women's movement of the late 1960s and early 1970s had almost no existence outside of these small consciousness-raising and action groups. But there were thousands of them. The groups had often sprung up spontaneously, and only in the major cities were some of them able to join together into loose, decentralized federations. The strength of such decentralized organization lay in the intense commitment to the goals of the movement that the groups generated, the courage they gave their members to demand changes in the way their friends, colleagues, bosses, husbands, and parents treated women, and the creativity they fostered, not only in poetry, painting, and protest, but also in changing one's own life. Kochen and Deutsch, and also Bennis and Slater, tell us that the more an organization must rely on creativity, innovation, adaptation to change and speed of reaction, the more it benefits from decentralization.[5] When the radical women's movement exploded with new ideas and new energy, that explosion was directly linked to extreme decentralization. It put the women's movement on the front page of national magazines and newspapers, revolutionized public opinion on women's issues from 1968 to 1972, and even brought new words, new usages, and new taboos into the English language.

Yet decentralization was at odds with coordination, particularly at a national level, and particularly over long periods of time. The one women's organization that survived this era and continued to grow, namely NOW, had a relatively centralized structure.[6]

The women's movement's use of consensus also created commitment and solidarity—important virtues in a "fighting" movement. One woman describes the joy of resolving conflict in a meeting right after the women who worked for a radical newspaper had taken over the paper:

> It was such an exciting meeting—almost everybody talked—there were about thirty women in the room—and it went from about a total split to finally someone saying, "Listen, if we can't do that we don't deserve the paper," and then everybody saying, "Right on!" It was one of the few meetings where it goes around and then people just really come together and say "Far out!" You know it's right. It was such a *high* . . . it was wonderful. It was such a high.

But while consensus can inspire and bind together a group of equals with common purposes, it can also suppress real conflict to the advantage of those with greater self-confidence and verbal aggressiveness. Thus, in a mixed group of men and women a consensual procedure may mean that the women subtly lose out.

The same is true for direct assembly government in general. In a government by direct assembly, decisions are made not by representatives, but by the citizens gathered together in a meeting hall. Some New England towns still run their affairs this way; some of these towns are so small that all the adult citizens can come together in one room to vote the amount they will tax themselves and to decide, for example, whether or not to institute zoning, or whether to make parents pay individually when their children ride the school bus. On the radical Left, some "alternative" organizations also run this way, with all members of the workplace making decisions together, in assembly. In the late 1960s and early 1970s I surveyed a number of town meetings and egalitarian workplaces, in order to identify the two most "participatory" for detailed study.[7] Even in the most participatory town and workplace, though, not everyone participated equally in these assemblies. In both settings the working class, the newcomers, the younger people, and those most distant from the polity's centers of communications attended less often and spoke less at the meetings than did the middle class, the oldtimers, the older people, and those who lived or worked near centers of communications.[8]

In both assemblies—the town meeting and the crisis center—women attended meetings as often as men but spoke less. At the town meeting, women spoke only one quarter of the time, made only 8 percent of the major statements of opinion, and initiated not one of the ten controversial exchanges. At the crisis center, with the exception of one extraordinarily verbal woman, women also spoke less. On a checklist of traits and attitudes associated with greater power at the center, women in this workplace fell significantly behind men on only two, but these both involved verbal insecurity.[9]

In short, although ironically women usually do better in academic tests of verbal ability than do men, in a face-to-face assembly, where people must use those verbal skills to influence others, today's women lose out.

The women's movement of the late 1960s and early 1970s demonstrated the strength, at least in some circumstances, of anarchist forms. But before thinking of adapting these forms to the larger polity, women should understand how the forms reflect and perhaps accentuate the disadvantages of those already disadvantaged. In the classic "form of freedom"—the face-to-face assembly—the interests of the disadvantaged, including the working class and women, are not usually protected equally.

This pattern of disadvantage is not confined to women. It recurs for almost all disadvantaged groups. Whenever inequality emerges in a society, the dominant groups will normally have greater influence in setting the norms of that society. It will then be difficult, in the personal, face-to-face atmosphere of an assembly, for the less advantaged to speak out, and their listeners will often discount in advance what they have to say, because their tone of voice and style of behavior does not carry authority.

Moreover, even in the most egalitarian societies certain forms of inequality will probably persist. Some people will continue to live and work closer to the hub of central communications, some will have more friends active in the community, some will have more verbal skills, and some will enjoy responsibility more than others. These people, generally more at ease in the assembly, will either subtly or more crassly dominate the proceedings.

What is to be done about these inequalities depends on whether one assumes underlying conflict or underlying harmony in the community making potential decisions. If on a given set of issues the interests of the members of the polity conflict, then the democratic goal should be to make sure that the interests of the disadvantaged (women, for example) are represented equally.

This is the underlying theory behind what I call "adversary democracy." It is the theory behind majority rule: When no individual is acknowledged to have rights or knowledge superior to any other, and when conflict cannot ultimately be resolved by continuing debate, then all parties will consider the outcome legitimate if each individual has a vote of equal weight and the issue is settled by the preponderance of votes. In adversary democracy, when there is no "right answer," the equal power of each individual is a necessary weapon for protecting interests equally. Accordingly, when interests conflict, referenda and proportional representation will be more likely than open debate in a face-to-face assembly to make the interests of the disadvantaged count equally in the final outcome.

However, if the interests of the members of the polity coincide on a given set of issues, then the democratic goal should be to come to the "best" decision. This is what I call "unitary" democracy, a form of democracy practiced in the West before the seventeenth century, and still practiced in most non-European countries. The theory of unitary democracy assumes underlying common interests among the citizenry. When everyone has common interests, no one's interests are hurt when certain kinds of people participate more than others. Enough people must speak from each vantage point to get all the relevant insights and suggestions onto the table, but this goal does not require equal participation. For example, if the interests of men and women are the same on any issue, it will not hurt women's interests if few women speak, as long as the men and women who do speak express the ideas nonspeakers would have come up with.

This point, however, brings up a second goal of participation. Participation is a device not just for ensuring everyone equal influence over an outcome, but for developing thoughtful, active citizens, who understand when their interests really conflict with those of others, and who are involved enough in their common life to contribute to the greater good of all. If some people rarely or never participate in political life, they are less likely to develop sides of themselves that will be important both to them and to the community. Referenda and representation do not solve this problem. Neither, unfortunately, do face-to-face assemblies. Instead of being encouraged to speak by the theoretically open character of the debate, a habitual non-participant is as likely to be threatened, bored, or otherwise alienated by a face-to-face meeting.

The best response to the goal of self-development is to rely not on large face-to-face assemblies, but on primary-group meetings (twelve persons or less) and on the wide diffusion of small, responsible jobs. Small primary group meetings help people explore what they think about an issue, find support for underdeveloped powers of self-expression and analysis, and develop the initiative for action. Unfortunately, in a context of genuine, irreconcilable conflict, small groups have two drawbacks. They divide minorities so that the minority members cannot give one another adequate support. And they make the enemy human, which can either weaken one's resolve to fight or provoke one to irrational, sometimes destructive, behavior. Thus, for most developmental purposes the small group must have some basis in common interest. In a context of conflict, working within a small group that must negotiate potential conflict with another group helps people become more aware of their real interests. Finally, creating many small jobs with formal responsibility for others helps those who do these jobs become aware of other people's needs and understand different points of view. It also develops self-respect when one does well, and realistic self-criticism when one fails.

If the goal is developing the faculties of the participants, assemblies should try to break up regularly for small-group discussion. This may not increase equality in participation,[10] but it gives each person a greater chance to be active. When the assembly must meet only as a whole, habitual non-participants can sit together, talk quietly among themselves, and possibly meet before and after. These tactics can offset the intimidating character of the larger meeting and contribute to the greater awareness of the disadvantaged.

At one point New York's Redstockings invented a "disk system," by which each woman entering a meeting took twelve disks. She had to spend one each time she spoke and was forbidden to speak after the twelve were spent. This technique had the advantages of making everyone conscious of inequalities in participation and of making the less aggressive members more conscious of their opportunities to speak. It had two disadvantages. First, when interests came into conflict, the tactic was not likely to reduce inequalities of influence. Although everyone at the meeting continued to have one vote, the more powerful always had, in addition, their networks of friends and their command of persuasive rhetoric. Second, in moments of common interest, the tactic probably obstructed ordered and careful debate on the best solution by forcing people with the most to contribute to save their disks rather than making useful, short interventions. It also tended to focus the group's interest on the frequency with which people spoke instead of the quality of what they said.

Redstockings probably instituted this system to achieve a third and final goal of participation—equal respect, or equal status, among the members. If some members consistently speak out while others stay silent, the speakers can gradually become a status elite and the nonspeakers come to feel less than equal. In the radical women's movement of the late 1960s and early 1970s, this concern for equal respect was greater than the concern for either protecting interests equally or developing individual abilities. Women wanted to create communities based on the bonds of friendship, which requires equal respect.[11] "Sisterhood" thus demanded equality, while differences in status tore the bonds apart.

But face-to-face assemblies are not the best vehicle for reinforcing equality of respect. Time limitations and the demands of consecutive debate will always create a distance between the small groups of speakers and the many who are silent—a distance that inevitably grows more pronounced as the assembly gets larger. Small primary groups and the diffusion of small formal responsibilities are more effective tactics for maintaining equal respect than are frequent face-to-face assemblies.

Face-to-face assemblies are less the forms of freedom or equality than the forms of community. Despite all their drawbacks in promoting the equal protection of interests, self-development, and equal respect, assemblies of modest size (say less than 200) can put each member palpably in touch with everyone else. They allow nuances of understanding that can only come from seeing another's face and posture, or hearing the inflections of her voice. They let waves of emotional communion flow as difficult or risky decisions are made; and long after the assembly's end, they bind together the people who were there through the common memory of what they did together. If such meetings continue year after year, they create an accumulation of memories that lets each member see the community as a whole in her mind's eye, feel its many sides and its central pulse, and make its collective good her own.

The organizational forms that feminists use for social change should depend on the context. In *external* politics, when women's groups make demands on the system that other groups resist, the movement should not try to replace representative institutions with direct democracy. Rather, it should aim its major political efforts at achieving greater representation of women's interests in the areas where they most conflict with those of men. This is not necessarily a matter of having more women in high places. Women legislators do not always represent women's interests better than men do. The women's movement should aim at electing women or men who will represent women's interests best in the major areas of conflict.

In *internal* organization, women's groups should continue to rely on small primary group organization, which contributes to self-development and to mutual support in outside conflict. They should also build extensive experience in formal representation, both for self-development and for the cadre this experience can train for outside conflict. They should not abandon face-to-face assembly, but use it sparingly, primarily to build community. They should be willing to use consensual, face-to-face institutions for issues on which there is an original conflict of opinion but also the possibility of an eventual genuine solution that is in the common interest, and should switch to majority-rule institutions like referenda or representation when a genuine conflict of interest underlies the conflict of opinion.

In short, feminists should not decide that there is only one democratic "form of freedom." They should examine the degree to which interests converge or conflict among the people making a decision, and then choose the institutions and tactics that best fit the underlying distribution of interests.

Notes

1. While I know no published description of decision-making in Spanish collectives, telephone interviews with the authors of three books on the anarchists indicate that anarchist collectives in the Spanish civil war made decisions by consensus when convenient, but had no ideological problem about resorting to majority rule whenever a difficult conflict arose. The authors in question are: Sam Dolgoff, author of *The Anarchist Collective: Worker's Self-Management in the Spanish Revolution, 1936–1939* (Montreal: Black Rose, 1974), Martha Ackelsberg, Department of Political Science, Smith College, author of "Revolution Begins at Home" (forthcoming), an examination of social and political practice in anarchist collectives during the Spanish civil war, and Jerome R. Mintz, author of *The Anarchists of Casas Viejas* (Chicago: The University of Chicago Press, 1982). Fred W. Thompson, a long-time member of the Industrial Workers of the World (I.W.W.), makes the same point regarding the early Wobblies (telephone conversation with the author).

2. Murray Bookchin, "The Forms of Freedom" (1968) in *Post-Scarcity Anarchism* (Berkeley, Calif.: Ramparts Press, 1971), 168. Bookchin concludes:

> The factory committees, which will almost certainly be the forms that will take over industry, must be managed directly by workers' assemblies in the factories. By the same token, neighborhood committees, councils and boards must be rooted completely in the neighborhood assembly. . . . The specific gravity of society, in short, must be shifted to its base—the armed people in permanent assembly.

Against "the intermediary of representatives," see Pierre-Joseph Proudhon in *General Idea of the Revolution in the Nineteenth Century* (1851), reprinted in *The Essential Works of Anarchism*, ed. Marshall S. Shatz, (New York: Quadrangle Books, 1972), 88–89; on "the inherent vices of the representative principle," see Peter Kropotkin, *The Conquest of Bread* (1892), reprinted in Shatz, *The Essential Works of Anarchism*, 205.

3. The power of a small discussion group in helping change behavior was early demonstrated by Lewin in a series of experiments during World War II to discover the most effective way of persuading women to give their children cod-liver oil. See Kurt Lewin, "Forces Behind Food Habit and Methods of Change," *Bulletin of the National Research Council* 108 (1943): 35–36, reprinted in *Group Dynamics: Research and Theory*, ed. Dorwin Cartwright and Alvin Zander (N.Y. Harper and Row, 1953). More recently, encounter, gestalt, and other therapies have effectively utilized the same technique. On the Chinese use of the small group for directed behavior change, see Robert Lifton, *Thought Reform and the Psychology of Totalism* (N.Y.: Norton, 1962). One might even hypothesize that the more a revolutionary movement demanded internal as well as external change, the more it would rely on small-group organization.

4. See, for example, Jo Freeman, "The Tyranny of Structurelessness," *Berkeley Journal of Sociology* 17 (1972–73): 151–64.

5. Warren G. Bennis and Philip E. Slater, *The Temporary Society* (N.Y.: Harper and Row, 1969); Manfred Kochen and Karl W. Deutsch, "Toward a Rational Theory of Decentralization," *American Political Science Review* 63 (1969): 734–49.

6. NOW adopted the consciousness-raising group, but let it run no more than a limited period of time, and restricted its autonomy. Even in NOW there has always been much controversy over the permissible degree of centralization. NOW remains a great deal less centralized than, say, the NAACP.

7. These cases, and the method of their selection, are reported in my *Beyond Adversary Democracy* (N.Y.: Basic Books, 1980—Chicago: University of Chicago Press, 1983).

8. Mansbridge, *Beyond Adversary Democracy*, 99–111, 184–209, 306–21.

9. "Articulate people intimidate me," and "I express myself well in words." See Mansbridge, *Beyond Adversary Democracy*, 105–06, 191–94. See p. 358 for the checklist of reported personality attributes by gender.

Women at the crisis center spoke less than men in spite of much raised consciousness on the subject. Some of the women at the center, organized in an active and militant support group, had raised the issue of women's lower verbal participation, and many of the men subsequently had made conscious efforts to break themselves of their habits of interrupting women or assuming they as men would speak first.

Don H. Zimmerman and Candace West, "Sex Roles, Interruptions and Silences in Conversations," in *Language and Sex*, ed. Barrie Thorne and Nancy Henley (Rowley, Mass: Newbury House, 1975), 105–29, present evidence that among mixed-sex college-age couples, men commit 75 percent of the "deep interruptions."

10. For example, the crisis center I studied usually broke its large assembly down into small groups of less than 15 people for discussion. However, the one time that I measured speaking in these small groups, the association between advantaged status and speaking was no smaller than in the larger assembly.

11. See Robert Brain, *Friends and Lovers* (N.Y.: Basic Books, 1976), 20; Mansbridge, *Beyond Adversary Democracy*, chap. 2 and 3.

29

Learning Pluralism: Democracy and Diversity in Feminist Organizations

Carmen Sirianni

With the beginning of its second wave, and especially its more radical variants since the late 1960s, feminism has been concerned with redefining democratic community on more participatory grounds. To this end, organizational processes, deliberative styles, and communicative ethics have been refashioned. Initially, little was distinctively feminist in this, as young women's movement leaders drew upon the models of the "beloved community" they had been practicing in the Student Nonviolent Coordinating Committee (SNCC) or the "participatory democracy" of the Students for a Democratic Society (SDS), the major black and white student movement organizations, respectively. To be sure, there was a feminist subtext from the beginning. Ella Baker, middle-aged granddaughter of a rebellious slave minister and chief staffer who had organized the central offices of the Southern Christian Leadership Conference (SCLC) before being displaced by yet another male minister, had articulated an approach to facilitative group leadership that was an alternative to both the bureaucratic form of the National Association for the Advancement of Colored People (NAACP) and the charismatic form of the male preachers who dominated SCLC. Baker argued that "you must let the oppressed themselves define their own freedom" and nurtured in SNCC an organizing style that recognized leadership inchoate in every community and in every individual. Through her influence on SNCC activists, and both directly and indirectly on SDS leaders, Baker can be said to have been the midwife of participatory democracy in the student movements of the 1960s. When Mary King and Casey Hayden confronted both student organizations with their own strictures on female leadership and began to form a separate movement in the process, it was to the teachings of Ella Baker that they turned, as well as to the experience they had gained in facilitative leadership among hundreds of indigenous "mamas" turned community activists across the South.[1]

However, despite this clear inspiration from an African American woman with years of activist experience and an explicit critique of male leadership, only with the development of a separate women's liberation movement in the late 1960s did participatory democratic community began to acquire explicitly feminist emphases. A feminist ideal soon emerged that stressed egalitarian participation, democratization of all leadership roles, elimination of all competitiveness in organizational life, careful listening, respect for the experiences of all women, self-transformation, and autonomy through intimate sharing and small-group support. In short, what later came to be called a distinctively, though not exclusively, female "ethic of care" in feminist theory was grafted onto a radically egalitarian version of participatory democracy and community.

Ironically, at this very time participatory democracy in SDS was unraveling through the pull of its own ambiguities and contradictions, not the least between its civic republican and existential variants, and beloved community in SNCC had given way to authoritarian and dogmatic sectarianism as its redemptive ethos proved incapable of accommodating a plurality of activist styles or democratic leadership transitions.[2] This would not have been a surprise to competitive elite theorists of democracy, who warned of the totalitarian potential of too much participation.[3] But some in the student movements were themselves beginning to develop a coherent critique of the excesses and ambiguities of participatory democracy. And by the end of the 1960s a number of political theorists had begun to articulate a pluralist version of participatory democracy that valued participation and self-management in expanding democracy and yet recognized limits and decried excesses, arguing instead for fundamentally plural democratic forms, decision criteria, styles of citizenship, and degrees of commitment. Robert Dahl and Michael Walzer, in particular, affirmed important elements of what I would call participatory pluralism, simultaneously broadening pluralist theory to accommodate the participatory revolution of the era, yet critiquing any pretense to singular democratic forms or ideals of citizenship.[4]

This rethinking of participatory democracy as the ideal and singular form of democratic community had no discernible impact on the organizational development of the radical women's movement at the time. Few prominent women's movement leaders seem to have been aware of it, and those who may have been did not cite this literature, either because they saw it as alien or feared that others in the movement would view it as such.[5] It is hardly a surprise that the movement, far from transcending the problems of participatory community that had plagued the student movements, recapitulated many of them, and some in even more extreme forms precisely because of the movement's distinctive feminist emphases.

Yet, if one of the central justifications for participation in political theory has been its educative impact on participants,[6] the feminist movement might be said quickly to have generated internal learning processes enabling it to refine the meanings and forms of participatory community. After presenting the ideal of democratic community and feminist process that emerged in radical women's organizations, I will argue that this learning has pointed predominantly, though not entirely or consistently, in the direction of participatory pluralism. As a result of having to confront issues of democratic representativeness, informal tyranny, imposed sisterly virtue, distorted communication, forced consensus, democratic accountability, and strategic efficacy, the movement was compelled to rediscover and relearn many of the lessons of pluralist theory. Not only did its own internal resources prove quite substantial for this task, but distinctively feminist emphases on care and difference more recently have enabled feminism to expand the range of issues that a participatory pluralism must confront, even if some of the movement's own innovations remain quite problematic and theoretical issues yet unresolved.

Feminist Process:
The Emergence of an Organizational Ideal

Neither SNCC nor SDS was able to respond effectively to the feminist critique that emerged in 1964–65. SNCC was rent by black-white sexual tensions on staff, and by fierce conflict between the "freedom high" and "structure" factions. SDS's not inconsiderable capacities for organizational learning and political debate about the meanings and forms of democracy were overwhelmed by the massive influx of new recruits with the escalation of the Vietnam War, and the competitive male intellectual styles that alienated many women in early SDS gave way to even more offensive macho styles of the newly arrived anarchist "prairie dog" leaders. Women's leadership styles, which had begun to come into their own in community organizing projects, were further marginalized by the antiwar emphasis on large mobilizations and rallies, and draft resistance accorded the male experiences of vulnerability and heroism a privileged role in movement culture and personal politics. Campus SDS chapters, which might have served better for sustaining and feminizing the ideals of participatory democracy, were often dominated by male cliques. As Sara Evans notes, "stardom was increasingly defined by glamour and rhetorical verbal skills, and the talents that could prove effective in small groups or in community organizing had little place in the broader movement."[7]

As a consequence, many women moved outside and began to redefine participatory group dynamics with distinctly feminist emphases. Consciousness-raising (C-R) groups and small collectives that combined CR with political projects were the primary forms for this in the late 1960s and early 1970s, although citywide women's liberation unions often established a broader framework for feminist participation on the bases of small groups. C-R philosophy and techniques were drawn from a variety of sources: the "speak bitterness" campaigns of the Chinese revolution, SDS "Guatemala Guerrilla" organizing, SNCC and Economic and Research Action Project (ERAP) personal discussion styles, and experiential learning in the Mississippi freedom schools. Kathie Sarachild, who is widely credited with developing specifically feminist C-R techniques and who had herself been a Freedom Summer volunteer in 1964, urged women to scrap the old theories and build feminist theory and politics on the basis of personal experience: "In our groups, let's share our feelings and pool them. Let's let ourselves go and see where our feelings lead us. Our feelings will lead us to ideas and then to actions."[8]

Sharing would help define common problems and dispel self-blame. Personal revelation was especially appropriate when the oppressed were in intimate relations with their oppressors.[9] The authority of personal experience recognized that all women had something to say about oppression and so had the right in women's groups to attentive listening and moral support. These would not only yield insight but transform the passive into self-confident activists, even leaders. These early C-R experiences were the practical loci for feminist theorists' later insight that autonomous selves are formed not in isolation but in supportive relations, in contrast to the view of liberal theory of the individual and individual rights.[10] Indeed, if every woman were seen as a potential leader, as Ella Baker and Mary King would have it, then leadership roles should be widely dispersed, skills shared, power diffused. Mutually supportive participation at the small-group level could have educative and transformative effects, and prefigure a society based on non-hierarchical relationships.

Hundreds of thousands of women took part in these small groups in the late 1960s and early 1970s, and many testify to the educative and empowering effects they had on their lives. As Evans has noted, "they provided a place, a 'free space,' in which women could examine the nature of their own oppression and share the growing knowledge that they were not alone. The qualities of intimacy, support and virtual structurelessness made the small group a brilliant tool for spreading the movement. Anyone could form a group anywhere: an SDS women's caucus, a secretarial pool, a friendship circle, a college dorm, a coffee klatch." Their spontaneous and contagious formation was later given an added boost when the National Organization for Women (NOW), the major arm of the mainstream women's movement, began officially propagating them, indeed, becoming their primary proponent, after initially believing that they would divert women's energies away from political action. Many chapters institutionalized CR courses with specific topics, and the Los Angeles NOW Consciousness Raising Committee distributed a sixty-page C-R handbook.[11]

Small participatory groups, often set up as collectives, have been particularly suited to a variety of women's self-help, service, and cultural projects. Women's health collectives have aimed to disperse knowledge and skills widely, and thus demystify medical expertise for both staff and patients to enable women to gain greater control over their own bodies. In this they have spearheaded a broader critique of professional ideologies and practices that disempower those they are supposed to serve. Perhaps the most famous of these is the Boston Women's Health Book Collective, which published *Our Bodies, Ourselves* in 1973 (and a subsequent 1984 edition), a book that has had an important democratizing impact on the construction of medical knowledge and the delivery of services in traditional as well as alternative settings. The shelter movement for battered women has also frequently used the democratic collective, and other participatory forms, because in the process of establishing active engagement and equal respect among staff and residents, the latter are provided with a living alternative to the domination they have experienced and the passivity of mere victim status. In one shelter studied by Noelie Maria Rodriguez, all members of the staff had at one time been victims of battering or incest, and most had themselves been residents of the shelter. Although some board members have professional credentials, none are required for regular staff. Current and past residents are active in all aspects of decision making, from hiring and administration to program details, and communication among staff and residents is continuous and open. Staff members serve as role models of those who have been able to redefine their lives without violence and victimization, and residents support and empower each other through peer counseling. Participation is meant to be empowering and therapeutic at the same time, and to serve as an alternative to the professional social-service model.[12]

Internal Critique of Structureless Democracy and Sisterly Virtue

The feminist movement's acute attention to group process, however, quickly began to generate a trenchant critique of small, relatively structureless groups. Jo Freeman's 1972 essay "The Tyranny of Structurelessness," which had been circulating before its publication in several places, was the most important document in triggering a process of critical reflection that has been going on ever since.[13] Diffuse participatory methods, according to Freeman, often do little really to democratize power and can, in fact, make those who wield the most influence in an organization even less responsible and less accountable to members. The refusal to name leaders often means that the membership is also unable to name the elites that emerge informally and that in many cases constitute oligarchic enclaves. Informal dominance is based on networks not all that different than old boys' networks in how they operate, a great irony for a movement that historically has sought to democratize power by formalizing methods of selection and decision making. Entry into informal networks is often based on friendship, marriage to New Left men with valued resources (mailing lists, presses), or on appropriate class, racial, and educational backgrounds and personally attractive styles. Some become de facto leaders simply by their ability and willingness to invest the most time, thereby creating the problem of representativeness that had deeply concerned both Dahl and Walzer. As Ann Popkin noted in her study of the Bread and Roses collective in Boston, this presented a real problem for women with full-time jobs, who often felt marginalized from the inner circle of "heavies" (the word members chose to describe the reality of power they felt proscribed from naming directly), or for those who had multiple political commitments. Formally democratic mechanisms were not available to control the power cliques, and the informal norms of steep time investment made it difficult for women with multiple commitments to achieve recognition as serious feminists with a role to play in formulating program and political direction.[14]

Communicative and decision-making processes could also be distorted by certain egalitarian procedures and personalized styles. Redstockings of New York, for instance, devised a system of equalizing opportunities to speak by distributing twelve disks to each member, one of which was forfeited each time a person spoke. As Jane Mansbridge has pointed out, this helped make women conscious of inequalities among themselves and alerted the more aggressive to the limits on their speech. But it did not reduce inequalities of influence, since the more powerful still were able to mobilize support networks and command through rhetoric when members' interests came into conflict. When interests tended to converge, it actually obstructed careful debate on the most optimal solution by discouraging short, helpful comments by those with most to contribute. And it tended to orient people to the frequency rather than the quality of speech.[15] Expressive personal styles, such as prefacing comments with "I feel" or "it freaks me out that," often sowed confusion or concealed political direction in the guise of openness. At mass meetings of women's unions such styles made it difficult to pursue orderly discussion or get people to respond sequentially to another's arguments. Decisions were often not carried out because of free-flowing discussion or the absence of minutes, which were seen as distinctly bureaucratic. Lack of formal structure made some feel even more inadequate and disempowered, since it appeared that all could speak and be listened to equally, and hence fear of speaking or lack of persuasiveness was more easily perceived as one's own personal failing. In many cases egalitarian styles bred conformity and stifled dissent by branding it "unsisterly" to challenge another woman's ideas or to claim individual authorship of an article. In denying a proper place for political and personal competition, which were viewed as peculiarly male, suppressed anger and hostility often came in through the back door in ways that were destructive of democratic process and personally hurtful. The result, as Karen Hansen has argued, was "an environment where only the brave, the politically correct, or the thick-skinned would speak. Many women described the mass meetings as almost unbearable."[16]

Personal politics in the small groups could become particularly oppressive, even totalitarian, according to Freeman and others, on issues of sexual preference. As many lesbians stepped out of the closet, lesbianism came to be interpreted not only as a right of sexual preference but as a political choice and as a criterion of feminist trustworthiness. Those who chose not to become a "woman-identified woman" nor to explore full sexual love and commitment were often seen as compromised or, worse yet, as traitors to other women. This sisterly version of Rousseauian virtue was often enforced through small-group process with particular vehemence, causing much personal trauma, even nervous breakdowns, and leaving the feminist identities of many committed activists shattered. Even where sexual preference was not at issue, politicizing the personal often meant escalating the emotional risks one was expected to take and exposing one's personal life to the continual scrutiny of the group. Just as existential daring infused the student movement's interpretations of participatory democracy, so did intense emotional risk taking become a standard for participatory openness and sisterly virtue in the radical women's movement. Many women recognized this to be a "perversion of the 'personal is political' argument" and resisted the creeping notion that "a woman's life is the political property of the women's movement," but not before many women's groups were destroyed in the process of learning how to draw the boundaries.[17]

The radically participatory and egalitarian ethos entailed profound ambivalence about leadership, and those who took initiative often received confused and contradictory messages about their efforts. On the one hand, they felt that the movement expected them to speak at local gatherings and national conferences, since moral pressure to be available and preach the gospel whenever needed was great. They were expected to provide theoretical analysis and strategic guidance, and their essays and books were enthusiastically welcomed and debated. On the other hand, they were accused of being elitist when they did take initiative or enter the limelight, of being manipulative when they did formulate plans and develop strategies, of being on a "male trip" of rational analysis when they did generate and debate theories.[18]

Ambivalence about leadership was so deep, and egalitarian impulses so strong, that many groups could not sustain a rational debate about what democratic leaders should be like or how the movement might produce them. If leadership potential was present in all women, many groups reasoned, then any woman should be able to run a mass meeting, every woman should be interested in theory, and no woman need be trained to manage an organization. One faction among the Feminists from New York tried to prescribe at the Second Congress to Unite Women in early 1970 that "*everyone* in the movement must be in groups which operate COLLECTIVELY (i.e. use the LOT SYSTEM)," and that no woman could speak before the media unless chosen by lot or could earn a living from writing or speaking about women's liberation.[19]

The results of these attitudes were often quite debilitating. Organizational structurelessness bred a peculiarly destructive psychodynamics of leadership trashing. Since competitive impulses could not be recognized and legitimated, they also could not be easily contained and channeled. Those who felt guilty and self-hating for asserting themselves, fearful of being accused of elitism, envious of others who achieved recognition, or inadequate for being unable to live up to the ideal of all women as leaders or theorists, could project their unwanted feelings onto the "heavies" by caricaturing and trashing them, disempowering them even as they expected to be empowered by them. The result was a dampening of initiative among many, as Linda Gordon has noted of Bread and Roses, or complete, though usually temporary, withdrawal from the women's movement, thus creating leadership vacuums and depriving the movement of much-needed talent. The first generation of leaders, in particular, suffered so greatly from what they called the "trashing" and "witch hunts" that they were almost completely decimated. Naomi Weisstein, for instance, who had felt profoundly empowered by her experience in supportive small groups in the late 1960s and who had successfully overcome her terror of speaking before large audiences to become a brilliant orator, felt that, by being trashed as an elitist star, the women's movement had "given her a voice and then taken it away again." And as in SDS and SNCC, the inability of the movement to name leaders who could be held accountable made it all that much easier for the media to choose its own stars to put on the cover of *Time* magazine or the CBS evening news, creating even more resentment toward them and reinforcing their sense that they were "feminist refugees" who should try to reach other women through the media and not the movement. As Freeman has argued, "the movement's greatest fear became a self-fulfilling prophecy. The ideology of 'structurelessness' created the 'star system' and the backlash to it encouraged the very kind of individualistic nonresponsibility that it most condemned."[20]

Structurelessness also left the larger feminist organizations vulnerable to control by disciplined sectarian groups. With membership open and criteria loose, leadership chosen according to who was willing to put in the most time, and meetings run haphazardly without previously circulated agendas or recorded attendance and minutes, cadre organizations could assert disproportionate influence by packing the mass meetings with women not previously active in chapters, volunteering a great deal of time in the office and propounding their own line as if it were that of the feminist group as a whole. In some cases, not only were the dominant sentiments of the group not well represented but views contrary to feminism itself were propagated. These unwelcome results of loose inclusiveness confronted feminists with severe challenges to their innocent notions of sisterly solidarity and open participation, and forced them to pose the questions explicitly: "What demos?" "Whose voice?" By what criteria is membership established and the right to speak in the name of others bestowed? Is having one's name on a list enough to qualify for membership, or does one have to be active in a chapter, pay dues, or subscribe to a particular program or ideology? And how does one demonstrate commitment and belief? Practically, these questions presented women's groups with the option of purging members of political sects, which was an agonizing decision that many saw as inherently antifeminist, and which paralyzed various groups and exhausted their leaders. Not a few dissolved shortly after such membership crises.[21]

The tension between prefigurative and strategic orientations, which Wini Breines sees as having been the key unresolved tension in the student movement, thus manifested itself in the participatory politics of the women's movement as well.[22] Structureless groups aiming to prefigure a utopia of radical equality in their internal process had a difficult time setting priorities or following through on decisions. Many socialist feminist unions paralyzed themselves in the elusive search for the ideal project. Internal crises produced continual fragmentation. And the groups that resisted formalizing structures for organizational maintenance were the very ones that spent the most time and effort on revising their structures and trying to maintain their organizations, time that was drained from actual or planned projects and effective political work.[23]

The tensions, however, were not just between the prefigurative and the strategic, but within those very processes imagined to prefigure the ideal. As Naomi Weisstein and Heather Booth noted in 1975, "our organizations and our alternate institutions die from internal bleeding long before they succumb to external pressure."[24] Informal dominance, expressive manipulation, leadership trashing, false consensus, enforced sisterly virtue—all these were problems that, to a considerable degree, were generated by the very attempts to prefigure an ideal of participatory openness and egalitarian process. And many were eventually contained only by elevating strategic considerations to a higher level of priority in women's organizations. The fault line between the prefigurative and the strategic cannot serve metanarratively to map the fundamental dilemmas of democratic participation, feminist or otherwise, since faults crisscross each of these in many directions and generate multiple tensions within and between them. And although the prefigurative ideal continues to reappear in feminist theory and feminist organizations, often in strikingly unitary form, the critique generated within the movement itself has created an increasingly profound capacity to manage, and imagine, a multiplicity of tensions and a plurality of forms.

Formalizing Structures:
Dilemmas of Empowerment

Concerns with personal self-development and calculations of political efficacy, which have served as important justifications in political theory for increased participation,[25] further anchored the emerging critique of structureless democracy in the women's movement. Since the radical women's movement of the late 1960s and early 1970s was largely a youth movement, it is not surprising that many activists, like those in SNCC and SDS, eventually began to formulate plans for lifetime commitment and to distance themselves from forms of organization that colonized so much time, excluded familial and career obligations, or exposed them to premature burnout. The attrition rate in small collectives was always quite high, reflecting de facto strategies for self-development and efficacy via exit. But choices were increasingly made in good conscience once the time and wage costs of egalitarian work were framed within the broader critique of the feminine volunteer syndrome that would deny women independent careers. And such concerns were often shared by poor, working-class, and Third World women activists, who found the egalitarian rejection of formalized authority and professional status to serve well neither their own developmental needs nor the practical delivery of services to their communities. In fact, the structureless democratic ideal has often proven rather exclusivist for those who do not have white middle-class privileges to fall back on, and making room for increased race and class diversity in the women's movement has meant revising what had appeared to be unambiguously egalitarian and prefigurative.[26] As careers, political and otherwise, have opened up for women generally, feminist activism imagines itself less singularly within an egalitarian form of participatory democracy. Myra Marx Ferree's comparative study of the women's movements in the United States and the Federal Republic of Germany shows the more autonomist and collectivist women's movement in the latter to be revising its structures and outlook as careers and political opportunities begin to open up for women. And many of the more radical feminist proponents of egalitarian collectives in the United States have never been that interested in maintaining the organizations they set up; often they quickly move on to new projects as part of their own "careers" in innovation, albeit not without excoriating those who compromise the ideal in order to stabilize their achievements.[27]

The movements against domestic violence and rape are cases in point. In the early 1970s shelters for battered women and rape crisis centers were frequently structured as democratic collectives heavily dependent on volunteer efforts and with little formalization of authority or division of labor. They developed critiques of male violence and practical methods of empowerment that eschewed the passivity of social-service client models. But as demand increased, many were forced to close or cut back services. Staff members were burning out and moving on, and volunteers had always been a relatively uncertain resource. Those committed to stabilizing and even expanding services, and to using the cumulative experience developed by the movement to empower women against violence, increasingly opted to formalize structures. Staff were paid, and increasingly well, as a way of securing long-term commitment and upgrading services, and more women of color and working-class women were recruited and retained as a consequence. Board structures were formalized to provide broader skills and political influence, and fund-raising activities were given new emphasis. Funding from state agencies came to be seen not just as a cooptative trap, but as an opportunity to expand services and transform the way various agencies defined battering and rape. As Nancy Matthews has shown, state funding, as well as the support of more hierarchical organizations such as SCLC and the YWCA, were crucial in some instances to broadening the anti-rape movement to minority communities and to overcoming the exclusivist practices of collectives staffed by radical white feminists. The anti-rape movement in Los Angeles has become multiracial and multicultural, with resources provided by the state and other organizations, yet it has creatively modified bureaucratic requirements to resist tendencies to parcel out the victim's needs according to staff structure and to turn the victim into a client. Barbara Levy Simon shows how staff members rebelled against the structureless democracy and the radical feminist director of a local rape crisis center in order to check the informal tyrannies and exclusivist practices based on friendship cliques, racial identity, and sexual preference, to stabilize and upgrade services, and to transform police practices and media coverage. Institutionalization did not lead to a modification of goals in a conservative direction, as Weber and Michels might have predicted, but to an expansion of goals and enhancement of internal democracy, while a sense of community that allowed the center to resist cooptation was maintained. One broad survey of rape crisis centers finds much structural diversity, although the original collective model had become "virtually extinct" by the 1980s, without, however, leading to a decline in political activity and education concerning rape. The shelter movement has also increasingly moved away from the democratic collectivist form to create "modified collectives" and "modified hierarchies" that can reap the benefits of more formalized structure while still broadly sharing information and decision making and remaining committed to the feminist goals of empowering battered women.[28]

Choices to formalize and expand activities reflect the dilemma "empower whom?" Implicitly, if not always explicitly, shelter and anti-rape activists have decided that empowering women who had been victims of violence was not served well by imagining that they could simultaneously empower all staff members and volunteers equally in the running of the shelters and crisis centers. The two goals of empowering women were in tension, rather than in sisterly harmony, and the participatory ethos has come to be modified. Formalizing authority and tasks, stabilizing staff and services, modifying the collective form, and developing a politics for state funding and educating bureaucrats have come to be seen as more effective ways of empowering the many victims of male violence.

Such tendencies in the women's movement, which became more prominent already by the mid-1970s, have not left it less democratic or more subject to oligarchical tendencies. In fact, formalized organizations have often resulted in greater internal democracy. Formal elections, priorities agreed upon and clearly delimited by vote, committee structures to ensure follow-up, and other routine practices have counteracted tendencies of informal leaders and nonelected activists to determine the agenda. As Staggenborg's comparison of the more formalized Chicago NOW chapter and the more radically egalitarian Chicago Women's Liberation Union, as well as her comparison of pro-choice organizations, has shown, institutionalization has not inevitably meant less radical goals, although it often entails narrowing to an organizationally manageable number of them.[29] Formalized structures have also made possible the participation of a wider variety of women, including those who cannot afford the high time costs of engagement, hence pluralizing feminist citizenship styles in ways that have been of central concern to Dahl and Walzer.

Although in 1968 NOW resisted radical attempts to have its officers chosen by lot and to rotate all positions frequently, the vast influx of younger members in the early 1970s and the rapid proliferation of chapters led it to incorporate much of the ethic of participatory democracy. Local chapters have a great deal of autonomy, engage in grassroots activism, and conduct much of their internal affairs according to informal and egalitarian norms. Consciousness raising became an important part of NOW activity in the 1970s and shaped the communicative ethics of political work in chapters. Nonauthoritarian and supportive styles of empowerment and self-development, consensus seeking and mutual understanding, helpful and noncompetitive ways of expressing criticisms and of listening to others have characterized chapter work. The National Consciousness Raising Committee advises the board at the national level, as well as national officers and the general membership, and currently conducts annual meetings to confront issues such as racism and homophobia within the organization. Much opportunity exists for lateral communication among chapters and committees, and information is widely disseminated rather than monopolized by the central offices. Albeit a large national organization, with over 280,000 members and 700 chapters, NOW functions in a manner that is quite decentralized, open, mobilized at the grass-roots level, and attentive to internal democratic and feminist process.[30]

Movement organizations with formalized structures have significantly greater capacities to sustain coalitions, since they can maintain more effective contact with delegated representatives from a variety of groups. Even simple things like being able to meet downtown at a convenient time in the middle of the day give paid staff members a significant advantage over grass-roots volunteers in coalition work. If alliances among diverse groups of women with multiple interests and identities are central to postmodern feminist politics, as Nancy Fraser and Linda Nicolson have argued, then we must pay increasing attention to those organizational features that facilitate and sustain coalitions. In this sense, formally democratic and representative structures seem to be as key to a postmodern feminism as to a democratic pluralism.[31]

Care, Commonality, and Difference:
Dilemmas of a Feminist Postmodern Pluralism

The National Women's Studies Association (NWSA) is another organization that has developed national representative structures while continuing to innovate in ways that are responsive to feminist concerns with differences among women and to the practical meaning of an ethic of care in organizational life. It provides a nice case study of more recent attempts to recognize rights of differentiated citizenship on the basis of distinctive group identities in feminist organizations.[32] Since its founding in 1976 NWSA has progressively formalized its structure and delineated its hierarchy, which consists of an annual delegate assembly of 150, a coordinating council of twenty-four that meets semiannually and can now initiate legislation, a steering committee of five that convenes between these semiannnual meetings, and a national coordinator.[33] Greater hierarchy was a response to some of the usual problems of an effective executive and daily administration, as well as to the relatively chaotic yearly meetings of the delegate assembly that were vulnerable to disruption by small vocal minorities whose demands were perceived as coercive. But while creating greater formal hierarchy, the association in its meetings at the various levels has tried to achieve consensus, wherever possible, and one-person-one-vote representation has been modified by a weighted voting system based on caucuses, such as women of color, lesbians, and others. Although NWSA is premised on a commonality among all women, it also recognizes basic differences in experiences and types of oppression, and special mechanisms necessary to achieve inclusiveness. Members of caucuses, and especially the women of color caucus, are overrepresented in the delegate assembly and the coordinating council, and this is justified in various ways: to ensure that all views are represented adequately, to lower the costs and increase the benefits of joining for previously underrepresented groups, and to provide the special access to insight that particularly oppressed groups possess. As Robin Leidner points out, following Mansbridge's analysis in *Beyond Adversary Democracy,* these reasons draw upon both unitary and adversary democratic arguments: unitary, to the extent that airing all relevant perspectives and having access to special insight can serve the common interests of all women; and adversary, insofar as the aim is to represent all possible constituents, rather than just current members, by altering the cost-benefit structure of joining. But unitary processes, especially in face-to-face settings, also represent what Carol Gilligan calls an ethic of care. NWSA caucus processes are concerned not just with an ethic of justice or rights to formal equality and fairness but with whether some individuals and groups feel hurt by decisions and ignored as distinctive constituencies. This ethic of care recognizes that all are diminished by the oppression of others, that all are responsible for one another and have a positive duty to give voice to those who are especially oppressed.[34]

This system of representation addresses the dual problem of commonality and difference among women in a creative way, and yet it is an unstable accomplishment, marked by continual conflict and revision. There remain multiple sources of tension, as Leidner's analysis so clearly demonstrates. First, no unambiguously clear criteria of special oppression exist, and in an organization where all members feel oppressed as women, caucuses have begun to proliferate as a way of giving voice to all those who feel the need for distinctive representation. Thus women's studies program administrators and Jewish women have formed caucuses, although others believed that these groups were already well represented. Caucuses have also formed for poor and working-class women, community college women, preK-12 educators, and others, with options for multiple caucus membership and hence multiple weighting of votes. Here the adversary logic of self-identified corporatist group representation competes with that of distinctive types and degrees of oppression whose special insight aims to produce unitary outcomes. And to the extent that some, such as program administrators, do not feel that the politicized criteria for representation have served the interests of academic programs, they have recently begun to hold separate conferences and could conceivably shift the emphasis of their activity outside the perhaps functionally too inclusive NWSA structure.

Second, the unitary caring model can stifle dissent, since those who disagree are often made to feel morally inferior, especially if disagreement is with those designated as having distinctive oppression and special insight. Guilt serves as a powerful weapon, above and beyond the weighted voting, but it also has generated considerable resentment among those who do not have the same access to it, and who often see the views of the majority overridden by smaller groups who wield it at will. Furthermore, I would add, those who resist guilt and appeal to an ethic of rights and fairness of representation in NWSA may feel themselves to be just as motivated by care for the constituencies of women they serve and the important yet still fragile programs they nurture. Resentment over the asymmetrical uses of guilt causes some to exit, or to reduce their participation, thus adding yet another potential source of concern about democratic representativeness.

Third, the meanings of equality that are invoked are varied and shifting, and in the heat of conflict often confused. Sometimes arguments are made for equal power of all individuals, and sometimes for all groups. At other times the emphasis shifts away from equal power to equal satisfaction or equal outcomes, which would entail much more radical concessions by majority to minority views about what constitutes feminist activity or what programs should receive priority. Equal satisfaction, as Leidner argues, is a radical expectation that strains to the limit a heterogeneous organization, and one premised on equality among individual women.

This case illustrates several general challenges of a feminist politics of participation. First, there are new, even postmodern, twists to the old problem of defining "what demos?" An organization that aspires to be inclusive in the face of obdurate exclusionary practices in the broader society must engage in various kinds of imaginary indexing of the missing voices. Who is missing and who should speak for them? Weighted group voting becomes one way of doing this. But the gap between the present and the absent provides a permanent source of tension, since imagining the missing citizens is at once a source of uncertainty and a claim to disproportionate power. Furthermore, if we admit the logic of difference into systems of representation, can we legitimately limit it to certain groups agreed to be especially disadvantaged, or must we open it up to all who *define themselves* as groups in need of distinctive voices? And by what criteria can we limit it, especially if, as in feminist movement organizations, virtually all members feel oppressed and work in various other institutional settings where they experience disadvantages of voice? Feminists can draw upon certain resources to limit the logic of proliferating demands for group representation, for example, distinctive critiques of racism and homophobia. But their own common identity as women who are oppressed, together with the very multiplicity of settings in which they work, point in the direction of unrestricted self-definitions of legitimate group voice. The latter might also occur as a method of regaining the relative weight of voice lost by some because of the initial modifications of one-person-one-vote principles, and so be driven by the logic of power balancing as much as identity, thereby introducing further ambiguity and tension into the logic of representation.

Furthermore, the various rationales for weighted group voice can have different implications for the norms of democratic discourse. Adversarial justifications for numerically privileging a group to lower the costs and increase the benefits of participation for current and future members of that group do not, of themselves, tend to privilege individual speakers. They are relatively compatible with universalist premises of democratic discourse, which guarantee no special insight to a particular individual's speech outside of a dialogue with others, and view truth as a function of the content of speech rather than the specific identity, racial or otherwise, of the speaker. But unitary justifications that appeal to special access to insight in the interests of all and that buttress this with the weapon of guilt are more likely in practice to conflate the privilege accorded the group with the privileged utterances of an individual who speaks in its name, generating a much more profound source of tension with the norms of open dialogue and fallible speech. And this is further exacerbated if the individual speaks in the name of a united and disciplined caucus. This tension can be profoundly educative, to the extent that majority groups feel compelled to recognize insights of minority ones and to accept them as being in the common interest, and to the extent that minority groups learn to admit fallibility without increasing their vulnerability. But it can also be diseducative to the extent that some come to feel that controversial issues are determined by appeal to insight that is above challenge, thereby corrupting a key premise of democratic dialogue.

Recent controversy over the firing of a paid black staff member in the national office of NWSA reveals how precarious some of these representational strategies are.[35] The women of color caucus at the national convention in 1990, privileging the account of this staff person and arguing her right to fully self-determine her own conditions of work, escalated its demands for representation to 50 percent of positions on all bodies as the only way to overcome the racism alleged to dominate the entire organization, and others proposed to further remove any pretense to one-person-one-vote by adding to this self-designated majority the weighted votes of other oppressed groups. Not all women of color agreed with this position, and some argued forcefully that limits on speech in personnel matters should be respected rather than dissolved in an open convention discussion. But such dissenters themselves felt silenced by the caucus, which made appeals to a fundamentalist analysis of racism as all-pervasive, thereby dismissing previous antiracist work of NWSA and denigrating those women of color who had been elected to serve on its governing bodies as having been hand-picked and coopted by white women, who were in turn holding hands with white male power in the universities. The complex organizational structure, which had evolved partly as a response to the demands for distinctive group voice, was now condemned as having been designed to mystify women of color and impose hierarchy on grass-roots activists. When substantial voting margins rejected the nonnegotiable demands to reinstate the fired staffer, dismiss the entire leadership, and ban them from future positions for five years, the women of color caucus resigned, though attempts are now under way to put some of the organizational pieces back together again.[36]

Though some, such as Iris Young, have made an important theoretical argument for differentiated citizenship and group representation, in contrast to traditional universalist conceptions that ignore or suppress difference, the dynamics in NWSA and other organizations attempting to accommodate multicultural claims alert us to the hazards of emphasizing difference, privileging particular voices, and modifying universalist principles of speech and representation, especially when these are attached to strong claims for weighted voting, veto power, and the like. In fact, some of the lessons of participatory democratic pluralism learned in earlier years have now come into profound tension with the issues being raised by multicultural pluralism and differentiated citizenship, and no easy theoretical or practical resolution is yet apparent.

Learning Feminist Pluralism

Over the past quarter of a century the women's movement has been engaged in complex learning processes about the meanings and forms of participation. This has involved rediscovering and relearning many of the lessons of pluralist theory while expanding its limits and providing the basis for a distinctively feminist participatory pluralism. Striking is how quickly the feminist movement began to articulate issues at the heart of pluralist theory, and yet how little guidance it sought in the writings of Dahl, Walzer, or Kaufman, whose critical appreciations of participatory democracy appeared just at the point when the radical women's groups were beginning to wrestle with their own internal dynamics. Although Jo Freeman's "The Tyranny of Structurelessness" first appeared in late 1972, many of its themes were actively discussed at conferences and in women's groups at least as early as the spring of 1970. Undoubtedly some of the soul searching within the remnants of SDS, as represented in Richard Rothstein's compelling critique of participatory democracy that had emerged from Chicago activist circles overlapping Freeman's, had some influence here, and vice versa. But it was largely on the basis of their own experiences that radical women's groups discovered the problems of informal tyranny and cadre control in the absence of formal representation and accountability. They came to recognize the legitimacy of plural citizenship styles among women with varied commitments, as opposed to the exclusion as less committed of those who could not make similarly intensive time investments. They questioned whether unstructured expressiveness was more confusing than clarifying for democratic discourse. They resisted the enforcement of new forms of sisterly virtue and false consensus. They learned how to nurture leadership among distinctive individuals rather than trashing it in the name of the diffuse leadership of all. As they grew older and began to confront the possibilities of feminist commitment over the life course, they began to appreciate the tensions between egalitarian democracy and their own self-development and political efficacy.

These learning processes in the younger and more radical wing of the women's movement drew upon resources in feminist group dynamics built up over several years. They were facilitated by the existence of organizations like NOW that were staffed by women with more established careers and experience in a variety of democratic political organizations, and that simultaneously resisted the extreme anti-organizational tendencies in the radical branch and yet rather quickly made room for participatory styles, consciousness raising, and feminist process. Some activists were members of NOW and various radical groups simultaneously. The organizational conditions for intergenerational learning about democratic participation were considerably more favorable than they were for SNCC or SDS. In addition, by the early 1980s theoretical contributions, such as Mansbridge's *Beyond Adversary Democracy* and her subsequent essay "Feminism and the Forms of Freedom," while recognizing the strengths of unitary democracy, offered feminism and other movements for face-to-face democracy a bridge to political theory that was deeply pluralist in spirit.[37]

Of course, in a movement as diverse and innovative as the women's movement, we see no single learning trajectory, no set of common lessons that all have recognized equally or common problems that all have resolved fully. By the early 1970s, as Freeman has argued, both NOW and many in the radical groups were beginning to recognize that different styles, perspectives, and forms of organization were not weaknesses but strengths that allowed the movement to reach different constituencies and serve different functions. Staggenborg's recent analyses show that successful social movements are likely to include a variety of types of organizational structures, each making different kinds of contributions. Formalized and centralized movement organizations, like the Chicago NOW chapter, are more likely to maintain themselves and the movement over a number of years and to bring about specific policy changes in institutional arenas. Decentralized and nonbureaucratic organizations, like the Chicago Women's Liberation Union, on the other hand, are more likely to develop innovative tactics and alternative institutions that in turn provide cultural resources for future mobilizations.[38]

Nonbureaucratic organizations have also provided the most vibrant settings for learning to participate, even when some of the lessons women learned resulted from painfully negative experiences, and when they subsequently left to work in more established organizations or to form new ones with more formalized structures. Difficult to imagine are the distinctive emphases on listening, empathy, empowerment, and attentiveness to difference, even in these formal settings, had it not been for the early and, in some sectors of the movement, repeated attempts to prefigure egalitarian participation. Prefigurative democracy is perhaps educative for the very reason that it *is* a double-edged sword, with the energy and vision of utopianism, as well as its pitfalls and illusions. In a democratic culture such as ours, which has broadly framed the historical context of participatory learning and has provided multiple options for engagement and few restrictions on exit, the repressive aspects of participatory utopianism that have so worried some competitive elite theorists appear relatively minor.

But feminist theory and organizational practice have not simply rediscovered and recast problems central to pluralism, they have enriched and expanded our understanding of them considerably. Feminists have increasingly come to question forms of organization, such as the small democratic collective, if these can be reproduced only through processes of homogeneous recruitment and thus exclude those of different cultural and sexual orientations or disadvantaged racial and economic backgrounds. What initially was, in many parts of the movement, the unitary and hegemonic ideal has been dislodged in favor of a multiplicity of forms aimed at ensuring inclusiveness and not presuming resources that might make that ideal work. Furthermore, a politics of diversity can no longer be presumed to result simply from the free flowering of democratically decentralized units, but must concern itself with how to form and maintain coalitions among women with different identities, perspectives, and interests. In this, formalized and sometimes centralized, albeit democratically representative, organizations generally prove superior. Feminists have increasingly attempted to incorporate a recognition of difference into the heart of the communicative process itself, avoiding a lazy, even relativist accommodation of adversarial interests and striving to make this recognition serve common interests in women's, and human, liberation. Group representation, weighted voting, and strong claims to special insight, and hence special obligation to listen and question majority perspectives, have become important ways of pluralizing democracy, challenging privilege, and compelling genuine deliberation. A distinctively feminist argument for multivocality has emerged, and this now needs to be linked to organizational analyses that recognize the multiplicity of structural forms and participatory arenas necessary for articulating different voices.

And "a different voice" of care has also enriched a pluralist conception of process by theorizing the submerged practices and discourses of nurturance, relatedness, and empathy often associated with women. But where these are linked in a privileged fashion with the unitary ideal of the democratic collective, the pluralist impulses of feminism are themselves in danger of becoming submerged and flattened. Kathy Ferguson's global critique of bureaucracy in favor of anarcho-feminist collectives that embrace the whole person, embody unambiguous caring and trust, and emphasize process over outcome is the most striking example of this tendency to translate Gilligan into narrow organizational terms. As Patricia Yancey Martin has argued, we need much more nuanced and dimensional concepts of bureaucracy, as well as of feminist organizations, than Ferguson provides, including a renewed emphasis on feminist outcomes rather than such exclusive focus on internal structures.[39]

An ethic of care can at best provide ambiguous and often contradictory guidance for organizational process and structure. Those rape crisis centers and battered women's shelters that choose to formalize authority and limit unstructured participation do so in the name of providing effective care. Those in NWSA who resist overpoliticizing decision-making processes and modes of representation do so in order to be able to nurture often fragile women's studies programs that serve the needs of many. Care, in short, is subject to multiple and conflicting interpretations and provides no unambiguous guidance for democratic process or organizational goals. And we cannot imagine equity and autonomy in complex societies without using universalistic ethics of justice and rights. As Mansbridge notes, "it is too easy in some feminist visions to mistake the corrective for the whole story, or to mistake the stress on nurturance or empathy for the conclusion that all human relations can be encompassed in nurturance."[40] Metanarratives elaborated from Gilligan's important distinctions and grafted onto those of anarchist or radical democratic theory do not help further the project of providing effective capacities for plural voice, but threaten to constrict them and to truncate the educative processes that have been going on for several decades.

A feminist theory of participation is confronted with its own set of perhaps irreducible paradoxes and permanent tensions. Illusions of the singular ideal of fully egalitarian, diffuse, nurturant, and transparent relations are unable to sustain themselves, even as they often prove educative and provide resources for further democratization. Managing commonality and difference is an unstable achievement open to pragmatic solutions that themselves generate new conflicts and problems. Key questions admit no unambiguous answers: what (missing) demos?

Empower whom? Care how? Weight voice how much? Delimit difference where? The innovativeness of feminist practice is to pose these and other questions in ways that pluralize more profoundly the ways in which we imagine citizens in a postmodern participatory democracy.

Notes

Acknowledgments: The following people provided welcome suggestions and critical insight: Karen Hansen, Jenny Mansbridge, Peter Conrad, Shula Reinharz, Claire Reinelt, Andrea Walsh, Robin Leidner, and Ian Shapiro.

1. Ella Baker, "Developing Community Leadership: An Interview," in Gerda Lerner, ed., *Black Women in White America: A Documentary History* (New York: Vintage, 1973), 345–52; Mary King, *Freedom Song* (New York: Morrow, 1987), chaps. 12–13.

2. James Miller, *"Democracy Is in the Streets"* (New York: Simon and Schuster, 1987); Emily Stoper, *The Student Nonviolent Coordinating Committee* (New York: Carlson, 1989).

3. See Carole Pateman, *Participation and Democratic Theory* (Cambridge: Cambridge University Press, 1970), chap. 1.

4. Robert Dahl, *After the Revolution?* (New Haven: Yale University Press, 1970); Michael Walzer, "A Day in the Life of a Socialist Citizen," in *Radical Principles* (New York: Basic Books, 1980), 128–38; see also Arnold Kaufman, "Participatory Democracy: Ten Years Later," in William Connolly, ed., *The Bias of Pluralism* (New York: Atherton, 1969), 201–12; Carmen Sirianni, *Participatory Democracy and Empowerment* (Cambridge: Cambridge University Press, forthcoming).

5. Jo Freeman is the one feminist leader to have been influenced, directly and indirectly, by Dahl, Walzer, and others, as will become apparent below, but even she fails to cite their work. Interview with Jo Freeman, Washington, D.C., 15 February 1992.

6. Pateman, *Participation and Democratic Theory*.

7. Sara Evans, *Personal Politics* (New York: Vintage, 1979), 176.

8. Quoted in ibid., 214.

9. Jane Mansbridge, "Feminism and the Forms of Freedom," Chapter 28, above.

10. Jennifer Nedelsky, "Reconceiving Autonomy: Sources, Thoughts and Possibilities," *Yale Journal of Law and Feminism* 1 (1989): 7–36; and Jane Mansbridge, "Feminism and Democratic Community," in *Democratic Community: NOMOS XXXV*, ed. John W. Chapman and Ian Shapiro (New York: New York University Press, 1993), 339–95.

11. Evans, *Personal Politics*, 215; Jo Freeman, *The Politics of Women's Liberation* (New York: McKay, 1975), 86; Anita Shreve, *Women Together, Women Alone* (New York: Viking, 1989).

12. Noelie Maria Rodriguez, "Transcending Bureaucracy: Feminist Politics at a Shelter for Battered Women," *Gender and Society* 2:2 (1988): 214–27.

13. Freeman, *The Politics of Women's Liberation*, chap. 4. This version is an expansion of "The Tyranny of Structurelessness," which appeared in *Ms.*, The Berkeley Journal of Sociology, and at least one collection on radical feminism in the early 1970s.

14. Ann Popkin, "Bread and Roses" (Ph.D. diss., Brandeis University, 1978), chaps. 4–5; "The Social Experience of Bread and Roses: Building a Community and Creating a Culture," in *Women, Class, and the Feminist Imagination*, ed. Karen V. Hansen and Ilene J. Philipson (Philadelphia: Temple University Press, 1989), 182–212.

15. Mansbridge, "Feminism and the Forms of Freedom," Chapter 28, above.

16. Karen Hansen, "Women's Unions and the Search for Political Identity," in *Women, Class, and the Feminist Imagination*, ed. Hansen and Philipson, 227; Popkin, "Bread and Roses."

17. Anne Koedt, quoted in Freeman, *The Politics of Women's Liberation*, 134ff.; Miller, *"Democracy Is in the Streets."*

18. Hansen, "Women's Unions," 223; Todd Gitlin, *The Whole World Is Watching* (Berkeley: University of California Press, 1980), 156.

19. Alice Echols, *Daring to Be BAD* (Minneapolis: University of Minnesota Press, 1989), 204–10, quotation on 207.

20. Naomi Weisstein, quoted in Evans, *Personal Politics,* 223; Freeman, *The Politics of Women's Liberation,* 121; Linda Gordon, untitled history of Bread and Roses, quoted in Popkin, "Bread and Roses," 156; Maren Lockwood Carden, *The New Feminist Movement* (New York: Russell Sage, 1974), 87ff.; Echols, *Daring to Be BAD,* 204–10.

21. Suzanne Staggenborg, "Stability and Innovation in the Women's Movement: A Comparison of Two Movement Organizations," *Social Problems* 36:1 (February 1989): 75–92; Freeman, *The Politics of Women's Liberation,* 129ff.

22. Wini Breines, *Community and Organization in the New Left,* 2nd ed. (New Brunswick, N.J.: Rutgers University Press, 1988).

23. Staggenborg, "Stability and Innovation"; Hansen, "Women's Unions," 219ff.

24. Naomi Weisstein and Heather Booth, "Will the Women's Movement Survive?" *Sister* 4 (1975): 1–6.

25. Pateman, *Participation and Democratic Theory*; Carol Gould, *Rethinking Democracy* (Cambridge: Cambridge University Press, 1988).

26. See Susan Schechter, *Women and Male Violence* (Boston: South End Press, 1982), 108, 249; Stephanie Riger, "Vehicles for Empowerment: The Case of Feminist Movement Organizations," in *Studies in Empowerment,* ed. Julian Rappaport, Carolyn Swift, and Robert Hess (New York: Hayworth, 1984), 99–117.

27. Myra Marx Ferree, "Equality and Autonomy: Feminist Politics in the United States and West Germany," in Mary Fainsod Katzenstein and Carol McClurg Mueller, eds., *The Women's Movement in the United States and Western Europe* (Philadelphia: Temple University Press, 1987), 172–95.

28. Nancy Matthews, "Surmounting a Legacy: The Expansion of Racial Diversity in a Local Anti-Rape Movement," *Gender and Society* 3:4 (December 1989): 518–32; Elizabethann O'Sullivan, "What Has Happened to Rape Crisis Centers? A Look at Their Structures, Members and Funding," *Victimology* 3:1–2 (1978): 45–62; Barbara Levy Simon, "In Defense of Institutionalization: A Rape Crisis Center as a Case Study," *Journal of Sociology and Social Welfare* 9 (1982): 485–502; Janet Gornick, Martha Burt, and Karen Pittman, "Structure and Activities of Rape Crisis Centers in the Early 1980s," *Crime and Delinquency* 31 (1985): 247–68; Susan Schechter, *Women and Male Violence,* 98ff.; for a particularly interesting analysis of a statewide movement to transform official practices while maintaining significant shelter autonomy at the local level, see Claire Reinelt, "Moving onto the Terrain of the State: The Battered Women's Movement and the Politics of Engagement," in Myra Marx Ferree and Patricia Yancey Martin, eds., *Feminist Organizations: Harvesters of the New Women's Movement* (Philadelphia: Temple University Press, forthcoming).

29. Staggenborg, "Stability and Innovation"; Staggenborg, "The Consequences of Professionalization and Formalization in the Pro-Choice Movement," *American Sociological Review* 53 (August 1988): 585–606.

30. Maren Lockwood Carden, *The New Feminist Movement* (New York: Russell Sage, 1974), chap. 9; Freeman, *The Politics of Women's Liberation,* chap. 3.

31. Nancy Fraser and Linda Nicolson, "Social Criticism without Philosophy: An Encounter between Feminism and Postmodernism," in Linda Nicolson, ed., *Feminism/Postmodernism* (New York: Routledge, 1990), 35.

32. For a general argument along these lines, though one with somewhat different organizational requirements than those of NWSA, see Iris Young, "Polity and Group Difference: A Critique of the Ideal of Universal Citizenship," *Ethics* 99:2 (January 1989): 250–74; an explicitly postmodern reading is more apparent in her "The Ideal of Community and the Politics of Difference," *Social Theory and Practice* 12:1 (Spring 1986): 1–26, reprinted in Nicolson, ed., *Feminism/Postmodernism,* 300–23.

33. Robin Leidner, "Stretching the Boundaries of Liberalism: Democratic Innovation

in a Feminist Organization," *Signs* 16:2 (1991): 263–89. Leidner does not consider the most recent changes in this essay, but the logic of her argument is nonetheless relevant here.

34. Jane Mansbridge, *Beyond Adversary Democracy* (New York: Basic Books, 1980); Carol Gilligan, *In a Different Voice* (Cambridge: Harvard University Press, 1982).

35. See the accounts in *Sojourner: The Women's Forum,* August 1990, pp. 8–9; October 1990, pp. 9–12; and *off our backs,* August–September 1990, pp. 1, 10–25.

36. For the most recent developments in NWSA, and their significance for democratic theory, see Robin Leidner, "Constituency, Accountability, and Deliberation: Reshaping Democracy in the National Women's Studies Association," *NWSA Journal* 5:1 (Spring 1993): 4–27; and Carmen Sirianni, "Feminist Pluralism and Democratic Learning: The Politics of Citizenship in the National Women's Studies Association," *NWSA Journal* 5:3 (Fall 1993): 367–84.

37. Mansbridge, *Beyond Adversary Democracy,* and "Feminism and the Forms of Freedom," Chapter 28, above.

38. Freeman, *The Politics of Women's Liberation,* 83; Staggenborg, "Stability and Innovation," 90.

39. Kathy Ferguson, *The Feminist Case against Bureaucracy* (Philadelphia: Temple University Press, 1984); Patricia Yancey Martin, "A Commentary on *The Feminist Case against Bureaucracy* by Kathy Ferguson," *Women's Studies International Forum* 10:5 (1986): 543–48; and "Rethinking Feminist Organizations," *Gender and Society* 4 (1990): 182–206.

40. Jane Mansbridge, "Feminism and Democracy," *The American Prospect* 1 (Spring 1990): 132.

30
Internal Organization and Social Structure in Community Organizing: The Case of ACORN

Gary Delgado

In our cities, in our states,
We're the ones that pay the freight,
But the rich folks go rolling along.

Keep us divided, whites from blacks,
Moderate and poor on different tracks.
And the rich folks go rolling along.

—ACORN Marching Song
(to tune of the Caison Song),
ACORN songbook, 1982

To assess the prospects of the Association of Community Organizations for Reform Now (ACORN), it is necessary to examine its internal organization, its staff-leadership-membership relations, its choice of issues and means of achieving its goals, its ideology, and its resources—and to observe how, in these various aspects, it interacts with the dominant external social structure.

The Social Composition of ACORN

In most community organizations the roles of members, leaders, and organizers are markedly different. When asked to differentiate between group leaders and community organizers, Zach Pollett, regional director for six ACORN states, smiled: "Why, leaders lead and organizers develop leaders."[1]

Reprinted from Gary Delgado, *Organizing the Movement: The Roots and Growth of ACORN* (Philadelphia: Temple University Press, 1986), pp. 179–210, 248–50. © 1986 by Gary Delgado.

Indigenous Leadership

Most of the community organizing literature is in agreement on a number of points regarding the role of leadership. First, leadership should be indigenous, composed of people from the neighborhood. Second, leaders are not born but developed, usually by organizers. Third, leadership is not structural; it is a function. As Meg Campbell writes in "The ACORN Maintenance Model":

> Leadership is something you do rather than a position or title you hold. It is something that happens in a group not a particularly designated person with certain qualities. Leadership, then, is responding to the current needs of the group in such a way that the group is helped to go on with whatever task it has and to have its own needs met at the same time. A person is a leader when s/he offers help or services to a group in a way the group can receive.[2]

Within this short definition lie all the problems and contradictions of the organizer-leader dichotomy. The organizer who creates a formal structure with definitive participatory roles may then render the formal structure irrelevant in a particular situation by defining the terrain of discussion or steering the group toward a particular issue. "Responding to the current needs of the group" is, of course, a matter of judgment, and implicit in Campbell's statement is a notion of who has the real power to determine the appropriateness of a specific response: the organizer.

The organizer training schools are unanimously agreed that developing indigenous leaders is the toughest task of the organizer. Mike Miller has written that organizers find leaders by discovery (listening to what other members of the community say about a particular person) and observation (watching leaders in meetings and while working within the group).[3]

"Leaders are developed through experience, mainly the experience of action," maintains Mark Lindberg of the New England Training Center. Therefore, he continues, the organizer should

1. give potential leaders a job;
2. create obligations for potential leaders;
3. when possible, let people's peers convince potential leaders to act;
4. when necessary, manipulate the situation;
5. to get people into action, heighten their emotions;
6. when possible, pick a leader who is directly affected by the issues;
7. graduate leaders to new levels of experience.[4]

Steve Max of the Midwest Academy adds, "Developing leaders is like teaching singing, acting or painting. You can't create talent where none exists, but you can shape and develop what talent there is."[5]

None of the literature minimizes the importance of training leaders; in fact, it takes special care to define leadership development as the most important part of an organizer's job. Neil Gilbert, for instance, writes:

> Recruitment is a singularly arduous chore in a professional movement aimed at the poor; not only are the organizers outsiders, but the individuals they are seeking to enlist are predominantly nonparticipants. The task is difficult, but not insurmountable. Indigenous leaders may be uncovered and trained; and less articulate and less motivated members of the target population may be stimulated to participate. This process, however, is long-range, involving a concentrated commitment of time and energy, with no guaranteed payoff.[6]

What happens when leaders do get "developed"? One example of a seasoned leader is Willard Johnson, former chairman of Arkansas ACORN, a retired railroad blacksmith whose "enthusiasm for socialism," according to a *New York Times* interview, "is about as deep as Barry Goldwater's."[7] After becoming a member of the Quorum Court in 1974, Johnson won a seat on the Little Rock Planning Commission. While he did talk out of one side of his mouth about the importance of the free enterprise system, in an interview I conducted with him in July 1979 he also talked about how his position on the Little Rock Planning Commission has allowed him to keep a freeway from being built through the center of town and to make sure that residential neighborhoods were not down-zoned for commercial interests. Johnson is very clear about his blue-collar status: "I'm the only peasant down there at City Hall. . . . My background is different, most of the other commissioners have had an educational advantage that I haven't had—they move in different social circles."[8]

Paul Cox, an ACORN leader in New Orleans and a tugboat captain, was moved to work for lifeline utility rates "because the company is a damn monopoly."[9] And in Bridgeport, Connecticut,

> Tom and Cathy Leehy of Remington Street said they have been fighting by themselves to no avail for better traffic signals and more signs in their neighborhood after their child was hit by a car. "At least we'll attempt as a group," said Leehy.
> "Before ACORN we all used to sit in front of our TVs at night and wait for something to happen."[10]

The good stories of leadership development are plentiful enough, yet clashes between staff and leaders have also affected the dynamic of developing the organization. For example, Bill Brookerd, former chair of Nevada ACORN, resigned in 1979 because he claimed he never had access to copies of the ACORN organizing model or financial information. Similarly, R. Walker, a former ACORN member and currently a Pine Bluff, Arkansas, alderman, recalls having floor fights with organizer Madeleine Talbot over access to membership lists and dues receipts.

Both of these incidents were coupled with charges of "organizer manipulation."

Barbara Friedman, a former ACORN trainer, remarked: "Manipulation can be an unrealistic hangup. A good professional organizer can tell early on who would make the best officer. We use common sense and try to be sensitive to the feelings of the members, but we don't agonize and torture ourselves."[11] Friedman's approach is eminently practical, but how does it merge with the official line that "members run the organization"? It is clear that organizers play a role in choosing and developing group leaders; in selecting potential candidates, they look for specific skills such as the ability to talk to people in the neighborhood, being articulate, having time and energy and demonstrated ability to accomplish tasks. Because of ACORN's organizing approach, however, prior leadership of a community group (as opposed to a labor or church organization) might actually rule out a candidate as an initial leader of an ACORN group. Extensive experience with a left political formation that had a "developed" ideological framework would almost certainly eliminate a neighborhood resident as an ACORN organizer's (and almost any community organizer's) candidate for a leadership position in a new ACORN group because of the possibility that such a leader would be pushing another organization's contradictory agenda. As a result, ACORN leaders with little or no prior leadership experience of any sort are very often voted into office by ACORN members.

This is both a plus and a minus for the organization. It is a plus because the leaders are truly indigenous grass-roots people who can usually be developed effectively within the ACORN structure. It is a minus because very often such leadership brings no close connection to an existing infrastructure, and because people without previous organizational experience are less likely to challenge the assumptions and assertions of ACORN organizers, at least initially. Thus, while it is true that members do run the organizational meetings and take part in decision making, it is equally true that the parameters of these discussions are set by the organizers. Given their experiential base, indigenous leaders are not in a position to challenge these parameters.

This rather obvious tension in the organization has manifested itself in several ways. First, seasoned ACORN leaders have repeatedly questioned the organization's commitment to hiring and training indigenous leaders as organizers. Rathke and others have articulated the hope that the sons and daughters of present members would choose to become staff organizers, but thus far ACORN has not achieved this goal. The problems of recruiting members as organizers include low staff salaries, class and racial differences that are actually exacerbated by the leader-organizer role relationship, and the inability of the organization to provide a social and cultural support system for nonwhite and low-income staff.

ACORN's difficulty in this area is not unique. In the context of another community group in Pittsburgh, Neil Gilbert observes:

> As organizers, nonprofessionals are often better equipped than the professionals for recruiting low-income participants, securing their trust, and activating their will to cooperate. The crucial factor is not the hiring of indigenous leaders, but the capacity in which they are employed. In Pittsburgh, the philosophy and structure of the program dictated that these individuals be skimmed off to expedite services rather than to organize a movement. As a result, *whatever time and effort went into recruitment and indoctrination were quickly dissipated* [emphasis added].[12]

Though ACORN is unlikely to hire members to expedite services, it has occasionally—conscious of the need for constituent representation on the staff—precipitously thrust leaders into staff positions when they were neither technically nor ideologically prepared. The resulting level of friction was not simply over questions of access to information, manipulation, or even recruitment. These are, of course, vital issues. But more fundamentally, there are class and race differences between organizers and members that are generally not successfully overridden by any unifying, comprehensive ideology.

Scholar-activist Tim Sampson has written of "the need of the professional to define him or herself as of the people they are working with rather than a breed apart,"[13] but the predominant tendency in the world of community organizers, and particularly in ACORN, is to apply a rigorous division of labor. Citizen Action Program (CAP) leaders in Chicago, interviewed by Joan Lancourt in 1976, observed:

> The organizers did not speak in public, did not get their names in the paper . . . did not speak at meetings. [They] did the preparation work . . . research, getting the fliers out, arranging the meeting place . . . making sure people were coming . . . getting there early to set up the chairs. All that kind of stuff. Gradually, in the better CAP organizations more and more of that was transferred to the leadership.[14]

In my own interviews with ACORN leaders I ran into an interesting set of perceptions. When asked to describe the staff functions, all eighteen leaders talked about "technical assistance and/or resource development." Yet when pressed, all but two admitted that virtually all the ideas for tactics and strategy in their last organizing campaign came from the organizer. Within ACORN, as within most large community organizations, organizers do in fact call the shots in terms of organizational direction; the organization has in fact become a staff oligarchy. That development is understandable: with greater size and complexity, increased specialization, and departmentalization, it is simply not possible for all members to possess enough of the relevant information for informed decision making; therefore, communications increasingly flow from the top down.[15] Why, then, the ideological commitment to "the people decide"?

The history of community organization shows that, for the most part, there was no leader-organizer dichotomy in the early days of either the labor movement or the civil rights movement. The twin roles were actually developed in the early community organizations to address the question of the role of "social work" professionals in ghetto communities. The question surfaced anew in the civil rights movement when the need arose to define a principled role for people outside the constituency immediately affected: progressive whites. The role dichotomy was further reinforced in the merger of the Alinsky-founded Industrial Areas Foundation (IAF) with the Chicago Students for a Democratic Society (SDS) in the Citizen Action Program, where former SDSers felt compelled to define separate roles for organizers and leaders.

Within ACORN, the problems of class and race differences between leaders and staff also exist, but the leader-organizer role separation has defined interaction in an acceptable manner. In a frank moment, however, one organizer reflected, "It certainly is true that the organizer-leader thing is somewhat of a game—but it's a game that forces me to remember who I am and where I come from, a game I know how to play. Anyway, until I hear about another set-up that doesn't completely allow organizers to run roughshod over people, it's the only game in town."[16]

Given this situation, a fundamental question about the staff-leadership structure is this: has the indigenous leadership ever made a transition to exercising real political power, either through the formal leadership role or through taking over staff positions? For the most part, leaders who have joined the staff have actually had less power in the organization in their new positions. Very often the power of leaders is based on their relationship with a particular group. Joining the staff negatively affects that relationship. Becoming "paid staff" instead of "first among equals" in the community can set up real barriers between leaders-turned-organizers and their former constituents. Moreover, power on the ACORN staff is based on a number of other variables: seniority, the demonstrated ability to produce organizational victories, the ability to articulate a position or organizational direction and organize the staff to pursue it, and, perhaps most important, political proximity to the staff leadership.

Leaders joining the staff, with few exceptions, have been unprepared to deal with multilevel nuances, direct argumentative style, and protracted (often three-day and -night) meetings. Although leaders have been able to push issues and agendas on a local level, no one leader has had a significant impact on the organization without the direct collaboration and support of the senior staff. This is not to say that ACORN's leaders do not influence the organization's direction; an example of a member-leader groundswell was the Jesse Jackson endorsement. However, even that endorsement—though initiated by activist leaders—was discussed, planned, and operationalized by the staff.

This observation points to an underlying structural fact: organizers, given their background, have had, in the words of the ACORN People's Platform, "the chance to be rich" and have chosen instead, at least temporarily, to work for what most members consider "beer money." Part of the ideological contradiction is that middle-class organizers who have rejected the organization's avowed goals of gaining economic benefits cannot blatantly direct low-income members who in fact enter the organization to make the system work in their interest.

In part, this motivational rift stems from the fact that some ACORN members are uncomfortable with the organization's tactics. On a more basic level, however, the cleavages between leaders and organizers are a reflection of differences in class, race, and sex between ACORN members and staff.

The Staff

ACORN's 50,000 members are 70 percent black and Latino, 70 percent female, and almost all from the working class (or reserve labor). In contrast, the 150-member staff is almost all white, about half female, and for the most part, from upper-middle-class families. Most organizers have college degrees, about 15 percent from elite institutions. Though these statistics do not, of themselves, reveal anything but a contrast between the backgrounds of the staff and members, closer examination of the 1982 staff reveals that: of the nine field operations directors, all are white and two are women; four (all men) graduated from Ivy League colleges; three of the four directors of project categories—national operations, campaign operations, internal operations, and the United Labor Unions—are men; and all four graduated from elite institutions, two from Ivy League schools.

In small-group discussions in the 1979–80 year-end/year-beginning meeting that included over 120 ACORN staff members, the primary reason given for working for ACORN, at salaries of $4,000–$8,000, was that the kind of organizing ACORN was involved in really worked. In keeping with the ACORN line "mouth—good; action—better," organizers came to ACORN to be part of something that worked.

But how long do organizers stay? ACORN recruits some sixty to seventy-five per year, most of them fresh out of college. The majority, probably 70 percent, do not make it through the first three months, often being surprised by the sheer amount of work, the discipline, and the number of times people will assure them that they will "definitely be there" for a meeting and then fail to appear. Those who progress through the first drive usually begin to reevaluate their commitment again at six months. This time the question is more likely to be: "Can I really become an organizer?" About four out of five trainees who make it through three months will stay through their first year's commitment. After a year, the major question becomes: "Do I really want to organize with ACORN?" Unfortunately, once again, the fallout at this stage is great: almost half of the remaining trainees will leave, usually to work in social-change jobs "where the money is better and the hours are fewer."

There are, of course, other career junctures in ACORN. The decision to have or expand a family may influence an organizer to resign, while the recent decision of three key staff people to "take a break" after ten years reflects the pace and constant demands of the organization. In sum, the rate of turnover, especially initially, is quite high.

Nevertheless, ACORN has probably produced more trained local organizers than any other network of community organizations, and many continue to do social-change work. Ann Lassen, a former ACORN recruiter, explained, "We look for people who are right out of college who want experience, or people who don't like traditional jobs and are searching for something more creative." When asked about the ability of ACORN to recruit people from low-income backgrounds, Lassen admitted problems. "But it isn't just the money," she added. "The work schedule, collecting money from members, the level of responsibility required of new recruits is fairly intimidating to everyone—people with little experience with that kind of time and energy commitment to work usually don't last."[17]

What kind of people do last through the rigorous recruitment and training process? Kopkind writes:

> The organizers come from out of state, for the most part: Steve Holt and Meg Campbell, for instance, went to Harvard and Radcliffe, and both taught in Massachusetts before settling in Arkansas. Barbara Friedman went to the University of California at Berkeley, heard about ACORN in a Vocations for Social Change publication, and came to Little Rock to check it out; she stayed. The out-of-state organizers seem to have come with no heavy ideological baggage. They are not radical intellectuals who see their work "among the people" as direct steps to a predictable revolution. They clearly express a radical sensibility; most are recognizable children of the movements of the sixties, but not adherents to particular sects. Perhaps they are the kind of people who would have been Peace Corps volunteers in 1963. But the social history of the last decade has given them a different political context for their interest in community development.[18]

Examples include Phil Moore, who used to work in Boston but moved to Detroit to put his planning degree to better use; Val Orselli, who came to work for ACORN after reading about the organization in *Working Papers;* and Terry Sheehan, who came as a VISTA volunteer and stayed on "to do some real organizing."[19] Though the managing editor of the *Pine Bluff* (Arkansas) *Commercial* has called ACORN organizers "damn Yankee know-it-all kids who would come in and tell us how to run things,"[20] Denver city councilman Sal Carpio says, "They're pros—they really push to keep everybody on their toes."[21]

In part, this push comes from the example set by ACORN's thirty-six-year-old chief organizer, Wade Rathke. Rathke is a native of New Orleans, where he attended Benjamin Franklin High School, a public school that caters to children with IQs of at least 120. His mother, a junior college administrator, holds a Ph.D. in English, and his father is an accountant for a large oil company. Rathke fits the profile of the young radical. While he did spend two years at Williams College as a member of the local SDS chapter, he also worked as a draft counselor, rock band manager, and journalist. Lanky and red-headed, with a prominent Adam's apple, Rathke is prone to pithy, down-home proverbs and cowboy boots. Though many activists describe him as arrogant and obnoxious, even his enemies in the organizing world will grudgingly admit his accomplishments. Faith Evans, former director of the Commission on Racial Justice of the United Church of Christ, calls Rathke "arrogant but effective,"[22] while Andrea Kydd, former administrator and trouble-shooter in the VISTA program, through which ACORN received grants, and current director of the Youth Project, a national foundation, views Rathke as "the only organizer from this period who ever really built something substantial."[23] As Cockburn and Ridgeway write, "To an outsider, ACORN's politics seem relatively limited. Rathke himself has the organizational reputation of being a kind of loner, playing the world of citizen politics rather in the manner of a general in a Pentagon war room."[24]

Military, gawky, arrogant—all these adjectives describe Rathke. He has also been called by other activists "piercingly analytical," "an organizational genius," and charismatic."[25] When asked to describe in terms of his own roots his future vision for ACORN, Rathke will point to an eclectic concoction: his admiration for the populist Non-Partisan League, the Southern Tenant Farmers' Union, and Huey Long's Share Our Wealth clubs, as well as his own involvement in the welfare rights movement and George Wiley's new majority: the Movement for Economic Justice. His politics? Like most community organizers, Rathke avoids labels. On various occasions he has claimed to be "just good at what I do—moving an agenda for low- to moderate-income people to take back what's rightfully ours." When asked what is rightfully theirs, Rathke smiles, "Why, everything!"[26] On the question of ideology, Rathke has said, "Our membership aren't out there in the clouds somewhere saying this is the way the world should look in 100 years. Our philosophy is very closely related to our membership's daily life experience. There's no ideology that instructs what we do. People make decisions and they start moving."[27]

The question of who makes decisions to move whom is clearly a subject of debate. In my view ACORN reflects the shortcomings of an organization that is controlled by white middle-class male progressives. These shortcomings are evident and may be analyzed in two areas: the development of issues within the organization, and the recruitment, development, training, and advancement of other than white male staff.

Issues and Infrastructure

Issues ACORN has addressed include redlining, school closings, taxes, utility rates, housing, and welfare, all of which have a fundamentally economic dimension. However, with a constituency that is 70 percent women and 70 percent black and Latino, the organization has purposely avoided issues that reflect other than economic inequalities—questions of gender and race. One consequence of this choice is that the organization has been unable to develop a staff infrastructure supportive of women and people of color.

Women's Issues

ACORN is quick to point to the obvious—the prevalence of women in key leadership and staff positions. The number of women leaders is not unusual, however: most community organizations, indeed most progressive organizations, are composed predominantly of women. As Komarovsky writes:

> The home is regarded as primarily the sphere of the woman rather than of the man. Consequently, when a rent increase or a deterioration in services impinges on the home, it is usually the woman's task to deal with it since it lies within her sphere. This pattern holds true more frequently in working-class than in middle-class households because of the greater separation of the roles typically found there. Building organization mobilization is commonly based on a network of social ties within a building which women, whether employed outside the home or not, are much more likely to form.

Along the same lines, Rubin adds, "Building organizations, like PTA's, provides an acceptable avenue for social action, since activities outside the home are seen as threatening by a significant minority of working-class husbands."[28]

Although ACORN does follow this pattern, it has not addressed the issues that are raised by progressive women's organizations: day care, equal wages, reproductive rights. When asked about this gap, Rathke replied, "It's never come up. If a local group wants to take up the issue of abortion, that's their prerogative. We have had a group in Memphis address the question of rape—in a public school situation where a young woman was raped, we went after the principal on how he dealt with her."[29] Subsequently, ACORN has initiated anti-rape campaigns in Boston, New Orleans, and Detroit. Although this direction is important, it still remains the exception rather than the rule in ACORN. Seth

Borgos, responding to the question of why ACORN has not been active around reproductive rights issues, answered, "It might split our constituency—many of our black members are not for it."[30] While both Rathke's and Borgos's explanations sound reasonable, they do not take into account the fact that many issue campaigns are developed by the ACORN research department and "sold" to organizers in various locations. Moreover, it is important to note that ACORN did not, for instance, endorse the Equal Rights Amendment until it was clear that without such endorsement the Texas Women's Political Caucus initially would not back the ACORN People's Platform.

On the staff level, women who were once organizers argue that the atmosphere within ACORN was relatively unsupportive to women—or to men with families—and that although many women had titles of power within the organization, none had serious control of major decisions.[31] Former ACORN staff member Madeleine Adamson writes, "The turnover rate for all organizers is high. For women, it appears to be even higher. The reasons are varied but a few stand out. They have to do with lifestyle—the difficulty of integrating any other interests in life with organizing, particularly having a family, and with the difficulty of competing in what is still a male-dominated field."[32]

ACORN has a significant number of women organizers. As in many cases, however, numbers do not tell the full story. In my view the assessment of the former organizers is correct. Although women do have a semblance of power within the organization, they do not in fact have power on the staff: on a staff of over 150, fewer than five women have access to major decision making. Male dominance in ACORN, therefore, is expressed two ways: first, structurally, in the issues it chooses and by not supporting the ability of people with families to work within the organization; second, informally, through the "old boys' network" that does make decisions.

Racial Issues

ACORN has a line: "Rather than organizing around racism, we involve our members in campaigns that affect all low- and moderate-income people, building solidarity." Echoing the line, ACORN leader Willard Johnson notes, "There's something about ACORN . . . it doesn't make any difference what a person's skin is. That's one benefit I think I've gotten out of ACORN. Our people have common problems and they try to help one another, not kick them in the butt because they're black or Catholic or something."[33] Former organizers Meg Campbell and Barbara Friedman have argued:

> We could have gotten hundreds more members with a racist position, but we kept it what it was, political and economic. After all, the issue never was "integration."

> We don't cut issues racially where that isn't relevant. There's no point in constructing rhetorical enemies who cannot be defeated. Short of race warfare, black people cannot triumph over whites; but whites and blacks can win against real estate agencies or real estate boards, and they do. Winning is what is important in organizing, and it's almost an obsession with ACORN.[34]

ACORN's approach to issues of race is exactly in line with the rhetoric of the Alinsky organizations. Lancourt writes:

> The closest the black organizers came to using the racial issue itself as a rallying point was in their tactical use of rhetoric to awaken black pride. Specific contests were most often defined as community control versus outside control, or lack of institutional accountability. That outside control and institutions were white was implicit, but issues of racism were acted upon in the context of more and better jobs, education, or housing rather than solely black versus white.[35]

In fact, in an interview in *Just Economics* in 1979, IAF director Ed Chambers advocated getting minority organizers working in white communities "because they never really integrate all the universals until they understand the majority culture."[36]

But ACORN, IAF, and Citizen Action do not always simply merge race and class; they avoid racial issues. In one early campaign, notes Martin Kirby:

> ACORN issued a 19-point list of questionable aspects of the highway situation. Only two points were concerned with race. It was pointed out that the highway would "slash through neighborhoods and increase busing." The question was also raised as to why a paragraph in a preliminary draft of the project's Environmental Impact Statement had been stricken from later versions. The missing paragraph said that the highway at one point would "penetrate an area in which intensive efforts have been taken to produce a racially integrated neighborhood." Such intrusion could very possibly result in the complete disruption of these efforts, resulting in the complete isolation of all-black neighborhoods.[37]

To ACORN's credit, the organizing staff did support the 1979 effort of a group in Star City, Arkansas, to desegregate a laundromat, but that action was initiated by black leaders and members in a town that had no organizer.

The avoidance of racial issues within the organization has both internal and external implications. In avoiding issues of race, ACORN has been unable to form linkages with single-issue minority groups organized around desegregation, police brutality, or saving vital services. This position has also had its effects on the recruitment of staff:

> For young Blacks, if you want to get into what's happening in your community, an ACORN or a Fair Share is not the place to do it. People still do not, in the Black community, believe that the primary reason for

discrimination is economic or class; they believe it is racial. People will join ACORN but when you talk about what young Blacks want to organize, they want to organize something that deals specifically with racial issues as sort of the focal point for the organization.

Second, the organizations are inadvertently racist. . . . I don't mean they're anti-Black or anti-Hispanic but what they do is they treat everybody the same way. If you don't take into account the fact that there are real differences culturally you're going to have problems. For instance, for any white person who comes on staff, there are natural social relations. If a Black organizer comes on a staff where there are few other Black staff, the social relations have to come from that very small group or from the constituency and that messes with the whole organizer/leader dichotomy. That causes role confusion for people. They get confused about who they are, what they're doing, because the hierarchy is reflective of essentially what society is; it's all white and mostly male.[38]

Within the ACORN staff, formal decision making takes place on several levels. Approaches to local campaigns are discussed between local organizers and their regional directors before options are presented to local boards. In the setting of national priorities, a prerequisite to action is the development of a written memo presenting the pluses and minuses of a proposed action, a set of organizational options, and a list of proposed first steps. Although demonstrated ability to articulate the plan and proximity to key staff play a part in an organizer's ability to get a memo discussed at a national or regional staff meeting, it is my experience that, once on the agenda, the plan usually gets thorough discussion, and staff will take some action. Still, though these discussions tend to be reasonable forums for airing ideas, they also tend to be most accessible to those who have the experience in the organization and the developed conceptual skill to write, organize, and fight for a particular direction. Structurally, the people in the society and in the organization who are in the best position to operate in this context are white males.

It should be noted that although my discussion of the disproportionate percentage of white males in positions of power centers on ACORN, this situation reflects the reality of most left or liberal organizations. Within ACORN a number of attempts have been made to address the problem, including the use of salary differentials and other incentives for minority recruits. The most successful initiative, however, has been the recruitment of young minority organizers to the affiliated union staff, where the hierarchy is less developed and the variety of work sites available for organizing allows for the development of many organizing approaches.

While all the large community organizing networks have attempted to initiate recruitment programs to remedy the small proportion (less than 10 percent nationwide) of minority organizers on their staffs, they have done so without attempting to address their fundamental assumptions that (1) economic issues subsume issues of race and gender; (2) organizers must be trained in the dominant culture even to work in their own communities; and (3) the structure of the organization need not change in order to successfully bring in people of color. Until these assumptions are questioned, such efforts will continue to be unsuccessful.

With regard to issues of both race and gender, ACORN and the other community organizing networks replicate and reproduce the values of the dominant society and culture. In fact, with the exception of the explicitly political demands ACORN has made on the Democratic party, the organization is susceptible to the criticism of economism—to reducing all issues to their lowest possible denominator: money or benefits. This reductionist tendency carries over from the way in which issues and campaigns are framed into two other areas of internal development: internal solidarity and ideology.

Internal Solidarity

Internal solidarity is a key variable in predicting the ability of any organization to be successful and to survive. Solidarity or *esprit de corps* may be thought of as the development of feeling among members on behalf of the organization resulting in a sense of common identity, the development of in-group/out-group relations, and general commitment to defend the group.[39] It is important to note, for example, that there appears to be little difference in the socioeconomic status of members and leaders. The majority of ACORN's twenty-six-member board are neither college educated nor employed in white-collar jobs.

Amitai Etzioni has observed that two factors predict the difficulty in socializing members into an organization: the selectivity of the organization's recruitment process, and the degree to which the organization's values and norms are concomitant with society's as a whole.[40] Lancourt, noting that the Alinsky citizen-action organizations, at least, are fundamentally system affirming, writes, "The major socialization tasks appear to have been making the existing social values of participation and democratic decision-making operative."[41]

I do not agree with Lancourt's conclusion that community organizations are fundamentally system affirming. Struggles over the allocation of urban space, service cutbacks, welfare, and housing put community organizations on the front lines of battles for state-controlled resources. Moreover, community organizations create a contradictory system of social practices that validates oppositional behavior.

In addition, I would argue that the membership selection process is an important factor in building group solidarity. Mancur Olson's influential book *The Logic of Collective Action* argues that a group will not reach its full mobilization potential unless its members are provided with "selected (material) incentives."[42] As economistic as I have conceded ACORN's approach to be, the recruitment of stable leadership in the organization points to, if anything, the opposite conclusion: people join and maintain connection with the organization because of nonmaterial feelings of solidarity with other members and because of an identification with the collective actions of the organization.

My own experiences with this issue may illustrate the point. When first organizing in a new neighborhood in Little Rock, I discovered that people on the south side of a specific street had a tremendous drainage problem: when it rained, their homes were flooded. This problem was discussed extensively at two house meetings prior to the first neighborhood meeting, where I expected a large turnout from among the families affected by the flooding. On the evening of the meeting the group did indeed choose to work on drainage as one of their initial issues; however, of the sixty-odd people in attendance, only eight were from the affected blocks. The issue was actually raised and carried by an elderly black man, elected vice-chair of the group, whose own home was not at all affected by the flooding.

After the meeting, Mr. Higgins, the new vice-chair, invited me to his home for coffee. Sensing my disappointment over the turnout of people affected by the chosen issue, he explained to me that "sometimes people aren't able to do for themselves, even if they know what's right . . . in those times it's the duty of people like you and me to help them out if we can." Mr. Higgins's comments, especially significant to a young organizer who had been beaten over the head with the notion of "self-interest," make my point. Certainly there are people who join ACORN to gain a direct benefit. Those who stay and particularly those who go on to become leaders, however, do so more from a sense of solidarity with other low-income people and with the organization than for the potential material benefits the organization may bring them.

Another, less altruistic reason for joining and maintaining connection with the organization is the recognition members and leaders receive, both internally and externally. Very often, ACORN members do not get positive reinforcement for their ideas or efforts in the society at large. ACORN provides a forum where they may develop leadership skills and receive recognition. As the organization's current national board president, Elena Hanggi, notes: "Empowering the majority of people in the U.S. to exercise control over every facet of their lives means having poor people in positions of power."[43] To train ACORN leaders to develop the skills necessary for actually exercising power, ACORN has developed a formal structure described as follows in a recent report of the New World Foundation:

> Issues to be addressed by a neighborhood chapter are decided on by that chapter. For city-wide issues, the city board and the local chapters will both discuss them. If there are favorable responses to a city board proposal at the local chapters, the board will then set strategies, agendas, and time-lines. National decisions are made via a similar two-way flow of information, proposals, responses and action.

Each ACORN chapter's chair becomes their representative to a city board. If ACORN is in more than one city in a state, chapter representatives make up the State Executive Board, which, in turn, selects two delegates to the National Association Board. If ACORN is only in one city in a state, the city board will perform the same functions as a state board.

The National Association Board defines the national organization's policies and sets priorities. It meets twice a year and selects an Executive Committee which meets an additional two times a year. The Executive Committee is composed of regional representatives and the Board selected officers of President, Vice-President, Secretary, and Treasurer. The Association Board also has a Subsidy Committee selected by the President to oversee local budgets and allocate canvass funds.[44]

A monthly leadership publication, *¡Vamonos!,* is distributed to leaders and staff, and a quarterly newsletter, *USA* (the *United States of ACORN*), is mailed to members. In addition, cultural solidarity is developed through the self-consciously organized social efforts that take place at state and national conventions, and the writing, singing, and distributing of ACORN songs by group members. Three themes generally recur in the songs: the growing power of ACORN, the solidarity of "the people," and the definition of the enemy. These examples are chosen from the ACORN songbook of 1982:

ACORN Anthem *(to the tune of "Yankee Doodle")*

The politician woos my vote;
He promises perfection.
The vows compiled are neatly filed
Until the next election

We belong to ACORN now;
We're alone no longer.
All of us we'll raise a fuss
Our voices stronger, stronger.

ACORN Organizing Song

Aren't you tired of seein' the way that your own country's being run?
For the sake of Monster Profit, they would even steal your son.
And if you think it's bad, well, buster, you can bet it will grow worse.
So you better start to organize, or empty out your purse!

ACORN Marches On *(to the tune of "Battle Hymn of the Republic")*

Mine eyes have seen the glory when the people stand as one.
We have scattered all the bureaucrats and put them on the run.
But even with our list of wins our work has just begun.
The ACORN marches on.

There's Republicans, there's Democrats, I don't know which is worse,
Cuz the elephants they kill my job; the donkeys kill my purse.
Well, it's time to take those fossil groups and pack them in a hearse
As ACORN marches on.

Many of the forty-two songs reflect the organization's struggles with utility companies, politicians, and corporate elites, but these are not the only "outsiders." Until very recently (with the 1984 Alliance for Justice coalition effort), part of the ACORN family's self-image was that of the only legitimate representative of low- and moderate-income people. While externally, this perception may have been rightfully interpreted as organizational arrogance, internally the belief ACORN was the only legitimate, multiracial, low-income organization with a tactically militant stance has been a prevalent and, I would argue, sustaining factor throughout most of the organization's existence. This sense of organizational integrity is integrally linked with the most elusive element in the glue holding the organization together: ACORN's ideology.

Ideology

ACORN's formal ideology is eclectic and populist: the chance to be rich; the right to be free. The closest ACORN has come to spelling out an ideology is in the set of organizing principles articulated by Rathke in 1978, which list ACORN's responsibility to "(1) organize the maximum number of low- and moderate-income people possible; (2) organize whatever individual and multiple constituencies possess the maximum ability to win change at any given place or at any given time; and (3) win the maximum amount of political power possible to be exercised by our constituency and their organization."[45] As opposed to pure ideology, then—which Schurman defines as a set of ideas designed to give an individual a unified, conscious worldview—ACORN has developed a practical ideology, "a set of ideas designed to give individuals rational instruments for action. It provides the norms or rules which prescribe behavior. In offering a prescription of 'how to get there from here,' the practical ideology has direct action consequences."[46]

In describing the operation of such a developmental, practical ideology, Perlman writes, "Each victory on each issue may not be earth-shattering, but the cumulative picture is one of ongoing progress. . . . Even . . . where the achievement may only be temporary . . . people are beginning to understand the issues, to see how power and politics operate, to grasp both the potentials and limitations in collective action and to feel a new sense of self-esteem."[47] And ACORN training director Meg Campbell has written, "This *idea of being organized* in a constituency-based organization . . . is more important than the particular issue we work on. Again, we might lose or we might win, and still the *need to be organized* remains."[48]

The question, then, is how does this practical ideology shape organizational development? Are democratic principles, an internal commitment to power, and an organizational commitment to organize "anything that moves" sufficient? The commitment is certainly necessary. Many groups reach a low level of political access; co-opted leaders or organizers are bought off, and the organizing stops. Nouveau populists, including Harry Boyte and Lawrence Goodwyn,[49] would also argue that these populist commitments are sufficient for building a class-based movement, while Piven and Cloward's *New Class War*[50] pictures a battle between capitalism and democracy, with democracy vaguely depicted as the focus of populism.

ACORN's contribution has been to concretize a number of left populist ideas, mostly related to the socialization of basic goods and services, coupled with a strong dose of radical democracy as evidenced by the platform's references to representation on regulatory and corporate boards and by the organization's consistent involvement in the electoral process. On a local level this approach has certainly worked. Father Blitz, an ACORN supporter and director of the Office of Peace and Justice for the Catholic diocese of Little Rock, notes, "When Wade [Rathke] first started in this state, ACORN was a real threat to the system. They went through a stage of being called communist etc. You don't hear that much any more. Many of the people that criticized ACORN initially are now supporters."[51]

ACORN's avoidance of formal ideology is related to another factor in its potential to survive and to be successful in the political arena: the ability to mobilize resources.

Resource Mobilization

In social science literature, discussions of resource mobilization deal with many of the areas already discussed in this chapter: internal solidarity, ideology, and the means employed by "resourceful actors" to effectively garner resources.

As has been illustrated, ACORN's tactics often draw fire from the press as well as adversaries. In fact, since the tactics of confrontation have become routinized, some adversaries have used an ACORN-initiated action to attack ACORN. An example of this occurred at the 1975 hearings on lifeline utility rates in Arkansas:

> Les Hollingsworth, a black city councillor, introduced the ACORN proposal. Mayor Wimberly took the microphone to argue against it. His earlier friendliness vanished, the color rose in his cheeks, and his hands shook. "This public hearing would only serve to give this organization a platform. And who are they? I have never seen a group so secretive. They refuse to tell where their money comes from. Those who set it up bring papers for others to read. In seven years, I have never known the real leaders of ACORN to come forward and make a statement."[52]

The question raised by Wimberly reinforces the explanation of the leader-organizer dichotomy and in addition raises the question of finances. The organization's survival depends on ACORN's ability, each year, to raise a high percentage of its budget by internal means—a budget that, between 1975 and 1981, rose from $250,000 to $2.3 million. Over that six-year period the percentage of internally raised money increased from 27 percent in 1975 to 62.4 percent in 1981, with the dues per organizer per month averaging $379.

There are three sources of internal financing: (1) membership dues, which account for 45 percent of the organization's income; (2) grass-roots fund-raising activities in the form of raffles, bake sales, community fairs, and the like; and (3) door-to-door canvassing—essentially, soliciting funds in more middle-class neighborhoods to support ACORN's work on specific issues, thus broadening the organization's support base without recruiting middle-class patrons to the membership ranks or leadership positions. ACORN's ability to finance itself internally is far from the norm for movement organizations, and its finances have occasioned much external comment and concern.

In 1984, 85 percent of the budget came from internal finances. ACORN has also initiated an allied business operation that is currently involved in selling paper to nonprofit organizations in three cities, and is looking into the possibility of setting up housing and heating oil-buying cooperatives. Formally, membership is involved in the budget process through monthly local board budget meetings, the preparation of budgets by city and statewide budget and fund-raising committees, and an evaluation by a national subsidy committee. Since some areas project a surplus, some a balanced budget, and others a deficit, the subsidy committee, in this relatively new system, determines

> how to allocate canvass income which comes from canvass campaigns conducted by separate canvass staffs in non-ACORN neighborhoods. Income raised through canvasses doesn't go to the locals that raised it, rather, it goes into a national pool distributed by the subsidy committee. The delegates must defend their states' financial performance to the other delegates. If local leaders find themselves with a shortfall in the course of the year, they must go to the subsidy committee seeking either an emergency loan or a revised subsidy.[53]

This process is quite important for ACORN, not only because national foundations are shying away from grass-roots organizing as a priority but also because ACORN's receipt of government funds made the organization a ready target for the New Right. *Conservative Digest* listed ACORN as one of "175 leftist groups that get your money"—that received government funds in 1981 ($231,370 in fiscal year 1980–81, according to an ACORN financial report dated 7 January 1981). The *Digest* objection to ACORN, however, was less its source of money than its political philosophy of using "food-buying clubs to build the necessary social bonds for people to struggle in the political and social arena."[54] Although the magazine did list every group with even vague political leanings—including the American Bar Association and the National Wildlife Federation—ACORN's name on the roster and its featured place in the exposé suggest that as the organization gets larger and particularly as it expands its electoral activity, its ability to develop government or private foundation resources will decrease. ACORN's staff, therefore, has increasingly begun to institutionalize internal fund raising, and the organization predicts 90 percent self-sufficiency by 1986.

While supporting 85 percent or more of the budget through internal means is impressive, fund raising is, at this point, still chiefly the responsibility of the staff. Not only does this fact sometimes contribute to staff-leadership conflict, since all ACORN finances are centralized in New Orleans, but it has also increased the tasks of already overburdened organizers and taken time away from other aspects of organizational development. ACORN cannot maintain its level of actions and, at the same time, increase its self-sufficiency without increasing the membership's involvement and commitment to internal financial development.

ACORN's Potential: The Organizational Ledger

This examination of ACORN's methods and development leads to the following conclusions:

Model. The ACORN model has allowed ACORN to replicate units of organization in forty geographic areas. The initial organizing drive results in the formation of a structure through which a local group can act, but also sets up staff-leadership role divisions that continue to prove problematic. Though the model has been used successfully, the ratio of members to organizers (approximately 450 to 1) has led many new organizers to resign, being unable to keep up the pace.

Staff. Although the staff within the ACORN-affiliated Service Employees Union is about 60 percent black, the staff of ACORN continues to be young, white, well-educated, and poorly paid. On one hand, after fifteen years of organizing, ACORN has developed considerable staff depth and expertise. On the other hand, the lack of formal ongoing training, the inability to maintain staff cadre, and the lack of success in hiring people at the state or national level who have not come up through the staff ranks have made the maintenance of staff continuity difficult. In addition, the latent organizational structure that points to staff oligarchy, male dominance, and a heavy dependence on Rathke as the organization's chief strategist—even as both staff and leaders articulate a commitment to ACORN as a participatory democracy—inhibits both the straightforward development of staff people as leaders within the organization and the ability of the indigenous leadership to challenge organizational direction. This situation, however, may also be changing, since twelve-year veteran Steve Kest in September 1984 assumed the role of executive director of ACORN, in which he handles external contacts, while the internal job of chief organizer, long held by Rathke, is now divided among three other people.

Leaders. The leadership pool reflects the general constituency. However, with the exception of association board members, indigenous leaders do not take part in the initial debates concerning organizational direction. They therefore tend to have less investment in the organization. Although the leadership training and delegation of financial responsibility to local leadership has mitigated against this trend, local leadership remains the organization's largest underutilized resource.

Electoral Strength. ACORN claimed that 150,000 registered after the 1984 campaign. A June 1985 mailing to supporters pointed to the possibility of local campaigns to elect an ACORN supporter as the first black mayor of Bridgeport as well as electoral drives in St. Louis, Pittsburgh, Little Rock, and New York City. With the Democratic party in shambles nationally, it is unclear how significant local electoral victories may be in building ACORN's party presence. However, each of the proposed drives is linked to a local group demand that will make candidate accountability, or lack of it, clear to local members.

Issues. Although ACORN has posited the need since early 1979 to develop a civil rights thrust in the Latino community, no campaign plan has materialized. However, beginning in 1982 the organization did move several local campaigns on budget cutbacks. In addition, the organization has started new coalition initiatives in the peace and labor communities. These efforts, coupled with the reinitiation of low-income campaigns (squatting actions and agreements with developers in three cities to hire local low-income residents), and a noticeable recognition of women's issues (the Spring 1985 issue of the *United States of ACORN (USA)* headlined, "ACORN declares War on Rape"), may well have moved the organization into a position to work with a broad variety of groups and constituencies.

Reputation. ACORN has the reputation of being unwilling to work with other local community groups. While relations with unions (in particular) and with churches are good, winning the support of the local community organizing competition will not be easy. Outside the community organizing networks, ACORN's consistent militance has earned it a reputation for tough, uncompromising, and creative actions, which the organization is beginning to transform into more national media coverage. ACORN's national lobbying efforts have also been enhanced by moving all the research and publications staff to Washington, D.C.

Ideology. In the past few years a number of internal memos have identified ACORN as "left" and have advocated strategy in terms of class conflict. Though the staff of the organization still resists labels, most of the staff people were comfortable with defining the organization as "anticorporate" and in favor of economic democracy.[55] However, while finally placing itself on the left, ACORN has staunchly resisted the question "left of what?"

Internal Solidarity. Although the organization still tends to be weak in terms of developing an internal alternative culture, the evolving radio stations in two states have forced questions of culture and ideology to become part of staff and leadership discussions. With regard to finances, ACORN stands head and shoulders above any other community organization, with 85 percent internal funding, through dues (45 percent) and a combination of grass-roots events and canvassing.

External Response. Movements on the left have received the most attention from the state, followed by those on the right, with little attention being paid to movements or organizations in the center. Thus ACORN's ideological neutrality, down-home Americanism, and dogged assertions that all it wants is its fair share—coupled with its folksy acronym—have until recently rendered it relatively safe. However, the use of VISTA volunteers in some of its more abrasive actions, the undisguised political nature of its 1980 and 1984 campaigns, and the recent decision to step out as a movement builder are making ACORN more susceptible to government harassment (since 1978 the association has been audited three times, and organizer arrests have gone from one in the first nine years to over forty in the past two years), as well as penetration from the organized left.

Constituency. ACORN has a large working-class, 70 percent minority constituency of roughly 60,000 members in twenty-seven states. The new campaigns (jobs and squatting) have appealed to younger constituents, but the age of most members is above thirty-five. The current organizational base is established in forty urban and rural areas. ACORN's "penetration" strategy has resulted in the initiation of a sister union affiliated with the AFL-CIO, two radio stations with pending applications for thirty more, and applications for three low-power TV stations.

In summary, the organization has done an effective job of mobilizing human, financial, and external political resources to represent the interests of low-income people. In terms of ideological development—

which ACORN partisans argue is unnecessary—although ACORN has not developed a structured ideology, that lack of definition has probably been appropriate for organizational development to this point. Further expansion and development, however, may require a more specific ideological position.

ACORN's premise has been that the building of collective oppositional experience is more important than formal ideological articulation. This has been a fruitful approach to developing both organizers and leaders, but it does not take people far enough along to sustain them over time. The organization's four-year-old leadership school may increase participants' skills so that agenda-setting and financial development can become more the responsibility of the indigenous leadership. Yet it is characteristic of ACORN to view this problem and attempt to solve it on the leadership level without making the same sort of in-service training formally available to ACORN staff. Without restructuring leadership responsibilities and increasing internal skills and political development for both leadership and staff, the organization may not be able to maintain present staff levels, or generate the new staff expertise necessary to expand the organization.

Notes

1. Conversation with author, June 1979.
2. Meg Campbell, "The ACORN Maintenance Model" (mimeographed, no date), ACORN Archives.
3. Mike Miller, "Leaders and Their Self-Interest," handout no. 5, Organize Training Center, San Francisco.
4. Mark Lindberg, "How Community Organizers Develop Community Leadership: Seven Principles" (New England Training Center, mimeographed, no date).
5. Steve Max, "Four Steps to Developing Leaders" (Midwest Academy, July 1973), 1.
6. Neil Gilbert, *Clients or Constituents* (San Francisco: Jossey-Bass, 1970), 70.
7. *New York Times,* 14 October 1976, ACORN Archives.
8. Conversation with author, July 1979.
9. Conversation with author, June 1979.
10. *The Telegram* (Bridgeport, Conn.), 4 September 1979, ACORN Archives.
11. Cited in Andrew Kopkind, "ACORN Calling: Door to Door Organizing in Arkansas," *Working Papers,* Summer 1975, p. 19.
12. Gilbert, *Clients or Constituents,* 161.
13. Timothy J. Sampson, "Role of Professionals in Movement Organizations" (mimeographed, author's files, December 1980).
14. Joan Lancourt, *Confront or Concede: The Alinsky Citizen Action Organization* (Lexington, Mass.: Lexington Books, 1978), 134.
15. Ibid., 122.
16. Conversation with author, July 1979.
17. Conversation with author, May 1979.
18. Kopkind, "ACORN Calling."
19. Conversation with author, August 1979.
20. *Austin American Statesman,* 25 July 1979, ACORN Archives.
21. *Denver Post,* 12 August 1979, ACORN Archives.

22. Conversation with author, August 1980.

23. Conversation with author, July 1979.

24. Alexander Cockburn and James Ridgeway, "Is There Hope for the 80's?" *Village Voice,* 26 March 1979.

25. Author's conversation with ACORN leadership, October 1979.

26. Conversation with author, August 1980.

27. In *Austin American Statesman* (July 25, 1979), ACORN Archives.

28. Both Komorovsky's *Blue Collar Marriage* (1964) and Lillian Rubin's *World of Pain: Life in the Working Class* (1976) are cited in Ronald Lawson and Stephen Barton, "Sex Roles in Social Movements," *Signs* 6, no. 2 (Winter 1980).

29. Conversation with author, August 1979.

30. Conversation with author, April 1979.

31. Essentially, the percentage of women in key positions on the staff of the organization has not increased.

32. Madeleine Adamson, "Women Organizers Spell Out Concerns," *Just Economics* (n.d.), 10, ACORN Archives.

33. *Arkansas Democrat,* 19 March 1978, ACORN Archives.

34. Cited in Kopkind, "ACORN Calling."

35. Lancourt, *Confront or Concede,* 104.

36. Madeleine Adamson, "Organizing Needs Affirmative Action," *Just Economics,* Spring 1979, p. 14.

37. Martin Kirby, *Southern Voices* 1, no. 2 (May–June 1974).

38. Adamson, "Organizing Needs Affirmative Action," 12.

39. Barry Mclaughlin, *Studies in Social Movements* (New York: Free Press, 1969), 14.

40. Amitai Etzioni, *A Comparative Analysis of Complex Organizations* (New York: Free Press, 1961), 250, cited in Lancourt, *Confront or Concede,* 210.

41. Lancourt, *Confront or Concede,* 120.

42. Mancur Olson, *The Logic of Collective Action* (Cambridge, Mass.: Harvard University Press, 1965).

43. Cited in Jack L. Brummel, "An Organizational Profile of ACORN" (New York: New World Foundation, 1984).

44. Ibid.

45. Wade Rathke, "Drawing the Line," *Just Economics* 5, no. 8 (November 1977), and 6, no. 1 (January 1978).

46. Franz Schurman, *Ideology and Organization in Communist China* (Berkeley: University of California Press, 1968), 22, 38, 39.

47. Janice Perlman, "Grassrooting the System," *Social Policy* 10, no. 2 (September/October 1976): 20.

48. Campbell, "Principles and Foundations," in "The ACORN Maintenance Model," 3.

49. Harry Boyte's and Lawrence Goodwyn's writing, including Boyte's *Backyard Revolution* (Philadelphia: Temple University Press, 1980) and Goodwyn's *Populist Moment* (New York: Oxford University Press, 1978), tends to equate democratic processes and anticorporate sentiments with revolutionary potential. This position dominates in community organizing circles.

50. For a critique of Frances Fox Piven and Richard A. Cloward, *The New Class War* (New York: Pantheon, 1982), see Gary Delgado and Howard Winant, "The End of Reaganism?" in *Socialist Review* 66 (November/December 1982).

51. Cited in Brummel, "An Organizational Profile."

52. Cited in Bo Burlingham, "They've All Gone to Look for America," *Mother Jones* 1, no. 1 (February/March 1976).

53. Brummel, "An Organizational Profile."

54. "How Washington Funds the Left," *Conservative Digest* 8, no. 4 (April 1982). This entire issue was devoted to listing left-liberal groups that received government money. ACORN was mentioned four times.

55. Conversation with author, November 1982.

31
Fishbowl Planning: Environmental Regulation, Economic Development, and Democratic Technique

Daniel Mazmanian and Jeanne Nienaber

The single Army Corps of Engineers district to require an elaborate program of broad participation in all its planning studies is the Seattle District, which has achieved the active involvement of a variety of interest groups through a continual exchange of views and information in workshops, public meetings, and the preparation of study brochures. Such "fishbowl" planning, as it is called, combines procedures used in other districts—for example, the close coordination with other agencies and local governments that characterized the San Francisco District's Wildcat and San Pablo creeks study, the Kansas City District's use of work groups in the L-15 study, and the exhaustive public consultation and publications achieved by the Buffalo District during its Cleveland-Akron and Three Rivers Watershed study. Why the fishbowl program was adopted and how well it has fared is illustrated in the controversy surrounding the Corps' proposed dam and reservoir for the Middle Fork of the Snoqualmie River in northwestern Washington.

Flood Control on the Middle Fork of the Snoqualmie River

In general, the controversy, which began in the late 1960s, pits recreationists, conservationists, and the governor of Washington against local developers, many property owners within the Snoqualmie River basin, and the Corps of Engineers. At the same time, the seemingly mutual objective of environmentalists and farmers is to preserve the greenbelt nature of the basin, but their strategies for achieving this objective have

Reprinted from Daniel A. Mazmanian and Jeanne Nienaber, *Can Organizations Change? Environmental Protection, Citizen Participation, and the Corps of Engineers* (Washington, D.C.: Brookings Institution, 1979), pp. 132–57, by permission of the Brookings Institution.

turned out to be diametrically opposed. The environmentalists are against the construction of a dam and reservoir on the Middle Fork because it would destroy the last remaining free-flowing and unspoiled wild river in the region. They also believe that the mitigation of flooding in the basin will without doubt lead to the commercialization and urbanization of the last greenbelt and recreational area on the fringe of the Seattle metropolitan area. Proponents of the project counter that property owners and farmers in the basin will be able to fend off the encroachment of the expanding metropolitan community and maintain the open-space character of the land *only* if the farmland is provided with relief from floods and protected from speculative buying through zoning for agricultural use. Otherwise, rising property values and in turn rising property taxes will compel residents of the basin to sell their holdings to subdividers and speculators.

Finally, the controversy brings to the fore one of the most tenacious problems associated with virtually every Corps flood-management study. Despite extensive efforts to include new publics in the agency's planning process, to encourage the presentation of new information, and to respond to changing social values, the Army engineers seem unable to overcome their traditional, almost instinctive, affinity for structural alternatives. Thus they did not approach the issue of flooding on the Middle Fork of the Snoqualmie River as impartial technicians weighing the costs and benefits of both structural and nonstructural alternatives. Rather, their intention was to build dams and reservoirs. Public pressure alone forced the Corps to change its proposal for a dam and reservoir on the Middle Fork *and* a dam and powerhouse on the North Fork to "only" a proposal for a dam on the Middle Fork (planning the North Fork dam was deferred for further study), to an even more compromised plan today. Moreover, it was left to the initiative of aroused citizens to propose most of the nonstructural alternatives to a dam or dams.

Characteristics of the Snoqualmie River Basin

Originating at a 6,000-foot elevation on the western slope of the Cascade Mountains, the Snoqualmie River drains nearly 700 square miles of the southeastern, or upper part, of the Snohomish River basin in northwestern Washington.[1] The basin is mountainous along the eastern boundary and has rolling hills in the western portion. The three forks of the river—the North, Middle, and South—all flow generally westward to a junction downstream from the town of North Bend, forming the Snoqualmie River proper. Shortly thereafter the river drops 268 feet over Snoqualmie Falls and flows northwesterly through the small communities of Fall City, Carnation, and Duvall, joining the Snohomish River near Monroe. It then empties into Puget Sound at Everett. The drainage area upstream from the falls is commonly known as the Upper

Valley, and the 40-mile stretch from below the falls to the Snohomish River is known as the Lower Valley.

The mean annual precipitation for the basin is 92 inches, with about 75 percent occurring from October through March. Thus the basin typically experiences extensive winter flooding, followed by lighter spring floods. It is these floods, so far unchecked, that have kept the basin in its essentially agricultural and relatively undeveloped state.

The Snoqualmie River basin has many outstanding natural features that make it a prime recreational area. The floodplain is the last remaining open space on the outer limits of the heavily populated Seattle metropolitan area. Its natural recreational attractions are the waterfall and the upper reaches of the river that provide clear mountain streams running through heavily forested areas. Stream fishing and canoeing can be enjoyed in a near-wilderness setting. As the Seattle District has recognized, "The rugged topography and scenic attractions within the basin are valuable environmental resources within an hour's driving time of the Seattle-Tacoma metropolitan area."[2]

The basin, however, is not in a rustic or wilderness state but supports thriving agricultural, dairy, and lumbering enterprises, as well as some manufacturing in North Bend. Increasingly, it has become a favorite retreat for the nearby urban dwellers as well. The estimated population of the entire Snohomish basin in 1969 was 214,000, while the adjacent Seattle metropolitan area boasted a population of 1.5 million.

Seattle District's Proposed Plan

Although flood management along the Snoqualmie River had been discussed for decades, the most recent debate over the need for a dam and reservoir began after a major storm in the western Cascade Mountains in 1959 caused flooding along the Snoqualmie, Skykomish, and Snohomish rivers. The storm produced flood stages in a relatively short period of time and substantial overbank flooding, causing great damage to residences, agricultural lands, utilities, and levees. The disastrous effects of the flood on residents living on the floodplain prompted the Washington State Legislative Council to seek federal assistance in developing a long-range flood management program for the basin. Some combination of structural flood protection devices, including a dam, was implied in the request.[3]

Resolutions adopted in 1960 by the Senate and House public works committees authorized the Corps to study means of providing federal flood protection assistance. Over the next nine years the Corps, in consultation with local King County officials, devised a plan for flood protection that included a dam and reservoir on the Middle Fork and a dam and powerhouse on the North Fork of the Snoqualmie River. The Corps held public hearings in 1961 and again in 1967, and the study was concluded in 1969.[4] The hearings were essentially gatherings of friends and neighbors and were dominated by the Corps and proponents of the plan. By 1967 most of the plan had been completed, and since it had received little opposition in the meetings, the Seattle District anticipated minimal resistance to it. Conditions changed rapidly in the late 1960s and early 1970s, however.

Recreationists and conservationists did not become involved in the project study in its early stages because they lacked broad-based organizational support for their position and thus felt they would be impotent in a confrontation with the Corps. (The Corps' greatest work load is in the North Pacific States.) The Sierra Club was following the evolution of the study with some displeasure, but it was not a potent political force in the Seattle area at that time.[5] But in 1968 the passage of a $100 million transit, park, and open spaces bond issue by the people of the Seattle area activated the environmental movement. Opposition to the Middle Fork dam and the fight to preserve the Snoqualmie River basin as the last greenbelt adjacent to the metropolitan area soon became the issue of the environmentalists.

It is important to remember that Congress had not authorized the construction of flood control devices in 1960, only a project study. The Seattle District, like any other Corps district involved in a study, would have to obtain many approvals before its proposal could actually be implemented, including that of the North Pacific Division of the Corps; the Board of Engineers for Rivers and Harbors (BERH) in Washington, D.C.; the Office of the Chief of Engineers (OCE); the governor; the secretary of the army; and the Office of Management and Budget. Only then could the Corps ask Congress for the authority to begin construction.

By December 1969 the report of the district office on flood management on the Snoqualmie River had been approved by the division and submitted to the BERH and the OCE. The local and regional offices recommended to the BERH and OCE that the construction of a multipurpose dam and powerhouse be started immediately on the North Fork. The district stated its position as follows:

> The storage in these projects *would control floods in sufficient degree to allow urban and suburban use of the valleys* in the vicinity of Snoqualmie Falls and the town of North Bend [the Upper Valley]. Downstream from Snoqualmie Falls, flood control would be sufficient to reduce flood damages to farms and roads and permit reasonable agricultural returns. The downstream flood plain below Snoqualmie Falls could be managed within the limits of flood protection provided thereby retaining its attractive environmental qualities. By these means, about 15,000 acres of flood prone land would be preserved for open space and agriculture. Also, the increased production from these lands would partially compensate for the loss of agricultural production resulting from continuing *loss of agricultural*

lands in the basin to urbanization and industrialization. Recreation facilities on the reservoirs would serve the increasing demands of the adjacent metropolitan areas. The enhancement of fisheries both in the reservoir and downstream would provide additional sports fishing. Low flow augmentation from reservoir releases would increase the commercial production of fish. Power output and water supply from the North Fork project would serve growing demands of the area.[6]

The first estimate, using 1969 prices, of the cost of the proposed plan was approximately $49 million. The cost to the federal taxpayers was $46.3 million for construction and $94,000 annually for operations, maintenance, and major replacements. At an interest rate of 4⅞ percent and an evaluation period of 100 years, the benefit-cost ratio was 1.8 to 1.

The Seattle District recommended land-use zoning, which would restrict development on the floodplain, as a means of minimizing future flood damage to property. This recommendation, however, was offered as a suggestion to the local people, not as part of the federal funded program, since land-use regulations come under the purview of state and local governments. Critics of the plan have argued that the suggested restriction of development on the floodplain through zoning directly contradicted the district's basic commitment to the development of the basin: almost 50 percent of the benefits attributed to flood control in the proposal would result from protecting future residential development.[7]

Alternative flood management solutions examined but rejected by the district included levee and channel improvements along the Snoqualmie River below Snoqualmie Falls. These would speed the floodwaters past the farmlands along the Snoqualmie but would cause increased damage downstream along the unprotected portions of the Snohomish River.[8] A diversion of floodflow from the Snoqualmie River and the Sammamish River basin to Puget Sound was ruled out as too costly. Floodplain evacuation was eliminated as unfeasible, given the level of investment in properties already situated on the floodplain, and the construction of single-purpose flood control storage sites could only be partially justified by benefit-cost criteria.

The BERH Review

The Seattle District chose an inappropriate time to forward its recommendation to the BERH for review. By late 1969 the Sierra Club, League of Women Voters, Audubon Society, Washington Kayak Club, Alpine Lakes Protection Society, and various other groups had informally banded together to become a potent force behind the cause of wilderness and recreation protection in the Northwest. Possibly even more important, however, the movement had become a national one by this time; both Congress and the president were becoming sensitized to the environmental issue.

When the Seattle District submitted its recommendation to the BERH, it also circulated a public notice (required with the submission of all studies) stating that until mid-February 1970 the BERH would afford interested parties an opportunity to furnish additional information about the proposal. Opponents of the dam and reservoir capitalized on this opportunity and flooded the BERH with letters. Because of the large response, the BERH extended the time allowed for comment for another month. Then, given the controversial nature of the proposal and the interest in the environment prevailing in Washington, D.C., the BERH made an unusual request by asking the Seattle District to hold another public hearing on the proposal so that BERH members could attend. The importance of this unprecedented move by the Corps' own review board was not lost on either proponents or opponents of the project.

The format of this unusual hearing was arranged by the Seattle District. Brock Evans, the Northwest regional vice-president of the Sierra Club, was invited to take a half hour to present the views of the opponents. Scott Wallace, long-time resident of the Snoqualmie Valley, a King County commissioner, a member of the Valley Greenbelt Association, and one of the leading spokesmen for the dam and reservoir, was invited to take equal time to present the views of the proponents. Otherwise, the hearing would be open to anyone who wished to speak. The district attempted to structure the hearing so that the Corps would appear to be impartial. In fact, however, the Seattle District was obviously partial to the dam proposal.

The Public Hearing

The hearing, held at a county park recreation center in North Bend on the evening of 6 March 1970 and attended by over 1,000 people, served to emphasize the broad public concern about the project and how severely the issue had polarized the community. It also provided the first point-by-point account of the opponents' arguments.

Those opposing the construction of the Middle Fork dam and reservoir revealed their prime concern: the preservation of the Snoqualmie Valley as an agricultural greenbelt. Eleanor Lee, president of the Puget Sound League of Women Voters, argued, for example: "Regardless of the Corps' very good intentions, the feeling of security provided by the dam is bound to increase the pressure for more intensive use of land in the flood plain." Furthermore, the "proposal will encourage land-use development inconsistent with the current Comprehensive Land-Use Plan of King County, which shows Snoqualmie Valley in agriculture/ flood plain use except for established communities. The proposal is also inconsistent with the Open Space Agreement accepted by members of the Puget Sound Governmental Conference."[9]

Opponents repeatedly referred to the rapid urban and industrial development that had occurred in the nearby Green River Valley after the construction of the Howard A. Hanson Dam. Joan Thomas of the Washington Environmental Council cited a similar occurrence in the Sammamish basin, where in 1963 a modest flood control project was initiated to protect farmers from flooding. "The land was zoned agricultural land, it was open space, and the project went ahead . . . So what happened after the project was completed? The price of land, which had been selling for about $2,000 an acre, is now an average of $10,000 an acre, and are the farmers getting out of the land? Yes, they are, if there's any land left, it's becoming industrial, developed for industry."[10]

Brock Evan's approach was to marshal a string of professionals to lay before the BERH the technical deficiencies of the proposal being made by the district engineers. Earnest Gayden, a professor of urban planning at the University of Washington, pointed out that the Seattle District had calculated as a benefit the projected urban development that would occur on the floodplain but had failed to include as a cost the losses that would result from withdrawing the land from good agricultural use. "If one takes the population projections which are used to justify this kind of project, then one must also take into account the needs of this same future population for milk, meat, and good local produce."[11] William B. Beyers of the University of Washington questioned the district's computation of recreational benefits for the project, finding them highly arbitrary and overstated.

An issue arising over every Corps project is the extent to which the project will produce net national benefits. This goes to the heart of the problem with benefit-cost ratios, which are supposed to index these local, regional, and national benefits. Gardner Brown, Jr., an economist at the University of Washington, questioned the legitimacy of using land enhancements in the valley resulting from the project as net national benefits.

> For years, the Corps has argued that flood control brings about a more intensive use of the flood plain. "More intensive" naturally means more economic activity which gives rise to land enhancement benefits, and in this case amounting to $118,000 annually over fifty years proposed for the Middle Fork project. These benefits should not be claimed in general because they are not national benefits. Additional growth due to the flood control aspects of the projects represents a relocation of economic activity from elsewhere in the economy. It may be a regional benefit; it is not a national benefit.[12]

If one accepts Brown's reasoning, then the project benefits cannot be included as part of a project's national economic benefits. Yet this was the main reason for asking federal taxpayers to pay the lion's share of the costs of the dam, as it is in most of the Corps's dam projects. Referring to a number of other alleged overstatements of benefits, Brown concluded that a more realistic benefit-cost ratio would be 0.9 to 1, about half of that estimated by the Seattle District.

Jerry Parker, associated with Urban Planning in Seattle, was the last of Brock Evans's panel of experts to speak. He focused on the position taken by the Corps and the local proponents that the greenbelt nature of the Snoqualmie Valley could be sustained and even enhanced by the dam. This position, he argued, contradicted the Corps' own calculations that the project "can only be justified over a 50-year period when you assume the intense growth of the flood plain and the residential use."[13]

The frustrations and anxieties of the proponents of the project continued to mount as they listened to this presentation by a host of professionals. Local proponents saw these professionals as outsiders who had no vested interest in the valley, who did not have to live through the agonizing floods, who had not been around during the previous decade when all the details of the proposal were being hammered out, and who were attempting to undermine a project the local proponents wanted very much.

Kirk Smith, Scott Wallace's first speaker and owner of a small publishing firm in Fall City, lashed out:

> We think that the people who are going to be most affected by the Snoqualmie River are the people who live here and none of the [previous] speakers or anyone else, I suspect, is really going to propose that we move the towns of North Bend and Snoqualmie off this river, for up to now I've heard no proposal protecting the thousands of people who live in those towns. I am impressed by our own state officials who come out and tell us that they don't think this dam is a good idea, even though that may not be their special interest. Bert Cole, God bless him, he's a Democrat, thinks the hills should be built on, and that's fine. Much against the will of the people who live there, he's already proposed the leases of state land for an explosives factory at Preston. Mr. Levy, our county councilman, and God bless him, he's a Democrat too, says don't move too fast, let's take a few months and maybe a few years, because it would be worth that not to let the Lower Valley go industrial.
>
> I submit it might be worth more to have something on Snoqualmie to stop heavy water in the event of a disaster or potential flood to save people and their homes and their institutions.[14]

Commenting on the opposition's expert testimony, he continued, "As far as I'm concerned, Mr. Evans and the university folk can argue with the experts of the Army Corps of Engineers as long as they wish—go to it—but I would like to see an answer to a need of people in the Snoqualmie Valley, and that's why I am the most firm supporter of the Middle Fork Dam."[15]

The proponent's central theme, aside from assailing the character and motives of the academics and the conservationists, was that the project would *guarantee* the preservation of the basin as an agricultural greenbelt—an objective repeated time and again—and not the reverse. Sympathetic consideration should be given to the people who had to bear the cost of flood damage.

Richard Zemp, North Bend planning commissioner, said that proponents were "aware that environmental hysteria" was causing "dizziness" to characterize "the majority of otherwise sensible people." Nonetheless, he felt compelled to argue that the environmentalists were simply confused, that in fact the proposed project was the best means to the ends espoused by them, and that they did not realize that correcting "the bad effects of nature, for instance flooding," could serve a positive end. He also said that the proposed project was "the best method of preserving the existing environment in Snoqualmie and Snohomish Basin, and the existing environment is the present social and economic culture long established in the Snoqualmie Valley."[16] The choice, therefore, was not between development and the greenbelt; it was between rampant flooding, the destruction of homes and property, and declining agricultural profitability, on the one hand, and the preservation of the Middle Fork as a free-flowing river, on the other hand.

Richard Holt, a North Bend attorney, agreed with many others that a compromise solution was possible and that if the dam, which had been proposed for valid reasons and in the expectation of many benefits, was built, strong legislation could "preserve the things that the Sierra Club and the other people are talking about."[17]

The problem, of course, was that zoning legislation did not yet exist. Opponents therefore felt that it would be folly to go ahead with the construction of the dam before they had ironclad legal guarantees that further development of the floodplain would be prohibited. Once the dam was constructed, property values in the basin would inevitably soar; the owners then would resist any agricultural zoning or land-use restrictions that in effect would deny them a great windfall profit.[18]

In summarizing the frustration of the opposition George B. Yount, a resident of Snohomish County, stated:

> My view at least is that the citizen is really getting the short end of the stick here. He's gone to the polls and expressed his views to save the open space [the 1968 bond issue] and he is met by a government agency unwilling to heed the vote. An aroused citizenry sees the rape of the land they love and protests in books, periodicals, and television, in the streets, and even at hearings such as this. Your answer is that it isn't in the best interest for all concerned. It is for the economy. My answer is that this project not only benefits too few, but it is a sacrifice too great for the public to bear.[19]

After more than six hours of nonstop presentations, all seventy persons who had anything to say had been heard. A wealth of information had been presented in support of both positions, although not necessarily in a coherent and organized fashion, and the preferences of the local residents, recreationists, property owners, and environmentalists had been made exceedingly clear. It is somewhat surprising, therefore, that General William F. Cassidy, then chairman of the Board of Engineers for Rivers and Harbors who had traveled over 3,000 miles to have a close look at the sites affected by the proposal and to learn how the local citizens felt about the issues, found the hearings so utterly disappointing.

> We got a lot of opinion, a lot of emotion, but very little in the way of fact. In my mind a good many of the people who talked had not even read the report [three-volume technical report prepared by the Corps], not analyzed [it]; they only picked pieces out of it and out of the news to justify their opinion. . . . There was a great deal of error and misinformation . . . presented here. The Board is not in the position to try and make a judgment from that kind of supposed information.[20]

What General Cassidy apparently had been looking for but had not found was hard information upon which the board could make its decision. The obvious conclusion is that what may be hard information to some is not to others. General Cassidy was clearly of the school that believes that facts based on feelings are not hard enough.

The Project Stymied

Upon returning to Washington, D.C., General Cassidy, along with the other board members (all generals in charge of divisions), decided that the proposal recommended by the Seattle District should go forward. In their letter to the chief of engineers they simply brushed aside the seeming contradiction between developing the Snoqualmie Valley and preserving it as a greenbelt. "The Board notes that there is a real need in the Snoqualmie River valley for flood control and for preservation of the greenbelt of agricultural land below the Snoqualmie River. The proposed dam and reservoir project on the Middle Fork of the Snoqualmie River serves this end."[21] In other words, for reasons that remain unclear the board concluded that the opponents' demand for a greenbelt really did not apply to the Upper Valley. While the Upper Valley would be open for development, the Lower Valley—if appropriate land-use regulation was adopted—could be maintained as a greenbelt.

When asked by the chief of engineers to review the project proposal, Governor Daniel J. Evans of Washington in turn asked the director of the state Department of Ecology to prepare a position for the state. An environmental review team was assembled and ultimately recommended that the project not be authorized. The governor accepted the team's advice and informed the chief on 23 November 1970: "It is the recommendation of the review team and my recommendation that the Middle Fork project not be authorized at this time." Instead, he suggested that "an in-depth study of all available alternatives and combinations of alternatives should be undertaken by the Corps of Engineers in concert with the appropriate agencies of the State of Washington."[22] The message was clear: the Corps would have to reach an accommodation with the opposition forces or there would be no project.

This was a dramatic setback for the Corps. The chief would never go over the head of the governor and recommend the project to Congress. Thus with the power of the governor behind them, the environmentalists achieved a major victory. In view of the district's many activities, however, it might be able to tolerate the loss of one project. But the environmentalists were on the warpath, and, having experienced one important victory, could they be satisfied? Wouldn't they press on to bring the entire construction program of the Seattle District to a halt?

The Advent of Fishbowl Planning

Governor Evans's decision not to endorse the proposal marked a turning point in the flood protection program for the Snoqualmie. It also marked a turning point for the Seattle District. Just before the governor's decision on the Middle Fork, Colonel Howard L. Sargent became district engineer of the Seattle District. Realizing the dire implications of the decision, Sargent decided to accept the governor's invitation to undertake a restudy. This would demonstrate both the district's continuing concern with the problems of the people in the river basin and its open-mindedness in considering all possible alternative solutions.

More important, Sargent viewed the restudy as an opportunity to implement a truly comprehensive public participation and open planning system that he had developed while in a management assignment at the Pentagon. It was called fishbowl planning, a sufficiently radical concept to have had little chance of adoption in more tranquil times. With little to lose and much to gain, however, the district staff, under the leadership of Sargent, underwent an almost complete about-face in the conduct of its planning.

Sargent first met with the governor to determine specifically what additional alternatives he wished to have studied. An agreement was reached on the subject of the restudy and on having it conducted by a study team composed of members of both the Corps and the state Department of Ecology. This was unprecedented. Not only were two agencies, one federal and one state, going to undertake a study jointly, but the two involved had previously been archenemies. (The Department of Ecology's review team, after all, had recommended that Evans veto the original Corps proposal.) The agreement of January 1971 between the two agencies called for the participation of the public through Sargent's fishbowl planning technique in reviewing four basic alternatives, including the original Middle Fork proposal. The plan for the restudy was then agreed upon by the OCE. Funding was appropriated by Congress in the budget for fiscal year 1973, and the restudy began in September 1972.[23]

The basic objective of fishbowl planning, as envisioned by Sargent, is "to insure that planning for public-works projects is highly visible to all interested organizations and individuals."[24] Concerned citizens were to be involved in the planning process from the beginning. Throughout the planning process citizens serve as a check on agency planners and contribute ideas, insights, and alternatives of their own. The program was designed to satisfy both the desire of citizens for participation in agency decisions and the necessity, strongly felt by Sargent, to check the subtle biases that agency planners inevitably introduce into proposals. The district could then render decisions on the proposals on the basis of all the facts.

The four formal or procedural components of fishbowl planning are workshops, public meetings, citizen committees, and a brochure on the study. The public meetings provide a forum for citizens, organizations, and agencies to discuss alternative solutions under consideration in a study. Workshops are smaller gatherings where more informal and particularized discussions take place, and ideally, citizens volunteer to conduct them. The citizen committees are in a sense organizational appendages to the Corps. They are composed of community and organization leaders who can maintain contact with the broader public, mobilize it for meetings, and so on.

The study brochure is an essential, and perhaps the most innovative, component of fishbowl planning. It serves as the central study document, which is available throughout the study, and is continually being modified and updated. It provides a written record of *all* the alternative solutions ever suggested by citizens, agencies, or whomever. As new alternatives are suggested, they are added in subsequent editions of the brochures, of which there are six or seven throughout the life of the study. Even if an alternative is rejected at some point, it is not deleted. Rather, it is retained as proof that it has been examined. The brochures serve as a forum for rational debate about the alternatives. An alternative is described in summary fashion on one page; on the next page a pro and con list is provided. Any person or organization can enter a position. Their names are included with their statements, letting everyone know where they stand. Each edition of the brochure contains a list of the names of all persons who have made comments on the study. Sargent felt that this helps "identify groups that should be participating—but aren't."[25]

Another section of the brochure "identifies the one or two alternatives selected for technical checkout, such as geology, hydrology, or a prediction of effects on fish and wildlife. The District Engineer discusses each alternative in turn, giving reasons for selecting or rejecting the alternative for the detailed checkout."[26] As the result of the checkouts become available, they are incorporated into the brochure and ultimately become the basis for the district engineer's recommendation to higher authorities.

In all, there is a considerable difference between traditional Corps planning and fishbowl planning. Procedurally, the latter includes fifteen separate activities designed to draw the public into the planning process; only three of these activities—two public meetings and formal-letter notification of its intentions to other public agencies—were included in traditional Corps planning.

The Joint Study

In one important respect the restudy of the Middle Fork project differed from Sargent's idealized outline for fishbowl planning. The joint study effort did not begin from scratch with a public meeting to determine the concerns and preferences of all interests, with no alternatives presented by the planners. Instead, the Seattle District and the Department of Ecology decided between themselves which alternatives to include in the study and selected four: two versions of the district's original multipurpose dam and reservoir proposal along with a recommendation for a land-use management system; a system of setback levees, floodway acquisition, and a land-use management system; and a totally nonstructural approach utilizing floodway easements and flood insurance.[27] The general public first knew of these alternatives in the initial edition of the study team's brochure.

The study team's decision to review only four alternatives was made for the sake of expediency, but conservationists saw it as an indication of the Corps' unwillingness to entertain all potential alternatives. Obviously a great deal of distrust still existed. The alternatives became the central issue at the initial public workshop held at North Bend on 3 October 1972, following the publication of the first edition of the study brochure. Thirty-six persons attended, representing all contending factions. The representative of the Puget Sound League of Women Voters requested that consideration be given to other alternatives that might be proposed by participating agencies or groups.

Public Consideration of the Restudy

The first large-scale public meeting to discuss the restudy was held in North Bend on the evening of 9 November 1972. Tempers had cooled in the two and a half years since the BEHR's public hearing, but the issues remained controversial nonetheless. One hundred and twenty persons attended the two-hour meeting (only a fraction of the thousand who attended the six-hour hearing in March 1970). The joint study team members shared the task of bringing the public up to date on their agreements and indicating what they intended to do next. The discussion of the alternatives was basically a rehash of the views expressed at the 1970 hearing, except that this time it centered on why the study team had limited itself to only four alternatives.

Edward Delanty of the Washington Kayak Club noted that "several other potentially viable alternatives" were not being considered. He pointed out that the town of Snoqualmie and part of North Bend constituted the major flood-prone residential areas on the upper floodplain. Therefore, "Why wasn't an alternative being considered which leveed these areas and nothing more? Has the cost of relocating the developments in the upper flood plain, coupled with limited levee work, been considered?" He went on to suggest that participants be permitted to present alternatives and that impact statements be prepared for the alternatives, as called for by the state's new Shoreline Management Act of 1971.[28]

The study team may have restricted itself to four alternatives, but as members claimed at the hearing, they had no intention of excluding the consideration of others. Thus Sydney Steinborn, chief of the Engineering Division for the Seattle District, expressed the team's desire to include in its report to the governor as many alternatives as were proposed. He answered Delanty by saying: "We want those who are proposing alternatives to come to us and take the initiative and we will have mini-workshops on alternatives. We hope to have this in January, so those of you who have alternatives continue to make them known."[29] The problem was whether the time and money available to the study team was sufficient for it to consider other alternatives. As Corps people often lament, public participation is very costly.

What came of the first public meeting, then, was the promise to incorporate additional alternatives into the study report. The burden of examining additional alternatives, however, would fall, not on the study team, but on those proposing them. Recreation advocates and conservationists would thus be given their first opportunity to make a constructive contribution to the decision-making process. Rather than being cast in the negative role of opposing the structural solutions, they now had the opportunity to come up with serious nonstructural ones.

The Mini-Workshops

The second workshop of the study was held in late January 1973 and was attended by some ninety persons. At the request of citizens who were concerned with the study but who lived outside the floodplain, this workshop was not held at North Bend but at Bellevue Community College on the eastern fringe of Seattle.

The issue of considering other alternatives had now been resolved. Dates were announced for a series of mini-workshops of the type promised by Steinborn at the public meeting in November. The workshops would be sponsored by various organizations and persons in the community; the study team would attend, but only in a consulting capacity. As it turned out, most of the mini-workshops were arranged by the groups opposed to the original dam proposal, although the sessions were attended by proponents as well.[30]

The first mini-workshop was conducted by Steven Doyle of the Duvall Valley Commission and was attended by approximately thirty persons. Marvin Vialle, the study coordinator representing the Department of Ecology, and Frank Urabeck, the study coordinator from the Seattle District, reviewed the four original alternatives. The sessions prompted questions about the effects of flooding on floodplains and about the environmental effects of the various alternatives. The second mini-workshop focused more narrowly on the need for, and likelihood of, land-use management systems that could complement the various alternatives being considered. In addition, the state and local laws that pertained to land-use regulations in the Snoqualmie River basin were reviewed.

The third mini-workshop shifted back to North Bend and was sponsored by David Osterholt of the Sierra Club. It was devoted to new alternatives proposed by the Sierra Club and the Alpine Lakes Protection Society (ALPS) that appeared in the next (fourth) edition of the study brochure. The Sierra Club had three suggestions: (1) a comprehensive system of floodplain management permitting current uses of the floodplain to continue but prohibiting new buildings and landfills (this became alternative 5); (2) a plan for evacuating the floodplain requiring the permanent evacuation of all habitable structures within the floodway area that were subject to deep and fast-flowing water (alternative 6); and (3) a plan that called for the rigorous application of state and local laws, such as the state's Shoreline Management Act of 1971, that apply to floodplains (alternative 7). ALPS suggested two other alternatives; a comprehensive plan to reduce the level, frequency, and siltation of floods by improving logging practices throughout the Snoqualmie River basin (alternative 8); and the placing of riprap along all sections of the Snoqualmie River banks that are subject to severe soil erosion, together with some local dikes and levees (alternative 9).

The valley farmers attending the mini-workshop felt that none of the five alternatives offered that evening were viable means of reducing flood damage. They persisted in their belief that this could be accomplished only with a dam.

The fourth mini-workshop was devoted to a presentation by Wolf

Bauer, long-time conservationist of the region. He argued that turning the Snoqualmie River valley into a European-type resort area would permit it to retain its open-space character while remaining economically viable through tourism and recreation.

The fifth mini-workshop considered an alternative proposed by the Washington Kayak Club. This plan called for designating segments of the Middle Fork above North Bend as "wild, scenic, and recreational rivers" under either a national or state river system; establishing an open-space zone over the 23,000 acres of the Snoqualmie River floodplain; building levees to protect the town of Carnation against the 100-year flood; and allowing setback levees above the falls (alternative 10).

Following these five mini-workshops, the last of the three previously scheduled general workshops was held in North Bend on March 13. It served as a summary session during which all the new alternatives were reviewed. During the sixth and final mini-workshop held the following week, the Department of Ecology reviewed the legislative aspects of each of the alternatives.

The Final Public Meeting

If General Cassidy had sat through the second and final public meeting of the restudy, held at North Bend Elementary School on the evening of 1 May 1973, surely he would have been appalled. Three years had elapsed since the BERH hearing, and barely one "new fact" or the kind of "hard information" on which the Corps could make its decisions had been uncovered. There were more alternatives and more rapport and mutual respect between state agencies and the Corps, between the conservationists and the Corps, and between the proponents and opponents of the dam and reservoir project. But positions on the original Seattle District proposal remained unchanged. Thus, although the continual constructive interaction of the fishbowl planning process resulted in the participants' greater appreciation for one another's views, it did not result in any new substantive information or a consensus.

Proponents had not been persuaded that the dam inevitably meant development and the end of the greenbelt nature of the valley. Bill Reams, King County councilman, made this clear.

> I have been on the Council for four years and have sat in on many of the meetings, a couple of them with the Department of Ecology, several meetings with our own flood control people, and several that we have had at the King County Council. The Council almost unanimously has voted to reaffirm the sponsorship of this project. We only had one Councilman dissenting. . . .
>
> We are committed to keeping the Snoqualmie Valley in its natural state and keeping the people on the land that have been on the land for the last 80 to 90 years, and we feel that in this discussion the best way to keep the

people on the land and allow them to continue farming is to allow this dam to be built. We think that by eliminating some of the severe flooding we will allow people who are having a tough time now, making it, to continue farming.[31]

Some attendees once again reminded the audience that floods were a severe hardship for those who had to endure them, and that therefore the dam should be built. Scott Wallace, after assailing the motives of Brock Evans (who had since moved out of the Seattle area), went on to say:

> I don't question the integrity of the opponents of the dam or of their methods or their feelings, they are natural, but the thing that disturbs me a little bit is that they will not honor the years of toil, the thousands and thousands of dollars spent by bona fide organizations, the counties, the state, the federal government and all of these other agencies that have worked on this project for 25 years from its first conception to try to come to a reasonable solution to a problem.[32]

After all, he argued, it was not as though they did not have the same goal in mind.

> The people that have cleared this valley and make it the greenbelt that all of you admire and . . . want to preserve . . . have a common goal: we want to preserve the greenbelt. The county has moved forthrightly to zone it for agricultural, established a floodplain over zone, and this is the use that it will be put to, and as we said in our position paper, our arguments for the dam are very simple, but the arguments against the dam are based on three false assumptions, and I reiterate again those assumptions are, one, the dam will foster . . . industrialization similar to that in the Green River basin, . . . two, the dam reservoir will destroy part of the river and part of the wilderness area, and . . . three, . . . by constantly advancing dubious alternatives the dam will be buried and the valley saved by doing nothing.[33]

So, again, one of the strongest proponents stressed his view that the recreationists were nothing but obstructionists, and misguided ones at that.

Naturally the environmentalists expressed their continuing belief in the social and environmental hazards of building a dam. The Washington Environmental Council endorsed alternative 10, as did the Washington Kayak Club and the Lake Washington Branch of the American Association of University Women. ALPS endorsed its own proposal, alternative 9.

A number of local opponents of the dam and reservoir took the opportunity to voice their views at this meeting, something that had rarely occurred during earlier meetings. The most damning of these came from Jesse Petrich, a real estate salesman from North Bend, and concerned the motives of at least some of those advocating the dam. "The gentleman alongside of me down there, I sold a piece of property of his the other day, and he says, 'Are you against the dam? Gee, if we had that dam my property would be worth twice as much, three times as much, because they could have built on all 650 feet of the river.' "[34]

Windfall profits—the motive the environmentalists believed to be behind much of the support of the dam but could never document—was finally raised by one of the local residents themselves.

Petrich related a similar episode.

> A funny thing happened today. A lady friend of my daughter's was waiting at the house for her when I got home from the office, and I had never met her before, and right away we got in an argument about this. She started to tell me about a dear friend of hers who had 12 or 13 lots down here on the river and . . . couldn't build on them because of the floodplain controls. And I said, "You know what it appears to me? She bet on the wrong horse. . . . She bought a bunch of them to hold and go up in value and make a little money, and she gambled and lost, and let her take it." And boy, she flounced out of the house madder than a wet hen, but that's the way I feel. . . . I think we can get along without a dam.[35]

There were also a number of pleas, however, for a more sympathetic understanding of the flood victim's position. Richard Zemp, for one, was convinced that the proposed dam was vital to the area and was willing to give up his holdings as a sign of his good faith. He owned about a mile of riverfront property in the Upper Valley and offered to make it available for sale (at market value) or to trade it for land held by the government so that the property could be set aside in its natural state. He reasoned that everyone would lose if a compromise could not be reached. Without some agreed-upon plan, he said "We are going to have a haphazard pattern of growth and development, and erosion and flood damage is going to continue. Let's stop the bickering and let's come to some kind of conclusion that we can lay on Governor Dan's desk and say O.K., now you have some viable alternatives."[36]

Zemp could not have been more correct in his estimation of what it would take to get an affirmative response from the governor. But a viable alternative, or even several from which to choose, was not to emerge from the restudy effort.

The Restudy Ends

This last public meeting was followed by the publication of the final version of the study brochure in June 1973. The brochure had by then grown from the original eleven pages to seventy, most of which were devoted to a description of the eleven alternatives.[37]

The study team also terminated its activities and submitted its report to Governor Evans in June. The report included a copy of the final brochure, assorted correspondence, new data papers that had been completed during the restudy, and a summary of the evolution of the restudy. But it did not contain a recommendation by the team favoring one, or even a select few, of the eleven alternatives. Neither the team members nor the broader public had reached anything close to a consensus. The study team did feel, however, that a compromise might have been worked out if there had been just a little more time. After six months of fishbowl planning the contending factions had finally overcome their initial distrust of one another and the agencies involved and had seriously begun to search for some sort of reconciliation. This essentially was their message to the governor. The report states: "While respective positions of proponents and opponents relative to the original Middle Fork proposal did not appear to have changed during the course of the workshops and public meetings, some indication toward compromise was indicated in the public participation period."[38]

Since Governor Evans had suggested the restudy, he was obligated to comment on it. He was not at liberty, however, to give his approval to the Corps to proceed with any of the alternatives. The Corps had formally presented only one proposal to him, the one the chief had asked the governor to comment on back in 1970. After reviewing the restudy, the governor advised the Corps that he had again concluded that the environmental risks associated with the Corps' proposal for a dam and reservoir were unacceptably high—therefore, no project.

Local pressure and the Corps' continuing interest in attending to the problem of flooding in the Snohomish River basin kept the issue alive. In 1973 the Community Crisis Intervention Center of St. Louis offered to mediate between the opponents and proponents. Governor Evans accepted the offer, and the mediation effort, begun in the summer of 1974, resulted in a plan agreed upon by the Sierra Club, the Washington Environmental Council, the valley farmers, the League of Women Voters, and the basin communities.

The items in the plan that fell under the purview of the Corps were the construction of a multipurpose storage dam on the North Fork of the Snoqualmie River (a dam much smaller in scale and storage capacity than that originally proposed by the Seattle District for the Middle Fork), the modification of the Seattle reservoir on the South Fork of the Tolt River to include flood storage, and setback levees for the towns of North Bend and Snoqualmie. Other features of the plan that were the responsibility of state and local governments called for the purchase of development rights in the floodplain to ensure its rural status, the creation of several public parks in the floodplain, and the protection of the plain where the Snohomish River spills into Puget Sound.

Governor Evans appointed an interim citizens' committee to oversee the implementation of the agreement, and the district office undertook a preliminary feasibility study of the portions of the plan that it would be responsible for. The district found the projects economically justifiable, but just as its study was being completed, a new governor was elected who asked to review the mediated plan. In July 1977 Governor Dixy Lee Ray endorsed the plan and encouraged the Corps to proceed with its feasibility study. However, she also virtually reopened the entire issue by asking that the future of the Cedar River basin (adjoining the Snohomish basin to the south and west) and the long-range water supply needs of Seattle be incorporated into the planning effort. This expanded study, initiated by the Corps and the State of Washington, is scheduled for completion in late 1981. Clearly the controversy is far from over.

Fishbowl Planning Appraised

What can be learned from the fishbowl experience? To begin with, the fishbowl process during the restudy departed in some ways from Sargent's plan, usually in innovative responses to unanticipated problems. For example, a second agency was made a part of the study team, a condition that was required by Governor Evans and one not typical of other Corps studies or of any other government agency's project studies. In addition, the mini-workshops were ad hoc, the result of the desire of citizens to offer alternatives the study team had neither the time nor resources to consider.

Second, Sargent did not consider fishbowl planning simply a strategic response to the controversy over flood management along the Snoqualmie River; he saw it as a format for all agency planning efforts. Therefore, since late 1970 it has been formally required for all Seattle District studies and has become fairly well institutionalized throughout the district.

Despite the inability of fishbowl planning to bring about a consensus on a single alternative in the Middle Fork study, the program is considered worthwhile by the district and by most outside observers. This may be partly because fishbowl planning did not begin with the same basic goal as that of the Office of the Chief of Engineers. It was hoped that in the new era of public participation the chief's guidelines would achieve a clear consensus among all those concerned by facilitating the resolution of conflict.[39] In contrast, fishbowl planning was designed to improve communication among all concerned parties, with the hope that this would lead to greater flexibility on the part of the proponents of each alternative and an atmosphere in which proponents could be encouraged to accommodate the concerns of others, thereby expanding the extent of mutual interest.[40] This may seem a subtle distinction, but as noted earlier, under the OCE guidelines planners were told—and had come to expect—that an elaborate public participation program would produce a consensus on an alternative that all parties accepted as the best solution. Fishbowl planning holds out no such promise; the important point is that it is not judged a failure if a consensus does not emerge.

In sum, the foremost payoff of fishbowl planning in the Middle Fork study was the respect the Corps' Seattle District won from even its strongest critics for opening the decision-making process to such an extent. This had never been attempted before.

Notes

1. The description of the basin is from U.S. Department of the Army, Corps of Engineers, Seattle District, *Snoqualmie River, Washington: Report on Flood Control and Other Improvements* (October 1969), vol. 1, chap. 2.

2. Ibid., 67.

3. Peter Tice Finden, "Analysis of Flood Management Alternatives Proposed for the Snoqualmie River Basin and the Related Public Study" (master's thesis, University of Washington, 1973), 15.

4. Ibid.

5. Interview on 23 January 1974 with Brock Evans, who served as Northwest regional vice-president of the Sierra Club from 1967 to 1972.

6. Seattle District, *Snoqualmie River*, 42–43 (emphasis added).

7. Statement of David G. Knibb, chairman of the Seattle Chapter of the Alpine Lakes Protection Society, in U.S. Department of the Army, Corps of Engineers, Seattle District, transcript of public meeting on the Middle Fork project, Snoqualmie River, Wash., held at North Bend, Wash., 6 March 1970, p. 134.

8. Curiously, the problem of downstream flooding associated with the construction of levees seemed to have escaped the Corps engineers involved in the L-15 study.

9. Seattle District, transcript of public hearing, 6 March 1970, pp. 46–47.

10. Ibid., 65.

11. Ibid., 75.

12. Ibid., 85.

13. Ibid., 93.

14. Ibid., 96.

15. Ibid., 98.

16. Ibid., 101–2.

17. Ibid., 114.

18. Fifty percent of the floodplain was in the hands of 5 percent of its residents (ibid., 193).

19. Ibid., 194.

20. Ibid., 200–201.

21. Letter, chairman of the Board of Engineers for Rivers and Harbors to the chief of engineers, 28 April 1970, p. 8.

22. U.S. Department of the Army, Corps of Engineers, Seattle District and State of Washington, Department of Ecology, *Middle Fork Snoqualmie River Joint Study: Report to Governor Evans* (June 1973), 2.

23. The cost-sharing agreement of the restudy called for the Corps to contribute $40,000 and for the state to contribute $14,000.

24. Colonel Howard L. Sargent, Jr., "Fishbowl Planning Immerses Pacific Northwest Citizens in Corps Projects," *Civil Engineering* 42 (September 1972): 54–57.

25. Ibid., 56.

26. Ibid.

27. Setback levees are those constructed some distance from the edge of the watercourse to contain floodwater within a broad natural channel. A floodway easement is acquired by a public body for the purpose of allowing floodwaters to pass without interruption beyond that caused by existing structures. Title to property, however, remains with the private owner.

28. Seattle District, transcript of public meeting on the Middle Fork project, held at North Bend, 9 November 1972, 49–50.

29. Ibid., 51.

30. The discussion of the six mini-workshops is drawn from Seattle District and Department of Ecology, *Joint Study*, sec. 5.

31. Seattle District, transcript of public meeting on the joint study held at North Bend, 1 May 1973, 15–16.

32. Ibid., 37.

33. Ibid., 37–38.

34. Ibid., 27.

35. Ibid., 28.

36. Ibid., 56.

37. Seattle District and Department of Ecology, *Joint Study*. The eleventh alternative was not discussed earlier, because it was suggested quite late in the restudy by a resident of North Bend. It called for channel modification to reduce flooding in the Upper Valley.

38. Ibid., 4.

39. U.S. Department of the Army, Corps of Engineers, Office of the Chief of Engineers, "Water Resources Policies and Authorities: Public Participation in Water Resources Planning," EC 1165–2-100 (28 May 1971).

40. U.S. Department of the Army, Corps of Engineers, Office of the Chief of Engineers, "Investigation Planning and Development of Water Resources: Public Involvement in Planning," SDR 1120-2-1 (10 November 1971).

32

Beyond NIMBY: Participatory Approaches to Hazardous Waste Management in Canada and the United States

Barry Rabe

Both Canada and the United States have stumbled badly in recent decades in attempting to design policy that can lead to the safe and efficient disposal of hazardous wastes.[1] These wastes pose a fundamental dilemma for both nations in that any disposal facility will likely impose high costs on those communities surrounding the facility that is constructed. At the same time, the siting and operation of a facility will offer widely dispersed benefits to all who escape these costs and continue to enjoy the advantages of life in a society that generates abundant

Reprinted from Barry G. Rabe, "Beyond the NIMBY Syndrome in Hazardous Waste Facility Siting: The Albertan Breakthrough and the Prospects for Cooperation in Canada and the United States," *Governance: An International Journal of Policy and Administration* 4, no. 2 (April 1991): 184–206. © 1991 Research Committee on the Structure and Organization of Government of the International Political Science Association. Reprinted by permission of Basil Blackwell.

quantities of these wastes. In both nations what is commonly referred to as the NIMBY (not in my back yard) syndrome prevails, in which those communities faced with a proposed site take aggressive collective action and thwart the proposal. As a result, the volumes of wastes increase and the types of waste requiring special disposal or treatment proliferate, with the political systems of both Canada and the United States appearing increasingly unable to break through this logjam.

This article considers some of the reasons that prevailing approaches to siting repeatedly have failed to produce agreements. It also explores alternative policy approaches that may prove more successful in transcending NIMBYism. In particular, the breakthrough case of Alberta, which achieved a siting agreement in 1984 and opened a new, comprehensive waste disposal and treatment facility in 1987, is examined in considerable detail to determine whether it was a political fluke or if it offers lessons for future siting efforts.

This analysis draws heavily on the growing body of scholarship on policy cooperation in considering the Alberta agreement and its prospects for replication. As Paul Quirk has noted, political science has generally failed "to identify the conditions for cooperative resolution of policy conflict" (Quirk 1989: 908). However, increasingly mature thinking about policy cooperation is evident in both institutionalist and game theoretic perspectives. Applied to cases such as hazardous waste facility siting, it suggests that meeting the following conditions can enhance the prospects for a cooperative outcome: creation of new governmental institutions with capacity for conflict mediation; provision of extensive opportunities for public participation early in the policy-making process; development of economic and related incentives to make cooperation more attractive to integrally involved groups and individuals; recruitment of credible and capable policy professionals to guide policy making on complex policy issues and build public trust; and cultivation of governing norms to guide citizen conduct and assure widespread policy support and compliance.

The Problem of Hazardous Waste and
Alternative Approaches to Siting

Hazardous waste defies precise scientific definition, exact estimation of public health risk through various routes of exposure, or technological agreement on the safest methods for disposal or recycling.[1] All of these factors contribute to the widespread public fear of these wastes and the difficulty in reaching agreement on their safe management. The classification systems for measuring the volumes of these wastes and their toxicity have improved in recent years, particularly in the United States. A series of recent government-sponsored studies suggests that between 250 and 275 million metric tons—or about one metric ton per person—of hazardous waste are generated in the United States each year (Conservation Foundation 1987: 158–60). No comparable estimate exists for Canada. A tabulation of recent provincial estimates suggests that approximately 5 million metric tons are generated in Canada annually, but this is in all likelihood a significant underestimation of the total volume.

Regardless of the total volume of wastes, it is commonly agreed that disposal and treatment supply fall far short of demand. Many hazardous waste disposal facilities were closed in the 1980s because of unsafe treatment practices and fears of environmental and public health dangers in the event of continued facility operation. Only a handful of new facilities were opened in either Canada or the United States in the past decade, and the majority of these are relatively modest in scope. Many of these new facilities have merely expanded the capacity of existing facilities, as in Michigan, or will treat only select types of wastes, as in Quebec.

Swan Hills, Alberta, a town of 2,396 people that is 209 kilometers northwest of Edmonton, remains the only community in Canada or the United States to accept a comprehensive hazardous waste facility in the 1980s. It features multiple treatment and disposal methods and has potentially expansive treatment capacity. However, even this facility will not handle all Albertan wastes, much less those of neighboring provinces or states, allowing it to make only a modest contribution toward total continental hazardous waste management needs. As one of the most comprehensive surveys of hazardous waste generation and management capacity in the United States noted in 1989:

> Once again, almost no new waste management capacity came on-line in the past year . . . the amount of waste management capacity that has actually become available during the past year is relatively small and is primarily directed at high-energy, liquid wastes. Thus, net waste management capacity for other types of wastes has continued to decrease, albeit more slowly, for a sixth year. (McCoy and Associates, 1989: 1–2)

With the lone exception of the Alberta facility, the Canadian situation is very similar. As a result, the single case of cooperation in Alberta will have to be replicated frequently in future years if adequate disposal capacity is to be developed.

Subnational governments in Canada and the United States dominate siting policy because of the absence of national siting legislation in both nations. Subnational authority remains somewhat more dominant in Canada, consistent with the constitutional deference to provinces on natural resource matters. These moderate differences in degree of decentralization are reflected in Figure 32–1 with the American and Canadian cases occupying different parts of cells 2 and 4. The 1988 Canadian Environmental Protection Act may begin to chip away at provincial powers in hazardous waste management, although this remains highly unlikely. The American states must contend with the

Figure 32-1
Typology of Hazardous Waste Facility Siting Policy
in Canada and the United States

	Centralized	Decentralized
Regulatory	1 (US HLRW)	2 Florida Ontario New Jersey New York (US LLRW) Alberta
Market	3 (Canada LLRW)	4 Minnesota Manitoba Michigan British Columbia Massachusetts Quebec North Carolina Saskatchewan

Centralized—national government dominant in siting process
Decentralized—state/provincial government dominant in siting process
Regulatory—government agency/agencies make main siting decisions
Market—private site developers make main siting decisions
HLRW—high-level radioactive waste
LLRW—low-level radioactive waste

regulatory structures imposed by the Resource Conservation and Recovery Act (RCRA). This legislation provides uniform national standards and permit guidelines for hazardous waste management, and has attempted to shift states away from land-based disposal methods. However, it operates on a conjoint basis, and more than forty states have acquired authority to operate RCRA permitting programs. Moreover, RCRA does not in any way establish a process for hazardous waste facility siting, leaving this matter almost entirely up to the states.

Given this latitude from federal legislation, Canadian provinces and American states have devised a wide array of policies to attempt to overcome this dilemma, few of which have demonstrated much promise to date. A fundamental dividing line between the varying approaches that have been adopted by individual provinces and states involves the nature of governmental involvement, as noted in Figure 32–1. Provinces such as Ontario and states such as Florida, New Jersey, and New York (cell 2) rely upon provincial or state environmental and natural resource agencies to make the main siting decisions and impose them on local communities. Under these "regulatory" approaches, governmental officials weigh a number of siting criteria—technical, economic, social, and political—and decide what type of facility is necessary and where it should be located. Local governments and the general public may be consulted at varying points of the process, but the final decision rests with provincial or state officials. A variety of coercive or consensusseeking methods may then be used to either force construction of the new facility or gain local support for it. Private corporations may be included on a contractual basis. They may be hired to construct and operate the facility after the provincial or state officials have decided its location, the wastes that will be accepted, and the methods that will be used for their disposal or treatment.

By contrast, provinces such as British Columbia, Quebec, and Saskatchewan and states such as Massachusetts, Michigan, and North Carolina give their public officials a far more passive role in the siting process (cell 4). Private sector initiative drives the siting process under this "market" approach. After establishing general guidelines for safety, provinces or states wait to receive proposals from private facility developers to specify the site, the types of wastes to be accepted, and the nature of the facilities to be constructed. These private developers work directly with communities that would "host" the site, often negotiating the terms of agreement with little or no direct involvement from provincial or state officials. In the absence of proposals from the private sector, no new facilities will be developed.

Both regulatory and market approaches have consistently failed to produce agreements on hazardous waste facility in both nations. Among regulatory approaches, even the existence of a dominant governmental authority is insufficient to overcome local resistance. In fact, it often triggers enormous public distrust of any governmental role in siting. Among market approaches, the attempt to establish a workable bargaining process in the absence of a substantial governmental role faces similarly rigid public resistance. Private site proponents repeatedly withdraw their proposals in response to fierce local outcry.

The Emergence of Cooperation in Alberta

The record of governmental efforts to site hazardous waste facilities is a gloomy one, although a few Canadian and American cases have deviated from the NIMBY pattern. The most noteworthy of these involves Alberta's novel approach to siting and its major siting breakthrough. The Alberta Special Waste Treatment Centre near Swan Hills has proven a model of private, provincial, and local government collaboration, antithetical to the pattern common in most other provinces and states that have attempted siting. As noted in Figure 32–1, the Alberta approach defies categorization in either the regulatory or market cells of the typology and in many respects constitutes a hybrid strategy. Both Manitoba and Minnesota have modeled their new siting programs after Alberta and will be a test of its replicability to other subnational units.

The Swan Hills case is intriguing not only for its seeming transcendence of NIMBYism but also for its alternation of the traditional structure of the siting process and nature of interactions among key participants. Under many current approaches to siting, a conflict emerges that resembles a one-shot, zero sum game such as prisoner's dilemma. In such cases interaction between factions ends rapidly, as local communities "defect" rather than pursue cooperative strategies in conjunction with waste facility proponents.

Alberta has countered this pattern by transforming the siting process into an open-ended, non–zero sum game that, at least in the case of Swan Hills, has resulted in multiparty cooperation. In the parlance of game theory, the case appears to most closely resemble an assurance game, where both factions prefer negotiation to conflict and both expect to receive optimal payoffs if they can cooperate. The Alberta case is consistent with the pattern noted by scholars who suggest that, under certain circumstances, it is possible to devise processes that lead to cooperative interaction, even among parties with considerable reason to be skeptical of one another and incentives to take adversarial actions (Hardin, 1982; Bendor and Mookherjee, 1987; Axelrod, 1984; Keohane, 1984; Oye, 1985; Rabe, 1986; Gillroy, 1990). Although the Alberta siting case may ultimately prove a fluke that cannot be replicated elsewhere, it does indicate that hazardous waste facility siting need not always be an intracable problem. It also suggests that careful attention to the conditions necessary to foster cooperative outcomes may be able to transform the process.

Such conditions are consistent with lessons for policy cooperation drawn from the modest but maturing political science literature on this topic. Some of these lessons are derived from institutionalist analyses which stress creation of new governmental institutions that can mediate factional conflict, establishment of mechanisms for meaningful public participation well before final decisions must be made, and development of competent and credible policy professionals to oversee policy and build public trust. Lessons drawn from game theoretic analyses of cooperation offer some similar insights, but they also emphasize the importance of altering payoffs through incentives that give communities greater reason to consider cooperation and the development of norms to generate a collective sense of responsibility for waste generation as well as guide citizen, corporate, and governmental conduct.

Beyond the Failed Market Approach

Alberta seemed a most unlikely candidate to break through the NIMBY syndrome in the early 1980s. The province began the decade with a market approach to hazardous waste facility siting that closely resembled the policies of British Columbia, Michigan, North Carolina, Quebec, and Saskatchewan. That approach met a familiar political response as Alberta's market-driven efforts resulted in a pair of private site proposals that were spurned in short order by fierce local opposition. In response, the province placed a moratorium on the siting of hazardous waste facilities in 1980 and established a provincial Hazardous Waste Management Committee to study the problem and devise an alternative siting process.

The committee operated in the absence of any structured process for siting or provincial regulation of hazardous waste management, having been encouraged to design a novel approach. Its report provided the basic structure of the approach that was ultimately embraced by the Alberta legislature. This new approach emphasized volunteerism, as only communities offering to host a site would be considered as candidates. In addition, private developers would be asked to propose facility plans to provincial authorities. At the same time, the new Alberta approach established a major provincial role through establishing siting criteria and educating the public as to the nature of the hazardous waste problem and alternative remedies. It also was designed to allow provincial authorities to make the final decision on site selection and the private corporations to be involved in construction and operation of the site and ultimately to play a direct role in the management of the facility. This blending of features resulted in a systematic role for government in the hazardous waste siting process that was unprecedented among all other provinces and states.

Siting criteria were applied through constraint mapping, which ruled out parcels of Albertan territory that were deemed inappropriate for various physical, biological, economic, social, and political reasons. Contrary to siting efforts in other provinces and states that used constraint mapping, these efforts in Alberta were shaped through exhaustive consultation with the public. This was an important part of a process that provided for extensive public participation at each stage.

The Alberta approach also involved a potpourri of general informational meetings and frequent sharing of technical and related reports with community organizations. The province established a host of liaison and other committees that were intended to foster regular and direct communication between public, provincial, and private corporation, and crown corporation representatives at every stage of the siting process. In the early stages of the site selection process Alberta Environment officials hosted more than 120 meetings in every county, municipal district, improvement district, and special area in the province. These meetings responded to citizen questions, provided briefings on the hazardous waste situation in the province, and offered general information on the types of criteria that can be used in a siting program

(McQuaid-Cook and Simpson, 1986: 1031–36). Those communities that expressed interest in possible participation continued to have far-reaching access to provincial officials and hazardous waste data. Communities that expressed an interest in this activity were offered a detailed provincial analysis of their area, which could prove useful to them in considering the viability of a hazardous waste site as well as potential landfill sites or other land uses. Fifty-two of a possible seventy jurisdictions requested these assessments, and they were invited to volunteer to further explore the possibility of hosting a site.

Fourteen communities requested further consideration, although nine were subsequently eliminated on either environmental grounds or in response to vocal public opposition. Five communities remained eager to pursue the possibility of further involvement. All of them held plebiscites in 1982 that drew heavy voter turnout and overwhelmingly approved the idea of hosting a hazardous waste facility. Seventy-nine percent of Swan Hills voters supported the facility proposal in a plebiscite in which 69 percent of eligible voters participated. The town was selected by Alberta Environment as the site of a comprehensive waste facility in March 1984. Community leaders from the town of Ryley, which is 85 kilometers southeast of Edmonton and has 500 residents, were very outspoken in registering their disappointment in not being selected as site host.

Swan Hills proved attractive to provincial policy makers because it was relatively close (209 kilometers) to the major metropolitan area of Edmonton and linked to this area by highway. At the same time, unlike Ryley and other candidate sites, Swan Hills had no immediate neighboring communities, so its acceptance of a facility did not require gaining the support of any nearby towns. Swan Hills also was eager to diversify its economy, which was previously reliant on oil and natural gas extraction, and attract investment for long-term economic development. Like many small Albertan—and Western Canadian—towns of this period, the Swan Hills' unemployment and bankruptcy rates increased rapidly in the late 1970s and early 1980s (McParland, 1981). The other four communities that held plebiscites over siting were also eager for economic development and diversification but were not in as serious an economic downswing as Swan Hills.

Local political leadership played a pivotal role in building public trust in the provincial siting process and support for pursuing the waste management facility. They emphasized the economic development potential, the voluntary nature of the siting process, and the fact that the proposed facility was part of a comprehensive provincial waste management strategy. Upon initial discussion, many Swan Hills residents expressed alarm and formed citizen opposition groups. "When I brought the idea back to council, I was almost run out of town on a rail," explained Margaret Hanson, the mayor at that time. But after the council embraced the idea, they formed a citizens committee to hold regular public meetings prior to the plebiscite. These gatherings were held every week over a twelve-week period, and every Swan Hills resident was actively encouraged to attend at least two of them. All relevant provincial and local officials were available at these meetings to discuss any aspect of the proposal. "We became taxi drivers, dishwashers, babysitters, whatever it took to get everyone out," recalled the former mayor of council-led efforts to build support for the proposal. "We divided up the phone book and called everyone to town" (Houston, 1990). Such extensive deliberations also served as a forum to consider—and refute—claims from national and international environmental groups such as Greenpeace that the facility would pose dire environmental and public health consequences if accepted.

Local leaders also attempted to defuse opposition by highlighting the slipshod, unsafe waste disposal practices previously used in Swan Hills and the province. There had been recent revelations of hazardous wastes being intermingled with garbage in area landfills and extensive dumping of oil industry wastes into ditches and waterways. "It's better to get rid of it properly," explained a local newspaper editor (Bohn, 1986). He emphasized that many Swan Hills residents were very familiar with such shoddy waste disposal practices in Alberta and gradually came to perceive the facility as providing a safer method of addressing a major local problem as well as a potential economic stimulus. These extensive public deliberations differed markedly from those over similar proposals in other provinces and states in their thoroughness, openness, and ability to foster an atmosphere of trust.

They also made possible an extensive public review of possible economic and social advantages that might be generated by acceptance of the facility. Swan Hills leaders argued that the construction of a facility with an anticipated $45 to $50 million in capital costs and creation of an estimated fifty-five new jobs would boost the area economy and its capacity to attract desired developments, such as a new hospital. In addition, the crown corporation provided the following: $105,000 to cover expenses incurred by Swan Hills for town meetings, consultation with outside experts, and travel expenses; funding to enable the town to hire a permanent consultant to evaluate monitoring data; subsidized housing for approximately thirty-five family units; and purchase of a van to provide transportation for Swan Hills residents to the site, which is twenty kilometers northeast of the town. The private corporation responsible for development and operation of the facility supplemented these benefits with the following: approximately $65,000 to support various local activities, including golf course development as well as other educational, sporting, and cultural activities; planting 400 trees for town beautification; and a special medical surveillance program for all facility employees. It has also provided such symbolic forms of compensation as making headquarter offices available for public meetings, sponsoring a hockey school, and donating a bear rug to the town council chambers.

The process of finding a host community went hand in hand with a provincial search for private firms to construct and operate the facility. The Alberta legislature created a provincial crown corporation, the Alberta Special Waste Management Corporation, in 1982 and also began in that year a national and international competition to attract private proposals for site development and management. This resulted in nineteen proposals, which were later winnowed to four finalists. One month after Swan Hills was selected as the site acceptable to both provincial and local constituencies, Chem-Security Ltd. (later purchased by Bow Valley Resource Services Ltd.) was selected to build and operate the facility. Representatives from both the private and crown corporations sought a high public profile in Swan Hills, attempting to maintain public trust and support for the project.

The Swan Hills Special Waste Treatment Centre opened in September 1987, with capacity to incinerate organic liquids and solids, treat inorganic liquids and solids, and landfill contaminated bulk solids. The center is expected to process approximately 15,000 to 20,000 metric tons of hazardous waste each year, although its potential capacity is significantly greater. It is the most comprehensive treatment facility ever constructed in Canada or the United States, given the breadth of treatment approaches and types and volumes of waste that it can handle. The center is expected to preclude any need for an additional major facility in the province, the central component in a comprehensive provincial waste management and waste reduction system that also includes regional facilities for storage and ultimate transfer to Swan Hills.

The Swan Hills experience is unique not only in its ability to foster sufficient cooperation to attain a siting agreement but also in its fundamental transformation of the siting process. It suggests that it may be possible to overcome the problems that have been so rampant in both regulatory and market approaches. In at least the instance of Swan Hills, this alternative approach has transformed siting from a fierce conflict that quickly produces an unresolvable disagreement to a more prolonged bargaining process that culminates in an agreement acceptable to all participants. Some of the most crucial components in this transformation include the following.

Tripartite Management and Governance
New, intermediary institutions have often served to transform highly conflictual situations into more cooperative ones. For example, Robert Keohane argues that new, multinational institutions have played a

pivotal role in fostering cooperation in an era in which no single nation or institution is likely to enforce agreement through hegemonic power (Keohane, 1984). New institutions may be needed to transform the siting process, distinct from traditional agencies within individual states and provinces that lack public credibility, meet stiff resistance, and repeatedly fail to attain agreement. The introduction of a crown corporation into provincial hazardous waste management appears to have contributed to the cooperative outcome in Alberta. This corporation assumes a number of the important responsibilities delegated to either private developers or regulatory agencies in most states and provinces (Laux and Molot, 1988). It provides for direct governmental oversight of facility operation and also affords uniquely direct public financial and technical assistance to private corporations responsible for site development and management. As a 1981 government report endorsing the crown corporation concept noted, the corporation

> would provide effective evidence of an arm's length position relative to government and industry . . . while allowing various government departments to continue their particular regulating, inspecting and monitoring functions. . . . [T]he public would be more likely to trust the administration of a crown body. Industry has indicated that if allowed to operate facilities in a free market environment, they too could function efficiently under such administration. Therefore, both concerns are met. (Alberta Hazardous Waste Team, 1981)

Under this tripartite system the Alberta Special Waste Management Corporation is responsible for overseeing numerous aspects of the provincial waste management system, including plant design and construction, provision of 40 percent of construction and operating costs plus operating loss subsidies to the private corporation, control of all provincial transfer and collection points, collection of 40 percent of revenues generated by the facility, provision of utilities and highways for the facility, and ongoing research, monitoring, and technological appraisal. Its also owns the site, which it leases to the private firm for a minimal fee. In turn, Bow Valley Resource Services provides 60 percent of the construction funds and operating costs and handles day-to-day operation of the facility.

The crown corporation is distinct from Alberta Environment and related provincial agencies, which set regulatory standards that specify the ways in which respective wastes are to be treated. Alberta Environment also provides a system for registering these wastes and punishing regulatory noncompliance by either the crown or private corporations. At the same time that the Swan Hills siting decision and Bow Valley Resource Services selection were made, Alberta was devising one of the more comprehensive hazardous waste regulatory systems of all the Canadian provinces, and it was to be implemented by these agencies. In addition to regulating waste management, provincial agencies provide a number of requirements and incentives for waste generators to alter their production processes in order to recycle or reduce the volumes (or toxicity) of the wastes that would otherwise be sent to Swan Hills.

Public Participation

The notion of any significant public role in the siting of hazardous waste facilities in Canada and the United States has become synonymous with protests that ultimately thwart siting agreements. Neither regulatory nor market approaches have found mechanisms of public participation that provide citizens with opportunities that enable them to influence policy and encourage them to cooperate. As Gary Davis has noted, common participatory measures such as formal adjudicatory hearings and informal public comment sessions "are usually held too late in the process to really make any differences in the facility siting decision and both tend to create hostility and discourage cooperation" (Davis, 1987: 29).

Creation of meaningful methods of public participation may thus be pivotal to any future breakthroughs. Prolonged political dialogue may be essential to defuse the adversarialism so common in NIMBY-type situations and to move toward more unitary processes of conflict resolution (Mansbridge, 1980; Williams and Matheny, 1994). Moreover, multiple participatory mechanisms and outlets may be necessary if participation is to have a significant impact (Mazmanian and Nienaber, 1979; Gormley, 1989).

The Alberta approach offered a multidimensional system of participation that was clearly more substantial, and more likely to build public trust, than the ones developed in the other provinces and states that were examined. Ontario and Florida, for example, have attempted to impose sites and have provided only perfunctory opportunities for public input. Explosive political conflict has gridlocked both siting processes. Alberta also surpassed the limited participatory opportunities provided in market-oriented approaches, such as in British Columbia and Massachusetts, where citizen involvement was minimal or nonexistent until after a community was confronted with a site proposal.

This level of participation has continued into the operational stage, through a number of formal and informal mechanisms designed to maintain communication between Swan Hills residents, provincial authorities, and representatives of the crown and private corporations. The Swan Hills Special Waste Liaison Committee was formed in 1985 and meets regularly with members of the Alberta Special Waste Management Corporation and Bow Valley Resource Services. One member of the Swan Hills council is appointed to the crown corporation board, and facility managers maintain a high profile in the community and its schools. Observers of the public participation processes consistently emphasize that it was essential to encourage this openness at an early stage and maintain it throughout, making possible a bargaining process that resulted in settlement and has preserved trust in the initial years of operation (Simons, 1988).

Compensation

Many provincial and state approaches to hazardous waste facility siting have been premised in part on the notion that host communities might agree to accept a proposed site if generous compensation packages were provided. Such packages could offer commitments of health and safety protection, economic subsidies, or support for necessary services such as transportation and education, and they could be agreed upon through negotiation (Portney, 1985; Mitchell and Carson, 1986). The notion of devising methods of compensation to defuse NIMBYism is consistent with lessons offered by game theorists, who suggest that tinkering with the level of payoffs and the structure for their distribution may result in unexpectedly stable, cooperative outcomes (Axelrod, 1984). In the process, highly regulatory and redistributive policies that local communities would normally resist might become more palatable if seen as facilitating local economic and social development.

Merely allowing for compensation to be discussed and provided does not result in cooperation, despite such an assumption by many provinces and states. By contrast, Alberta Environment, the Special Waste Management Corporation, and Bow Valley Resource Services proposed a host of compensatory benefits at a very early stage in the process—and offered them in a very concrete manner—rather than wait for the advanced stages of deliberation over a specific site. Swan Hills officials contend that the economic impact of the facility has been considerable and has served to solidify public support. The facility has helped Swan Hills overcome declines in oil and gas extraction industries, providing eighty-six new jobs and luring new industries eager to locate near the comprehensive waste disposal facility. Swan Hills has enjoyed prosperity in the years following facility approval, with major increases in housing starts, a $5-million upgrade of water supply facilities, the opening of a modern 25-bed hospital, construction of a major new office complex, and planning for a major industrial park in the 1990s. Swan Hills has also begun to lure hundreds of tourists each year, most of them eager to visit the facility. This has proven a completely unexpected aspect of economic development attributable to the agreement.

Policy Professionals

Policies that involve redistribution and regulation invariably lead to political conflict. They often require the guiding hand of nonelected public officials—or policy professionals—to facilitate bargaining, agreement, and implementation (Peterson, Rabe, and Wong, 1986). This is particularly important in hazardous waste facility siting, where political saliency and conflict are extremely high and the credibility of environmental regulatory agencies has often been suspect (Price, 1978; U.S. Office of Technology Assessment 1985; 1988). As William Lyons and colleagues have noted, "the public has lost faith in those responsible for waste disposal—whether they are private chemical companies or public agencies . . . and is no longer willing to defer responsibility to 'experts' " (Lyons, Fitzgerald, and McCabe 1987: 89).

The loss of credibility of Alberta environmental officials helped undermine the province's market approach of the 1970s. A 1979 report of the Alberta Environment Research Secretariat indicated that provincial officials were "being seen as aligned with private industry in favour of waste management facilities, as opposed to being neutral" (Krawetz, 1979: 10). This perception, along with the other important factors, served to scuttle facilities proposed in Fort Saskatchewan and Two Hills. This ultimately led to the abandonment of the province's market approach in favor of one that established a crown corporation with functions that could be clearly distinguished from those of environmental regulatory agencies.

The Swan Hills case has resulted in a remarkable coalition between leaders from each of the key components of the tripartite system and local government officials. A major conflict did emerge in 1985 over the role of the crown corporation, resulting in the controversial dismissal of the crown corporation chair by the Alberta environmental minister. This threatened to return Alberta to the adversarial days of the late 1970s, although the quick appointment of a highly regarded replacement as chair defused the situation (Glenn, Orchard, and Sterling, 1988: chap. 3, pp. 4–5). Important leadership has been provided by a number of key provincial officials with extensive experience in natural resources management and considerable public prominence. Elected Swan Hills officials have provided a solid base of support, with the former mayor and council playing a pivotal role in promoting the project and devising a public participation process that could garner trust.

Developing Governing Norms

Norms that guide behavior and lead to a collective willingness to address the problem of hazardous waste management have been notably lacking in most provincial and state siting efforts. A norm functions in a particular social setting insofar as individuals can be expected to act in certain ways and be punished when they fail to act in these ways. Norms may be buttressed by laws but take on a self-policing characteristic that is often fundamental to cooperative interaction and implementable policy (Axelrod, 1986). With regard to hazardous waste, neither Canada nor the United States has devised generally acceptable understandings of what constitutes appropriate and inappropriate conduct either individually or by private or governmental organizations. Moreover, there is as yet no great likelihood of punishment in the event of defection from the norm or refusal to make constructive contributions to resolution of the hazardous waste problem. This has led to extensive illegal dumping in both nations and explains the proliferation of abandoned sites that has necessitated, in the United States, the creation of a multi-billion dollar "Superfund" to facilitate highly expensive site cleanup. It has also encouraged exportation of wastes to developing nations, which has mired both nations in embarrassing foreign policy conflicts upon revelation of haphazard dumpings in heavily populated areas abroad.

Alberta has not resolved this issue but has taken unusual steps to begin to develop governing norms through its massive information and educational efforts. "The public needed to be able to identify with the problem before ever considering any responsibility in developing a solution," noted one analyst (Simons, 1988). Alongside these efforts, the comprehensive nature of the system to regulate waste management and promote waste reduction is intended to provide an overarching framework in which all Alberta citizens can begin to understand their personal contributions to the problem and their potential role in its resolution. These efforts have only begun to lead to norm development that might facilitate a collective sense of responsibility for the hazardous waste problem, but they appear to surpass those that have been attempted in the other provinces and states that were examined. Furthermore, Alberta's distinctive political culture may gave it certain advantages over many other provinces and American states in developing such norms. This culture has been highly supportive of natural resources extraction as a tool of economic development and may be more trustful of private and provincial leaders than other, eastern provinces or many American states (Gibbins, 1980; Richards and Pratt, 1979).

Limitations and Uncertainties

The ratification of a siting agreement and the opening of a comprehensive waste treatment center are surprising developments given the acrimonious pattern of hazardous waste facility siting in Canada and in the United States. However, the real tests of the effectiveness of the Alberta approach will be the environmental, economic, and political performance of its hazardous waste management system over time and the experience of other provinces and states that emulate its unique qualities. Some initial concerns that have emerged in the Alberta program suggest that its implementation may indeed be smoother than that of other provinces and states but will not be foolproof. At the same time, the Alberta approach has already begun to diffuse beyond the province's boundaries, having had significant influence on new policies devised in neighboring Manitoba and Minnesota. These cases offer some early indication of the approach's likely effectiveness when it is replicated elsewhere.

The Dangers of Capture

Regulatory theorists have long warned that outward signs of collaboration between regulatory agencies and regulated parties can result in capture of the former by the latter (Lowi, 1969; McConnell, 1966; Stigler, 1975). Canadian environmental regulatory policy in recent decades has been far more deferential to the preferences of private and public organizations that contribute to environmental contamination than has American policy. The relative absence in Canada of environmental advocacy groups or a strong national government presence in regulation has often resulted in harmonious—but arguably captured—regulatory relationships (Rabe, 1989).

This more cooperative form of policy making is, in the eyes of many analysts, more efficient in economic terms and every bit as effective in protecting the environment and public health than the more adversarial American approach (Vogel, 1986; Brickman, Jasanoff, and Ilgen, 1985). For example, Thomas Ilgen's comparative analysis of chemicals regulation in Canada and the United States emphasizes the relative merits of the Canadian approach (Ilgen, 1985). But this regulatory style may not be acceptable in the adversarially oriented American states and those more economically developed provinces, such as Ontario, that have increasingly embraced an American command-and-control approach to environmental regulation. Moreover, this more cooperative style of policy making has regularly failed to overcome NIMBYism in hazardous waste facility siting in a variety of other provinces.

The more cooperative approach may also lead to more superficial forms of public participation than would first seem likely, given the proliferation of meetings, outreach efforts, and citizen involvement opportunities in Alberta hazardous waste management. For example, the Alberta Hazardous Chemicals Advisory Committee, which coordinated the assessment of the provincial Hazardous Waste Regulation and its amendments, is dominated by industry representatives. More than half of the committee's members are from the private sector, with the remainder from provincial agencies or municipal associations. This complete absence of environmental advocacy group representation is characteristic of environmental policy making in the province, as the major North American organizations have only a minimal presence in Alberta. It is also consistent with repeated pledges by Alberta environmental officials to consult closely with the regulated community and not allow hazardous waste regulations to thwart economic development. In such a setting, capture could emerge once the political flames of NIMBYism have been contained, particularly if a community such as

Swan Hills became economically dependent on the continued operation of the facility (Crenson, 1971).

Planning Pitfalls

The early experience of the Swan Hills facility may underscore the difficulty that a provincial or state government may face in assuming responsibility for all aspects of waste management. Since the facility opened, it has received more incinerable solids and less materials for physical and chemical treatment than had been anticipated. These surprises can be attributed in part to the fact that the province was so eager to get a comprehensive facility sited that the Swan Hills treatment center was "designed, built, and opened before the final hazardous waste regulations were promulgated and before authorities had any reliable data on the waste types and volumes being generated" (Glenn, Orchard, and Sterling, 1988: chap. 3, p. 6). Moreover, Alberta Environment has continued to prove far more reluctant than American states (under the prodding of the U.S. Resource Conservation and Recovery Act) to require waste generators to provide detailed waste production data to the province. This has made the projection of waste disposal needs a highly uncertain process.

As a result, Alberta has found its share of treatment center costs to be much higher than originally anticipated. The province provided $32.7 million to Bow Valley Resource Services to cover operating losses during the first two years of operation, and such subsidies are expected to continue for at least five more years. Moreover, the underutilization of certain components of the comprehensive facility has led Alberta officials to take a more receptive view toward importation of certain nonprovincial hazardous wastes to bring the facility up to capacity and trim operating losses. An original selling point of the comprehensive facility was its anticipated capacity to give Alberta complete control over its own waste management and the autonomy to restrict waste importation from other provinces and the United States. In fact, a 1985 Ontario highway spill of a truck destined for an Alberta storage facility led the Alberta environment minister to ban further acceptance of out-of-province PCB wastes (Glenn, Orchard, and Sterling, 1988: chap. 3, pp. 6–7). This was rescinded, however, when Alberta agreed to incinerate substantial PCB residues from a major 1988 fire in St-Basile-le-Grand, Quebec, a policy shift triggered in part by economic considerations.

The Swan Hills facility is far too new for any definitive analysis of its economic efficiency, capacity to respond to provincial waste disposal needs, or ability to protect the environment and public health. But its early difficulties illustrate some of the potential pitfalls that may occur when an individual province or state attempts to sponsor and manage its own facilities and relies on a comprehensive central facility to serve as the system's focal point.

Replicability

Alberta's unique approach to hazardous waste facility siting will have significance for all of North America only if it proves worthy of emulation elsewhere and can in fact be adopted by other provinces and states. The capacity of the Alberta approach to be replicated elsewhere with success is already being tested in a neighboring province and state. Manitoba and Minnesota have abandoned their ineffective siting efforts and borrowed heavily from Alberta in establishing new approaches to siting. Thus far, the Manitoba case is the more promising of the two and may well lead to a major siting agreement in the early 1990s. Like Alberta, it has established a crown corporation and an extensive public participatory process that invites local communities to volunteer as possible hosts for a comprehensive facility. Much like Alberta, Manitoba has a far-reaching system of hazardous waste regulation and offers numerous incentives to stimulate waste reduction. Thus far, it has met most of its early timetables without NIMBY-like explosions.

Five communities had expressed strong interest in hosting a facility, although the Rural Municipality of Rossburn dropped out of contention after a January 1990 referendum was defeated. Among the remaining communities, the City of Winnipeg and the Local Government District of Pinawa are thought the most likely candidates. The Winnipeg metropolitan area generates more than 80 percent of the province's hazardous waste, and a nearby site would limit the dangers and costs associated with long-distance waste transport. Pinawa, a town of 2,100 residents located ninety kilometers northeast of Winnipeg, has appeared most eager to acquire the facility. It has a sizable concentration of technically skilled residents accustomed to environmental risk since the primary employer is the Whiteshell Nuclear Research Establishment. Pinawa leaders view the hazardous waste facility as a potential source of economic diversification.

The Minnesota experience suggests, by contrast, that the Albertan model may not be so fully—or successfully—transportable to American soil. The state abandoned its politically disastrous regulatory approach in 1986 through amendment of the Minnesota Waste Management Act. Much like Alberta's approach, the new legislation sought local voluntarism through a series of public participation mechanisms and compensation packages. It simultaneously pursued the selection of a site and the recruitment of a private firm for site development and management. Although it did not establish an equivalent of a crown corporation, it does provide for possible state financing and ownership of any facility. This would give Minnesota a far greater role in hazardous waste management than most other states. Minnesota also made other adjustments, such as agreeing to eliminate incineration from any comprehensive facility, because of widespread public opposition around the state. It also must operate within the confines of fairly exacting waste management criteria that are imposed by the national RCRA program. This leaves state officials far less bargaining room than in Alberta or Manitoba (Reinke, 1988).

The politics of facility siting under this approach have proven far less harmonious in Minnesota than in Alberta or Manitoba. They seem far less likely to result in a siting agreement. Fifteen Minnesota counties expressed early interest in the possibility of accepting a site. Many of them were economically depressed areas and were attracted by the possible compensation packages and potential economic stimulus that a site might provide. Each of these counties received $4,000 per month from the state, and the four finalists were scheduled to receive $150,000 per year for two years to assist them in technical reviews and in other ways.

A much more adversarial process has emerged in Minnesota than in Alberta. Fourteen of the counties dropped out, and the one that remains, Red Lake in the northwestern part of the state, may follow this pattern. Local and national environmental advocacy groups proved quite active and encouraged counties to withdraw their offers of participation. Moreover, the staff of the Waste Management Board became divided and suffered major turnover, severely damaging the credibility of the board. Public trust further eroded when the media revealed that the private firm that was selected to build a facility if a site was agreed upon has a poor environmental safety record in other states. In short, there are strong signs of NIMBYism in Minnesota, despite its emulation of the Albertan process. However, the Minnesota experiment deviated from the Alberta approach in several critical respects, including less extensive public participation processes, the absence of a crown corporation, and less comprehensive compensation packages. Further experimentation among states is necessary to determine whether the Alberta approach is in fact replicable in the United States.

Conclusions

Hazardous waste facility siting poses a series of fundamental political problems that are common to Canadian provinces and American states. The prevailing policy approaches of the 1970s and 1980s have repeatedly failed to produce significant siting agreements. By contrast, an alternative approach has been devised in Alberta that has resulted in a major siting breakthrough. This case meets a number of important conditions on the attainment of policy cooperation that are established by the growing body of scholarship on that subject. The Alberta approach may warrant emulation elsewhere and has already served as a model adopted by one neighboring province and one neighboring state. Of course, it should not be viewed at this early stage as either flawless or capable of easy transborder diffusion. Though the initial political agreement is noteworthy, the mere construction of a comprehensive facility does not guarantee technological effectiveness, long-term economic efficiency in waste management, or protection of the environment or public health. Nonetheless, the case suggests that the NIMBY syndrome need not be insurmountable and that careful attention to the institutional, economic, and social aspects of the siting process can enhance the likelihood of cooperation.

Notes

Acknowledgment: Funding for this research was provided by a grant from the Canadian Studies Faculty Research Grant Program. Research assistance was provided by Richard Compton, Debbie Cosans, Margaret Daniel, Laura Flinchbaugh, Elizabeth Lowe, Jessica Miller, Marion Perrin, Pamela Protzel, and Robin Norton. Both sources of support are greatly appreciated. I am also grateful to Colin Campbell, John Gillroy, Philip Mundo, Paul Quirk, Mark Schneider, Eric Uslaner, Kathy Wagner, Kenneth Warner, and two anonymous reviewers for their helpful comments on earlier versions, and to Becky Pace for diligent word processing.

1. The word *hazardous* is generally synonymous with the word *toxic* in both Canada and the United States. Individual provinces and states tend to define hazardous, as opposed to solid or radioactive wastes, in somewhat different ways. Over time, however, the definition provided by the U.S. Resource Conservation and Recovery Act (RCRA) has become dominant. This legislation defines hazardous waste "as a solid waste or a combination of solid wastes that, because of its quantity, or physical, chemical, or infectious characteristics, may cause, or significantly contribute to, an increase in mortality or an increase in serious irreversible, or incapacitating reversible, illness; or pose a substantial present or potential hazard to human health or the environment when improperly treated, stored, transported, or disposed of, or otherwise managed." Solid wastes may be deemed hazardous under RCRA if they exhibit one or more of the following four characteristics: ignitability, corrosivity, reactivity, or toxicity (Fortuna and Lennett, 1987: 26–27).

References

Alberta Hazardous Waste Team. 1981. *Hazardous Wastes in Alberta.* Edmonton: Alberta Environment.
Axelrod, Robert. 1984. *The Evolution of Cooperation.* New York: Basic Books.
———. 1986. "An Evolutionary Approach to Norms." *American Political Science Review* 80:1095–1111.
Bendor, Johnathan, and Dilip Mookherjee. 1987. "Institutional Structure and the Logic of Ongoing Collective Action." *American Political Science Review* 81:129–54.
Bohn, Glenn. 1986. "Where Waste Finds a Home." *Vancouver Sun,* 22 November:B1.
Brickman, Ronald, Sheila Jasanoff, and Thomas Ilgen. 1985. *Controlling Chemicals: The Politics of Regulation in Europe and the United States.* Ithaca: Cornell University Press.
Conservation Foundation. 1987. *State of the Environment: A View Toward the Nineties.* Washington, D.C.: Conservation Foundation.
Crenson, Matthew A. 1971. *The Un-Politics of Air Pollution: A Study of Non-Decision-making in the Cities.* Baltimore: Johns Hopkins University Press.
Davis, Gary, with Mary English. 1987. "Statutory and Legal Framework for Hazardous

Waste Facility Siting and Permitting." Paper presented at the Workshop on Negotiating Hazardous Waste Facility Siting and Permitting Agreements. Arlington, Va.

Fortuna, Richard C., and David J. Lennett. 1987. *Hazardous Waste Generation: The New Era*. New York: McGraw-Hill.

Gibbins, Roger. 1980. *Prairie Politics and Society: Regionalism in Decline*. Toronto: Butterworths.

Gillroy, John M. 1990. "Moral Considerations and Public Policy Choices: Individual Autonomy and the NIMBY Problem." Paper presented at the Annual Meeting of the Midwest Political Science Association. Chicago, Ill.

Glenn, William M., Deborah Orchard, and Thia M. Sterling. 1988. *Hazardous Waste Management Handbook*, 5th ed. Don Mills, Ontario: Southam.

Gormley, William T., Jr. 1989. *Taming the Bureaucracy*. Princeton: Princeton University Press.

Hardin, Russell. 1982. *Collective Action*. Baltimore: Johns Hopkins University Press.

Houston, Maureen. 1990. "Arm-Twisting Recommended." *Winnipeg Free Press* 14 April:3.

Ilgen, Thomas. 1985. "Between Europe and America, Ottawa and the Provinces: Regulating Toxic Substances in Canada." *Canadian Public Policy* 13:578–90.

Keohane, Robert O. 1984. *After Hegemony*. Princeton: Princeton University Press.

Krawetz, Natalia M. 1979. *Hazardous Waste Management: A Review of Social Concerns and Aspects of Public Involvement*. Edmonton: Alberta Environment Research Secretariat.

Laux, Jeanne Kirk, and Maureen Appel Molot. 1988. *State Capitalism: Public Enterprise in Canada*. Ithaca: Cornell University Press.

Lowi, Theodore J. 1969. *The End of Liberalism*. New York: Norton.

Lyons, William, Michael R. Fitzgerald, and Amy McCabe. 1987. "Public Opinion and Hazardous Waste." *Forum for Applied Research and Public Policy* 3:89.

McConnell, Grant. 1966. *Private Power and American Democracy*. New York: Knopf.

McCoy and Associates, Inc. 1989. "1989 Outlook for Commercial Hazardous Waste Management Facilities: A Nationwide Perspective." *The Hazardous Waste Consultant*, March/April:1–13.

McParland, Kelly. 1981. "Oil Cuts Drain Town's Lifeblood." *Edmonton Journal* 10 July:B1.

McQuaid-Cook, Jennifer, and Kenneth J. Simpson. 1986. "Siting a Fully Integrated Waste Management Facility." *Journal of the Air Pollution Control Association* 34:1031–36.

Mansbridge, Jane. 1980. *Beyond Adversary Democracy*. Chicago: University of Chicago Press.

Mazmanian, Daniel, and Jeanne Nienaber. 1979. *Can Organizations Change?* Washington, D.C.: Brookings Institution.

Mitchell, Robert Cameron, and Richard T. Carson. 1986. "Property Rights, Protest, and the Siting of Hazardous Waste Facilities." *American Economic Review* 76:285–90.

Oye, Kenneth A., ed. 1985. *Cooperation under Anarchy*. Princeton: Princeton University Press.

Peterson, Paul E., Barry G. Rabe, and Kenneth K. Wong. 1986. *When Federalism Works*. Washington, D.C.: Brookings Institution.

Portney, Kent E. 1985. "The Potential of the Theory of Compensation for Mitigating Public Opposition to Hazardous Waste Treatment Facility Siting: Some Evidence from Five Massachusetts Communities." *Policy Studies Journal* 14:81–89.

Price, David E. 1978. "Policy Making in Congressional Committees: The Impact of 'Environmental' Factors." *American Political Science Review* 72:548–74.

Quirk, Paul J. 1989. "The Cooperative Resolution of Policy Conflict." *American Political Science Review* 83:905–21.

Rabe, Barry G. 1986. *Fragmentation and Integration in State Environmental Management*. Washington, D.C.: Conservation Foundation.

————. 1989. "Cross-Media Environmental Regulatory Integration: The Case of Canada." *American Review of Canadian Studies* 19:261–73.

Reinke, Dan. 1988. "Development of a Stabilization and Containment Facility in Minnesota." Paper presented at the Air Pollution Control Association Annual Meeting. Dallas, Tex.

Richards, John, and Larry Pratt. 1979. *Prairie Capitalism: Power and Influence in the New West.* Toronto: McClelland and Steward.

Simons, C. S. 1988. "Public Participation in Swan Hills—A Success Story." Paper presented at the Air and Waste Management Association Annual Meeting, Pacific Northwest International Sections. Whistler, British Columbia.

Stigler, George J. 1975. *The Citizen and the State.* Chicago: University of Chicago Press.

U.S. Office of Technology Assessment. 1985. *Superfund Strategy.* Washington, D.C.: U.S. Office of Technology Assessment.

————. 1988. *Are We Cleaning Up? 10 Superfund Case Studies.* Washington, D.C.: U.S. Office of Technology Assessment.

Vogel, David. 1986. *National Styles of Regulation: Environmental Policy in Great Britain and the United States.* Ithaca: Cornell University Press.

Williams, Bruce A., and Albert A. Matheny. 1994. *Democracy, Dialogue, and Social Regulation.* New Haven: Yale University Press.

About the Editors

Frank Fischer is Professor of Political Science at Rutgers University and has also taught graduate and undergraduate courses on organizations and public administration at New York University and the Free University in Berlin. Among his books are *Technocracy and the Politics of Expertise* (1990), *The Argumentative Turn in Policy Analysis and Planning* (coedited with John Forester, 1993), *Confronting Values in Policy Analysis: The Politics of Criteria* (coedited with John Forester, 1987), *Politics, Values and Public Policy* (1980), and *Evaluating Public Policy* (1984). A frequent guest of the Wissenschaftszentrum für Sozialforschung (Science Center for Social Research) in Berlin, he is currently engaged in a comparative study of environmental regulation and administration in Germany and the United States. He also serves as book review editor of *Industrial and Environmental Crisis Quarterly*.

Carmen Sirianni teaches graduate and undergraduate courses on organizations, political sociology, work, and gender in the sociology department at Brandeis University. He has taught at Harvard University, Northeastern University, the State University of New York at Binghamton, Merrimack College, and the University of Genoa. He is coeditor (with Paula Rayman) of the Labor and Social Change series of Temple University Press. Currently he is completing a book entitled *Participatory Democracy and Empowerment* for Cambridge University Press, and a collection of essays entitled *Rethinking Radical Democracy,* as well as editing (with Cameron Macdonald) a volume on service work. His previous books include *Workers' Control and Socialist Democracy: The Soviet Experience* (Verso, 1982), *Work, Community, and Power: The Experience of Labor in Europe and America, 1900–1925* (edited with James Cronin, Temple University Press, 1983), *Worker Participation and the Politics of Reform* (Temple University Press, 1987), and *Working Time in Transition* (edited with Karl Hinrichs and William Roche, Temple University Press, 1991).